Reference and Information Services

LIBRARY SCIENCE TEXT SERIES

Audiovisual Technology Primer. By Albert J. Casciero and Raymond G. Roney.

The Collection Program in High Schools: Concepts, Practices, and Information Sources. By Phyllis J. Van Orden.

The Collection Program in Schools: Concepts, Practices, and Information Sources. By Phyllis J. Van Orden.

Developing Library and Information Center Collections. 2d ed. By G. Edward Evans.

The Humanities: A Selective Guide to Information Sources. 3d ed. By Ron Blazek and Elizabeth Aversa.

Immroth's Guide to the Library of Congress Classification. 4th ed. By Lois Mai Chan.

Information Sources in Science and Technology. By C. D. Hurt.

Introduction to Cataloging and Classification. By Bohdan S. Wynar. 7th edition by Arlene G. Taylor.

Introduction to Library Automation. By James Rice.

Introduction to Library Science: Basic Elements of Library Service. By Jesse H. Shera.

Introduction to Library Services for Library Technicians. By Barbara E. Chernik.

Introduction to Public Services for Library Technicians. 4th ed. By Marty Bloomberg.

Introduction to Technical Services for Library Technicians. 5th ed. By Marty Bloomberg and G. Edward Evans.

Introduction to United States Public Documents. 3d ed. By Joe Morehead.

The Library in Society. By A. Robert Rogers and Kathryn McChesney.

Library Instruction for Librarians. 2d rev. ed. By Anne F. Roberts and Susan G. Blandy.

Library Management. 3d ed. By Robert D. Stueart and Barbara B. Moran.

Micrographics. 2d ed. By William Saffady.

Online Reference and Information Retrieval. 2d ed. By Roger C. Palmer.

Problems in Library Management. By A. J. Anderson.

Reference and Information Services: An Introduction. Richard E. Bopp and Linda C. Smith, General Editors.

The School Librarian as Educator. 2d ed. By Lillian Biermann Wehmeyer.

The School Library Media Center. 4th ed. By Emanuel T. Prostano and Joyce S. Prostano.

The Social Sciences: A Cross-Disciplinary Guide to Selected Sources. Nancy L. Herron, General Editor.

Reference and Information Services
An Introduction

General Editors:

RICHARD E. BOPP
University of Illinois
at Urbana-Champaign

LINDA C. SMITH
University of Illinois
at Urbana-Champaign

LIBRARIES UNLIMITED, INC.
Englewood, Colorado
1991

LIBRARIES UNLIMITED, INC.
P.O. Box 3988
Englewood, CO 80155-3988

Library of Congress Cataloging-in-Publication Data

Reference and information services : an introduction / general
  editors, Richard E. Bopp, Linda C. Smith.
    xx, 483 p. 19x26 cm. -- (Library science text series)
    Includes index.
    ISBN 0-87287-875-9 (cloth) -- ISBN 0-87287-788-4 (paper)
    1. Reference services (Libraries) 2. Information services.
I. Bopp, Richard E. II. Smith, Linda C. III. Series.
Z711.R443   1991
025.5'2--dc20   91-14086
                                                    CIP

CONTENTS

Part I
Concepts and Processes

Part II
Information Sources
and Their Use

PREFACE

Reference and Information Services: An Introduction is designed primarily to provide the beginning student of library and information science with an overview both of the concepts and processes behind today's reference services and of the most important sources consulted in general reference work. The editors believe there is a need for a reference text that goes beyond the study of the tools and interview techniques used at the reference desk. Consequently, this text offers chapter-length discussions of the principles and goals of library instruction, of training and continuing education for reference staff, of the evaluation of reference services, and of the management of these services. It also includes a chapter on unique approaches that are useful when serving people belonging to any of several large segments of the population, such as children, the elderly, and those with disabilities.

The text gives roughly equal space to concepts and to sources. The first ten chapters deal with concepts and are topical. Chapter 1 introduces and briefly describes important reference services as they are practiced in most general reference settings today. It also offers a brief history of reference services and a glimpse at likely future developments. Chapter 2 provides a philosophical rationale for the desirability of these services and the general goals of reference services. Chapters 3 through 10 discuss important areas of reference activity and introduce the concepts underlying their current practice. In many cases, specific applications in different types of libraries are pointed out.

Chapter 11 serves as an introduction to the remainder of the text. It describes the general principles and sources for selecting and evaluating reference tools and the principles for building a reference collection. Chapters 12 through 20 discuss the characteristics and uses of particular types of reference tools; a number of general titles of each type are described, with the most important receiving the most detailed descriptions. Rather than merely describing reference tools, however, these chapters emphasize the formulation of strategies for effective use of specific sources or groups of sources. Each chapter concludes with a description of a librarian's strategy for answering a fictitious but realistic reference question in the context of a particular library setting.

The internal organization of the chapters also requires mention. Chapters 12 through 20 have identical structures, with discussion falling under the following headings: Uses and Characteristics, Evaluation, Selection, Important General Sources, Search Strategies, and, following Notes and a List of Sources, Additional Readings. Chapters 1 through 11 also offer Additional Readings, which, along with the Notes, can be used to delve further into topics discussed in those chapters.

To complement the text and to highlight certain topics, boxes are used throughout this book (numbered consecutively within each chapter). In the chapters on sources, the boxes are used primarily to present scenarios illustrating specific search strategies which can be followed when dealing with certain kinds of reference questions. In the chapters on concepts and processes, the boxes are of several types. Some present a situation or problem which the reader is invited to consider and, possibly, discuss in a group setting. Others highlight information which the author has chosen to present in graphic or outline form or as an extended quotation or definition. In the sources chapters, figures are used to illustrate important features of the reference tools discussed; these are also numbered consecutively within each chapter.

A goal of this text is to integrate discussion of related topics as much as possible. For instance, individual electronic reference sources are discussed, not in a separate chapter, but with other sources of the same type. (Chapter 5 deals with the general types of electronic sources and with general searching principles.) A number of the search strategies presented in the sources chapters attempt to show how print and electronic sources can be used together, in a complementary fashion, in the provision of reference service. There are also numerous cross-references throughout the book, referring the reader to chapters where other aspects of a given topic are discussed.

Throughout the text, terms that may be new to the reader are defined as they are introduced. Consequently, the editors see no need for a separate glossary. The indexes provide comprehensive access to discussions of particular concepts and types of sources, as well as to all titles mentioned in the text. However, titles found only in the Notes or in the lists of Additional Readings are not indexed.

Some mention should be made of the multiauthored nature of this text. When the editors first talked about the need for a new reference text more than two years ago, it was clear that the task was too large for two authors to complete successfully. Discussions with colleagues produced a number of additional individuals interested in the project, and others have joined since that time. The editors believe that the variety of perspectives the numerous authors bring to the text works to the advantage of the reader, who benefits from the diverse experiences in reference work reflected in different chapters. While most authors are currently affiliated either with an academic library or with a graduate school of library and information science, several have worked previously in either public, special, or school libraries. While the general format of the text, particularly in the chapters on sources, has been imposed on the authors to provide overall consistency in the text, each author has a unique style and viewpoint. At the same time, each chapter has been read and edited by both editors, who have sought to eliminate any serious gaps or inconsistencies in the text which might result from the fact that so many individuals have been involved in its creation.

It is hoped that this text will be useful, not only to students of library and information science, but also to practicing librarians who seek to review basic reference principles and sources. The editors welcome any comments and suggestions regarding ways in which the text might be improved.

RICHARD E. BOPP
Reference Librarian and Associate Professor of
Library Administration, University Library
University of Illinois at Urbana-Champaign

LINDA C. SMITH
Associate Professor
Graduate School of Library and Information Science
University of Illinois at Urbana-Champaign

ACKNOWLEDGMENTS

Many individuals have assisted either the editors or one of the authors in one or more of the many tasks involved in the creation of this text. We would like here to express our thanks both to these friends and colleagues and to others whose contributions, though perhaps more subtle, are also deeply appreciated.

At Libraries Unlimited, Inc., we are indebted to Bohdan Wynar and David Loertscher for their careful reading of the manuscript and many helpful suggestions. Rebecca Morris Kelley has patiently guided us through the final editing and preparation of the book, Judy Gay Matthews designed the book, and Kay Minnis did the typesetting. Our thanks to all of them.

A number of individuals helped one or more authors by performing background research or bibliographic work. These include Michele Arms, Carol Elsen, Tania Gottschalk, Eric Loehr, Melissa Ritter, Anne Shaughnessy, and Sandra Wolf. We are grateful for their conscientious assistance.

Lisa Boise, Carol Elsen, Janice Johnson, and David Micko assisted with the physical preparation of the manuscript or accompanying illustrations; our thanks to them as well.

We also wish to thank Jennifer Halla, Amy Huck, Eric Loehr, and Carol Tenopir, who read one or more chapters at the draft stage and offered valuable ideas for improvement.

Finally, to our families, friends, and colleagues who listened to and supported us during the two years of work leading to this text's publication, we are eternally grateful.

LIST OF CONTRIBUTORS

Bryce Allen
Assistant Professor
Graduate School of Library and
    Information Science
University of Illinois at Urbana-
    Champaign
Chapter 8

Betsy K. Baker
Reference Department Head
Northwestern University Library
Evanston, Illinois
Chapter 2

Susan E. Bekiares
Documents Library Head and Associate
    Professor
University Library
University of Illinois at Urbana-
    Champaign
Chapter 20

Richard E. Bopp
Reference Librarian and Associate
    Professor
University Library
University of Illinois at Urbana-
    Champaign
Chapters 1, 14

David A. Cobb
Map and Geography Librarian and
    Professor
University Library
University of Illinois at Urbana-
    Champaign
Chapter 17

Prudence Ward Dalrymple
Assistant Professor
Graduate School of Library and
    Information Science
University of Illinois at Urbana-
    Champaign
Chapter 4

Leslie Edmonds
Coordinator of Youth Services
St. Louis Public Library
St. Louis, Missouri
Chapters 3, 10

Constance A. Fairchild
Reference Librarian and Assistant
    Professor
University Library
University of Illinois at Urbana-
    Champaign
Chapter 15

Frances F. Jacobson
Librarian
University High School Library
University of Illinois at Urbana-
    Champaign
Chapters 10, 16

Josephine Z. Kibbee
Head of Reference and Assistant
    Professor
University Library
University of Illinois at Urbana-
    Champaign
Chapter 9

David N. King
Assistant Professor
College of Library and Information
    Science
University of Kentucky
Chapter 2

Kathleen M. Kluegel
Reference Librarian and Assistant
    Professor
University Library
University of Illinois at Urbana-
    Champaign
Chapter 5

Martha Landis
Senior Special Collections Bibliographer
    and Associate Professor
University Library
University of Illinois at Urbana-
    Champaign
Chapter 18

Susan Miller
Coordinator of Bibliographic Instruction
    and Assistant Professor
Milner Library
Illinois State University
Normal, Illinois
Chapter 12

Maureen Pastine
Director
Central University Libraries
Southern Methodist University
Dallas, Texas
Chapter 2

Carol Bates Penka
Reference Librarian and Assistant
    Professor
University Library
University of Illinois at Urbana-
    Champaign
Chapter 18

Linda C. Smith
Associate Professor
Graduate School of Library and
    Information Science
University of Illinois at Urbana-
    Champaign
Chapters 11, 19

Patricia F. Stenstrom
Library and Information Science Librarian
    and Associate Professor
University Library
University of Illinois at Urbana-
    Champaign
Chapter 13

Ellen D. Sutton
Assistant Education and Social Sciences
    Librarian and Assistant Professor
University Library
University of Illinois at Urbana-
    Champaign
Chapters 3, 10

Lizabeth A. Wilson
Head, Undergraduate Library and
    Associate Professor
University Library
University of Illinois at Urbana-
    Champaign
Chapter 6

Beth S. Woodard
Central Information Services Librarian
    and Associate Professor
University Library
University of Illinois at Urbana-
    Champaign
Chapter 7

CONCEPTS AND PROCESSES

1 □

HISTORY AND VARIETIES OF REFERENCE SERVICES

Introduction

What are *reference services*? One widely accepted answer to this question is presented in box 1.1. In this text, the focus is on both the personal assistance provided to library users (e.g., the reference interview) and the organized services provided to groups of users (e.g., instruction). Attention is also paid to behind-the-scenes activities, such as training and collection development, which are necessary antecedents to the provision of reference services.

■ ━━━━━━━━━━━━━━━━━━━━━━━━━━━━━━━━━━ ■

1.1
One Definition of Reference Service

I represent reference *work* to be the personal assistance given by the librarian to individual readers in pursuit of information; reference *service* I hold to imply further the definite recognition on the part of the library of its responsibility for such work and a specific organization for that purpose. In short, we are willing to give help, and what is more, consider such help an important enough part of our obligations to justify training and assigning staff especially for this work.
— Samuel Rothstein
"Reference Service: The New Dimension in Librarianship"[1]

Reference services, concepts, and processes can be viewed from a variety of perspectives, and they differ in varying situations. School librarians practice reference work in a somewhat different manner than do librarians who work in other institutions or in business settings (special librarians); reference services provided in academic libraries differ in some respects from the reference services offered in public libraries. The size and characteristics of the potential user groups vary greatly. A librarian in a special library may serve 30 professional users, while a school librarian may have 300 children who regularly visit the library. Academic reference librarians may be responsible for providing service to thirty thousand students, faculty, and staff, while a public library reference department may have three hundred thousand potential users in its service area. It is nevertheless true that certain identifiable activities are found to some degree in the reference services provided at most, if not all, libraries. These activities are the subject of this book, and they are introduced in this chapter.

Reference librarianship—the professional specialty which has reference services as its focus—had its origins in the second half of the nineteenth century, partially in response to one of that era's most important accomplishments, the spread of education. As more people were educated, educational institutions grew in size, and the size and complexity of libraries grew as well. At the same time, changes in educational practices required more students to use their college libraries.[2] As the educational level of the general population rose, more people also came to public libraries to use the collections there. Because these individuals were not skilled in library use, the need for an intermediary between library users and library collections was gradually recognized. That intermediary was a librarian, and, within a short time, a *reference* librarian.

The state of reference librarianship today is similar, in one respect at least, to the state of Western society in the nineteenth century: that is, it is in the midst of radical change, more so than at any time in its history. Just as the economic and technological forces of the Industrial Revolution transformed Western society during the nineteenth century, so is the electronic revolution of today transforming the nature and practice of reference librarianship. This is an age of transition, and the options and opportunities in reference work are greater than at any time in its 100-year history. Significant changes have already taken place. In most libraries, reference work today is very different than it was only twenty years ago. The future, although not entirely clear, offers many exciting possibilities.

It is helpful to view reference services in several contexts: their history, current practice, and likely future developments. Current practice will be described in every chapter of this text; some chapters also look to the future and/or summarize past developments of specific reference activities. This chapter contains a brief and general overview of a variety of reference services as they developed in the past, as they are practiced and discussed in the present, and as they may evolve in the future.

Varieties of Reference Services

Although reference services are changing in dramatic ways, their basic character—the provision of assistance to individuals seeking information—remains stable. Traditionally, this assistance has occurred in library buildings and has involved the use of library-owned materials. In the past twenty years, it has increasingly involved the use of information sources not owned by the library, such as online databases, as well, and it may take place outside as well as inside the library. Still, the great variety of reference services can be viewed, as Samuel Rothstein discussed them in 1961, as involving three basic functions: the provision of information; instruction in the use of libraries and information sources; and guidance in the choice of library materials.[3]

These three basic types of reference services can be fairly easily distinguished in theory, but in practice they are often conducted together: that is, one interaction with one patron at one point in time may include elements of all three types. The types are defined here, and the various activities of each type are briefly discussed in the following sections. An *information service* is one which provides the answer to a user's question or information need, regardless of its complexity or the length of time it takes the librarian to find the answer. An *instructional service* is one which teaches individuals how to locate information themselves, or assists them in choosing and using reference tools, whether these tools be reference books, online databases, or a card catalog; it may also teach them how libraries are organized and how librarians can assist them. *Guidance* is similar to instruction, but has historically had a somewhat different focus; it advises and assists users rather than teaching specific skills. Generally, the librarian helps the user choose appropriate books, periodical articles, or other materials to meet personal, recreational, or educational goals. As the scope of instruction has broadened in recent years, the distinction between guidance and instruction has become less clear.

Information

Information services take a variety of forms, from the simple provision of an address or telephone number, to the tracking down of an elusive bibliographic citation, to the identification and delivery of documents about a specific topic. Although an increasing number of answers to information requests are retrievable by electronic means, information services in most settings still depend primarily upon printed tools for their effectiveness. The evaluation, selection, and maintenance of a reference collection suited to the information needs of the library's users, activities which are generally referred to as *collection development*, are discussed in chapter 11.

Ready reference questions. One of the most basic information services is the answering of ready reference questions. A ready reference question is a question that can be answered, quickly, by consulting only one or two reference tools. It is generally a request for factual information, such as an address, the spelling or definition of a word, a date or place of an event, or something about the life or career of an individual. A ready reference question could also be a request for brief information about an organization, such as a brief description of the organization's origin, purpose, and activities. Another common question concerns whether the library owns a specific book or journal.

Ready reference questions constitute the majority of questions received at most reference desks in public and academic libraries. The tools—both printed and electronic—for answering these questions are quickly learned by the novice reference librarian, and providing answers to these questions soon becomes routine. In some libraries, two separate information service points are maintained: an *information desk* to handle ready reference questions, and a *reference desk* to deal with more difficult and time-consuming questions. Since ready reference questions are such a major component of reference work, it is wise to remember that each question, no matter how routine, is of importance to the user who asks it, and that meeting the information needs of each library user is the goal of an effective reference service.

Bibliographic verification. Another frequently offered information service is bibliographic verification. This is similar to ready reference, except that it provides facts about publications rather than about events, people, places, or organizations. Bibliographic verification typically requires the librarian to search the printed or electronic versions of standard bibliographic tools, such as indexes, catalogs, bibliographies, and library and union catalogs (discussed in chapters 5, 18, and 19), to "verify" that the user's information about a document (i.e., a bibliographic citation) is correct and complete. The neophyte may well wonder why this is such an important part of reference work. The reason is that the habits of students, researchers, and the general public often do not lead to the gathering of complete bibliographic citations. Unfortunately, publications such as newspapers and magazines, and even scholarly books and articles, do not always give complete information about the materials they discuss—complete enough to find those materials in a library or at a bookstore. In addition, students working on assignments may not have written down complete or accurate information about the publications their teachers want them to read, or the teachers may not have given them accurate information. Finally, because of the importance in the scholarly world of the "invisible college"—an informal network of colleagues with similar research interests—many citations are gathered by a researcher in a context that does not always lead to the researcher coming to the library with complete information about the publication which a colleague has recommended. It becomes the librarian's job, in these situations, to try to find complete and accurate information, so that the patron can obtain a copy of the desired book or article.

Bibliographic verification involves using what information is available to the librarian to find the missing information. Occasionally, the librarian will discover, during the search, that the information provided by the reader was not only incomplete but inaccurate as well. At the end of the verification process, the patron will generally have the information needed to locate the item in the library, obtain it on interlibrary loan, or order it at a local bookstore.

Interlibrary loan. Bibliographic verification often leads to an interlibrary loan request if it is determined that the library does not own the item needed by the user. Interlibrary lending of materials has been practiced in American libraries for many years. Because obtaining the document needed by the user is a logical extension of identifying that document (verification), interlibrary loan (ILL) has generally been regarded as a reference function, and it has often been handled by the library's reference department or by a separate department closely associated with the reference department. The ILL process itself includes an important reference function: the borrowing library must carefully verify the bibliographic information about the item requested before the request is forwarded.

The growth of electronic shared cataloging networks, such as OCLC, RLIN, and WLN,[4] has made the interlibrary loan process faster and easier. Thirty years ago, most ILL transactions were manually verified and transmitted by mail. Today, however, when the borrowing and lending libraries both belong to such an electronic network, or to one created for other purposes, the borrowing library may be able both to verify the citation and to place the loan request electronically. When a shared cataloging network is used to request a book, the cataloging record already in the network serves as verification (journal articles, of course, do not have cataloging records, so they still must be separately verified). Also, the request is transmitted instantly; as a result, the library patron should receive the material faster. Even if the borrowing and lending libraries do not belong to the same shared cataloging network, electronic resources can be used to speed the transaction. If only the borrowing library belongs to a shared cataloging network, the necessary verification can be conducted electronically, a process which is generally faster than manual verification using printed tools. Or, if the two libraries both have access to an electronic mail system, the ILL request can be transmitted instantly.

The transmission of interlibrary loan requests using a telefacsimile (fax) device is also gaining favor among libraries.[5] This technique speeds up the transaction in those cases where the borrowing and lending libraries do not belong to the same electronic network. The rapid growth of electronic and telefacsimile communication between libraries suggests that these are becoming the primary methods for transmitting ILL requests.

Information and referral services. Just as reference librarians can identify resources in other libraries which can be borrowed for the user, they can also identify community resources and agencies which can provide the user with needed services or with information which the library does not possess. In the late 1960s and 1970s, the concept of an information and referral service (I & R) developed in a number of public libraries. As defined by Thomas Childers, I & R has as its goal "facilitating the link between a person with a need and the resource or resources outside the library which can meet the need."[6] Outside resources may include social service agencies, community organizations, government offices, or individuals. To support an I & R service, a library generally maintains "a *resource file* — a current list of resources and information pertinent to them."[7] This file may be a manual file or a locally produced database accessed by a microcomputer. This file is the major information tool which the reference librarian consults to refer users to outside agencies that can assist the users further. The file may also be used by the librarian to assist local agencies in identifying resources for their clients; in one study, however, individual users far outnumbered agency users.[8] Most I & R services are designed primarily to direct individuals in the local community to the agencies appropriate to their needs (see box 1.2).

■ ══ ■

1.2

The Public Library as Information Center

There is an obvious need for some institution to be responsible for supplying information that will guide the public through the maze of government and private service agencies spawned by our complex society. Not knowing where to start in their search for information or direct assistance, all too commonly, people are shunted around from one waiting line or telephone number to another. Many become too discouraged to continue what seems like a futile pursuit. Whenever I & R service is introduced in public libraries, it proves to be extremely helpful and is invariably used extensively.

The public library has the capability of serving as the first-stop center for all information needs. Not only can it lend books, it can expand its reference service to link people to the information or practical assistance they need wherever the source exists, in or out of the library. The demonstrated need for this service, together with a growing recognition of the public library's broader information capability, are inspiring increasing numbers of public libraries to consider utilizing traditional professional skills to "index the community."

— Clara Stanton Jones
"The Public Library as the Comprehensive
Community Information Center"[9]

There are two basic types of I & R services: those which only provide information about agencies, and those which provide information and make direct referrals to agencies. Those which provide an agency name, address, and telephone number to the user, along with some information about the agency, are the easiest for a library to set up and maintain; however, the librarian usually never finds out if the referral was successful. I & R services which actually contact the agency to verify that it can and will assist the individual require much more time and effort in organizing material, training staff, and coordinating service with local agencies. However, the success rate of referrals using this approach — and, therefore, the effectiveness of this reference service — can be much higher than for other types.[10] A national survey by Childers, in the late 1970s, found that most public libraries that offer I & R services provide information only rather than actual referrals, although many libraries did acknowledge giving advice along with information on local agencies.[11]

Cooperative reference service. Another form of referral in reference work is the referring of a user's reference question to another library. This occurs often in small or specialized libraries, when the reference librarian exhausts the sources available. At this point, the question can usually be referred to another library which, under a cooperative agreement, pursues the question further.

The organization of cooperative reference services of this nature varies. Local libraries participating in a consortium may refer reference questions among themselves, and services of this kind are also usually organized at the state level. One of the more highly developed cooperative reference programs is that in Illinois, which has a statewide network comprised of libraries of all kinds. The state is divided into eighteen regional systems. Each system contains a headquarters library with its own reference collection and staff. Reference questions are referred to this library from any participating library in the system. If the question cannot be answered by the headquarters staff, it is referred to one of the four Illinois Research and Reference Centers (IRRCs). These centers are located in the Illinois State

Library, in the Chicago Public Library, and in two academic libraries—the University of Illinois at Urbana-Champaign and Southern Illinois University at Carbondale. Reference staff members in the IRRCs have direct access to the large collections of their host libraries, and can answer most questions not answerable at the local or system level.

Much cooperative reference service is handled in a more informal manner. The telephone is often the librarian's most useful reference tool. When the answer to a question is elusive, the librarian can call another library and ask a reference librarian there for assistance. In these situations, it is often advantageous to let the users convey their information needs directly to the second librarian. On other occasions, however, if the first librarian has done a considerable amount of work on the question, the librarian may be in a better position than the user to describe the question and relate what sources have already been checked. Experience, and the policies and procedures followed by the library or reference department, are the best guides to use in any given situation.

Whether formal or informal channels are used to refer a question to another library, the librarian who first receives the question must carefully and thoroughly discuss the question with the user. Unless the patron talks directly to the second librarian by telephone, the second librarian can deal only with the question as it is communicated by the librarian who initiates the referral. If this communication is erroneous or incomplete, the user may not receive the answer sought. Although such questions are often renegotiated later, this is time-consuming both for the user and for the librarian. As with interlibrary loan interactions, accuracy on the part of both the patron and the librarian is necessary for a successful outcome.[12]

Research questions. Both ready reference and bibliographic verification interactions may evolve into yet another major information service, the provision of research assistance. This service, when compared to answering ready reference questions, may require considerably more time and effort from the librarian. The user's information need is broader; the questions asked are usually more complex or less concretely defined. Several sources may need to be checked before the complete answer is found. It may not even be immediately apparent to the librarian which type of reference tool is likely to contain the needed information. In this case, an intermediary source, such as a guide or index to reference tools, must be consulted to obtain a list of likely sources.

The librarian must, when providing research assistance, carefully review the question with the user, to ensure that the question is completely understood by both parties. This interactive process, called a *reference interview*, is described at length in chapter 3. The reference interview is necessary to clarify many reference questions, because the user's information need may be broader than initially conceived. The need may also be of sufficient complexity that the librarian must ask a series of questions about it before enough is understood to begin thinking of appropriate sources to search. As the search progresses, both the question and possible answers are further discussed. The conscientious librarian ensures that the patron is completely satisfied with the information provided before ending the interaction.

Often, during a reference transaction of this nature, either the librarian or the patron must interrupt the search process to attend to other activities. The handling of this situation depends to some degree upon the service policies of the individual library. The librarian may work further on the question as time permits and call the patron by telephone at a later time. If the patron has more time but the librarian does not, the librarian may advise or instruct the patron how to continue the search. This latter scenario is most likely in an academic or school library, but may occur also in a public library. In special libraries, it is generally assumed that the librarian will continue the search and deliver the information as soon as possible.

Selective dissemination of information. A form of continuing research assistance which has been developed and refined in the past thirty years is selective dissemination of information (SDI). SDI is a customized reference service; it is offered most frequently to researchers who use academic or special libraries (see box 1.3).

■ ═══ ■

1.3

Customized Services in Special Libraries

When the clientele is limited to a particular organization, special libraries often develop close working relationships with their users and are able to identify, not only on an organizational basis but also on an individual basis, the type of information needed and how it should be delivered. Thus services can be closely tailored to fit the needs and working habits of the users.

— Elin B. Christianson
"Special Libraries"[13]

Alternately, it may be referred to as a *current awareness* service, because it is designed to keep researchers aware of current developments as reflected in the literature of their fields. The researcher describes for the librarian an ongoing information need, and the librarian creates a profile of the information to be delivered to the researcher on an ongoing basis. SDI may involve something as simple and routine as providing the researcher with copies of tables of contents from selected journals received by the library. On a more advanced level, it involves delivering to the researcher recently published articles on a specific topic, or at least a list of citations to those articles. This can now be accomplished electronically. The librarian can access appropriate databases online, conduct a search that matches the profile of the researcher's information need, and request (online) that the same search be repeated each time the database is updated. The resulting citations can be mailed to the librarian or directly to the researcher. Although the automated approach to SDI takes very little time and is preferred by many librarians, manual SDI programs — which provide greater flexibility and may be offered for free — can still be effective.[14]

Database searches. The character and importance of electronic database searching as a reference service are discussed at length in chapter 5. Here, suffice to say that the proliferation of databases remotely searchable with a computer terminal and a modem attached to a telephone line has allowed librarians to identify certain kinds of information more quickly and more comprehensively than was previously possible. Companies that specialize in the management of electronic databases offer to libraries, for a fee, access to electronically retrievable information in a wide variety of disciplines. The information these databases contain is of two basic types: bibliographic and nonbibliographic. The bibliographic information consists of citations to literature such as books, journal articles, research reports, and other documents. The nonbibliographic information is varied; some databases provide statistics, others offer summaries of news events, directory information, or other factual data. A growing number of databases provide the full text of documents ranging from encyclopedias to scientific journals.

In reference work, database searches can be performed either in a ready reference transaction or in the provision of research assistance. In a ready reference interaction, the librarian may dial onto a database to find a fact or a statistic. This quick and closely circumscribed search can be fully and easily integrated into routine reference service. When providing research assistance, however, the librarian uses a computer search most frequently to provide the patron with comprehensive information about a topic or with a comprehensive list of citations to literature on that topic. This service requires a careful reference interview and an online session that often involves a search of several databases. Consequently, it usually must be offered, by appointment, in a separate location from the reference desk. Although it may be feasible to offer on-the-spot searches of this nature in some settings or at certain times, it is often impossible to integrate this service into the normal flow of reference work as efficiently as reference librarians might like. In fact, a recent study of online searching in public libraries showed that online searches conducted in a location other than the reference desk were generally more successful.[15]

Other forms of database searching provided by reference librarians include searches of local and regional online catalogs, national shared cataloging networks, and locally produced databases. The growing number of CD-ROM workstations,[16] which allow library users to perform their own electronic database searching, adds to the impact the electronic revolution has had on reference services. Database searching, in all its forms, greatly increases the reference librarian's ability to meet users' information needs completely and efficiently.

Information brokering. An important consequence of the increasing number of online databases and the expansion of the kinds of information accessible via computer and telephone lines is the ability to gather information independent of a library. For centuries libraries have, along with governments, been the primary custodians of information. The fact that libraries collected printed books and journals in numbers beyond the budgets of either individuals or businesses meant that individuals or businesses in search of information went to libraries to find that information. Now, however, many individuals and most businesses have access to much information, particularly current information, online. Although this has freed business from dependence on libraries, it has also freed librarians from that same dependence. Some librarians have found it challenging and profitable to leave their library jobs and set up their own information services, offering to gather, evaluate, and package information for their clients for a fee. These professionals are generally referred to as *information brokers*.

Information brokering is one example of the fact that online searching skills make librarians essential even when libraries are not. The increasingly sophisticated knowledge and skills required to retrieve comprehensive and accurate information from among hundreds of online databases, coupled with the demand for that information, have made information brokering profitable. Individuals needing specific, hard-to-find information, and businesses needing large quantities of information quickly and accurately, turn to information brokers for assistance. These brokers may locate information on an occasional basis, or they may develop close and lasting business relationships with their clients, providing SDI services, consulting on information needs or programs, and performing ready reference services or any number of related activities. Like special librarians, they go beyond informing their clients of the existence of information sources; to be successful, they often must deliver either the documents themselves or analytical abstracts or summaries based on a reading of a number of printed or full-text online sources.[17]

Instruction

Instruction is a major component of reference service in academic and school libraries and an important aspect of reference work in most public libraries. It is also found in varying degrees in different kinds of special libraries. Instruction is conducted with individual library users and also with groups of users. Three of the most frequent forms it takes are: teaching how to use the library effectively; suggesting specific strategies to be used in locating information; and instructing in the use of specific information sources.

Instructional activities have often been viewed as an alternative to information services—teaching users how to find information, rather than finding it for them. This approach is sometimes necessary, for instance, with class assignments, when the number of users seeking information exceeds the reference staff's ability to research each question individually. However, instruction is increasingly viewed in a broader context. The sources of information in our society, both printed and electronic, are rapidly growing in number and complexity. Users who are unaware of the existence, content, and organization of these sources may never know the extent of available information about a topic of interest to them. The need for instruction that explains how information is organized and how it can be effectively accessed and used—what is described in chapter 6 as "information management education"—has become clear to the library profession. A policy statement adopted by the Council of the American Library Association in 1980 states that "it is essential that libraries of all types accept the responsibility of providing people with opportunities to understand the organization of information."[18] The statement goes on to urge all libraries "to include instruction in the use of libraries as one of the primary goals of service."[19]

Basic types of instruction are described briefly in this chapter. The role of instruction in reference work is discussed fully in chapter 6.

One-to-one instruction. Helping an individual library patron understand the organization and use of the library's collection is the oldest and still most commonly practiced form of instruction. It usually evolves naturally out of a reference interview, particularly in cases in which the person is using the library for the first time or is conducting research which requires use of unfamiliar reference tools. In the first case, the librarian typically explains the organization of the library and how to use the catalog which provides access to its collection. When instructing in the use of printed tools, librarians must inform users as to the organization and scope of each tool and explain how to access the relevant information in it. This is best taught by example: the librarian demonstrates the use of the tool by finding relevant citations or data, and makes sure the user understands the process well enough to continue the search.

Increasingly, one-to-one instruction involves helping users learn how to search electronic databases, such as the library's online catalog or a bibliographic database at a CD-ROM workstation. Although both of these computerized tools may be designed to be user-friendly, there are inevitably ambiguities or questions that cannot be answered by either online or printed aids. Again, demonstrating a successful search is a more effective teaching technique than merely telling the user how to conduct one.

As is pointed out in chapter 6, one-to-one instruction can now be accomplished effectively at a computer terminal, as well as in person. Computer programs can provide physical orientation to the library and instruction in the use of important library resources. Printed guides can also be stored in a computer's memory, from which they can be downloaded and/or printed out by individuals who access the computer from locations outside the library.

Group instruction. In many situations, a number of individuals are new to a community, whether that community be a town, an academic institution, or a private or public organization. It is more efficient to introduce these individuals to the library in a group, rather than one by one; hence the popularity of the *library tour* or *orientation program*. It is important that new users learn the locations of important library units and equipment, and that they meet, whenever possible, the reference staff who are there to serve their information needs. While printed guides, computer programs, and audio or video presentations can all add significant information to a library orientation, the human touch provided by a personal tour is the most effective way truly to *welcome* individuals to the library and encourage them to contact the librarians for assistance in the future.

In school and academic settings, librarians, working with teachers, often speak to all the students in a specific class who will be using the library for a research assignment. At its most basic level, *course-related instruction*, this talk may consist of a tour of the library, along with an introduction to reference sources in the subject areas covered by the course and suggestions as to their effective use in research. When teacher and librarian work together in designing the library-use activities of a course, a higher level of instruction, *course-integrated instruction*, can result. Here, the library instruction becomes a required part of the assignment, and the librarian acts more as a teacher: discussing the assignment, suggesting strategies for meeting the objectives of the assignment, and discussing reference sources as tools to be used in meeting those objectives.[20] Although course-related instruction is valuable, and is still widely practiced, instruction librarians are moving away, whenever possible, from talking about information sources as ends in themselves, in favor of "a problem-based approach to information gathering" in which sources "serve a secondary role ... as examples of items useful to patrons in the search for information."[21] This kind of discussion is facilitated by course-integrated instruction, in which the librarian's expertise is recognized by both teacher and students as an essential component of the course.

New forms of group instruction have emerged in recent years. One example is workshops for college faculty to teach them concepts and methods of electronic database searching. The number of such programs is likely to increase as more sources of information become accessible to users outside the confines of the library building.

Guidance

The guidance function of reference service, though not as often discussed in the library literature as information and instruction, has just as long a history. During the first half of the century, it was prominently represented in public libraries in the form of readers' advisory services. Though these services have been less visible in recent years, the guidance function survives in libraries in other forms, such as bibliotherapy in special libraries and term-paper counseling in school and academic libraries. Furthermore, as more information retrieval occurs outside libraries, the guidance function of reference service may increase. Even when librarians are no longer in control of the access to information sources, they still are likely to understand better than many users the principles and techniques of information storage and retrieval. Consequently, the guidance function may again gain prominence in the electronic age, in the form of information consulting. However, instead of guiding library users in the choice of books and other reading material, librarians will be guiding them in the choice of electronic information sources.

Readers' advisory services. It could be argued that readers' advisory services most clearly reflect the goals of the late nineteenth-century librarians who developed the concept of personal assistance to readers. Samuel Green, whose 1876 article, "Personal Relations Between Librarians and Readers," is generally credited with stimulating the development of reference services, placed great emphasis upon helping readers choose the books best suited to their interests, needs, and reading level.[22] The need for such a service was gradually recognized in public libraries. Although the first readers' advisory department was not established until 1923 (in the Chicago Public Library), there was a clear precursor of this service as early as 1885, when the St. Louis Public Library created the position of "library hostess."[23]

The classic readers' advisor interviewed library users to understand their needs and goals, and then chose library materials that would fulfill those needs and goals. In many cases, a formal reading list was prepared for the user. Readers' advisors also sometimes provided current awareness services and library-use instruction to assist readers in using the library and keeping aware of new books in their fields of interest.[24] Readers' advisory services proliferated rapidly in the 1920s, had their "golden age" in the 1930s, declined in the 1940s, and all but disappeared in the 1950s, their essential functions taken over by general reference librarians or subject specialists.[25] Their spirit survives, however, in other forms of guidance, such as term-paper counseling in academic libraries. In some public libraries, readers' advisory services still seek to help users identify fictional and other recreational materials to satisfy their individual interests and tastes.[26]

Bibliotherapy. Bibliotherapy is a more specialized form of guidance, related in its goals to readers' advisory work but generally practiced in a group. Though not, strictly speaking, a reference service, it has been practiced alongside traditional reference services and readers' advisory services in programs such as the Counselor Librarianship Project at the Chicago campus of the University of Illinois in 1951.[27] Originally, bibliotherapy involved using directed reading to aid in a physical or emotional healing process. Today, bibliotherapists use literature, film, or other media chosen for their appropriateness to the needs of the group, to assist the personal growth and/or rehabilitation of group members through discussion of the material read or viewed.

Practitioners have distinguished two primary types of bibliotherapy: clinical and developmental.[28] *Clinical bibliotherapy* is used by doctors and hospital librarians with persons who have emotional or behavior problems, such as mental patients, to encourage self-understanding or behavior change. *Developmental bibliotherapy* is used with normal individuals in schools or in public libraries to promote self-knowledge, personal growth, and the successful completion of "developmental tasks" associated with various life stages. Clara Lack, who has practiced bibliotherapy in both hospital and public library settings, encourages public libraries to adapt the techniques of developmental bibliotherapy and create "readers' discussion groups" in which literature can be used as a basis for examining both individual and societal values and goals.[29] Although bibliotherapy requires specialized training and is not widely practiced, continuing interest in its techniques and goals is demonstrated in recent articles by Arleen Hynes and Alice Smith.[30]

Term-paper counseling. Another form of guidance is *term-paper counseling* (sometimes called *term-paper assistance* or *research consultation*). Although generally discussed in the literature as a form of instruction, it is treated here as a guidance service because of its parallels to the readers' advisory services formerly offered extensively in public libraries. Term-paper counseling, like the readers' advisory service, is usually offered at a location other than the reference desk, where the librarian can spend more time guiding each student on an individual basis. Like users of a readers' advisory service, the consumers of term-paper assistance approach the term-paper counseling desk or office, on their own initiative, to seek assistance in reaching a specific goal attainable only through the use of library materials (in this case, the completion of a research paper). The librarian considers each student's needs, assesses the student's understanding of library use and search strategies, and provides individualized guidance regarding which library tools should be consulted to find appropriate sources of information on the student's topic. The librarian will probably write down a list of reference sources to be checked, much as the readers' advisor would compile a list of suggested readings on a topic.

Term-paper counseling programs are very widespread in academic libraries. Some are offered year-round; others are offered only at the peak term-paper-writing times of each semester. Either way, these programs offer a level of flexibility and individualized attention which is not usually available either at the reference desk or in group instructional programs.[31] *Term-paper clinics*, which consist of group instruction in library-use and research skills, may be offered in addition to or instead of the individual assistance provided in term-paper counseling sessions.[32]

Research advice and consulting. These two activities are discussed together because they share the same basic characteristics. In each case, the librarian provides guidance regarding a project which a user (or client) is pursuing. Whether in a formal consulting agreement or in a reference-desk encounter, librarians are approached for advice because of their expertise in the area of information retrieval and management. In some cases, a consultant may be asked to participate in the implementation of the librarian's recommendations. In others, and in research assistance situations, advice is the only commodity the librarian is asked to provide.[33]

Consultants may be information brokers or they may be full-time librarians. Their availability as consultants is made known to clients through publicity or some other means (for example, the *Directory of Library and Information Professionals*[34] indicates if the individuals listed are available for consulting). After negotiating, both client and consultant sign a formal contract specifying the purpose of their relationship and what is expected of each party. Generally, the consultant writes a report recommending specific courses of action to help the client reach the stated goals. Muriel Regan lists implementation of computerized reference services, evaluation of reference services, design of a reference area, and similar projects as possible consulting opportunities for the reference librarian.[35]

Research advice may be offered in a normal reference-desk encounter, or by appointment with a reference librarian or information specialist. The user is interested in pursuing research on a given topic—for example, genealogical research—but does not know how to proceed. The librarian is approached for advice. Many public libraries offer research advice to users who are investigating their family histories. The librarian typically offers advice on how to conduct this kind of research, suggests sources of information, and explains to the user how to obtain documents that are not in the local collection. In an academic library, research advice is frequently offered to faculty and students. In addition to providing information on the topic and instruction in the use of relevant reference tools, the librarian offers guidance on the most effective strategy for locating further information, recommending specific tools, special collections, or electronic resources as options for proceeding with the research project.

Developments in the History
of Reference Services

Early History

Charles Bunge noted that historians of reference services usually trace modern concepts of reference work to Samuel Green's 1876 paper, "Personal Relations Between Librarians and Readers,"[36] later published in *American Library Journal* (now *Library Journal*).[37] Until that time, Bunge writes, libraries concentrated on acquiring and organizing materials, and library users were expected to find what they needed independently.[38] Green's paper is both quaint and surprisingly modern in its concept of reference work. It is interesting to note that all three reference functions—information, instruction, and guidance—are touched upon in Green's paper. He advised librarians in public libraries that many patrons, particularly working men and businessmen, have neither the knowledge nor the time to search for the information they need, so the librarian should find the information and present it to them. When young people come to the library to work on school assignments, Green advised instruction in the use of encyclopedias and indexes to books, along with an invitation to ask for assistance if the needed information is not readily found. He also pointed out that librarians are frequently asked for guidance in the choice of recreational reading materials or in the conduct of research into specific topics. In all of these cases, Green pointed out, individuals do not know how to use a library effectively on their own, as do scholars. He also noted that friendly and effective assistance to users will bring citizens to the library and cause the community to view its public library as indispensable.[39]

Green's ideas were presented at a time when printed library aids, such as the dictionary catalog, the Dewey Decimal Classification system, and periodical indexes, were also beginning to make it easier to find information in the library and within library materials. Although some librarians regarded these aids as sufficient, during the 1880s and 1890s the need for special full-time staff trained in the principles of assisting library users in their search for information gained wide recognition and acceptance. This new activity, initially called "assistance to readers," was known by the 1890s as "reference work." By 1883, public libraries in several large cities offered classes for "reference assistants." In 1887, the first library school opened at Columbia College. By 1900, many public libraries had reference rooms, where reference materials were available on open shelves and reference librarians were ready to provide assistance in the use of library materials.[40]

The Twentieth Century

During the first half of the twentieth century, the concepts and practices of reference work were expanded, and specialized services such as readers' advisory and bibliotherapy (discussed earlier) were developed. Early in the century, public library reference departments began answering information requests by telephone. About the same time, they began providing reference services in branch libraries, in addition to those offered in the reference room of the central library.[41] In public libraries, the establishment of separate collections, in areas such as business, science, music, and art, began as early as 1913. A similar trend in academic libraries occurred in the 1930s, when some libraries created separate units to serve faculty and students in specific subject departments.[42] In both types of libraries, a consequence of this departmentalization was the need for reference librarians with appropriate subject backgrounds. This evolution of subject departments has continued to the present day, contributing to a lively discussion as to whether centralized or decentralized reference services are the most effective mode of service (see chapter 9).

At the same time, the growth of *special libraries*—libraries established to serve primarily employees of the institutions which created them—exerted a profound effect upon the concepts and practices of reference work. The idea of special libraries developed in the early years of the century, beginning with the establishment of the Legislative Reference Service of the State of Wisconsin in 1900. Based on that example, special libraries were later created in industrial research laboratories, businesses, and health care institutions. The significance of special libraries for the development of reference service was that, unlike other libraries, special libraries existed primarily to provide service rather than to build and house collections.[43] This freed the special librarian to pursue a higher standard of reference service, based on "a detailed knowledge by the librarian of the information needs of the clientele, ... a willingness to seek out needed information from any source, and an ability to synthesize or otherwise to prepare information for use by the client."[44] This approach to reference work emphasized information functions almost exclusively, rather than the guidance and instruction functions which had predominated in the early development of reference services in public and academic libraries.

The Issue of Levels of Service

The growth of special libraries and the evolution toward subject departments in academic and large public libraries presented the library profession with a different concept of reference work. Rather than assisting users in finding information, reference librarians, in this view, should determine a user's information needs, use their bibliographic and subject expertise to locate the needed information, analyze the value of the information retrieved, and then present it to the user. The coexistence of this new concept of reference work with the traditional concept of primarily providing only assistance to users was first discussed by James Wyer, in his 1930 text, *Reference Work*.[45]

Wyer surveyed the literature of reference services and identified three "distinct conceptions" of reference work: conservative, moderate, and liberal. These three concepts vary in their outlooks regarding "the kind and amount of service ... which properly may be given to patrons."[46] The *conservative* approach to reference services emphasizes assistance to users, as the users conduct their own information searches. To do more than assist is to do the users' work for them; instead, the librarian should instruct users so that they will become more proficient and independent researchers. The answering of ready reference questions is still viewed as the librarian's province, but for complicated, time-consuming questions, users should be helped in their searches. It is argued that no library has the staff to answer completely the information needs of every patron who approaches the reference desk. Therefore, quick factual questions can be handled by the reference librarian, but research is the user's responsibility, and the librarian's role must be limited to the provision of assistance, instruction, and suggestions.[47]

The *liberal* view, which Wyer called "ideal" and hoped would one day be practiced in all libraries, argues that the library should "wish to find or create ways and means to satisfy every questioner."[48] The reference librarian should make every user's information need the librarian's responsibility, not the user's. As Green argued in 1876, the liberal view claims that the user cannot be expected to understand how to access the increasingly complex array of reference tools. However, rather than attempting to teach the user, the librarian should personally research each question and deliver the answer to the user. The reference librarian is thus presented as an expert in the field of information retrieval; the user is presumably happy with the service received and views the library in a more positive light.

The *moderate* concept of reference work was viewed by Wyer in 1930 as a compromise, and it has been described in less charitable terms since.[49] Not comfortable with the conservative view, but believing they lack the resources and/or the expertise to implement the liberal view, practitioners of the moderate approach to reference services offer varying degrees of service to different users at different times. The amount and kind of service are likely to vary according to how busy the reference desk is,[50] but may also be influenced by the status of the questioner or the way in which the question is received.[51] The moderate concept of reference services could thus be viewed as emphasizing expediency and the need for users, in many but not all cases, to learn how to use reference tools themselves. On the other hand, many reference librarians would argue that what is referred to as "moderate" is actually the maximum service they can provide, because of time, budget, equipment, or skill limitations, rather than because of an unconstrained decision to limit the services offered to users.

Discussion of optimal kinds and levels of reference service continues today. In the past twenty years, however, the significant impact of electronic reference resources on the retrieval of information and the enormous burgeoning of interest in instructional services have changed somewhat the focus of the discussion. The plethora of electronic reference tools available to the reference librarian has enormously increased information retrieval capabilities. At the same time, users can, if they possess a computer, modem, and some searching knowledge, access many databases independently, without involving a librarian in the information retrieval process. To some, this means that librarians must offer the maximum level of services or risk losing their clientele. To others, this is an opportunity for further instructional activities. In a sense, the debate over levels of service has been transformed into an "instruction versus information" debate. As Brian Nielsen pointed out, this debate centers on the role of the reference librarian as an intermediary, with the information advocates emphasizing this role as desirable and the instruction supporters claiming that information retrieval and use are essential life skills which should be taught to all interested individuals.[52] In practice, most librarians simply agree that a variety of services, carefully and intelligently geared to the actual needs of specific user groups, can effectively demonstrate their value to their public.

Library Systems and Networks

Reference work has been enriched since the 1960s and 1970s by the growth of state, regional, and local library consortia and systems, and by the development of electronic shared cataloging networks at the national level. Both have made it easier to locate needed sources in other libraries, and the cataloging networks in particular are very useful for bibliographic verification questions.

Library consortia and systems represent attempts by all kinds of libraries to improve their services to their users through cooperative activities in collection development, reference services, and document delivery. Most notable has been the growth of state and regional systems. The characteristics of these systems vary from one state to another. In some cases, membership is restricted to libraries of one type (e.g., public libraries), while in others all kinds of libraries are included. The model of cooperative reference services followed by library systems in Illinois (described earlier in this chapter) may occur to varying degrees in the systems created in other states.[53]

These systems are very helpful to smaller libraries, although users of larger libraries also benefit from easier access to specialized materials in the collections of other system members. The advantages to reference librarians are many, particularly since the recent creation of online union catalogs for many of these systems. If a user's information need cannot be met with the tools at hand, the reference librarian can consult the online union catalog to identify relevant materials in one of the other libraries in the system. Typically, these titles can then be charged to the user and expeditiously delivered to the requesting library.

A concomitant development has been the growth of national electronic shared cataloging networks, such as OCLC and RLIN. For the purposes of reference work, these networks function as online union catalogs for the member libraries (at least for materials cataloged since each library joined), and they allow the reference librarian quickly to verify the user's citation and determine where a copy may be obtained. Sometimes, in fact, they help librarians find the items in their own libraries, as in the case of a user whose citation is to a title which is part of a series: if the library has cataloged the item only by series title (which is unknown to the user), a check of RLIN or OCLC by the title of the individual piece will (if another library cataloged this title separately) lead the librarian to the series title by which the item is retrievable in that library's own collection. OCLC and RLIN can also be used to identify specific editions of a work, or to locate other works by a particular author, beyond those listed in a single library's catalog.

■ ══ ■

1.4

Reference Services Yesterday and Today

Comparing past and present reference practices can be both interesting and informative. One way to do this is to browse through a reference services textbook from an earlier era and compare it to this text. A good choice might be Margaret Hutchins' *Introduction to Reference Work*, published in 1944.[54] Another valuable exercise is to think back to your childhood experiences in libraries. Do you remember times when a librarian in your school or public library assisted you in finding information or in using the library?

Based on these exercises, how do you feel reference work has changed in the past twenty years, or in the past fifty years? How has it remained essentially the same?

Some Current Trends and Issues

Librarianship is a vibrant profession, constantly changing in response to new societal and technological developments. Reference librarians care deeply about providing services of high quality, services that meet the information needs of their users and are perceived by the users as satisfying those needs. How best to achieve these objectives in a rapidly changing environment, with limited personnel and financial resources, is not always clear. Thus, reference librarians, like all professionals, have differing opinions about how their work should be conducted. These differences are reflected in the published literature of librarianship. This section introduces the reader to four recent developments in reference services and discusses some of the issues related to these developments, in order to provide a context for understanding concepts discussed in other chapters.

Electronic Reference Services

The computer has revolutionized access to information in libraries of all kinds and sizes. Online catalog terminals and indexes on CD-ROM workstations allow users to search databases in their entirety, saving the users the task of searching numerous catalog drawers or annual volumes of printed indexes. The results can often be printed out, saving the users the drudgery of writing out each citation they wish to pursue. Increasingly, libraries (particularly academic libraries) are also providing—at the same terminals used for online catalog searching—free access to externally produced databases covering journal literature.[55] Specialized, locally produced databases allow retrieval of previously hard-to-find facts, addresses, or bibliographic information. CD-ROM workstations offer users free and direct access to electronic databases which, if searched by a librarian in a dial-up search session, might require users to pay the cost of the search. Almost 1,400 commercial databases are now available in CD-ROM format.[56] Some libraries have begun receiving and answering reference questions by electronic mail.[57] While some users still exhibit uncertainty or distrust, a new computer-literate generation has come to appreciate the power of electronic retrieval and to expect the opportunity to search a given tool electronically rather than in printed format.

What does this mean for reference librarians? For one thing, it means the ability to answer many questions faster and more easily. For example, it is many times faster to find either a citation for a specific dissertation, or citations for many dissertations in a given subject area, electronically than to search the annual printed index. It also boosts the professional standing of the librarian with library users. Library users familiar only with traditional library services are amazed and impressed when the reference librarian, without leaving the desk, moves quickly and confidently from one online database to another to find an elusive citation or to print out the full text of a periodical or newspaper article. Both the speed of dial-up retrieval and the convenience of CD-ROM searching help users appreciate the value of libraries as sources of information.

It is undeniable that the computer has increased the cost of providing reference service. Although the cost of dial-up searches is often passed on to users, the expenses of CD-ROM workstations, which are considerable, are borne by the library. Also, despite the user-friendly nature of these workstations, patrons often need assistance to use them effectively, and the equipment frequently needs maintenance and resupply. The growing profusion of electronic sources—at the same time important new printed reference tools are also being published—places an additional burden on the librarian to maintain professional skills and knowledge. The benefits of electronic searching, however, are generally regarded as far greater than the problems they create, and the advantages to users are so great that reference librarians (and library administrators) generally eagerly embrace each new application of this technology.

Electronic searching, while boosting the power and importance of reference librarians, has also appeared to some to be a potential threat to that importance. Users can now retrieve information on their own, without coming to the library or engaging the services of a librarian. During evening and weekend hours, users can search Dialog's "Knowledge Index" databases or those on BRS/After Dark at rates cheaper than those available to librarians during business hours. As more information is made available directly to consumers, will libraries and librarians be seen as less worthy of financial support?[58]

Several responses to this question are possible. One is that, even if individuals have the ability to access databases directly, they may not have the expertise and background to use them knowledgeably, accurately, and efficiently. The trained librarian does, however, possess those qualities. Secondly, if libraries can find a way to offer online searching services to the public at no charge—as they have always done with printed tools—they can maintain their value to sophisticated users while also assuring that their traditional role of providing information regardless of the user's financial status continues. CD-ROM databases appear to be an effective response of this type; they offer users free electronic searching within the library.[59] Another option for librarians is to use their skills to facilitate electronic searching by users through instruction programs. Information management education, discussed further in chapter 6, seeks to share with users a librarian's knowledge of and experience in the organization and retrieval of information. The status of librarians as experts and as professionals remains intact, and their importance is recognized, but they function as guides, yielding control of the actual search and retrieval process to the individuals who will ultimately use and benefit from the information retrieved.

Reference Service Effectiveness

The evaluation of reference services—question-answering, instruction, and database searching, among others—has elicited much interest in recent years. Evaluation of instructional programs has been seen as increasingly vital, and it is discussed further in chapter 6. The area in which the most startling results have occurred has been the evaluation of the handling of factual questions at the reference desk. The technique used (discussed further in chapter 8) is unobtrusive evaluation, that is, evaluation conducted without the knowledge of the reference staff to whom the questions in the study are posed.

Ironically, at the same time that the computer has given greater retrieval power to the reference librarian, unobtrusive studies of reference staff have generally shown that only 50 to 60 percent of ready reference questions posed at reference desks are answered correctly.[60] These findings have disturbed many in the profession, and they have given rise to a number of observations and suggestions (including the observation that the effectiveness of reference service is based upon more than the answering of factual questions).[61] Joan Durrance, in a study that defined success not in terms of accuracy but in terms of the client's willingness to return to the same librarian in the future, points out how factors in the reference environment often contribute to negative perceptions on the part of library users.[62] Ian Douglas believes that reference service effectiveness can be improved if librarians carefully notice which questions lead to "unsatisfactory outcomes" and pursue activities, such as further acquisition of or training in the use of specific types of reference tools, to attempt to deal with such observed failures.[63] It has become clear that reference desk services, to be more effective, must be observed more carefully, discussed more thoughtfully, and supported more fully by staff development and continuing education activities for reference staff.

Burnout

It is pointed out in chapter 7 that staff development and continuing education activities are also valuable weapons against a common malady among reference librarians: burnout, an overwhelming feeling of frustration, apathy, and exhaustion regarding one's work.[64] The causes and pervasiveness of burnout among reference librarians have been variously described in recent literature. William Miller sees the problem as resulting from too many new services and activities—online searching, instruction, committee work—added to traditional reference desk service, with no increase in staff to handle the new activities.[65] Charles Bunge writes of "a gap between the ideals of reference librarianship that [librarians] believe and espouse and the realities of reference service that can be practiced."[66] Box 1.5 summarizes the contributions of the reference librarian, the job, the library user, and the organization to the development of burnout symptoms.

■ ══ ■

1.5
The Genesis of Burnout

Many information professionals, fresh from graduate school, enter their first job filled with enthusiasm, eager to make a difference and to help people meet their information needs.... New librarians are not on the job for long, however, before they realize that their own needs and expectations do not always match the needs and expectations of their organization or their clients. Workloads are often too heavy for the time allotted; staff are expected to perform many jobs simultaneously; positive feedback, from either clients or the organization, is usually scarce.... Many organizations don't give staff a chance for input into their own destinies. These are some of the chronic stresses that can turn enthusiasm into stagnation, frustration, and eventually, apathy.

— Mary Haack, John W. Jones, and Tina Roose
"Occupational Burnout Among Librarians"[67]

Many coping mechanisms have been suggested for overcoming these feelings and regaining a positive outlook toward the job. The organization can assist by offering reference librarians options such as job sharing and job exchange, and by encouraging librarians to undertake new and different assignments periodically to assure that their jobs do not become too routine or lacking in challenge.[68] The training and development techniques described in chapter 7 are designed to support employees and feed their self-esteem and self-confidence. The reference manager can also attempt to keep reference desk hours at a reasonable level, so that staff are not burned out by excessive contact with the public.

These methods depend on the concern and flexibility of the organization. Individuals also have the ability to heal themselves and to aid in maintaining the professional health of their colleagues. They can develop support systems with colleagues, and can avoid becoming overextended by learning to decline jobs and to give up overly demanding job responsibilities.[69] They can also free themselves of timetables that are too rigid and from the trap of trying to live up to someone else's expectations.[70] It also helps to exercise regularly, to dissipate job tensions, and to attend workshops and conferences to expand professional contacts and exchange information and ideas.[71]

As Tina Roose pointed out, those who are burned out were all once on fire.[72] Avoiding burnout requires thinking carefully and positively about oneself and one's work, avoiding excessive commitments while doing one's best to achieve reasonable yet challenging goals. Sharing both one's excitement and one's frustrations with trusted colleagues, and maintaining an objective interest in serving the needs of one's users, while steadily learning new ways to serve those needs, can help one stay on the course of job satisfaction and professional growth.

The Use of Nonprofessionals in Reference Service

Closely related to both burnout and the effectiveness of reference service is the increasing use of nonprofessionals in reference work. These nonprofessionals may be permanent paraprofessional staff, graduate students in library and information science who hold assistantships in the library, or part-time college undergraduates. Nonprofessionals can help professional reference staff fend off burnout by staffing the reference desk or by handling ready reference and directional questions at a separate information desk. Because they generally have not completed a full formal educational program in reference service, a carefully designed training program for them is necessary if they are to provide accurate and effective service.

The use of nonprofessional staff in reference service has been called "one of the hottest topics of debate in the literature of librarianship."[73] It has been argued that a large majority of the questions asked at a typical reference desk could be successfully answered by well-trained nonprofessionals.[74] The concern of many in the profession, however, is that nonprofessional staff may lack the knowledge and experience to recognize when a seemingly simple question hides a different or more complex information need which the user either does not recognize or does not realize is within the power of the librarian to answer.[75] One study showed that patrons reported that their information needs were satisfied less often when they were helped by a nonprofessional staff member than when a professional assisted them.[76] Others have responded that, with proper training and support, nonprofessionals at a reference desk or at a separate information desk can effectively determine when a question is within their level of expertise and when a referral to a professional librarian is desirable. A critical factor in the success of nonprofessionals may be the presence of a professional librarian or other staff member nearby who is readily available for consultation or referral.[77] In these situations, nonprofessionals supplement and complement professional reference service, but are not expected to replace it.

■ ══ ■

1.6

Setting Up an Information Desk

You have been asked by the head of your library's reference department to take responsibility for setting up an information desk to take some of the pressure off the very busy reference desk. The information desk will be staffed by a variety of part-time individuals, primarily paraprofessional staff from other library units and graduate students from a nearby library school. The department head would like to see a draft of a planning document in a month.

What factors should you consider in deciding where to place the desk and how to design it? What kind of training program should you propose? What policies and procedures will be necessary to guide the staff who will work at the new information desk? How can you and the department head most effectively gain your colleagues' support for this new endeavor? Do you feel confident that this project will be a success for both staff and library users?

When carefully trained and properly supported, nonprofessionals working in a busy reference setting can allow the professional staff to focus on those questions requiring an in-depth reference interview and/or extensive experience and knowledge of reference resources. Thus, librarians can spend more time on those questions that truly require the level of training, knowledge, and skills that only professionals can offer.[78] They can contribute in a major way to the provision of high-quality service and to the prevention of burnout. As Martin Courtois and Lori Goetsch wrote, "Properly trained nonprofessionals with an understanding of reference service and a clear-cut referral relationship may enhance the job roles of both nonprofessionals and professionals."[79]

The Future of Reference Services

What is the future of reference work? Many visions have been presented, a few of which can be traced through the notes and additional readings for this chapter. The following is not a comprehensive summary of these visions, but an assessment based both on the literature and on some of the current trends in reference services discussed above.

To some degree, the future depends not on librarians but on the economic health of society and decisions made by its voters. All public libraries and many school and academic libraries depend on the public's willingness to be taxed to support them. Librarians can, of course, influence the attitude of voters by providing needed materials and services, so that their value to society is as clear and as substantial as possible. To do this effectively, it is essential that user needs and preferences be kept in the forefront when reference services are planned and evaluated.

It has been often noted that this is an information society. The increased availability and importance of information have created a demand for more, as various consumer and self-help movements emphasize personal knowledge and competence in place of excessive dependence on doctors, lawyers, and other experts.[80] Many in the library profession have seen this as a golden opportunity for librarians to assume a central and highly important role in society.[81] One of the most promising movements in this direction is seen in the information and referral services offered by many public libraries, which seek to make the library the primary source of community information. An increasing number of academic libraries are making electronic versions of encyclopedias, dictionaries, periodical indexes, and other reference works available on their online catalog terminals, so that users may have easy access to various important sources of information at one location.[82] Both of these developments show that libraries are providing free access to sources of information beyond the materials in their own collections. They indicate that future reference librarians will function as guides to the broader world of information, not just as interpreters of books and magazines in a particular library.

There is no doubt that expanding electronic applications will continue to contribute to the improvement of reference services. For busy faculty or community and business leaders, it will often be more convenient to submit questions by electronic mail than by telephone (just as it is more convenient now to use the telephone than to go to the library). Reference librarians in the future will undoubtedly answer many questions either by electronic mail or by faxing the answer to the user's telefacsimile machine. Direct user access to free and convenient database searching, whether on CD-ROM or on locally mounted databases, is another example of the expanded reference services made possible by electronic technology. Although these systems are costly, their popularity makes it likely that the funds will be found to increase the number and kinds of databases that libraries will offer to their users.

Many writers have argued that the new electronic resources will lead to an expansion of the guidance and instructional roles of reference librarians in the years ahead. As more electronic reference tools are made available, there will be a need for a knowledgeable professional to help the user choose from the many options. This fact will lead to increased librarian participation in the research process, as the greater variety of resources makes it impossible for most individuals to master all the titles they need to use. Reference librarians will assume the role of guide and instructor, helping the user to choose among the available resources, teaching the use of these resources, and advising the user when a search mediated by a librarian is preferable.[83]

Numerous writers have also suggested that reference librarians should develop a more professional relationship with their users. These writers urge public and academic librarians to move closer to the model practiced by special librarians, offering more sophisticated and customized services on a continuing basis. It has also been suggested that reference librarians get outside the library more often, to study and eventually to anticipate the information needs of their users. Related to this view is the questioning of the viability of the reference desk as the library's primary service point.[84] The concept of reference librarians meeting with users by appointment in private offices, where more extensive discussions of user goals and needs are possible, seems to hold increasing appeal.

If reference librarians are to spend their time in offices, whether in the library or out in the community, there will be a need for more instructional handouts and computer-assisted instruction programs, as well as for more nonprofessional staff to handle the many ready reference questions that will still require attention. It has been suggested that the ratio of nonprofessional to professional staff in libraries will need to double, and that libraries— particularly academic libraries—will need to give up their reliance on collection size as a measure of greatness, and concentrate more on measuring success in terms of access and services.[85] It remains to be seen whether most libraries will possess both the will and the wealth to provide the funds and training time required to create reference services in which simple and repetitive questions can be handled by nonprofessional staff, the most basic library-use instruction can be provided by computer programs, and reference librarians are freed to deal with truly challenging questions and significantly to expand the range of services they are capable of providing to their users.

■ ━━ ■

1.7

Two Views of the Future for Public and Academic Reference Work

Richard De Gennaro on Public Libraries:
I can see us going more into providing to users, through branch libraries, information about jobs, about social services, information that people are going to need to help them get on with their lives. This means going beyond some of the traditional library services for recreation and for education.

And we're also coming to a point where the library's role will be to help people find what kind of training for jobs is available, what kind of organizations are available to help people to find out about these questions. A good deal of that is already going on, and by 1998 we'll be doing more of it, and it will become a more important part of our function.

Evan Farber on Academic Libraries:
The reference function in the future, particularly in academic libraries, will be somewhat like a reader's advisor. The basic questions will be mostly answered by technology, particularly by expert systems, other forms of computer-assisted instruction, artificial intelligence.

Librarians will act much more as individual reference librarians, helping people evaluate their searches, shape their searches. They will act, in a sense, much more as information advisors for individuals and let the technology do the searching for the information.

—Richard De Gennaro and Evan I. Farber
In *Libraries in the '90s: What the Leaders Expect*[86]

Notes

1. Samuel Rothstein, "Reference Service: The New Dimension in Librarianship," *College & Research Libraries* 22 (January 1961): 12.

2. Samuel Rothstein, "The Development of the Concept of Reference Service in American Libraries, 1850-1900," *The Library Quarterly* 23 (January 1953): 7-8.

3. Rothstein, "Reference Service," 12-13.

4. These are acronyms for Online Computer Library Center, Research Libraries Information Network, and Western Library Network, respectively. These networks are discussed further in chapters 5 and 18.

5. Leslie R. Morris and Patsy Brautigam, *Inter-Library Loan Policies Directory*, 3d ed. (New York: Neal-Schuman, 1988), vi.

6. Thomas Childers, *Information & Referral: Public Libraries* (Norwood, N.J.: Ablex, 1983), 1.

7. Ibid., 1.

8. Ibid., 215.

9. Clara Stanton Jones, "The Public Library as the Comprehensive Community Information Center," in *Public Librarianship: A Reader*, ed. Jane Robbins-Carter (Littleton, Colo.: Libraries Unlimited, 1982), 128.

10. Robert Croneberger, et al., "The Library as a Community Information and Referral Center," in *Public Librarianship*, 479.

11. Thomas Childers, "Trends in Public Library I & R Service," *Library Journal* 104 (October 1, 1979): 2035-39.

12. For further reading about cooperative reference, consult: Tina Roose, "Reference Services — An Essential Type of Resource Sharing," *Catholic Library World* 52 (February 1981): 286-90; Beverly P. Lynch, "Networks and Other Cooperative Enterprises: Their Effect on the Function of Reference," *RQ* 15 (Spring 1976): 197-202.

13. Elin B. Christianson, "Special Libraries," in *ALA World Encyclopedia of Library and Information Services*, 2d ed. (Chicago: American Library Association, 1986), 782.

14. Kathleen Strube and Carol M. Antoniewicz, "Manual Selective Dissemination of Information from Journal Holdings of an Academic Medical Library," *Medical Reference Services Quarterly* 7, no. 1 (1988): 1-8.

15. Janice Helen McCue, *Online Searching in Public Libraries: A Comparative Study of Performance* (Metuchen, N.J.: Scarecrow Press, 1988), 136.

16. See chapter 5 for a discussion of compact disc-read-only memory (CD-ROM) workstations.

17. Introductions to the information brokering option can be found in: Karen Smalletz, "Information Brokering," *Bulletin of the American Society for Information Science* 14 (April/May 1988): 28; Mick O'Leary, "The Information Broker: A Modern Profile," *Online* 11 (November 1987): 24-30.

18. Quoted in Carolyn A. Kirkendall and Carla J. Stoffle, "Instruction," in *The Service Imperative for Libraries: Essays in Honor of Margaret E. Monroe*, ed. Gail A. Schlachter (Littleton, Colo.: Libraries Unlimited, 1982), 42.

19. Ibid.

20. Concise descriptions of course-related and course-integrated instruction are provided in Anne F. Roberts and Susan G. Blandy, *Library Instruction for Librarians*, 2d rev. ed. (Englewood, Colo.: Libraries Unlimited, 1989), 69-70.

21. Francesca Allegri, "Course Integrated Instruction: Metamorphosis for the Twenty-First Century," *Medical Reference Services Quarterly* 4 (Winter 1985/86): 59.

22. Samuel Swett Green, "Personal Relations Between Librarians and Readers," *Library Journal* 1 (October 1876): 74-81.

23. Rhea Joyce Rubin, "Guidance," in *Service Imperative*, 95.

24. Ibid., 96-97.

25. Ibid., 98-99.

26. Joyce G. Saricks and Nancy Brown, *Readers' Advisory Service in the Public Library* (Chicago: American Library Association, 1989), 6.

27. Clara Richardson Lack, "Can Bibliotherapy Go Public?," *Collection Building* 7 (Spring 1985): 28; Rubin, "Guidance," 108.

28. Lack, "Can Bibliotherapy Go Public?," 28-30; Rhea J. Rubin, "Uses of Bibliotherapy in Response to the 1970s," *Library Trends* 28 (Fall 1979): 242-45.

29. Lack, "Can Bibliotherapy Go Public?," 27.

30. Arleen McCarty Hynes, "Bibliotherapy—The Interactive Process," *Catholic Library World* 58 (1987): 167-70; Alice G. Smith, "Will the Real Bibliotherapist Please Stand Up?," *Journal of Youth Services in Libraries* 2 (Spring 1989): 241-49.

31. Kathleen Bergen and Barbara MacAdam, "One-on-One: Term Paper Assistance Programs," *RQ* 24 (Spring 1985): 333-35.

32. Callie B. McGinnis, "Columbus College's Term Paper Clinic: A Ten-Year Tradition," *The Georgia Librarian* 25 (Winter 1988): 188-90.

33. Muriel Regan, "Library Consulting: Challenge, Autonomy and Risk," *The Reference Librarian* 22 (1988): 220.

34. *Directory of Library and Information Professionals*, 2 vols. (Woodbridge, Conn.: Research Publications, 1988).

35. Regan, "Library Consulting," 220.

36. Green, "Personal Relations," 74-81.

37. Charles A. Bunge, "The Personal Touch: A Brief Overview of the Development of Reference Services in American Libraries," in *Reference Service: A Perspective*, ed. Sul H. Lee (Ann Arbor, Mich.: Pierian Press, 1983), 2.

38. Ibid.

39. Green, "Personal Relations," 74-79.

40. Louis Kaplan, "The Early History of Reference Service in the United States," *Library Review* 83 (Autumn 1947): 286-90; Thomas J. Galvin, "Reference Services and Libraries," *Encyclopedia of Library and Information Science*, vol. 25 (New York: Marcel Dekker, 1977), 211.

41. Bunge, "The Personal Touch," 3.

42. Galvin, "Reference Services and Libraries," 214.

43. Ibid., 215-16.

44. Bunge, "The Personal Touch," 3.

45. James I. Wyer, *Reference Work: A Textbook for Students of Library Work and Librarians* (Chicago: American Library Association, 1930), 6-13.

46. Ibid., 6.

47. This discussion of the three concepts draws heavily on Wyer, *Reference Work*, 6-13, and on Galvin, "Reference Services and Libraries," 217-20.

48. Wyer, *Reference Work*, 9.

49. See, for example, Rothstein, "Reference Service," 14; and William A. Katz, *Introduction to Reference Work*, 5th ed., vol. 2 (New York: McGraw-Hill, 1987), 53-55.

50. Katz, *Introduction*, 53-55.

51. Rothstein, "Reference Service," 14-15.

52. Brian Nielsen, "Teacher or Intermediary: Alternative Professional Models in the Information Age," *College & Research Libraries* 43 (May 1982): 183-91.

53. Library organizations—consortia, networks, systems—in the United States and Canada are listed in the *American Library Directory* (New York: Bowker, annual).

54. Margaret Hutchins, *Introduction to Reference Work* (Chicago: American Library Association, 1944), 214p.

55. See the June 1989 issue of *Information Technology and Libraries* for several articles addressing this development.

56. This is the number of databases listed in the 1991 edition of *CD-ROMs in Print* (Westport, Conn.: Meckler, 1991), 450p.

57. Examples are given in Christine M. Roysdon and Laura Lee Elliott, "Electronic Integration of Library Services through a Campuswide Network," *RQ* 28 (Fall 1988): 82-93; and Ellen H. Howard and Terry Ann Jankowski, "Reference Services via Electronic Mail," *Bulletin of the Medical Library Association* 74 (January 1986): 41-44.

58. One version of this concern is summarized in James Rice, "The Golden Age of Reference Service: Is It Really Over?," *Wilson Library Bulletin* 61 (December 1986): 17.

59. Rice, "Golden Age," 18.

60. A number of these studies are summarized and criticized in Ian Douglas, "Reducing Failures in Reference Service," *RQ* 28 (Fall 1988): 94-101. Douglas also offers practical suggestions for improving reference performance.

61. Ibid., 94-95. Reactions of several librarians are provided in Peter Hernon and Charles R. McClure, "Library Reference Service: An Unrecognized Crisis—A Symposium," *Journal of Academic Librarianship* 13 (May 1987): 69-80.

62. Joan Durrance, "Reference Success: Does the 55 Percent Rule Tell the Whole Story," *Library Journal* 114 (April 15, 1989): 31-36.

63. Douglas, "Reducing Failures," 98.

64. Tina Roose, "Stress at the Reference Desk," *Library Journal* 114 (September 1, 1989): 167.

65. William Miller, "What's Wrong with Reference," *American Libraries* 15 (May 1984): 303-6.

66. Charles Bunge, "Potential and Reality at the Reference Desk: Reflections on a 'Return to the Field,'" *Journal of Academic Librarianship* 10 (July 1984): 131.

67. Mary Haack, John W. Jones, and Tina Roose, "Occupational Burnout Among Librarians," *Drexel Library Quarterly* 20 (Spring 1984): 67.

68. Miller, "What's Wrong," 321.

69. Mary Van Orsdol, "Burnout and Rejuvenation," *The Unabashed Librarian*, no. 61 (1986): 20.

70. Nathan M. Smith, Nancy E. Birch, and Maurice P. Marchant, "Stress, Distress, and Burnout: A Survey of Public Reference Librarians," *Public Libraries* 23 (Fall 1984): 85.

71. David S. Ferriero and Katharine A. Powers, "Burnout at the Reference Desk," *RQ* 21 (Spring 1982): 277.

72. Roose, "Stress," 167.

73. Marjorie E. Murfin and Charles A. Bunge, "Paraprofessionals at the Reference Desk," *Journal of Academic Librarianship* 14 (March 1988): 10.

74. Jeffrey W. St. Clair and Rao Aluri, "Staffing the Reference Desk: Professionals or Nonprofessionals?," *Journal of Academic Librarianship* 3 (July 1977): 153.

75. Egill A. Halldorsson and Marjorie E. Murfin, "The Performance of Professionals and Nonprofessionals in the Reference Interview," *College & Research Libraries* 38 (September 1977): 385.

76. Murfin and Bunge, "Paraprofessionals at the Reference Desk," 10-14.

77. Ibid., 14; Beth S. Woodard, "The Effectiveness of an Information Desk Staffed by Graduate Students and Nonprofessionals," *College & Research Libraries* 50 (July 1989): 463.

78. St. Clair and Aluri, "Staffing the Reference Desk," 153.

79. Martin P. Courtois and Lori A. Goetsch, "Use of Nonprofessionals at Reference Desks," *College & Research Libraries* 45 (September 1984): 391.

80. See, for example, John Naisbitt, *Megatrends: Ten New Directions Transforming Our Lives* (New York: Warner Books, 1982), chaps. 1 and 6.

81. One example of this view is expressed in Thomas T. Surprenant and Claudia Perry-Holmes, "The Reference Librarian of the Future: A Scenario," *RQ* 25 (Winter 1985): 234-35, 238.

82. A chart of the databases offered at seven academic libraries and the Colorado Alliance of Research Libraries (CARL) is provided in William Gray Potter, "Expanding the Online Catalog," *Information Technology and Libraries* 8 (June 1989): 101-2.

83. Surprenant and Perry-Holmes, "The Reference Librarian of the Future," 236-37.

84. Two articles by Barbara J. Ford are important here: "Reference Beyond (and Without) the Reference Desk," *College & Research Libraries* 47 (September 1986): 491-94; and "Reference Service: Past, Present, and Future," *College & Research Libraries News* 49 (October 1988): 578-82.

85.   Irene Hoadley, "The World That Awaits Us: Libraries of Tomorrow," *Wilson Library Bulletin* 61 (October 1986): 24-25.

86.   Richard De Gennaro and Evan I. Farber, as quoted in *Libraries in the '90s: What the Leaders Expect*, eds. Donald E. Riggs and Gordon A. Sabine (Phoenix, Ariz.: Oryx Press, 1988), 5, 6.

Additional Readings

Bunge, Charles A. "Potential and Reality at the Reference Desk: Reflections on a 'Return to the Field.'" *Journal of Academic Librarianship* 10 (July 1984): 128-32.
   A library school professor summarizes his perceptions of reference work in the 1980s gained during a sabbatical year spent working at reference desks in an academic and a public library. The primary focus is the causes and cures for disparity between the service librarians would like to provide and the service they in reality are able to provide.

Green, Samuel Swett. "Personal Relations Between Librarians and Readers." *Library Journal* 1 (October 1876): 74-81.
   Although some of Green's values and opinions may be found objectionable by some of today's reference librarians, his classic statement of the rationale for the development of reference services is still worth reading.

Hernon, Peter, and Charles R. McClure, eds. "Library Reference Service: An Unrecognized Crisis — A Symposium." *Journal of Academic Librarianship* 13 (May 1987): 69-80.
   These six articles address the meaning and significance of unobtrusive testing which indicates that only 55 percent of factual reference questions asked at public and academic library reference desks are answered correctly. While the issues raised by such studies are important, the article by Childers enumerating the many kinds of reference services not evaluated in these studies makes the word "crisis" seem overly dramatic.

Miller, William. "What's Wrong with Reference: Coping with Success and Failure at the Reference Desk." *American Libraries* 15 (May 1984): 303-6; 321-22.
   This is one of the most honest and provocative articles in recent years on the topic of reference work. Miller argues that the newer, more innovative reference services, such as online searching and instruction, coupled with static staffing levels, have overloaded the librarians in many reference departments and caused dissension in their ranks.

Murfin, Marjorie E., and Lubomyr R. Wynar. *Reference Service: An Annotated Bibliographic Guide.* Littleton, Colo.: Libraries Unlimited, 1977. 294p.
   This work lists and annotates more than 1,250 books and articles dealing with reference and information services. A supplement, published in 1984, describes some 1,600 additional titles published during the years 1976 to 1982.

Nielsen, Brian. "Teacher or Intermediary: Alternative Models in the Information Age." *College & Research Libraries* 43 (May 1982): 183-91.
   Although he addresses the issues involved in the information-versus-instruction debate, Nielsen's primary purpose is to ask reference librarians to re-think their relationships with their user groups. He looks for a new role model to replace both the intermediary/expert model and the teacher model.

Potter, William Gray. "Expanding the Online Catalog." *Information Technology and Libraries* 8 (June 1989): 99-104.
   Potter's essay is the lead article in a special issue on "Locally Loaded Databases in Online Library Systems." It provides a summary of and an introduction to the succeeding articles, most of which report the experiences of several libraries which have made various electronic databases available on the same terminals used for online catalog searching. Another overview article, Charles Bailey's "Public-Access Computer Systems" (pp. 178-85), discusses current as well as projected future developments in electronic end-user searching.

Public Library Association, Community Information Section. *Guidelines for Establishing Community Information and Referral Services in Public Libraries*. 3d ed. Chicago: American Library Association, 1989. 25p.

This work provides brief guidelines for setting up an I & R service and for selecting and training staff to deliver the service successfully to public library users. Its current, extensive bibliography of published materials on this topic is particularly valuable.

Riggs, Donald E., and Gordon A. Sabine. *Libraries in the '90s: What the Leaders Expect*. Phoenix, Ariz.: Oryx Press, 1988. 197p.

This interesting volume is based on separate personal interviews with twenty-five prominent librarians, from various library settings, regarding their expectations for the course of library services and library education in the 1990s. Several chapters deal directly or indirectly with the future of reference services.

Saricks, Joyce G., and Nancy Brown. *Readers' Advisory Service in the Public Library*. Chicago: American Library Association, 1989. 84p.

This book describes how an effective readers' advisory program offering assistance in the selection of fiction materials can be organized, promoted, and delivered. The authors emphasize preparation in the areas of patron interviewing, knowledge of useful reference sources, and an understanding of various categories of popular fiction.

Schlachter, Gail A., ed. *The Service Imperative for Libraries: Essays in Honor of Margaret E. Monroe*. Littleton, Colo.: Libraries Unlimited, 1982. 215p.

Essays in this tribute to the University of Wisconsin Library School professor focus on the reference functions of information, instruction, and guidance, as well as on a fourth function, called "stimulation" (i.e., to use libraries). There are also chapters on education for reference work and on evaluation of reference services.

Stieg, Margaret F. "Technology and the Concept of Reference, or What Will Happen to the Milkman's Cow." *Library Journal* 115 (April 15, 1990): 45-49.

The author argues that the Victorian values which led to the creation of reference services in the nineteenth century are, in our computerized age, still the "essential identity of reference work." Although the information sources may be vastly different now, the same commitment to personal service and empathy with users is necessary for effective reference interactions.

Vavrek, Bernard, issue ed. "Current Trends in Reference Services." *Library Trends* 31 (Winter 1983): 361-510.

Individual articles in this issue provide overviews of reference services as currently practiced in academic, public, school, and special libraries. Among the specialized articles are one on online searching in reference and one on education for reference librarianship.

2 □

TOWARD A PHILOSOPHY FOR REFERENCE SERVICE

Introduction

For many, *philosophy* is the realm of questions without concrete answers, the world of ineffable ideas and improbable theories, where consensus is consumed in endless debate and inoperable designs. Even its etymologic derivation, compounded from the Greek words *philo* and *sophia*, and usually translated as "the love of wisdom," suggests preoccupation with archaic purposes and dusty methods, outdistanced by the pace of modern society in this contemporary information age, as irrelevant to the achievement of practical library tasks as cosmology is to the conduct of business.

How far from the truth such notions are. Philosophy is not only inescapable, but necessary. It pervades every decision and every action of every individual, family, social group, institution, profession, organization, and society. Every decision and every action is an expression of beliefs and values and ideals, a concrete explication of philosophy applied to practical affairs. Philosophy is the fountainhead from which professional practice flows. In fact, *profession* means to openly declare a belief. Professional practice is a philosophy enacted. To neglect philosophy is to abandon basic principles and reasoned action to the random forces of expediency and whim. This is as true of librarianship as it is of professions such as medicine and law.

Libraries are institutions created and maintained for a purpose. They reflect fundamental social values, beliefs, ideals, and needs. Librarianship has been described as a theory-poor profession, a result of inadequate attention given to explication of basic principles and professional values. In fact, librarianship is rich in philosophical tradition, and professional practice involves commitment to fundamental social and ethical ideals. This chapter offers a brief introduction to the philosophical foundations of librarianship and the practical application of that philosophy in reference services. Within that context, it offers an overview of some important issues and controversies surrounding contemporary reference and information services.

Historical Antecedents

More than any other profession, with perhaps the exception of law, librarianship is subject to prevailing cultural, political, and social forces. The great libraries of ancient times, such as those of Ashurbanipal in the seventh century B.C. and the Alexandrian Library four centuries later, reflected the cultural glory and progressive aspirations of societies at their pinnacle. They served not only the archival, economic, and administrative needs of government, but also the educational, cultural, and religious needs of the citizenry, and were open to scholars and educated visitors from all over the civilized world. At the height of its democratic flowering, all citizens of Greece had access to the libraries of its major cities. The first public library in Rome, conceived by Julius Caesar before his death and established by Gaius Asinius Pollio around 35 B.C., was described by Pliny with the phrase *ingenia hominum rem publicam* ("human intelligence and natural capacities made public"). In contrast, after the collapse of the Roman Empire, monastery and church libraries often maintained only a small portion of their collections for public use. The few university libraries were open to scholars and students, but most of the libraries of medieval Europe were cloistered realms intended to serve the purposes of the church and royalty, hoarding guarded secrets and rare intellectual treasures.[1]

Library historians suggest that the public library as it is understood today was born in the early nineteenth century. Throughout ancient and medieval times, libraries could be used only by an educated minority within limitations imposed by social conditions, prevailing conventions, and institutional controls. Relatively few people could read. Collections were acquired to meet the needs and aspirations of a designated populace, and materials were relatively rare and valuable; hence, restrictions on access were common.[2] However, the very same limitations exist even today. More people are able to use libraries today than in the past, because a greater proportion of the population is literate, but libraries are still used primarily by an educated minority, even in open societies. Collections are larger, more diverse, and more accessible today because books and other materials are more abundant and more replaceable. Even so, collections are still expensive to acquire and maintain; political, social, and institutional considerations still influence selection of materials; and restrictions on borrowing privileges and use of services still exist. Thus, it might be argued that the noticeable differences between the libraries of the past and those of today are but a matter of scale: more readers, more books, more libraries, more library users.

Nevertheless, significant changes did occur in libraries during the 1800s. As institutional products of the cultural and political environment within which they exist, libraries reflect the ideals and purposes of society. The social, intellectual, and political movements of the later Renaissance through the Enlightenment were instrumental in the evolutionary course of librarianship. It was during the nineteenth century that those seminal philosophical ideas which had overthrown governments and precipitated dramatic social restructuring during the previous century exerted their influence on librarianship, coming to fruition with the public library movement, the reformation of academic librarianship, and the birth of special librarianship. Now, over two centuries later, those same fundamental ideals continue to guide modern librarianship.

Philosophical Foundations

The latter part of the seventeenth century and the eighteenth century are commonly referred to as the *Enlightenment*. It was a period during which the cultural, social, religious, economic, political, and intellectual movements of the Renaissance coalesced in the writings of John Locke, David Hume, Voltaire, Montesquieu, Jeremy Bentham, Adam Smith, Jean-Jacques Rousseau, and others. The influence of Enlightenment thought, combined with the unique circumstances that had arisen in the American colonies, was a powerful philosophical elixir. The innovative and radical ideas of American figures like Jefferson, Madison, Franklin, and Paine found their way back to Europe.[3] This period is also frequently referred to as the *Age of Revolution*, because it was a time during which philosophy inspired radical change. The newly evolving ideas became the cornerstone of the Bill of Rights and the establishment of constitutional monarchy in England; the Declaration of Independence, Bill of

Rights, and constitutional government in America; and the Declaration of the Rights of Man and of the Citizen and the revolution in France.

At the core of the philosophy of the Enlightenment was rationality as the defining quality of human beings; that is, the single most important characteristic which distinguishes humans from other animals is their ability to reason. Although individuals may differ in the circumstances of life, each is born a *tabula rasa*, capable of learning, making good judgments and fair decisions, and living a productive and moral life. In the "state of nature," an allegorical construct used to describe human society without government, people guide and monitor their own conduct, improving their circumstances and contributing to the shared course of society. One enjoys fundamental "natural rights" to life, to pursue one's own well-being unhindered, to freely exchange knowledge and the products of one's labor, and to freely espouse one's ideas and personal beliefs, constrained only by respect for the same equal rights of others. In society with others, people enter into a "social contract," an allegorical construct used to describe the relationship between individuals and established government. The contractual purpose of government, posited in the notion of natural law, and the only legitimate basis for use of power by government, is to protect the inherent rights of individuals from the encroachment of others. Government consequently has no inherent rights of its own, even to continue in existence, except those powers invested in it by the people. Thus, it may undertake social programs and provide services if they are for the good of all and if the permission of the populace is specifically granted.[4]

An essential requisite for social self-government, intellectual progress, economic development, and religious toleration, of course, was an informed populace. Freedom of speech and the press, facilitating the uninhibited flow of knowledge and ideas, was necessary to this end. In America, the constitutions of the various states and the amendments to the federal constitution were unequivocal on this matter (see box 2.1). So completely obvious was the need for protection of free speech and the press, as well as other rights expressed in the Bill of Rights, that the framers of the Constitution initially omitted them and, even when they were proposed, argued against adopting the amendments as unnecessary. So immersed were they in the natural rights philosophy of the day that, from their vantage, the government had only those powers specifically outlined in the Constitution and so did not have the power to do any of the things forbidden in the amendments.[5] The French had taken a more moderate course in their Declaration of the Rights of Man and of the Citizen, allowing for exceptions to the freedom of speech and the press to be determined by the courts. In effect, despite the original absolute prescription against abridgement of those rights, much the same has occurred in the United States. As a result, those who express unpopular ideas, whether political, social, religious, artistic, or personal, are constantly embroiled in confrontations with those who would censor them.

■ ══ ■

2.1

Some Constitutional Protections of the Free Press[6]

"That the freedom of the press is one of the great bulwarks of liberty, and can never be restrained but by despotic governments."
—Constitution of Virginia, Bill of Rights
June 12, 1776

"The liberty of the press is essential to the security of freedom in a state, it ought not, therefore, to be restricted in this commonwealth."
—Constitution of Massachusetts
A Declaration of the Rights of the Inhabitants
June 15, 1780

"Congress shall make no law ... abridging the freedom of speech, or of the press...."
—Constitution of the United States, Amendment 1
1789, ratified 1791

"The free communication of thoughts and opinions is one of man's most precious rights. Every citizen may therefore speak, write, and publish freely; except that he shall be responsible for the abuse of that freedom in cases determined by law."
—Declaration of the Rights of Man and of the Citizen
Presented to the National Assembly, August 1789
Preamble to the Constitution of France, 1791

A second requisite, if the populace were to be capable of informed and knowledgeable self-governance, was education. Each person had the capacity to learn, to make wise judgments and decisions, to guide an independent course, and contribute to society. Formal education is not a prerequisite for the exercise of basic common sense, but innate capacity can be enhanced and perfected through training and education, and an informed citizenry is a literate citizenry. Public education systems had been established in France and Germany early in the nineteenth century. The United States and England followed their example within a few decades. The public library movement was a part of that educational enterprise (see box 2.2).

2.2

On the Library as an Educational Institution

Belief that universal education is essential for the welfare of the republic; belief in the power of books as a deterrent from vice and a source of education and culture; all this had entered into formation of social libraries, apprentices' and mercantile and young men's libraries, and school-district libraries. To this had been added a slowly growing conviction that only a free library could meet the needs of modern society; a library which should ignore the distinctions of class which had long retarded a sense of community solidarity and had left the intellectual wants of many to the mercy of charity; a library offering equal privileges to all the residents of the community maintaining it.

— C. Seymour Thompson
Evolution of the American Public Library, 1653-1876[7]

More recent explications of natural rights, not specifically enumerated as such in any of the original doctrines, but rather implied by other rights, are those of equality and privacy. The basic equality of all people was, of course, a fundamental foundation of social contract theory, as is apparent in the texts of the American Declaration of Independence and the French Declaration of the Rights of Man and of the Citizen. Unfortunately, just as Aristotle had compromised his philosophy to accommodate the prevailing inequality of women and slaves in ancient Greece, so too many of the American theorists, however committed personally to the abolition of slavery and recognition of the equal rights of women, settled initially for compromise in founding the new government. Attempts to eradicate the inequities, begun in earnest in the 1800s, have been complicated by the difficulty of defining exactly what is meant by *equality* and how it might best be guaranteed.

The right to privacy has presented even greater difficulty. Since it is not specifically mentioned in founding documents or supporting philosophical writings, its definition by the courts has been slow and complicated. It has been variously related to the First Amendment, recognizing the right to free speech; the Fourth Amendment, guaranteeing the protection of person and property from unlawful search and seizure; the Ninth Amendment, extending protection to other rights not enumerated in the Bill of Rights; and the Fourteenth Amendment, assuring due process. That the right to privacy, particularly in the form of professional confidentiality, exists is rarely questioned. However, the scope of the right to privacy, the extent of protection to be accorded, and the circumstances which constitute invasion of privacy remain vague and ill-defined.

Philosophy of Library Service

The historical importance of natural rights philosophy cannot be minimized. The impact of that philosophy on the development of libraries and the philosophy of library service is equally significant. Through that philosophy, the library as an institution becomes an incarnation of democratic ideals and values, and the services provided by libraries become a public espousal of belief and commitment to the philosophical principles upon which democratic institutions are based. Many of the particulars of that philosophy can be found in the American Library Association's "Policy Manual," published each year in its *Handbook of Organization*.[8] Five basic tenets of that philosophy, outlined in the "Library Bill of Rights" (box 2.3), the "Code of Ethics" (box 2.4), and other related policies adopted by the American Library Association (box 2.5), are especially apparent.

First, libraries exist for the purpose of information and enlightenment. They are institutions with an educational and informational mission.[9]

Second, libraries recognize the basic human capacity of reason and judgment. They should guard against prejudicial selection policies, exclusion, restricted access, labelling or proscription of controversial materials, and specifically extend access to all points of view, however controversial or unpopular.[10]

Third, libraries are dedicated to preserving intellectual freedom. The role of libraries is that of an instrument for the protection of freedom of expression and the free access to ideas, and any attempts at censorship should be resisted.[11]

Fourth, libraries recognize basic human equality, and do not deny or abridge access or service because of origin, age, background or views.[12] Moreover, access to information or services in publicly supported libraries should not be limited by the ability to pay.[13]

Fifth, libraries should protect the confidentiality of their clientele.[14]

2.3
Library Bill of Rights[15]

The American Library Association affirms that all libraries are forums for information and ideas, and that the following basic policies should guide their services.

1.   Books and other library resources should be provided for the interest, information, and enlightenment of all people of the community the library serves. Materials should not be excluded because of the origin, background, or views of those contributing to their creation.

2.   Libraries should provide materials and information presenting all points of view on current and historical issues. Materials should not be proscribed or removed because of partisan or doctrinal disapproval.

3.   Libraries should challenge censorship in the fulfillment of their responsibility to provide information and enlightenment.

4.   Libraries should cooperate with all persons and groups concerned with resisting abridgment of free expression and free access to ideas.

5.   A person's right to use a library should not be denied or abridged because of origin, age, background, or views.

6.   Libraries which make exhibit spaces and meeting rooms available to the public they serve should make such facilities available on an equitable basis, regardless of the beliefs or affiliations of individuals or groups requesting their use.

— Amended version as adopted by ALA Council
January 23, 1980

■ ═══ ■

2.4

ALA Code of Ethics[16]

    1.   Librarians must provide the highest level of service through appropriate and usefully organized collections, fair and equitable circulation and service policies, and skillful, accurate, unbiased, and courteous responses to all requests for assistance.

    2.   Librarians must resist all efforts by groups or individuals to censor library materials.

    3.   Librarians must protect each user's right to privacy with respect to information sought or received, and materials consulted, borrowed, or acquired.

    4.   Librarians must adhere to the principles of due process and equality of opportunity in peer relationships and personnel actions.

    5.   Librarians must distinguish clearly in their actions and statements between their personal philosophies and attitudes and those of an institution or professional body.

    6.   Librarians must avoid situations in which personal interests might be served or financial benefits gained at the expense of library users, colleagues, or the employing institution.

—Adopted by ALA Membership and Council
June 30, 1981

Reprinted by permission of ALA.

2.5
Selected ALA Policies[17]

50.4   Free Access to Information

The American Library Association asserts that the charging of fees and levies for information services, including those services utilizing the latest information technology, is discriminatory in publicly supported institutions providing library and information services.

52.6   Instruction in the Use of Libraries

In order to assist individuals in the independent information retrieval process basic to daily living in a democratic society, the American Library Association encourages all libraries to include instruction in the use of libraries as one of the primary goals of service.

53.1.1   Challenged materials which meet the criteria for selection in the materials selection policy of the library should not be removed under any legal or extralegal pressure.

53.1.2   Expurgation of any parts of books or other library resources ... is a violation of the Library Bill of Rights....

53.1.4   Denying minors access to certain library materials and services available to adults is a violation of the Library Bill of Rights....

53.1.5   Evaluation of library materials is not to be used as a convenient means to remove materials presumed to be controversial or disapproved of by segments of the community.

53.1.6   Restricting access to certain titles and classes of library materials for protection and/or controlled use is a form of censorship.

53.1.7   Labeling certain library materials by affixing a prejudicial label to them or segregating by a prejudicial system is a practice which seeks to close paths to knowledge; such practices violate the Library Bill of Rights.

53.1.11   Diversity in Collection Development

Access to all materials legally obtainable should be assured to the user and policies should not unjustly exclude materials even if offensive to the librarian or the user.

Reprinted by permission of ALA.

Although many of the policy statements of the American Library Association specifically address issues of censorship and access to materials, it should be noted that the principles upon which these policy statements are founded apply equally to reference service. In fact, as a part of its policy statement on diversity in collection development,[18] the fundamental iteration of service philosophy, equally applicable to both reference and collection development, is presented: "Intellectual freedom, the essence of equitable library services, promotes no causes, furthers no movements, and favors no viewpoints. It only provides for free access to all expressions of ideas through which any and all sides of a question, cause, or movement may be explored."[19]

Some Practical Problems

The philosophy of reference service in all types of libraries derives from the same source and is based on the same principles. However, the interpretation and practical application of those principles present problems, and the solutions arrived at in different types of libraries do not always coincide. Several instances in which the interpretation and application of principle to practice present problems exemplify this difficulty, as discussed further in chapters 5, 6, and 8.

The traditional purpose of reference service has ostensibly been to assist individuals in their use of the library's collection and the variety of information resources available. Its primary goal was to assure that users obtained the information they required. However, the extent to which the librarian should participate in the process of information seeking has been an issue of some contention. In many libraries, particularly public and academic libraries, the role of the reference librarian as typically defined is to assist individuals in the use of reference tools, including searches of bibliographic databases. It is then left to the user to decide which of the items identified might be of great enough potential value to consult. The actual information required to answer a query would be provided only if it were available in a readily accessible reference tool. In some libraries, most commonly in special libraries, the role of the reference librarian extends much further. The librarian often selects material for the user on the basis of its appropriateness and quality, and may even provide summary reports gleaned from the best available information resources. In this capacity, the librarian serves as a quality filter, making judgments about the value of information for the user. Many libraries would find it practically impossible to offer such personalized service to their users even should they desire to do so. However, beyond the issue of feasibility is a problem of philosophical import: the notion of neutrality as a principle of professional practice. Should librarians make value judgments about the quality of information and make decisions for users about the appropriateness of sources? To what extent does the quality filtering process entail censorship? Should librarians instead remain neutral and nonjudgmental, offering equal access to all information sources regardless of quality? To what extent is neutrality a disservice to those who are less library-literate or less capable of making informed decisions about the sources of information they consult?

Personal reference service and instructional services have coexisted in most academic and many public and special libraries for many years. In fact, point-of-use instruction in the use of reference tools and library resources is so integrated with reference service that it is often difficult to distinguish between them. It has been argued, however, that the primary responsibility of the librarian is to provide the information required by users, and that more formalized instruction, especially group instruction, constitutes an abrogation of reference responsibility. Thus, as a matter of policy and principle, formalized instruction may not be offered.[20] Conversely, it has been argued that, as educational institutions, it is the responsibility of libraries to contribute to the challenge of assuring an informed citizenry. Consequently, educating citizens in the use of libraries and the information resources at their disposal may be considered even more basic a service than traditional reference service in some libraries.[21] In some libraries, educational services now include instruction in matters beyond library use, extending into the realm of personal information management and the use of information technology.[22] The practical problem of offering services beyond the capabilities of staffing is one of management. Of greater philosophical import is the issue of the primary role of the library: informational or educational. To what extent does instruction constitute an abrogation of the professional responsibility of the librarian to provide *personal* guidance and assure that users successfully meet their information needs? To what extent does query-centered reference service contribute to the mission of a more information-literate populace? Does either the failure to provide instruction or the extension of instruction at the cost of comprehensive reference service constitute a disservice to those who are less library-literate and less capable of making informed decisions about information resources?

The quality and effectiveness of both reference and instructional services have become a matter of concern in recent years. Research into the needs of library patrons and their use of libraries, and evaluation of library services provide valuable insights necessary for assessment and improvement. Among the most effective techniques are those involving unobtrusive study of users, either directly through observation or indirectly from library records, and the performance of librarians.[23] The practicality and benefits of unobtrusive research methods are of managerial importance when the studies are conducted at the institutional level; they are of general research interest when undertaken on a larger scale. A larger philosophical question is the issue of privacy and confidentiality. To what extent do surveillance of users during their visits to the library, and study of records of their queries and use of materials, constitute an invasion of privacy? To what extent is unobtrusive study of reference or instructional activities invasive? To what extent can the practical benefits in improved service, if any, justify the invasion of privacy, if any?

The technological developments of recent decades have extended the reference resources of libraries to include electronic databases. Most academic and public libraries provide online search services on a cost recovery basis, charging fees to recover the communication and vendor-imposed costs incurred. Charging users for library services is a matter of practical concern, of course, but the issue of philosophical import is the effect of fees for service on access to information. The position of the American Library Association on this issue is clear. A second issue concerns the study of transaction logs in online catalogs and electronically compiled circulation records. The possible intrusions on personal privacy entailed are similar to those discussed previously. A third philosophical issue concerns the extent to which the librarian may, intentionally or not, become a nonneutral quality filter during a search of electronic databases.

As a final example of problems in the application of the philosophy of reference services, many libraries categorize their users, extending different levels of reference service to those in different categories. It is not uncommon for academic libraries to distinguish between undergraduate and graduate students, faculty and researchers, administrators and staff. In public libraries, it is not uncommon to distinguish between the business community, city administrators, students, and other constituencies. In law and medical libraries, it is not unusual to distinguish between professional clientele, lay users, and administrators. In many cases, such distinctions are made for practical purposes. However, the philosophical question is the basic principle of equality of access to information as a fundamental requisite for a democratic society. To what extent does the categorization of users and differentiation between groups conflict with that basic principle?

Conclusion

No solutions to these and other problems related to the interpretation and application of the philosophy of reference service are offered here. If they were not extremely complex, they would already have been resolved. Moreover, it is important to keep in mind not only that libraries differ in their interpretations of the broad principles that guide their services, but also that in any setting ideals cannot always be achieved. The financial support for a library, its level of staffing, and its institutional mission contribute to any decisions about services. Private libraries and libraries serving a special group often find it necessary to shape policy in ways that are appropriate for their own environments. Many of these policies and decisions are reasonable and justifiable.

It is also important to realize, however, that every decision and every activity that occurs in a library has philosophical implications. If decisions are made and activities are pursued entirely on the basis of practicality and expediency, then principle is in danger of being subordinated and perhaps compromised for the sake of pragmatics. The expediency of removing a controversial book from the collection because of pressure involves submitting to censorship; so too does the expediency of discouraging a troublesome patron, or offering preferential service, or abandoning a complex reference problem because of time limitations, or charging for services, involve issues of principle. Referring to the fundamental philosophical foundations upon which libraries and their services are based may not always provide clear answers, and different libraries may come to different conclusions concerning interpretation of principles and their application to services, but conscious attention to principles offers a source of continuing guidance for professional practice.

Notes

1. James Thompson, *A History of the Principles of Librarianship* (London: Clive Bingley, 1977), 62-71.

2. Ibid., 65-66.

3. The most basic source on the Enlightenment remains Peter Gay's two-volume work, *The Enlightenment, An Interpretation* (New York: Knopf, 1967-69).

4. Brief discussion of these ideas and many of their proponents can be found in the eight-volume *Encyclopedia of Philosophy* (New York: Macmillan, 1967).

5. For example, see Thornton Anderson, *Jacobson's Development of American Political Thought: A Documentary History* (New York: Appleton-Century-Crofts), 204.

6. The full text of American documents can be found in Francis N. Thorpe, ed., *The Federal and State Constitutions, Colonial Charters, and Other Organic Laws* (Washington, D.C.: U.S. Government Printing Office, 1909). The full text of the French "Declaration of the Rights of Man and of the Citizen" appears in Norman L. Torrey, ed., *Les Philosophes* (New York: Capricorn, 1960), 284-87.

7. Quoted in Thompson, *Principles of Librarianship*, 70.

8. *ALA Handbook of Organization* (Chicago: American Library Association, 1990-91).

9. ALA "Policy Manual," sections 53.1, 52.6.

10. Ibid., 53.1, 53.1.1, 53.1.2, 53.1.5, 53.1.6, 53.1.7, 53.1.11.

11. Ibid., 53.1, 53.1.2, 53.1.6.

12. Ibid., 53.1, 53.1.4.

13. Ibid., 50.4.

14. Ibid., 52.4.

15. *ALA Handbook of Organization*, 256.

16. Ibid., 260.

17. Ibid., 253-57.

18. ALA "Policy Manual," section 53.1.11.

19. *ALA Handbook of Organization*, 258.

20. Constance Miller and James Rettig, "Reference Obsolescence," *RQ* 25 (Fall 1985): 52-58.

21. Mimi Dudley, "A Philosophy of Library Instruction," *Research Strategies* 1 (Spring 1983): 58-63.

22. A continuing column on "Information Management Education" appears in *Medical Reference Services Quarterly*.

23. The ethical difficulties presented by unobtrusive studies pervade all the social sciences. For a discussion of the problem, see Terry Pinkard, "Invasions of Privacy in Social Science Research," in *Ethical Issues in Professional Life*, ed. Joan C. Callahan (New York: Oxford University Press, 1988), 225-30.

Additional Readings

Bekker, Johan. "Professional Ethics and Its Application to Librarianship," Ph.D. diss., Case Western Reserve University, 1976. 458p.

    Bekker offers a stern critique of the American Library Association's Code of Ethics. He explores the common attributes found in the codes of ethics of a wide variety of professions and presents recommendations for a more useful code of ethics for librarianship.

Callahan, Joan C., ed. *Ethical Issues in Professional Life*. New York: Oxford University Press, 1988. 470p.

    Although this collection of readings is not specifically oriented toward librarianship, many philosophical positions and problems are common to a variety of professions. This volume includes valuable discussions of ethical and legal issues, as well as sample codes of ethics.

Encyclopedia of Philosophy. 8 vols. New York: Macmillan, 1967.

    Expert, yet readable, summary entries accompanied by references make this a valuable starting point in philosophy. Discussions pertinent to the philosophical foundations of librarianship include "Rights" (7:195-99), "Natural Law" (5:450-54), "Social Contract" (7:465-67), "Enlightenment" (2:519-25), and the entries for notable individuals of the age.

Hauptman, Robert. *Ethical Challenges in Librarianship*. Phoenix, Ariz.: Oryx Press, 1988. 110p.

    Hauptman considers many of the ethical issues confronting librarians today, and criticizes the current American Library Association's Code of Ethics.

Lindsey, Jonathan, and Ann Prentice. *Professional Ethics and Librarians*. Phoenix, Ariz.: Oryx Press, 1985. 103p.

    A collection of commentaries by librarians and library educators, most of whom suggest improvements to the American Library Association's Code of Ethics.

THE REFERENCE
INTERVIEW

Introduction

Broadly defined, a *reference interview* is a conversation between library reference staff and a patron for the purpose of clarifying patron needs and aiding the patron in meeting those needs. This process ranges from a brief directional encounter to an ongoing interaction when the patron needs assistance on a research project. The personal communication styles of the participants in the reference interview, the needs of the patron, the collection available for use, and the policies and procedures of the institution all influence how formal or informal the interview may be, but it is distinguished from general conversation between staff and patron because it has a specific purpose and structure.

In the reference interview, the librarian's goals are to determine what information the patron needs, how much information is needed, the depth or sophistication of the need, and what information format is most appropriate for or preferred by the patron. To meet these goals, the librarian may need to ascertain what the patron already knows about the topic, the source or context of the request (such as a homework assignment, personal interest, or background information for a job interview), the amount of time available to the patron for answering the question, and, if applicable, how much money the patron is willing to spend to cover the costs of services requiring a fee, such as online searches or photocopying.

In any library setting, a variety of questions are likely to be asked. Some may be very straightforward, and require only brief confirmation leading to short, factual answers; others will require a fairly comprehensive search of available literature on a sophisticated or obscure subject. The latter type of inquiry often requires an extensive interview process in which the subject is increasingly better defined (for the librarian and, in some cases, for the patron as well), and a number of intermediate answers and avenues for searching are needed.

The reference department may have policies regarding the level of service it will offer to patrons as a general rule (that is, to what lengths the librarians should go in answering a given type of inquiry). As described in chapter 1, a *conservative* level of service defines the reference interview as direction to a source or minimally helping the patrons to help themselves. A *moderate* level of reference service involves some instruction in the types of sources and their use while providing answers to the patron's questions. A librarian providing a *liberal* level of service consistently provides the answer or sources of the answer.[1] A liberal approach could include remaining with the patron throughout a lengthy search process, and the development of customized bibliographies.

Expediencies such as limited staff and resources, or elements of the particular situation surrounding an inquiry, often determine the level of service provided to a patron in a given instance. In any case, the nature of the patron's need, along with factors such as amount of staff time available to each patron, the expertise of the staff, and the number and appropriateness of available sources, determine the level of interviewing provided at the reference desk.

The reference interview includes question negotiation, location of the answer or otherwise meeting the patron's information need, and communication of the answer to the patron (or otherwise effecting successful closure of the interview). Frequently a patron's question to the reference librarian does not represent the true needs of that patron. The librarian must then, through a variety of types of questions, define the subject, scope, and, if possible, purpose of the patron's inquiry. Once the question is well understood, the librarian needs to determine the degree to which the question can be answered by developing a successful and efficient search strategy. Once the answer has been found, the librarian has to communicate the information to the patron and confirm that the information actually satisfied the patron's needs.[2]

A successful interview may not conclude with the complete fulfillment of the patron's information need (the full and complete answer to the inquiry). In their textbook on the reference interview, Elaine and Edward Jennerich refer to success as an intangible element.

> Many successful interviews may conclude without the patron finding the necessary information. Perhaps the information does not exist in the format the patron wants, or the library cannot supply the information.... In any event, a successful interview is one in which the patron feels satisfied that the librarian has given undivided attention and provided competent services. This may be quite different from what a librarian has traditionally considered successful — that the question has been answered completely.[3]

Joan Durrance has also taken issue with the use of accuracy as the primary measure of the success of the reference interview, stating that, "Given the nature of the environment, accuracy may not be the most appropriate measure of success."[4]

To better understand the reference interview process, librarians must consider both verbal and nonverbal communication issues, as well as the ways in which environmental factors, such as the physical arrangement of the reference area, affect the interview. The librarian needs to develop the skills or techniques called for in each of the three steps of the interview. In addition to learning the basic principles of the reference interview, librarians should be aware that they may encounter specific types of interviews which will require adaptation of general interviewing techniques to the specific need of the patron. Some librarians have an intuitive grasp of the nature of the reference interview, but it is nevertheless helpful to examine communications issues, interviewing skills, and types of interviews to learn more about the process.

Communication Issues

The reference interview may be viewed as a communication system in which librarians receive or decode messages; process messages; and encode or provide responsive messages.[5] The librarian and the patron may to varying degrees be viewed as joint administrators of the system, in which each has separate and distinct responsibilities for the complete exchange of information. The reference interview is part of a larger human communication and information-seeking context which includes the user's conceptual framework and the information system's organization and language.[6]

As participants in this communication system, reference librarians are concerned with verbal and nonverbal communication and the environment in which the interview takes place. The most obvious elements in a reference interview focus around verbal communications: what is said and what is heard or understood by both patron and librarian. Librarians should realize that patrons may encounter numerous barriers in their attempts to communicate effectively during reference interviews. Patrons may have little knowledge of the subject of the inquiry, the library's collection, or how to use reference tools. In addition, they may be uneasy about asking questions or talking to library staff members, and reticent to reveal the true question because of its sensitive nature.[7] Patrons may perceive the librarian as unapproachable (too busy, preoccupied, or intimidating).

Most of these barriers can be overcome during the reference interview through verbal reassurances or mediation. Librarians should help patrons feel comfortable in communicating with library staff. Interviewing and search strategies need to be tailored to the patron's particular circumstances, and questioning is essential to help the librarian adequately serve the patron. In cases in which a patron is unable to articulate or formulate the need, because of a lack of knowledge about a subject, the librarian can suggest general or subject-specific encyclopedia articles as a first step in a multi-step interview process.

Patron perceptions of staff functions, the purpose and organization of a library, and the approachability of staff are often factors in patrons' success or failure in meeting their information needs. In a study at Syracuse University's Carnegie Library, researchers found that about half the patrons interviewed had specific questions they were working on, but only 35 percent of those who had questions would ask a librarian for help. The major reasons given for not asking librarians were: (1) dissatisfaction with past service; (2) the perception that the question was too simple or trivial; and (3) a desire not to bother the librarian.[8] Reference librarians may also have to be concerned about what is *not* being asked if they are to assure success for the library's patrons.

Several nonverbal communication techniques will help reference staff be approachable and capable of interacting positively with patrons. A pleasant, welcoming expression and a calm, direct manner generally increase approachability. Some patrons are reluctant to interrupt a librarian who is reading while at the reference desk, though apparently on duty. Subjects in a recent study conducted by Joan Durrance reported that "the librarian's body language or manner conveyed a message that what had been going on was of more importance than the interrupting question."[9] Bunge and Murfin found that the activity in which the librarian was engaged when approached seemed to influence the success or failure of the interview.[10]

Eye contact is an important communication element in Western society. Although staring should be avoided, eye contact communicates attentiveness. Being at eye level, whether seated or standing, is conducive to communication, and can contribute to a more egalitarian atmosphere than a situation in which only one of the parties is standing. A respectful, even tone of voice should be maintained. Often it is helpful to establish rapport with the patron before beginning the interview. This may be done by informal conversation, including a brief salutation. Informal conversation may give the librarian needed time to focus on the individual patron. Moving from behind the desk toward the patron, or asking that a patron be seated next to the desk, is a signal to patrons that the librarian's attention and a certain amount of time are reserved for them.

Although communication skills are necessary to an efficient and productive reference interview, it is important that the librarian have a genuinely helpful attitude and a basic commitment to individual growth and pursuit of knowledge. This is not a matter of interview style, but a subtle, underlying philosophy that leads to effective service delivery, rather than just the accoutrements. Humanism extends the principle of caring for people to caring for them on their own terms, and thinking about their needs from their point of view. All inquiries should be taken seriously and at face value, at least initially, even if further negotiation is obviously needed.

3.1
Human Relations Skills

Learning to interact effectively on a one-to-one basis with another human being is not only a matter of learning body postures or appropriate phrases. Although these skills are part of handling the interview in a meaningful way, it is important to remember that we are dealing with humanism in bringing people and information together. Librarians should not regard the development of interpersonal communication skills solely as a means to further library public relations.... Effective public relations may very well be a side benefit of a staff trained in effective human relations skills, but personal growth and philosophical attitude, in addition to interviewing skills and a knowledge of resources must be taught as an integrated cohesive whole. To fail to understand interpersonal communication in reference as humanistic theory is to fail those individuals who come to the library seeking knowledge.

—Helen M. Gothberg
"The Beginnings"[11]

The physical setting of the reference area conveys messages to the patron as well. Librarians frequently have little control over the interior design of their institutions, including the amount of space available for and the appearance of the reference area, but it is important to maximize comfort and efficiency. Librarians should consider the following:

1. Is the primary reference service point visible and its function clearly labelled?

2. Is there adequate signage in the library so the patron can find the reference area?

3. Is the reference area aesthetically attractive and free of clutter?

4. Is seating available for patrons and staff alike? Is a writing surface available? Are counters at the appropriate height for jointly consulting reference tools?

5. Are reference tools, including referral forms and instructional handouts, close to the interview area? Are online catalog or other computer terminals used in reference activities convenient to the interview area?

6. Can furniture be placed so as to reduce the number of interruptions during the interview? Is extraneous noise controllable?

7. Is space available for more private interviews when necessary?

Often the space available for reference service is not lavish, but it is important to optimize available space through careful planning, in order to improve communication and promote positive interaction between staff and users.

Reference librarians need to be skilled communicators to provide effective service to patrons. This requires being articulate, approachable, and capable of sending appropriate messages by their appearance and that of their work space.

3.2
Communication Skills

[It is the work of reference librarians to give] assistance to the library user who wishes to tap the library's resources. These resources and the structure which houses them tend to be complex and difficult to use. Frustration upon the part of the library user—low or high in magnitude—often results from attempts to extract from the library what is required. Time constraints and anxiety caused by the need for the information can be added to the frustration. The outcome is an uneasy human being who tends to flounder. To contact and inform this person successfully, the reference librarian needs to be skilled in the art of communication.

—Virginia Boucher
"Nonverbal Communication"[12]

Interviewing Skills

In addition to a general understanding of the role of communication in the reference interview, there are specific techniques that will help reference staff manage a successful patron interview. The basic pattern of the reference interview has three elements: questioning, locating the answer, and communicating the answer (figure 3.1). The use of informal communication in this process can set the tone and facilitate the transition between stages.

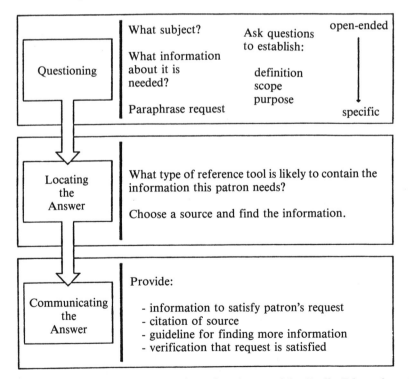

Fig. 3.1. Elements of the reference interview (prepared by Leslie Edmonds and Ethan Edwards).

Informal Interaction

Informal conversation, both initially and at the conclusion of the more formal portion of the interview, enables the librarian to focus on each patron as an individual, even during extremely busy times at the reference desk. A greeting provides the opportunity for the librarian to acknowledge and make initial contact with the patron, and to make the transition from one patron to another. Informal conversation can build rapport and establish a working relationship with the patron, and it also enables the patron to see the librarian as an individual. At the close of the interview, it affords the librarian the opportunity to encourage the patron to come back and seek assistance again. This helps to avoid making patrons feel that they are being dismissed.

Questioning

The key element of the reference interview is questioning, or question negotiation. "One of the most important tasks of a librarian who acts as an intermediary between the inquirer and the system is query negotiation – determining what the inquirer really wants to know."[13] The patron may have a single question that accurately and completely represents the information need, in which case the entire interview process may consist only of verifying that the answer meets the need as stated by the patron. However, patrons may not clearly state their information needs, or they may not have completely formulated their questions and need help in doing so. Because the librarian's first task is to establish patrons' true information needs, it is often necessary to use a series of interview questions.

During the interview, the librarian makes a series of choices regarding what topics to address by questioning, which may include the following:

1. The problem or situation surrounding the need (why the question is being asked), which may assist in determining the true subject of the request.

2. The subject of the question, including its relationship to other areas.

3. Requirements to answer the request (such as amount of information or desired format).

4. External constraints, such as the amount of time the user has to spend, deadlines for the needed information, and the availability of materials.

5. Patron variables (also called internal constraints), such as aptitude, reading ability, and level of motivation.

6. Prior search history (what the patron has already done to locate the desired information; what the patron already knows about the subject).[14]

Brenda Dervin and Patricia Dewdney presented a model of users' information-seeking behavior which they call the "sense-making model," in which patrons, in trying to do something they want or need to do, encounter a gap that needs to be filled. In order for that gap to be filled by the reference librarian, it is helpful to know the context of the need, or the purpose to which the resulting information will be put.[15]

It should be remembered that even seemingly straightforward and simple requests for information may not reflect the true needs of the patrons. Patrons may put questions in a form they think the library can answer because of preconceptions concerning factors such as the ability of the librarian, reference practice, or the structure of information (how information is packaged for consumption). Robert Taylor introduced the concept of the *compromised* question: a user's question which is altered according to what the available sources of information are expected to offer.[16] Such preconceptions may be erroneous, but it is important for librarians to realize that all users arrive at the reference desk with their own frames of reference, which include a set of assumptions or preconceptions. The librarian needs to avoid preconceptions and should test any assumptions made prior to or during the reference interview. These assumptions may be very useful in the interview situation, because they may offer clues for further exploration about the inquiry or the inquirer, but they should be tested during the question negotiation process so that false conclusions do not lead to answers that do not meet the patron's need.

In any inquiry, it is important initially to take the question at face value and negotiate it from that standpoint. The main purpose of the interaction is to respond to the patron's need as efficiently and completely as possible. Robert Hauptman cautions the librarian to avoid unnecessary and possibly counterproductive interviewing.[17] If, however, in the course of verifying or rephrasing the question, it is determined that the real question is different from that stated, that is the time to begin a more extensive questioning process. In all conversations with patrons, it is important to use clear, direct sentence structure and avoid the jargon of the library and information science field. Use of encouraging questions or comments, such as "Can you give me an example?" or "I see what you mean"—probably a natural activity of most librarians—facilitates the questioning process, encouraging the patron to continue to explain the need.

Two major types of questions are generally employed in the reference interview: *open-ended* or *open* questions, which invite the patron to describe the need and its context; and *closed* questions, which ask the patron to make a definite (often "either-or") response, and are useful in clarifying definitions or eliminating false leads.

Generally, the interview should progress from open questions to more narrow and direct questions, as the librarian feels that the patron has identified the true request. Open questions frequently begin with words such as *what*, *where*, and *how*. For example, one might ask a patron who has asked for information on elections, "What kind of election information might be helpful?" rather than, "Do you want election results of local or national offices?" (It could be that the patron really wants the definition of *electoral college*.) Open questions can include questions related to why the patron wants certain information. However, the use of professional judgment is especially important in eliciting the purpose or reasons for an inquiry; in some cases, clarification may best be sought through statements rather than questions: "It would help me to know what this information might be used for" or "If this is for a term paper, you might try...." The librarian should not try to determine a patron's purpose in asking a question if it is obvious from the interaction that knowing the purpose is entirely unnecessary. In addition, the patron has every right to refuse to divulge the purpose behind a question, even though this may limit success in having it answered.

While closed questions can be extremely useful at certain points in the interview process, the overuse of closed questioning can inhibit discussion and elicitation of useful information concerning the patron's need. Dervin and Dewdney stated that "regardless of the interrogator's intent, a closed question always restricts the freedom of the user's response.... All closed questions involve a judgment already made by the librarian of what is relevant to the user. Frequently, the closed question involves an attempt by the librarian to match the user to the more familiar parts of the system."[18] Librarians may tend to categorize their inquiries in terms of the types and forms of information available in known reference tools and other sources, while assuming that these forms are the most useful to the requester. Assumptions about requirements to fill a stated need and knowledge of reference sources should not preclude adequate question negotiation.

"Neutral questioning is a strategy for conducting the reference interview in a way that allows the librarian to understand the query from the user's viewpoint. Neutral questions are open in form, avoid premature diagnosis of the problem, and structure the interview along dimensions important to the users."[19] Neutral questioning, a subset of open questioning, can help to establish the reference setting as neutral territory and the interview as a shared responsibility of the patron and the librarian, lessening the potential for an imbalance of power between librarian and patron.

Open questions reveal possibilities for more discussion; closed questions focus narrowly and directly on a particular subject or source. Questions such as "Do you want to know how we elect the U.S. president?" or "Did you want to look at the recent issues of *Time* covering the election?" focus on particular solutions to patron questions. As the interview moves toward closure, it is appropriate to narrow the scope of questions, although one may appropriately suggest that a broader subject will yield more material on the required subject. Of course, open and closed questions will be intermingled in the course of the interview, as various ideas and procedures are explained and then confirmed or rejected. The movement from open to closed questions describes only the general shape of the interview.

Mary Jo Lynch reports that only 8 percent of questions asked in a sample of interviews she collected were classified as open; 90 percent were clearly closed questions; and 2 percent fell into neither category and were termed "intermediate," because they acted primarily as a bridge or clarifier for the patron's query.[20] It is inadvisable to assign a correct proportion of closed to open questions in an interview, as each inquiry, situation, and participant varies. Lynch asserts that "the value of an open or a closed question depends entirely on the interviewer's purpose and the amount of time available."[21] Subsequent researchers argue that the use of open questioning, at least initially, can actually shorten the time of a successful interview.[22] In any case, librarians need to be more aware of open questioning as a standard technique for reference interviewing.

Effective questioning requires good listening skills. Through active rather than passive listening, the librarian becomes more involved in the communication process and relies less on an assumed understanding of the patron's need.[23] *Active listening* involves paying close attention to all that a patron is saying, with the goal of subsequently paraphrasing the patron's request. This act of paraphrasing is useful in order to verify definitions and the scope of the patron's request during the course of the interview, and should become standard interviewing practice. Without full understanding of the patron's need, it is unlikely that the librarian will be successful in meeting that need.

Locating the Answer

Conducting an appropriate search for information is a reference skill separate from interviewing (see chapter 4). It is important to realize, though, that continued communication with the patron is important during this phase of librarian-patron interaction. In many libraries and for many types of requests, the actual search for information is performed by the patron. Likewise, in some situations the librarian may work with a patron for an extended length of time, and the search may take them to various parts of the library. The process of "inclusion" was researched by Gillian Michell and Roma Harris, who found that certain categories of patrons were more likely to rate librarians as competent if the patrons were included in the reference process.[24] Whatever the degree of involvement in the actual search process, the librarian should determine whether the patron needs assistance in finding items in the library or instruction in the use of access tools, such as the library's catalog or indexes.

Clarity is an important concern when giving directions. The librarian needs to be aware of how much information the patron can understand or remember at one time. Directions should avoid jargon or acronyms. When sending patrons in search of materials, the librarian might supply titles, call numbers, and the like to patrons in writing, or encourage patrons to take notes. If an online library catalog or periodical index is used, a printer may be available for producing a printed citation that the patron can take to another service point, such as the circulation desk.

For some searches, the librarian may answer the question for the patron. In such cases it is not necessary to share the search strategy used, but it is important for the patron to know when and where the information or material will be available and if charges will be incurred. It may be important for the patron to know in what format the information will be (some patrons refuse to read microfilm, for example) or if material is noncirculating. Although it does not matter for purposes of this discussion who will actually locate the answer for the patron, it is important to invite the patron to ask more questions or to revise the request as the search progresses.

Communicating the Answer

Providing the information or other form of the answer to the patron completes the reference process only if the answer proves satisfactory to that patron. Communicating the answer sometimes involves more than simply providing the information requested.[25] Additional or qualifying information may have been elicited during the search process. The librarian needs to convey the answer in a form that is both focused and complete, and to relate it directly to what was learned about the inquiry during the questioning stage of the interview. When librarians cannot locate complete answers, they must ensure that patrons understand that they are giving partial information and why. In communicating an answer, one should always cite a source of the answer, verify that the information is satisfactory to the patron, and suggest guidelines for finding more information on the original topic or related topics, if this is appropriate to the question asked.

Librarians need to adapt this model of interviewing to each patron's inquiry. It is not necessary to have a full interview with a patron who is a knowledgeable library user and needs only directional assistance. However, librarians should, under most circumstances, conduct at least minimal interviews to verify patrons' requests, even when it appears that patrons know what they want and are quite capable of articulating their needs. Most libraries are too busy, during many times of the day, for librarians to feel comfortable taking the time to do complete interviews. Although compromises have to be made, librarians can develop techniques to expedite interviews. By recognizing that there are several types of reference questions requiring different types of responses, librarians can become skilled at tailoring the interview to the question.

Types of Interviews

Because one goal of the reference interview is to ask appropriate questions and to make efficient use of both staff and patron time, it is helpful to adapt the basic model of the reference interview to the specific inquiry. A successful interview is tailored to each patron, but an interview style can be developed for the common types of patron requests. Library policy may dictate which particular kinds of questions the reference staff should attempt to answer and the extent to which the staff should offer service. Policy may also influence how the reference interview is conducted. What follows is a brief discussion of various types of information services (introduced in chapter 1) commonly offered in libraries and information centers, and some specific concerns for the reference interview presented by each type.

Ready Reference

Ready reference service usually includes responses to short, factual questions, and ordinarily involves the use of a basic tool such as a directory, almanac, encyclopedia, dictionary, or handbook. Ready reference service may also include directional assistance ("Where can I find the business department?"). The goal in ready reference is to give accurate information in a short time period, so the reference interview should be as simple as possible. Simple confirmation of what information is needed and a clear indication of the answer are what is most often called for. It is important, however, to confirm that the patron's information need has been met, in addition to answering the specific question asked. For example, it might be helpful to ascertain that the patron who wants the business department is indeed looking for information located in the business department, before giving directions.

Common sense may dictate the source of a particular piece of information, but it is important to verify facts in appropriate sources even if the reference librarian is sure of the answer. Obviously, when giving directions to locations within the library, it is not necessary to produce a map to prove that the answer is accurate. However, it is good practice actually to consult sources for definitions, statistics, ratings, and other factual information. When referring patrons to a source, the patron should be asked to return if the desired information is not obtained from that source.

Research Projects

At the other end of the spectrum is the interview with a patron who identifies the need as a research project. Research usually involves in-depth coverage of a topic, multifaceted questions, the need to consult multiple sources, and analysis of the information presented. The reference interview with a researcher is frequently a cumulation of several interactions over several hours, days, weeks, or longer. Such patrons will probably have a series of questions as they progress with their search. To avoid duplication of effort over time, it is important to encourage patrons to keep track of sources used or avenues taken during the course of the research interaction. In some cases, the librarian can keep a written record of sources suggested to a patron or procedures already tried if that librarian expects to be working with the patron again. It is also an important part of the interview strategy to give appropriate amounts of information in each interview session and to encourage patrons to continue to ask questions as research progresses.

Selective Dissemination of Information (SDI)

Selective dissemination of information (SDI) is a reference service through which the library staff notifies a patron about new sources of information on a subject of ongoing interest to the patron. This service is often computerized, and may involve analysis of the contents of periodic and monographic publications.[26] An interview for an SDI service should involve asking the patron to identify subject areas with as much specificity as possible and/or to identify particular publications, whether journals or works by particular authors or publishing firms, to be reviewed regularly by library staff. The SDI interview can be enhanced by a printed list of possible subjects for searching, such as the thesaurus of a particular subject database, or a list of journals available. An evaluation interview should be done after the first SDI is delivered, and at least annually after that, to ensure that the materials or citations forwarded to the patron are indeed helpful. SDI services are frequently offered to patrons who do not come to the library, so the interview may take place over the telephone or by mail rather than in person. Verbal (including written) cues take on increasing importance with telephone or mail requests for information, as nonverbal cues are unavailable.

Readers' Advisory

During a readers' advisory interview, the librarian is asked to give evaluative recommendations of particular titles to meet a patron's need. Often this takes the form of recommending "good" recreational reading, but readers' advisory service can also include finding appropriate materials to meet a nonfiction request. The librarian may rely on published reviews, best-seller lists, or personal reading when giving these recommendations.

During the advisory reference interview, it is important to ask questions that help define the patron's own evaluative structure. Patrons may not be particularly clear about what they consider to be good books, so the librarian may have to develop questions about patrons' reading habits to obtain adequate information to make successful recommendations. By asking what books the patron has read recently and enjoyed, what genres or subjects the patron reads regularly, or the kinds of materials the patron does not like, the librarian will be able to get a sense of direction from the patron. Open questions in this type of inquiry can best elicit information about personal taste. It may be useful or even necessary to ask about the purpose for which the patron is looking for information. For example, it might be helpful to know whether the person requesting a good introduction to ancient history is working on a class assignment or planning a trip to Greece.

When communicating suggestions to a patron, it is important, if possible, to provide either a brief oral summary or a review or annotation of the book so that the patron is given a chance to make informed decisions about the titles recommended. It is also good practice to give the patron a choice of several titles. The librarian may be able to get a better sense of the patron's preferences by seeing which books are accepted and which rejected.

Information and Referral/Community Information Service

The purpose of a community information service is to supply information that will guide patrons through a maze of government or private service agencies or ephemeral community information.[27] Information and referral services are described in chapter 1. Generally, information and referral (I & R) involves helping library users receive assistance or other information from appropriate local, state, or federal service agencies or informing them about community resources, such as cultural or educational resources. Requests may spring from personal crises ("Where can I get a hot meal?") or otherwise express an immediate need ("My son needs a Social Security number by the fifteenth. Where do I go to get him one?"). Timeliness is an essential element of answers to such requests. Effective, discreet questioning is extremely important in the I & R interview. It is essential to establish when the patron needs the information and to deliver the most recent (and still valid) information to the patron. It may be necessary to verify information by calling local agencies to confirm facts.

In the case of crises or sensitive requests, it is important to assure patrons that questions are held in confidence and that privacy will be respected. It is also important for the reference staff to understand how much help to give. If a person is requesting medical or legal advice, it is important to be clear and sympathetic, but to do no more than refer the patron to published sources or to agencies that can give the patron appropriate and informed professional help. Clarifying the nature and scope of the request is especially important in I & R requests. In sensitive situations, neutral questioning may be a particularly useful technique, as it emphasizes pragmatic solutions to the requester's needs. When communicating the answer, the librarian should write down information, such as addresses or phone numbers, as well as alternative sources of further information, and state the source of information. If it is not practical to verify the source of information when communicating an answer, the librarian should instruct the patron to verify that the answer given is current and otherwise accurate.

Individual Instruction

When interviewing a patron, it is important to assess whether the patron needs instruction in using the library or specific reference tools. Depending on the type of library, the library's policy on instruction, and the amount of time available, the reference librarian should be ready to incorporate instruction in the use of the library's catalog and other reference tools into the interview. In many reference interactions, the librarian will end up giving the patron citations to sources or helping the patron to develop a search strategy rather than providing a simple answer to a question. In the course of the interview process, it is wise to ask patrons if they would like assistance in using a particular source, or if they are finding the needed information. The librarian should also be prepared for the patron who asks for instruction directly.

In a school library, the instructional interview might take the form of shaping students' research behavior, through a series of questions designed to help them achieve manageable topics for term papers. In a special library, the interview may include descriptions of available resources or databases, and the kinds of information they provide, to help the patron make informed choices in using these resources.

In instructional or teaching interviews, librarians must be careful to avoid jargon, to explain and/or demonstrate each step, and to use examples. Librarians can supplement spoken instruction with written instructions prepared for commonly used tools. In the case of some electronic reference products, the librarian can be on call to interpret instruction that is available online. Librarians can also help patrons learn to do research by providing a reference model. By explaining the steps required to answer a question, and including patrons in the search process, the librarian can help patrons comprehend how to use these techniques themselves. It helps the patrons to see how the reference librarian works.[28] The amount of instructional information included in the reference interview depends on the type of question and the patron's sophistication and interest in instruction, as well as the library's policy for offering instruction and the expediencies of the situation.

Database Search Interview

The primary task of the database online search interview (discussed in more detail in chapter 5) is to translate the research topic or need for factual information into key words and phrases which can then be converted, when appropriate, into the controlled vocabulary of the specific database and developed into an efficient search strategy. The major portion of the online search interview is conducted prior to the search in order to minimize online time, and therefore cost, incurred by the patron. Sometimes the only online search interview is conducted prior to the search, and the results are mailed to the patron, who may or may not contact the librarian after receiving them. Depending on the topic, the time available, and the parties involved, it may be extremely helpful for the patron to be present during the actual search in order to clarify concepts and interpret results as the search progresses, as it is not always possible to predict the shape a search will take online.

The online search interview should include an explanation of controlled vocabulary and Boolean logic (discussed in chapters 4 and 5), and a full description of the expected product, costs, and time factors (such as delays in the receipt of citations printed offline). It is important to confirm that an online search is appropriate to the specific query and to ensure that the patron has been made aware of possible manual alternatives.

The interview associated with CD-ROM database searching can be more relaxed and extensive, because charges are not incurred directly during the search process. CD-ROM searching is conducted primarily by the patron, so the search interview frequently includes teaching the patron how to operate the equipment and perform the actual search, in addition to explaining terminology and developing a search strategy with the patron. The interview is likely to have several stages. During a pre-search interview, the theory is explained and the procedure outlined; then, during the search, the librarian may be called upon to reiterate or explain procedures or results. After the search, patrons may ask that results be interpreted or that they be given suggestions for other terms or strategies. It is good practice to check on the first-time CD-ROM user during the search, at least subtly, as this is when such explanations will probably make the most sense to the patron; it will also encourage searchers to return to library staff members for any assistance or interpretation of the process or results along the way or after the search. CD-ROM users often return to use the system again, so initial instruction is a good investment of time and effort.

Librarians customarily require a formal appointment for purposes of discussing an online electronic search with the patron; CD-ROM searching is ordinarily set up as a self-service operation, with user assistance provided by the reference staff. Although many CD-ROM products provide online or printed instructions or other documentation, these are not always effective for the particular search situation. It may not be clear to the patron what decisions need to be made or how to make them. The length and depth of the CD-ROM interview, as well as the number of interviews during the search process, will vary with the skill of the user, expediencies of the particular situation, and the policies and philosophy of the institution. (See chapter 5 for a full discussion of electronic reference services.)

Telephone Interview

Not all questions asked over the telephone are easily answered over the telephone. Most libraries have policies that limit telephone reference to "short, factual information questions which do not require extensive reading or interpretation on the library staff member's part."[29] Most libraries develop procedures to call patrons back later with information that is not immediately available in a ready reference collection, and to give priority to serving patrons in the library before answering telephone requests.

The structure of a telephone interview is similar to that of an in-person interview. However, nonverbal communication cues are not available over the telephone, so the librarian should carefully and frequently confirm and paraphrase a telephone request. Verbal courtesy and a pleasant tone of voice are essential. It may be necessary to set up a time to return the patron's call to communicate the answer or even to negotiate the question. When communicating an answer, including referrals to other agencies, it is important to cite sources for the answer, and to ask the patron to confirm that the correct information has been transmitted. The librarian may choose to send the patron the answer in printed form (in the form of a written message, photocopy, or facsimile) as an alternative to calling back or as a follow-up to a verbal answer.

Interviews Involving Problem Patrons

Reference librarians may be faced with handling problem patrons or situations, and the resulting interaction could be termed a type of reference interview. Patrons who are angry or dissatisfied with the library or a particular library transaction should be treated with respect, and the interview should focus on the problem and the solution to that problem, if possible. It is important for the librarian to articulate, or rephrase, the patron's problem in most cases to assure the patron that the librarian is listening and understands the nature of the problem. Empathy can be constructive even when the problem cannot be rectified by the librarian. Reference librarians should understand the degree to which they can become involved productively in a particular encounter, which requires an awareness of pertinent library policies and the role of various library administrators in the mediation process.

Librarians should remain as calm and courteous as possible when handling complaining patrons, and should learn diplomacy in refusing unreasonable demands. They should answer any questions they can when patrons express complaints, but the primary purpose of such interactions is to discover points of agreement and ways in which the library *can* accommodate the patron in more appropriate ways. It may be necessary to inform patrons of the library's formal procedures for handling such complaints.

Patrons who are aggressive to staff or other patrons, or who exhibit abnormal behavior (staring at other patrons, for example), are frequently the most difficult to handle. In such cases, librarians may need to consult superiors or seek help from library security or police. Arguing with an already angry, upset, or perhaps unstable patron is not likely to improve the situation. All comments should be direct, calm, and polite. Obviously, it is important to assess each situation accurately and fairly before entering into any type of negotiation with a difficult patron or in any emergency situation.

Conclusion

The reference interview, be it one sentence or an extensive conversation, is an essential element of reference service. As libraries, information centers, and information systems become more varied and complex, patrons' reliance on librarians to help them find needed information efficiently grows as well. Librarians need to use the good judgment that comes from practical experience with patrons to know when to use the basic model of questioning, locating the answer, and communicating the answer, and when to adapt or change procedures to fit the patron and the question asked. The reference interview is a key element in the librarian's role as intermediary between a patron's need for information or service and the information system. While knowledge about resources (such as reference sources, the library's collection, or community resources), information systems and organization, library policies and staff functions, and subject areas are all essential to meeting the patron's information needs successfully, the ability to conduct an effective reference interview enables the librarian to successfully match that knowledge with the patron's particular information need.

Notes

1. William A. Katz, *Introduction to Reference Work*, 5th ed., vol. 2 (New York: McGraw-Hill, 1987), 53-54.

2. Ethan A. Edwards, *Library Information Exchange: Investigation and Model Utilizing NovaNET, Final Report* (Champaign, Ill.: Lincoln Trail Libraries System, 1990), 60-61.

3. Elaine Zaremba Jennerich and Edward J. Jennerich, *The Reference Interview as a Creative Art* (Littleton, Colo.: Libraries Unlimited, 1987), 8.

4. Joan C. Durrance, "Reference Success: Does the 55 Percent Rule Tell the Whole Story?," *Library Journal* 114 (April 15, 1989): 31.

5. Randall P. Harrison, *Beyond Words* (Englewood Cliffs, N.J.: Prentice-Hall, 1974), 48.

6. Charles A. Bunge, "Interpersonal Dimensions of the Reference Interview: A Historical Review of the Literature," *Drexel Library Quarterly* 20 (Spring 1984): 10. Here Dr. Bunge is describing a key concept from Robert S. Taylor, "Question-Negotiation and Information Seeking in Libraries," *College & Research Libraries* 29 (May 1968): 178-94.

7. Ellis Mount, "Communication Barriers and the Reference Question," *Special Libraries* 57 (October 1966): 576-77.

8. Mary Jane Swope and Jeffrey Katzer, "Why Don't They Ask Questions?," *RQ* 12 (Winter 1972): 163-64.

9. Durrance, "Reference Success," 34.

10. Charles A. Bunge and Marjorie E. Murfin, "Reference Questions—Data from the Field," *RQ* 27 (Fall 1987): 15-18.

11. Helen M. Gothberg, "The Beginnings," *The Reference Librarian* 16 (Winter 1986): 16-17.

12. Virginia Boucher, "Nonverbal Communication and the Library Reference Interview," *RQ* 16 (Fall 1976): 27.

13. Brenda Dervin and Patricia Dewdney, "Neutral Questioning: A New Approach to the Reference Interview," *RQ* 25 (Summer 1986): 506.

14. Marilyn Domas White, "The Dimensions of the Reference Interview," *RQ* 20 (Summer 1981): 374; and "Evaluation of the Reference Interview," *RQ* 25 (Fall 1985): 78.

15. Dervin and Dewdney, "Neutral Questioning," 507-9.

16. Robert S. Taylor, "Question-Negotiation and Information Seeking in Libraries," *College & Research Libraries* 29 (May 1968): 182.

17. Robert Hauptman, "The Myth of the Reference Interview," *The Reference Librarian* 16 (Winter 1986): 47-52.

18. Dervin and Dewdney, "Neutral Questioning," 508.

19. Ibid., 506.

20. Mary Jo Lynch, "Reference Interviews in Public Libraries," *The Library Quarterly* 48 (April 1978): 131.

21.   Ibid., 135.

22.   Dervin and Dewdney, "Neutral Questioning," 512.

23.   Nathan Smith and Stephen Fitt, "Active Listening on the Reference Desk," *RQ* 21 (Spring 1982): 247.

24.   Gillian Michell and Roma M. Harris, "Evaluating the Reference Interview: Some Factors Influencing Patrons and Professionals," *RQ* 27 (Fall 1987): 95-103.

25.   Edwards, *Library Information Exchange*, 61.

26.   Carol Berger, ed., *Library Lingo: A Glossary of Library Terms for Non-Librarians*, 2d ed. (Wheaton, Ill.: C. Berger & Co., 1990), 19.

27.   Clara S. Jones, ed., *Public Library Information and Referral Service* (Syracuse, N.Y.: Gaylord, 1978), 26.

28.   Paula Montgomery, "Modeling Effective Reference Behavior," *School Library Media Activities Monthly* 4 (November 1987): 34.

29.   Bill Katz and Anne Clifford, eds., *Reference and Online Services Handbook: Guidelines, Policies, and Procedures for Libraries* (New York: Neal Schuman, 1982), 316.

Additional Readings

Bunge, Charles A. "Interpersonal Dimensions of the Reference Interview: A Historical Review of the Literature." *Drexel Library Quarterly* 20 (Spring 1984): 4-23.
    Bunge's article is a bibliographic essay providing a historical overview of the literature on the reference interview.

Dervin, Brenda, and Patricia Dewdney. "Neutral Questioning: A New Approach to the Reference Interview." *RQ* 25 (Summer 1986): 506-13.
    The authors describe the strategy of neutral questioning as a means of understanding the query from the user's viewpoint.

Jahoda, Gerald, and Judith Schiek Braunagel. *The Librarian and Reference Queries: A Systematic Approach*. New York: Academic Press, 1980. 175p.
    This work analyzes the reference process, including query negotiation and relevant communication models, and offers techniques to improve the reference interview.

Jennerich, Elaine Zaremba, and Edward J. Jennerich. *The Reference Interview as a Creative Art*. Littleton, Colo.: Libraries Unlimited, 1987. 107p.
    This textbook provides fairly comprehensive coverage of techniques and skills needed for the reference interview, including attention to training nonprofessional staff in interviewing and the place of library education in training librarians to perform reference interviews.

Katz, Bill, and Ruth A. Fraley. "Reference Services Today: From Interview to Burnout." *The Reference Librarian* 16 (Winter 1986): 1-312.
    This entire issue of *The Reference Librarian* is devoted to issues in reference service. The first section, entitled "The Reference Interview and Communication Challenges," contains several articles specifically addressing the reference interview. Particularly informative is "How to Find Out What People Really Want to Know" by Catherine Sheldrick Ross, which contains a thorough discussion of open and closed questioning.

Mount, Ellis. "Communication Barriers and the Reference Question." *Special Libraries* 57 (October 1966): 575-78.

Various types of communication problems encountered in the reference interview, with suggestions for handling them, are presented in question/answer scenarios.

White, Marilyn Domas. "The Dimensions of the Reference Interview." *RQ* 20 (Summer 1981): 373-81.

_____. "The Reference Encounter Model." *Drexel Library Quarterly* 19 (Spring 1983): 38-55.

White's model of the reference interview focuses on the content, rather than the form, of the interview, and takes into account issues of human information processing. She offers a conceptual approach to categorizing interviews for the question negotiation process.

BIBLIOGRAPHIC CONTROL, ORGANIZATION OF INFORMATION, AND SEARCH STRATEGIES

Introduction

All too often, individuals studying to become reference librarians assume that the principles and practice of cataloging, as well as the philosophical underpinnings of bibliographic control, are subjects merely to be endured until learning about the real business of reference work. Nothing could be further from the truth. The premise of this chapter is that a basic understanding of the principles of bibliographic control, as well as a basic knowledge of the way in which these principles are employed to provide access to documents, is essential to effective reference service. To provide answers to questions posed at the reference desk, at the catalog, at the searcher's workstation, or via telephone or electronic mail to users located outside the library, the reference librarian must first understand how various kinds of documents are organized and what tools are available for consultation during the search process. Searching is easier when the librarian is familiar with the various strategies that can be employed to make searching effective and efficient. These strategies can also be demonstrated to patrons through bibliographic instruction or point-of-access assistance, and they can be incorporated into the design of printed and electronic materials to aid the user.

The process of organizing information to make it available to persons seeking to use it is known as *bibliographic control*, and it is an activity basic to librarianship. Indeed, the history of librarianship in the United States is closely associated with the development of bibliographic organization schemes, such as Melvil Dewey's classification scheme, and the extensive bibliographic activities of the nation's libraries, such as the Library of Congress, the National Library of Medicine, and the National Agricultural Library. Since the nineteenth century, considerable time, money, and effort have been expended to design, implement, and maintain local, regional, national, and international systems of bibliographic control, to ensure that the universe of published information is made accessible.

While the concept of bibliographic control is simple, the practice of organizing information is complex and can be confusing both to beginning librarians and to library users. The universe of published materials may be partitioned in several ways: by publishing mode (e.g., books versus articles); by format (e.g., print versus electronic); or by subject area (e.g., general versus specific subject). In this chapter, two main approaches to organizing materials are presented as ideal types: catalogs and indexes. The bibliographic principles underlying their design are discussed. The process of searching for information by applying the principles of bibliographic control is described, and general search strategies are explained.

■ ══ ■

4.1

Defining Bibliographic Control

"The bibliographic universe is not under bibliographic control until anyone can discover those of its inhabitants that will suit his or her purposes."

—Patrick Wilson
"The Catalog as Access Mechanism"[1]

The phrase *bibliographic universe* refers to the totality of published items, regardless of date, format, or location. *Bibliographic control* refers to the organizing of these items, or rather the organizing of the representations of these items, so that they may be identified and located. The most common methods of ordering and providing access are by author, by title, and by subject.

The Library Catalog

The catalog serves as the primary means of access to a library's collection. Catalogs represent the holdings of a particular library at a particular geographic location or locations. Although the cataloging records that comprise a library's catalog may be drawn from one of the shared cataloging networks such as OCLC or RLIN, the catalog itself is specific to that particular library's collection. Bibliographic records are selected from the national database and may undergo modifications, such as the addition of a local call number or volume holdings statement. Consulting a national database answers the question: Does an item exist? Consulting the library's catalog answers the questions: Does the library own the item? and Where can the item be found? Occasionally, the catalog of a very large or specialized library collection can serve both functions: for example, the catalog of the National Library of Medicine can tell whether an item exists and at least one location where it may be borrowed, if it is not available locally.

A library's catalog is cumulative, including all materials held in a collection, regardless of date of publication or date of acquisition. In large libraries or library systems, the contents of the catalog may be a combination of several branch or departmental libraries. In these instances, the catalog is known as a *union catalog*. (Local circumstances may preclude representation in the catalog of all holdings of all libraries within a system. When the catalog is not fully representative, this fact should be made clear to users and librarians.)

The catalog is composed of representations of bibliographic objects, including books, journals, phonograph records and cassettes, maps, and other nonprint items. These representations are called *bibliographic records*. In a card catalog, the bibliographic record is printed on a set of cards; in an online catalog, the bibliographic record consists of machine-readable information encoded in digital format. The machine-readable version of a bibliographic record conforming to certain standards for content and structure of the data is called a *MARC* (MAchine-Readable Cataloging) record.

There are three major types of access points in a catalog: author, subject, and title. For any given item, there will be three types of access points, with one or more entries per access point. In a card catalog, this means that a card is created for the author(s), for the title(s), and the subjects (usually two or three subjects as described by subject headings). The subject headings are selected from established subject heading lists—the *Library of Congress Subject Headings* (LCSH),[2] or the *Sears List of Subject Headings*,[3] for example—during the cataloging process. The use of standardized lists ensures that the terminology and format of the headings remain consistent. An additional card is created to be filed in the shelf list, which provides control over the collection and access by classification number. A single item, then, is represented by several cards or access points. The number of cards and the access points themselves can be determined by examining the *main entry* card, which lists each card that has been created for the item. A card set for the book *The Happy Bookers* appears in figure 4.1.

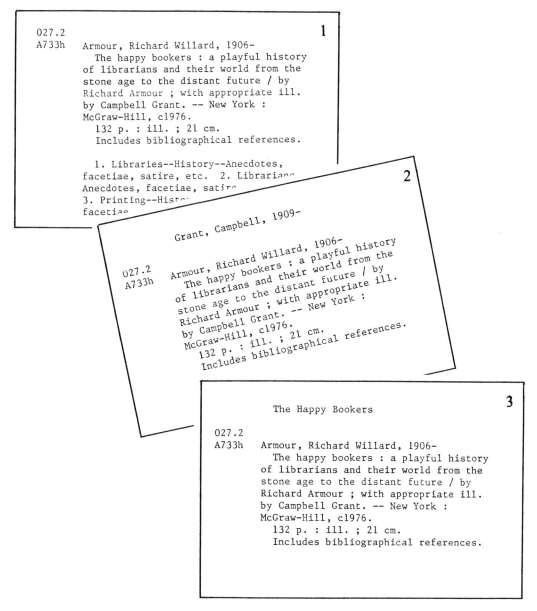

Fig. 4.1. Set of catalog cards. 1. The main entry card lists or *traces* all the other cards in the card set. One card is filed for each of the subject headings and added entries, plus one additional main entry card used for the shelf list. 2. Additional card or *entry* for the illustrator. 3. Title card. 4, 5, 6. Subject heading cards.

(Figure 4.1 continues on page 62.)

Fig. 4.1 — *Continued*

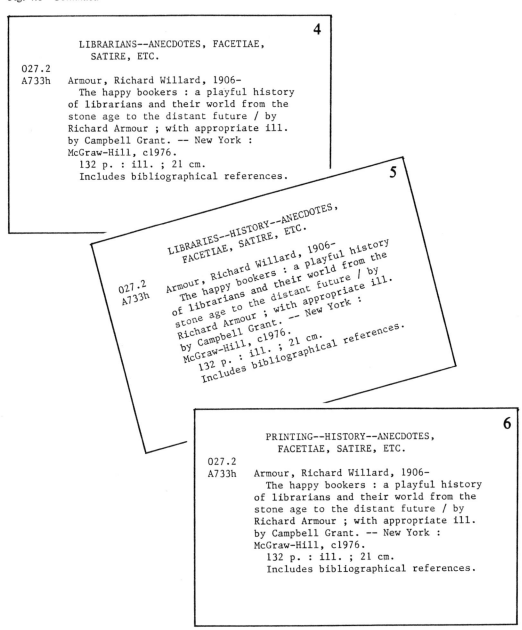

This information, particularly the subject tracings, can be very useful, because it shows how the cataloger has chosen to represent that particular item and can suggest terminology to use in searching. The ability to gain an overview of the full bibliographic record is a particular advantage of the card catalog over a printed index. Unfortunately, this advantage is often ignored by the catalog user (patron and reference librarian alike), and even by the catalog creator, when the information is included on only one of the cards of the set (the main entry card).

Indexes

Just as it is essential to understand some basic principles of cataloging, it is important to understand some basic principles of indexing. This need is even more critical in order to understand issues arising from converting print to electronic media and merging indexing and cataloging files. Indexes serve to locate information within a document. The most familiar index is the one found at the back of a book, which is used to find where certain topics are discussed within the text itself.

The indexes discussed in this chapter are indexes to published periodical literature. This kind of index is produced on a regular schedule (typically on a monthly, quarterly, or annual basis) and provides access to the topical contents of a group of publications. The group of publications that is indexed may be determined by a variety of criteria; topic, language, publication type, and country of origin are some of the most common criteria. For example, the *Readers' Guide to Periodical Literature*[4] indexes a group of popular magazines published in the United States. *Education Index*[5] includes only publications whose primary focus is education, while *Index Medicus*[6] indexes medical journals published throughout the world in a variety of languages. The criteria used in selecting materials to include for indexing are usually explained in the introductory pages of the index and are essential reading for effective use of the index.

Indexes are published in book or electronic form, and may cumulate yearly or for longer time periods. Most indexes are arranged in alphabetical order by subject, and some provide a separate listing by author. Some indexes do not provide title access to materials. Unlike a library catalog, the domain of an index is unrelated to the library's collection. From the searcher's perspective, then, an index represents what has been published in a particular subject area during a specified time period; in order to determine whether a particular library holds an item, some additional searching must be undertaken. Though this may seem quite obvious, it becomes less clear when online or CD-ROM (compact disc-read only memory) indexes are presented to the user alongside or through the same terminal as an online catalog. For example, users may confuse a CD-ROM version of an index such as *Education Index* with the online catalog, because both are accessed through a microcomputer located in the same or adjacent areas in the library. In libraries where databases are loaded onto the same computer as the online catalog, it is even more important to distinguish between the function of a catalog and an index. Unless this distinction is made very clear, patrons may expect to obtain all the items listed in an index, just as they would expect to locate all the items listed in a library's catalog.

Principles of Bibliographic Control

Despite the differences between catalogs and indexes, some underlying principles of bibliographic control are held in common. These are physical arrangement, collocation and authority control, and depth and comprehensiveness of indexing. Each of these principles is defined and discussed in the following sections.

Physical Arrangement

For purposes of discussion, the catalog may be regarded as a file, a group of objects arranged in an arbitrary or meaningful order. An example of a file arranged in arbitrary order is a dictionary catalog in which the records are arranged in alphabetical order. An example of meaningful order can be found in a classified catalog in which the records are arranged by classification number to reflect a subject arrangement.

In a classified catalog, materials on similar subjects are filed together as they would appear on the shelf according to the classification plan. Users of a classified catalog must consult a schedule or plan to determine the appropriate class numbers for a particular topic before beginning to search, in much the same way as the index of a book is consulted to locate discussions of a particular topic. Classified catalogs are seldom used in the United States, but are more common in Europe. In a dictionary catalog, the searcher may approach the file directly, as one might consult an encyclopedia or a dictionary. Dictionary catalogs are of two types: integrated and divided. In an *integrated* catalog, one must look at only one place in the catalog, that is, in one alphabet. This can be confusing when the same word serves as a title, an author, and a subject, particularly in large research collections. In a *divided* catalog, one alphabetic arrangement is used for authors and titles, and another for subjects. In this arrangement, books *by* an author and books *about* an author are not filed next to one another, but are filed in entirely separate alphabetic sequences. For example, a play by Shakespeare would be in the author/title alphabetic sequence, but a book about Shakespeare's plays would be in the other. A biography of Shakespeare would appear in the subject catalog—but, if the title of the biography were "Shakespeare," it would also appear in the author/title sequence.

■ ═══ ■

4.2

Undeserved Success in Catalog Searching

Although divided catalogs are usually understood to assist the user, particularly when files are large, this advantage sometimes goes unrecognized and unappreciated by catalog users. For example, in a recent study in which students were asked to search for topical information in a divided card catalog, one undergraduate conducted all five searches in the author/title catalog. The research assistant (a library school student) who observed this phenomenon later reported: "He never discovered that there was another section of the card catalog dealing with subjects. Based on his lack of understanding of the catalog, he shouldn't have been successful in finding materials. But the irony is, he found about as much as those students who conducted their searches in the subject catalog!"

As card catalogs are converted to electronic formats (online catalogs), questions of physical arrangement of the file may become moot, because the information is stored in computer files in a location remote from the searcher. Separation of author, title, and subject are created not by the physical arrangement of the cards, but by the search command structure.

Some of the characteristics of both dictionary and classified arrangements have produced interesting problems and attempts at new solutions in the online environment. For example, the ability to browse through a meaningful order (typical of a classified catalog) is supported in some experimental catalogs by providing a classification schedule such as the Dewey Decimal System along with the catalog records. Searchers can browse the classification schedule onscreen in order to gain a sense of related topics. In other catalogs, related subject headings are displayed for browsing.

The physical arrangement of indexes reflects many of the same principles as the catalog. In most indexes, arrangement by subject is paramount. This is most often accomplished through a dictionary arrangement, such as that found in *Library Literature*,[7] although some indexes, such as *Library and Information Science Abstracts*,[8] use a classified arrangement. These two approaches are illustrated in figures 4.2 and 4.3.

Information retrieval

   See also
   Information needs
   Subject access

Bierbaum, E. G. A paradigm for the '90s: in research
   and practice, library and information science needs
   a unifying principle; "least effort" is one scholar's
   suggestion. bibl *Am Libr* 21:18-19 Ja '90
Rethinking the library in the information age, v II;
   a summary of issues in library research; edited by
   Anne Mathews. U.S. Office of Educ. Res. & Improvement, Office of Lib. Programs, 555 New Jersey Ave.,
   NW, Washington, D.C. 20208-1430 1988 224p charts
   [for sale by the Supt. of Docs., Congressional Sales
   Office, U.S. G.P.O.]
UK Online User Group. State of the Art Conference
   (2nd: 1986: Bristol, England). Online information
   retrieval in practice; proceedings of the 2nd UK Online
   User Group State of the Art Conference, Bristol, 1986;
   edited by Linda Dorrington. Taylor Graham 1987
   158p

Aims and objectives

Bookstein, A. Set-oriented retrieval [expanded version
   of paper presented in the 11th International conference
   in research and development in information retrieval]
   Inf Process Manage 25 no5:465-75 '89
Molholt, P. A. Research issues in information access.
   (*In* Rethinking the library in the information age,
   v II. U.S. Office of Educ. Res. & Improvement, Office
   of Lib. Programs 1988 p93-113)

Fig. 4.2. Entries from *Library Literature*
(February 1990). Reprinted by permission of
The H. W. Wilson Company.

**ZjVrm — Searching. Recall *and* Precision. Government
   department libraries. Education libraries. Netherlands. Ministry
   of Education. ADION**   90/3147
   ADION onderzocht: de ontsluiting in het ADION-systeem; precision
en recall. [ADION investigated: subject access in the ADION system;
precision and recall.] Hilde Ongering, Gerhard J.A. Riesthuis. *Open*, 21
(7/8) July/Aug 89, 261-264. tables. 6 refs.
   In the Netherlands the Ministry of Education and Science asked the
Amsterdam University Study Group on Books, Libraries and Information
Science to examine the precision and recall levels of its automated
information   system   ADION   (Automatisch   Documentatie-   en
Informatiesysteem   voor   Onderwijsliteratuur   in   Nederland/Automatic
Documentation and Information System for Educational Literature in the
Netherlands). The ADION data base at Sept 88 contained approximately
39,000 records, to which some 125 new records are added weekly. A list
of 60 search topics was compiled and each topic was searched by both an
educational researcher and an information specialist and the results
compared. Despite deficiencies in the thesaurus used the results showed a
70% precision/recall rate. (P.W.)

**ZjVrqOtc — File organisation. Relational data bases. Data base
   management systems**   90/3148
   Complex view support for a library database system. Hideki
Nishimoto, Shoji Ura. *Information Processing & Management*, 25 (5)
1989, 515-525. illus. tables. 14 refs.
   Describes an interface mechanism called 'complex view support', to be
used with a relational data base system (RDBS) in supporting an
increasingly complex distributed environment in automated library systems.
Until now, an RDBS has not been suitable for library management work
such as cataloguing and retrieval because of the restriction that the data
should be in the form of flat tables. However, the RDBS potential, which
provides flexibility in sharing, recovery, and security, in addition to
storing and managing large data banks efficiently, has become even more
attractive in the modern library system. (Original abstract—amended)

Fig. 4.3. Entries from *Library
and Information Science
Abstracts* (March 1990).
Reprinted with the permission
of Library Association Publishing, London.

ZjVs — Searching. Strategies   90/3149
   Set-oriented retrieval. A. Bookstein. *Information Processing &
Management*, 25 (5) 1989, 465-475. 14 refs.
   In the recent past information retrieval methodologies have been
based on retrieving documents one at a time. Introduces a set-based
retrieval which is consistent with the single-document or sequential
methods and defines a precise model of the set-oriented approach.
(Original abstract—amended)

Other indexes use a divided approach, separating the subject section from the author section. An example of this approach is *Index Medicus*. Finally, indexes often have supplementary sections in which different types of entries are included. *Library Literature* lists book reviews separately, and *Index Medicus* has a section listing review articles that precedes the main subject index. Familiarity with several indexes and their various features can often save time, and is important for efficient searching.

Collocation and Authority Control

A basic tenet of cataloging is the principle of *collocation*, which means that similar materials are gathered at a single location. In other words, one of the functions of cataloging is to ensure (as much as possible) that all materials by Shakespeare are filed together, and that all materials about aardvarks are located at the same point in the file. While this may seem quite simple and obvious, the cumulative nature of the catalog, combined with the practice of using popular (and therefore changing) terminology for subject headings, makes collocation difficult to achieve in most library catalogs today.

From their inception, catalogs were designed to be searched directly by the library user, and are presumed to be self-explanatory. The use of popular words and terms as subject headings facilitates searching directly without first consulting a list of subject headings or requiring any specific training or subject expertise. Multiple word phrases are sometimes combined and inverted for purposes of collocation; for example, "Insurance" and "Insurance, medical" are filed next to each other. When terminology changes, cross-references are added to the catalog so that intellectual links are made between the new and old terms, even though the cards themselves are not physically refiled.

An essential method of achieving collocation is maintenance of *authority control*, both name authority control and subject authority control. For example, name authority control ensures that all existing permutations of an author's name—P. S. Winnicott, Pamela Smith Winnicott, Pamela S. Winnicott, or Pamela Smith if Winnicott was a name acquired or dropped by a change in marital status—are linked so that all the works written by this individual are gathered at a particular location in the catalog. Similarly, subject authority work ensures that the subject headings assigned to the work are indeed correct and in current use, and that any cross-references that have been established are noted (see figure 4.1). For instance, subject catalogers must make sure that the subject heading string "Libraries—History—Anecdotes, facetiae, satire, etc." is used, rather than "History of libraries," and that an indication of a cross-reference to terms used earlier is included, so that all works concerning "Libraries—History" can be located from a single entry point in the catalog. The maintenance of linkages between terms is referred to as the *syndetic structure* of the subject headings. The sheer size of the bibliographic universe and the complexity of modern knowledge (the "information explosion") have made authority control one of the biggest challenges in cataloging today.

In indexes, the terms used to represent the contents of a document are called *descriptors*; the descriptors that are used for an index constitute its *vocabulary*. This terminology is also often controlled by the use of a *thesaurus* which lists terms that can be assigned to bring out various aspects of a document's contents. Because indexes are frequently confined to a specific subject area, the terms used as descriptors may be rather technical and highly specific.

Terms in a thesaurus are linked by references indicating relationships such as broader term, narrower term, and related term. Although the most recent edition of the *Library of Congress Subject Headings* includes Narrower Term/Broader Term designations, it was not designed to function as a true thesaurus.[9] While the difference between a subject heading list and a thesaurus is debated among librarians, one difference is that the syndetic structure of a thesaurus is more rigorous and hierarchical than that of a subject heading list.

Another difference lies in the way in which a thesaurus is constructed. Many thesauri are created as reflections of the nature of the subject field itself. They are representations of knowledge within a specific subject area. The topics and their interrelationships are represented through terms regardless of the existence of documents within those areas. Other thesauri are more like subject heading lists, in that terms are introduced by virtue of *literary warrant*: that is, they are derived from the published literature itself. When a term has been used sufficiently to warrant its use in a subject heading or as a descriptor, it is considered for inclusion in the list.

■ ══ ■

4.3

Two Approaches to Building a Thesaurus

There are, of course, two methods of thesaurus construction which I choose to call stalactitic and stalagmitic. The stalagmitic is the way Taube and I went about constructing our index — down on the floor of the cave among the documents, slowly building towards the ceiling. The stalactitic seems to be much more fun — one convenes groups of experts who hang up on the roof of the cave, twittering and chirping among themselves but as far away from the actual documents as they can get.

Stalagmitic thesauruses can be constructed either by humans or computers working with actual terms in text; stalactitic thesauruses only by committees of experts. And if a thesaurus has a smooth machine-produced regularity, with all terms expanded equally, it was probably produced by subject specialists jealous of the importance of their field; if it is full of charming irregularities, with some terms almost ignored and others expanded to almost tedious depth, it was probably produced by machine, faithfully reflecting the charming irregularities of the authors.

— Harold Wooster
"A Naive Look at Subject Analysis"[10]

The use of a *standardized* or *controlled vocabulary* supports the same function in indexing as the collocation function of subject authority control in cataloging. Both indexing and subject cataloging have as their goal the grouping of similar items using standardized vocabulary. Correct, consistent use of authority control and controlled vocabulary provides quality control; these techniques ensure that materials are represented reliably and consistently, so that the user may depend on consistent results when using proper search and retrieval techniques.

Depth and Comprehensiveness of Indexing

Perhaps the most distinctive feature of an index compared with a catalog is its depth and comprehensiveness of indexing. Indexing is most often associated with articles, whereas cataloging is associated with separately published works such as books. The bibliographic record for cataloging is standardized on a national, even international level, while the indexing record, known as the *unit record*, may differ from index to index. Despite these differences, however, one of the most important elements of the unit record is the set of descriptors used to describe the conceptual contents of the document. Many more descriptors are used to describe the contents of an article; a ten-page article may have ten descriptors associated with it, while the average number of subject headings applied to a book is less than three. One implication of this difference is that, based on probability alone, a given item will be located more easily in an index than in a catalog.

Subject headings sometimes capture more than one concept per heading by pre-coordinating the terms. For example, a book entitled "Children's Books and Magazines: A Market Study" is about the children's book publishing industry. The subject heading for this book is "Children's literature—Publishing—United States." The concept "children" is pre-coordinated with the concept "literature" to make the subject heading "children's literature." Other types of literature may also be represented by pre-coordinated headings. Further, the subject heading for this book is composed of another term, "publishing," and finally, the geographical location "United States." While all these terms further describe what the book is about, they do not serve as access points except in electronic formats, such as an online catalog, in which keyword searching is available.

In printed indexes, however, each descriptor indicates an access point. If a record has ten descriptors associated with it, that item will appear in the index at ten different locations. In printed indexes, unlike card catalogs, the descriptors attached to the item are not usually listed as part of the entry in the index. It is therefore impossible to see what other aspects of an article have been brought out by the indexer.

In online and some CD-ROM systems, however, the searcher can request that the descriptors be displayed. Examining the descriptors can often provide insight into other aspects of a topic covered by an article, or can suggest additional terminology to be incorporated in a subsequent search. Figure 4.4 shows the descriptors from the CD-ROM version of ERIC and the subject headings for the same item in a catalog.

```
ERIC:

        College and University Library Services for the Handicapped Student in
     Texas.
        Thomas, James L., Ed.
        North Texas State Univ., Denton, School of Library and Information
     Sciences.  1978.
        49p.
        Descriptors: *Academic Libraries; Directories; *Handicapped Students;
     Library Equipment; *Library Facilities; *Library Services; Questionnaires;
     Surveys
        Identifiers:  *Texas


Card Catalog:

     027.7
     C686          College and university library services
                   for the handicapped student in Texas
                   / edited by James L. Thomas. --
                   Denton, Texas : Texas Library
                   Association, 1978.
                   vi., 41 ℓ ; 28 cm.

                   1. Libraries and the physically
                   handicapped.  2. Handicapped--Education
                   --Texas.  3. Libraries, University and
                   college--Texas.  I. Thomas, James L.
```

Fig. 4.4. Same report as listed in ERIC and in the card catalog.

Models of Searching

In the past two decades, electronic data storage techniques have been applied to create online and CD-ROM versions of both bibliographic indexes and library catalogs, providing unprecedented opportunities for librarians and researchers to observe how people actually search. In this section, several models of the searching process are described, as are the ways in which the bibliographic control properties of indexes and catalogs can be exploited by these models.

Models of searching can be categorized in a variety of ways: manual or online, ideal or real, catalog or index. Some search models assume that information retrieval can be modeled using mathematical or system analytic formulas. Others suggest that modeling the actual searching behavior of users and librarians is a more useful approach. Still others focus on the differing functions of catalogs and indexes.

Modeling the search process can be helpful in designing bibliographic instruction or in helping searchers improve their results. The growing availability of direct patron access to electronic information systems such as CD-ROM and online catalogs has stimulated interest in modeling the search processes of casual (untrained) users as well as those of librarians. As mentioned earlier, the blurring of distinctions between indexes and catalogs that has occurred in the online environment has also challenged previous assumptions about search patterns.

One way of improving the information search is through education and training (user education provides the focus for chapter 6). Both librarians and users can be taught to search more effectively, and they can be given hints as to ways in which they can improve their results. These hints are known as *heuristics* or *tactics*. Articles describing such tactics are frequently published in the library literature, particularly in journals dealing with online searching.

Another way of improving searching is through system design. Appropriate didactic interventions, such as "help" screens, can be built into the system interface, or machines can be programmed to modify strategies automatically to achieve better results. Increasingly, librarians are taking an active role in creating or adapting systems to meet the needs of their users.[11] Although system design is not discussed in this text, one should be mindful of one question: should librarians teach users to adapt to the system (i.e., learn how to use a system that is not entirely natural) or should librarians design systems that adapt to the user? The traditional approach to assisting users in improving their search results has been instruction. Such instruction can make the encounter between librarian and user more personal, yet it is time- and labor-intensive for both librarian and user. On the other hand, standard systems of bibliographic organization used by most libraries provide consistency to users and also enable cooperative activities among many libraries. The system design approach may lead to proliferation of diverse systems of varying quality; nevertheless, effective system design may empower users to pursue their searches independently and free librarians from repetitive instructional tasks.

Examining the search patterns of both librarians and users in order to improve information access is an important research area in library and information science. Early research focused primarily on patterns displayed by reference librarians in answering questions from printed sources, but recent work has examined searching behavior of librarians conducting online searches. Studies have looked at such factors as individual differences, cognitive style, and differences between new and experienced searchers.[12]

As libraries provide more and more opportunities for patrons to access electronic information systems directly, the need for both instruction and assistance, by either humans or machines, will surely expand, as will interest in modeling the user's search process. The study of both cognitive and affective aspects of the search process encourages librarians to become more aware of user needs, and enables them to make appropriate interventions to facilitate searches. For example, research examining the need for users to engage in reformulating their requests based on feedback from an information system may lead to systems that prompt the user to examine subject headings as a source of additional searching terms.[13] By studying how students feel at various stages of preparation of a term-paper bibliography, librarians may become more aware that searching for information is not solely an intellectual process; it may be accompanied by feelings of anxiety, confusion, relief, disappointment, or confidence.[14]

The use of expert systems to support and enhance both librarians' and users' searching is a recent development that holds great promise. Since design of expert systems in reference begins with a clear understanding of search processes, careful observation of the search processes of both reference librarians and users is a logical place to start.[15]

Manual or Online

One of the earliest search models was developed in 1936, by Carter Alexander.[16] This model of searching lays out the steps taken in conducting a manual search in a reference collection, much as a flowchart does, but with far less complexity. The model describes six steps: clarify the question, select the type of material to answer the question, prioritize the sources within the type, locate and search, evaluate, and repeat if necessary. The model assumes familiarity with the reference collection, or at least the types of materials contained within that collection. In other words, this model assumes at least a working knowledge of the materials in part 2 of this text. The model is general enough that it can be adapted to the electronic environment in which databases, rather than printed materials, are reviewed. It does not address selection of terminology for the search (discussed in a later section of this chapter).

Some models of searching apply equally well to online and manual environments. For example, Bates's tactic called TRACE is well-suited to searching both card and online catalogs.[17] To TRACE means to use the information already found to derive additional search terms, and to examine the way in which the document has been represented. In a catalog search, the searcher uses the subject tracings as potentially relevant headings in refining the search. Examining the subject tracings on catalog cards is an excellent (though often overlooked) way to improve a manual search; when an online catalog is designed to display the subject tracings, this same technique can be used. In printed indexes, the list of descriptors is not displayed and TRACE cannot be used. In an electronic environment, however, TRACE may be used by displaying the field(s) in the unit record that list the descriptors used. Some system designers have incorporated the TRACE tactic as a feature of the interface. In such systems, the user is prompted to ask for a listing of the descriptors with the suggestion that they be incorporated into the search.

4.4

A Model of the Search Process

A patron has come to the reference desk with the question: "I need to know about neural nets."

Step 1: *Clarify the question.* Find out what domain of knowledge the term comes from—physiology, psychology, computer science? What does the inquirer plan to do with the information; at what level of detail is the information needed?

Step 2: *Select the material(s).* Determine whether the term has been established long enough to appear in standard reference books, such as encyclopedias and dictionaries of the subject field, or whether recent issues of an index must be examined. Consulting the subject heading list to determine whether the topic appears as a subject heading that can be searched in a catalog is also appropriate. Consideration of a database search also occurs at this stage, and may be appropriate if the term is too new to appear as a subject heading or descriptor. Knowledge of the reference collection and its contents is critical to success.

Step 3: *Prioritize the sources* identified in the order of their likelihood of containing the answer. In the case of the neural net question, one criterion for prioritizing might be the level of detail desired and the level of understanding exhibited by the patron. For a layperson, a quick search in a general periodicals index or an up-to-date encyclopedia would be a good first priority.

Step 4: *Locate the sources.* Are they in the reference area? Are they owned by the library, or is it necessary to call another location or refer the patron to another location?

Step 5: *Search the materials* you have selected until a suitable answer is found, or until you are sure that an answer cannot be found there. This process is evaluative, since the determination of suitability varies with the librarian's assessment of the user's information need.

Step 6: *Evaluate*, and *repeat* if necessary. The searching process is cyclic, and may require asking the patron for further clarification, for more time, or whether a referral to another library would be desirable.

Ideal or Real

The contrast between the ideal and the real in search models recognizes that, while models of searching are useful for conceptual and pedagogical reasons, most librarians do not follow the ideal model exactly. In the online world especially, the contrast between the ideal and the real can be understood by looking at the origins of computerized information retrieval. The first computer systems were developed in part for mathematical and data processing applications, so it is not surprising that the first attempts to apply computers to problems of information storage and retrieval were based on mathematics, particularly set theory. Mathematics is an exact or "pure" science, which contrasts with the ambiguity and inexactitude of language. While there are no doubt a number of implications that can be drawn from the mathematical origins of computer-based information retrieval, in contrast to the humanistic origins of most library organization schemes, three of the most important are discussed here: exact matching, Boolean logic, and flowcharting.

Exact matching refers here to the unambiguous way in which computer operations are performed. All text is stored in a computer in binary form as a series of zeroes and ones (bits). During a search operation, the computer scans text files bit by bit, comparing the terms used in the request with the terms available in the file. Just as numbers are unambiguous, the binary nature of computer design leaves no room for "maybe" or "almost" or "not quite." Terms must match exactly in order for them to be retrieved; thus, this process is referred to as exact match.

Another fundamental characteristic is the use of *Boolean logic*, a method of analyzing a problem by manipulating groups (or sets) of items. When the groups or sets are taken as a whole and considered together using the Boolean operator OR, the result is a *union* of the sets. The union of the sets includes all the items from each set. When sets are compared in terms of the elements they share in common using the Boolean operator AND, one finds the *intersection* of the sets. The intersection of two (or more) sets is thus the group whose members share at least one common element with the members of the original group(s). As discussed in more detail in chapter 5, the ability to use Boolean operators to manipulate sections of computerized information files is regarded by most librarians as fundamental to computerized information retrieval systems today. This is because Boolean operators maximize the power of online retrieval by enabling searchers to express a series of requirements for the items they wish to retrieve. The technique of combining terms at the time of the search is called *post-coordination*, as contrasted with *pre-coordination*, in which a string of terms is linked by the indexer or subject cataloger at the time the item is entered into the system. Because post-coordination is under the control of the searcher, this approach gives greater power and flexibility to the search. Any terms can be linked through post-coordination, so the search can be tailored to the requester's query. In quickly changing fields such as science, the ability to combine terms in ways not previously thought of is particularly attractive.

Despite the importance that librarians place on using Boolean operators in developing search strategies, Boolean logic is difficult for the average person to understand and apply.[18] For example, when searching for articles about black Americans, most people string together a list of synonyms by using the conjunction AND: Blacks and Black Americans and Negroes and African-Americans. In Boolean logic, however, this list has an effect the opposite of what was intended, because it requires that *all* the terms be present for an item to be retrieved. Since indexers and catalogers use only one term to represent the concept of racial identity, and since other parts of the bibliographic record are likely to express the concept only once, such a search statement will retrieve nothing, because it is overly restrictive. The correct approach would be to use the Boolean operator OR: Blacks or Black Americans or Negroes or African-Americans, thus allowing the presence of *any* of the terms to lead to retrieval.

A third approach to search models that derives from this framework is flowcharting. While helpful in graphically displaying the sequence of steps in an information search, one of the drawbacks of elaborate flowcharts is that when they attempt to address all exigencies, they become so complicated that it is difficult to follow them exactly. They therefore are rarely validated through actual practice, and remain ideal rather than real models. Figure 4.5 contains an excerpt from one flowchart of the reference process that encompasses three pages.[19]

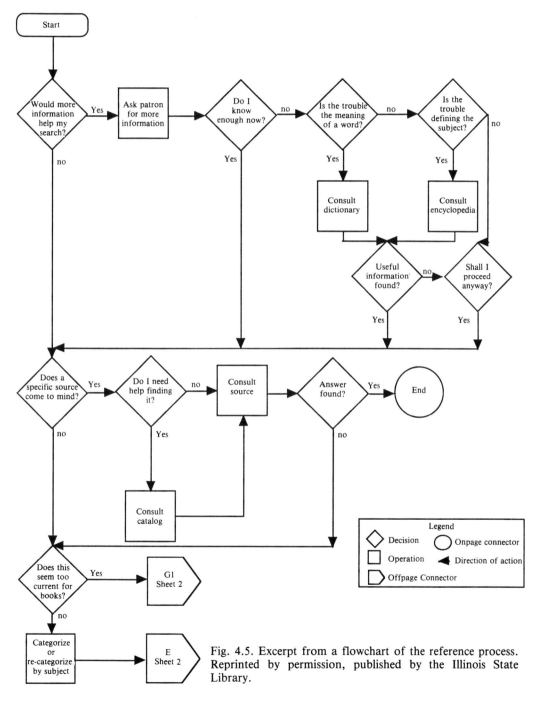

Fig. 4.5. Excerpt from a flowchart of the reference process. Reprinted by permission, published by the Illinois State Library.

Catalog or Index

Models of searching based on the type of bibliographic tool employed may differ in several dimensions, because of fundamental differences in how each is expected to function for the user. For example, one function of a catalog is to serve as a location device. Once searchers determine that an item is owned by the library, and find a shelf location, they may browse the shelf location for similar items. The success of this strategy depends upon the accuracy with which a subject classification number has been assigned. Despite the cataloger's commitment to collocation, a fully comprehensive search is not generally the only measure of success in a catalog search. Of equal interest to many patrons is whether the book is physically present and available for borrowing. Of course, availability of the periodicals listed in an index is also important to the patron; however, the index is not expected to reflect a specific library's collection, but rather a domain of knowledge.

Because of the different functions of catalog and index, the models used to describe a typical search have been assumed to differ as well. Generally speaking, the index search is conducted to identify items about a particular topic, and is therefore inherently a subject or topical search. Both the records loaded into a database and the format of a printed index place primary emphasis on subject access. In a catalog, however, it has generally been assumed that most searches are *known-item* searches through which users seek to locate particular items about which they possess some specific information—an author or a title, for instance. In this model, the user enters the catalog, identifies the item, and goes to the shelf to locate it. The search may be broadened by browsing the shelves nearby, using the subject classification scheme to identify more items. This model may be described as moving from the specific to the general.

Since the introduction of online catalogs, however, the assumption that most catalog searches are for known items has been challenged. Beginning with Karen Markey's work in the early 1980s, many studies of users' behavior in searching library catalogs have revealed that users frequently approach the online catalog as they would approach an index to search for information on a topic.[20] This change in our understanding of how people view catalogs, together with the widespread adoption of online catalogs, has stimulated considerable thinking and research into the problem of subject access in library catalogs.

In an index, the searcher moves from the general topic to a specific aspect of the topic. In some indexes, the entries are arranged to reflect a hierarchical structure, with more general articles first, followed by more specific aspects listed underneath. Notice the sub-headings for specific aspects of "Economic development" in figure 4.6, from the *Social Sciences Index*.[21] However, the physical items may or may not be present in the library where the searcher is conducting the index search, so the bibliographic descriptions must stand for the items themselves. This is one of the reasons for including more subject descriptors in an index than in a catalog. The searcher identifies items on a similar topic by scanning the index page. In an index or online database search, the searcher has no physical location like a shelf to browse, so all scanning must be done within the index itself, either on the printed page or on the screen. The need to scan pages at several different concept "locations" when searching a multifaceted topic in a printed index shows clearly why the ability to combine concepts through Boolean operators is so highly prized by online searchers. For example, had the patron wanting information on neural nets further specified that she wanted to know how neural net theory affected the design of expert systems and artificial intelligence by computer programmers in Japan, the librarian might have to pursue searches on four additional concepts: expert systems, artificial intelligence, computer programmers, and Japan. Boolean operators enable this search to be expressed in a single search statement: neural nets AND (expert systems OR artificial intelligence) AND computer programmers AND Japan.

Economic development—*cont.*

Nicholas Kaldor's contribution to the analysis of international monetary reform. S. Griffith-Jones. bibl *Camb J Econ* 13:223-35 Mr '89

The politics of growth: strategic interaction and economic performance in the advanced industrial democracies, 1974-1980. P. Lange and G. Garrett. bibl *J Polit* 47:792-827 Ag '85; Discussion. 49:242-74 F '87; 50:677-704 Ag '88; 51:646-61 Ag '89

Productivity growth, convergence, and welfare: what the long-run data show. W. J. Baumol. bibl *Am Econ Rev* 76:1072-85 D '86; Discussion. 78:1138-59 D '88

Property relations and economic development: the other land reform. D. W. Bromley. bibl *World Dev* 17:867-77 Je '89

The shifting patterns of sectoral labor allocation during development: developed versus developing countries. K. Pandit and E. Casetti. bibl *Ann Assoc Am Geogr* 79:329-44 S '89

Socialism and the demands of development. S. Amin. *World Marx Rev* 32:36-9 My '89; Discussion. 32:66-8 Jl '89

Third World trades ideas [symposium of the Chinese Association for International Understanding] Li Bin. *Beijing Rev* 32:12 My 8 '89

Transportation and world development. W. Owen. *Ekistics* 53:362-6 S/O-N/D '86

What and where is political economy? review article. M. Moore. *J Dev Stud* 25:583-9 Jl '89

What's still wrong with the World Bank? D. Bandow. *Orbis* 33:73-89 Wint '89

World variation in human welfare: a new Index of development status. R. J. Tata and R. R. Schultz. bibl maps *Ann Assoc Am Geogr* 78:580-93 D '88; Discussion. 79:609-15 D '89

Congresses

The futures of development. Qin Linzheng. *Futures (Engl)* 21:94-7 F '89

Environmental aspects

Aid and the environment. R. W. Bradnock. il *Geogr Mag* 61:supp1-4 D '89

Capitalism and the environment. P. M. Sweezy and H. Magdoff. *Mon Rev* 41:1-10 Je '89

China's environmental prospects. B. Boxer. *Asian Surv* 29:669-86 Jl '89

Ecological modernization of industrial society: three strategic elements. U. E. Simonis. il *Int Soc Sci J* 41:347-61 Ag '89

Environment and security. N. Myers. *Foreign Policy* no74:23-41 Spr '89

Global impoverishment, sustainable development and the environment: a conceptual approach. G. C. Gallopin and others. il *Int Soc Sci J* 41:375-97 Ag '89

Greener faces for its greenbacks [World Bank] *Economist* 312:41-2 S 2 '89

Growth can be green: how to be clean and prosperous too. *Economist* 312:12-13 Ag 26 '89

Inheriting the earth [sustainable development concept] *Economist* 312:77 S 16 '89

The state in environmental management: the ecological dimension. K. J. Walker. *Polit Stud* 37:25-38 Mr '89

'Sustainable development' and the environment; review article. H. Brookfield. *J Dev Stud* 25:126-35 O '88

History

Nineteenth-century development experience and lessons for today. C. T. Morris and I. Adelman. bibl *World Dev* 17:1417-32 S '89

Prometheus unbounded: global perspectives on economic growth prior to the industrial revolution; review article. R. A. Dodgshon. *J Hist Geogr* 15:189-92 Ap '89

International aspects

Democracy, economic development, and income inequality. E. N. Muller. bibl *Am Sociol Rev* 53:50-68 F '88; Discussion. 53:794-806 O '88; 54:865-71 O '89

The development of international inequality 1960-1985. H. Theil. bibl *J Econom* 42:145-55 S '89

The economics of development: a survey. N. Stern. bibl *Econ J* 99:597-685 S '89

Level of development and income inequality: an extension of Kuznets-hypothesis to the world economy. R. Ram. bibl *Kyklos* 42 no1:73-88 '89

Taxation, aggregate activity and economic growth: cross-country evidence on some supply-side hypotheses. R. B. Koester and R. C. Kormendi. bibl *Econ Inq* 27:367-86 Jl '89

Maps

Mapping for world development [Peters projection] P. Vujakovic. bibl maps *Geography* 74:97-105 Ap '89

Fig. 4.6. Entries from *Social Sciences Index* (April 1989 to March 1990). Reprinted by permission of The H. W. Wilson Company.

Strategies for Bibliographic Searching

Based on the preceding discussion of search models, this section describes some simple strategies for bibliographic searching. A *search strategy* is defined as a conscious approach to decision making in order to achieve certain specified objectives. Although the study of search strategies is often closely associated with research into individual differences in learning or problem-solving styles (cognitive styles), search strategies can be learned and consciously applied as the situation requires. Individual differences may account for preferences in searching, but they should not be allowed to restrict or inhibit the searcher's ability to employ a variety of techniques while conducting a search for information.

Librarians are called upon to advise and instruct library users at a variety of levels and in a variety of settings (see chapter 6). They play an active role in the evaluation of reference materials of all types, and may also be involved in the selection or evaluation of particular online or ondisc systems or products (see chapter 11). In order to determine how a product supports or encourages appropriate use, it is necessary to understand and articulate the basic principles of searching. In an attempt to remain unrestrictive and to accommodate diversity in user need, type of question, type of source, institutional setting, or personal style, these principles are described at a general level that differentiates them from heuristics or searching "tips" that apply to specific situations. For these, the reader is referred to the current library literature, wherein descriptions of such techniques appear regularly.[22]

Two strategies, specific-to-general and general-to-specific, enable the searcher to exploit bibliographic structure in order to achieve an objective. These strategies may be applied to solving problems such as vocabulary selection and reference tool selection. Other strategies assist the searcher in capitalizing on specific system properties to improve the efficiency and quality of an information search. Two such properties are context and feedback.

The Specific-to-General Approach

The *specific-to-general approach* is defined as a search in which the searcher has a known, relevant item in mind and wishes to find others like it. For example, when a requester knows the author and title of a book, and wishes to find similar books by different authors, subject headings can be examined and then used to locate additional items. As pointed out earlier, this strategy works well in bibliographic systems that display descriptors, such as card catalogs and online databases and catalogs, but cannot be employed in most printed indexes, as they do not display descriptors.

■ ══ ■

4.5
Finding Related Items

Suppose the user has just finished reading the book *Dreams of Reason: The Computer and the Rise of the Sciences of Complexity* by Heinz Pagels. She would like to continue reading in the same area, but she has no idea how to go about finding books on similar subjects. By looking up the book in the catalog, she discovers that the subject headings applied to the book are Science — Philosophy, Complexity (Philosophy), and Computers and civilization. Since her interest is really in the effects of computers on peoples' lives, she decides to look further under the subject heading Computers and civilization. Using the library's online catalog, she finds that there are 140 books with that subject heading. By browsing through the list, she finds the following books: *The Mind Tool: Computers and Their Impact on Society, Competing Visions, Complex Realities: Social Aspects of the Information Society*, and *Computers and the Social Environment*. These will be a good start for a further reading program.

The first step is to locate the known item in the file. Assuming the information about the known item is complete and correct, locating the item in the file can usually be done through an author or title search. While an author/title search is not always easy, especially when the file is large or the entry is complex (for corporate authors, such as those for United States government agencies, for example), it is usually straightforward and unambiguous. Once the record is located, the searcher may examine the subject terms assigned to the work and proceed immediately to incorporate those terms in a subsequent search for more items. This direct entry into an information file eliminates the need to think of possible subject terms on one's own, and also makes consulting a thesaurus or list of subject headings optional. Of course, the terms located initially may also be used as entry terms into a thesaurus or list of subject headings. One of the reasons the specific-to-general approach works well is that it provides a specific, unambiguous entry point of known accuracy into an information file.

When used in an online database search, this technique is usually called *citation pearl growing*. The initial citation is the point of entry, or seed of the pearl, and the search is expanded outward by selecting subject terms from the descriptor fields of the unit record. The successive expansions constitute the layers of the pearl. Another example of this strategy in online searching is the most-specific-facet-first approach. For instance, a proper name or a highly specialized term or phrase is used as the entry point. Because most online systems allow searchers to enter free text or keywords, almost any specific term can be used as an entry point. If the retrieval is sufficient and of good quality, the search can be terminated; if larger retrieval is desired, both free-text terms obtained from titles or abstracts and controlled vocabulary terms obtained from lists of descriptors can be added to expand the retrieval.

Citation indexing, discussed in more detail in chapter 19, also works on the same principle. A specific known item is used as an entry point to the index or database, and other items, assumed to be similar in subject matter because their authors cite the known item, can then be located. Citation searches may result in somewhat different retrieval, since it is the judgment of the authors of the works themselves, rather than the judgment of the indexers, upon which the links between items are established. Acknowledging the diversity of both indexing practices and citation habits, fully comprehensive results may be achieved only by conducting multiple searches using both indexing and citation links.

Still another example of the specific-to-general approach is reflected in search request forms or in queries in reference interviews in which requesters are asked to supply a known citation as a starting point. Here, the requester makes the judgment as to the relevance of a particular item to the topic of the request (the information need). Such information may be invaluable to the searcher in fully understanding what is meant by the patron's information request and in resolving any potential ambiguities.

General characteristics of the specific-to-general approach are its highly interactive quality and the need for continual review of results. With this degree of interactivity, however, there is always the danger that the searcher will become lost or distracted during the search; therefore, it is essential to know when to stop expanding the search and cycling through the process.

The General-to-Specific Approach

The key to effective searching when moving from the general to the specific is the syndetic structure that provides a logical overview or map of the concepts and vocabulary of a particular topic area. Since items are indexed to the most specific aspects of a topic, it is crucial to determine the correct level of specificity. This can be obtained quickly and easily by scanning a thesaurus. For example, the thesaurus used in indexing medical literature, known as *Medical Subject Headings* (MeSH),[23] provides terms for the leg bones of the human body. The four bone terms listed are femur, fibula, patella, and tibia. Articles dealing with fractures of the fibula would therefore be indexed at the most specific level — fibula and fractures. The femur, however, has an additional level of specificity that describes two particular locations on the femur: femur head and femur neck. A fracture of the femur that is located at the head of the femur must therefore be indexed at the most specific level — femur head and fractures. The best (and sometimes only) way to determine the level of specificity is to consult the thesaurus. Some thesauri (and MeSH is an example of such a thesaurus) provide a display of terms in a hierarchical structure. In MeSH, this display is known as the *tree structure*, shown in figure 4.7, p. 78. The alphabetical listing and the tree structure can be used together to determine the correct level of specificity. In the alphabetical listing, an interpretive note is made at "leg bones," and the appropriate place in the tree structure is indicated by means of an alphanumeric code: A2.835.232.484. As pointed out earlier, some indexes incorporate syndetic structure either through classification or by the arrangement of items under a heading, or both.

MUSCULOSKELETAL SYSTEM
  SKELETON
    BONE AND BONES
      FOOT BONES (NON-MESH)
        TARSAL BONES

TARSAL BONES	A2.835.232.262.710
CALCANEUS	A2.835.232.262.710.300
TALUS	A2.835.232.262.710.780
HYOID BONE	A2.835.232.409
LEG BONES (NON MESH)	A2.835.232.484
FEMUR	A2.835.232.484.247
FEMUR HEAD	A2.835.232.484.247.343
FEMUR NECK	A2.835.232.484.247.510
FIBULA	A2.835.232.484.321
PATELLA	A2.835.232.484.624
TIBIA	A2.835.232.484.883

Fig. 4.7. Tree structure from *Medical Subject Headings* (MeSH).

A further enhancement to some online systems (such as MEDLINE, the online version of *Index Medicus*) is an *explode* feature that captures several terms at various levels within the hierarchy below the starting term with a single command. Once a term is located in the hierarchy, it may be exploded, and the search expanded very quickly; this can be done without sacrificing precision, since it is possible to determine ahead of time which terms will be included. In the example used in the previous paragraph, an online searcher can explode the term *femur*, thereby capturing all articles dealing with the femur, the femur head, and the femur neck. The explosion may also occur higher up in the tree, capturing all the terms for leg bones; in this case, though, the term "leg bones" is not a permitted descriptor, and so the numeric code A2.835.232.484 for leg bones must be entered instead.

Unfortunately, not all bibliographic systems have thesauri, nor are the thesauri always readily available in libraries. Sometimes the list of subject headings used in a specific index is published in one section of the printed index or can be purchased separately; all too frequently, it is not. For example, the list of subject headings used by the *Readers' Guide to Periodical Literature* is not available, nor is the list for *Library Literature*. The absence of these lists makes it impossible for either librarian or user to scan a list of headings to select appropriate candidates. Furthermore, it is difficult to grasp either the scope of the subject matter or the syndetic structure of the index, because only those headings for items appearing in that volume are displayed in each volume of the index. An additional barrier to the general-to-specific approach is the number of subject heading schemes and controlled vocabularies that populate the bibliographic universe. These controlled vocabularies differ in degree of specificity, frequency of updating, availability, and structure. The librarian functioning as a generalist must cope with several different controlled vocabularies on a daily basis.

A single controlled vocabulary that encompasses many subject areas and is in widespread use (such as *Library of Congress Subject Headings*) provides consistency for librarians and users, but specialized thesauri developed by subject experts provide a greater degree of flexibility and specificity. In some specialized areas, there has been an attempt to rationalize controlled vocabulary to provide consistent access across a number of indexes. The thesauri for the *International Nursing Index*,[24] the *Cumulative Index to Nursing and Allied Health Literature*,[25] and *Hospital Literature Index*[26] are all modeled after the Medical Subject Headings used by *Index Medicus* and, where practical, share the same terminology.

In addition to moving up and down a hierarchical list of descriptors, syndetic structure supports moving horizontally through the use of cross-references and *see also* references. As pointed out earlier, one of the advantages of a controlled vocabulary is *collocation*: gathering similar works together despite individual variance in title words or abstracts. Once the searcher has arrived at the correct location in an information source, the list of descriptors may be scanned to select more specific items.

One of the difficulties, however, is selecting the correct terminology in order to arrive at the desired spot in the file. In a system without cross-references, the searcher must use the allowed term (in the correct spelling and grammatical form) in order to locate any materials. Maintaining at least a minimal number of cross-references is essential to successful controlled-vocabulary searching, because the cross-references support a greater number of entry points, increasing accessibility. Cross-references permit the searcher to move from an entry term that is *not* used to a controlled vocabulary term that *is* used. Using an incorrect term results in no retrieval (manual or online), creating the usually false impression that nothing exists on the given topic.

The ability to allow users to map their terminology to the system's is so important that various schemes for enhancing the number of entry points have been proposed. Some of these involve providing expanded lists of words that can be used as entry points (sometimes called "super thesauri"), encouraging reference librarians to add cross-references to catalogs, and allowing users to add their own terms to local databases.[27] While these ideas remain largely experimental, they serve to focus attention on an important problem in searching.

Context and Feedback

The preceding discussion suggests that the specific-to-general approach is particularly well-suited to electronic environments (online, CD-ROM), while the general-to-specific approach works best when the searcher can gain a quick overview of a topic, usually through scanning a printed source. This contrast highlights the importance of context in developing a search strategy. In printed sources, displays of syndetic structure inform the searcher of the context in which terminology is to be understood, as well as creating a visual map of the structure of a discipline. In online sources, however, these visual cues are not available. As anyone familiar with the English language can attest, context plays a major part in resolving ambiguity when terms have several meanings. For example, *stress* can be understood in a psychological context ("stressed out" from exams), in a physical context (metals undergo stress), or in a medical context (stress as exertion).

The effect of ambiguity on searching can be profound, particularly in large online systems (catalogs or databases that contain files covering many disciplines). Entering the term *stress* (meaning psychological stress) in an online catalog will retrieve a large number of items, but only a portion of them will deal with psychological stress. In some systems, the only way to determine which ones are relevant is to display all the items (no small task when 300 items are retrieved). Reviewing a few items and discovering that some of them deal with stress in metals will reveal semantic ambiguities, however, and indicate that another concept or term must be added in order to limit the search to the appropriate subject area. A very easy way to do this is to use Boolean AND with a psychological term, such as *role conflict*, which fixes the search in the appropriate context, where further refinements can take place. This model for searching is often called the *building-block approach*, and is widely used in online searching.

In online databases where the subject content is consistent throughout the file, a different strategy is necessary. For example, in PsycInfo (online version of *Psychological Abstracts*[28]) the use of a general psychological term would be unnecessary, as the psychological context is implicit. In fact, including general psychological terminology in a search in PsycInfo may be counterproductive, because indexing of articles is done at a specific level. It is unlikely that such a general concept would be indexed, and therefore the search would retrieve little or nothing. This tactic is sometimes ironically referred to as *overspecifying* a search. What this means is that the searcher has not taken into account the implicit context of the file, and has constructed a redundant search strategy.

■ ━━━ ■

4.6

Effects of Failing to Recognize the Context of a Search

In looking for articles about the psychological effects of child abuse, the searcher selects an appropriate database (PsycInfo) but fails to recognize that virtually all articles in this file deal with psychological aspects of phenomena. The searcher correctly uses the descriptor *child abuse*, which retrieves 2,647 articles, but also chooses to create a free-text phrase *psychological effects*, which retrieves 816 articles. (A discussion of the use of free text and controlled vocabulary in online searching is covered in chapter 5.) When the two search statements are combined, the result is 13 articles. These 13 articles might well be relevant, but it is likely that the number of relevant articles is much greater. The searcher's requirement that the words "psychological effects" appear in the bibliographic record has resulted in an unrealistically restricted retrieval. Two alternative approaches should be considered: either conduct a manual search of *Psychological Abstracts* under the descriptor *child abuse*, or attempt to gain greater understanding of additional parameters of the search through a more in-depth reference interview.

The importance of context is often overlooked, because it is often taken for granted. The tremendous growth of online searching, wherein contextual clues are all but lost, has served to reemphasize the potential value of context in resolving ambiguity and in providing clues as to meaning and direction in searching. The context provides a kind of feedback that is invaluable to the searcher. Feedback as to the progress of a search, particularly in an online environment, has come to be a valued component of system design. Features such as menus that assist the searcher in formulating (and reformulating) a search strategy, help screens that can be invoked by the user as needed, and display of retrieved items in order of their relevance to the query are becoming more common as online system designs continue to evolve.

Although online feedback may be more explicit, subtle forms of feedback can be observed in printed formats. Hierarchical displays in indexes, evidence of the scope of an area such as the amount of catalog space or the number of pages in an index allocated to a particular topic, and even the age of the catalog cards themselves often exert a subtle influence on the direction of a search. By recognizing the existence and value of feedback in refining or changing direction in a search, librarians can become aware of the role feedback plays in their own search strategies, and they can also incorporate feedback mechanisms in the programs and systems they provide to users.

Choice of Reference Tool

Little has been said so far in this chapter about the choice of reference tool. Selecting an appropriate reference tool or database affects the search strategy; together, tool selection and search strategy determine the effectiveness of the search. Strategies that are appropriate for the various types of tools discussed in part 2 are presented along with the tools themselves. There are some intermediary tools, however, that deserve mention.

Printed guides to reference works, such as the well-known Sheehy's *Guide to Reference Books*[29] assist the searcher in identifying appropriate sources. Recognizing the value of syndetic structure, the *Guide* uses a classification by both subject area and type of tool. The approach employed by the *Guide* is general to specific, providing a visual map of a field through which one may navigate. Such an approach provides a good overview of the structure of a subject field and of the variety and scope of reference materials that are available.

On the other hand, the number of reference tools included in the *Guide* continues to expand rapidly, and only the most comprehensive reference collection is likely to own most of the tools described. Some libraries annotate the *Guide* with their holdings to simplify locating tools in the reference collection. Other libraries create keyword indexes or small databases that contain descriptions of their reference holdings. These can be consulted quickly in order to determine which books are on hand to answer a particular type of question, and can be searched by keyword so that librarians can locate books easily, even if they cannot recall the titles.[30]

On a more elaborate level, expert systems are being designed to lead the librarian or the user through a series of steps that will assist in locating the appropriate book to consult to find a particular piece of information. These developments stem from the recognition that librarians, like many other professionals, have a limited capacity to remember all the resources available to them, and therefore wisely rely on intermediary assistance to ensure that they have not overlooked an important source of information.

Other tools are available to assist the online searcher in selecting the appropriate database(s). They are discussed in depth in chapter 11, but because they constitute a source of information parallel to printed guides to reference sources, and because tool selection is of critical importance to effective search strategy, they are mentioned briefly here. Sources such as the *Directory of Online Databases*[31] and its companion volume *Online Database Selection*[32] provide a good overview of the growing number of databases available. In addition to these printed tools, both DIALOG and BRS allow a searcher to enter a specific term to see how many times that term appears in the various databases. By observing the frequency of occurrence of a term, the searcher can estimate the likelihood that a search on that topic will be fruitful in a particular database. As mentioned earlier, this strategy works best with a specific term, since more general terms are often implicit in a subject-specific database. Such implicit concepts are not indexed, and therefore no matches will occur.

Summary and Conclusion

An understanding of the way in which the bibliographic universe is organized is essential to effective, efficient searching. The two primary types of access mechanisms discussed in this chapter are library catalogs and indexes, each of which is presented as an ideal type: catalogs providing access to a particular library's collection of books, and indexes providing access to articles in a particular subject area. In actuality, each of these types exists in less pure forms, and the distinctions between them are becoming less clear-cut, particularly when they coexist in the same electronic environment. Despite—and perhaps because of—the increasing complexity of the bibliographic world, it is important to keep in mind the fundamental principles of bibliographic control such as access, physical arrangement, collocation and authority control, and depth and comprehensiveness of indexing.

Exploiting the power of bibliographic organization to conduct effective, efficient searches takes practice and experience. Thinking critically about the process as one goes along, as well as observing the behavior of others (librarians and users alike), can yield valuable insight into how best to assist and instruct others to find information. While detailed models of the searching process still have not been developed, two general strategies for searching—specific-to-general and general-to-specific—can be used effectively. The selection of appropriate reference tools, a critical component of the success of a search, can be made easier by consulting bibliographies of reference works, and the selection of appropriate terminology can be facilitated by sources that link various controlled vocabularies. The application of online and computer technologies has affected the bibliographic world, both by making it more complex and by offering librarians the challenge and the means to improve access to information.

Notes

1.   Patrick Wilson, "The Catalog as Access Mechanism: Background and Concepts," *Library Resources & Technical Services* 27 (January/March 1983): 4-17.

2.   U.S. Library of Congress, Subject Cataloging Division, *Library of Congress Subject Headings*, 12th ed., 3 vols. (Washington, D.C.: Library of Congress, 1989).

3.   Minnie Earle Sears, *Sears List of Subject Headings*, 13th ed., ed. Carmen Rovira and Caroline Reyes (New York: H. W. Wilson, 1986), 681p.

4.   *Readers' Guide to Periodical Literature*, 1900- (New York: H. W. Wilson, 1905-).

5.   *Education Index*, 1929- (New York: H. W. Wilson, 1932-).

6.   *Index Medicus* (Washington, D.C.: National Library of Medicine, 1960-).

7.   *Library Literature*, 1921/32- (New York: H. W. Wilson, 1934-).

8.   *Library and Information Science Abstracts* (London: Library Association, 1969-).

9.   Mary Dykstra, "LC Subject Headings Disguised as a Thesaurus," *Library Journal* 113 (March 1, 1988): 42-46; and "Can Subject Headings Be Saved?," *Library Journal* 113 (September 15, 1988): 55-58.

10.   Harold Wooster, "0.46872985 Square Inches—A Naive Look at Subject Analysis," in *Digest of 1970 Annual Meeting* (Philadelphia: National Federation of Science Abstracting and Indexing Services, 1970), 41-48.

11.   Examples of locally produced interfaces are discussed in Brian Nielsen, "Roll Your Own Interface: Public Access to CD-ROMS," *Database* 12 (December 1989): 105-9; and William H. Mischo and Melvin E. DeSart, "An End User Search Service with Customized Interface Software," in *Twenty-Fourth Annual Clinic on Library Applications of Data Processing, Questions and Answers: Strategies for Using the Electronic Reference Collection*, ed. Linda C. Smith (Urbana-Champaign, Ill.: University of Illinois at Urbana-Champaign Graduate School of Library and Information Science, 1989), 188-204.

12.   Christine L. Borgman, "All Users of Information Retrieval Systems Are Not Created Equal: An Exploration into Individual Differences," *Information Processing & Management* 25, no. 3 (1989): 237-51; Carol Hansen Fenichel, "Online Searching: Measures That Discriminate Among Users with Different Types of Experience," *Journal of the American Society for Information Science* 32 (January 1981): 23-32; and Tefko Saracevic and Paul Kantor, "A Study of Information Seeking and Retrieving. III. Searchers, Searches, and Overlap," *Journal of the American Society for Information Science* 39 (May 1988): 197-216.

13.   Prudence W. Dalrymple, "Retrieval by Reformulation in Two Library Catalogs: Toward a Cognitive Model of Searching Behavior," *Journal of the American Society for Information Science* 41 (June 1990): 272-81.

14.   Carol Collier Kuhlthau, "Developing a Model of the Library Search Process: Cognitive and Affective Aspects," *RQ* 28 (Winter 1988): 232-42.

15.   John Richardson, Jr., "Toward an Expert System for Reference Service: A Research Agenda for the 1990s," *College & Research Libraries* 50 (March 1989): 231-48; Marty Kesselman and Sarah Barbara Watstein, "Artificial Intelligence and Expert Systems: Part II," *Library Hi Tech Bibliography* 4 (1989): 1-9; and Charles W. Bailey, Jr., Jeff Fadell, Judy E. Myers, and Thomas C. Wilson, "The Index Expert System: A Knowledge-Based System to Assist Users in Index Selection," *Reference Services Review* 17, no. 4 (1989): 19-28.

16.   Carter Alexander, "Technique of Library Searching," *Special Libraries* 27 (September 1936): 230-38.

17.   Marcia J. Bates, "Information Search Tactics," *Journal of the American Society for Information Science* 30 (July 1979): 205-14.

18.   Christine L. Borgman, "Why Are Online Catalogs Hard to Use? Lessons Learned from Information-Retrieval Studies," *Journal of the American Society for Information Science* 37 (November 1986): 387-400.

19.   Charles A. Bunge, *Professional Education and Reference Efficiency*, Research Series no. 11 (Springfield, Ill.: Illinois State Library, 1967), 44-46.

20.   Karen Markey, *Subject Searching in Library Catalogs* (Dublin, Ohio: OCLC Online Computer Library Center, 1984), 176.

21.   *Social Sciences Index* (New York: H. W. Wilson, 1990), 490.

22.   Examples of such articles appear regularly in the journals *Online* and *Database*, among others, and a number have been reprinted in *Database Search Strategies & Tips: Reprints from the Best of Online and Database* (Weston, Conn.: Online, Inc., 1988).

23.   U.S. National Library of Medicine, *Medical Subject Headings*, 1963- (Washington, D.C.: National Library of Medicine, 1963-).

24.   *International Nursing Index* (Philadelphia: American Journal of Nursing, 1966-).

25.   *Cumulative Index to Nursing and Allied Health Literature* (Glendale, Calif.: Glendale Adventist Medical Center, 1961-). Titled *Cumulative Index to Nursing Literature* prior to 1977.

26.   *Hospital Literature Index* (Chicago: American Hospital Association, 1955-).

27.   Marcia J. Bates, "Subject Access in Online Catalogs: A Design Model," *Journal of the American Society for Information Science* 37 (November 1986): 357-76.

28.   *Psychological Abstracts* (Lancaster, Pa.: American Psychological Association, 1927-).

29.   *Guide to Reference Books*, 10th ed., ed. Eugene P. Sheehy (Chicago: American Library Association, 1986), 1,560p.

30.   Evan I. Farber, "A Keyword Index to the Reference Collection," *American Libraries* 18 (June 1987): 440-41.

31.   *Directory of Online Databases* (New York: Cuadra/Elsevier, 1979-).

32.   *Online Database Selection: A User's Guide to the Directory of Online Databases* (New York: Cuadra/Elsevier, 1989).

Additional Readings

Bates, Marcia J. "Idea Tactics." *Journal of the American Society for Information Science* 30, no. 5 (September 1979): 280-89.

_____. "Information Search Tactics." *Journal of the American Society for Information Science* 30, no. 4 (July 1979): 205-14.
These two articles set forth the concepts of *search tactics*, defined as moves made to further a search, and *idea tactics*, defined as ways of generating new ideas or solutions to problems in information searching. Together, these articles describe a psychological approach to search strategy that is similar to the approach taken in this chapter.

_____. "Search Techniques." *Annual Review of Information Science and Technology* 15 (1980): 139-69.
In this article, Bates provides a review and synthesis of literature in the field of search strategy, both manual and online, through 1980.

Cochrane, Pauline A. *Redesign of Catalogs and Indexes for Improved Online Subject Access: Selected Papers of Pauline A. Cochrane*. Phoenix, Ariz.: Oryx Press, 1985. 484p.
This collection draws together both indexes and catalogs, showing how the problem of subject access manifests in each type.

Cochrane, Pauline A., and Karen Markey. "Catalog Use Studies—Since the Introduction of Online Interactive Catalogs: Impact on Design for Subject Access." *Library & Information Science Research* 5 (1983): 337-63.
This review focuses on methods and directions in research on searching online catalogs.

Cutter, Charles A. *Rules for a Dictionary Catalog*. 4th ed., rewritten. Washington, D.C.: Government Printing Office, 1904. 173p.
This early work sets forth the principles to which library catalogs still adhere.

Hafter, Ruth. "The Performance of Card Catalogs: A Review of the Research." *Library Research* 1 (Fall 1979): 199-220.

Krikelas, James. "Catalog Use Studies and Their Implications." *Advances in Librarianship* 3 (1972): 195-220.

_____. "Searching the Library Catalog: A Study of Users' Access." *Library Research* 2 (1980-81): 215-30.
An acquaintance with studies of catalog use as provided in these literature reviews will serve to point out the challenges inherent in the study of search strategies. Because both catalogs and indexes are designed to be searched by library users as well as librarians, the insights gained from catalog use studies can introduce the ways in which librarians have conceptualized the relationship between design and use of bibliographic tools.

Wilson, Patrick. "The Catalog as Access Mechanism: Background and Concepts." *Library Resources & Technical Services* 27 (January/March 1983): 4-17.
    Wilson takes a conservative position regarding the role of the library catalog, suggesting that its function is primarily as a local finding device, and argues against providing the enhanced subject access to materials that is advocated by many.

ELECTRONIC
REFERENCE SERVICES

History and Development
of Electronic Resources

In large part, the history of electronic resources for reference begins with the development of computer-assisted typesetting and printing. The publishers of indexing and abstracting services first used computers to print their paper products. They created magnetic tapes that were interpreted by a computer and drove their printers. These magnetic tapes could also be read by computers for other purposes. Companies and government agencies, such as the National Library of Medicine, developed computer software that could read and manipulate the information on these tapes in new ways. This software allowed reference librarians in those organizations to ask the computer to "search" for an indexed term or group of terms to see if there were articles cited on these tapes which would meet the information needs of their patrons. In the beginning, computers required so much time in the processing of these requests that they were done on a delayed basis, called *batch processing*. A request was submitted to the computer center on one day and the results were made available the next day. If there were any typographical or logical errors in the request, they had to be corrected and the request resubmitted for processing, thus delaying the results for another day.

During the 1960s and 1970s, computer power, speed, and memory all increased, as did the ability to communicate with computers over existing telephone wires, rather than having each terminal directly wired into the main computer. Information service companies, such as Dialog Information Services, which had been created to serve the information needs of a single organization or agency, made their computerized files available to other libraries on a contractual basis. The number of computerized files, called *databases*, grew from a mere handful in the early 1970s to the hundreds available today. Reference librarians all over the world now possess the power to use simple computer terminals or complex computer workstations to connect with computers located almost anywhere. Librarians can select, from among the many hundreds of databases available, those which contain the needed information. They can then process their inquiries online and receive the needed information directly on their equipment, or have it printed in a preferred format and sent to the librarian or the patron as desired. This use of electronic resources is known as *online searching*. It is just one of several systems of electronic resources available to reference librarians.

Databases

The term *database* needs to be explored more fully if one is to gain an understanding of and appreciation for it. The initial focus here is on bibliographic information, but many other types of information and databases are created and used. A database starts when a publisher creates a format for information. This information might be a bibliographic citation, a statistical table, or a biographical fact, to name a few. The publisher determines which elements of information are important, how these elements are to be displayed or printed, and which elements can be manipulated by the computer. Machine-readable files of this information are created in the form of computer tapes or discs. Once the data is in machine-readable form, the file can be put to multiple uses. One of the principal uses is to print a publication, such as an index or abstract, which is sold or distributed to the organization's members or subscribers. Another use is as an internal information database for the organization's own use; the telephone directory is an example of this process. A telephone company compiles data from its customers and puts the data into machine-readable form. This electronic version is used to create the published directories that are sent to the telephone company's customers and to subscribing libraries. A second use is for the telephone company's information operators as a machine-readable database. A third use, of most interest to reference librarians, is the leasing or sale of these files to external information service companies.

Information service companies are sometimes called *vendors*, to distinguish them from the organizations that create the databases, which are called *producers*. A few organizations, such as the National Library of Medicine, serve both functions. Vendors serve as a link between the databases and those who use them. Using their own software and its associated search language, these companies make further decisions about which data elements are important, how to format each data element, which elements will be retrievable or searchable, and which elements will merely be displayable at the terminal or printable. These decisions are extremely important to database users, since they determine the ways in which these databases can be searched.

One way to think about databases is to consider the card catalog as a nonelectronic database. Each card in the catalog is one record. The format of the card imparts information. The style shows whether the author name or the title is more important. The card indicates whether the item is a book, a serial, or a set of related items. It identifies when the item was created. Some data elements on the card are just for display or printing, such as illustration information, size, and number of pages. Other elements are searchable, such as the title, author, and subject headings which are shown in the tracings at the bottom of the card. Some elements, such as series information, are searchable in some cases but not in others. The first word of each of the headings that can be searched is an *access point* to that record.

The card catalog is a valuable reference resource, but it shows the limits of printed materials. A card catalog exists in only one place. Each card is filed only under the first word of the heading. Cards from the catalog cannot be pulled, compared, and sorted to produce lists of materials best suited to the needs of the patron. The catalog user must check one or more headings and scan the cards one by one, looking for all the relevant features.

Searching Capabilities

When a card catalog or other printed reference source is converted to electronic form, it is fundamentally altered by the expanded searching capabilities and speed of the computer. The static format of the printed tool is transformed into a series of dynamic access points. The power of the computer to scan, list, combine, and reorder information is great, and seems to grow each day. The speed of processing is increasing as well. Personal computers now measure their speed in MIPS (million instructions per second), with some of the faster machines currently rated at over 8 MIPS. Large mainframe computers are correspondingly faster. Size and speed allow the computer to manipulate perhaps its most important tool in database handling: Boolean logic.

Boolean Logic

Boolean logic is a form of symbolic logic named after George Boole, the nineteenth-century English mathematician who developed it. Boolean logic allows one to create and combine sets of items that meet criteria specified by the user. Boolean logic uses common words as logical operators in very specific ways. These *Boolean operators* are *AND*, *OR*, and *NOT*.

The Boolean operator *OR* is used to make a more inclusive set by making an item eligible if it meets at least one of the stated criteria: an item would be included in a set if it meets condition A *or* condition B. In creating a set of citrus fruit, for example, one might use the Boolean string: oranges OR grapefruit OR lemons OR limes. This set is more inclusive than a set which has a single criterion for acceptance, e.g., oranges. One way to visualize Boolean logic is with *Venn diagrams*. In these diagrams, shadings indicate the results of each of the operators. The Venn diagram for OR is shown in figure 5.1.

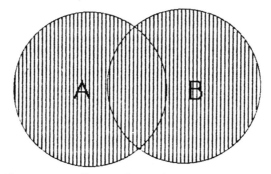

Fig. 5.1. Venn diagram for Boolean operator "OR."

The Boolean operator *AND* is used to make a more restrictive set by requiring that an item must meet both the conditions stated to be included in the final set: an item would be included only if it meets both condition A *and* condition B. One could use the Boolean AND to create a set containing only those books written by Isaac Asimov which contained the word "robot." The Boolean string would be: Isaac Asimov AND robot. The Venn diagram for AND is shown in figure 5.2.

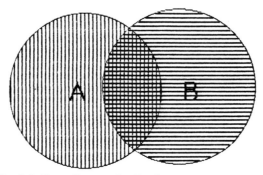

Fig. 5.2. Venn diagram for Boolean operator "AND."

The Boolean operator *NOT* is also used to make a more restrictive set. It excludes items meeting condition A that also meet condition B. To create a set of trees that are not deciduous, one would use the Boolean NOT to exclude deciduous from the final set. The Boolean string would be: trees NOT deciduous. The Venn diagram for NOT is shown in figure 5.3.

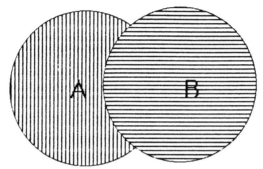

Fig. 5.3. Venn diagram for Boolean operator "NOT."

Boolean operators form the essential machinery for making computerized information retrieval precise and effective. With Boolean logic, in theory, one could manipulate databases containing a million records to produce the single item that contains all of and only the information specified by the user.

Truncation

Another capability for database manipulation occurs because of the computer's vast list-making potential. It can compile a set of materials that meet multiple criteria simultaneously. The term *truncation* refers to shortening a word or eliminating some characters from a longer term to pick up variants. It is a form of the Boolean operator OR. In truncation, the computer is told to put into a single set all those items that share a common sequence of characters, even if they do not share all the same characters. For example, in searching for the truncated term "librar," the computer is asked to make a set of items which contain the term "library" or "libraries" or "librarians" or "librarian" or "librarianship."

Truncation can take place to the left, to the right, or in the middle of the core characters. Truncation can also involve the replacement of several characters or a single character. In the previous example, the truncation occurred to the right of the core characters, and is thus called *right-hand truncation*. It can be further described as a *multiple-character truncation*. If the truncation occurs to the left of the core characters, it is *left-hand truncation*. An example of left-hand truncation with the core characters "ship" would retrieve, at least, a set of records containing the terms "librarianship" or "guardianship" or "statesmanship" or "leadership" or "steamship." When truncation occurs in the middle of the core characters, it is called *internal truncation*. An example of internal truncation would be "Labo@r," where "@" is the internal truncation symbol. If this is a single-character substitution system, in which the symbol can stand for either nothing or a single character, this term would pick up everything in the set "labor" or "labour." If it is a multiple-character system, in which the symbol can stand for more than one alternate character, the set could include "labor" or "labour" or "laborer" or "labourer." Frequently, systems allow one to select a single-character or multiple-character truncation method in order to tailor the search to one's needs. Truncation allows the user to acknowledge and compensate for some amount of uncertainty in the source information, as well as for other, more predictable variations in the database.

Displaying the Index

An additional feature of electronic access to reference sources is the ability to see a range of terms in a context. This is a function of the computer's ability to build and display multiple indexes to a single database. A primary index, called the *inverted index* or *inverted file*, is built on an alphabetical basis, in which each retrievable word in the database is listed in a single sequence. In part, this inverted index allows the computer to manipulate the file at incredible speeds. It goes directly to the term requested, which is linked to the records containing that term. Without the inverted index, the computer would have to scan the entire database looking for the requested sequence of characters. The main inverted file is called the *basic index*. In an operation which may be called "browse" or "expand" or "neighbor," the computer displays the requested section of the basic index, as shown in figure 5.4. This allows one to see a term while it is surrounded by the terms immediately preceding and succeeding it alphabetically. Often, there is an identification of the number of records in the database which contain that term. This feature allows one to identify the most productive terms to retrieve a concept, brings to the eye some of the perhaps unanticipated terms which are in close proximity, and can also allow one to preview the effects of truncation.

```
?E DATABASE

Ref    Items        Index-term

E1        47        DATABANKS

E2         1        DATABAS

E3       728        *DATABASE

E4         1        DATABASED

E5       506        DATABASES

E6         2        DATABASICS

E7         1        DATABASING

E8         2        DATABLE

E9         2        DATABOOK

E10        3        DATACIDE
```

Ref = Number   Items = Number of items including that term

Fig. 5.4. A portion of Social SciSearch's basic index on DIALOG.

An additional aspect of the basic index allows for great precision in identifying material. Each term in the basic index has markers that show its position in the record. Most computer retrieval systems allow a searcher to specify a particular positional relationship between two terms, termed *proximity*. A system will have a set of specialized proximity operators that name the positional relationship needed. For example, to specify that two terms must be right next to each other, one could use an "adjacency" operator. One could also specify that the terms be within a determined number of words, or in the same sentence, field, or paragraph. In this way, a searcher can specify that the system retrieve only those items which contain a phrase, such as "quality circles," even if that phrase is not a descriptor in the database.

A variation of the basic index occurs in databases that have a controlled indexing vocabulary. In these databases, the producers create and maintain a list of subject headings, called *descriptors*, which must be used by the indexers to identify the subject of the item. Frequently, these descriptors are linked with other related subject headings through the use of concepts such as "related term," "broader term," and "narrower term." When such relationships exist among the descriptors in a vocabulary list for some subject, the result is called a *thesaurus*. In some databases, an index of the descriptors is created. In others, the thesaurus itself is an index, with the related terms identified and directly retrievable. Figure 5.5 is an example of an online thesaurus display.

```
?E (DATABASES)

Ref     Items    Type    RT    Index-term
R1      2938             20    *DATABASES   (COLLECTIONS OF INFORMATION..)
R2      0        U       1     DATA BANKS
R3      0        U       1     DATA BASES (1969 1981)
R4      59       N       6     BIBLIOGRAPHIC DATABASES
R5      15       N       2     FULL TEXT DATABASES
R6      8        N       3     NUMERIC DATABASES
R7      316      N       7     ONLINE CATALOGS
R8      93125    B       10    DATA
R9      4078     B       23    INFORMATION SOURCES
R10     10918    R       48    COMPUTERS
R11     2999     R       36    DATA PROCESSING
R12     57       R       4     DATABASE DESIGN
R13     309      R       10    DATABASE MANAGEMENT SYSTEMS
R14     67       R       4     DATABASE PRODUCERS
R15     232      R       10    ELECTRONIC PUBLISHING
R16     4248     R       20    INFORMATION RETRIEVAL
R17     1572     R       18    INFORMATION STORAGE
R18     2840     R       8     LIBRARY COLLECTIONS
R19     142      R       12    ONLINE VENDORS
R20     1002     R       11    RESEARCH TOOLS
R21     1469     R       15    SEARCH STRATEGIES


Ref = Number    Item = Number of items including that term

Type = Relationship to base term    U = Used For    N = Narrower term

B = Broader term    R = Related term    RT = Number of terms

related to that term, e.g., DATABASES has 20 related terms.
```

Fig. 5.5. Online thesaurus terms from ERIC on DIALOG.

In addition to the alphabetical base of the basic index and the relational base of the thesaurus index, there can be other bases for indexes in a single database. In databases that contain numbers, some indexes may show these numbers in a meaningful, numerically based order. For example, in business directories containing sales data, there may be an index that shows sales in order from largest to smallest, or there may be scales of magnitude for sales figures, showing the ranges.

A database might also have terms in it which have more meaning if they are selected into yet another kind of index, one in which the function of the term is made explicit. For example, an author's name has more meaning, perhaps, or is more easily manipulated, if it can be seen in the context of other authors' names. One could pick out variations of a single author's name if this list is organized on a surname-first basis, as shown in figure 5.6. Similarly, the name of a company might be more useful if it appears in a context of other company names or variants.

```
ROOT  MCCLURE-CHARLES


R1     MCCLURE-CHARLES                1 DOCUMENT

R2     MCCLURE-CHARLES-J-R            1 DOCUMENT

R3     MCCLURE-CHARLES-R            33 DOCUMENTS
```

Fig. 5.6. An author display from ERIC on BRS.

The power of the computer to create, manipulate, display, and retrieve these mutliple indexes to a single file is very important to users. When this is combined with the power of Boolean logic, it multiplies the possibilities for creatively manipulating databases to retrieve needed information.

Electronic Resources for Reference Service

The world of electronic reference resources contains a wide variety of information types as well as several channels for information delivery. In this section, the focus is on the type of information only. Modes of information delivery are discussed in the next section of this chapter.

Bibliographic Databases

The most common reference resource, and the one most people think of when they think of electronic reference resources, is the bibliographic database. These *bibliographic databases* are the machine-readable form of indexes and abstracts. In bibliographic databases, the base record is a citation to an article, book, chapter, or paper. The citation may include an abstract or summary of the item. The citation may include subject headings selected by the database producer. Author, title, and source information are generally available and searchable. Some bibliographic databases include notes, augmented title words (when the original title is uninformative), or translated titles (if the original is in a language other than English). Publication type, date of publication, and language of the material are all additional information about an item which may or may not be available or searchable. Most, but not all, bibliographic databases correspond directly to a printed index or abstract.

Bibliographic databases cover an enormous range of subject disciplines and areas. Some databases (e.g., Dissertation Abstracts Online) are multidisciplinary in scope but limited to a particular document type. Others are very focused in subject coverage but are inclusive of a wide range of formats (e.g., BioBusiness). The coverage of other databases is determined by the source of the material; for example, the U.S. Government Printing Office has a database covering its material published since 1976. These titles are just a very small sample of the more than 500 databases generally available to reference librarians in the United States.

This great wealth of databases is both a strength and a weakness. The diversity is a strength when a reference librarian is seeking information on a subject that is well covered in one database. It is a weakness when a topic is partially covered by several databases, each with its own subject headings, structure, dates of coverage, rules for inclusion, and so forth. It is difficult for a reference librarian to keep all potentially useful databases and their idiosyncrasies in mind when trying to determine the best source and strategy to use to answer a query. Instead, reference librarians depend on written guides and handbooks to databases, such as *Computer-Readable Databases: A Directory and Data Sourcebook* or the *Directory of Online Databases*,[1] to assure selection of the most appropriate information source.

One common aspect of bibliographic databases is the general absence of material published before the mid-1960s. It is typical for a database to go only as far back in time as the date it was first created using machine-readable techniques. Conversion of older material into machine-readable form is a costly undertaking, and few database producers have done it. One exception is Dissertation Abstracts Online. Its coverage goes back to 1861 in its electronic form, because its printed cumulative index was created as a machine-readable file in 1973. In general, however, recent material is far more likely to be available through an electronic resource than is older material.

Nonbibliographic Databases

The term *nonbibliographic database* is used to describe a variety of databases which are distinguished from bibliographic databases by content, style, or format. Some examples of nonbibliographic databases are described in this section.

Full-text Databases. A rapidly growing area of electronic resources for reference is *full-text databases*. In full-text databases, the base record is the full paper or document or article itself, with the associated bibliographic citation information, rather than a citation to a paper or other document located outside the database. Full-text databases are a clear outgrowth of the ability of computers to store and manipulate very large files of information. Some full-text databases are primarily newswire services, such as AP and Reuters. Some newspapers are also available as full-text databases, such as the *Washington Post* Electronic Edition. Others are "journal" files (e.g., *Harvard Business Review*), with entire journals as the database. Some full-text databases include many journal titles in a single file, as does Magazine ASAP. Still others are general information sources, like the *Academic American Encyclopedia*. A growing number of full-text files are professional literature databases, which include the full texts of many journals in a particular discipline, for fields such as pharmacy, medicine, and law. With full-text databases, reference librarians and others have immediate access to entire records that might not be readily available in print. This can serve a library well when an item not in its collection is needed, and the time frame of the reference query does not allow for requesting the item from another library.

Numeric Databases. The term *nonbibliographic databases* also includes databases composed primarily of numbers. These are commonly referred to as *numeric databases*, in which tables of statistics are the base record, along with the citation to the printed counterpart, if any, from which these tables have been drawn. These numeric databases come both from federal government agencies (e.g., the Bureau of Labor Statistics) and from the private sector (e.g., ECONBASE). Like full-text databases, these databases are self-contained universes of information. The reference librarian requiring data can turn to these files and fill the information need without consulting printed sources. The advantages to the patron, who can get the required information without going to a specialized library or the central library building, are enormous.

Graphics Databases. An unusual type of database which can still be described as non-bibliographic is a *graphics database*. These databases have graphic representations as a key element of their base record. One such graphics database is TRADEMARKSCAN-FEDERAL, which contains images of U.S.-registered trademark designs (i.e., logos, stylized writing, non-Roman characters, and symbols) along with corporate information about the trademark owners. The benefits of these graphics representations in a database are substantial. In the case of trademarks, since so much of the trademark information is contained in the stylized visual elements, "seeing is believing." The differences between two symbols described in words may seem slight, but, when compared visually, these differences are substantial and meaningful.

Chemical structures are an element in another type of graphics database. Chemicals that have similar or identical elements have remarkably different properties when arranged in different structures; thus, the graphics portion of the record may be very important to the reference patron.

Directory/Address Databases. Yet another type of nonbibliographic database is the *directory/address database*. In these files, the base record is a name, address, and telephone number. Often, these databases have a business focus, as in the D&B — Dun's Electronic Business Directory, which lists approximately eight million businesses. In these business directories, there is additional information related to such factors as business activities, employees, and size of firm, which may be of interest to patrons using the file. For the reference librarian, the address and telephone number are frequently the critical elements needed for the hard-to-locate firm. Other directory databases have different bases for inclusion, as does the Encyclopedia of Associations. In most cases, virtually all the elements in the record are searchable, from zip code to area code, as well as size of business, parent company, and others. Given the highly restricted access points in most telephone or business directories, the greatly increased number of access points in many electronic directories provides valuable reference capabilities.

Nontraditional Electronic Resources

Some electronic resources, although not originally designed for reference service, are nevertheless used effectively as reference tools.

Bibliographic Utility. *Bibliographic utilities* are large databases of shared cataloging information created by the combined efforts of large libraries, such as the Library of Congress, the British, Canadian, French, and German national libraries, and contributing member libraries in the United States and Canada.

Bibliographic utilities have at the heart of their databases a set of bibliographic records in machine-readable form, called *MARC format*. MARC stands for *MA*chine *R*eadable *C*ataloging, and it is both a standard format and a set of records conforming to that standard. In 1968, the Library of Congress developed the first MARC format for monographs in English. Since 1968 for monographs in English, and since other dates for other types of material and other languages, the Library of Congress has created cataloging records in the MARC format. These MARC records are created on machine-readable magnetic tapes and are sent to bibliographic utilities, where they are processed and made available to subscribing or participating members. This form of distribution resembles that previously outlined for other reference databases.

The major shared cataloging networks in the United States are RLIN and OCLC. RLIN is a product of RLG (Research Libraries Group) which, as its name suggests, is composed of major research libraries in the United States and Canada. The OCLC bibliographic utility is a product of OCLC, Inc. OCLC is composed of many individual libraries, state libraries, and library systems, networks, and consortia. The members of the bibliographic utilities contribute their acquisition and cataloging records in MARC format to the database. In this instance, libraries are database producers as well as database users.

The advantages of this process of shared cataloging for member libraries are clear. Each time any library creates an acquisition or catalog record, the results of that intellectual endeavor are shared with the other members. The buying or cataloging library inputs the data it knows about the item. Other libraries call up that record, modify it if necessary to fit their needs (while leaving the original record intact), and print it or have it stored on a magnetic tape and sent to them for their own catalog systems. Because this process happens online, a record is available virtually instantaneously to all.

OCLC and RLIN have cataloging and acquisitions librarians and staff as their primary creators and users. Although reference librarians are a very small part of the bibliographic utilities universe, this does not lessen the impact of bibliographic utilities for reference service. To cite just one example of this impact, the availability of millions of bibliographic records in a single file, with numerous access points, has transformed the process of *bibliographic verification* through which a reference librarian confirms and clarifies the information a patron provides about a particular item. In the print universe, because of the static nature of the medium and the varied coverage of printed bibliographies, a reference librarian had to determine the likely format (e.g., serial, series, or monograph), medium (e.g., print, microfiche, or microprint), date, and country of origin of an item before beginning the search. The outcome and length of the search would depend on how accurately these facts had been determined. A single misinterpreted clue could lead the reference librarian on a long, frustrating chase. In the electronic universe of bibliographic utilities, because of the wholly cumulative nature of the files, misinterpretation of these clues provides, at worst, a few moments of unproductive searching. If the information provided by the patron contains misspellings, the alternative access points provided usually allow successful retrieval in spite of inevitable patron errors.[2]

In addition, different libraries observe different cataloging practices. An item which is treated as a part of a series in one library can be given full separate monographic cataloging in another. This means that the reference librarian can electronically find full bibliographic information, whether the patron presents the citation as a monograph or as part of a series. As a further advantage to the reference librarian, once the citation has been discovered on the network, the additional, new, or corrected information can lead to discovery of the item in the home collection. Figure 5.7, page 96, is an example of a verification search on OCLC, which demonstrates the ability of the system to retrieve an item when the patron knows part of the title and the surname of the third of three authors.

Each of the bibliographic utilities provides holdings information, which identifies libraries in the system which own the item. This can help patrons locate the needed item in a nearby collection or assist in the interlibrary loan process.

Local or System Catalog. Another electronic resource for reference is a direct outgrowth of the bibliographic utility. This resource is the *local* or *system catalog*. A variety of names are used to identify the electonic catalog, including *OPAC* (Online Public Access Catalog), *PAC* (Public Access Catalog), and *LIS* (Library Information System). These terms focus on the public nature of the electronic catalog, as opposed to a system restricted in large part to library staff. In the electronic catalog, the bibliographic records that a library has created in machine-readable form are processed, loaded onto rapid-access storage devices, and made available through a computer system. Sometimes the catalogs of the member libraries in a library system or a library network are combined into a single electronic catalog. A *search engine* – that is, software to search the catalog – is developed or acquired and modified to the local environment. A *user interface*, meaning commands or menus to communicate between the user and the search engine, is developed. Terminals or workstations are provided for the public to use while searching the catalog. The aim of all these efforts is to create an electronic catalog that has a fast and effective search language understandable by the public which uses it, and that is capable of handling many users simultaneously.

```
SWIC,FIRS\+

UIU - FOR OTHER HOLDINGS, ENTER dh DEPRESS DISPLAY RECD SEND
OCLC: 15224502      Rec stat: p Entrd: 870204          Used: 891129
Type: a Bib lvl: m Govt pub: s Lang:  eng Source:    Illus: a
Repr:    Enc lvl:    Conf pub: 0 Ctry:  cau Dat tp: s M/F/B: 10
Indx: 1 Mod rec:    Festschr: 0 Cont: b
Desc: a Int lvl:    Dates: 1988,

   1 010        87-5073
   2 040        DLC $c DLC
   3 020        0520059077 (alk. paper)
   4 043        n-us---
   5 050 0      HQ759.98 $b .R56 1988
   6 070 0      HQ759.98.R5
   7 072 0      U400
   8 082 0      306.8/74 $2 19
   9 090           $b
  10 049        UIUU

  11 100 10     Rindfuss, Ronald R., $b 1946-
  12 245 10     First births in America : $b changes in the timing of
               parenthood / $c Ronald R. Rindfuss, S. Philip Morgan, Gary
               Swicegood.
  13 260 0      Berkeley : $b University of California Press, $c c1988.
  14 300        xi, 291 p. : $b ill. ; $c 24 cm.
  15 490 1      Studies in demography ; $v 2
  16 504        Bibliography: p. [251]-275.
  17 500        Includes indexes.

  18 650  0     Family demography $z United States.
  19 650  0     Parenthood $z United States.
  20 650  0     Fertility, Human $z United States.
  21 700 10     Morgan, S. Philip.
  22 700 10     Swicegood, Gray, $d 1950-
  23 830  0     Studies in demography (Berkeley, Calif.) ; $v 2.
```

Fig. 5.7. An author-title search and corresponding record on OCLC. Reprinted with permission of OCLC Online Computer Library Center.

    The advantages to reference librarians of the electronic catalog are easy to see. The library's own collection is one of its most important reference resources, in part because helping users find specific items or items about a subject in the home collection is one of the most frequent reference interactions. The electronic catalog provides enhanced access to that collection. Boolean logic, additional search access points, and merging of multiple types of material in one catalog are all advantages when dealing with collection queries. In addition, if the catalog is a system-wide or a network-wide one, the additional material that can be identified and made available to local patrons is valuable. For example, in the University of Minnesota's LUMINA system, the number of records available through the system-wide catalog in 1989 was 1.9 million records for all official roman-alphabet titles.[3]

■ ══ ■

5.1

The Law of the Instrument

If a new tool has been acquired, everything must be processed with that tool. This law is best demonstrated by a two-year-old and a hammer. The next best demonstration is the computer: if one acquires a computer, everything needs to be computerized.

Locally Developed Reference Resources. The final type of electronic resource for reference to be discussed here is the *locally developed reference resource*. This term includes any machine-readable file that the reference library or the larger institution has loaded on any computer that is locally controlled. The computer may be anything from a small desktop computer to a large mainframe computer located in another building or city.

The most common electronic reference resource is the *local reference file*, an electronic form of the "home-grown" reference file that reference librarians have always developed to answer the problematic questions that appear with some frequency at their particular reference desk. These locally developed files frequently are filled with information about the library and its special collections and services, the city, local institutions and organizations, people, and other facts which are hard to find in regular reference sources or come up so frequently it is useful to have the information at the ready. The local reference file is often on cards, in a notebook, or in a vertical file collection. With the advent of computers located on the reference desk, reference librarians began looking at the possibilities of creating electronic versions of their local reference files. Using file management, database management, or other information-handling programs, local files were converted to machine-readable form and loaded into the reference computer.

With these files now in electronic form, many of the difficulties of a manual file are solved. Indexing and retrieval aspects which are difficult to develop and maintain in a printed file become very easy to do on a computer. Frequently, all the words in the text become retrieval points, and the file is fully indexed. It is very easy to correct and update using these programs with the files, since one can often do a global search-and-replace function. In this way, all occurrences of the old term(s) are found and replaced by the new term(s); for instance, Senator X with address Y in all the locations in the file is easily replaced by new Senator A with address Z. Often these files can be called to the screen with a few keystrokes, quickly searched, the results printed on an attached printer, and the answer handed to the patron in a minute or two. Because these files can easily be enlarged and updated, each reference librarian can add information as it is discovered. Thus, these local reference files become more comprehensive and more dynamic as electronic resources for reference.

Information Delivery Systems for Reference

In the current environment, several delivery systems are available for electronic reference resources. The salient aspects of each of these delivery systems are described in this section. Some of the factors which can be important in the selection of information delivery systems for a particular reference setting are also presented.

Online Retrieval Systems

Online retrieval systems are the primary delivery system for most electronic resources. In an online system, a computer or terminal in the reference library is used to communicate with large, vendor-operated computer hosts, which may contain many hundreds of databases. The local computer or terminal uses a modem (abbreviated from *modulator-demodulator*) which translates digital computer signals to an analog signal that telephone lines can carry. These signals run through a system of telecommunication computers that form networks across the country. These telecommunication networks carry the signals from the local library to the desired computer, perhaps located thousands of miles away. At the host computer, another modem retranslates the telephone signals back into digital signals. This process, which may sound a little cumbersome, in fact takes a second or less to accomplish. The term *online* indicates that both the local computer or terminal and the host computer are in active communication at the time of the search. This distinguishes it from the batch-style computer interactions described in the early part of this chapter. In the online information retrieval process, the librarian selects the relevant search terms, types them into the terminal, and sees the results immediately. This information loop is repeated and modified until the desired results are obtained.

Online retrieval as an information delivery system has several advantages for the reference librarian. First, it uses equipment that is widely available and relatively inexpensive. Frequently, the reference library has the necessary equipment for use with its own online catalog, and with very inexpensive modifications can use it for online information retrieval. This makes the system within the fiscal reach of most libraries. A second consideration is flexibility. A library can choose to use one or several information service companies. A library can choose to use a single database or hundreds of databases. Typically, a library has to pay only for actual use of a system, so there is little, if any, up-front cost. Box 5.2 shows the cost elements of online search systems. A third consideration is the amount of information available. With vendors such as DIALOG, BRS, WILSONLINE, ORBIT, and the National Library of Medicine, thousands of databases and millions of records are available at almost literally the touch of a button. Bibliographic utilities such as OCLC and RLIN are also available through the online retrieval system, providing access to millions more bibliographic records.

■ ══ ■

5.2

Cost Components of Online Search Services

The following are elements of online searching with some ranges of costs. Different systems select and package these costs in different ways.

Vendor subscription charges:	$0-150/year
Telecommunication charges:	$6-15/hour
Vendor system charges:	$10-35/hour
Database royalty charges:	$0-200 + /hour
Citation royalty charges, online:	$.00-.85 + /citation
Citation royalty charges, offline:	$.00-.85 + /citation
Vendor shipping or minimum offline charges:	$0-10/transaction

Because online information retrieval systems operate nearly instantaneously, use equipment that is relatively inexpensive, and provide access to millions of records, this approach has gained the widest acceptance in providing electronic resources for reference service.

The online information delivery network has some drawbacks as well as advantages in the reference setting. Because most system charges are based on usage, as shown in box 5.2, costs are difficult to predict, and therefore difficult to budget for. In addition, although many databases are common among the several information service providers, some databases important to a library are available on only one system. This means that a library needs to choose between missing access to some databases or selecting two, three, or more vendors. Each of the online information service companies uses a different search language. As a result, it is sometimes a challenge for a reference librarian to remember each system's commands, particularly those commands that must follow a precise formula, such as print commands. Even within a single system, there are variations among databases. The online systems try to create consistency across the databases within the system, but one will still find authors' names, or other data elements, treated rather differently from one database to the next, as shown in figure 5.8.

```
                    WILSONLINE:  Library Literature

USER: NBR SMITH, LINDA (AU)

              pstg     (Category) Term        File: LIB     Category: AU
              ----     ---------------
      1         1      (AU) SMITH, KEVIN
      2         1      (AU) SMITH, KEVIN, DIRECTOR OF LITERACY VOLUNTEERS
                            OF NYS, INC.
      3         1      (AU) SMITH, L.
      4         1      (AU) SMITH, LAURIE E.
      5         1      (PS) SMITH, LILLIAN H.
      6        16      (AU) SMITH, LINDA C.
      7         1      (AU) SMITH, LINDA-JEAN
      8         2      (AU) SMITH, LOTSEE PATTERSON
      9         1      (AU) SMITH, LOUISE

              BRS:  Library and Information Science Abstracts

ROOT SMITH-LINDA

      R1   SMITH-LINDA            2 DOCUMENTS
      R2   SMITH-LINDA-A          1 DOCUMENT
      R3   SMITH-LINDA-C          2 DOCUMENTS
      R4   SMITH-LINDA-E          1 DOCUMENT
      R5   SMITH-LINDA-J          4 DOCUMENTS
      R6   SMITH-LINDA-K          1 DOCUMENT
      R7   SMITH-LINDA-L          4 DOCUMENTS
      R8   SMITH-LINDA-M          2 DOCUMENTS

                    DIALOG: ERIC

?E AU=SMITH, LINDA C

Ref    Items     Index-term
E1        8      AU=SMITH, LEWIS B.
E2        3      AU=SMITH, LEWIS H.
E3        1     *AU=SMITH, LINDA
E4        1      AU=SMITH, LINDA ANDERSON
E5       14      AU=SMITH, LINDA B.
E6        8      AU=SMITH, LINDA C.
E7        1      AU=SMITH, LINDA C., COMP.
E8        2      AU=SMITH, LINDA C., ED.
E9        9      AU=SMITH, LINDA H.
```

Fig. 5.8. Author searching in different files on three systems.

As a consequence of this variation within and across systems, the searcher has to prepare carefully for each search by verifying how each of the data elements is formatted, indexed, and labeled, or risk missing relevant material by inadvertently using the wrong search approach. This may produce searches that are less effective, more expensive, or both. As an added difficulty, the reference librarian using these systems is acutely aware of the connect costs accruing with each keystroke, which put a great deal of emphasis on efficiency. This fiscal pressure can interfere with a feeling of ease in using these resources. As a final consideration, since much of the equipment which is needed to access these systems is also used for other reference work, such as searching the online catalog, it can be awkward to switch from one application to another. Reference librarians must weight all these factors in the context of their own situations to arrive at appropriate decisions regarding use of online systems as an information delivery mode.

Optical Disc Systems for Reference

The term *optical disc* refers to an electronic storage medium which is produced and read by means of laser technology. The material stored on these discs can be text, numbers, graphics, or a combination of all of these in digital form. "Optical discs can be classified according to their use as storage memory: read-only, write-once, or erasable memory."[4] Each of these types of discs uses a special reading drive in association with a computer or workstation. In read-only memory discs, the data is embedded into the storage medium at the time of production. Read-only discs include compact discs (CD), such as CD-Audio, CD-ROM, CD-I (Compact Disc Interactive), and videodiscs. In write-once discs, the discs are prepared to accept data during production, but the actual writing to the discs occurs in a read/write optical drive of the user. Each segment of the disc can be written on only once, because the process of writing in these systems changes the physical medium permanently. Write-once discs include WORM (Write-Once Read-Many or Mostly) and CD-PROM (Compact Disc Programmable Read-Only Memory). Erasable optical discs would be similar to today's magnetic disks, capable of being written and read many times, but they are still in the experimental stage.

Of these discs, the most important for reference service and for libraries in general are CD-ROM. One research group, Link Resources, predicts a CD-ROM market of $900 million per year in 1991.[5] Videodiscs are of secondary importance, and the other optical discs have not yet made an impact.

Each CD-ROM disc stores approximately 550 million bytes of information. Some videodiscs hold 1 gigabyte of information (1,000,000,000 bytes). For comparison, a standard 5.25-inch floppy disk holds 360,000 bytes, and a high-density 3.5-inch disk holds 1.2 million bytes. A standard piece of paper stores the equivalent of approximately 250 bytes. Thus, the vast storage capacity of optical discs is a very strong asset in the delivery of electronic resources for reference.

In appearance, CD-ROM discs are identical to compact discs available for audio systems, while videodiscs are about as large as an audio record album. In this section, CD-ROM will be the focus, because database producers, database vendors, and other information industry organizations have developed many systems for CD-ROM and there are many others under development.

These CD-ROM systems are distributed to users and mounted on CD-ROM stations. The basic elements of a CD-ROM station include a disc drive to read the CD-ROM, a personal computer or workstation to run the disc drive, and a search language to manipulate the data on the CD-ROM. A printer is often associated with a CD-ROM station. Sometimes all the associated equipment is leased from the database producer as part of the subscription package to the CD-ROM product. In other cases, the equipment is owned by the library and only the discs are acquired on a subscription basis. As part of the subscription to the service, database producers update the disc(s) at regular intervals, typically by replacing the entire disc with a new disc containing the original material plus the update.

The range of products that has been developed for CD-ROM is broad and varied. Among them are the Bible and its associated reference works; the InfoTrac family of CD-ROM databases; the McGraw-Hill Scientific and Technical Reference Set (including, among other titles, the *McGraw-Hill Concise Encyclopedia of Science and Technology*); Newspaper Abstracts; OCLC's Search CD450, with segments of its online union catalog and subject-related indexes; the Census of Agriculture from Slater Hall; and a prototype CD-ROM system from the National Oceanic and Atmospheric Administration with historical weather data. These are in addition to the more traditional indexes and abstracting services, such as Readers' Guide, PAIS, MEDLINE, and ERIC. Some of these titles are available from several different producers, while others are produced by a single company.

In a reference library, a CD-ROM station provides the user with the ability to search the index, abstract, or other reference tool directly, an activity termed *end-user searching*. CD-ROM search software often provides the user with much of the power of multiple indexes and Boolean logic available in the commercial online search environment, without its time and cost pressures. In end-user searching, the users are able to explore the database, following leads as they are discovered, and printing out citations during the search. CD-ROM search software is designed to be *user friendly*, that is, to be easily understood and implemented by the searcher. Printed user aids and self-contained help screens help the user discover effective search techniques. Many systems offer two or more levels of searching, designed to meet the needs of novice searchers as well as those of the more experienced. For the novice, there might be a series of menus with simple questions to answer, which lead the user to select from a single displayed array of index terms. For the more experienced searcher, there might be a command-driven option which provides more searching power, greater efficiency in handling citations, or just faster searching.

For the reference librarian making decisions about information delivery systems, CD-ROM systems have some clear advantages. In contrast to the online information delivery systems previously discussed, CD-ROM systems have a single fixed subscription price for unlimited use. This simplifies budgeting, since the annual costs are known in advance and do not vary with use. Each library can select the system or group of systems which meets the needs of its users and fits within the acquisitions budget. Each CD-ROM system or station stores thousands of citations on a single disc, so that the patron can search the equivalent of a dozen volumes of an index simultaneously. Since the systems are designed to be end-user systems, a reference librarian does not have to be a search intermediary for each patron. It also allows the system to be used whenever the room is available for patron use, rather than limiting it to whenever a librarian can be scheduled. With careful planning and equipment acquisition, a library can provide multiple-user stations or multiple-system stations, so that each CD-ROM gets maximum use and patrons get maximum access. As an additional advantage, patrons *enjoy* using CD-ROM systems. It allows them to be in charge of their own searches, relieves them of the burden of writing down their own citations (with their inevitable errors), and provides them with many more citations in less time than a manual search. These citations can be printed on paper or can be *downloaded* (written) to the user's own diskette for later handling and printing.

CD-ROM presents its own set of disadvantages as well, which must be weighed against the advantages in any selection/evaluation process. As a rule, CD-ROM systems tend to be expensive, an average of 176 percent of the cost of the corresponding print tool.[6] The late development of standards for the logical representation of data on CD-ROM discs, often referred to as the *High Sierra standard*,[7] has resulted in a degree of incompatibility among CD-ROM systems. Some CD-ROM systems, developed before the High Sierra standard, have not conformed to it. There is now an additional international standard (International Organization for Standardization: ISO 9660) to create consistency across systems. Others conform to the High Sierra standard, but use software or indexing systems which make them incompatible with other systems. Some pieces of CD-ROM equipment, like drives, are incompatible with some varieties or generations of computer equipment. All CD-ROM systems are intended to be user friendly, but some are more successful in their design than others. In CD-ROM systems with different search levels, the levels frequently have little in common, so it is difficult for the patron to develop the skills needed to use the higher levels successfully. This results in the patron either remaining at an unsophisticated level, and perhaps having research impeded, or needing individualized training and instruction in the higher search techniques. CD-ROM systems in which there is a skills ladder are rare. Searching procedures vary widely, so a user of multiple systems is sometimes confused by the very different capabilities, style, and look of the systems. In addition, because CD-ROMs are still at an early point in their product life cycle, many CD-ROM systems undergo frequent and far-reaching revisions and upgrades. Some CD-ROM tools become an entirely different product only a few months after purchase. These frequent changes make it difficult to maintain current user aids. Not all CD-ROM systems make it clear to the patron (or the reference librarian) what the database contains, in terms of degree of coverage of the listed journals, the dates of coverage, and the like. Very often the CD-ROM and the online version of the same database vary significantly from one another and from the printed version as well. One of the ways in which they vary the most is in frequency of updates. An online database tends to be updated at least as frequently as the paper version is published, while the CD-ROM version is updated on a quarterly, semiannual, or annual basis. As a result of all these factors, making subscription decisions about CD-ROM products and services requires intensive investigation and cross-checking of information from a variety of sources. Once selected, CD-ROM systems often require significant modifications to work well with the library's existing equipment, and the nature of these adjustments may tax the skills and time of the librarian in charge of the project. It is at this point that many reference librarians discover another difficulty about many CD-ROM systems: the producing company provides inadequate technical support, technical support is lacking altogether, or one must pay for technical support. This is in marked contrast to the online vendors, which have a tradition of providing free, excellent support for their users. As a consequence of all the many positive and negative factors, CD-ROM has most often found a niche in the reference service spectrum as a complement to, rather than as a replacement for, online information delivery systems.

Locally Loaded Databases

One of the earliest means of access to databases is now regaining its position in the marketplace. This is the locally loaded database. In the early days of machine-readable files, locally loaded tapes of databases were the only means of access to these files. This automatically restricted access to those relatively few reference librarians who were located in an environment able to support this system. Locally loaded databases became a less viable option with the proliferation of other databases, the increasing size of databases, and the formidable task of local development of software to search these files. The current computer environment within libraries has created new opportunities to overcome these obstacles. Many libraries have developed online catalogs, with large, fast computers serving the system. These online catalogs have powerful search languages with which to manipulate the large files. Thus, two major difficulties have been solved: storage capacity and search language. The issues that remain are resolved in varying ways by each library or system that loads databases locally. Because locally loaded databases require substantial computing resources, the projects typically involve a larger unit than an individual library. A campus, a library system, or a library consortium is needed to supply the funds, personnel, and number of users. This section outlines some of the issues and decisions, with a view to illuminating the current picture of a rapidly growing, rapidly changing field of electronic reference resources.[8]

A typical library system might identify one, or perhaps two or three, database(s) which would meet the needs of a large portion of its user community. Once selected, the databases are acquired, processed by the system's software, loaded onto disk storage units, and made available for searching through the local network. Each of the steps in that sequence, including the selection of the databases, is a result of a complex decision-making process. In any environment with a diverse user community, such as a college campus, there are a great many databases vying for selection. Choosing among them, weighing such factors as costs, potential use, and size of the databases, is a difficult task. Further questions about how many years of a database to load, whether to include only those items held by the library, and whether to limit the database by language must be resolved. Deciding whether to use the online catalog's search engine or to acquire a commercially available one has further ramifications for how these locally loaded databases will be used. Determining the hardware configurations, anticipating storage requirements, and predicting system response time is a process of some uncertainty. The final step of the process — making the databases available to the library's user community — has additional ramifications. Database producers require that access to these databases be limited to the primary user community, while a library's online catalog is usually available to anyone with a modem. Creating mechanisms invisible to primary users to filter out the external users is a challenge.

Other steps in this process include creating a *user interface*, a program that works between the user and the online catalog/database system; creating user aids to explain the products; and alerting the user community to the availability of the services. The remaining difficulty, proliferation of databases, is solved through selectivity. Each organization selects a few databases which serve a large portion of its primary clientele. Locally loaded databases are an option for librarians located in a computer-rich environment, but they form just part of the electronic access picture. In an article describing locally loaded databases at the University of Pennsylvania, Emily Fayen noted that the library needs to make MEDLINE available in three electronic formats for the library's users: CD-ROM as a teaching tool, three years of the English-language-only portion of MEDLINE locally loaded for the large majority of users, and online for the researcher with a need for a comprehensive search of the entire file.[9]

One might wonder why a library would wish to load externally produced databases alongside its online catalog. In large part, it is a question of access. The online catalog, since it is distributed across the library in as many locations as the library has terminals or ports, provides increased access to the library's book collection. Patrons far away can browse the catalog. In addition to the spatial meaning of *access*, the online catalog has also increased intellectual access to the catalog. Many more indexed terms and many more ways to manipulate the records add up to increased access. This increased access to the book collection has led to raised expectations for access to the rest of the library's collection. Tyckoson estimated that most library catalogs, whether on cards or online, index only 2 percent of the works in a collection[10]; improved access to the remaining 98 percent is a goal any library would wish to meet. Locally loaded databases are one way to provide that improved access.

For the reference librarian, having some databases loaded as part of or alongside the online catalog creates a very rich service environment. Because they are locally mounted, searching or printing the databases incurs no additional costs. Librarians and patrons are free to explore the databases in search of the needed item or research materials. If the databases are matched against the holdings of the library, then the retrieved material is known to be available. In any case, these local databases can hold the key to the less accessible parts of the library's collections. Some libraries, in addition to loading external databases, also create and load machine-readable files of special collections or nontraditional materials. This adds to the comprehensiveness and the utility of the system for reference service.

Integrating Electronic Resources
into Reference Service

That electronic reference resources are used in reference settings is evident. What is less evident are the interactions among the several components and the consequences for reference service.

Reference Service Environment

For the purposes of this discussion, the reference service environment consists of the physical surroundings of the reference service point, the equipment used in the provision of services, the reference staff, the materials budget, and the reference service policies. This reference matrix is a dynamic, interlinked one, with changes in any area affecting and shaping each of the others. Electronic reference resources must fit into this context for effective integration into the reference process.

The physical environment can be considered first. The reference desk is a possible location for some of the electronic resource equipment. If the reference desk is a location for an online catalog, with a basic cathode ray tube (CRT) terminal connected to a mainframe computer, some equipment (a modem and switch box for example) could be added to allow it to connect also to an online service. It is likely that, without any equipment modification, the terminal could be used to access any locally loaded database. If the online catalog equipment is a personal computer, then, with a very small outlay for a modem and communication software, this computer could be used to link to an online service or to a locally loaded database. If there is no electronic equipment at the reference desk, then space, esthetic, and efficiency considerations would play a role in the location of the computer/terminal for reference. If equipment is far away, hard to get to, or under the jurisdiction of others, such as an adjacent interlibrary loan department, integration of electronic resources into reference service is very difficult. On the other hand, if the equipment is close at hand or even at the reference desk, ease of access contributes to the integration.

For purposes of discussion, it will be assumed that a personal computer has been acquired and is located on or near the reference desk. If it is to be used to gain access to online information delivery systems, there are some additional considerations which can contribute to the successful integration of the service for reference. There are a variety of software packages which facilitate log-on procedures, and others which continue past the log-on stage to help users select databases and formulate search strategies. These packages are called *front-end* systems when they are located at the user's equipment. They are called *gateways* when they are located between the user's equipment and the information service provider. These front-end/gateway systems shift part of the burden of remembering search system protocols and language from the user to the software. In reference settings where many staff members are at the reference desk, or where a wide range of experience in online systems exists among the staff, these front-end/gateway systems can provide valuable assistance in equalizing access to electronic resources. If the equipment at the reference desk is multipurpose in nature, the ease with which one is able to change from one function to another will greatly affect the degree of integration achieved. Selecting software that facilitates this switching function, and is itself easily manipulated, is an effective strategy in designing a reference environment for electronic resources.

In addition to equipment and software, a variety of supporting resources are needed to integrate electronic information products and services into the reference setting. One of the central requirements is the education and training provided to the reference librarian. A broad range of education and training options is available to the reference librarian. These include courses in electronic resources from library and information science programs, training programs offered by information service providers, in-house training offered by experienced librarians to their colleagues, videotapes on electronic resources designed to be used in the library's video center, and self-instruction through use of training manuals and literature. In most situations, reference librarians become acquainted with electronic resources through a combination of all of these methods. Once the essentials of the appropriate resources are acquired, there will be a need for maintenance and updating of these skills. Typically, a reference librarian will read (or more likely, scan) literature created by the information service providers, and browse current journals on the topic, such as *Online*,[11] *Database*,[12] *Online Review*,[13] or *CD-ROM Professional*,[14] as well as attending workshops and similar programs offered by the library's or system's staff. The main component of all these training activities is time. It takes time and commitment to keep abreast of the electronic information industry. This large investment on the part of individual librarians, and the concomitant investment by the library, is a necessary part of the process of integration of these electronic resources. It is expected, of course, that the rewards to the librarians and their patrons will include more effective and efficient service than is possible without these electronic resources.

An additional facet of the integration process is the fiscal or budgetary one. All the electronic resources previously described, and all the delivery systems, require some expenditure of funds. Some of these expenditures are nearly invisible, such as for electricity to run any equipment. Some of these expenditures are quite visible, such as for the purchase of a CD-ROM workstation. Each reference library's unique mix of staff, user community, and resources determines the appropriate mix of electronic and traditional materials to fulfill the reference service goals within budgetary constraints. Some external considerations also play a role. Some funding sources have restrictions on the type of materials for which their money can be used. For example, some public materials funds cannot be spent on things that are not "books," so they could not be spent on electronic resources at all. Other, less restricted funds can be spent on CD-ROM or locally loaded products, but not on online access to databases, because online access does not create an object. In some cases, the reference department is free to offer any electronic service, providing the users cover all costs of the service. In others, staff money is reallocated to support some electronic resources, in part because of the efficiencies in using electronic rather than printed reference tools.

Ready Reference Applications

At the beginning of this section, it was noted that the reference environment was an interlinked matrix of factors. This is particularly evident in the area of reference service policies covering the use of electronic resources. The desire to offer patrons the highest possible service favors extensive use of multiple electronic resources. The requirement that the library provide its services within a finite budget limits this use. The service policy developed by the reference staff assures that the access to the resources balances the two opposing tendencies. A library might determine that two CD-ROM systems would meet the needs of a significant share of the user community and that all access to these systems should be free, including printing. The policy might further stipulate that for those whose immediate reference needs are not met in this way, a limited fund would be earmarked for ready reference use of electrronic resources by reference librarians to access online information sources. Typically, the reference service policy spells out in some detail the expected uses and limits on ready reference queries, because of the pay-per-use aspects of most online information services. The policy must ensure that ready reference resources are allocated appropriately across the fiscal year.

The process of codifying the general parameters of questions appropriate for ready reference searching will depend in part on the climate in the particular reference setting. If the setting is resource-rich, with machines on every table, a fairly extensive ready reference budget in place, and a highly trained staff available, the kinds of questions that seem appropriate for ready reference searches will be very diverse. In other settings which lack some or most of the resources just described, the kinds of questions deemed appropriate will be fewer. In almost any setting, bibliographic clarification and verification fall within the realm of ready reference questions. If a patron comes to the reference desk with an incomplete or uncertain citation, the choice between a few minutes of online search time and several minutes (or hours) of manual searching is clearly in favor of the online session. Other questions fall along a spectrum from very likely to quite unlikely. One of the more likely questions might be a search for the address for a small business. A reference librarian could search one of the electronic business directories effectively, rather than searching manually through perhaps ten or twelve national business directories, state business directories, and telephone directories for the likely geographic area. A question that would be much less likely is a request for all the critical articles about a literary work. Each library chooses its own balance point on the spectrum.

A typical rule of thumb in any setting concerns who makes the choice of the electronic resource. If the librarian chooses the resource, it is probably part of a ready reference search; if the patron must request the electronic resource, it generally is not. Another useful rule of thumb is visualization of the results of the search. If the results can be foreseen as a set with a single item in it (i.e., "the answer"), it is a ready reference search; if the results would be a set with multiple items, it is not.

In any use of electronic resources for ready reference, efficiency is an important goal. Efficiency includes the librarian's time, the patron's time, and the computer's time. In an effort to achieve this efficiency, many reference librarians use brief memory aids. Usually, these aids are in addition to the more formal guides provided by the electronic information service companies. Sometimes these aids are as simple as a card with file names and numbers taped to the reference desk. In other cases, the library develops single-page search guides to the databases used for ready reference. In some settings, since librarians each know their own search needs best, each develops a unique *aide de memoire* for problematic situations.

There is a need for easy-to-use resource selection aids as well. A reference librarian must identify and choose, from among the very large number of databases and services available, the one which best suits the librarian's skills and the patron's query. Because several databases may apply to the appropriate subject area, the details about coverage and inclusiveness must be determined before selection. Database catalogs, indexes, and guides need to be supplemented by briefer, more focused summaries. Typically, these summaries are created in the form of a features table, limited to those databases included in the reference library's pool of potential resources, like the hypothetical one in box 5.3. Together, ready reference search policies, resource guides, and search aids result in a setting that enables efficient and appropriate ready reference searching.

■ ══ ■

5.3

Features Table — Current Events Files

Database Name/ID	System	Dates of Coverage	Content
WONDERFUL	Q	1979-Current	Journals
PRETTYGOOD	Z	1985-Current	Newspapers
USEFUL	T	1979-1988	Reports

Extended Electronic Search Services

In this section, the focus is on searches requiring a more comprehensive approach to and use of the available electronic resources. These comprehensive searches done on behalf of a patron are termed *retrospective searches*, *bibliographic searches*, *online searches*, or *mediated searches*. *Online searches* is the term used here to identify searches in which the reference librarian serves as an intermediary between the patron and the electronic resource. This shift from ready reference searches, which are conducted as an integral part of the reference process, to mediated searches, which are conducted for the benefit of the recipient of the service, has several consequences. Some of the consequences fall into the reference service policy arena; the others into an area that can be termed *reference processes*, that is, the interaction between the librarian and the patron. The first to be addressed are the policy concerns.

One of the first consequences to be considered is financial. Extensive use of online resources creates significant costs for the library. The determination of who is responsible for paying these costs is an issue with which reference librarians have struggled from the earliest days of providing online services. This philosophical discussion is termed the *fee-or-free issue*. At its core, the fee-or-free conflict poses the choice between the library offering online searches free to its users and paying for these services from its budget, or offering the service at a price to those who can afford it and will directly benefit from it, relieving the budget of a cost that often benefits relatively few of its patrons. As a philosophical issue, this has been and likely will continue to be discussed in the literature, at conferences, and in professional forums for the foreseeable future.[15] As a practical matter, the library makes the best decision it can in the face of conflicting considerations, and sets its service policy accordingly. Box 5.4 shows some alternatives to consider in this process.

■ ══ ■

5.4

Charging Alternatives for Online Searches

A reference librarian proposes subscribing to an online service to provide bibliographic searching to the patrons of the library. The proposal includes some choices for funding the possible searches. These choices are:

1. Charge all users of the service the full cost of the search, but not for the equipment, staff time, and paper, which are absorbed in the library's operating budget.

2. Charge all users of the service the full cost of the search, including a portion of the overhead and staff time.

3. Charge different users for different proportions of the costs, depending on perceived ability to pay. For example, local business might be charged 110% of all costs, the library's primary user community might be charged 75%, students 50%, and senior citizens 15%. The hope is that the business charges will cover the costs of the subsidies to the other groups.

4. Make no charges to anyone, with the cost of the service covered by reducing expenditures in other areas.

What are some of the consequences of each of these choices? Are there other charging systems which can be developed to meet other criteria?

Libraries must also determine to whom the service will be offered. This determination is frequently connected to the charging policy, as it directly affects access to resources. A library frequently will choose to offer online services only to its primary user group, in recognition of the resource-intensive nature of the service. In other situations, a library might need to offer this service to a much more diffuse community of users, to meet its obligations as a publicly funded library, as just one example. Some information service companies have user group requirements as well. For example, some database producers may restrict the access to their databases to an identifiable subscriber group.

Another service issue to be considered is who will conduct these searches. The intermediary is expected to make the necessary online decisions that will best fulfill the patron's request. There is extensive discussion in the library literature about whether the search intermediary should be a *generalist* (a reference librarian with a typical reference librarian's skills, duties, and attributes) or a *specialist* (a reference librarian who has reduced duties elsewhere to accommodate the time required to master the searching skills for online searches). This is another way to ask if online searches are a natural extension of the everyday reference activities of assisting patrons in finding the materials they need, or are in some way different from these activities, because of the greater responsibility the intermediary has for serving in place of the patron.

In a typical reference service encounter, the librarian does not take the responsibility for selecting the items that the patron will use from an index. Offering suggestions for selection criteria to be implemented by the patron is a more typical activity for the reference librarian. In an online search, the determination for inclusion or exclusion of items is largely performed by the intermediary. Each library offering online services has to determine whether the resources necessary to make each generalist an effective search intermediary are available and are best spent in this way. Alternatively, if online searching is viewed as an activity that is best performed by one or a few specialists, does this create a technologically elite group within the reference staff?

A further variation of the generalist-or-specialist issue is the centralized or local service concern. If a library has determined that it is more appropriate for online search services to be offered by specialists, then that specialization can be carried further by establishing a special unit which conducts these online searches apart from any reference service point. This search unit might be staffed entirely by librarians who are search intermediaries in the fields of inquiry served by the library. This organizational structure would further remove online searching from the realm of the reference room and reference librarian. This separation of online searching from regular reference functions was perhaps more common earlier, when such services were only beginning to be offered, than it is currently. It is also more likely to occur in those libraries which offer online searches for a fee than those in which it is free. By creating a separate unit to do the fee-based online searches, the library allows reference librarians to continue to offer all their services free. In a few situations, separating any fee-based services from the rest of the library's services is required to satisfy legal considerations.

These philosophical issues and their resolution form the framework for reference search service policies. There is a great deal of variation in online search policies among libraries. However, in spite of the policy variations, the reference processes associated with online searching are largely identical, and are discussed in the next section.

The Search Interview

The reference process for online searching begins with a patron whose information need can be satisfied with an online search. The search might be requested by the patron, or the need for it could be identified during a traditional reference interview. In either case, the reference librarian who will be performing the search conducts a search interview with the patron.

In the course of a fairly structured search interview, the reference librarian discovers the patron's parameters for the search by asking the following kinds of questions. At the same time, the librarian shares with the patron the dimensions of what an online search can and cannot do.

1. Is the search part of the research needed to write a term paper, an article, a bid for a contract, a business report, or a dissertation, or is it a personal interest? This will help determine the overall framework for the search.

2. Is it essential that as much information as possible be gathered about the topic, or can the needs be met with a smaller set of material? Some search needs can be met with one database; others require two or more to complete the search.

3. Is it more important to cover the most recent material, or is currency not as important as breadth of coverage? In some fields, the most current information is available in separate databases. In other fields, one might choose one database for its currency and another for its range of coverage.

4. Is there a type of literature that is critical to the research (e.g., patents)? Frequently there are databases which cover a particular type of literature, such as dissertations, newspapers, or government reports, that can be essential to a search.

5. Is the language of the material important to the researcher (e.g., is only material in English needed)? Sometimes language requirements play an important role in database selection and manipulation.

6. Are there geographical requirements for the search? If the patron needs material from or about a country or region, or if the patron wishes to restrict the material to a particular population, this can be an important factor to consider.

7. At what level of specialization will the material be most useful? For example, a student who is beginning to research a new topic will need to start with material that is less specialized than the business person who is searching for information on products and competitors.

8. What fiscal resources are available for the search? This can affect several searching parameters, ranging from database selection to output formats.

9. Is this a one-time search, or part of a series of searches on the same topic? Some searches will be constructed differently if there will be a series of searches with chances for evaluation and refinement between sessions. (Sometimes patrons do not know until they see the results if there are gaps in the retrieval that need to be covered, so even searches conceived as single sessions can change into multipart searches.)

10. What time constraints does the patron have for the use of the information? If waiting for the search results to be printed by the host computer and mailed takes longer than the patron has available, then choices about alternative output modes need to be considered.

These elements of the search interview might be termed the *externals*, that is, important elements of search decisions but largely external to the search topic itself. The next set of considerations deals more directly with illuminating and clarifying the search topic. The clarification process takes the form of a verbal duet between the searcher and the patron.

The searcher asks a question, the patron responds, and then the searcher rephrases the response in order to assure that the response has been understood. With each iteration, this communication loop refines the topic for the searcher and for the patron as well.

Because the primary search operators are the Boolean AND, OR, and NOT, using Venn diagrams as a mechanism for clarifying the search topic is very effective. It can help the patron visualize the search process and the likely outcomes of search decisions. In fact, the Venn diagram is often presented as part of a search request form (an example is shown in box 5.5) as an aid to the patron in the initial step of the search process.

At the heart of the search interview, the librarian tries to help the patron articulate the central element(s) of the search topic. One of the ways to ascertain this is to ask what concept must be present for the item to be of any interest. This step is further developed by identifying synonyms for the central concept. This is followed by the development of the second (and third, and so on) central concept and its synonyms.

■ ═══ ■

5.5

Search Request Form

This is an example of part of a search request form, showing the relationship between the Venn diagram and the search concepts.

The search analyst retrieves citations relevant to your topic by creating sets and using computer (Boolean) logic. An online search can retrieve citations containing all of the important search concepts. In the following schematic diagram, only those citations in the fully shaded portion would be considered relevant in a search with three main search concepts.

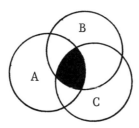

In the following sections, please identify the key concepts in your search topic and list any synonyms or other closely related terms under each concept.

Concept A: _____   Concept B: _____   Concept C: _____

Synonyms: _____   _____   _____

_____   _____   _____

_____   _____   _____

_____   _____   _____

_____

An effective strategy to employ during a search interview is to have a patron visualize the titles of a few items that would be considered perfect. Such titles, whether or not they exist, can provide a useful target for the searcher, and provide further feedback to the searcher in understanding the patron's topic.

At this point in the search interview, the intermediary and the patron should have a much clearer perception of the search topic and the resources available for it, as the sample search interview in box 5.6 illustrates.

■ ══ ■

5.6

Search Topic Before and After Search Interview

Patron: I am interested in the doctor-patient relationship.

Searcher: What about the doctor-patient relationship most interests you?

Patron: I'm wondering if male and female doctors treat their male and female patients differently.

Searcher: You are most interested in how sex differences might affect doctor-patient relationships.

Patron: Yes. I also wonder if the doctor's specialty makes any difference, so I want to find out if there are any studies about doctors who specialize in family practice.

Searcher: So, you want to find out if there are studies which compare doctor-patient relationships across specialties, with a particular interest in family practice.

Patron: Yes, that's right.

Searcher: Some of the relevant literature might be written in foreign languages. Would you be interested in those?

Patron: No, I only want English-language material for this paper, since I am mainly interested in U.S. doctors.

Searcher: I think we will be able to limit the material to English for you. Are you most interested in material published in the last few years, or do you want older material to see if things have changed over the years?

Patron: Since this is just a paper for my psychology class, I don't need every-thing ever written. I think I'll stick to recent articles, from the last three to five years.

Searcher: To sum up, you want recent, English-language articles on the sex-related differences in doctor-patient relationships, comparing, if possible, other specialties to physicians in general or family practice.

Patron: That's it exactly. When can we get started?

Database Selection

With a clear understanding of the search topic and the additional dimensions of the search, the searcher needs to identify and select the database(s) that will provide the most effective results. Through the use of the same guides and handbooks that would be used for ready reference searching, the searcher will identify a few databases that seem to hold the most promise. Several techniques can help the librarian select among the different databases.

A review of the database guides provided by the vendor will help determine the appropriateness of a database, as these guides typically have detailed descriptions of subject coverage. The librarian would review these descriptions to see if the search topic is among the primary subject areas, or if it falls into a more peripheral position.

If the database warrants further consideration, the thesaurus for that database might be examined to see if there are good matches between the patron's concepts and the controlled vocabulary. Frequently, an absence of parallel or synonymous terms suggests some incompatibilities between topic and database. The searcher and the patron together can identify the descriptors that come closest to the search concepts.

Another aspect of database selection is the material covered. Often the guides list the journals contained in the database. These lists can be consulted if the patron is aware of one or more titles that are important in the subject area.

Search Previews

As a final step in database selection, a searcher can use an online preview. Most online systems have a feature that allows the searcher to see the number of matches (postings) of a term or group of terms in several databases simultaneously. In DIALOG, this is called DIALINDEX; in BRS it is CROSS; and in ORBIT it is the Database Index. These files contain the indexing terms and the postings for these terms in all the databases in each system, though they do not contain any of the database contents. Because the vendors have created these files to assist in effective searching, the costs for searching them are very low. In each of these systems, one can choose a subject category created by the vendor, or individual databases, or a combination of the two. A limited search strategy can be executed against these databases and the results displayed. These results can help the searcher make the final database selection. In addition, since the results of each search are known, fairly accurate cost estimates can be developed for each database.

Search Strategies

In any reference situation, the reference librarian can imagine a set of materials that will meet the needs of the patron. The steps that the librarian takes to help the patron find that set of materials is the *search strategy*. In most manual searches, this strategy remains at an informal level, as the librarian thinks, "We'll start with the author index of this tool, since the patron has a specific author in mind." In the more constrained field of online searching, search strategies tend to be more formally developed, and are often written down, at least in part. Using Boolean logic, database thesauri, the database contents and structure, and the patron's information needs, the searcher will outline the steps expected to retrieve that ideal set for the patron online. This process is fundamental, since 90 percent of an online search occurs before logging on.

Each searcher, however, also realizes that, with few exceptions, the goal of retrieving all of and only the ideal set of materials remains largely unattainable. Most of the decisions a searcher makes in the search strategy are made to achieve the appropriate balance between two goals of information retrieval: precision and recall. *Precision* refers to getting only relevant material. *Recall* refers to getting all the relevant material. In a world in which language was unambiguous, and where indexing was perfect, precision and recall would be the same. For the rest of us, because language is ambiguous and indexing imperfect, precision and recall are largely incompatible goals. For example, the word *program* is used to represent at least three rather different concepts. This affects precision, since a search on the term *program* for one of these concepts will retrieve unrelated material that refers to either of the other two meanings of the term, and thus reduce precision. On the other hand, because of synonyms and changes in terminology over time, there are often a multitude of terms available to describe a single concept. Searching for every possible term to achieve perfect recall is a demanding task. As a result, search strategies are a compromise between precision and recall.

The searcher can use the online preview as a final stage in search strategy development. By seeing the postings of the terms and the effects of combining terms logically, some unanticipated consequences of the strategy may reveal themselves, or some potential lines of development may be explored in a very low-cost setting.

Search Sessions

At this point, the searcher is prepared to conduct the online search. In some settings or situations, the patron will be with the searcher at the time of the search; in others, the search will be done without the patron present. In either case, the patron has been included in the process, in terms of decisions that will be made online to achieve the best search. When patrons are present, they may be consulted about particular choices. When they are not present, the searcher has to make decisions based on options identified to the patrons during the search interviews.

Since the searcher makes the majority of concept development and decision-point choices before beginning the online search, few unanticipated situations should be encountered during the search. Most search sessions involve refinement or minor modification of the search strategies to create the desired results. If the search session begins to have intermediate outcomes markedly different from those planned, it may very well indicate that the search should be stopped and redesigned with the new information taken into account. More typically, the search conforms to expectations and the searcher and patron are both satisfied with the results.

Most searches have one or more sets of output as an end result. If the search has been done on a computer, rather than on a terminal, there is more flexibility about the forms of output. In the main, output can come as an *offline printout*, which is printed in batch mode by the host computer and mailed to the searcher, or as an electronic stream, captured by the searcher's computer on a disc, termed *downloading*, for later printing. Frequently, the offline print is less expensive, in part because no connect time is associated with the host computer's printing, and in part because the citation charges associated with offline prints are sometimes lower. However, the downloaded form can be less expensive if the system uses minimum printing charges for offline prints, or if the citation charges are lower for online prints, or if there are mailing charges. These factors will play a role in determining the most cost-effective choice for obtaining search results. In addition, the patron's time frame can affect these decisions.

Post-Search Follow-Up

For the most part, the results of a search consist of citations to journals, monographs, or other forms of research literature. The patron will need some assistance in dealing with these citations. In some cases, the only need is to identify the salient parts of the citation form, or how the citations to different kinds of material may be readily identified. In others, the patron may need to be told the several steps to follow to acquire the needed materials through an interlibrary loan office. Some searchers, when dealing with downloaded citations, repackage them in different ways to make them more usable by the patron. This can range from having the output sorted on some useful criterion, such as the source journal, to adding the library's call number to the citations. In any case, it is incumbent on the searcher to ensure that the patron has a full understanding of the printout and its use.

Current Awareness Service

If the patron has a continuing information need, the searcher can suggest that a current awareness service might be available and appropriate. The most common term for a current awareness service is *selective dissemination of information* (SDI), introduced in chapter 1. Typically, to set up an SDI, a search profile is created on the host computer. This profile is then run against each update of the database as it is loaded. Citations on this update that match the search terms in the SDI profile are printed and mailed to the patron. In this way, the patron is automatically kept aware of current developments of interest. In general, the vendors of online services set the charges for an SDI to cover the search costs and the printing of a small set of items for each update. If the number of citations matching the profile exceeds the prepaid number, additional charges may be incurred. An SDI service is most often utilized by advanced researchers to help them keep current in their fields.

An online search can be an exhilarating reference encounter. The patron becomes aware of the skill and knowledge required to perform an effective search. The reference librarian almost always learns a good deal about a new field or area. There is often a sense of an information partnership, with the librarian and the patron both investing time and energy, and both gaining information in return.

Direct Patron Access to
Electronic Resources

In this section, the focus shifts from librarian-mediated use of electronic resources to direct patron use of these resources, termed *end-user searching*. End-user searching is most often associated with CD-ROM systems, but it can also apply to patrons' use of locally loaded databases or other online systems. Several vendors offer an additional online service aimed directly at the end user. DIALOG offers Knowledge Index, while BRS offers BRS/AfterDark and BRS/Colleague. H. W. Wilson offers end-user searching as a component of its CD-ROM search systems, with the search created at the CD-ROM workstation and executed online. These systems are primarily menu-based in design, rather than the command-driven style of the full service. End-user systems have a limited number of databases available and are sometimes available only during "off-peak" hours. As a result of these factors, the vendors can set the costs of these systems lower than those of the full-service versions. The vendor may base the charges on connect time, or may set a flat fee. Some libraries have chosen to make these end-user online search systems available through the library, while other libraries have chosen to make only information about these systems available, leaving patrons to make their own subscriptions.

For the reference librarian, end-user searching presents service opportunities and challenges. The service opportunities lie in the power that the patron has available to search and retrieve information electronically. The most basic elements of electronic reference sources, such as cumulative indexing, ease of printing citations, and the ability to browse a range of subject terms, are features largely unavailable in their printed counterparts. More advanced features like Boolean operators and truncation are even further removed from the patron's interactions with comparable printed sources. The patron using electronic resources, therefore, is given a sense of control of the search process that is highly rewarding.

The service challenges are largely in the realm of instruction. The first element of instruction in these self-service systems is helping patrons identify the best resources for their needs. Experience has shown that patrons are as likely to sit at an inappropriate workstation as at an appropriate one. This selection problem is better understood when one realizes that the names of the CD-ROM systems or stations and the database names within the various menus facing the patron mean little to most patrons. As a result, many librarians create point-of-use signs, brochures, and handouts, with the aim of linking patrons with the right resources. These signs often go unread or are misunderstood. The challenge is even greater for resources, such as locally loaded databases, which are often used in remote locations, far from any opportunities for guidance in the selection process.

A related service challenge is assisting patrons' understanding of the coverage of the database or system. A patron may choose to use a database on CD-ROM and never realize that there are significant differences between the printed tool and the CD-ROM version with the same title. A patron may not notice that only the last three years of a database have been locally loaded, or may not realize that more years are available in alternative formats. Designing informational screens or printed guides that can communicate this information succinctly and attractively is very difficult.

There are also challenges in assisting the end user to interpret the output and match it to the available resources. The patron may be able to find the items that are owned within the library, but may not know about services, such as interlibrary loan, that make resources available from a larger bibliographic universe.

These service challenges will be of increasing importance, because growth in end-user searching seems a near certainty. Use of both CD-ROM systems and locally loaded databases is increasing rapidly, and there is similar growth in the use of end-user online systems. The user community served by reference librarians could become increasingly invisible, served indirectly through help screens and search guides, and, perhaps more directly, through electronic correspondence (*e-mail*) using the library's computer system.

A Look at the Future of Electronic Reference

One could imagine that reference librarians, having access to millions of records, with the power of Boolean logic and the speed of the current computer generation, have solved all the information retrieval problems facing them. Unfortunately, this is not yet true. The lack of standardization among the multiple systems and services requires reference librarians to invest a great deal of time and energy in learning the variations, and also results in a certain amount of inefficiency in using them. One can hope that standardization of terminology and formats will become more widespread in times to come.

One reason to be hopeful is that the systems available now resemble one another more than they did in earlier versions. Some companies build recognition of alternate commands into their software, so that, in large part, one can use similar language across multiple systems. There is growing recognition on the part of the information industry that standardization of terminology and command structure can lead to increased user satisfaction. In addition, current developments in the area of standardization by national and international organizations, such as the National Information Standards Organization – Z 39 (NISO) and the International Organization for Standardization (ISO), are providing a basis for standardization in the form of a Common Command Language.[16] There is also reason to believe that the next generation of search software will have full recognition of alternate command languages built in, so that the individual searcher can use a "native" search language in "alien" territory. The translating aspect of the computer will result in identical retrieval with either search language.

Technological Uncertainties or
Orphan Technologies

As the events of the last decade have shown, development and change are the hallmarks of electronic reference resources. Several technologies have emerged to provide previously unavailable resources in new ways. Some of these have lasted for only a very short time. One example of a technology that filled its niche for a very short time is *COM*, computer output on microform. In this sytem, machine-readable files were printed by the computer on microform – sometimes microfiche, sometimes microfilm designed to be mounted on very fast microfilm readers – at frequent intervals. Microform was chosen because of the much lower expense and smaller space required, as compared to paper. As each update was printed, previous updates were discarded. Because of the combination of inexpensive updates and the availability of machine-readable cataloging records, COM catalogs were chosen by many libraries as an alternative to printed card catalogs. Nevertheless, a look around libraries today reveals very few COM catalogs, even though the lower cost and other factors remain valid. The improved access provided by online catalogs has relegated COM catalogs to a footnote in library technology. As orphan technologies go, COM was a relatively inexpensive trip down an unproductive development branch. Microform readers and printers can be used for other materials in the library; the machine-readable files were used to create public access catalogs. Thus, very little was lost. Libraries may not be so fortunate in their next selection of technology.

Reference librarians know that the lifespan of any index is infinitely long. Indexes printed in 1607 are still used today, and will be used in the year 2091. Print technology has lasted through a much changed world. The indexing technology mode of the current era is CD-ROM. Many indexing and abstracting databases are available in that medium. Many other full-text, graphics, and numeric databases are also available or are in development for CD-ROM. When an index is available in print and in CD-ROM, some libraries have chosen to subscribe only to the CD-ROM version. Typically, the current CD-ROM disc contains the most recent few years of the index. The most common method of updating a CD-ROM file is for the producer to send the current disc to the subscriber, and the subscriber to send the superseded disc back to the producer. As discs fill, older material "falls off" the end. It is not yet clear if archival discs of the complete file will always be made or will be made available. Given the long life of an index and the relatively short lifespan of any generation of electronic technology, there are long-term concerns about the future of these indexes. If CD-ROM turns out to be a side branch on the developmental tree, what are the consequences for reference service? Will reference librarians have to maintain orphaned equipment well into the next century to read the indexes of the 1980s and 1990s? (Librarians who are still using aging and failing microprint equipment to read the READEX microprint files know some of the difficulties of orphan technologies.) Or will there be unfillable gaps in the indexes? If CD-ROM is on the main trunk of development, it is more likely that the succeeding generation of equipment and technology will incorporate CD-ROM technology to the degree necessary transparently to accommodate current media. The question of the availability of archival files remains a vital one in either scenario.

There are related concerns for online information services. Currently, there is a commitment to maintain all the files back to record number 1. As these files grow, and as use of the older material decreases, will the commitment continue? Will the very limited use of older files justify maintaining them forever? What will the alternatives be for information service companies, reference librarians, and people with the need to use these items?

Future Developments in Electronic Reference Services

There are many developments in the realm of electronic resources for reference that hold promise for the future of reference service. One of the more exciting concepts is the growing availability of *hypertext*. This programming environment allows the linking of related concepts and information in a multilayered database through a computer workstation. Reference tools would no longer have to be single-dimensional, linear works. Instead, the "see" and "see also" concepts could have a dynamic link from the text. The user could, by pressing a button, go instantly to an explanation of a concept, to a bibliographic reference, or to a graphics display. *Hypermedia* is a further expansion of hypertext, and can include links to audiovisual materials. Reference tools using hypertext or hypermedia are currently in an early state of development, but the rapid rate of development in general in this field holds promise for reference as well.

Another development which may yield a new generation of electronic resources for reference is the Compact Disc—Write-Many-Read-Many (CD-WMRM) system of data storage. Unlike CD-ROM, CD-WMRM would allow the user to add data to the disc with equipment available at a reasonable cost. This would allow the reference department to add local call number information to a commercially available database, for example. The possibilities presented by this hardware, with its vast storage capacity and the flexibility for local augmentation, are very exciting.

The saying, "May you live in interesting times" holds both threat and promise. The reference librarian in the era of electronic resources for reference lives in very interesting times indeed.

Notes

1. Kathleen Young Marcaccio, ed., *Computer-Readable Databases: A Directory and Data Sourcebook*, 7th ed. (Detroit, Mich.: Gale Research Inc., 1989), 1,646p. This directory, which is updated at irregular intervals, contains listings and descriptions of computer-readable databases. It includes multiple indexes by subject, producer, and vendor. The *Directory of Online Databases* (New York: Cuadra/Elsevier) is published quarterly, with two volumes and two supplements per year. (Volume 1, no. 1 appeared in the fall of 1979.) It provides information on a wide variety of databases, their sources, and availability.

2. Beverly Kooi, Richard E. Schultz, and Robert Baker, "Spelling Errors and the Serial Position Effect," *Journal of Educational Psychology* 56 (1965): 6.

3. "University of Minnesota Completes Online Catalog," *Library Journal* 114 (September 15, 1989): 19.

4. Ahmed M. Elshami, *CD-ROM: An Annotated Bibliography* (Englewood, Colo.: Libraries Unlimited Data Book, 1988), xii.

5.   Charles Oppenheim, *CD-ROM: Fundamentals to Applications* (London: Butterworths, 1988), vi.

6.   Norman Desmarais, *The Librarian's CD-ROM Handbook* (Westport, Conn.: Meckler, 1989), 174p.

7.   Ibid., 19.

8.   For a fuller discussion of locally mounted databases, the June 1989 issue of *Information Technology and Libraries* is a special issue on "Locally Loaded Databases in Online Library Systems."

9.   Emily Gallup Fayen, "Loading Local Machine-Readable Data Files: Issues, Problems, and Answers," *Information Technology and Libraries* 8 (June 1989): 137.

10.   David Tyckoson, "The 98% Solution: The Failure of the Catalog and the Role of Electronic Databases," *Technicalities* 9 (February 1989): 8-12.

11.   *Online* (Weston, Conn.: Online, Inc., 1977-).

12.   *Database* (Weston, Conn.: Online, Inc., 1978-).

13.   *Online Review* (Oxford, England: Learned Information, 1977-).

14.   *CD-ROM Professional* (Weston, Conn.: Pemberton Press, 1988-).

15.   John M. Budd, "It's Not the Principle, It's the Money of the Thing," *Journal of Academic Librarianship* 15 (1989): 218-22.

16.   Margaret Morrison, "The NISO Common Command Language: No More 'German to the Horses,'" *Online* 13, no. 4 (July 1989): 46-52.

Additional Readings

Baker, Betsy, and Kathleen Kluegel. "Availability and Use of OCLC for Reference in Large Academic Libraries." *RQ* 21 (Summer 1982): 379-84.
   This article documents the widespread use of OCLC in Association of Research Libraries academic reference departments despite often-difficult physical access to the database. It provides an analysis of OCLC holdings by date and type of material as an indication of its reference value. It further describes some of the improved access available in the online utility.

Desmarais, Norman. *The Librarian's CD-ROM Handbook*. Westport, Conn.: Meckler Corporation, 1989. 174p.
   This book provides a good background to the whole area of CD-ROM-based information systems. In addition to describing the hardware and software issues, Desmarais covers selection and management issues. The book then identifies individual CD-ROM products which are reference works, abstracts, and indexes. It further identifies a variety of products which are more specialized but could be of reference interest in some situations.

Kesselman, Martin, and Sarah B. Watstein, eds. *End-User Searching: Services and Providers*. Chicago: American Library Association, 1988. 230p.
   This collection of articles addresses the full range of issues surrounding end-user searching. It discusses planning, training, and selection and use of these systems, both online and disc-based services.

Lathrop, Ann, comp. *Online and CD-ROM Databases in School Libraries: Readings*. Englewood, Colo.: Libraries Unlimited, 1989. 375p.
   Lathrop's book of readings includes important articles on every issue concerning use of electronic resources in school libraries. It has sections on instructional strategies, management, products, and resources, among others. Although school libraries are the focus of the articles, librarians in other settings could find valuable insights among this fine collection.

Nielsen, Brian. "Allocating Costs, Thinking About Values: The Fee-or-Free Debate Revisited." *Journal of Academic Librarianship* 15 (1989): 211-17.

In this article, Nielsen reviews the history of the fee-or-free debate. He then examines that debate within the value structure of librarianship and challenges the "information as commodity" perspective that underlies much of the discussion.

Palmer, Roger C. *Online Reference and Information Retrieval*. 2d ed. Littleton, Colo.: Libraries Unlimited, 1987. 189p.

Palmer's text describes information processing and retrieval from record creation through indexing and retrieval, using extensive examples from a variety of information service providers.

Sieburth, Janice F. *Online Search Services in the Academic Library: Planning, Management and Operation*. Chicago: American Library Association, 1988. 331p.

This very thorough examination of online search services focuses on the academic setting, but most, if not all, the issues have applicability across the library spectrum. Each library can take these sound discussions of the topics and apply them to the local environment. The numerous samples of budgets, search requests, and statistical gathering forms are the successful survivors of evolutionary design, and are well-suited to local adaptation.

Tenopir, Carol. *Issues in Online Database Searching*. Englewood, Colo.: Libraries Unlimited, 1989. 188p.

Tenopir has written extensively about current issues in online searching in library literature. This book is an updated and revised collection of some of these columns, arranged by general subject area. They provide the reader with thoughtful and lively perceptions on a wide variety of topics.

6 □

INSTRUCTION AS A
REFERENCE SERVICE

Instruction has become a fundamental function of librarianship. Once regarded as an extra, even frivolous, adjunct to reference service, instruction is now considered a basic library service. In 1980, the American Library Association published a policy statement which concluded that instruction in libraries should be considered by *all* types of libraries as one of their primary goals of service.[1] Rare is the reference librarian, bibliographer, or even cataloger who does not have some responsibility for staff or user education. Librarians are increasingly involved in user education as libraries move into an age when one no longer needs to be physically within the walls of the library to locate and use information. At one time, users were required to visit the library to use the card catalog, to leaf through the periodical indexes, and to browse the bookshelves. With increased computer networking, telecommunications, commercially available databases, dial access, and the proliferation of information resources outside the domain of the library, greater and greater capability for information retrieval is put in the hands of the user. Librarians must take on more responsibility for advising users on the appropriate systems, advocating equal access for users, and educating users in the retrieval, use, and management of information. The responsibility for educating users in information management, particularly in the framework of reference services, is the focus of this chapter. This chapter defines *instruction*, discusses instruction as a reference service, highlights the history of instruction, outlines practical applications and implementation, and suggests future challenges.

What Is Instruction?

What is instruction? In defining *instruction*, a statement on librarians and instruction made in 1876 by Otis Hall Robinson is as cogent and appropriate today as it was over one hundred years ago. During the Conference of Librarians (the forerunner of the American Library Association's Conference) held in Philadelphia in 1876, a group of distinguished librarians was asked to respond to the paper, "Personal Intercourse and Relations Between Librarians and Readers in Popular Libraries," authored by Samuel Green, the librarian of the Public Library of Worcester. Robinson, then head of the University of Rochester Library, responded in what has become a pioneering statement on librarians as teachers:

> I wish his paper could be read by every librarian and every library director in the country. A librarian should be more than a keeper of books; he should be an educator. It is this that I had in mind yesterday when I spoke of the personal

influence of a librarian to restrain young persons from too much novel-reading. The relation which Mr. Green has presented ought especially to be established between a college librarian and the student readers. No such librarian is fit for his place unless he holds himself to some degree responsible for the library education of the students. They are generally willing to take advice from him; he is responsible for giving them the best advice. It is his province to direct very much of their general reading, and especially in their investigation of subjects, he should be their guide and friend. I sometimes think students get the most from me when they inquire about subjects that I know least about. They learn how to chase down a subject in the library. They get some facts, but especially a *method*. Somehow I reproach myself if a student gets to the end of his course without learning how to use a library. All that is taught in college amounts to very little; but if we can send students out self-reliant in their investigations, we have accomplished very much.[2]

As Harold Tuckett and Carla Stoffle noted in their 1984 essay, "Learning Theory and the Self-Reliant Library User," Robinson's statement is noteworthy both in defining instruction and in setting an agenda for librarians:

... not only does it clearly suggest the appropriateness of the librarian's active participation in the educational process, but it also posits an essential goal of bibliographic instruction, namely, "self-reliance" on the part of library users.[3]

Today, instruction in the use of libraries goes beyond the walls of the library to the broader concept of instruction in the use of information. As the amount of information continues to expand, and as radical changes are made in the way in which information is stored, organized, accessed, and used, it has become increasingly apparent that individuals need instruction not only in the use of libraries, but in the general handling and use of information. The American Library Association Presidential Committee on Information Literacy calls for individuals to be information literate, to participate fully in the information society. A key portion of the committee's report is presented in box 6.1.

6.1
Information Literacy

To be information literate, a person must be able to recognize when information is needed and have the ability to locate, evaluate, and use effectively the needed information. Producing such a citizenry will require that schools and colleges appreciate and integrate the concept of information literacy into their learning programs and that they play a leadership role in equipping individuals and institutions to take advantage of the opportunities inherent within the information society. Ultimately, information literate people are those who have learned how to learn. They know how to learn because they know how information is organized, how to find information, and how to use information in such a way that others can learn from them. They are people prepared for life-long learning, because they can always find the information needed for any task or decision at hand.

— American Library Association
Presidential Committee on
Information Literacy, *Final Report*[4]

Information literacy has become a widely and often vigorously debated topic both inside and outside librarianship. In her article, "Information Literacy or Bibliographic Instruction: Semantics or Philosophy," Lori Arp presents a reasoned case for carefully considering the possible implications of embracing the notion of information literacy.[5] She cautions that, by definition, the term *information literacy* implies hierarchical ordering of skills and mandated testing. She notes that by accepting information literacy, librarians must decide to order skills they do not yet agree upon and to expect competency-based testing. Given the highly charged political connotation of the word *literacy*, librarians must be careful about making too many claims about their ability to produce that which they cannot measure or prove.

Instruction is, then, as Robinson encouraged in 1876, the American Library Association Presidential Committee on Information Literacy reiterated in 1989, and myriad instruction proponents have practiced in between, the teaching of individuals to become self-reliant information users—"successful bibliographic problem-solvers who learn through informa-tion use."[6]

Numerous terms have been used for instruction in libraries and information, most notably: (1) *library orientation*; (2) *library instruction*; (3) *bibliographic instruction*; and (4) *information management education*. At first glance, the variant terms may appear to be semantic hairsplitting. However, the different terms reflect the evolution of the theory and practice of instruction.

Library Orientation

Library orientation comprises service activities designed to welcome and introduce users and potential users to services, collections, the physical layout of the building, and the organization of materials. In his 1981 text, *Teaching Library Use*, James Rice defines library orientation as the first level of instruction with modest objectives:

1. To introduce users to the physical facilities of the building itself.

2. To introduce the departments or service desks and the appropriate staff members.

3. To introduce specific services, such as computer searches, book talks, or inter-library loan.

4. To introduce library policies, such as overdue procedures, or the hours the library is open.

5. To introduce the organization of the collection with the specific goal of reducing user anxiety about trying to locate materials.

6. To motivate users to come back and make use of the resources.

7. To communicate an atmosphere of helpfulness and friendliness.[7]

Most libraries offer some form of library orientation, most commonly manifested as librarian-guided tours. Although library tours have become a mainstay of user services, library orientation is not limited to a librarian guiding users through the reference room and on past the circulation desk. Library orientation can take the form of video productions, handouts, written guides, and computer programs. Self-guided audio tours have proven to be a viable, effective alternative to the cattle-herding of large tours.[8] Electronic bulletin boards, advances in microcomputer software (hypertext, for example), and interactive video technology also allow librarians to enhance orientation.

■ ═══ ■

6.2

Sample Library Orientation Program for a College Library

1. Library tours (offered by librarians and through audiotape)

2. Electronic kiosk (an interactive video computer station which greets the patrons as they enter the library; offers various orientation options — maps of the facilities, listings of special collections, introduction to the staff, news of the day, etc.)

3. Electronic bulletin board (available through dial access; provides library hours, downloadable handouts, suggestion box, message center, etc.)

4. Printed guides and handouts

5. Library booth at student, residence hall, and university events and information fairs

6. Signage

7. Faculty open house

8. Newsletter

Library Instruction

Library instruction refers to instruction in the use of libraries, with an emphasis on institution-specific procedures and collections. The term reflects an emphasis on the library as defined by its physical walls. Rice defines library instruction as the second level of instruction.[9] Focusing on in-depth explanation of library materials, library instruction has concentrated on tools and mechanics, including techniques in using periodical indexes, reference sources, card and online catalogs, and bibliographies. Some typical objectives of a library instruction program include:

1. To learn to use the *Readers' Guide to Periodical Literature*.

2. To be able to find books on a subject through the card catalog.

3. To be able to use microforms and the appropriate reading equipment.

4. To be able to use a specific reference tool, such as the *Encyclopaedia Britannica* or a *Who's Who*.[10]

Library instruction can take the form of lectures, discussions, workbooks, media presentations, computer-assisted instruction, and handouts.

Bibliographic Instruction

Bibliographic instruction (BI) has been increasingly used since the mid-1970s to refer to any activities, aside from reference interviews, which are designed to teach learners how to locate information.[11] In contrast to library instruction, bibliographic instruction goes beyond the physical boundaries of the library and beyond institution-specific confines. Proponents of bibliographic instruction suggest that the term better reflects the teaching that needs to be undertaken. With the increasingly complex bibliographic apparatus, the proliferation of information sources, and pervasive information technologies, BI librarians have moved toward a problem-solving rather than a content- or institution-oriented approach to instruction. The 1980s saw the emergence of the "second generation" of bibliographic instruction, with an emphasis on a conceptual approach based on learning theories.[12]

The conceptual approach to bibliographic instruction results in teaching principles rather than specific methods, such as focusing on how to use the *Readers' Guide* or how to check out a book. The intent of teaching principles of information organization and retrieval is to provide learners with the knowledge to function in a broad range of situations. Bibliographic instruction can be carried out using a variety of methods, including media productions, computer-assisted instruction (CAI), lectures, discussions, simulations, and workbooks.

■ ══ ■

6.3

Sample Bibliographic Instruction Program at a University

1. Library tours (while part of orientation, fundamental to providing a physical context for future BI)

2. Videotape presentation of research strategy

3. Research skills textbook written for the specific institution

4. Expert system for identifying general materials on a topic

5. Online catalog workshops

6. Research skills classroom instruction (number of sessions depends on needs of students)

7. Term-paper research counseling

8. Reference desk service

Information Management Education

The term *information management education* emerged from medical librarianship in the early 1980s. Nina Matheson and John Cooper proposed that librarians had a critical responsibility for creating systems and information environments that facilitate information retrieval and use by individuals.[13] Information management education refers to instructing users in the identification, retrieval, evaluation, and use of information. The operant notion is management of information by the individual. Traditionally, librarians have avoided assisting users in the actual use of information. Librarians have viewed their responsibilities as ending once the information is in the hands of the user.[14] Information management education demands that librarians instruct users in how to use and manage information, departing from their traditional role as mere providers. Information management education as carried out in many medical libraries can entail teaching physicians how to organize their reprint files, instructing health care professionals how to search MEDLINE, or advising nursing students on how to analyze a patient care problem and where to go for the appropriate information.

■ ═══ ■

6.4

Sample Information Management Education Program in a Medical Library

1. Orientation (audio and video tours; storyboard floor plan)

2. Workshops (on topics such as professional files, searching MEDLINE, Grateful MED, telecommunications, text management, downloading, word processing, managing departmental collections)

3. Course-integrated instruction

4. Credit courses

5. Brown-bag and breakfast seminars

6. Computer-assisted instruction

School librarians have also been active in developing instructional programs that replace the traditional library instruction goals of merely teaching physical access to information. In 1988, the American Association of School Librarians and the Association for Educational Communications and Technology published the important work, *Information Power: Guidelines for School Library Media Programs*, which reflects the emerging emphasis of going beyond the location of information to information analysis.[15] The authors of *Information Power* present three major precepts for school library media programs:

> The information curriculum includes instruction in accessing, evaluating, and communicating information and in the production of media.

> The information curriculum is taught as an integral part of the content and objectives of the school's curriculum.

> Library media specialists and teachers jointly plan, teach, and evaluate instruction in information access, use, and communication skills.[16]

Developments in Instruction as a Reference Service

Are reference and instruction diametrically opposed? Must it be either reference or instruction? Does instruction detract from or enhance the quality of reference service? Is instruction merely an adjunct service to the reference desk? Or is reference adjunct to instruction? Reference and instruction are intrinsically linked, complementary, and intertwined user services. To separate instruction from reference is to do a disservice to users.

Some suggest that reference service is the most intimate method of instruction. In some instances, the one-to-one assistance a user receives from the reference librarian may well be the most effective form of instruction. Leaving instruction to the reference desk does pose some problems, however. Instruction at the reference desk presupposes that a patron will approach the desk and ask a question. What happens if there is one librarian and ten persons in line? Instruction might be abandoned in favor of the expedient answer. Reference service is typically tied to a place and set hours. How do remote users get help when they dial into the online system, do not get the desired results, and the reference desk is closed? The limitations of the reference desk often create barriers to instructing patrons when they need it.

Reference and instruction services are developed in response to the user's information needs, the financial and personnel resources of the library, and the institution's priorities. Both reference and instructional services are basic components of user services. They should complement, enhance, and support one another.

A shift is taking place in reference and instructional services. Moving away from a focus on the librarian as the provider of information, many libraries are emphasizing information independence training for users. This shift is occurring for sevaral reasons:

1. Libraries are recognizing that not all user needs can be addressed through traditional reference service.

2. An information society requires a citizenry capable of accessing, evaluating, and using information.

3. Reference desk service cannot effectively handle the increased demands for assistance.

4. Individuals prefer to be independent researchers rather than dependent on someone behind a desk.[17]

5. The breakdown of the geographic barriers to information and resources demands an alternative to traditional reference desk service.

6. Individuals are moving away from institutional help to self-help.[18]

Reference and instructional services are currently being reexamined and questioned by the profession. How do libraries provide services to remote or invisible users dialing into library systems? How are computer skills best taught? How can CD-ROM technology be integrated into user education programs? What impact have networks, resource sharing, and telefacsimile (fax) had on reference services? Both traditional reference desk service and instruction are undergoing dramatic changes as a new paradigm of user services is created.[19]

Highlights of the History of Instruction

Although many assume that instruction is a recent outgrowth of reference services, instruction and reference services developed simultaneously as responses to patrons who were unable to use libraries organized with the specialist in mind. It is true that the last twenty years have seen accelerated advances in the theory and practice of instruction, but instruction as it exists today can be traced back over a hundred years. The history of instruction can be broadly divided into four periods: (1) the professor-of-books period, 1850 to 1920; (2) the foundation period, 1920 to 1970s; (3) the decade of acceptance (1980s); and (4) the second generation of bibliographic instruction from the late 1980s to the present.[20] From its roots in the nineteenth century to the second generation of today, instruction has reflected changes in education, society, and the structure of information.

Period 1: 1850 to 1920. Instruction in the use of libraries had its beginnings in the nineteenth century, when librarians were true generalists who informally served patrons as teachers. In 1858, the great philosopher and generally learned man, Ralph Waldo Emerson, called for libraries to appoint a professor of books. The "professor of books" mentality was based on a world of general, broad-ranging knowledge.

The late nineteenth century saw a move away from generalist education, as specializations and disciplines began to develop with the professionalization of scholarship. During this period, libraries concentrated on building book collections to support the trend in scholarship. Librarians were regarded primarily as selectors and custodians of books. Responding to the scholar's need for unique titles, libraries focused on providing improved access through detailed cataloging and precise organization. Librarians created elaborate organizational systems and minimized their interaction with users.

This approach may have served the scholar, but it certainly did not respond to the growing numbers of undergraduates confused by the burgeoning collections and complex organizational systems. By the early 1880s, Columbia, Cornell, and Michigan were offering lectures on books and library use.[21] While most college libraries taught the undergraduate through informal instruction at the reference desk, one college librarian stands out for his trailblazing efforts. Azariah Root, Oberlin College librarian, conducted a continuously running library instruction program from 1899 to 1927 in which students were introduced to library systems, resources, and the history of the printed work.[22] Led by Samuel Green's efforts at Worcester Public Library, public libraries chose to instruct patrons by offering personalized reference service, particularly in fiction.[23] Public and academic libraries dabbled in instruction through lectures and at the reference desk as responses to a changing clientele and increased information resources.

Period 2: 1920 to 1970. During the 1920s and 1930s, proponents of instruction began to look outward to the larger educational community and to join in the enterprise of educating students. Louis Shores spearheaded an effort known as the "library arts college," which challenged the prevalent notion of research librarianship with the pioneering concept of educational librarianship.[24] Shores's teaching library concept is without question a direct ancestor of the client-centered library of today. Another instruction pioneer, Harvie Branscomb, endorsed integrating the academic library into the educational mission of the university in his 1940 work, *Teaching with Books.*[25]

During the early 1960s, a remarkable experiment was directed by Patricia Knapp at Monteith College at Wayne State University.[26] The Monteith College Library Experiment provided discipline-specific library instruction as an integrated part of the curriculum. Knapp was successful in furthering the idea that the library should be the center of learning. Even though the experiment only lasted for two years, Monteith provided a model and inspiration for library instruction practitioners to follow.

The social upheaval of the 1960s was felt in libraries as well as in society. Students mandated educational reform. The information explosion took on great proportions. Students historically excluded from higher education were arriving at the university in large numbers. Teachers began abandoning textbooks and encouraging independent inquiry and research papers. Librarians asked if libraries could not be more than mere repositories for the relics of civilization. One way librarians began responding to these myriad forces was actively to advocate instruction in libraries and library use.

Librarians moved away from their historical role of custodian, cataloger, and keeper of books to that of educator and facilitator. Instruction programs sprang up throughout the United States in a true grassroots movement. Professional groups were formed, conferences and workshops were held, articles were written by the score, and guidelines and standards were authored. Particular efforts and programs served as models of success: Earlham College, Sangamon State University, University of Texas at Austin, UCLA, University of Wisconsin at Parkside, and Ohio State University, to name a few. During the 1970s, practitioners continued to be concerned with "how to do it good" at their local institutions, including issues of faculty involvement, marketing, evaluation, in-service training, and institutional acceptance.

Perhaps one of the most significant developments of the 1970s was the shift away from tool-based to concept-based instruction. Librarians began to recognize that teaching specific, discrete tools such as the *Readers' Guide* or the *Oxford English Dictionary* did little to prepare a student for beginning research in mechanical engineering the next semester.

Librarians began to experiment with how to teach students to develop, use, and evaluate a *search strategy* – a systematic plan for identifying, locating, and evaluating information. Librarians also discovered that users learned transferable information skills more readily when using conceptual frameworks and a cognitive approach to research skills instruction.[27] Mary Reichel in particular spearheaded the movement away from tool-based instruction.[28] Cerise Oberman drew upon the work of Piaget in applying learning cycles to bibliographic instruction.[29] New theories were developed, explored, debated, upheld, and discarded in the 1970s, the decade which leaders in the field have called a time of ferment and development.[30]

Period 3: The 1980s. During the 1980s, bibliographic instruction became an accepted public service in most libraries. The Council of the American Library Association published a landmark policy in 1980 marking the official acceptance of BI in the profession.

> Instruction in the use of libraries should begin during childhood years and continue as a goal of the formal educational process in order to prepare individuals for the independent information retrieval essential to sustain life-long professional and personal growth.

> It is essential that libraries of all types accept the responsibility of providing people with opportunities to understand the organization of information. The responsibility of educating users in successful information location demands the same administrative, funding, and staffing support as do more traditional library programs. The American Library Association encourages all libraries to include instruction in the use of libraries as one of the primary goals of service.[31]

It became rare that a job announcement for a reference or public service position did not include instruction responsibilities.[32]

The decade of acceptance was also a decade of challenges for instruction librarians. The major challenges included how to educate librarians for BI, the proliferation of information technologies and their impact on BI, the effective measurement and evaluation of instruction, the application of learning theory to BI, and liaison to educational groups outside of librarianship.

Period 4: The Second Generation. Having established itself as a field with its own literature, organizations, theory, conferences, standards, folklore, and history, bibliographic instruction is now moving into what is being called the *second generation*.[33] The second generation of BI librarians have a firm foundation on which to stand as they look to a future concerned with information literacy, remote access to information, and significant demographic changes.

Individuals in a knowledge-based economy need to be information literate. They need to be able to analyze problems critically, identify information to answer the questions, evaluate the information, and synthesize it during the creation of new knowledge.

Remote access to libraries and information continues to increase because of an expanding home and office computer hardware base and great changes in telecommunications. The library is no longer defined by its physical walls, but by its services and staff expertise.

A variety of demographic shifts are occurring in the United States, as this country increasingly becomes a multicultural society. As the median age of Americans increases, demographers suggest that the labor force will look decidedly different in the year 2000 than it did in 1991, containing an increasing number of women, nonwhites, and newly arrived immigrants. African-Americans are entering the labor force twice as fast as whites, and the number of Hispanic workers could increase at four times the rate of whites.[34] New immigrant groups from Asia, South America, and Central America are entering the United States in record numbers.[35] Additionally, the U.S. marketplace is no longer based on a national structure, but has become internationalized into the global economy.

These three influences combine to challenge the practitioners of the second generation. Librarians will have to address information handling, encourage information self-reliance, and support information adaptability. Emerging learning technologies, such as interactive video and expert systems, will be exploited by librarians using electronic media to enhance learning. One of the great challenges for the present generation will be to ensure that technology, called the great equalizer by some, will not become the great unequalizer, creating a class of information have-nots. Pluralism and diversity in society need to be reflected in libraries. Librarians will seek to encourage diversity in staffing, in collections, and in learners.

Librarians find themselves involved with a wide variety of instructional activities, whether in a university or college library, a school library, a public library, or a special library. Each setting and the clientele served demand different instructional responses from the library.

Academic librarians are actively engaged in classroom instruction in information retrieval skills, authoring hypermedia instruction programs, teaching CD-ROM, developing and testing interfaces for computer systems, designing instructional programs for multicultural learners, setting up in-house staff training programs for BI, exploring expert systems to enhance instructional opportunities, serving on curricular reform committees, and building partnerships with teaching faculty. With an unmanageable and still-increasing amount of information available on virtually every topic, students are often overwhelmed and find themselves unable to make informed decisions about information use. Bibliographic instruction librarians are increasingly involved with teaching students to develop the critical thinking skills necessary to be successful self-reliant information users.[36]

School librarians are actively involved in *resource-based teaching*, which uses a variety of sources rather than a prescriptive textbook to teach a unit or subject. They are involved with the school's teachers and administrators to integrate information instruction into the curriculum from kindergarten through high school. They are interested in a taxonomy of information skills and how children can best attain those skills. They teach the value of information, not just in the school environment, but for consumer decisions, college selection, and solving personal problems.

In the public library, bibliographic instruction most commonly manifests itself as programming and outreach. Public librarians organize seminars on specific topics for out-of-school adult learners on such subjects as taxes, small businesses, getting published, selling and buying a home, and retirement planning. For school-age children, public librarians often cooperate with school districts to develop joint instruction to prepare students for such perennial events as science fairs. Public libraries are in a unique position when it comes to serving the instructional needs of the aging. For many senior citizens, the changing face of the public library brought on by automation can be particularly disorienting. Bibliographic instruction for older patrons in the use, application, and misuse of technology is an important mandate.

Special librarians, particularly medical librarians, have always kept instruction librarians looking to the future. Special librarians are particularly concerned with information handling and management. It is not unusual for a special librarian to instruct patrons in how to organize reprint and personal files, how to select the most appropriate database management software, how to search commercial databases, and how to dial up a remote information resource. Special librarians were the first group of librarians to become involved in what is referred to as *end-user instruction*. End-user instruction is concerned with teaching patrons (the end users of the information) how to search a database for themselves, bypassing the librarian as a search intermediary. Special librarians are often actively involved in designing information retrieval systems and user interfaces that facilitate searching of complex databases.

Librarians, whether in academic, school, special, or public library settings, are increasingly involved in user education, and are challenged to develop effective and creative approaches to educating the user at the most appropriate time in the most appropriate way. The second generation of BI librarians has its work cut out for it in the 1990s. At few times in library history has there been such a strong need for leadership that establishes a responsive and assertive agenda for library action, and instruction librarians are a pivotal force in that undertaking.

Practical Applications of Instruction

Regardless of the type of library, content to be taught, administrative organization, age of users, or experience of the learners, the following elements must be addressed in the development of instructional services or programs: (1) needs assessment; (2) goals and objectives; (3) learning theory; (4) instructional method; (5) presentation or teaching techniques; (6) structure of instruction programs; (7) administration; and (8) evaluation. Five scenarios describing situations in which these elements can be applied to develop instruction programs are interspersed with the text in this section.

Needs Assessment

Conducting a needs assessment prior to the actual instruction is crucial to ensuring a responsive and appropriate teaching program. Needs assessment is much like a consumer analysis, market survey, or community analysis, as it provides evidence for informed decisions, helps safeguard against false assumptions and myths, and provides a basis for building a program. Needs assessment must be ongoing to respond to changes in user groups, information structures, and resources. Assessment of both external factors and internal factors needs to be conducted in order to ascertain the information needs of users and the library's ability to meet them.

External Assessment. An external assessment includes reviewing elements outside the library which will affect instruction, including: (1) society; (2) the community; (3) the institutional context; and (4) the users or learners. Box 6.5 lists questions that need to be asked and information sought to answer them.

■ ═══ ■

6.5
External Assessment Questions

1. *Society*

   What expectations does society have for libraries and learning?

   What does society expect the library to do?

   Where is the library placed in the educational community?

2. *Community*

   What libraries and information centers exist in the community?

   What are the local resources beyond libraries?

   What is the level of cooperation among libraries?

   Do users have access to other libraries and resources?

3. *Institutional Context* (e.g., company, system, university, school, hospital)

   What is the educational and service philosophy of the institution?

   What are the institution's priorities for the library?

   What are the goals of the institution?

4. *Users or Learners*

   Who are the users?

   Who are the non-users?

   What is the experience and background of users?

   What about remote or invisible users?

   What are the learner's constraints? Cognitive level? Age? Disabilities?

   How many learners are there?

Internal Assessment. An internal assessment involves evaluating the resources of the library in relation to providing instruction and examining current instructional efforts. Box 6.6 lists questions that should guide an internal assessment.

■ ═══ ■

6.6
Internal Assessment Questions

1. *Resources*

   What are the library's priorities?

   What are the instructional skills and talents of the staff?

   Does the staff have the expertise to teach?

   What are the staff attitudes toward instruction?

   Is there administrative support for instruction?

   Can the collection absorb increased demands that instruction will create?

   What are the strengths and weaknesses of the collection?

   Does the library have appropriate space (e.g., classrooms) for instruction?

   Does the library have the necessary equipment (e.g., overhead projector, Datashow, videocassette recorder, chalkboard)?

   Will the library provide financial support for the program?

2. *Current Situation*

   Is any instruction being conducted?

   How is instruction currently administered?

   What type of instruction is in place?

Methods of Assessment. To answer the questions posed, the librarian must gather information from as many diverse sources as possible. Much information is readily available, but some must be gathered through conducting original surveys.

Four major mechanisms can provide information: literature surveys, surveys and questionnaires, observations, and testing. *Literature surveys* include research into local and institutional sources, such as archives, college catalogs, annual reports, statistical summaries, and promotional brochures, as well as use of national and international sources, such as clearinghouses and publications in library science and related fields.[37] The literature of management, education, cognitive science, and computer science is particularly rich with cogent publications for bibliographic instruction practitioners. *Surveys* can be conducted which ask users about their needs and preferences, or which ascertain staff attitudes toward instruction. Merely astutely *observing* from the reference desk, in the stacks, or near online catalog terminals can provide strong anecdotal evidence of user needs. Lastly, users can be *tested* on what they already know. Testing is particularly helpful when standards and goals can be articulated.

The data gathered using these four methods generates a profile of the information needs of the user and the library's ability to meet those needs. The profile is the first step in developing instruction. It allows the librarian to identify the user group to target for instruction. When initiating instruction, it is wise to identify a pilot group instead of trying to fill the needs of the entire clientele. Pilot programs facilitate evaluation and control any damages or disasters.

6.7

Scenario 1: Instruction for International Students

You are one of four librarians in an academic engineering library. You spend a lot of time at the reference desk and you have observed an increasing number of international students using the library, some of them not very successfully. You have also observed that few of the students avail themselves of reference service, choosing rather to ask fellow international students for assistance. As the percentage of international engineering students, particularly those from Asia, continues to grow, you are becoming increasingly concerned about the library's ability or inability to reach and serve these students.

After discussing your concerns with your colleagues, you are asked by the head of the library to develop a user education program for international engineering students. You do not quite know how you will identify your target group, what you will teach, or how you will structure the program, but you are willing to give it a try. Your colleagues are willing to help implement the program, but, like everyone else, they are overextended and cannot be counted on to do extensive teaching. Someone suggests that there must be resource people and units on campus, such as the Office of International Students, that can provide valuable assistance. Outline your approach.

Goals and Objectives

Goals and objectives do not guarantee successful instruction, but the lack of them could mean failure. The best instruction is based on clearly articulated goals and objectives. Writing goals and objectives is a skill that may be frustrating at first to acquire, but is an essential skill for good instruction.

Goals and objectives serve both the instructor and the learner. For the instructor, objectives focus instruction, guide instruction and structuring of content, and provide a mechanism for measurement and evaluation. For the learner, objectives give direction, set clear expectations, increase motivation, focus time, and allow for self-monitoring of progress. For both learner and instructor, objectives create a mutual understanding of content, expectations, and outcomes. It is important that objectives be written before the content or teaching method is selected.

There are three types of objectives: (1) general objectives; (2) terminal objectives; and (3) enabling (or behavioral) objectives. *General objectives* describe the overall goal of a program and what the entire program is designed to achieve. *Terminal objectives* break down the general objectives into more specific meaningful units. *Enabling objectives* define specific knowledge or skills necessary to achieve the terminal objective; they describe the behavior of a person who has mastered the material. Enabling objectives have four elements: (1) the learner; (2) the performance (observable behavior); (3) conditions (situation statement); and (4) criterion (acceptable behavior). Examples of the three types of objectives appear in box 6.8.

■ == ■

6.8

Sample Instructional Objectives

General: The user understands how information is defined by experts and recognizes how that knowledge can help determine the direction of a search for specific information.

Terminal: The user understands that the identification of a specific information source will depend on the individual question and the strategy devised.

Enabling: Wanting to locate "everything" on a certain topic, the user can correctly determine if the topic is too broad, and can discover this by first looking at the number of citations for that topic in a printed index.

To determine if the objectives are well-written and appropriate, answer the following:

Are the learning outcomes appropriate?

Are all logical outcomes appropriate?

Are objectives attainable?

Are the objectives in harmony with the philosophy of the institution?

Are the objectives in harmony with the principles of learning (readiness of learner, motivation, transfer value)?

Is the learner the subject of the objectives?

Librarians new to writing objectives should consult Robert F. Mager's *Preparing Instructional Objectives* for a lively, self-paced lesson that can easily be completed during one sitting.[38] In applying objectives to libraries, librarians will find a superb model in the statement developed by the Bibliographic Instruction Section of the Association of College and Research Libraries.[39] The model statement is unique in that the general and terminal objectives reflect both a cognitive approach to learning and the developments in information management. Its beauty is that it can be customized to a particular library, regardless of type, and to individual learners, regardless of experience, age, or background.

■ ══ ■

6.9

Scenario 2: Instruction for Secondary School Students

You are the only librarian in the school library and have been in the position for a little over six months. You feel very strongly that library and research skills should be part of every student's general education. In fact, you have always considered yourself a teacher-librarian. Unfortunately, your predecessor did not share your philosophies, so there is no existing instruction program. You are set on developing and implementing a course-integrated instruction program for grades seven through twelve (see box 6.12).

As a member of the curriculum committee, you are well acquainted with the educational aims of the school as well as its course structure. All students take English composition and literature courses each year, as well as core courses in the pure and applied sciences and social sciences.

You are concerned that frequent teacher turnover may cause some continuity problems when you implement your plan. Incidentally, many of the teachers have one-semester appointments as part of their student training in the College of Education. You are also fearful that the students are more computer literate than you are. Many have personal computers at home and are enthralled by their capabilities.

Outline your approach.

Learning Theory

The most effective instruction efforts take into account learning theory and consider individual styles of learning. It is essential that librarians become knowledgeable about learning theories, so that they can develop effective instruction.

What is learning? The generally accepted definition of *learning* is a relatively permanent change in a person's knowledge or behavior due to experience. Learning is a change in the content or structure of knowledge or in behavior. In learning, the cause of that change is experience, rather than drugs, psychological intervention, fatigue, or maturation. Learning theories continue to be developed and modified. As new theories are proposed and become fashionable, older theories are not necessarily discarded. Divergent theories exist simultaneously and are often considered equally valid in different situations. While there is no one definitive, exclusive learning theory, the two major schools of *behaviorism* and *cognitivism* have particular importance for bibliographic instruction practitioners.

Behaviorists, such as Ivan Pavlov, John Watson, Edward Thorndike, and B. F. Skinner, advocate an objectivist view of learning. Behaviorists focus on observable behavior or changes in actions. According to behaviorists, the human mind is a blank slate, and the individual a passive learner controlled by external forces. Learning, as explained by behaviorists, is an accumulative process, with one event building on a previous event.

Cognitivists, such as Jean Piaget and Jerome Bruner, focus on changes in knowledge instead of changes in behavior. Suggesting that the mind is endowed with an innate structure, rather than the behaviorist's blank slate, cognitivists believe that learning is facilitated when the learner has an understanding of the task to be learned.

Both schools have had an impact on bibliographic instruction. The influence of the behaviorist school on BI can be seen in the writing of goals and objectives, workbooks, linear-based computer-assisted instruction, and institution-specific instruction. The cognitive theory is reflected in the use of conceptual frameworks,[40] guided design,[41] and problem analysis.

Several factors need to be considered when determining how an individual learns: (1) cognitive development; (2) learning style; and (3) learning environment.

Cognitive development was divided into four stages by Piaget.[42] Stage one is called the sensorimotor period, and occurs from birth until about two years of age. An infant in the sensorimotor period learns through physical cues. From two to seven years of age, an individual moves through the preoperational period, which sees the development of language and perception. The concrete operational stage takes over until age eleven, during which time the individual begins to understand symbols, still learns by doing, and begins to be able to do elementary problem analysis. The final stage, which begins around the age of twelve years, is called formal operations, and allows for formulation, testing, and understanding of hypothetical situations. Some educators estimate that 30 percent of adults never fully reach the formal operational stage. Librarians need to be aware of where learners are in their cognitive development when devising instruction.

Each individual develops a preference for a *learning style* or a habitual manner of problem solving. Educators divide learner styles into field-dependent and field-independent and spontaneous and deliberate learners. The learning preference generally reflects child-rearing practices and socially acceptable practices. A field-dependent learner prefers learning by observing, is distracted by the surroundings, seeks guidance, and likes learning in groups. A field-independent learner tends to learn through question and answer, likes to work alone, and is analytical in problem solving. A spontaneous learner prefers complexity, suggests answers and solutions quickly, and uses nonlinear approaches. A deliberate learner prefers a step-by-step process, prefers discovery over being informed, likes order, and works in depth before moving on. These learning styles are not exclusive of one another. In fact, an individual can be a deliberate learner when faced with a new task and a spontaneous learner in another situation.

The environment greatly affects an individual's ability to learn. Physical constraints include perception, time, and mobility. Emotional constraints include motivation levels, persistence, responsibility, and structure. Sound, light, temperature, and space design are other environmental constraints affecting learning. The librarian must be cognizant of how these various constraints can adversely or positively affect an individual's ability to learn.

Instructional Method

After a needs assessment is completed, goals and objectives are written, and learning styles are examined, the librarian begins the process of deciding what *instructional methods* to employ. Marilla Svinicki and Barbara Schwartz present an extremely effective system for categorizing and selecting methods in their book, *Designing Instruction for Library Users*.[43]

Svinicki and Schwartz provide a continuum of instructional methods based on who or what determines the sequence of learning events. Based on the degree of control over learning, the continuum places the instructor in total control at one end (direct instruction) and the learner in total control at the other end (indirect instruction). Between the two extremes is semi-direct instruction, where learner and instructor share control of the instruction. Box 6.10 lists various instructional methods as they are placed in the continuum.[44]

■ ═══ ■

6.10

Instructional Methods Continuum

DIRECT	SEMI-DIRECT	INDIRECT
(Instructor Control)	(Shared Control)	(Learner Control)
Group Methods	**Group Methods**	**Group Methods**
1. Lecture	1. Lecture/Discussion	1. Discussion
2. Demonstration	2. Case study	2. Brainstorming
3. Media (video, slide-tapes, audio recordings)	3. Demonstration/Hands-on	3. Simulations
	4. Workshops	4. Games
Individual Methods	**Individual Methods**	**Individual Methods**
1. Text and guides	1. Workbook	1. Computer simulations
2. Handouts	2. Worksheets	2. Computer-assisted instruction (notably HyperCard-based programs)
3. Point-of-use (instruction given at place of use, such as a media tutorial on how to use *Psychological Abstracts* located next to that index)	3. Study guides	3. Contracting
	4. Programmed instruction	4. Projects (e.g., research paper, resource-based reports)
	5. Tutoring	
	6. Term-paper counseling	
	7. Computer-assisted instruction	

Direct Instruction (Instructor Control). The primary goal of direct instruction is the efficient delivery of information to the group or individual. In direct instruction, the learner is passive, sitting back and absorbing the lecture, the videotape, or the text. The instructor decides what material is covered and determines how to organize the information. The instructor is the focus of the learner's attention.

When instructors are in control, they can deliver much information in a relatively short period of time, which can often be quite desirable. Direct instruction is particularly useful for overviews and introductions, and it provides a method for giving leading-edge, unpublished information to students. If the instructor is a very good, enthusiastic lecturer, the direct instruction method can be inspiring and exciting, and can pique the learner's curiosity. In addition, the learner does not have to possess any high-level skills to learn in an instructor-controlled learning situation, other than being attentive and receptive. There are several disadvantages to direct instruction, most notably its unresponsiveness to individual learning styles. There is no opportunity for learner practice, feedback, or direct application of the information presented. In an instructor-controlled environment, the message is transmitted that there is only one correct way of seeing things. For the vast majority of learners, lectures fall at the bottom of the list of preferred ways to learn.

Semi-Direct Instruction (Shared Control). Semi-direct instruction involves the presentation of information by the instructor, followed by student practice or application. The instructor is responsible for the initial presentation of information through a demonstration, example, or reading. Under the instructor's direction, the learner completes tasks or answers questions which require application of the material. Semi-direct instruction demands greater involvement by the learner than does direct instruction. The learner becomes an active participant guided by the instructor.

In semi-direct instruction, more student participation is possible than in direct instruction. There is the opportunity for the instructor to provide the student with immediate feedback. The instructor can still maintain control of the learning experience, although not as tightly as in direct instruction. Semi-direct instruction does have the drawback of being time-consuming, both in student practice and instructor preparation. The learner may not have the necessary skills and knowledge to participate fully in this type of instruction.

Indirect Instruction (Learner Control). Indirect instruction is learning which the student directs. The instructor steps back from the podium, turns off the audiovisual equipment, and stops posing questions. The learner does the bulk of the postulating, analyzing, and, ultimately, learning. For the learner, indirect instruction promotes active learning and increases the motivation to learn through involvement and responsibility. Few curricular aids are needed in indirect instruction.

Indirect instruction is perhaps the most underutilized method, as many instructors do not have the skills or confidence effectively to facilitate indirect instruction, and they fear the unpredictability that is one of the major drawbacks of indirect instruction. Instructors must be poised, confident, and able to think on their feet when the unexpected happens. Indirect instruction can be extremely time-consuming for both instructor and learner. Not effective for large groups, indirect instruction is ideal for small, highly motivated groups of learners.

No one instructional method serves all situations. Commonly, more than one method is used during a single class session; for example, a class session might begin with a lecture, incorporate a video production, include a discussion, and end with a self-paced worksheet. A variety of teaching methods keeps learners involved, invigorated, and responsive. The beginning instructor will no doubt feel intimidated by using more than one teaching method. Moving from one method to another is a sophisticated teaching skill which the instructor will master over time. Only through experimentation, trial and error, innovation, and practice will the individual instructor find the mix that works for teacher and students alike.

■ ═══════════════════════════════════════ ■

6.11

Scenario 3: Business Information Seminars

You are one of ten reference librarians in a public library. Your particular area of expertise is business reference. Whenever patrons come in or call seeking investment, stock market, tax, or other related business information, they are almost automatically referred to you. You are finding it particularly difficult to handle the increasing level of questions and the seemingly unending demand for information about the economic outlook for literally hundreds of different companies. You are certain that many of the questions you answer are related to potential stock purchases; you have helped so many investors that you are beginning to feel you should take a cut of their profits.

You see two issues: (1) how to educate and train your colleagues in the reference department in business reference; and (2) how to instruct a nebulous group of patrons who demand an inordinate amount of your time in locating information about individual companies and economic forecasting. Your director is somewhat of a traditionalist and is dubious about initiating any user education programs. You see a definite need for business information seminars, and believe that you could market them successfully. A couple of the other reference librarians are supportive, but do not feel they can help to any great degree because they lack the subject expertise. What is your strategy for developing a program?

Presentation Techniques

Many librarians are called upon to give presentations to users as well as to colleagues, superiors, and subordinates. Presentation skills are so much in demand in librarianship, in a wide variety of circumstances, that librarians should develop their skills and welcome opportunities to practice these skills. How should the presentation be organized? What about notes? And the delivery? Gestures? Overheads? Handouts? There is so much to consider when teaching! The following brief lesson in presentations answers some of the questions.

The presentation itself is made up of three parts: the introduction, the body, and the closure. First, work on the body when writing a presentation. Next, prepare the closure. Often a speaker or instructor runs out of time and fails to summarize or close. At all costs, provide a summary. The audience needs to have a feeling of closure and of points being brought together. Last, write the introduction. The introduction should provide the learner with the motivation to listen to the body. The old directive about presentations is true:

> Tell them what you're going to tell them (introduction); tell them (body); tell them what you've told them (closure).

Good presentations are well organized and offer learners a scheme they can easily follow.

Notes are invaluable even to the most experienced speaker or lecturer. Outlines and phrases make better notes than verbatim monologue; nothing is more deadly than hearing an instructor read a lecture. Use only one side of note paper or cards; if notes are made on both sides, the flipping of the paper can be distracting to the audience. Numbering notes prevents disaster if the papers are dropped or reshuffled inadvertently. Notes need to be large and legible. What one can easily read in the still of an office may become illegible in front of a large crowd, when nerves take over. Margins can be used for keywords, questions, and directives to the instructor (e.g., breathe, pause, smile). Each thought should be finished on a single card. Extending an idea over several pages interrupts a natural flow when presenting. Properly prepared notes help the speaker control the situation.

Nonverbal communication is extremely important in teaching. Studies show that between 60 and 70 percent of what an audience notices is nonverbal. Appropriate appearance is essential to creating and maintaining audience receptivity; the instructor's appearance should not distract the audience from the content of the presentation. Instructors also need to be comfortable with their own appearance.

Eye contact is a way to involve the audience, but good eye contact does not mean staring at one person until he awkwardly averts his eyes. Talk to various sections of the audience, but do not move methodically as if watching a tennis match. Voice pitch and pattern can be used effectively for emphasis and variation. Gestures can also greatly enhance lecturing. The best gestures are big, meaningful, purposeful, vigorous, and complete. Gestures need to be well-timed but spontaneous. One very effective way to evaluate use of gestures is to watch a video recording of the lecture.[45]

Structure of Instruction Programs

As the field of bibliographic instruction has matured and developed, five major organizing structures have become dominant: orientation, course-related instruction, course-integrated instruction, team teaching, and separate courses. These structures reflect the manner in which the instruction is tied to the curriculum and the institution's educational goals. While the choice of the instructional method (direct, semi-direct, or indirect instruction) is dependent on the composition of the learner group, the library's facilities, the instructor's skills, the size of the group, and a myriad of other factors, the structure of the instruction program is dependent primarily on the level of interdepartmental and administrative support and cooperation.

The five structures generally defined by practitioners are shown in box 6.12.

■ ══ ■

6.12
Five Structures of Instructional Programs

Orientation: Activities designed to introduce and orient library users to services, facilities, and resources of a particular library.

Course-related instruction: Instruction that provides learners in a given course information skills demanded to carry out one or more activities of that course.

Course-integrated instruction: Instruction which is part of a course's objectives and essential to the knowledge of the subject. Integration takes place at the time the course is designed or modified.

Team teaching: Instruction which is designed, delivered, and evaluated by a librarian and classroom instructor together.

Separate course: Course taught by a librarian, whether for credit or not, that is considered part of the institution's curriculum.

The five structures are distinguished by the level of cooperation required among librarians, department faculty, and administrators. In selecting a structure for instruction, librarians must consider the political environment, current support, and the degree of interdepartmental cooperation. The five structures are predicated on the type of cooperation existing, with orientation requiring none on one end of the continuum, and separate courses requiring total cooperation on the other, with course-related, course-integrated, and team teaching in between. Librarians may be limited to a particular structure because of a low level or the complete absence of cooperation. As instruction programs develop and cooperation increases, the library can move from orientation to structures more closely tied to the institution's curriculum.[46]

Administration

Administration of instruction programs involves many issues and practicalities, including: (1) organizational structures; (2) personnel; (3) budgets and funding; and (4) marketing and public relations. The beginning librarian may not be responsible for the administrative details of a program. However, how those details are handled will greatly affect the ability of librarians to implement instruction.

Organizational Structures. The bibliographic instruction librarian works within two organizational structures, that of the larger institution and that of the library. Developing the skills to manage up, as well as down, is imperative to a successful program.[47] *Managing down* involves directing subordinates to carry out work. *Managing up* entails influencing superiors. Bibliographic instruction librarians need to become effective managers both upwards and downwards. The greater institution may be a college or university, a school system, a public library community, or a corporation. Within each institutional structure, the librarian must identify where policy, budget, and personnel decisions are made and how to actively influence those decisions.

To illustrate the importance of understanding the organizational structure and corporate rules of any institution, consider a typical university. Depending on whether the university is public or private, the governing body is usually a board of trustees or regents; sometimes appointed, sometimes elected, they are more or less responsible for guiding the university's development, policy, and educational philosophy. Charged with carrying out the board's advice is the university administration: the president or chancellor, the vice presidents or vice chancellors, the deans, and the department heads. Within the teaching faculty, a hierarchy based on appointment and tenure exists, led by the full professor, followed by associate professors, assistant professors, and instructors. Even within the ranks of students, most campuses place graduates above undergraduates in the hierarchy, as reflected in housing, enrollment, financial aid, and library policies. Within the library, a typical arrangement places the library director at the top of a staff pyramid of associate university librarians (AULs), assistant directors (ADs), department heads, librarians, support staff, and student assistants.

Within the university structure, as in any organizational structure in which librarians work, the librarian responsible for instruction has to determine where various decisions are made. Who sets priorities? Who makes personnel decisions? At what level are budgets allocated? Who controls curriculum decisions? Some answers may be readily available and clear-cut; other answers might be mired in institutional lore or affected by distinct personalities. The great challenge of administration is to work both within the official structure and within the informal systems of influence that exist in every institution—university, corporation, municipal government, or school.

Within the library, the responsibility of instruction can be organized in a variety of ways. Bibliographic instruction can be the responsibility of a discrete instruction department, the reference department, or subject specialists. Each organization has disadvantages as well as beneficial characteristics.

Establishing a separate unit devoted to instruction is unusual in academic and public libraries, but is becoming more prevalent in large medical libraries. A separate department allows the librarians to concentrate on user education and not be drained by other responsibilities. While a separate department establishes visibility for instruction, it also can isolate the librarians from other library services.

Typically, in academic and public libraries, instruction responsibilities are covered by the reference department. This organizational delineation is a natural outgrowth of the symbiotic relationship of reference and instruction. Needs assessment is a relatively simple operation when instruction is handled by the reference staff. Front-line librarians generally have an excellent sense of the instructional needs of patrons. Overwork and confusion of priorities are the major drawbacks of having the reference department be responsible for instruction.[48] If a reference department views its primary responsibility as providing desk reference, instructional efforts may be viewed as a lesser priority, and will receive less emphasis.

In many libraries, subject specialists or bibliographers are responsible for instruction. It is a reasonable extension of a specialist's position to incorporate user education duties. A subject specialist knows the literature of the field and has an in-depth understanding of the bibliographic apparatus. The subject specialist may, however, lack the teaching skills necessary for instruction.

In the one-person library, it goes without saying that the same person who selects the books, catalogs the materials, and provides reference service is also responsible for instruction. In many schools and corporate libraries, the organization scheme of the truly holistic librarian is the norm.

Organizational structures can facilitate or hinder instructional efforts. The successful instruction librarian learns how to maneuver within the structures, pinpoint how and where decisions are made, and influence those decisions.

Personnel. Without appropriate personnel, an instruction program is doomed. Recruitment and development of instructional staff are major issues in instruction. In many situations, the existing staff takes on instruction responsibilities. Because so few library schools have established programs in user education, the majority of librarians are ill-prepared for instruction.[49] School librarians with preparation in education may fare better, but they too often lack background in the theory of bibliographic instruction and its application. Because of this lack of expertise, libraries have established in-service training programs, and individuals seek out continuing education opportunities through conferences and regional courses. Recruitment of new staff with teaching experience is a possibility when positions turn over or new ones are created. When hiring an entry-level BI librarian, administrators expect the following skills and proficiencies:

1. Ability to select educational objectives for specific activities
2. Ability to select appropriate instructional methods
3. Knowledge of evaluation techniques
4. Teaching ability
5. Instructional media skills.[50]

When selecting a BI administrator, such as an instruction coordinator, search committees look for those who can:

1. Conduct needs assessment
2. Devise policies and plans
3. Acquire necessary staff and budget
4. Train and evaluate staff
5. Market bibliographic instruction
6. Conduct program evaluations.[51]

Instruction responsibilities are not the solitary domain of the professional staff. Support staff are often very involved in the implementation of instruction programs, in activities such as handout compilation, scheduling, marketing, and in some cases, delivery of the instruction. Instruction programs often increase the clerical workload and require a redirection of workflow and priorities. Clerical staff development is just as vital as continuing professional education.

Budgets and Funding. Without money, not much happens. Adequate funding needs to be allocated for instruction on a permanent basis. Funding is needed for staff, equipment, supplies, and materials. Funding can come from within the library and from outside sources.

The library's budget for instructional activities should be integrated into the operating budget. Bibliographic instruction librarians may be asked to document the need for funding. This can be done through producing annual reports and statistical summaries, gaining the recognition of the community, receiving grants and awards, and gathering letters of support.

Librarians should not miss the opportunity to apply for outside funding to enhance their budgets. Librarians can often receive matching funds from a teaching department, a private donor, or a local business. A variety of grants exist for innovation in libraries and instruction. Beward of the pitfalls of soft money, however: grant funding is for a finite period, and plans for how to fund a program permanently must begin before the grant runs out.

Marketing and Public Relations. Only recently has the library community begun to see itself as being in the business of marketing services. The marketing of bibliographic instruction involves educating potential users to the availability of instructional services.[52] Marketing can take place, for example, through an informal departmental liaison,[53] through an aggressive mailing campaign to promote term-paper counseling,[54] or by designing a handsome logo.

Bibliographic instruction can create an excellent mechanism for improving public relations. Public relations involves two-way communication between an institution and its clientele. Since instruction is predicated on communication, enhanced public relations are an extra benefit of BI. Librarians cannot sit back and passively wait for the public to recognize the library's efforts; they must use the marketing techniques at their disposal to ensure good relations.

6.13

Scenario 4: Instruction for End-User Online Searchers

You are the assistant librarian in a corporate library. One of your main responsibilities is conducting the thousand-plus annual online database searches for the research and development division, which is comprised of more than one hundred engineers and computer scientists. Hoping to provide better service to the department (and possibly be rewarded for your creativity), you think that the engineers and computer scientists would be better served if they did their own online searching. After all, there are plenty of terminals distributed throughout the buildings. Money is no object as long as the money spent saves time and improves the company's product.

The head of the library is dubious about your idea to train the engineers in online searching. She is fearful of losing her job because there will be nothing for her to do. You feel that her fears are unfounded, but you must be sensitive to her insecurities. You feel that training employees in end-user searching will free the librarians to expand information services. Where do you go from here?

Evaluation

Evaluation is critical to ensuring that instruction efforts continue to improve (see chapter 8). Evaluation is the art of asking questions and finding evidence to make informed decisions. The primary purpose of evaluation is to improve the quality of teaching for the learner's benefit.

Effective evaluation depends on several factors. In assessing the quality of instruction, the librarian must recognize that assumptions and values affect evaluation. The ability to assess quality depends on the quality of the questions, the quality of the evidence, and the quality of the reasoning. Good questions challenge values and assumptions, question performance, force judgments, and hold the instructor accountable to the learner. Good evidence provides meaningful answers, improves credibility, and forces decisions.[55]

Evidence can be gathered by observation, through surveys, by testing, and through documenting use. By observing learners, anecdotal evidence can answer the question of whether learners ask for help, use the information provided, or look bewildered. Surveys can ask what students learned, if they found it helpful, or if they used the information. Tests can ascertain if the learner can answer key questions or perform expected behaviors. Evidence of use can be gained by having the learner keep a journal or develop a strategy, or by examining the bibliography at the end of the student's term paper. Once evidence is gathered, a judgment must be made as to whether the instruction was of value to the learner. Judgments force decisions which lead to improvement in instruction. Evaluation must be ongoing to ensure responsive and continually improving instruction.

■ ═══ ■

6.14
Scenario 5: Instruction for an Elementary School Science Project

You are a new librarian in the Youth Services Department. You have been asked by the head of the department to develop a user education program directed at sixth to eighth graders preparing projects for the annual science fair held in the area middle schools each spring. The department head tells you that each March students come to the library in the evenings in search of materials for their science projects, as well as advice on how to display their work. The department feels that it has not been very effective in assisting the students, because it is ill-prepared to handle individual requests. She would like to change all that, and has asked you to develop a workshop on science-fair readiness for the students.

She reminds you that you will have to work with local school teachers, media specialists, possibly parents, and, of course, the other librarians in the department. You remember your own experience with a science fair in the seventh grade as an enriching and confidence-building experience. You want to ensure that these students feel the same way. Where do you start?

Future Trends and Challenges

Instruction is entering an exciting new era, receiving renewed impetus much as it did in the 1960s. Converging forces are creating new instructional needs. The national call for information literacy, rapidly changing information technologies, increased remote access to libraries and information, new demands on the citizenry of an information-based society, and the accelerated creation of new information demand that librarians take on enhanced roles as advocates for the user, information consultants, and educators. As advocates, librarians need to articulate user concerns during the development of information systems and policies. As consultants, librarians should advise and guide users in problem solving and provide an informed context for decision making. As educators, librarians are obligated to teach individuals to use systems as a means of managing the information process, and to facilitate the learning of principles and concepts which are transferred to diverse information settings. These roles are played both at the reference desk and in the bibliographic instruction classroom. Educating users to make full, judicious, and informed use of information is a fundamental responsibility shared by all librarians.

Notes

1. American Library Association, "Policy Statement: Instruction in the Use of Libraries," Council Document No. 45 (1980).

2. Otis H. Robinson, "Proceedings: First Session," *American Library Journal* 1 (1876): 123-24.

3. Harold W. Tuckett and Carla J. Stoffle, "Learning Theory and the Self-Reliant Library User," *RQ* 24 (Fall 1984): 58.

4. American Library Association Presidential Committee on Information Literacy, *Final Report* (Chicago: American Library Association, 1989), 1. For additional readings and discussion, see Trish Ridgeway's "Information Literacy: An Introductory Reading List," *College & Research Libraries News* 51 (July/August 1990): 645-48.

5. Lori Arp, "Information Literacy or Bibliographic Instruction: Semantics or Philosophy," *RQ* 30 (Fall 1990): 46-49.

6. Tuckett and Stoffle, "Learning Theory and the Self-Reliant Library User," 58.

7. James Rice, Jr., *Teaching Library Use* (Westport, Conn.: Greenwood Press, 1981), 5.

8. Charles Forrest and Mary Gassmann, "Development of a Self-Guided Audiocassette Tour at a Large Academic Research Library," *Research Strategies* 4 (Summer 1986): 116-24.

9. Rice, *Teaching Library Use*, 6.

10. Ibid.

11. American Library Association, Association of College and Research Libraries, Bibliographic Instruction Section, Policy and Planning Committee, *Bibliographic Instruction Handbook* (Chicago: American Library Association, 1979), 57.

12. Constance Mellon, ed., *Bibliographic Instruction: The Second Generation* (Littleton, Colo.: Libraries Unlimited, 1987), xiii.

13. Nina Matheson and John Cooper, "Academic Information in the Academic Health Sciences Center: Roles for the Library in Information Management," *Journal of Medical Education* 57, no. 10, pt. 2 (October 1982): 1-93.

14. James Rice, "The Hidden Role of Librarians," *Library Journal* 114 (January 1989): 57-59.

15. American Association of School Librarians and Association for Educational Communications and Technology, *Information Power: Guidelines for School Library Media Programs* (Chicago: American Library Association, 1988), 171p.

16. Ibid., 39.

17. Tuckett and Stoffle, "Learning Theory and the Self-Reliant Library User," 58.

18. John Naisbitt explores the shift from institutional help to self-help in *Megatrends: Ten New Directions Transforming Our Lives* (New York: Warner Books, 1982), ch. 6.

19. For a discussion of a new paradigm, see "The Future of Reference," *College & Research Libraries News* 50 (October 1989): 780-99; and Joanne Euster, "Technology and Instruction," in *Bibliographic Instruction*, ed. Constance Mellon (Littleton, Colo.: Libraries Unlimited, 1987), 53-59.

20. Mark Tucker delineates the first three periods in his "Emerson's Library Legacy: Concepts of Bibliographic Instruction," *New Directions for Teaching and Learning* 4 (1984): 15-24.

21. Kenneth Brough, *Scholar's Workshop: Evolving Concepts of Library Service* (Urbana, Ill.: University of Illinois, 1953), 152-55.

22. Richard Rubin, "Azariah Smith Root and Library Instruction at Oberlin College," *Journal of Library History, Philosophy, Comparative Librarianship* 12 (Summer 1977): 250-61.

23. Samuel Rothstein, *The Development of Reference Services Through Academic Traditions, Public Library Practice and Special Librarianship* (Chicago: Association of College and Research Libraries, June 1955), 22.

24. Louis Shores, "The Library Arts College, A Possibility in 1954?," speech delivered at the Chicago Century of Progress in 1934; later published in *School and Society* 4 (January 26, 1935): 110-14.

25. Harvie Branscomb, *Teaching with Books: A Study of College Libraries* (Chicago: Association of American Colleges, 1940), 239p.

26. Patricia Knapp, *The Monteith College Library Experiment* (New York: Scarecrow Press, 1966), 293p.

27. David F. Kohl and Lizabeth A. Wilson, "Effectiveness of Course-Integrated Bibliographic Instruction in Improving Coursework," *RQ* 27 (Winter 1989): 206-11.

28. Mary Reichel and Mary Ann Ramey, *Conceptual Frameworks for Bibliographic Education: Theory into Practice* (Littleton, Colo.: Libraries Unlimited, 1987), 212p.

29. Cerise Oberman and Katina Strauch, eds., *Theories of Bibliographic Education: Designs for Teaching* (New York: R. R. Bowker, 1982), 233p.

30. Carla J. Stoffle and Cheryl A. Bernero, "Bibliographic Instruction Think Tank I: Looking Back and the Challenge for Think Tank II," in *Bibliographic Instruction*, ed. Constance Mellon (Littleton, Colo.: Libraries Unlimited, 1987), 13.

31. American Library Association, "Policy Statement."

32. Mary Ellen Larson and Ellen Meltzer, "Education for Bibliographic Instruction," *Journal of Education for Library and Information Science* 28 (Spring 1987): 10.

33. Constance Mellon, "Introduction," in *Bibliographic Instruction*, xiii-xvi.

34. Diane Crispell, "Workers in 2000," *American Demographics* 12 (March 1990): 36-37.

35. Joe Cappo, *Future Scope: Success Strategies for the 1990s and Beyond* (n.p.: Longman Financial Services Publishing, 1990), 40-55.

36. For additional discussion of critical thinking, see Sonia Bodi, "Critical Thinking and Biblio-graphic Instruction: The Relationship," *Journal of Academic Librarianship* 14 (July 1988): 150-53; Eugene Engeldinger, "Bibliographic Instruction and Critical Thinking: The Contribution of the Annotated Bibliography," *RQ* 28 (Winter 1988): 195-202.

37. The National Library and Orientation Exchange (LOEX) serves as clearinghouse for BI materials. On request, LOEX will send practitioners sample scripts, videotapes, handouts, and the like. The address is LOEX Clearinghouse, Eastern Michigan University, Ypsilanti, MI 48197. The telephone number is (313) 487-0168.

38. Robert F. Mager, *Preparing Instructional Objectives* (Belmont, Calif.: Fearon Publishers, 1975), 136p.

39. "Model Statement of Objectives for Academic Bibliographic Instruction," *College & Research Libraries* 48 (May 1987): 256-61.

40. Pamela Kobelski and Mary Reichel, "Conceptual Frameworks for Bibliographic Education," *Journal of Academic Librarianship* 7 (May 1981): 73-77.

41. Cerise Oberman and Rebecca A. Linton, "Guided Design: Teaching Library Research as Problem Solving," in *Theories of Bibliographic Education* (New York: R. R. Bowker, 1982), 111-34.

42. Jean Piaget, *The Origins of Intelligence in Children* (New York: International Universities Press, 1952), 419p.

43. Marilla Svinicki and Barbara Schwartz, *Designing Instruction for Library Users* (New York: Marcel Dekker, 1988), 249p.

44. Ibid., 7. This is based on figure 2.1, with some modifications. Svinicki and Schwartz suggest that tutoring is an indirect method. This chapter places tutoring in the semi-direct method. See Lizabeth Wilson and Joyce Wright, "Term Paper Counseling: The Library's Tutorial," in *Integrating Library Use Skills into the General Education Curriculum*, ed. Maureen Pastine (New York: Haworth Press, 1989): 269-87. In addition, advances in nonlinear software, such as hypertext, allow the learner greater control over the instruction, placing computer-assisted instruction in both the semi-direct and indirect categories.

45. See Sandra Roger, "If I Can See Myself, I Can Change," *Educational Leadership* 45 (October 1987): 64-67; Mary Ann Ramey and Allan Spanjer, "Videotaping Bibliographic Instruction: A Con-frontation with Self," *Research Strategies* 2 (Spring 1984): 71-75.

46. Lori Arp and Lizabeth A. Wilson, "Structures of Bibliographic Instruction Programs: A Continuum for Planning," in *Integrating Library Use Skills*, ed. Maureen Pastine (New York: Haworth Press, 1989), 25-34.

47. John R. Darling and E. Dale Cluff, "Social Styles and the Art of Managing Up," *Journal of Academic Librarianship* 12 (January 1987): 350-55.

48. William Miller, "What's Wrong With Reference: Coping With Success and Failure at the Refer-ence Desk," *American Libraries* 15 (May 1984): 303-22.

49. See Rao Aluri and June Lester Engle, "Bibliographic Instruction and Library Education," in *Bibliographic Instruction*, ed. Constance Mellon (Littleton, Colo.: Libraries Unlimited, 1987), 111-24.

50. Ibid., 117.

51. Ibid.

52. Carolyn Kirkendall, ed., *Marketing Instructional Services: Applying Private Sector Techniques to Plan and Promote Bibliographic Instruction* (Ann Arbor, Mich.: Pierian Press, 1986), 157p.

53. Patricia Breivik, *Planning the Library Instruction Program* (Chicago: American Library Association, 1982), 121.

54. Kwasi Sarkodie-Mensah, "Making Term Paper Counseling More Meaningful," *College & Research Libraries News* 50 (November 1989): 912-15.

55. For more discussion on the objectives and mechanics of evaluation, see American Library Association, Association of College and Research Libraries, Bibliographic Instruction Section, *Evaluating Bibliographic Instruction* (Chicago: American Library Association, 1983), 122p.; F. Wilfrid Lancaster, *If You Want to Evaluate Your Library* (Champaign, Ill.: University of Illinois, Graduate School of Library and Information Science, 1988), 193p.

Additional Readings

American Association of School Librarians and Association for Educational Communications and Technology. *Information Power: Guidelines for School Library Media Programs*. Chicago: American Library Association, 1988. 171p.
    This is an especially valuable handbook for school librarians engaged in the development of school library media programs. Reflective of the leadership school librarians have taken in instruction, the book addresses missions and challenges of school libraries, the roles and responsibilities of school library media specialists, leadership, planning, management, personnel, resources, and association support. Of particular interest is the survey of school library media centers in appendix A.

American Library Association's Presidential Committee on Information Literacy. *Final Report*. Chicago: American Library Association, 1989. 17p.
    In its short seventeen pages, the *Final Report* of the Presidential Committee on Information Literacy convincingly presents the case for librarians taking a leading role in information education. Extremely well-written and engaging, the report creates a compelling case for information literacy in personal life, in business, and in citizenship. The committee's recommendations have far-reaching implications for all librarians, not just those involved with user education.

Beaubien, Anne K., Sharon A. Hogan, and Mary W. George, eds. *Learning the Library: Concepts and Methods for Effective Bibliographic Instruction*. New York: R. R. Bowker, 1982. 269p.
    Published as a companion volume to Bowker's *Theories of Bibliographic Education: Designs for Teaching* (1982), this book addresses the practical implementation of bibliographic instruction. As a guide to designing instruction programs, the book discusses goals and objectives, needs assessment, curricular design, administration, budgets, resources, and evaluation. Its uniqueness lies in the discussions of the research process in the humanities, social sciences, and history and how to teach those processes. The excellent chapter on planning the single stand-alone lecture or presentation is invaluable.

Brottman, May, and Mary Loe, eds. *The LIRT Library Instruction Handbook*. Englewood, Colo.: Libraries Unlimited, 1990. 125p.
    Created by the Library Instruction Round Table from a grant, the World Book-American Library Association Goals Award, this handbook and training manual covers development of library instruction programs in school media centers, academic libraries (graduate, four-year, and two-year), public libraries, and special libraries.

Clark, Alice S., and Kay F. Jones, eds. *Teaching Librarians to Teach*. Metuchen, N.J.: Scarecrow Press, 1986. 232p.
    Prompted by the need for continuing education designed to enhance and update the teaching skills of bibliographic instruction librarians, the editors put together a text which serves as a guide for in-service training programs. The book addresses education for bibliographic instruction, good teaching, objectives, motivation, and program evaluation. Linda Lucas's chapter on "Educating Librarians to Provide User Education to Disabled Students" challenges librarians to reevaluate services to diverse user groups.

Katz, Bill, and Ruth A. Fraley, eds. *Library Instruction and Reference Services*. New York: Haworth
    Press, 1984. 254p.
    This work (published simultaneously as *The Reference Librarian*, number 10) brings together
various, conflicting, and challenging views on the coexistence of instruction and reference. Two
divergent schools of thought are presented: one is typified by the firm commitment to the value and
importance of instruction, the other holds that instruction is not a library function. The chapters
discuss the continuum between the two schools with such topics as the symbiotic relationship of instruction and reference, teaching at the reference desk, instruction in public libraries, and instruction as an
enhancement of reference service.

Kirkendall, Carolyn A., and Carla J. Stoffle. "Instruction." In *The Service Imperative for Libraries:
    Essays in Honor of Margaret E. Monroe*, edited by Gail A. Schlachter, 42-93. Littleton, Colo.:
    Libraries Unlimited, 1982.
    Although now somewhat outdated, this essay remains one of the best surveys of bibliographic
instruction. In outlining the history and major movements in instruction, the authors emphasize educational theory in instruction and the importance of administrative support. This particularly cogent
review of user education in academic, school, public, and special library settings is completed with an
extensive classified bibliography.

McDonald, Frances Beck, ed. *The Emerging School Library Media Program*. Englewood, Colo.:
    Libraries Unlimited, 1988. 328p.
    With articles contributed by major figures in school librarianship, this collection illustrates the
instructional role of library media specialists. The authors reiterate the contributions librarians make to
the educational process.

Mellon, Constance A., ed. *Bibliographic Instruction: The Second Generation*. Littleton, Colo.:
    Libraries Unlimited, 1987. 204p.
    This work presents the writings of many practitioners whose ideas and research were responsible
for transforming bibliographic instruction from a haphazard, grassroots activity to an accepted,
integrated area of librarianship. The authors intended for the book to be a forum for first-generation
instruction librarians to discuss the issues, concerns, and challenges of instruction and subsequently
establish an agenda for the second generation. Noteworthy essays address librarians as teachers in the
information age, human aspects of library technology, education for bibliographic instruction, the
needs and feelings of beginning researchers, and the future.

Oberman, Cerise, and Katina Strauch, eds. *Theories of Bibliographic Education: Designs for Teaching*.
    New York: R. R. Bowker, 1982. 233p.
    This book represents the theoretical foundation for bibliographic instruction as a discipline and is
intended as a companion volume to the more practical *Learning the Library: Concepts and Methods for
Effective Bibliographic Instruction* (1982). The essays focus on the theory of information structure and
education principles. Emphasizing concept-based learning, the text encourages a shift away from tool-
based learning. Chapters of note discuss information problem solving, guided design, and teaching
information structure.

Pastine, Maureen, and Bill Katz, eds. *Integrating Library Use Skills in the General Education Curric-
    ulum*. New York: Haworth Press, 1989. 334p.
    This work (published simultaneously as *The Reference Librarian*, number 24) discusses some of
the major ideas underlying integration of library use skills and research methodologies into general
education programs. Patricia Breivik's essay, "Politics for Closing the Gap," is required reading for all
librarians committed to quality education. Book sections are titled: (1) Bridging the Gap Between High
School and College; (2) Library Skills in a Community College; (3) Library Skills in Colleges and
Universities; (4) Library Use Skills for Off-Campus Programs; (5) Issues Related to Microcomputers
and End-User Online Searching; and (6) Future of BI.

Reichel, Mary, and Mary Ann Ramey, eds. *Conceptual Frameworks for Bibliographic Education:
    Theory into Practice*. Littleton, Colo.: Libraries Unlimited, 1987. 212p.
    One of the keys to successful teaching is the ability to present ideas in an involving, memorable, yet
simple way. The primary focus of this book is how to create intellectual excitement by presenting

interesting and challenging material using conceptual frameworks. The chapters provide model presentations using systematic literature searching, search strategies in the social sciences, humanities, and sciences, and automated search processes.

Roberts, Anne F., and Susan G. Blandy. *Library Instruction for Librarians*. 2d ed. Englewood, Colo.: Libraries Unlimited, 1989. 257p.

This textbook provides both the mature instruction librarian and the library school student with a concise theoretical, practical, and historical guide to instruction. Written by practitioners, this how-to book is based on proven practices, and provides examples of curricular aids, a selective bibliography, and advice to the beginner.

Svinicki, Marilla D., and Barbara A. Schwartz. *Designing Instruction for Library Users: A Practical Guide*. New York: Marcel Dekker, 1988. 249p.

Directed primarily at the academic librarian who teaches information skills, this text can be used by those involved in user education in any setting. The authors provide a readily available guide to the instructional design process, including a practical system for categorizing instructional methods, a planning continuum, designing and sequencing instruction, learning theory applied to instruction, and assessing the effectiveness of instruction. Perhaps most helpful are the eight case studies in which the design matrix is applied. The authors end with their golden rules of instructional design.

TRAINING, DEVELOPMENT, AND CONTINUING EDUCATION FOR THE REFERENCE STAFF

Introduction

An efficient reference librarian, with excellent communication skills, a thorough knowledge of reference sources, and the ability to translate patrons' requests into the language of library resources and to use available resources appropriately, does not spring, fully armed, from the head of Zeus, as the fabled Athena did. While some people do have natural abilities in working with others and good instincts regarding how to approach reference service, all reference librarians need nurturing and training to expand and complement these innate abilities. Merely working with patrons and sources on a daily basis does not ensure that reference librarians are providing service to the best of their abilities. "When it comes to service, we haven't begun to take advantage of the improvement possibilities."[1]

New reference librarians begin their careers with only the required library school courses to support them, occasionally reinforced with paraprofessional or preprofessional work. Beginning reference courses in library schools generally cover specific reference sources, types of printed sources, reference query negotiation, selection and evaluation of reference sources, and manual searching strategies.[2] Only one of these five topics is directly related to the service aspect of reference work. To use this basic knowledge effectively, reference librarians must be trained to apply this professional education to a particular library setting. It is unreasonable to expect new graduates to perform today's sophisticated reference services successfully, or even adequately, without an investment of time and effort on the part of the employing library. These graduates need careful orientation, training, retraining, development, and continuing education to maximize their potential for providing effective reference service.

Reference librarians rarely see themselves as educators or administrators, even though they teach patrons every day and often perform traditional administrative functions such as supervising clerks, students, paraprofessionals, volunteers, or other librarians. These supervisory responsibilities usually include training others in some capacity. The average reference librarian usually does not fully comprehend this role in training, either as a recipient or as a facilitator for others. This chapter describes the role of training in preparing reference staff to provide effective service.

Most of the professional library literature about reference education focuses on library school education, but "the overwhelming preponderance of reference education, as it is actually *acquired* by North American librarians, goes on outside the accredited library schools and very little indeed has been written about it."[3] It was not until the use of para-professionals in reference service became more popular, and the results of unobtrusive testing (that only 55 percent of factual reference questions are accurately answered) shook the complacency of the profession's confidence in its ability to provide reference services, that more attention was paid to formal, on-the-job training in reference services.

When reference departments rely only on informal apprenticeships, serious gaps in reference staff training occur. Commonly, trainees, whether new reference librarians, reference assistants, student shelvers, or volunteers, learn a few specific tasks and never understand the rationale for what they are doing or how these tasks fit into the overall mission of the library. Employees not only need to be trained in specific skill areas related to their direct responsibilities, but also must have a knowledge base broad enough to understand the larger context. A broad knowledge base also allows them to learn new skills which they need to respond to the rapidly changing environment of reference and information services.

Today's reference staff are expected to handle changes that occur with increasing frequency. Reference personnel must live with uncertainty and must adapt to new management styles, changing library patron demands, and advances in technology. Adaptability is extremely important for reference librarians. Unless training ensures that librarians are committed to the value of reference service, are able to provide instruction to patrons regarding available services, and are flexible in responding to changes, reference librarians will be limited to using traditional tools, and they will not be able to approach reference service in the context of changed user needs or new technologies.[4]

The terms *training*, *education*, and *development* are often used interchangeably. Leonard Nadler introduced the term *human resource development* in 1969, and defined it as "organized learning experiences in a definite time period to increase the possibility of improving job performance or growth."[5] He went on to make fine distinctions between training, education, and development, which Suellyn Hunt further clarified for librarians: "Training = job-related learning experiences; Education = individual-related learning experiences; Development = organizational-related learning experiences."[6] The various aspects of these three activities are explored in this chapter.

Orientation

All staff members, whether part-time, temporary workers, or experienced individuals who plan to stay for a while, need *orientation*, or an introduction to the job environment. *Staff orientation* is "an initial training process designed to acquaint new employees with various aspects of the organization, including established goals, policies, and procedures; the physical environment; other personnel and working relationships, job duties and responsibilities; and fringe benefits."[7] Typically, this type of training is not transferable to another setting, and provides little that employees could use if they took jobs in other libraries. Box 7.1 provides an example of an orientation program.

Orientation provides a sense of support, defines the employee's singular role in the library, and establishes the individual as a part of the team. Dorothy Jones stressed that the training of new librarians should address the political setting, the work organization of the department, the details of each task, and the path to promotion and job retention.[8] The orientation program's ultimate goal is to promote a feeling of self-worth, a sense of belonging, an attitude of pride and confidence in both self and the library, and a desire to succeed. One objective should be to address typical issues and answer typical questions before they cause frustration or inhibit productivity. Enculturation should be a part of orientation programs: communicating the culture, expectations for dress and behavior (both the formal and the informal rules of behavior), and the importance of each individual in the organization.

7.1
General Orientation Checklist

Employee's Name:

Weeks 1-2

Orientation to Reference Department

1. Meet with library personnel office representative

2. Meet with trainer to cover such things as training plan schedule, employee's work area, review position's duties based on job description, and review job conditions and benefits: hours, vacations, sick leave, etc.

3. Organization and goals of Reference Department

   Reading material, such as New Employee Orientation Packet: IV. Reference, Reference Department Policies and Procedures Manual, and last year's departmental annual report

   Explanation of Reference's mission, goals, and expectations

4. Tour of Reference, introduction to each staff member below: (list departmental members, with job titles or area of responsibility)

   Location of important files or reading materials such as meeting minutes and staff newsletter

Orientation to Public Services

1. Read New Employee Orientation Packet: III. Public Services

2. Meet with assistant to head of public services

   — introduction to Public Services mission, goals, and policies

3. Tour of Public Services:

   — introduction to key staff, including heads of documents, circulation, and interlibrary loan

4. Location of facilities, files, etc.; including Photoservices and Microforms

Weeks 3-4

Orientation to General Library System

1. Read New Employee Orientation Packet: II. The General Library and Library Brochure

2. Tour of Main Library, Branch Library I, and Branch Library II

3. New Employee Coffee

Orientation to the Campus/Community

1. Read New Employee Orientation Packet: I. The Campus/Community

2. Attend the Campus Personnel Office's new employee orientation session

   — Adapted from worksheets provided in
   Painlessly Preparing Personalized Training Plans[9]

Socialization is also an important aspect of the orientation session. Employees need time to get acquainted with coworkers in an informal setting, to discuss their activities in an unstructured environment, and to reflect on and absorb what they have already been told. In any training program, reference staff, as well as staff in other departments with which the trainee comes in daily contact, should be formally introduced, but they should also have some opportunity to meet on a less formal basis, such as a coffee hour or other informal gathering. This is particularly important for reference staff who must work together as a team.

Orientation is only the first step in a continuing process. A positive, upbeat orientation program extending over a period of several weeks or even months can be very effective in helping the new employee to become an efficient, productive member of the library staff.[10] An effective period of induction will help the new staff member become more receptive to continuing training, absorb the details of the job, become a better team player, and feel comfortable in the new position.

Basic Training: Learning the Essentials

Basic *training* in job requirements is mainly concerned with helping staff members learn basic job skills, but it also covers some skills that employees may be able to take to other jobs. The *ALA Glossary* defines training as "the process of developing the knowledge, skills, and attitudes needed by employees to perform their duties effectively and to meet the expectations and goals of the organization. This diverse process, which may be performed by supervisors, fellow employees, and personnel officers, involves planning, preparation, execution, and evaluation."[11]

Defining Competencies

If supervisors fail to define performance expectations, employees will establish their own acceptable performance levels, either individually or as a group. Studies have shown that employees set unofficial guidelines for productivity for the group.[12] Staff members will observe colleagues and draw their own conclusions regarding what kind of behavior is expected.

The mutual development of performance expectations and objectives will avoid hidden expectations or standards. If clear standards and a specific model of performance are described, individuals will know what is expected of them and how they are to be evaluated. If librarians, or any group of library workers, are asked to participate in establishing these objectives, the objectives are more likely to be accepted by the group.

After a consensus of what constitutes adequate performance has been established, the next important step is to write a competency description, which describes the correct performance of a job and delineates behaviors that signal when it is done right. A *competency* is a person's knowledge, skills, or attitudes that enable him or her to function satisfactorily in a work situation, either alone or with others.

A number of competencies necessary for effective reference service have been identified. In a project designed to explore the environment in which information professionals work, to identify and define the competencies needed to work in that environment, and to stimulate discussion about the educational process, King Research, Inc. listed reference competencies generic to all work settings. Some attitudes identified include: like to help people, sensitive to others' needs, supportive of coworkers, patience, curiosity, and service orientation.[13] On a much more specific level, Ralph Gers and Lillie Seward listed minimum required behaviors in a reference interview, including: smiles, makes eye contact, gives friendly verbal greeting, is at the same eye level as patron in setting the tone of the interview.[14]

The UCLA Biomedical Library developed a training program for library school students involved in an internship program. Two separate components were identified: reference desk and online searching. The desk component included ten objectives; the first one, and its eight specific competencies identifying the relevant knowledge, skills, and attitudes, are listed in box 7.2.

■ ══ ■

7.2
UCLA Biomedical Library Reference Desk Competencies

Reference Desk Objective One

Conduct an effective reference interview, analyzing information needs, evaluating potential information sources, and providing appropriate direction to sources satisfying the user's request.

Competencies

1. Establish a working rapport with requesters, expressing interest in the requester's information need, and promoting confidence in the student's ability to answer the requester's need;

2. Analyze the requester's information needs by distinguishing each subject component and determining the logical relationship between components;

3. Determine the likely format(s) of requested information based upon the organizational structure of scientific literature;

4. Determine appropriate reference sources by comparing scope, arrangement, access points, and publication characteristics;

5. Determine the requester's level of library experience and the appropriate technical level of information required;

6. Select the most appropriate search strategy based on the above competencies, available resources, time constraints, costs, and the required amount of information;

7. Relate perspective and background on the choice of reference tools to the requester so that she/he understands why as well as how to use the most appropriate tool; and

8. Promote a satisfactory answer to each reference query by accompanying the requester through the initial step(s) of the search, encouraging additional questions, and providing follow up whenever possible.

— From Roberta Walters and Susan Barnes
"Goals, Objectives, and Competencies for Reference Service"[15]
Copyright by and reprinted with permission
of the Medical Library Association.

Some other reference competencies can be derived from the various functions performed by reference librarians. In the reference interview, reference staff need to have excellent communication skills, including listening, instructing others, or giving clear directions. When answering questions, librarians must know about available reference sources, be able to find proper sources to answer the question, be familiar with the library's collection, and use appropriate technology. Although these are only a few of the functions that reference librarians perform, they need to be competent in these areas.[16]

Assessing Training Needs

Reference departments frequently hire new staff members. Since no department has unlimited time or funds to train, it needs to determine how to get the most from training. Therefore, it is essential to conduct needs assessments. Needs assessment is important in order to plan, manage, and allocate scarce training dollars, as well as to evaluate training results. Training needs are competencies required or desired that have not yet been developed. Training should never be conducted without identifying its purpose or need.

There has been a great deal of discussion about what reference librarians need to know, from a general liberal arts and sciences background that gives a basis of knowledge to comprehensive knowledge of reference sources. A public service attitude, communication skills, teaching ability, an ability to evaluate information, a knowledge of the structure of literature, and the ability to formulate search strategies effectively are all aspects of reference service that most reference librarians would include as requirements.

Analyzing what goes on at the reference or information desk can be a good beginning for identifying needs of reference librarians or paraprofessionals. Reference interview techniques; knowledge of reference sources; ability to manipulate online and card catalogs, local files, CD-ROM stations, or online databases; and working as a team with colleagues, sharing knowledge in a constructive way, are all areas in which any staff member who works the reference or information desk should be competent. While analysis of reference desk activities is a good method for identifying basic training needs for new reference desk workers, many other techniques are available.[17]

Interviews, either with individuals or in groups, are particularly useful in determining the needs of experienced librarians.[18] From interviews, it may be determined that librarians have particular ongoing training needs, such as further practice in asking open-ended questions and achieving closure in the reference interview. Other areas in which experienced personnel generally identify training needs are in using new equipment or systems, learning new sources and tools, and reviewing little-used reference sources.

When skill deficiencies exist, certain questions must be answered to determine the best course of action. If the job is one the employee used to do, have procedures changed? If not, then feedback and practice may be the answer. If procedures have changed or it is a new job, then procedures may be simplified, training may be done on the job, or formal training may have to be arranged. If there is no skill deficiency, then the obstacles to adequate performance must be examined and corrected. One obstacle may be that procedures are unrealistic or have not been clearly communicated. Creating practice sessions, a job aid, or finding guide, or combining them, can be a more practical approach to helping people to perform complex tasks that are infrequently used. Some performance problems are associated with environmental or attitudinal factors that prevent or discourage optimum performance; not all deficiencies in performance can be addressed with training. Other techniques, such as providing feedback on observed behaviors or planning practice sessions, can also be used to improve performance at the reference desk.

7.3

Is This a Training Problem?

A large university reference department provides occasional reference assistance in using the library's collection of British Parliamentary papers. The staff has received training, which consists of reviewing the types of access tools, discussing formats, and examining a bibliography prepared by an experienced librarian. One particular staff member has trouble dealing with these questions. She ordinarily panics and turns to the person who prepared the bibliography. When that person is not available, she can generally muddle through to answer the question. Is this a training problem? What are the obstacles to adequate performance?

Writing Objectives for Training

If training objectives are to be useful, they must describe the kind of performance that will be accepted as evidence that the learner has mastered a particular task. This definition by behavior is used to measure whether the trainees have achieved the goal of the training and whether the training is successful.

There are three kinds of objectives: acquiring knowledge, learning skills, and reinforcing attitudes. Examples of knowledge in the reference setting include information and understanding about the reference collection, general collection, library services, and policies. Skills of reference librarians include the ability to translate that knowledge into performing tasks such as conducting reference interviews, instructing users, and communicating in a clear and concise way. Attitudes such as commitment and motivation are observable in the behavior of the reference librarian.[19]

For training as for bibliographic instruction (see chapter 6), in order for objectives to be useful, three elements are necessary: performance, conditions, and criterion.[20] Performance describes what is to be done—what the trainee should be able to do. Conditions describe the situation and the kinds of tools that can be used. Criterion describes the quality and quantity of work expected and the time allowed to complete the job. In reference work, this means the quality of service, including accuracy and completeness.

Selecting Methods

Selection of the most suitable instructional strategy is based on several considerations. One of the most important is congruency with the stated training objective. The strategy should recognize the need for trainees to respond and to receive feedback, should adapt to individuals' different learning styles, and should approximate what happens on the job. Factors that restrict the choice of strategy include the instructor's level of skill, the size of the group, costs, time, and equipment available.

Some methods are more suitable than others in helping trainees attain the intended objective. Objectives that stress knowledge acquisition, such as "describe the structure of biological literature," are most appropriately reached through lecture, discussion, and assigned readings. Lectures and films require only that people listen and watch, while programmed texts and computer-aided instruction are specifically designed to require that a choice be made before the trainee can move to the next question, page, or screen. Research has shown that programmed texts are the first choice of trainers for knowledge retention.[21]

Skills generally cannot be learned and applied without some sort of practice. While the general concepts behind the application of skills, such as the steps involved in the reference interview, can be learned through lectures, demonstrations, or other passive forms of teaching, reference staff must use a skill if they are to apply it consistently. Role playing, in which situations are outlined and individuals assume roles to try out behaviors in a realistic manner, is one technique that simulates the job environment. Other methods that simulate job behavior include case studies, management games, practice sessions, and workshops. Often, reference departments compile questions which have really been asked at their desks and assign trainees to identify sources to answer these questions.[22] If the training objective is to select an appropriate search strategy to find a known item in the online catalog, effective methods might include programmed instruction, or a combination of reading, lecture, and discussion, as well as practice sessions. Because this objective requires that a choice be made, a method requiring a response will be more effective.

The best training promotes self-discovery, recognizing that "the most important things cannot be taught but must be discovered and appropriated for oneself."[23] As an ancient proverb puts it: "Tell me, I forget. Show me, I remember. Involve me, I understand." Adults learn best with active involvement, by solving realistic problems. If adults work things out for themselves, they are more likely to be able to work out similar problems on the job. Active learning promotes the use of ingenuity and imagination rather than performance of a task in a set manner. Problem-solving skills can be learned effectively in this way, using case studies or in-basket exercises to simulate decisions that must be made on the job.

Attitudes can be influenced in a variety of ways, and experts differ in the approaches they suggest. With adults, interaction again is important, so sensitivity training, role playing, and discussion groups are useful means of changing attitudes. Trigger videos, or short episodes used to stimulate or trigger discussion, can raise a large number of issues, including sexual harassment, handling aggression or other problems, or behaviors that affect the image of the library.[24]

The availability or lack of experienced trainers, instructional space, facilities, equipment, and materials can do much to facilitate or hinder the training process, and all influence the choice of instructional strategy. The time and costs of development, the size of the group, and the learning styles of the trainee population also restrict the choices the trainer can make. A number of training experts have written excellent guides to facilitate selection of training methods for the new trainer.[25] Bibliographic instruction experts have also identified approaches to teaching library skills to patrons; these approaches transfer well to training situations.

Facilitating Retention of Skills

In learning almost any skill, people go through an awkward phase when the newly acquired skill does not feel natural and does not achieve results. This period, called the "results dip" or "incorporation lag," is particularly difficult.[26] Initially, when reference librarians attempt to substitute a new behavior for an old one, it feels uncomfortable and results suffer. Some studies have found that up to 87 percent of the skills actually acquired by a training program may be lost if attention is not paid to making sure that these skills are retained.[27] Combating the problem of transferring learned skills to the job environment can take several forms, both during the training itself and back on the job.

Techniques that simulate the behavior used on the job are more likely to teach skills that will actually be used on the job. The training program itself should include a sufficient amount of time to practice, which may be as much as a third of the instruction time.[28] Practice away from the job provides an opportunity to fail in a controlled environment without the normal consequences, a frame of reference for tasks to be performed, and an ability to apply new skills learned more easily and readily.

Role plays, while not a particular favorite with trainees, continue to be one of the best approaches to allow the learner to take part in a realistic, but simulated, and therefore nonthreatening, situation. Role plays are excellent ways to demonstrate appropriate techniques to use with problem patrons and in question negotiation. Role plays in isolation do not produce skilled performers. They do, however, help ensure that trainees learn the steps appropriate for skilled performance.

Drills, or short, repetitive exercises, can be used to master skills in small steps. As skills are practiced under a variety of circumstances, the trainee's ability to perform consistently improves. During these drills, trainees function as coaches for each other, helping to critique as each element or move is practiced and then combined into a series of moves. Drilling then provides confidence and "confidence builds 'ownership' of the skill. And ownership must occur *during* the training course in order for the skill to transfer to the real job."[29]

There are several other techniques which can be used during the training session to facilitate retention of skills learned. Action plans, where the participants reflect on program content and write goals of intended implementation, are useful techniques for maintaining behavior. These might take the form of a letter to oneself or an ideas-and-applications notebook. Other activities which can be incorporated into training sessions include guided practicing (as opposed to turning trainees loose for independent practice), and question-and-answer sessions which involve some sort of systematic pattern to include everyone.

One of the most important methods of facilitating retention of skills on the job is feedback. There are two basic types of feedback. The first recognizes good work, general competence, or exemplary performance, and encourages employees to keep up the good work. This kind of feedback is important in maintaining skill levels, because behaviors can lapse through lack of reinforcement. Addressing the upkeep of these strengths is as important as fixing problems. The other kind of feedback is improvement feedback, which sends the message that change is needed. This feedback calls attention to poor work, incompetence, or problem behavior.

Effective feedback is immediate, clear, accurate, specific, and positive. Behaviors should be reinforced as quickly as possible. Trainees need to be informed of the trainer's awareness of their behavior as soon as it happens, through attention, recognition, or praise. Negative feedback is better than no feedback at all, but positive feedback produces the best results. Employees tend to remember longest what they hear first and last in a message, and are more likely to apply suggestions if the feedback is personal and private. Approval of or agreement with ideas and behavior is communicated by the absence of feedback, so it is very important for people to be informed when their behaviors are not appropriate.

■ ══ ■

7.4   ?

Giving Effective Feedback

Mary, a new reference assistant, is handling the reference desk while the reference librarians are in an extended meeting. An abusive patron calls on the phone and demands to speak to a reference librarian. Mary tells the patron that none are available, and asks if she can help in any way. He curtly says no and continues to be abusive without actually swearing. Mary hangs up.

When the reference librarians return from their meeting, the patron immediately calls the reference head. After taking the call, John, the reference head, calls Mary into his office and says, "I hear you hung up on one of our patrons; tell me about it." Mary relates the story in detail. John says, "I think you did the right thing. No one should have to put up with that kind of abuse. However, based on what you told me, I think there may have been a better way to handle the situation. What do you think it might be?"

Was this feedback effective?

There are several ways to provide feedback on the job. Performance can be examined through personal diaries and self-reporting by individuals; through observations and interviews with supervisors, either informally or in a performance appraisal; or through buddy systems, support groups, coaching, or job aids. Very few of these methods have been reported as having been applied in reference settings. Coaching, which is basically one-on-one counseling, is one technique that has been used to provide feedback on reference staff performance in reference interviews, notably in public libraries. Coaching is one of the best ways to make sure that newly learned skills are transferred and maintained on the job, but it is a feedback technique that has only recently been applied in reference situations.

Alternatives to giving feedback include review sessions, which give trainees opportunities to refine and polish skills learned and encourage continued use of the skill; further practice time, such as that provided by database vendors who give free time or reduced rates on selected databases; or the use of job aids. The use of informational job aids or performance aids helps to transfer skills learned in training. The idea behind job aids is to eliminate the need for people to remember details, by providing assistance in the form of checklists, reference manuals, flowcharts, computer databases, templates for keyboards or telephones, and so on.[30] These performance aids give trainees a better chance to use new skills by providing the minimal guidance which is so badly needed in the early stages of attempting to apply a newly learned skill on the job.

Evaluating Training

Without evaluation, it is impossible to know whether the training program has done what it was designed to do. Has the performance of the reference staff member improved? If so, is it because of the training program? It is important to build evaluation into the program from the very beginning.

Who Evaluates? Experts suggest that evaluation be done by as many people as possible, to eliminate biases. This means that the supervisor, the trainer (if he or she is not also the supervisor), the employee who received the training, coworkers, and outsiders (who could be patrons) may be involved in evaluation.

Otherwise-excellent staff development programs often fail to provide built-in opportunities for participants' self-assessment. Thomas Shaughnessy argues that "staff development programs which include a self-assessment component should focus on providing each participant with the tools and materials necessary for the individual to test himself or herself and to score the test,"[31] in order to ease staff anxiety concerning test results and to increase accuracy of results. Videotaping has been suggested as "a useful, and surprisingly comfortable, self-evaluation technique, because it captures actions in context otherwise lost to the person acting."[32] The results of self-evaluations are difficult to validate, however, and should be used in conjunction with other approaches.

William Young believes that peers working together at a reference desk are in the best position to judge reference behaviors, and that this is the most promising and realistic approach to evaluating reference desk performance.[33] Behaviorally anchored rating scales (BARS) are frequently used to assist in defining degrees of performance on the job. Several libraries have used these satisfactorily. Most have extracted behaviors, skills, and knowledge from a service standard to create a checklist of desirable behaviors, such as a librarian asking for assistance in certain situations or suggesting alternative sources of information to the patron.[34] Figure 7.1 shows behaviorally anchored rating scales which are a portion of an instrument used in peer evaluations of an information desk staff in an academic library.

II. Interactions with Users	Seldom	Not Frequ. Enough	Sometimes	Frequently	Almost all the time	Cannot Respond
Maintains a professional posture						
1. Looks alert, confident, and interested						
2. Manifests openness (e.g., is approachable)						
3. Works to minimize initial barrier between patron and staff member						
4. Establishes good eye contact (e.g., looks up as patron approaches desk)						
Desk Service Priorities						
1. Gets people started						
2. Acknowledges the presence of users not yet served						
Effective Communication						
1. Uses good grammar						
2. Gears expression to user's understanding						
3. Avoids unexplained or unnecessary jargon						
4. Speaks in positive, relaxed, appropriately loud tone of voice						
Helps Shape Questions						
1. Listens well						
2. Seeks definitions						

Fig. 7.1. A portion of an instrument used in peer evaluations by staff at an information desk.

The supervisor's evaluation is the most subjective, and can be difficult to rely on in training situations, unless testing, observation, or interviews accompany it. Also, since supervisors have a number of other areas of job performance to attend to, the particular performance concerned with training may be difficult for them to determine.

Although library users' consistently high ranking of satisfaction with reference services calls into doubt their ability to evaluate reference performance,[35] it has been suggested that library users can evaluate librarians' attitudes, degree of self-confidence, and ability to instruct patrons in the use of reference sources.[36]

What Is Evaluated and How? Evaluating training can be very difficult. Decisions have to be made, not only concerning how to evaluate, but also on what can and should be evaluated. Four different levels can be evaluated in a training program: reactions, learning, job behavior, and results.[37]

Although attendees do not necessarily have to enjoy a session, it is important that a positive reaction to the training sessions occur if learning is to take place. A positive reaction to training is a precondition to learning, but it is not a guarantee that learning will transpire. Participants must feel a commitment to training—must feel it is valuable—in order to learn. Most often, reactions are assessed by rating scales for individual sessions. Verbal comments or nonverbal cues can also be observed. In order to supplement the attendees' comments, the supervisor or an observer should also record comments.

Learning—the acquisition of knowledge, skills, or attitudes—within the training context can be tested through programmed instruction, objective tests, essays, and pen-and-pencil tests. Testing may also be built into the training, such as judgment of performance in practice sessions or in-class exercises. In order to determine if skill improvement can indeed be attributed to the training program or if it results from outside influences, training experts recommend the use of pre-tests, post-tests, and control groups.[38] All those attending a training session, as well as those in a control group which does not receive training, are given a pre-test to see what skills and knowledge they already possess. After a period of time has elapsed since training was administered, both groups are again tested to see if skills improved through training, or merely from working on the job. Most librarians, of course, have difficulty finding the time to administer tests in this way.

Although trainees may learn the skills and be able to perform them in the training session, they may not be able to perform them on the job. If the trainee did achieve the criterion during training sessions, the application exercises may not have been similar to the on-the-job environment. For example, reference assistants may be able to search the online catalog correctly when given examples with the author and title identified, but may not be able to do so effectively on the job because they are unable to identify those key items from a citation that does not have these elements labeled. The evaluation itself can affect the result of training, so if trainers or supervisors wish to reinforce that training, they should use obtrusive methods, or testing that is known to the trainee. If it is important that outside factors be limited, unobtrusive methods, in which the trainees do not know they are being tested, should be used. Terry Weech and Herbert Goldhor have shown that reference librarians correctly answer a larger proportion of reference questions when they know they are being evaluated.[39] Chapter 8 discusses the advantages and disadvantages of unobtrusive and obtrusive methods in more detail.

When on-the-job benefits of training programs are hard to measure or are unclear, or when outcomes are not adequately measured with simple quantitative methods, as is the case in reference librarianship, interviews can be useful. Interviews and group discussions are more informal ways of assessing the effectiveness of a training program.[40]

The final results, or benefit to the organization, should be the last stage of evaluation. Benefits such as users' satisfaction with library service, or their ability to access needed information, are difficult to measure in themselves. If the goal is to determine the effect that training has had on these outcomes, it becomes even more complicated; for this reason, libraries rarely evaluate at this level.[41]

Beyond "Boot Camp":
Continual Learning

Training for reference staff should be a continuous process that is never really finished. Although the library can complete its induction phase to orient new staff members and finish on-the-job training for basic job skills, there is a constant need for staff to update their professional knowledge. Technological obsolescence can occur when individual competence holds constant while professional standards advance.[42]

There are many areas in which reference librarians need continual updating. New discoveries are made every day, and events occurring worldwide cause the world's knowledge to be in constant flux. The sources which record this information and tools which provide access to these sources are revised and updated, or appear in different forms. People are affected by these events and discoveries, so their needs, interests, and expectations change also. Reference librarians will always have to keep up with new information, new reference sources and access tools, and the changing needs of their patrons.[43]

Charles Bunge discussed methods which reference librarians use to update their reference knowledge and skills. The most frequently mentioned strategy is reading professional literature, followed by reference staff meetings, and staff sharing. He also mentioned attendance at conferences, workshops, and other meetings outside the individual's library as much-used methods for reference librarians.[44]

Two different approaches to lifelong learning can be identified. While both approaches use similar methods, and have similar purposes of improving the competence of individuals, each has a different focus. *Staff development* is organizationally centered and directed, while *continuing education* is individually centered and directed. They are, however, not mutually exclusive, and are in fact complementary approaches. Bunge's study of the updating strategies used by reference librarians pointed out that both approaches are actually beneficial in helping staff members avoid technological obsolescence, develop expertise and knowledge in specialized areas, and widen their experience and practical knowledge.

Staff development's goal is to improve the organization's effectiveness, or service to its patrons, by increasing the competence of its staff. Much of the training that has been discussed up to this point is encompassed by the term *staff development*; orientation and on-the-job training are certainly included. The library has a responsibility to improve staff performance, and it is to the library's benefit to produce employees who are committed to the library.

Merely providing the training for basic job skills is not enough. The library administration should provide continual training for reference librarians which develops and maintains competence, updates basic professional foundations, and introduces new concepts. Staff development should emphasize attitude shaping, people-handling skills, dealing with patron feelings, listening skills, and thinking on one's feet. The library should also help reference librarians deal with stress that accompanies any kind of front-line position. Tina Roose pointed out that "reference librarians are among the few researchers of this world who are expected to perform with an audience in the midst of many other demands and distractions."[45]

■ ═══ ■

7.5

Reference Service as Combat: Fighting Job Stress

Some experts suggest that jobs with a high emotional labor content, jobs where the performer's persona goes on the line time and time again at the customer interface, should be treated as combat. And like combat soldiers, people in high-stress service jobs need to be rotated off the front line frequently — and sometimes permanently. As one expert puts it, "In Vietnam we *knew*, come hell or high water, that after so many months, we were out of there. You need to do that for service people. They have to know there is a light at the end of that tunnel — and it isn't from an oncoming train."

— Ron Zemke
"Contact!"[46]

Burnout, a concept introduced in chapter 1, is not a problem unique to reference service providers, but it is very intense and pervasive.[47] It is important to note that the four stages of burnout — enthusiasm, stagnation, frustration, and apathy — start with enthusiasm. The challenge to libraries is to rekindle the fire of enthusiasm and not let it burn out, but to feed it with challenges, new environments, new information, and new techniques. Staff development and continuing education can provide the kindling for the fire by presenting new information and techniques of approaching the reference interview. When someone is removed from the desk, even temporarily, to attend a development activity, it gives that person breathing room and a chance to reflect upon what has happened. The sessions are intended to provide new insights into desk service, and new ways of coping with stress by improving knowledge, skills, or attitudes. Staff development programs that promote job rotation and which help service providers see their jobs as playing a role for the organization provide concrete assistance with job burnout and stress.

Individuals must also accept some of the responsibility for fueling the fire, by planning their own continuing education activities. Continuing education activities center on the individual's personal interests, and include those that promote personal development and growth as an individual, whether to increase personal job satisfaction or to prepare for a promotion.

Continuing education includes learning experiences which will (a) introduce new concepts and skills, (b) update basic professional foundations, (c) refresh or reemphasize aspects of professional training, (d) provide additional competencies to make career advancement or change possible, and (e) furnish the individual with an overview of his or her profession as a changing and evolving discipline.[48]

Opportunities for continuing education originate from many different sources. Courses offered at local junior colleges, colleges, or universities range from computer and software management courses and supervisory and teaching skills to subject-related topics which may or may not lead to an advanced degree. Outside groups, such as online database vendors, often offer basic and advanced training in the use of their software, with refresher courses and updates on specific databases. Library professional organizations make many contributions to continuing education for reference librarians. Local interest groups often provide forums for discussing mutual problems, challenges, and potential solutions with peers. State associations sponsor conferences, workshops, and programs in more convenient locations than many nationally sponsored programs. The American Library Association, as well as associations of special groups, provides numerous activities to promote the individual reference librarian's development (see box 7.6).

■ ══ ■

7.6

Selected American Library Association (ALA) Groups
Emphasizing Staff Development and Continuing Education

ALA Subcommittee on Continuing Education
> Develops policies and standards on continuing education within the association.

ALA Subcommittee on Education for Support Staff Issues
> Identifies issues relating to basic job preparation and continuing education for support staff.

Association of College and Research Libraries, Staff Development Officers of Large Research Libraries Discussion Group
> Provides a forum for discussion of mutual concerns on staff development.

Continuing Library Education Network and Exchange Round Table
> Provides a forum for those interested in continuing library education, training, and staff development.

Library Administration and Management Association Personnel Administration Section, Staff Development
> Facilitates and promotes effective staff development programs and the exchange of information and research.

Public Library Association

> Community Information Section, Education and Training
>> Promotes and offers learning opportunities in community information services.

> Community Information Section, Service Development
>> Assists libraries to develop and implement community information services and prepares aids for service development, training, and evaluation.

Reference and Adult Services Division, Evaluation of Reference and Adult Services
> Collects and disseminates information concerning evaluation and measurement of reference service.

> Performance Standards for Reference/Information, Librarians Discussion Group
>> Provides a forum for the exchange of information concerning performance issues in reference services.

> Machine Assisted Reference Service, Education and Training of Search Analysts
>> Addresses concerns of educating and training search analysts who use computer-based retrieval systems, including studying alternative methods and techniques.

The ALA Handbook of Organization[49] describes these and other groups more fully.

Conclusion

The results of a thorough and responsive training program which involves the staff in decision making and uses participatory educational methods will be a highly motivated staff who have high morale and good self-esteem, identify with their peers, cope with changes and stress, make fewer mistakes, and solve problems. On the other hand, unplanned, on-the-job training may result in ill-trained, unmotivated employees. There is a danger that necessary skills may not be learned, and also a danger that undesirable methods and approaches will be reinforced and low standards set. "Employees (new or old) learn, whether we wish it or not. If we are disorganized, indifferent, or sloppy in our approach, the employee will absorb the standards. No amount of future lecturing will erase these standards."[50]

Reference librarians have a responsibility to themselves and to the profession to improve their own knowledge, skills, and attitudes which influence their performance at the reference desk. They likewise have an obligation to those they supervise, however few there may be, and whether or not they are graduates of a library school program, to help those individuals improve their performance.

New library school graduates in their first jobs as reference librarians may find themselves in the position of hiring and training student shelvers. They have a responsibility to those students, and to the library, the library's patrons, and the library profession, to do the best job they can in training those students. Perhaps someday one of those shelvers may decide to become a reference paraprofessional or a reference librarian, and will also be committed to developing the skills of every person on the staff to the fullest capacity.

Notes

1. Karl Albrecht and Ron Zemke, *Service America! Doing Business in the New Economy* (Homewood, Ill.: Dow Jones-Irwin, 1985), 129.

2. Marsha D. Broadway and Nathan M. Smith, "Basic Reference Courses in ALA-Accredited Library Schools," *Reference Librarian* 25-26 (1989): 431-48.

3. Samuel Rothstein, "The Making of a Reference Librarian," *Library Trends* 31 (Winter 1983): 388.

4. Sheila D. Creth, *Effective On-the-Job Training: Developing Library Human Resources* (Chicago: American Library Association, 1986), 6.

5. Leonard Nadler, *Handbook of Human Resource Development* (New York: Wiley, 1984), 1.3.

6. Suellyn Hunt, "A Structure and Seven-Step Process for Developing In-House Human Resources Programs," *Bookmark* 41 (Summer 1983): 227.

7. Heartsill Young, ed., *The ALA Glossary of Library and Information Science* (Chicago: American Library Association, 1983), 214.

8. Dorothy E. Jones, "I'd Like You to Meet Our New Librarian: The Initiation and Integration of the Newly Appointed Librarian," *Journal of Academic Librarianship* 14 (September 1988): 222.

9. Donnagene Britt, Patricia Davison, and Judith Levy, eds., *Painlessly Preparing Personalized Training Plans* (Berkeley, Calif.: University of California Library, April 1982), 7-9.

10. Mary W. Oliver, "Orientation of New Personnel in the Law Library," *Law Library Journal* 65 (May 6, 1972), 140.

11.   Young, *ALA Glossary*, 231.

12.   F. J. Roethlisberger and W. J. Dick, *Management and the Worker* (Cambridge, Mass.: Harvard University Press, 1939), 522.

13.   Jose-Marie Griffiths and Donald W. King, *New Directions in Library and Information Science Education* (White Plains, N.Y.: Knowledge Industry Publications, 1986), 243.

14.   Ralph Gers and Lillie J. Seward, "Improving Reference Performance: Results of a Statewide Study," *Library Journal* 110 (November 1, 1985): 35.

15.   Roberta J. Walters and Susan J. Barnes, "Goals, Objectives, and Competencies for Reference Service: A Training Program at the UCLA Biomedical Library," *Bulletin of the Medical Library Association* 73 (April 1985): 161-63.

16.   For further discussion of areas of competency, see Anne F. Roberts, "Myth: Reference Librarians Can Perform at the Reference Desk Immediately Upon Receipt of MLS. Reality: They Need Training Like Other Professionals," in *Academic Libraries: Myths and Realities. Proceedings of the Third National Conference of the Association of College and Research Libraries* (Chicago: ACRL, 1984), 402.

17.   See Richard B. Johnson, "Determining Training Needs," in *Training and Development Handbook*, eds. Robert L. Craig and Lester Bittel (New York: McGraw-Hill, 1967), 16-33, for a discussion of alternative needs assessment techniques.

18.   Barbara Conroy, "The Structured Group Interview: A Useful Tool for Needs Assessment and Evaluation," *Mountain Plains Journal of Adult Education* 4 (March 1976): 19.

19.   Creth, *Effective On-the-Job Training*, 31.

20.   Robert F. Mager, *Preparing Instructional Objectives*, 2d ed. (Belmont, Calif.: Fearon Publishers, 1975), 21.

21.   John W. Newstrom, "Evaluating the Effectiveness of Training Methods," *Personnel Administrator* 25 (January 1980): 58.

22.   Julian M. Isaacs, "In-service Training for Reference Work," *Library Association Record* 71 (October 1969): 301.

23.   Donald A. Schon, *Educating the Reflective Practitioner: Toward a New Design for Teaching and Learning in the Profession* (San Francisco: Jossey-Bass Publishers, 1987), 92.

24.   Phillipa Dolphin, "Interpersonal Skill Training for Library Staff," *Library Association Record* 88 (March 1986): 134.

25.   Some of the following sources are extremely useful: Chip R. Bell, "Criteria for Selecting Instructional Strategies," *Training and Development Journal* 31 (October 1977): 3-7; Vernon S. Gerlach and Donald P. Ely, *Teaching and Media: A Systematic Approach*, 2d ed. (Englewood Cliffs, N.J.: Prentice Hall, 1980), 420p.; John W. Newstrom, "Selecting Training Methodologies: A Contingency Approach," *Training and Development Journal* 29 (October 1975): 12-16; William R. Tracey, *Designing Training and Development Systems*, 2d rev. ed. (New York: AMACOM, 1984), 503p.; and Marilla D. Svinicki and Barbara A. Schwartz, *Designing Instruction for Library Users: A Practical Guide* (New York: Marcel Dekker, 1988), 249p.

26.   Neil Rackham, "The Coaching Controversy," *Training and Development Journal* 33 (November 1979): 14.

27.   Ibid.

28.   Susan N. Chellino and Richard J. Walker, "Merging Instructional Technology with Management Practices," in *Strengthening Connections Between Education and Performance*, ed. Stanley M. Grabowski (San Francisco: Jossey-Bass Publishers, 1983), 12.

29.   James C. Georges, "Why Soft-Skills Training Doesn't Take," *Training* 25 (April 1988): 46.

30.   Ron Zemke and John Gunkler, "28 Techniques for Transforming Training into Performance," *Training* 22 (April 1985): 62.

31.   Thomas W. Shaughnessy, "Staff Development in Libraries: Why It Frequently Doesn't Take," *Journal of Library Administration* 9 (1988): 7.

32.   Judith Mucci, "Videotape Self-Evaluation in Public Libraries: Experiments in Evaluating Public Service," *RQ* 16 (Fall 1976): 33.

33.   William F. Young, "Methods for Evaluating Reference Desk Performance," *RQ* 25 (Fall 1985): 73.

34.   Diane G. Schwartz and Dottie Eakin, "Reference Service Standards, Performance Criteria, and Evaluation," *Journal of Academic Librarianship* 12 (March 1986): 6; and Mignon S. Adams and Blanche Judd, "Evaluating Reference Librarians Using Goal Analysis as a First Step," *Reference Librarian* 11 (Fall/Winter 1984): 141.

35.   William F. Young, "Evaluating the Reference Librarian," *Reference Librarian* 11 (Fall/Winter 1984): 123-24.

36.   Schwartz and Eakin, "Reference Service Standards," 4-8.

37.   Donald L. Kirkpatrick, "Techniques for Evaluating Training Programs," *Training and Development Journal* 33 (June 1979): 78-92.

38.   A. C. Hamblin, *Evaluation and Control of Training* (London: McGraw-Hill, 1974), 8.

39.   Terry L. Weech and Herbert Goldhor, "Obtrusive Versus Unobtrusive Evaluation of Reference Service in Five Illinois Public Libraries: A Pilot Study," *Library Quarterly* 52 (1982): 305-24.

40.   See Robert O. Brinkerhoff, "The Success Case: A Low-Cost, High Yield Evaluation," *Training and Development Journal* 37 (August 1983): 58-59, 61; and Sumru Erkut and Jacqueline P. Fields, "Focus Groups to the Rescue," *Training and Development Journal* 41 (October 1987): 74.

41.   Kirkpatrick, "Techniques for Evaluating Training Programs," 89.

42.   Elizabeth W. Stone, "Towards a Learning Community," in *Continuing Education for the Library Information Professional*, eds. William G. Asp, Suzanne H. Mahmoodi, Marilyn L. Miller, Peggy O'Donnell, and Elizabeth W. Stone (Hamden, Conn.: Library Professional Publications, 1985), 65.

43.   Charles A. Bunge, "Strategies for Updating Knowledge of Reference Resources and Techniques," *RQ* 21 (Spring 1982): 228.

44.   Ibid., 229-31.

45.   Tina Roose, "Stress at the Reference Desk," *Library Journal* 114 (Sept. 1, 1989): 166.

46.   Ron Zemke, "Contact! Training Employees to Meet the Public," *Training* 23 (August 1986): 44.

47.   See the following articles for discussions of burnout in librarians: Mary Haack, John W. Jones, and Tina Roose, "Occupational Burnout Among Librarians," *Drexel Library Quarterly* 20 (Spring 1984): 46-72; William Miller, "What's Wrong with Reference: Coping with Success and Failure at the Reference Desk," *American Libraries* 15 (May 1984): 303-6, 321-22; Sandra H. Neville, "Job Stress and

Burnout: Occupational Hazards for Service Staff," *College & Research Libraries* 42 (May 1981): 242-47; David S. Ferriero and Kathleen A. Powers, "Burnout at the Reference Desk," *RQ* 21 (Spring 1982): 274-79; Nathan M. Smith and Veneese C. Nelson, "Burnout: A Survey of Academic Reference Librarians," *College & Research Libraries* 44 (May 1983): 245-50; and Nathan M. Smith, Nancy E. Birch, and Maurice Marchant, "Stress, Distress, and Burnout: A Survey of Public Reference Librarians," *Public Libraries* 23 (Fall 1984): 83-85.

48.   Stone, "Towards a Learning Community," 62.

49.   *ALA Handbook of Organization* (Chicago: American Library Association, annual).

50.   Gordon F. Shea, *The New Employee: Developing a Productive Human Resource* (Reading, Mass.: Addison-Wesley, 1981), 61.

Additional Readings

Allan, Ann, and Kathy J. Reynolds. "Performance Problems: A Model for Analysis and Resolution." *Journal of Academic Librarianship* 9 (May 1983): 83-88. Reprinted in *Performance Evaluation: A Management Basic for Librarians*, ed. Jonathan A. Lindsey, 198-208. Phoenix, Ariz.: Oryx Press, 1986.
 Allan and Reynolds describe a flowchart for identifying appropriate solutions to performance problems in libraries. A series of questions helps identify major issues.

Boyer, Laura M., and William C. Theimer, Jr. "The Use and Training of Nonprofessional Personnel at Reference Desks in Selected College and University Libraries." *College & Research Libraries* 36 (May 1975): 193-200.
 Boyer and Theimer conducted a survey on reference staffing and found that while 69 percent of 141 libraries reported using nonprofessionals at reference desks, more than 80 percent of those did not provide formal in-service training.

Britt, Donnagene, Patricia Davison, and Judith Levy, eds. *Painlessly Preparing Personalized Training Plans*. Berkeley, Calif.: University of California Library, April 1982. 24p.
 Developed as an in-house tool, this packet is nevertheless a good starting point for others, as it outlines training procedures. It gives very useful and concise information on writing objectives. Examples are provided.

Casteleyn, Mary. *Planning Library Training Programmes*. London: Andre Deutsch Limited, 1981. 175p.
 Promoting the continual process of training for all library staff members, Casteleyn outlines a continuum, from induction courses through on-the-job training for nonprofessionals, preprofessionals, and newly qualified librarians, to continuing professional training. The duties of a library training officer, the equipment necessary to enhance the successful communication of information, and a checklist for planning training are discussed in some detail.

Conroy, Barbara. *Library Staff Development and Continuing Education: Principles and Practices*. Littleton, Colo.: Libraries Unlimited, 1978. 296p.
 Conroy describes how to plan, implement, and evaluate learning programs. Procedures, practices, and examples are given, with good bibliographies to provide further background reading.

Creth, Sheila D. *Effective On-the-Job Training*. Chicago: American Library Association, 1986. 121p.
 Creth presents a very concise overview of training needs, planning, implementation, and evaluation, with exercises and examples drawn from libraries. The two appendixes are particularly useful, containing excerpts of actual job training plans in libraries for different kinds of positions, and an orientation checklist.

Hunt, Suellyn. "A Structure and Seven-Step Process for Developing In-House Human Resources Programs." *Bookmark* 41 (Summer 1983): 227-32.
Hunt describes the basic plan for an effective on-the-job training program in libraries.

Jones, Dorothy E. "'I'd Like You to Meet Our New Librarian': The Initiation and Integration of the Newly Appointed Librarian." *Journal of Academic Librarianship* 14 (September 1988): 221-24.
Jones discusses the importance of introducing new librarians to the organizational culture, departmental objectives, work organization within the department, task details, and the path to promotion and job retention. She advocates careful preparation for and supportive introduction to the policies, procedures, methods, relationships, and attitudes of each unique situation.

Katz, Bill, ed. "Continuing Education of Reference Librarians," (entire issue). *Reference Librarian* 30 (1990): 1-273.
This issue of *Reference Librarian* covers a range of topics concerning training and continuing education of librarians. Several articles stress the need for adaptability and critical thinking skills.

"A Nexus of Education and Practice: The Residency Program at the University of Michigan Library." *Library Journal* 111 (February 15, 1986): 118-30.
Michigan's residency program is structured to help new graduates develop specialized experience peculiar to a research library environment. The program focuses on current issues, trends, and developments, and offers unique training opportunities rarely presented to professionals with little experience.

Stabler, Karen. "Introductory Training of Academic Reference Librarians: A Survey." *RQ* 26 (Spring 1987): 363-69.
Stabler surveyed 116 newly appointed reference librarians concerning the effectiveness of introductory training programs. The study found that many new reference librarians felt that their orientation programs were poorly organized, and listed the availability of a policies and procedures manual as the most frequent suggestion for improvement.

Tracey, William R. *Designing Training and Development Systems*. Rev. ed. New York: AMACOM, 1984. 503p.
This lengthy and detailed overview of every conceivable aspect of training is particularly useful for writing objectives, selecting appropriate media, and constructing evaluative instruments.

Warren, Malcolm W. *Training for Results: A Systems Approach to the Development of Human Resources in Industry*. Reading, Mass.: Addison-Wesley Publishing Co., 1969. 239p.
Warren's book is a good overall introduction to training that contains particularly good sections on orientation, defining training needs through evaluating present performance and establishing performance standards, selecting training methods, and evaluating training.

Woodard, Beth S. "A Selective Guide to Training Literature for the Reference Librarian/Trainer." *Reference Services Review* 17 (Summer 1989): 41-52.
Selected articles and books of use to reference librarians with training responsibilities are presented. Topics included are establishing an atmosphere that facilitates learning, assessing training needs, defining competent performance, writing clear and specific objectives, selecting methods used in training, maintaining skills and providing feedback, and evaluating the effectiveness of the training program.

EVALUATION OF REFERENCE SERVICES

Introduction

Evaluation of reference services literally means establishment of the *value* of the services offered. Value can sometimes be established in quantitative terms: for example, in information service to businesses, a dollar value is sometimes placed on the information provided.[1] In general, however, evaluation of reference and information services relates to the *quality* of the services, even when that quality cannot easily be measured in quantitative or monetary terms. Improving the quality of services (as opposed to the narrower idea of enhancing the value of services) is the objective of the evaluation of reference service. This chapter outlines techniques that reference librarians can use to establish the quality of their services.

Before examining these techniques in detail, it should be emphasized that quality of service is an everyday, common-sense idea. In fact, library users are continually evaluating the kind of service they receive. It is not too difficult to decide if one has received good service, whether it is in a retail establishment, a restaurant, or a library. Users soon form opinions that some librarians give better service than others, that some libraries are easier to use than others, or that some sources are more reliable than others. Evaluation of reference services can make use of this critical judgment on the part of users to improve the quality of the services.

Managers of reference and information departments are concerned with evaluating the services provided by their departments, but it would be wrong to think of evaluation as strictly a management function. In traditional industrial operations, quality control was typically a separate department, intended to check on the work done by line workers. However, in industry this separation of quality control from production has begun to be supplanted by organizational devices such as quality circles, in which workers suggest ways for improving the quality of the product. Industry has come to recognize that line workers have a primary responsibility for the quality of the product they produce. In professional service as well, separating evaluation from service provision is inappropriate. In recognition of this fact, a number of libraries have experimented with quality circles.[2] Although these experiments have produced some positive results, the implementation of quality circles in libraries has been quite limited.

However, specific organizational devices such as quality circles are not necessary to ensure that library professionals stay constantly concerned about the quality of the service they are providing. James Shedlock wrote that "Most professionals routinely ask themselves, 'Am I giving quality service?' This concern for quality is generally considered a mark of professionalism."[3] A concern with evaluation is an important part of a professional attitude,

171

or a professional approach, to library and information services. Reference and information workers must continually ask themselves (and their coworkers) questions about their work and about the tools they use. Every time a librarian comments on the relative usefulness of a reference work, evaluation occurs. Every time a librarian wonders, "How might I have handled that question better?," an evaluative attitude is displayed. If, on occasion, an information worker asks, "Should we really be answering that kind of question?," a more profound evaluation of service provision is being accomplished.

This professional concern for evaluation can be traced throughout the history of reference librarianship. Reference statistics have probably been kept as long as there have been reference departments. Such statistics provided a means to measure reference services, but more sophisticated means of evaluating reference work were not developed until the 1940s. It is not a coincidence that this period also marked the emergence of program evaluation in a variety of social programs.[4] In 1939, Edward Henry proposed criteria for evaluating reference collections and personnel,[5] and G. L. Gardiner traced empirical studies of reference back to 1943.[6] Large-scale awareness of the importance of reference evaluation really began in the 1960s. Samuel Rothstein played a major role in articulating this awareness in an important article in 1964.[7] Later in that decade, more sophisticated evaluation techniques, such as unobtrusive testing (discussed in more detail later in this chapter), began to evolve, and since then reference librarians have had a variety of ways to evaluate the quality of reference services.

In summary, evaluation is constantly carried out by professionals who are concerned about the services they provide. It is an essential component in a professional attitude toward library and information work. When managers of library and information departments become concerned with evaluation, mechanisms are put in place to channel and direct this concern about the quality of service. Structures for evaluation become part of the formal organization of the department. Procedures are established to carry out the evaluation in a regular and consistent manner, so that quality of service can be compared over time. The national concern for quality that is part of a professional attitude is thus channelled into techniques that accomplish evaluation in efficient and effective ways.

Why Evaluate Reference?

The importance of evaluation of reference and information services can sometimes be taken for granted. Nevertheless, evaluation is a costly activity: it takes resources that might be employed in other ways. One of the most costly aspects of evaluation is the staff time required to accomplish it. A librarian who is evaluating some portion of the collection, or who is analyzing the results of user questionnaires or conducting a community survey, is not available to deal with patrons' queries.

The benefits to be achieved by evaluation must be weighed against these costs. The most important motive for evaluating a library service is to improve the service. It follows that techniques must be used that will provide insights into how service can be improved. It is essential that all evaluation efforts be driven by a serious desire to provide better service to patrons. Evaluation that is not followed by improvement is wasted effort.

A second motive that can justify the effort, and the cost, of evaluation is to manage resources effectively. Both human and physical resources are essential to reference and information service, but there are frequently alternative ways of employing these resources in providing service. For example, it may be possible to use paraprofessional staff instead of professional staff in some aspects of service provision, or it may be possible to substitute a lower cost reference source for an expensive one. Evaluation can provide insights into the most efficient way of running a reference or information service.

Another motivation, one that Samuel Rothstein called a "hidden agenda" in reference evaluation, is political.[8] It is important that those who are responsible for providing funding for reference and information departments be made aware of the benefits achieved by those services. Those who are involved in service provision see evidence of the value of the service daily, as patrons are able to meet their information needs. They may take for granted that the service is worthwhile, and that it should be adequately funded. However, libraries seldom have a surfeit of funds. Instead of taking for granted the benefits of reference and information services, reference workers may be asked to justify their existence with hard data. The techniques of evaluation discussed in this chapter can provide the kind of evidence that will convince funding agencies to make adequate resources available.

What Can Be Evaluated?

The first task facing reference and information departments that want to establish a program of evaluation is to decide what aspects of their services are to be evaluated. One concept that may help in this decision is F. W. Lancaster's distinction between the *inputs* that go into provision of the service, the *outputs* in terms of service actually provided, and the ultimate *outcome* from that service (see box 8.1).[9]

8.1
What Can Be Evaluated?

1. Inputs

    Reference Materials:
        Reference books
        Online and CD-ROM sources

    Staff:
        Reference librarians
        Reference assistants

2. Outputs

    Factual questions answered (correctly, promptly)

    Instruction given

    Assistance in using library provided

3. Outcomes

    Information needs satisfied

    Library skills and knowledge improved

In many reference and information departments, programs may already exist to evaluate some of the *inputs*: the components that go into providing reference services. In particular, there may be established mechanisms for evaluating the text resources (the reference materials) in terms of their quality and coverage, and the human resources (the reference workers) in terms of their performance in providing reference services. This evaluation of resources constitutes the first level of evaluation.

However, making use of high-quality resources does not necessarily guarantee that high-quality services will be provided. A number of mechanisms to measure directly the quality of services (the *outputs*) have been tested in a variety of libraries. Typically, these measures focus on the reference transaction, in which questions are answered or instruction and assistance are provided. Evaluation of reference transactions constitutes the second level of evaluation.

Finally, there is a third level of evaluation. Even if the service is shown to be using high-quality resources (the first level), and to be doing a good job of dealing with individual transactions (the second level), the service as a whole may not be meeting the needs of its user community in an effective and efficient manner. Again, mechanisms exist that enable a library to assess the extent to which it is meeting the information needs of its community: in other words, the *outcome* of the service.

The section on evaluation techniques provides a more detailed outline of the ways librarians can assess the quality of their reference service at each of these three levels.

Standards
for Reference Service

An important question in establishing a program of evaluation for reference services relates to the standards against which service can be judged. In some industries, for example, it is possible to establish standard times for the various tasks involved in manufacturing products. These standards enable productivity to be measured. Similarly, quantitative standards can be established for the quality of the manufacturing (for example, machining a part to within one one-thousandth of an inch). In some library tasks, similar productivity and quality standards can be established; for example, standard times for filing a card or standards of accuracy for entering a record into a database. Because of the nature of the work, though, it is difficult to establish quantitative standards for reference work. Most reference librarians would agree that service should be accurate and complete, and that patrons' information needs should be satisfied. The difficulty comes in establishing a quantitative standard for each of these characteristics. Should accuracy attain 90 percent or 95 percent? Should the standard for patron satisfaction be set at 95 percent or 99 percent? Even when evaluation methods are used for measuring the accuracy of responses or the satisfaction of patrons, there is no clear way of establishing an accepted minimum standard of performance.

A number of standards for reference service have been devised, both by associations concerned with reference service, and by state and regional authorities.[10] These are usually very general in nature, and although they may sometimes suggest quantitative goals, they seldom provide a basis for detailed evaluation of a particular reference service. This means that libraries must set their own standards for quality reference service. One way of establishing such standards is to examine the results obtained by similar libraries. This in turn implies that similar or identical evaluation techniques must be used by a number of libraries, so that the results can be compared. In the absence of detailed standards for reference service, these comparative data are very important in understanding the significance of the results of evaluation.

8.2
Standards for Reference Service

The Ohio Public Libraries Standards for Reference Service has a provision that 80 percent of all reference questions should be answered on the same day. How do you suppose that percentage was chosen as a standard? Suppose a library attains a same-day response rate of 75 percent. Does it follow that the library is providing inadequate service? Suppose a library provides a same-day response rate of 90 percent. Does this mean that the librarians need not be concerned about improving the timeliness of their service? How would you go about evaluating the service of a public library reference department to see if the standard was reached?

Techniques of Evaluation

The techniques to be used in evaluation will vary depending on what is to be evaluated, the goals of the evaluation, and who is performing the evaluation. Although these techniques are not mutually exclusive – in fact, use of several techniques is often quite beneficial – they are distinguishable, and serve different purposes.

Level 1: Evaluation of Resources

Evaluation of Reference Collections. In chapter 11, criteria for the selection of high-quality reference materials are introduced. A reference collection should consist of the very best tools the library can afford. Nevertheless, selecting high-quality materials is not enough to ensure that the collection as a whole is of high quality. The quality and usefulness of materials must be assessed on a regular basis after they have been added to the collection. There are three criteria that are useful in this ongoing evaluation of reference collections: the extent to which the information included is up-to-date, the use that is made of the materials, and the reputation of the materials as indicated by their inclusion in standard lists (see box 8.3, page 176).

The first criterion for reference collection evaluation, the extent to which the materials are up-to-date, is important because the quality of reference materials can change over time. The information they contain may have been accurate when they were acquired, but now be incorrect. Older reference tools may be superseded by subsequent titles. Superseded editions are candidates for removal from the collection, and all older materials should be carefully scrutinized to ensure that the information they present is still accurate and useful.

The second criterion, the usefulness of the materials in the collection, is more general than the first criterion, and more difficult to implement. In addition to scanning the collection to ascertain the recency of its materials, it is possible to measure directly the usefulness of titles in the reference collection. A tally of materials being reshelved can be used to obtain an approximate measure of the use of those materials. Alternatively, reference staff can make a checkmark on a form inserted into each reference book every time they consult that title. Another technique is to affix adhesive colored dots to the spines of materials to indicate either reshelving or consultation by a reference staff person. These methods can give helpful quantification of the use of the materials in the collection.

■ ═══ ■

8.3
Evaluating Reference Collections

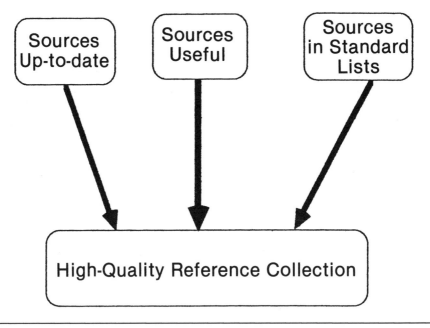

One can never rely solely on the demonstrated use of materials in evaluating materials in a collection. For example, patrons may be making use of obsolete materials because the library has not acquired more current tools. Materials may be little used because of lack of familiarity by reference staff or inadequate subject access provided by the library catalog. Demonstrated use should always be taken as only one factor, along with several others, in deciding whether to retain an item in the collection.

The third criterion is the reputation of the materials in the collection. This can be established by comparing the contents of the collection with standard lists. For example, the American Library Association produces, on a regular basis, a listing of *Reference Sources for Small and Medium-Sized Libraries*.[11] Christine Gehrt Wynar edited a *Guide to Reference Books for School Media Centers*.[12] Also useful are two compilations of reference books by Bohdan S. Wynar: *Recommended Reference Books for Small and Medium-sized Libraries and Media Centers*[13] and *Best Reference Books*.[14] Other standard lists of reference materials are covered in chapter 11. In all cases, these standard lists can be used to improve the quality of the collection, either by adding or removing titles. It is, however, important to exercise caution when using these lists. They are designed to be used by many libraries, and so do not take into account local variations in user populations and needs. Thus, the standard lists may omit items that are invaluable to a particular collection, while including materials that would be superfluous in another collection.

One basic assumption that guides the idea of reference collection evaluation is that there is an optimal size for a reference collection. A reference collection should be small enough so that reference staff can be reasonably familiar with all of the tools, the kinds of information they contain, and the kinds of questions they can answer. On the other hand, a reference collection should be large enough so that a reasonable proportion of patron inquiries can be resolved and answered quickly. Experience indicates that, especially for factual reference questions, a small, high-quality collection with which the reference staff is thoroughly familiar can be more effective than a larger collection. As high-quality materials are added to the collection, it is important to survey the collection and remove materials that are superseded, unused, or not recommended, so that the collection can remain at its optimal size, and so that books that are not frequently consulted in the reference collection can be made available for circulation to patrons.

Mechanisms for reference collection evaluation will differ from one library to another, but it is always desirable to make the reference staff responsible for the task. Frequently the collection is divided by topic area, with the staff member most familiar with a topic being given responsibility for that section. These specialists may suggest items for withdrawal from the collection, or for transfer to another part of the library. Some mechanism for consultation with the rest of the reference staff is important, so that all reference staff will know what is happening to the collection.

8.4
Evaluating Reference Books

A university library reference department has in its collection a multivolume encyclopedia published in the 1950s in the European duchy of Transmogrania. Of course it is written in Transmogranian, a language that none of the reference staff can read. This encyclopedia remains in the lists of reference works because it is a standard, authoritative work on all aspects of Transmogranian life and culture. A survey of the reshelving of reference works in the department shows that no volumes of this work were reshelved during the six months in which the survey was conducted. As always, the reference library is finding that its shelf space is inadequate, and one reference librarian suggests removing the encyclopedia from the reference collection. Would you: (1) keep the encyclopedia in reference, because it is a standard reference work; (2) transfer the encyclopedia to the general stacks, where it will become a circulating title; or (3) get rid of the encyclopedia by donating it to the only faculty member on campus who can read Transmogranian? Are there alternative solutions?

Evaluation of Reference Staff. Any library with a thoroughly developed personnel function will already have in place one of a number of techniques for conducting annual or periodic evaluations of its employees. Although a variety of personnel evaluation techniques exist, and can be found in any of the standard textbooks on library management or library personnel administration, evaluation of reference personnel poses special problems and challenges. Personnel evaluation normally takes into account two different criteria: the characteristics of the employee (in terms of qualifications for the position), and the employee's performance of the job itself.

The first criterion for reference staff evaluation is the extent to which employees possess characteristics that will make them good reference staff. However, it is difficult to establish a suitable list of employee characteristics against which reference staff can be evaluated. Young and Schwartz and Eakin give examples of the kinds of characteristics that can be taken as essential for good reference librarians.[15] Examples include approachability, knowledge of reference resources in the collection, and the ability to investigate a problem thoroughly. Even if a list of employee characteristics has been developed, it is sometimes difficult to test the extent to which librarians have those characteristics. How can one test such characteristics as approachability, or even something less subjective, such as the employee's knowledge of the reference collection?

The second criterion is how staff are performing in their jobs. The main problem with this criterion appears to be one of observation. Usually, an employee's supervisor is the one who conducts the evaluation, but it is frequently difficult for the supervisor to observe directly how well a reference librarian is performing. It may not be possible to observe in detail the interaction between a reference librarian and a patron without intruding upon that interaction. Other individuals, such as the librarian's coworkers or the users who are served by the librarian, may be in a better situation to observe how well the librarian is performing. However, obtaining the evaluations of these individuals may be difficult because of concerns about personal bias and confidentiality. It seems likely that, in many situations, the librarians themselves are in the best position to observe the quality of the service they are providing. Some libraries ask employees to evaluate themselves, and include this self-evaluation in the performance evaluation scheme.

The objective of reference staff evaluation is to help reference librarians and other reference workers to improve the level of their performance, and thus to improve the service offered. One model that has great potential in reference service is the Management by Objectives model. Here, the workers' characteristics and performance are evaluated by themselves and by others such as supervisors or coworkers. As part of the evaluation process, areas for possible improvement are identified, and concrete objectives are set for the coming year. The next performance evaluation will take into account the workers' objectives from the past year, and will provide feedback on how well those objectives have been achieved. It will then be possible to set new objectives for improved service in the following year. This process takes into account the capabilities of each worker, and uses an iterative process to create a high-quality reference staff.

■ ═══ ■

8.5

Evaluating Reference Librarians

In some libraries, salary increases are determined, at least in part, on the basis of merit. The theory behind merit increases is that the best employees should be rewarded for their efforts, while those who are providing less excellent service are given an incentive to improve. How might this work in practice? Suppose you are supervising a staff of ten reference workers, and only three of them can have merit increases. How would you go about selecting the three best employees? How would you explain to the rest of the staff the criteria upon which they were being judged? Could you implement a merit pay system in a fair and objective manner?

Level 2: Evaluation of Reference Transactions

Although the ongoing evaluation of resources such as collections and personnel is important, it provides only a partial perspective on the quality of reference service. To get a more complete picture, it is essential to evaluate what happens when the service is being provided. Katherine Emerson defined the *reference transaction* as "an information contact that involves the use, recommendation, interpretation or instruction in the use of one or more information sources or knowledge of such sources, by a member of the reference or information staff."[16] This transaction involves a complex encounter between the librarian and the user.

A typical reference transaction starts when a patron asks for some information or assistance. The information need may be clarified through a reference interview, and then the reference librarian does one or more of a wide range of activities: instruction, explanation, bibliographic searching, and examination of sources and tools. Finally, if all goes well, the information or assistance is obtained by the patron. Evaluation of such a complex transaction is difficult, and it is made more difficult by the fact that several transactions may be occurring simultaneously in a busy reference department. However, a number of techniques have been developed to try to evaluate the effectiveness of reference transactions in any library. These include unobtrusive evaluation, obtrusive evaluation by user surveys and other methods, and compilation of reference statistics.

Unobtrusive Evaluation. One way of simplifying the evaluation of reference transactions is to concentrate on one component of the transaction, or on one particular kind of transaction. One example of this simplification has occupied a great deal of the literature on reference evaluation in the past twenty years: unobtrusive evaluation.

Terence Crowley, in his 1968 doctoral thesis, developed a technique of unobtrusive evaluation of reference service, and Thomas Childers's thesis two years later refined the technique.[17] Proxy users were hired to approach library reference desks, either in person or by telephone, and to ask factual questions for which the correct answers had previously been established. From the responses received, it was possible to ascertain the proportion of correct responses given by various libraries. This evaluation was "unobtrusive" because the library workers who were being evaluated did not know that the experiments were being conducted. Later research by Terry Weech and Herbert Goldhor[18] established the value of this technique in providing an accurate picture of service provision, by demonstrating that when reference workers were aware that they were being evaluated, they correctly answered a larger proportion of the questions.

Since the pioneering work of Crowley and Childers, a large number of studies using unobtrusive evaluation have been reported in the literature. Kenneth Crews provides a good overview of this research.[19] A consistent pattern of responses has emerged. In responding to questions about facts, library reference departments give correct answers about 55 percent of the time. Naturally, this result has been a cause of considerable discussion among librarians who are concerned about the quality of service. It has also led to increased interest in methods of improving performance of reference staff (see chapter 7).

Unobtrusive techniques have been applied to studies of other aspects of the reference transaction. Questions requiring more detailed analysis have been asked, as well as questions that draw on specialized sources such as government documents. The extent to which reference staff conduct reference interviews, and the quality of those interviews, have also been studied using proxy users. Unobtrusive studies directed toward different classes of reference workers (librarians, library technical assistants, and student assistants) have been completed. A number of studies have used unobtrusive testing as a diagnostic tool within one library, for example, to determine areas in which staff training may be required.

Unobtrusive testing is now an established element in the evaluation of reference transactions. A number of concerns about the technique exist, however. Some feel that it is unethical to test a reference service in this way without informing the reference workers that such an experiment is being conducted. This concern may be more substantial when the results of unobtrusive testing are applied to individual workers rather than to the service as a whole. Another major concern relates to the fact that unobtrusive testing has been used primarily to examine one aspect of the reference transaction: the accuracy of responses to factual questions. It is important that the ability of reference departments to answer factual questions not be taken as indicative of all of the services they provide. For instance, other activities, such as providing detailed bibliographic assistance or instruction in library use, may be just as important in the reference department's service.

It is difficult to escape the consistent finding, from more than 20 studies, that has come to be called the "55 percent rule." Many comments about the "crisis" in reference service are based on the widely held opinion that reference service should be doing better than this. The results of unobtrusive testing have pointed out areas in which substantial improvement can be made in the service provided by library reference departments. Libraries are now turning their attention to staff training, collection improvement, and other techniques to improve the accuracy of responses to factual questions.

8.6
Unobtrusive Evaluation

As the supervisor of a reference department, you are concerned about the quality of service being offered. After reading the accounts of a number of unobtrusive tests of reference service, you decided to conduct such a test yourself. It has now been completed, and you have communicated the results to the reference workers. One of the reference librarians, discovering that his service has been evaluated unobtrusively at some time in the past two months, expresses considerable anger about the unobtrusive evaluation. First of all, he says that they are busy enough in the reference department without having these phony patrons to deal with as well. Secondly, he feels that the university students hired to ask the questions are not like real patrons: they do not have real information needs, so they cannot provide a realistic test of the librarians' ability to meet patrons' needs. In addition, the unobtrusive test pays attention to only one aspect of his work: the accuracy and completeness of the response. He feels that this is not a fair evaluation of his abilities as a reference librarian. But the thing that bothers him most about it is the sneakiness of the technique. Why can't they let people know before doing something like this?

What responses would you, as the supervisor, make to these criticisms? Do you think you could convince the librarian that unobtrusive evaluation is in fact a good idea?

Obtrusive Techniques: User Surveys. Among the obtrusive techniques of evaluating reference transactions, perhaps the most widely employed is user surveys. Here there is no element of surprise: the library staff know that a survey of users is being conducted. In fact, in most cases the library staff conduct the survey. Generally speaking, such surveys have asked patrons whether they found what they needed, whether they were satisfied by the service provided by the reference department, and whether the reference staff appeared efficient, friendly, and so on.

This approach shares the weaknesses of other survey techniques. First, what is being solicited is opinions rather than facts. Such opinions may be helpful and interesting, but they are not necessarily a reflection of reality. If 75 percent of patrons say they found what they needed, one should not assume that the reference department is functioning at 75 percent effectiveness. Users may understate or overstate their success depending on the state of their knowledge, the feeling they have about libraries or about the library staff, and other variables. User satisfaction questions are particularly prone to response bias on the part of users (that is, the respondents reply as they think they are expected to reply, not as they really feel).

Despite these shortcomings, user surveys can provide useful detail about the workings of a reference service. One of the best surveys has been developed and tested over a number of years in a wide variety of libraries: the Wisconsin-Ohio Reference Evaluation Program.[20] In this survey, after each reference transaction, the user answers one set of questions while the library worker answers a set of matching questions. The first advantage of this technique is that it provides a comparison between the opinions and perceptions of users and library staff about the transaction. The second advantage is that the questions are tied to a specific transaction, rather than being asked about service in general. This seems likely to reduce the chance of response bias. The third advantage of this survey instrument is that it has been used in a variety of libraries. The survey results from all of these libraries are available in a database, and it is possible to determine how the results from one library compare with those of similar libraries. Instead of having only a general idea about the reference service, a reference librarian can identify areas that need improvement, or areas of particular strength, compared with other libraries serving similar user groups.

In general, the task of questionnaire design is so tricky, and the likelihood of response bias so great, that libraries are well advised to avoid trying to create their own survey instruments. Using an expertly designed and thoroughly tested survey instrument like the Wisconsin-Ohio form can produce useful results; in-house forms may produce only vague and uncertain results.

8.7

Evaluation by Questionnaire

One questionnaire used to evaluate the service in an academic library contained the following question: "Please give a brief description of your last encounter with a reference librarian. What did you do? What did the librarian do?" The questionnaire allowed about half a page for a written response. What kind of responses do you think would be obtained from this question? How would you go about analyzing the responses to find out whether the reference department was providing high-quality service? What other purposes might this question serve? Try answering this question yourself. Do you think response bias might affect what you say?

Other Obtrusive Evaluation Techniques. Some suggestions for obtrusive evaluation of reference work have been tested experimentally, but have not yet been implemented in practice. Some researchers have made recordings of reference transactions, and have analyzed the recordings to ascertain the extent to which interview techniques, such as open and closed questions, were used (see chapter 3 for a discussion of these techniques), and how these techniques are associated with success in reference transactions. In other experiments, reference transactions have been videotaped and the effectiveness of the reference workers evaluated by peer judges. Although such techniques provide an unprecedented opportunity to observe and analyze in depth the performance of reference librarians and the quality of the service they are providing, a number of ethical and practical concerns have prevented use of these techniques in the working environment of reference departments.

Reference Statistics. Probably the oldest and most widespread technique of assessing reference work is to keep a tally of the number of questions that are answered during a given period at a given service point. Sometimes these tallies are analyzed by type of question asked (subject queries versus directional), and a few details may be recorded about the kind of answer that was given (for example, the time that was taken to answer the question). Reference statistics that result from the compilation of such tallies are useful for managers. They may provide the input needed to improve the scheduling of staff at service points, and they may provide data to justify the extension of reference service, but it is questionable whether reference statistics really provide any solid evaluation of the service provided.

Box 8.8 shows an example of a reference statistics tally sheet. Data collected on such a sheet can be used by managers to identify busy times, so that additional staff can be scheduled, or to identify the amount of individualized library instruction that is required at different times during the year, so that group bibliographic instruction can be implemented during periods of high demand.

■ ═══ ■

8.8

Example of a Reference Statistics Tally Sheet

Reference Desk
Daily Statistics

Day:
Date:

Record All Questions Here	9am-1pm	1pm-6pm	6pm-9pm
Reference			
Directional			
Additional Data: Mark When Appropriate			
Telephoned Questions			
Instruction			
Card Catalog			
Online Search			
Search Question			

Reference statistics, and their byproducts such as reference fill rates (the proportion of reference questions successfully answered) and reference completion rates (the number of reference questions completed on the same day), make assumptions about the quality of the reference work, but do not really measure that quality. Reference statistics usually cannot distinguish between a transaction that is successfully completed, and one in which the patron is not helped. Accordingly, it is correct to think of reference statistics as an important type of data collection for management of the service, but not as an evaluative tool.

8.9
Reference Statistics

Output Measures for Public Libraries[21] suggests the use of reference completion rate as a tool for assessing reference output. Is it possible that reference librarians might judge a question as completed but that the user might regard the response as incomplete? Paul Kantor[22] suggests a measure that depends on reference librarians' estimates of the success of the reference process. Again, is it possible that librarians might regard a transaction as being successfully completed, but the patron's opinion might differ? How might you try to improve these measures in order to get a more objective idea of completion rate or success rate?

Level 3: Evaluation of Reference Services

The third level of evaluation of reference services moves beyond individual reference transactions, and attempts to evaluate the extent to which the reference service is meeting its overall objectives. For this kind of evaluation to be possible, a statement of the goals and objectives of the reference department must exist. A typical statement of goals and objectives might include such functions as meeting the information needs of the user community and teaching the user community about the library and its services. The task of this third level of evaluation is to ascertain the extent to which the reference service is meeting those goals and objectives.

To evaluate how well reference services are meeting the information needs of the user community, it is necessary to survey the entire community in some reliable way to find out what its information needs really are, and whether the library is perceived as a source that can provide that information. Similarly, to find out the effectiveness of the reference service in teaching the community about the library, it is necessary to ascertain the extent of community knowledge about the library's services.

In dealing with these larger questions, other concerns may be addressed as well. It may be possible to identify population segments whose information needs are not being met by the reference service, or parts of the user community that show little awareness of the library's services. All of these concerns are addressed by a community needs analysis. A number of different techniques can be used to analyze the information needs of a community. *A Planning Process for Public Libraries*[23] gives an example of a telephone survey that can be used by a public library to ascertain the extent to which the citizens in the community know about and use the library's reference service. Other, less formal, techniques can also be used. For example, key informants from within the user community can be interviewed to determine the extent to which there are user needs that are not currently being met by the library's reference services.

One way of thinking about this level of evaluation is to see it as part of an ongoing planning process, in which all of the possible kinds of reference services are considered along with existing services. The kinds of questions that might be asked are: "Should we be answering the kinds of questions that we are currently answering?" and "Are there questions that we should be answering that we are not currently answering?" The community survey will give an idea of the amount of use currently made of existing reference services, and it should also identify areas of information need that the services are not currently meeting. This information can serve as input to the library's ongoing strategic planning process.

■ ═══ ■

8.10
Community Surveys

A public library's community needs analysis ascertains that 90 percent of the citizens of the community know about the reference service, and that 75 percent of the citizens approve of the work that the service is doing. However, only 23 percent of the citizens indicate that they have made use of the service in the past three years. What does this tell the library about the quality of its service? What additional questions does it raise? How might the library try to answer those questions?

The same survey shows that one of the main problems facing citizens in the community is obtaining affordable rental housing. Landlord-tenant disputes were frequently cited as an area in which the citizens find they need information. Should the library try to respond to this problem? What sort of information service might be helpful?

Related Issues

As libraries develop new services or provide services to special populations, suitable evaluation techniques must be devised. To ensure that evaluation is an ongoing activity, responsibility for implementing reference services evaluation must be clearly delineated.

Quality of Online Searching

In today's environment of rapid technological change, automation is affecting many aspects of reference service. With the introduction of electronic information storage and retrieval into the reference process, evaluation of reference service has acquired new dimensions. It is now possible to evaluate the content of databases, the quality of interfaces and retrieval techniques, and the performance of online searchers. While these kinds of evaluation are similar to those already discussed in this chapter, there are new challenges and opportunities associated with these issues.

Two main factors influence the quality of online searching: the systems being used to do the searching, and the people who are doing the searching. Librarians can evaluate the content of online databases using the same criteria as for printed reference tools: accuracy, completeness, authority, and so on. However, some databases are available through a number of vendors, each of which uses a different interface and command structure. This proliferation of database vendors has increased dramatically with the widespread use of CD-ROM storage. Thus, as described in chapter 11, librarians frequently have the opportunity to evaluate not only the content of the database, but also the interface, access points, and command structure through which they and their users search the databases. This means that evaluation of online/ondisc sources has a new dimension, and that librarians should be paying particular attention to the ease of use and effectiveness of interfaces and command structures when they are deciding which sources should be used in their reference service.

The area in which technological change has produced the greatest difference in the evaluation of reference service is in the creation of a special class of reference librarians: online searchers. Although online searchers are being superseded to some extent in some libraries and information centers by end-user searching, there remain many situations in which specialized service is provided by reference workers who have expertise in online retrieval of bibliographic citations and other information. It will be recalled that two key problems in evaluation of reference workers were the development of lists of desirable characteristics, and observing the actual performance of the workers. Online searching has changed that situation by providing a work situation in which certain necessary characteristics and skills are more easily defined, and in which observation may be easier.

Research has identified a number of the characteristics that lead to high-quality performance in online searching.[24] These characteristics range from cognitive skills in learning and problem solving to learned tactics for retrieving information. There are now some answers to the question, "What makes a good online searcher?," and these answers are more precise than the answers to the more general question, "What makes a good reference librarian?" At the same time, the online searching environment is more constrained than the general reference environment, and observation of the performance of online searchers may be easier as a result. For example, many online search departments use a search request form on which the user records the topic to be searched. Some libraries keep copies of the online search, containing not only the retrieved citations, but also the search strategy used to retrieve the citations. By matching the search request form with the copy of the search, it is possible to see how well a searcher has met the information need of the user.

Technological change has provided new challenges for the evaluation of reference tools and reference workers, but it has also provided new opportunities for the effective evaluation of reference services. It is essential that any plan for implementing new techniques of providing reference service include methods for evaluating the quality of the service provided.

8.11

Evaluation of CD-ROM Services

End-user searching provides tremendous opportunities for library patrons to satisfy their information needs, but it also can lead to a great deal of frustration on the part of users. Not only do they have to select the appropriate database and the best terms to do their search, but they must master a user interface that may be quite challenging. Your library is planning to implement end-user searching of bibliographic databases on CD-ROM. How can you evaluate the success of this technology in meeting information needs? How can you evaluate the quality of the training that is being offered to patrons who make use of this service? Suppose that five years from now you will be asked whether it is worthwhile to continue this program of end-user searching. What information will you need in order to justify the continuation of the program? How might this information be derived from your evaluation of the service?

Evaluation of Service to Special Populations

The user population being served by the reference or information service can influence the process of evaluating the service. The example used here is service to children and young adults, but similar concerns may be raised about service to a wide range of special populations, from homebound seniors to the socially disadvantaged. The special needs of these populations provide new criteria against which service can be evaluated.

In the area of evaluation of resources, it may be important to include characteristics such as patience and empathy with children in evaluating the performance of children's librarians. In evaluation of reference transactions, some of the techniques previously discussed may require adaptation. For example, children may not be able to complete a traditional user survey, or to act as surrogates in unobtrusive testing. Interviews with patrons may be the best way to evaluate the success of reference transactions in the children's reference department. At the third level of evaluation, evaluation of services in the aggregate, each of the programs of the children's department can be assessed against the department's goals. Some of the data used in this kind of evaluation can come from the children themselves: for example, from their willingness to return for additional programs. It may also be possible for library workers to assess how children's cognitive skills are developing as a result of library programs and activities. Still, the evidence of others who deal closely with the children is also important: for example, parents' opinions about the importance of library programs in the lives of their children, and teachers' assessments of the effectiveness of library programs in enhancing students' cognitive and academic skills.

This example demonstrates that providing reference services to special populations presents challenges for evaluators. Although the need for evaluation is as great as for general reference services, evaluation techniques may have to be adapted for effective use with the special population being served.

■ ══ ■

8.12
Evaluating Reference Services for Children

In many schools, students are given assignments that require them to make use of the school library. By examining completed assignments, a school librarian can ascertain the extent to which students are making successful use of the library. This provides a direct means of evaluating the quality of the information and instruction services of the school library. In a public library children's department, the librarian does not have such a convenient mechanism for evaluation. How would a children's librarian ascertain the quality of information and instruction services being provided by a public library? What evidence could be used to evaluate these services?

Organizing for Evaluation

There is no ideal organizational structure or mechanism for implementing reference evaluation. In a small library, one or two individuals may have responsibility for the entire reference service. At the other end of the spectrum, a large library may have hundreds of staff members providing reference service through a large number of service points. Nevertheless, there are some necessary conditions for the evaluation of all reference services. It is necessary for reference staff to have time to step back from the daily provision of services and to examine the service as a whole. There must be an opportunity for the setting and regular reexamination of the goals and objectives of the reference service. From this can come an understanding of the aspects of the service most in need of evaluation, and of evaluation techniques that may be applied to those areas.

It is also necessary to have the responsibility for evaluation clearly delineated, and written into job descriptions wherever appropriate. If this does not happen, then the reference staff will tend to think of evaluation as a good idea, but one that someone else will deal with. When any reference program is developed, an evaluation component must be included in the planning. For example, if a bibliographic instruction program is being developed, the librarians in charge must have from the beginning a clear idea of how the success of the program will be measured. Similarly, if the library is thinking of acquiring a new technology, such as CD-ROM databases, then an evaluation scheme that will assess the effectiveness of that new technology must be incorporated from the beginning. If a branch library is being opened in a new community, a plan for community needs analysis (with regular follow-up analyses) should be included in the planning for that branch.

If a library is providing services which are not being evaluated, then library workers have a responsibility to develop techniques of evaluation for them. Some libraries have started to do unobtrusive evaluation of their telephone reference service on a regular basis, and to chart the accuracy and completeness of the responses given over time. Other libraries have adopted a questionnaire approach to the regular evaluation of reference transactions. The key point is that evaluation should be an ongoing, regular part of the functioning of the reference department. Single, isolated attempts at evaluation can produce interesting results, but the value of these projects is soon lost. Ongoing evaluation provides the input necessary for continual improvement of the service.

Finally, it is necessary to bring together the librarians who are responsible for evaluation of reference service on a regular basis so that they can share their perceptions of the quality of service. In such meetings it is possible to develop means by which evaluation can be translated into improved service. As indicated at the beginning of this chapter, evaluation which does not lead to service improvement is probably a waste of effort. Again, it is important for the library staff to be able to take the time to obtain a perspective on the quality of the existing service, and to think of ways in which it can be improved.

Conclusion

All of the techniques and approaches to the evaluation of reference service described in this chapter have shortcomings. None of them provides a complete picture of the quality of the service. Accordingly, a thorough evaluation program will make use of a number of these techniques, in an integrated manner, to build up an overview of the effectiveness and quality of the reference service.

A multimethod approach to reference evaluation will include elements from all levels of evaluation. It is important to evaluate the inputs to reference service, including the reference collection and the reference staff. Similarly, it is important to obtain some idea of how well reference transactions are being completed. Finally, it is essential that the success of the reference service in meeting its overall goals and objectives be considered from time to time, through some sort of community needs analysis. Many libraries have some or all of these elements in place, and the challenge is to integrate the results of the different kinds of evaluation, and to respond to these results with effective action.

Evaluation is an essential component of service provision. It is the responsibility of every professional librarian to ensure that adequate resources are available for evaluation and improvement of the service, so that the reference service can fulfill its mandate of meeting the information needs of its patrons.

Notes

1. Readers interested in pursuing further the concept of the value of information can begin by examining these survey articles: Bonnie Cooper Carroll and Donald Ward King, "Value of Information," *Drexel Library Quarterly* 21 (Summer 1985): 39-60; Aatto J. Repo, "The Value of Information: Approaches in Economics, Accounting, and Management Science," *Journal of the American Society for Information Science* 40 (March 1989): 68-85.

2. See, for example, Nancy Hanks and Stan Wade, "Quality Circles: Realistic Alternatives for Libraries," *Show-me Libraries* 36, no. 9 (June 1985): 6-11; Janice DeSirey, Christopher Dodge, Nancy Hargrave, Randi Larson, and Susan Nesbitt, "The Quality Circle: Catalyst for Library Change," *Library Journal* 113 (April 15, 1988): 52-53.

3. James Shedlock, "Defining the Quality of Medical Reference Service," *Medical Reference Services Quarterly* 7 (Spring 1988): 49-53.

4. Jack L. Franklin and Jean H. Trasher, *An Introduction to Program Evaluation* (New York: Wiley, 1976), 233p.

5. Edward A. Henry, "Judging Reference Service," *Library Journal* 64 (May 1, 1939): 358-59.

6. G. L. Gardiner, "The Empirical Study of Reference," *College & Research Libraries* 30 (March 1969): 130-55.

7. Samuel Rothstein, "The Measurement and Evaluation of Reference Service," *Library Trends* 12 (January 1964): 456-72.

8. Samuel Rothstein, "The Hidden Agenda in the Measurement and Evaluation of Reference Services: Or, How to Make a Case for Yourself," *Reference Librarian* 11 (Fall/Winter 1984): 45-52.

9. F. W. Lancaster, *If You Want to Evaluate Your Library* (Champaign, Ill.: University of Illinois Graduate School of Library and Information Science, 1988), 193p.

10. See, for example, Suburban Library System, "SLS Minimum Reference Standards for Public Libraries," *Illinois Libraries* 70 (January 1988): 16-19; Marjorie E. Murfin and Charles Albert Bunge, "Responsible Standards for Reference Service in Ohio Public Libraries," *Ohio Libraries* 1 (March/April 1988): 11-13; James R. Rettig, "Public Service Standards for Libraries," in *Serials Standards: Development, Implementation, Impact: Proceedings of the Third Annual Serials Conference*, ed. Nancy Jean Melin (Westport, Conn.: Meckler, 1984), 27-38.

11. American Library Association, *Reference Sources for Small and Medium-Sized Libraries*, 4th ed. (Chicago: American Library Association, 1984), 252p.

12. Christine Gehrt Wynar, *Guide to Reference Books for School Media Centers*, 3d ed. (Littleton, Colo.: Libraries Unlimited, 1986), 407p.

13. Bohdan S. Wynar, ed., *Recommended Reference Books for Small and Medium-sized Libraries and Media Centers* (Englewood, Colo.: Libraries Unlimited, annual).

14. Bohdan S. Wynar, ed., *Best Reference Books, 1981-1985: Titles of Lasting Value Selected from American Reference Books Annual* (Littleton, Colo.: Libraries Unlimited, 1986), 504p. (The 1986-1990 edition was in press at the time of this writing.)

15. William F. Young, "Methods for Evaluating Reference Desk Performance," *RQ* 25 (Fall 1985): 69-75; Diane G. Schwartz and Dottie Eakin, "Reference Service Standards, Performance Criteria and Evaluation," *Journal of Academic Librarianship* 12 (March 1986): 4-8.

16. Katherine Emerson, "Definitions for Planning and Evaluating Reference Services," *Reference Librarian* 11 (Fall/Winter 1984): 63-79.

17. These theses were subsequently published as: Terence Crowley and Thomas Childers, *Information Service in Public Libraries: Two Studies* (Metuchen, N.J.: Scarecrow Press, 1971), 210p.

18. Terry L. Weech and Herbert Goldhor, "Obtrusive Versus Unobtrusive Evaluation of Reference Service in Five Illinois Public Libraries: A Pilot Study," *Library Quarterly* 52 (October 1982): 305-24.

19. Kenneth D. Crews, "The Accuracy of Reference Service: Variables for Research and Implementation," *Library & Information Science Research* 10 (July 1988): 331-35.

20. For a description of the development of this questionnaire, see Charles Albert Bunge, "Factors Related to Reference Question Answering Success: The Development of a Data-Gathering Form," *RQ* 24 (Summer 1985): 482-86; Marjorie E. Murfin and Gary M. Gugelchuk, "Development and Testing of a Reference Transaction Assessment Instrument," *College & Research Libraries* 48 (July 1987): 314-38.

21. Nancy A. Van House, Mary Jo Lynch, Charles R. McClure, Douglas L. Zweizig, and Eleanor Jo Rodger, *Output Measures for Public Libraries: A Manual of Standardized Procedures*, 2d ed. (Chicago: American Library Association, 1987), 99p.

22. Paul Kantor, "Quantitative Evaluation of the Reference Process," *RQ* 21 (Fall 1981): 43-54.

23. Vernon E. Palmour, Marcia C. Bellassai, and Nancy V. De Wath, *A Planning Process for Public Libraries* (Chicago: American Library Association, 1980), 304p.

24. See, for example, Carol Tenopir, "What Makes a Good Online Searcher?," *Library Journal* 112 (March 15, 1987): 62-63; Raya Fidel, "Individual Variability in Online Searching Behavior," in *ASIS '85: Proceedings of the 48th ASIS Annual Meeting*, ed. Carol A. Parkhurst (White Plains, N.Y.: Knowledge Industry Publications, 1985), 69-72; and Trudi Bellardo, "An Investigation of Online Searcher Traits and Their Relationship to Search Outcome," *Journal of the American Society for Information Science* 36 (July 1985): 241-50.

Additional Readings

Bone, Larry Earl, ed. "Community Analysis and Libraries." *Library Trends* 24 (January 1976): 429-643.
    This entire issue of *Library Trends* is devoted to community needs analysis. Included are general articles, case studies, and an excellent annotated bibliography.

Bunge, Charles Albert, and Marjorie E. Murfin. "Reference Questions: Data from the Field." *RQ* 27 (Fall 1987): 15-18.
    This article gives a good summary of some of the data collected by libraries using the Wisconsin-Ohio Reference Evaluation Program, and illustrates the usefulness of this evaluation technique.

Chelton, Mary K. "Evaluation of Children's Services." *Library Trends* 35 (Winter 1987): 463-84.
    This article covers program evaluation concepts and methods as applied to children's services. Chelton gives examples of the forms that can be used for evaluating children's programs.

Durrance, Joan C. "Reference Success: Does the 55 Percent Rule Tell the Whole Story?" *Library Journal* 114 (April 15, 1989): 31-36.
    Recognizing that accuracy of answers as revealed by most unobtrusive testing provides only a partial view of the quality of reference service, Durrance used unobtrusive observation to evaluate the setting of the reference transaction, the use of interviewing skills by reference librarians, and the interpersonal behavior of reference librarians.

Gorman, Kathleen. *Performance Evaluation in Reference Services in ARL Libraries*. Washington, D.C.: Office of Management Studies, Association of Research Libraries, 1987. 83p. [SPEC Kit 139.]
    This kit provides examples of the techniques and forms used for performance evaluation of reference staff in ARL libraries. It shows how various theories about performance evaluation can lead to different approaches to the task of evaluating the performance of staff.

Hernon, Peter, and Charles R. McClure. *Unobtrusive Testing and Library Reference Services*. Norwood, N.J.: Ablex, 1987. 240p.
    This is an important text on unobtrusive testing methods, providing a full discussion of many of the issues surrounding this type of evaluation. It also provides findings from unobtrusive tests conducted by the authors.

_____, eds. "Library Reference Service: An Unrecognized Crisis – A Symposium." *Journal of Academic Librarianship* 13 (May 1987): 69-80.
    Specialists in reference evaluation discuss the implications of evaluation findings for academic libraries.

Jennerich, Elaine Z. "Before the Answer: Evaluating the Reference Process." *RQ* 19 (Summer 1980): 360-66.
    Jennerich surveys the research on the reference process, and recommends that more attention be paid to this process in evaluation of reference services.

Kantor, Paul. "Quantitative Evaluation of the Reference Process." *RQ* 21 (Fall 1981): 43-54.
    Kantor presents a model for reference evaluation based on recording librarians' perceptions about reference transactions. This method is compared with other evaluative techniques in terms of both cost and effectiveness.

Nichols, Margaret Irby. "Weeding the Reference Collection." *Texas Library Journal* 62 (Winter 1986): 204-6.
    This is one of the very few articles that discusses the evaluation of reference collections. It is an excellent practical paper with many good suggestions for weeding reference collections.

Rodger, Eleanor Jo, and Jane Goodwin. "To See Ourselves as Others See Us: A Cooperative, Do-it-yourself Reference Accuracy Study." *Reference Librarian* 18 (Summer 1987): 135-47.
    This is one of the best in-house evaluation studies making use of unobtrusive testing. Particularly interesting is that the authors used a combination of accuracy and completeness in evaluating the answers provided by reference workers.

Van House, Nancy A., Mary Jo Lynch, Charles R. McClure, Douglas L. Zweizig, and Eleanor Jo Rodger. *Output Measures for Public Libraries: A Manual of Standardized Procedures*. 2d ed. Chicago: American Library Association, 1987. 99p.
    This is the standard handbook for data collection on the "outputs" of public libraries. It is worth reading critically to judge how the suggested procedures can assess the quality of reference services. Another aspect worth noting is the extent to which the output measures are based on self-reporting by librarians about their service.

Von Seggern, Marilyn. "Assessment of Reference Services." *RQ* 26 (Summer 1987): 487-96.
    This is an excellent annotated bibliography of many aspects of assessment of reference services, including many of the evaluative techniques discussed in this chapter.

9 ☐

ORGANIZATION AND MANAGEMENT OF REFERENCE AND INFORMATION SERVICES

Introduction

Given the rationale for offering reference services (outlined in chapter 2) and the types of services typically offered (outlined in chapter 1), how should a library best be organized to provide these services? Most libraries designate a specific area for reference books and generally offer reference assistance to patrons from a central location. Typically, in a library large enough to be organized into departments, the reference department holds responsibility for managing this collection and providing information and instructional services. This chapter, therefore, opens with a discussion of the typical context in which reference services are offered: the reference department.

Traditions rarely remain immutable, however, and the model of the central reference department, with the reference desk as the focal point of reference service, has perennially come under challenge. Are patrons better served (that is, have their information needs satisfied) by a central reference department or by more specialized departmental libraries? The efficacy of a centralized reference collection and services has been subject to considerable discussion, which is summarized later in this chapter. Likewise, one of librarianship's sacred cows, the reference desk, has engendered criticism. Does a reference desk offer the most visible and effective means of providing reference service, or does it underutilize staff expertise by encouraging directional and quick-answer questions? This chapter highlights key issues in these lively debates, for ultimately the quality of reference service is influenced not only by the collection and the expertise of reference librarians, but also by the context in which the service is provided.

In addition to the organization of reference services, this chapter discusses the administration of these services, from the perspective of the departmental manager. The role of the reference manager, and potential management models, provide the framework for a discussion of issues that affect each reference librarian who is a member of a department.

Reference Department

In reference departments, as in libraries in general, the organization chart is typically pyramidal, with staff reporting to the head of reference. In smaller libraries, the head reports immediately to the library director; in larger institutions, reference is usually part of a public services unit, which may include circulation and adult services. In this case, the head of reference reports to the director of public services, or to someone with a similar title or position.

This pyramidal model is deceptively simple, however, for within the reference department the organization more closely resembles a web. Reference departments vary in size from one or two librarians to more than twenty, and frequently provide services beyond their reference desks. Online searching and instructional services (described in chapters 5 and 6) have become logical extensions of the reference function, and are typically administered through the reference department. A 1985 survey of large academic libraries reported that reference departments may also be responsible for selection of the general library collection (62 percent of respondents), interlibrary loan (40 percent), maintenance of a government documents collection (30 percent), and maintenance of a separate microforms collection (19 percent), among other responsibilities.[1] Some of the activities for which reference departments are commonly responsible are shown in figure 9.1.

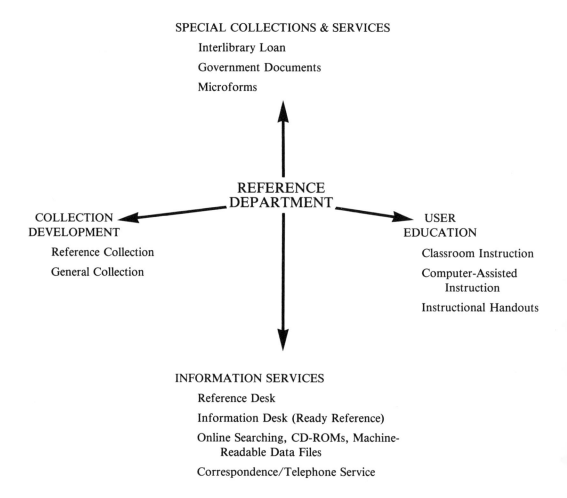

Fig. 9.1. Typical responsibilities of a reference department.

Thus, the reference department is a multifaceted organization, in which it is not uncommon for individual reference librarians to hold multiple responsibilities and to assume managerial roles for the administration of specific functions. Overall coordination is therefore necessary for the department to function smoothly and effectively. Before presenting a discussion of the role of the reference manager in pulling it all together, however, two critical issues relating to the organization of reference services are explored.

Centralized versus Decentralized Service

A single reference department is not necessarily a given. In larger libraries, the reference department may not be the only unit in which reference services are provided. With the trend towards more specialized services, many libraries, both public and academic, have developed departmental or special libraries which not only house subject collections, but also provide reference services for their clientele. The issue of centralized versus decentralized reference collections and services is not a new one. Writing almost a half century ago, Mary Barton, head of General Reference at the Enoch Pratt Free Library in Baltimore, referred to the "voluminous literature" on the advantages and disadvantages of decentralization.[2] Summarized here are the arguments from both sides.

Proponents of centralized reference services cite the advantages to library users. They argue that centralized reference services result in improved efficiency and fewer referrals elsewhere, since the reference collection and personnel are in one place. This becomes particularly critical given the increasingly interdisciplinary nature of research (e.g., anthropologists utilize both biological and social science literature). Extended service hours, particularly when budgetary considerations necessitate reduced hours in smaller units, and more consistent availability of professional staff (particularly on nights and weekends) likewise prove helpful to library users. From the perspective of the librarian, this model supports improved communication and more effective staff specialization. Librarians have the option of specializing in functions such as online searching, user education, reference collection management, or interlibrary loan, to maintain a high level of expertise and minimize the burnout associated with loss of control. The greater number of staff allows for more varied professional interests and activities and increased opportunities for in-service training and staff development. Centralization may offer economic advantages as well, by reducing the duplication of services and collections at multiple points, while freeing critical space for other uses.[3]

Proponents of decentralized reference services likewise cite the advantages to library users. They counter with arguments that subject departmentalization results in superior reference assistance, because subject specialists are better equipped to provide in-depth service. Because research processes are not identical in all fields (the archival research of the historian differs significantly from the utilization of current technical reports by the engineer, for example), librarians cannot be expected to be equally versed in research strategies and tools in the humanities, social sciences, and sciences. Moreover, with increasingly numerous and complex electronic databases, subject expertise is a valuable asset which the centralized model does not support. Proponents likewise argue that, within a smaller, more homogeneous unit, librarians enjoy greater autonomy and control. From an administrative standpoint, the smaller units offer greater opportunity for direct interaction, thus reducing the need for formal communication, management, and support activities.[4] Those who favor the decentralized model also cite the preferences of users for more focused units of library service and small, client-centered work groups.[5]

A final resolution to this debate may never be possible—nor need it be. Size of the collection, availability of staff, and the nature of users' information needs are but a few of the variables that influence the efficacy of either model. The question as to whether the "renaissance" librarian or the subject specialist provides a better model for service must ultimately be answered within the framework of each institution.

■ ═══ ■

9.1
Centralization versus Decentralization of Reference Services in a Public Library

A public library in a large metropolitan area has received funds to construct a new library building, which will offer considerably more space than the existing facility. At present, the library maintains one large, multidisciplinary reference collection, with a staff of ten professionals. Several of the librarians have expertise in online searching, while others pride themselves in their knowledge of the collection and the community. The administration is wrestling with the question of whether to retain the concept of a central reference department, or organize reference services along departmental lines, particularly for the business, local history, and music collections.

What advantages do centralization or decentralization have for patrons? For staff? For the administration?

Should a decentralized system still maintain a general reference department? What should its role be?

The Future of the Reference Desk

Whether reference services are centralized or decentralized, a concern still remains as to how those services will be provided. A primary objective in the administration of reference services remains the maximization of effective service. In most libraries, the route to accomplishing this goal has been to develop a central reference area, with staff and bibliographic resources dedicated to meeting the information needs of the library's users.

In reality, however, the ideal of the reference desk, staffed by competent professionals whose expertise is consistently utilized by informed library users, is at best elusive. Librarians may feel that their skills and expertise are atrophying when they are constantly faced with repetitive and routine questions, such as how to find a journal, or how to print citations from a CD-ROM station. Thelma Freides asserts that studies of user behavior indicate that users do, in fact, perceive the reference desk as intended for quick replies.[6] When the necessity arises for providing detailed bibliographic assistance or genuine research consultation (e.g., in facilitating term-paper research or assisting with genealogical queries), both patron and librarian experience frustration when competing with ringing phones and queues of patrons with short-answer questions.

Moreover, some have questioned whether the reference desk has made general users less self-sufficient and more dependent on library staff, and whether it offers a realistic means of providing public service for patrons, particularly in an electronic age. Would patrons be better served if more public service librarians applied their expertise to developing automated user aids, consulted on more effective computer interfaces, or developed in-house databases (such as an index finder) to provide improved access?[7] Does the reference desk represent an organizational fiction that pretends "we can do everything and do it well"?[8]

9.2

A Critical Mass or Trivial Pursuit?

"The reference desk represents the critical mass of resources—human, printed, and now electronic, configured for a convenient and predictable location so that library patrons can find the service and can find someone to help them."

—Patricia Swanson
"Traditional Models: Myths and Realities"[9]

"By establishing the desk as the focal point of reader assistance, libraries not only spend professional time on trivial tasks, but also encourage the assumption that the low-level undemanding type of question handled most easily and naturally at the desk is the service norm."

—Thelma Freides
"Current Trends in Academic Libraries"[10]

What, then, are alternatives to the traditional reference desk? In most instances, the solutions do not involve dismantling the reference desk, but rather supplementing it. Many libraries have turned to the model of a separate information desk to provide ready reference and catalog assistance. Staffed by competent and well-trained paraprofessionals and/or pre-professionals (such as graduate library school students), this alternative can help to relieve pressure on the reference desk by channeling away many directional and quick-answer questions. In some cases, implementing a separate telephone reference service can relieve the burden of answering the phone while assisting in-house patrons. On the other end of the spectrum, term-paper or research counseling, either by appointment or at a separately staffed desk, may give the opportunity to offer more in-depth research assistance than can generally be provided at the reference desk. Taking this idea further, the University of Michigan has implemented a reference "on-call" model, which uses librarians as off-the-scene resources. Scheduled regularly as back-ups, the librarians are called by the support staff at the information desk whenever a question requiring additional expertise or in-depth consultation arises, but they do not actually staff the desk.[11]

9.3

By Appointment or on Demand?

A busy chemistry library in a university serves over two thousand under-graduate students, two hundred graduate students, and thirty-five faculty members, with just one professional librarian. Her responsibilities include management of the library as well as collection development, online searching, and bibliographic instruction. She has two very competent paraprofessionals, a graduate assistant, and student workers of varying abilities. The reference needs of the clientele are considerable, from assistance in using *Chemical Abstracts* to help with complex citations to factual queries.

Should the library provide reference on demand (i.e., at a desk or on call)? By appointment? What are the advantages or disadvantages to the patron and to the librarian?

In what ways can the library organize to provide reference assistance?

Despite its drawbacks and limitations, most reference librarians will agree that the reference desk is alive and well. Judging from the sheer volume of action seen by the reference troops on the front lines, a retreat from this service could hardly be justified. The answer lies not in finding an alternative to the reference desk, but in developing an integrated system for addressing users' varied information needs, with the desk as a focal point. Staffing a reference desk need not preclude the development of microcomputer applications to assist in instruction or referral, nor does it preclude the availability of in-depth consultation. As the previous examples illustrate, with creativity and flexibility, reference librarians have begun moving towards a system of information services built around user needs and professional expertise, not just furniture.

Management of Reference Services

Whether reference services are to be centralized, and how the services are to be provided, are ultimately management issues. Defined in operational terms, *management* is the act of directing and organizing to accomplish a goal. The reference manager's concerns, therefore, focus upon working with the staff to accomplish the goals set by the department and by the library. Many of the topics discussed in previous chapters—the use of paraprofessionals, fees for service, and standards—are essentially management issues, involving decision making, coordination, communication, personnel administration, planning, and goal setting. The reference department is typically the arena wherein these concerns are raised, and the reference manager, as well as the dynamics within the department, play a critical role in determining how (or if) they are resolved.

In the following section, issues relating to the management of reference services are explored. Potential management models are presented, and the role of the manager is discussed.

Management Models

Nearly every aspect of a reference department's operation involves decision making: hiring new personnel, establishing policies, introducing new services, and purchasing new equipment or products. The manager is ultimately accountable for the department's performance and is responsible for the decisions which affect both the activities of the department and its personnel. How those decisions are made, however, can vary greatly, depending on the institution and/or the department head's management style. A full-scale discussion of management theory should be addressed in a management course; this discussion of management models borrows from the literature on management theory and puts it in the context of the reference department.

Hierarchical Management. Management models run along a continuum from authoritarian, in which the department head makes all the decisions, to collective, in which decisions are made by the group as a whole. The *hierarchical* model can be conceptualized as a pyramid, with all authority emanating from above. In this model, the department head alone holds the authority for making decisions. Simple from an administrative point of view, this approach offers the advantage of time savings by eliminating the necessity for lengthy meetings and consultations, and by substituting action for endless debate in the absence of consensus. This model, however, can have negative consequences for departmental morale and staff cooperation, when decisions are made in the absence of input. For instance, if budget cuts warrant the cancellation of titles, the manager may decide which titles to cancel. While this simplifies the decision-making process, the final decisions may well incur the animosity of the staff, who were unable to provide input. Maintaining the authority for decision making should not preclude adopting a consultative approach and seeking advice and input from the staff before making a decision.

Participatory Management. In recent years, the *participatory management* model has received much attention in the literature. In this instance, the manager chooses to allocate the right to make a particular decision to the staff. At the heart of participatory management is group decision making, and its effectiveness depends not merely on the administrative talents of the manager, but also on the dynamism and leadership within the staff.

Proponents of participatory management credit this model for improving job satisfaction and commitment and reducing factionalism and territoriality within the department. With greater input follows greater acceptance of decisions by the staff. Critics, however, counter that no relationship has been proven between participation in decision making and overall productivity. They cite reduced library effectiveness because of the additional time and money spent in reaching decisions. Moreover, consensus decision making produces fewer, more conservative results. If the decision of the group is ultimately not adopted by administrators, low morale is likewise a byproduct of this process.[12] Some decisions and situations lend themselves more easily to group decision making than others. To continue with the example of cancellation of reference titles, group decision making may not prove fruitful if the staff cannot reach a consensus.

Collective Management. *Collective management* of reference services represents the ultimate in democratic decision making. Unlike participatory management, in which the manager chooses to allocate the right to make a particular decision to the staff, in collective management the authority and responsibility for decision making rest with the department as a whole. Because of institutional realities and the weight of tradition in establishing administrative models, this management scenario is relatively uncommon in larger departments. Smaller units, however, may effectively utilize this model, as the scenario in box 9.4, page 198, illustrates.

■ == ■

9.4

Collective Management: A Case Study

As a solution to the temporary absence of the department head, in 1985 the Oberlin College Library reference department experimented with an alternative to the traditional management structure: collective management. Their concept of collective management required full participation by the professional reference staff in goal setting, long-range planning, and decision making. To simplify administration, they developed a position of reference manager who chaired staff meetings, represented the department in library-wide meetings, and wrote reports, but whose authority was defined by the group. This position rotated every two months, with each librarian serving at least once. Analyzing their experiences, they made the following observations:

Advantages include:

- greater control of the work situation
- excellent opportunities for staff development
- more involvement in the library as a whole
- stronger support for departmental goals and objectives
- increased staff enthusiasm

Disadvantages include:

- difficulty of group decision making in the absence of a consensus
- lack of financial reward
- inconsistency in managerial experience and skill
- added responsibility for the director or head of public services

Generally considered a success, the group concluded that an "especially important factor was our shared philosophy of academic librarianship and reference service."

— Cynthia Comer et al.
"Collective Management of Reference Services"[13]

Supervisory Rotation. Another alternative model is that of *supervisory rotation.* In this situation, librarians take turns serving as department head on a rotating cycle, thus providing each librarian (who meets established criteria) with the opportunity to manage the department. Not only a management training technique, this model offers advantages to the staff by increasing motivation, job satisfaction, skill versatility, and teamwork. Disadvantages include varying administrative ability levels among the staff and lack of continuity.[14] Though not a common model in libraries, supervisory rotation represents an innovative approach to encouraging the participation of each librarian in the administration of the department.

Role of the Reference Manager

While the decision-making aspects of the manager's responsibilities carry over into every aspect of the operation of the reference department, on a day-to-day basis, the reference manager must also pull together a diverse group of people and services. Though the components of the reference manager's role cannot really be isolated, the following discussion investigates specific aspects of that role, including coordination, communication, planning and goal setting, and personnel administration.

Coordination. One of the major responsibilities of the reference manager is to coordinate the functions of the reference department to ensure its smooth operation. As previously mentioned, in larger departments services can be broken down into separate components, such as collection development or online services, and each reference librarian can take on responsibility for a specific component. These coordinators then report to and work with the manager to resolve problems, assess the service, or plan for changes or future needs.

Coordination must also be done on a more specific level, involving the day-to-day decisions necessary for the overall functioning of the department. Scheduling and staffing the desk, allocating staff and resources for specific services or projects (e.g., online searching or the development of user aids), and implementing new services (such as electronic reference) all involve viewing a department's operation in its entirety. The manager must balance the ideal of fully meeting departmental goals with the reality of demands on the staff.

Another important aspect of coordination is ensuring consistency in service. Though staff members may exhibit different individual styles, policies and procedures must be followed consistently. From questions such as patron use of the departmental telephone, to priorities (such as in-person queries before phone requests), to the limits and level of service to provide (such as how far to go in pursuing genealogical queries), the reference department must present a united front, and all follow the same policies and procedures. While few would contest this logic, arriving at a cogent, comprehensive, and mutually agreeable statement (particularly of the policies) is easier said than done. Since neither staff nor library services remain static, policies and procedures must constantly be defined and refined, and new (or revised) policies and procedures must continually be developed in response to a changing environment. Codifying the resulting consensus into a manual can provide a useful statement and set of guidelines for staff to follow.[15]

Communication. Another critical function of the reference manager is to foster communication, both within the department and between the department and other units within the library, including the administration. Departmental meetings provide an important means of communicating information from the library's central administration, and also offer a forum in which staff members can discuss mutual concerns. Ideally scheduled on a weekly or bi-weekly basis, an agenda for these meetings might include a discussion of day-to-day issues, such as specific policies and procedures, problem patrons, or thorny class assignments. On another plane, the meetings provide an important opportunity for the department to engage in planning (e.g., for incorporating CD-ROM services) or goal setting (e.g., achieving competence in utilizing online sources for ready reference) for the department as a whole. The manager then serves as the vehicle for presenting the department's plans and needs to the library's administration.

Not all communication, however, can or should wait for a scheduled meeting. A significant amount of information often needs to be communicated on a daily basis, particularly to personnel at the reference desk. Since members of the department may work at night, or be otherwise involved in off-the-desk projects during the day, sharing information is not always easy. Provisions must be made for information to be shared between meetings. From reporting broken photocopiers (the bane of many a librarian's existence) to warning about an assignment for 300 freshmen given incorrect titles, a notebook at the reference desk can frequently save both frustration and duplication of effort — if everyone remembers to use it! Likewise, a bulletin board in the departmental office can communicate routine messages, upcoming meetings, whereabouts of staff members, or articles and continuing education opportunities of interest to the staff.

Effective communication is essential both within the department and between the reference department and other units within the library. As the representative of the reference department, the head is frequently the liaison between reference and technical services. Because the reference librarians interpret the catalog for the public, they rely heavily upon the work of their colleagues in technical services. Yet, relations between these departments have traditionally been strained, owing to the difference in perspective of their jobs.[16] Bridging the gap involves a broad understanding of the concerns and contributions of both the technical services and reference functions and a commitment to working toward a shared goal.

■ ━━━ ■

9.5
Us and Them?

And it came to pass that when Kutta the Book God had made the first Library, she saw that it was good. She called the librarians together and divided them as a herder divides the sheep and the goats. To the first group she spoke, saying, "You shall dwell in the light and serve the readers, and your glory shall be great." Then she turned to the second group and spoke, saying "You shall dwell in the darkness. Secret shall be your ways and hidden your practices. You shall not know the public, neither shall any reader know you. Go forth and classify."

— Michael Gorman
"On Doing Away with Technical Services"[17]

In a large library, communication between the reference department and other public service units is very important, particularly with regards to reference referrals. For instance, in a library system with separate departmental libraries, all reference personnel must be aware of hours of reference service, availability of online and CD-ROM services, and special collections and policies within libraries in the system. Undoubtedly, one of the major frustrations among library users is an incorrect referral, particularly one involving a trip across town or campus. All units providing reference service must be well informed and must communicate information with each other to facilitate their making appropriate referrals. Cooperation with other units in areas such as bibliographic instruction, reference collection development, and online searching is likewise critical. With a clear understanding of the complementary role each department plays, reference service is maximized, while unnecessary duplication of collections and related reference services is minimized.

Finally, the manager serves as liaison between the reference department and the library administration. The head presents to the administration the needs, concerns, and plans of the department, such as the necessity for more sophisticated equipment to facilitate electronic reference service. Likewise, the head communicates to the reference staff the central administration's concerns, whether involving budget cuts and retrenchment, or new directions and initiatives. Ideally, the reference manager participates on an administrative or advisory committee and represents the department directly in the library's planning and decision-making process. Because virtually every decision, from networking CD-ROMs to installing a security system, has ramifications for public service, input from those units working most directly with the public is essential.

Goal Setting and Planning. One of the most important responsibilities of the reference manager, according to Charles Bunge, is ensuring that the staff has a shared sense of the aims and purposes of the department, which then forms the heart of the planning process.[18] Specifying the mission of the department serves as a guide to the development of goals related to services, resources, and personnel. For example, if the mission of a library is to foster information literacy as well as providing reference services, the goals, and the means of achieving them, will reflect this objective. Planning then will proceed for services (bibliographic instruction programs, computer-assisted instruction), resources (user aids), and personnel utilization (instruction coordinators) which support the instruction mission.

No department, no matter how well run, can operate successfully without change. Not only do facilities (e.g., phone systems and furniture) become outmoded, but advances in technology, and the consequences of the information explosion, also mandate that the reference department keep pace with the present and plan for the future. Plans may be developed in response to a demonstrated need; for example, overcrowding in the reference room might necessitate a weeding project. Or they may anticipate a need, such as planning for providing online catalog assistance when a new automation system is introduced. No matter what the impetus, however, planning must involve setting goals and objectives which are consistent with the department's mission, and must involve all members of the department if staff support is to be forthcoming.

Aside from setting goals and objectives, and involving the department, the manager must in many cases take finances into account in the planning process. The degree of control which the department head exerts over the reference budget varies from library to library. In most instances, the reference book budget is under the direct control of the department, but the overall operating budget (salaries, supplies, equipment) may be centrally administered. Nevertheless, the reference manager must understand the overall budgeting process and be prepared to present a cogent proposal. For instance, in planning for security for the reference collection, the annual replacement cost of missing items (including staff time) must be calculated against the costs involved in the installation and maintenance of a security system. The entire project, however, depends on departmental and library priorities and the availability of funds.[19]

Personnel Administration. A large proportion of the reference manager's mental energy, if not time, is devoted to personnel administration. From hiring and staff development to evaluation, motivation, and conflict resolution, the reference head holds the responsibility for managing the human resources in the department—a responsibility far more complex than managing a collection or a budget.

The recruitment of new staff provides an excellent opportunity to shape the department. In some institutions, the head alone makes the hiring decision; in others, the head is part of a committee which makes a recommendation to higher administrators. In either case, hiring offers the opportunity to work towards establishing an effective and integrated department, filling existing gaps, and complementing strengths and specializations within the department. Aside from job-related characteristics, such as previous experience or language skills, an applicant's individual style must be taken into consideration. Reference work can be very ego-involving, and individuals who are highly competitive and judgmental can be a detriment to a work environment which depends on shared expertise and cooperation among colleagues. Thus, the astute search committee or department head will seek a candidate with a combination of intellectual ability (particularly reasoning skills and logic) and highly developed interpersonal skills. Once a hiring decision has been made, the new librarian must be integrated into the department and receive an appropriate orientation both to the library and to the department, including discussion of the department's procedures and its philosophy of service, as pointed out in chapter 7.

Continued professional development is essential for all staff members, if the department is to benefit from new developments in the field. These developments may involve the application of new technologies to reference work, such as the incorporation of online services into the reference environment, or innovations in library instruction, or emerging ethical concerns. Continued development of the staff, whether through in-house training or attendance at conferences and workshops, is essential for keeping the department at the forefront of reference work, both in theory and in practice. (For a more detailed discussion, see chapter 7.) In the well-administered reference department, continuing education maintains a high profile, and the staff benefits from new developments in the field.

In addition to hiring and training, the head of reference is also responsible for performance appraisal. Effectively undertaken, this evaluation provides the opportunity to establish and assess the individual staff member's goals, and reaffirms the department's objectives. Optimally, the overall effectiveness of the department is enhanced by encouraging activities which help achieve individual and departmental goals, and identifying areas which need improvement. (See chapter 8 for a more detailed discussion of the theory and practice of evaluation.)

As in any work environment, personnel problems will inevitably arise in a reference department, and their solution depends on the leadership of the manager as well as on dynamics within both the department and the institution. Much has been written about stress among public service librarians, with the common refrain being that an increase in demands and expectations (user education, online searching) without a concurrent increase in staff causes burnout. Another ubiquitous concern is loss of control. As institutions and collections grow in size and complexity, and as technology renders access to information seemingly limitless, it is difficult for the individual on the reference staff to feel confident or capable in all aspects of the job. Likewise, interpersonal conflicts and tensions among the reference staff, or grievances with the central administration, can have serious consequences for departmental morale. The reference manager must display sensitivity to the needs and limits of the staff, and establish realistic goals for the department, and must also possess skills in both problem solving and conflict resolution.

Developing Management Skills

As mentioned previously, situations frequently arise in which individual librarians must assume managerial roles for the administration of specific functions, such as coordinating online or instructional services or managing interlibrary loans. These librarians bear responsibility for daily operations, as well as the necessary training and staff development, budgeting, and planning. To the librarian without prior management experience, this can present an unanticipated challenge. While collective management or supervisory rotation provide on-the-job training for developing management skills, few librarians have the opportunity to profit from such experience.

How do managers learn to manage? Library schools generally offer courses in library administration, which can provide useful background and theory, but one cannot learn to manage in the sense that one can learn to conduct online searches. Moreover, the practicing librarian will no doubt be challenged with a variety of issues and situations not addressed in textbooks. From handling personnel problems, such as an uncooperative staff member, to planning for new services, such as answering reference questions electronically, the reference environment promises a constant challenge. Management skills and strategies may well be developed, however, and keeping up with the professional literature and taking advantage of continuing education opportunities are two important means of achieving professional growth.

Librarians are fortunate to have numerous professional support systems to foster the development of managerial skills. Professional associations, such as the American Library Association (ALA), provide several forums for the discussion of management issues. Though seemingly byzantine in its organization, ALA provides numerous avenues for professional development for the manager or potential manager of reference services. A variety of discussion groups, committees, and task forces provide opportunities for information exchange, foster research, and sponsor continuing education opportunities, mainly through programs at conferences. From staff development and evaluation to leadership training, professional involvement serves as a practical means of developing management skills. A sampling of opportunities offered by the American Library Association is provided in box 9.6.

■ ══ ■

9.6
Management Development and Support Activities
of the American Library Association

Reference and Adult Services Division

   Management of Reference Committee
      Identifies and studies issues relating to the management of reference services in all types of libraries.

   Evaluation of Reference and Adult Services Committee
      Concerned with qualitative evaluation and quantitative measurements of service.

Library Administration and Management Association

   Middle Management Discussion Group
      Provides a forum for examining and encouraging the improvement of middle management in libraries.

   Personnel Administration Section: Supervisory Skills Committee
      Addresses the ongoing personnel needs of library supervisors by providing support through programs, publications, and workshops.

American Association of School Librarians

   Supervisor's Section
      Provides a forum for discussion of the problems relating to all phases of school library supervision.

Association for Library Service to Children

   Managing Children's Services Discussion Group
      Addresses concerns relating to the management of children's services, and provides an opportunity for members to develop management expertise.

For more information on ALA's management activities, and how to get involved, see the *ALA Handbook of Organization*.[20]

Summary

Though reference librarians pride themselves on providing answers, there are no ready answers to the question of how to provide reference service most effectively, nor how best to manage a reference department. Whether centralized or decentralized, provided at a desk or in an office, the challenges of reference service require both effective leadership and staff dynamism if reference librarians are (to borrow from William Faulkner's well-worn phrase) to not merely endure, but prevail.

Notes

1. Paula D. Watson, *Reference Services in Academic Research Libraries* (Chicago: American Library Association, 1986), 49.

2. Mary Barton, "Administrative Problems in Reference Work," in *The Reference Function of the Library*, ed. Pierce Butler (Chicago: University of Chicago Press, 1943), 223.

3. See Thomas D. Watts, "A Brief for Centralized Library Collections," *Journal of Academic Librarianship* 9 (September 1983): 196-97; Jane P. Kleiner, "The Configuration of Reference in an Electronic Environment," *College & Research Libraries* 48 (July 1987): 302-13.

4. See Hugh Atkinson, "A Brief for the Other Side," *Journal of Academic Librarianship* 9 (September 1983): 200-201.

5. See Snunith Shoham, "A Cost-Preference Study of the Decentralization of Academic Library Services," *Library Research* 4 (1982): 175-94; Charles Martell, *The Client-Centered Academic Library: An Organizational Model* (Westport, Conn.: Greenwood Press, 1983), 136p.

6. Thelma Freides, "Current Trends in Academic Libraries," *Library Trends* 31 (Winter 1983): 466-67.

7. See Barbara J. Ford, "Reference Beyond (and Without) the Reference Desk," *College & Research Libraries* 47 (September 1986): 491-94.

8. William Miller, "What's Wrong with Reference: Coping with Success and Failure at the Reference Desk," *American Libraries* 13 (May 1984): 322.

9. Patricia K. Swanson, "Traditional Models: Myths and Realities," in *Academic Libraries: Myths and Realities, Proceedings of the Third National Conference of the Association of College and Research Libraries* (Chicago: Association of College and Research Libraries, 1984), 89.

10. Freides, "Current Trends in Academic Libraries," 466-67.

11. This model is discussed in Barbara Barton and Charles Bunge, "Paraprofessionals at the Reference Desk," paper presented at the Wisconsin Library Association Annual Meeting, October 27, 1989.

12. Nicholas Burckel, "Participatory Management in Academic Libraries: A Review," *College & Research Libraries* 45 (January 1984): 25-33.

13. Cynthia Comer et al., "Collective Management of Reference Services," *Library Administration and Management* 2 (September 1988): 191-95.

14. See Bob Perdue and Chris Piotrowski, "Supervisory Rotation: Impact on an Academic Library Reference Staff," *RQ* 25 (Spring 1986): 361-65.

15.   For specific examples of reference policies held by academic, public, and special libraries, see Bill Katz and Anne Clifford, eds., *Reference and Online Services Handbook: Guidelines, Policies, Procedures* (New York: Neal Schuman, 1982), 581p.

16.   For a more detailed discussion of reference/technical services relations, see Gordon Stevenson and Sally Stevenson, eds., *Reference Services and Technical Services: Interactions in Library Practice* (New York: Haworth Press, 1984), 176p. Also published as the *Reference Librarian* 9 (Fall/Winter 1983).

17.   Michael Gorman, "On Doing Away with Technical Services," *American Libraries* 10 (July/August 1979): 435.

18.   Charles A. Bunge, "Planning, Goals, and Objectives for the Reference Department," *RQ* 23 (Spring 1984): 306-15.

19.   For further discussion, see Ruth A. Fraley and Bill Katz, eds., *Finance, Budget, and Management for Reference Services* (New York: Haworth Press, 1989), 376p. Also published as the *Reference Librarian* 19 (Fall 1987).

20.   *ALA Handbook of Organization* (Chicago: American Library Association, annual).

Additional Readings

Cuyler, Alison E. "The Management of Library Reference Services: An Overview of the Literature." *Reference Librarian* 3 (Spring 1982): 127-47.
This review article includes a well-referenced bibliographic essay on issues relating to reference administration and management, from accountability to staffing. A selected, partially annotated bibliography of over 130 references (through 1980) includes sections on general management, personnel issues, statistics, budget, administration of online services, policies, and evaluation.

Hansel, Patsy J. "Administration of Reference Services in the Small Public Library." *Reference Librarian* 3 (Spring 1982): 113-20.
Focusing on the small public library, this article discusses issues involved in providing reference services with limited staff. The author offers strategies for staff development to provide for more effective reference and information services.

Katz, Bill, and Ruth A. Fraley, eds. *Reference Services Administration and Management*. New York: Haworth Press, 1982. 147p. (Also published as *Reference Librarian* 3 [Spring 1982].)
This collection of seventeen articles represents one of the few publications devoted to the specific issue of management of reference departments. Articles range from general concerns, such as guidelines for a beginning manager of reference, to specific topics, such as developing a policy manual. Anecdotal rather than scholarly, the articles nevertheless provide a practical look at reference management.

Kleiner, Jane P. "The Configuration of Reference in an Electronic Environment." *College & Research Libraries* 48 (July 1987): 302-13.
This well-researched article focuses the centralization versus decentralization debate on the reference department, in light of new electronic technologies. Both the positive and negative impact of centralization on staff and services are reviewed, and the rationale is presented for the move away from decentralized towards centralized reference services at Louisiana State University.

Library Administration and Management. Chicago: Library Administration and Management Association, 1987- . Quarterly.
Published by the Library Administration and Management Association of the American Library Association, this periodical addresses management and administrative issues for all types of libraries. The focus is practical rather than theoretical, and is intended for information sharing as well as discussion of topics of relevance to managers.

Ridgeway, Trish, Peggy Cover, and Carl Stone, eds. *Improving Reference Management*. Chicago: Reference and Adult Services Division, American Library Association, 1986. 73p.

This collection of papers is based upon a workshop sponsored by the Southeastern Library Association and the Reference and Adult Services Division of the American Library Association. Seven articles address typical management concerns, such as establishing standards, evaluation, burnout, utilization of paraprofessionals, and management techniques.

Thomas, Diana M., Ann T. Hinckley, and Elizabeth R. Eisenbach. *The Effective Reference Librarian*. New York: Academic Press, 1981. 214p.

Offering an overview of issues and concerns relating to the management of reference services, the chapter on administration includes a discussion of management systems, organization, goals and objectives, budgeting, and personnel administration.

Wheeler, J., and Herbert Goldhor. "Reference Services." In *Wheeler and Goldhor's Practical Administration of Public Libraries*, 160-87. Rev. ed. New York: Harper & Row, 1981.

This chapter addresses the organization and development of reference services in the public library, including relationships with other departments and libraries, staffing, training, collection development, services, and evaluation.

REFERENCE SERVICES TO SPECIAL GROUPS

Introduction

If *reference service* is defined as the individualized assistance given to a patron to provide needed information, one could argue that members of special groups might automatically or by definition receive good reference service. If the librarian is to meet individual needs, part of the reference task is to assess the individual patron's capabilities and develop a search strategy based on that assessment. By definition, every patron is special. Why, then, does service to special groups require discussion?

Developing special reference services for special groups is a corollary to developing services for the majority. As the reference librarian sets up standard service priorities, awareness will develop that exceptional or, in some cases, elusive patrons are not being served commensurate with their needs. Thus, beyond the provision of basic reference services for the obvious, primary group of users, librarians need to identify significant secondary or special groups of users with common needs, and adapt and adjust reference services to these special patrons. By anticipating group needs, librarians will be able more efficiently and less problematically to provide special reference services to each group. The ability to fill reference requests from members of special groups will increase when special techniques and collections are developed and specialized reference sources are collected. Collections for a particular group should include sources containing information on common interests or concerns of that group, and agencies should be identified which can be contacted for additional information or support. Specialized professional reference sources can provide reference librarians with information on materials or services which they could offer to special groups.

Libraries, particularly those supported by public funds, have a legal obligation to provide service without discrimination. The profession has created the *Library Bill of Rights* to emphasize further its commitment to fair use of resources and openness to all users (see box 10.1). Reference librarians also need to be aware of legal issues connected with confidentiality and censorship when serving special groups, particularly with information given to juveniles or other special groups, such as prisoners.

The basis of concern for reference services to special groups is ethical as well as legal. Reference librarians often must be advocates for patrons to ensure that they have equal access to information and materials.

■ ═══ ■

10.1
Library Bill of Rights

Article 5 of the Library Bill of Rights states that:

> A person's right to use a library should not be denied or abridged because of origin, age, background, or views.[1]

> — (Adopted June 18, 1948. Amended February 2, 1961; June 27, 1967; and January 23, 1980, by the ALA Council.)

Broadly interpreted, this article includes all persons, regardless of circumstance. In the interpretation of article five, the rights of minors to free access to libraries are explicitly defended:

> The American Library Association opposes libraries restricting access to library materials and services for minors and holds that it is the parents — and only parents — who may restrict their children — and only their children — from access to library materials and services. Parents who would rather their children did not have access to certain materials should so advise their children. The library and its staff are responsible for providing equal access to library materials and services for all library users."[2]

> — (Adopted June 30, 1972. Amended July 1, 1981, by the ALA Council.)

The special groups discussed in this chapter are differentiated on the basis of age (children, young adults, and the elderly); disabling conditions (physical and mental disabilities); language facility (non-English-speaking and the adult illiterate); and institutionalization (prisons, hospitals, and convalescent care). For each of these groups, defining characteristics of the group are described, reference techniques and policy issues associated with the group are discussed, and special reference tools are identified, when appropriate.

Within any library community, there may be other groups to be considered, and not every group discussed here would be of concern to every library. This chapter gives an overview of issues associated with reference services to special groups, and provides a model for developing specialized reference services to groups in any community. The assumption is that service to any one group is a microcosm of general reference service — that the basics of reference service are present and the task is to adapt good reference skills and collections to serve each group. The model for adapting reference services includes:

1. Assessing the problems a special patron experiences when trying to access information and service at the reference desk

2. Doing research that includes contact with associations and special service providers about how to improve services for special users (and to attract non-users)

3. Planning how to change the reference interview, collection development, and delivery of service

4. Training staff to work with patrons with special needs

5. Implementing periodic evaluation of reference services to special patrons.

Though school, public, academic, and special libraries may vary in the degree to which certain reference services are provided, elements to be considered for inclusion in an adequate configuration of reference services for special groups include:

- Informational services commensurate with the group's needs and abilities, such as ready reference, homework assignment help, personal research assistance, and information and referral services (see chapter 1)

- Readers' advisory service (see chapter 1)

- Instructional services which include assistance both in using materials and in understanding the information found (see chapter 6)

- Collection development to support informational and developmental needs of each group, including a good reference and circulating collection of materials at appropriate reading and cognitive levels in book and nonbook formats

- Interlibrary referral and loan services to supplement local sources, when necessary

- Solutions to problems of access caused by physical, cognitive, or emotional barriers.[3]

Reference Services
to Specific Age Groups

Three age groups are discussed in this chapter. As an introduction to thinking about differences in reference services called for because of age, the focus is on children, young adults, and the elderly. Service to adults is not addressed because the basic reference services described throughout this book focus on services to the general adult audience. For this discussion, *children* are defined as persons from birth to age fourteen, or infancy through junior high school, while *young adults* are defined as persons from ages twelve through eighteen, or junior high and high school students. There is an intentional overlap in the definitions of children and young adults to account for the variety of ways in which both public libraries and schools choose to serve the junior high or middle school person. The *elderly* include persons who are sixty-five years of age or older. While there is little literature on special needs of the elderly for library service, this is the fastest growing segment of our population, growing by about 30 percent in the last decade.[4] Undoubtedly, the library profession should begin to adapt reference services to meet the needs of this growing population.

Children

In addition to serving the children themselves, most reference services to children include assistance to parents, teachers, and other care providers. An adult is often the intermediary for the child's questions, and may need guidance in the use of materials housed in the youth services area of the public library or the school library media center. The parent, for example, can be extremely helpful in translating what a preschool child is actually asking for when she asks for the "choo choo" book (*The Little Engine That Could*[5]). The parent might have his own reference needs, such as interest in information on trends in children's publishing. Unfortunately, not all adults are clear or skilled translators of children's needs.

Thus, the reference librarian may need to develop skill at discerning a teacher's intent under-lying a school assignment to the student and then adapting it to the collection at hand, or may have to be able to separate parent and child long enough to find out what the child really wants to know or read (as opposed to what the parent thinks the child wants). In any case, children's reference service actually includes patrons of all ages.

Because of the emphasis on programming and fiction collection development in service to young children, preschoolers' information needs are often ignored. Young children have many questions and can develop interests in nonfiction topics. A collection of print as well as nonprint materials is necessary to meet the young child's needs for information. For example, a film or recording may help answer a preschooler's questions about what school is like. It is also important to be able to supply information that is simply stated, if, for instance, a young child asks about how to care for a family pet or about more serious issues such as dealing with death or illness. Librarians need to have commercially or locally produced bibliographies of picture and easy-to-read book titles available, for both reference staff and patrons to use, as subject cataloging of these materials is often inadequate.

When children enter school, their reference needs become increasingly influenced by class assignments. Also, as school-age children grow socially and intellectually, their personal interests become more individual and their reading and critical thinking skills allow them to use books and printed materials with increasing power and effectiveness. Because children develop at varying rates, it is important for the reference librarian to accurately assess the child's levels of skill and sophistication when answering questions or helping with homework research. Most school-age children have tremendous problems forming questions or identifying personal interests, so librarians need to perfect skills in interviewing children and eliciting accurate responses from them. Children, like patrons of any age, need a wide range of services. Typically, the school media center provides materials to meet the child's instructional needs, with the public library serving as backup.

Information Services for Children. Various surveys of children's reference questions show that they are predominantly school-related or stimulated by popular culture (television, movies, sports).[6] This being the case, there is a certain predictability for much reference work done with children, which allows the reference staff to plan ahead. It is not particularly easy to get teachers to warn librarians about the assignment needs of children, but often librarians can set up a system of communication whereby assignment sheets are copied and kept on file. Teachers can be phoned or approached informally with questions, and notations kept from year to year about the major assignments that are likely to return perennially. Strong communication links between school library media specialists and public library reference staff can help both institutions provide better reference service to school children. Also, some time spent in reading local and school papers and keeping up with movies, music, and youth culture will help librarians predict and relate to reference questions on personal interest topics.

Children often need information about community events and services. They also have limited choices for gathering such information, and may logically turn to librarians at the public library or at school for help. As with adult information and referral questions, children sometimes want to know factual information about the community (e.g., "Who is mayor of our town?"), or information on local events ("When does the Fourth of July parade start?"), or information on community resources ("Who do I contact to join the Boy Scouts?"). A community resource file that contains a section on children's activities will be extremely useful in answering this kind of question. Major metropolitan areas often publish guides to resources available for children; in smaller communities, local service agencies may provide such guides. When actually referring a child to call or contact someone outside the library, it is helpful to write out all the needed information and encourage the child to get a parent or other adult to help with the call.

If the child has a title request and the material is unavailable locally, the possibility of interlibrary loan should be explained. Because children often have no way to pick material up at a neighboring library, it is important to provide access to interlibrary loan delivery systems. Like most adults, children prefer to have material available at their local libraries or in their school collections, but in some cases they may be able to wait for interlibrary delivery. Local interlibrary loan service may have special limitations with regard to children. Sometimes schools are excluded from interlibrary loan policies and agreements, or internal public library policy may deny interlibrary loan privileges to patrons below a designated age.

Electronic reference services, with the exception of instruction in the use of the library's online catalog, are rarely provided to children. The reasons for this are both economic and pragmatic (provision of access to computerized information, particularly commercially controlled databases, is costly, and few online or CD-ROM databases provide elementary-level information). General encyclopedias online or ondisc are one type of source which would be accessible to children, and may be feasible in a public library already equipped to provide computerized reference sources to the adult population.

Ethics and Confidentiality. Children may request information on sensitive topics, such as sex or drugs. Reference librarians need to consult and interpret — and in some cases formulate — local policy related to the provision of information to minors on controversial topics. Some institutions are required to act *in loco parentis* (in the place of the parent), unless released from this status by particular parents with respect to their own children. The political or religious affiliation of some libraries may dictate local policy with regard to minors, and require library personnel to provide less than the Library Bill of Rights' intended level of access to information. For example, in a parochial school library, librarians may be restricted from providing information about abortion.

In the course of a reference transaction, a child may reveal a need for counseling, police protection, legal aid, or other social services. Again, children's access to these services is often limited, so they call on familiar adults for help. (See box 10.2.)

■ ━━━ ■

10.2

Child Abuse and Awareness: How Can Libraries Help?

In response to the question "do we really need child abuse materials and services in libraries?," the answer is a resounding yes. Increased awareness of the incidence of child abuse and neglect has concerned citizens and professionals scurrying to find appropriate resources that will help them answer questions for themselves, for their clients and for their families. In Illinois the Department of Children and Family Services received 70,000 reports of alleged abuse in 1986; this figure skyrocketed to 95,000 in 1988....

In many communities, the public library is the only place where resources ... on child abuse issues may be available. As demand for appropriate materials increases, librarians must be aware of trends and issues that are developing in this field. Social service professionals are interested in becoming more familiar with available lay materials suitable for adult or children's use, in receiving resource lists which can be used in counseling sessions, in increased access to sophisticated database searches, and in practical research trends; libraries are the logical resources to provide these services.

— Lincoln Trail Libraries System
"Children in Crisis: A Cooperative Library and Community
Agency Support for Abused and Neglected Youth"[7]

Librarians need to know who in the community provides these services to children, what library policy is about maintaining confidentiality, and what local and state law specifies about reporting information such as suspected child abuse. Because of the vulnerability of children, it may be necessary to call police, social workers, or parents on behalf of a child and balance this with the need to respect the privacy of the child. The ability to maintain confidentiality in a patron-librarian relationship is inextricably tied to legal issues. In a school library setting, the librarian is typically governed by the same regulations which govern all school personnel, designating them mandated reporters of certain kinds of information. For example, the Abused and Neglected Child Reporting Act of Illinois specifically states that the privileged quality of communication between designated employees and children does not apply in situations involving abuse and neglect.[8]

Readers' Advisory. While readers' advisory services to the general adult population (see chapter 1) have become less common in recent years, readers' advisory is an essential service for children. Whether asking for school-related information or a good book to read, children usually need some guidance in choosing materials. Readers' advisory service to children is enhanced when the librarian knows the local collection well, has specialized training in library materials for children, and is an active reader of the literature. When helping children with book selection, the librarian should determine the child's interests or needs (e.g., "Are there any books on moving to another town?"), the child's age or grade level, and some indication of the child's reading level. The child can usually articulate an interest, and most often will tell the librarian a grade level, but it may be a little more difficult to assess the child's actual reading level. School library media specialists may be able to check school records, while public librarians may have to ask parents or children what books they have been reading recently to get some idea of where to start. It is always wise to give children several choices of titles and encourage personal selection. This gives children practice in independent book selection, but also answers the need for some guidance from a knowledgeable adult.

Instruction for Children in the Use of Libraries and Materials. Often both formal group instruction and individual instruction are included as part of children's reference services. Traditionally, library instruction has been the responsibility of the school librarian. It is believed that integrating library skills in all areas of the curriculum, cooperation between librarian and teacher, and creative learning activities will provide children with the skills they need to succeed in school and become lifelong learners. It has not been demonstrated, however, that the skills learned in formal library instruction are effectively transferred by children to academic libraries when students reach higher education,[9] or that students can transfer skills from school to public libraries.[10] Particularly as public and school libraries begin to use online catalogs, instruction must be library-specific, as each library online catalog has unique design features. At the same time, though, the instruction needs to be generic (e.g., there is such a thing as an author name that can be searched). Part of the reference interview with young patrons should include an explanation of why and how reference tools are used. Children may need help in interpreting information once it is found. It is often a creative process to determine at what point library instruction related to homework assignments becomes doing the homework itself!

The Reference Interview. The reference interview is important for all patrons, but it is "particularly problematic when dealing with children who form their questions through limited vocabulary and sphere of experience."[11] Children should receive assistance in "identifying, locating and interpreting information."[12] The main vehicle for this is the interview. Good listening, a friendly, open demeanor, and clear, short explanations will help children express their needs for assistance and assure a successful search. Children often lack an intellectual context for their questions, so interviews with children may need to be more directive, with fewer open-ended questions and more explanation, than interviews with adults. For instance, children often come with a homework assignment question which is essentially the teacher's—the student acts as the messenger, not as a thoughtful (or even interested) inquirer. Also, children may not be accurate in their requests. Verifying spelling, proper names, and any facts presented in a child's question may be a good first step in an interview to ensure that both the librarian and the child are on track. Children also have difficulty following directions in sequence. A reasonable suggestion to a middle-grade child that includes three or four steps (go to the catalog, find the call number of this book, go to the proper place in the stacks, find the book, look in the index for your topic, and so forth) may be too difficult for the child to remember at that stage of development. The reference interview may have to be done gradually as the child works through the search step by step.

In addition to the problems of getting information from the child and helping the child absorb information from the librarian, time is short. Children have a short attention span, and are easily discouraged if a search is not successful on the first few tries. Again, a series of short exchanges may be more successful than one longer, more complete interview. The reference librarian needs to be good at juggling several searches-in-progress at a time, keeping track of where each child's search is. Children react to a positive attitude and praise, so efficiency may sometimes have to be sacrificed for friendliness.

Specialized Reference Sources. While there are relatively few reference sources for children to use themselves (reference titles are a very small part of the publishing market for children), there are a number of sources that help librarians and other adults to select children's materials and to provide good, accurate general reference and readers' advisory services to children.

Kenneth Kister's *Best Encyclopedias: A Guide to General and Specialized Encyclopedias* will help in selecting encyclopedias for children, and Carolyn Peterson and Ann Fenton's *Reference Books for Children* may be a helpful buying guide, particularly if it is updated. *Children's Catalog*, a Wilson publication, and Lois Winkel's *The Elementary School Library Collection: A Guide to Books and Other Media* both present fiction and nonfiction titles for a basic collection for children. The latter contains a separate section listing children's reference sources, and the former includes subheadings for types of reference sources in its index. The American Library Association, the National Council of Teachers of English, and other professional organizations regularly publish bibliographies of recommended titles for children. There are also several helpful book-length bibliographies on special topics in children's literature. For example, Joan Fassler's *Helping Children Cope* recommends titles on stressful topics such as death, illness, separation, and other kinds of change. Margaret Carlin, Jeannine Laughlin, and Richard Saniga have compiled *Understanding Abilities, Disabilities, and Capabilities*, a bibliography of children's books about individuals with disabilities. *Books for the Gifted Child*, Vol. 1, by Barbara Baskin and Karen Harris, and *Books for the Gifted Child*, Vol. 2, by Paula Hauser and Gail Nelson, recommend titles that are intellectually stimulating but age-appropriate for gifted children. Charlene Strickland's *Dogs, Cats, and Horses* defines a core collection of about 600 of the best books for children in grades 1-12. Two especially helpful indexes for children's books are Carolyn Lima and John Lima's *A to Zoo, Subject Access to Children's Picture Books*, and Sharon Dreyer's *The Bookfinder: A Guide to Children's Literature About the Needs and Problems of Youth Aged 2 to 15*, in four volumes. Both provide access to affective themes in children's literature. Aids for collecting and evaluating nonbook materials for children are also available.

The main types of reference works published for use by children are dictionaries and encyclopedias. There are also specialized indexes and directories which provide access to various types and formats of information or materials for children. Examples of these include *Index to Poetry for Children and Young People, 1964-1969* and its supplements; Carolyn Peterson and Ann Fenton's *Index to Children's Songs*; *Science Fair Project Index, 1973-1980* and its sequel; and *The Complete Directory to Prime Time Network TV Shows, 1946-Present*, by Tim Brooks and Earle Marsh.

Young Adults

Young adult (YA) reference services are comprised of essentially the same components as children's reference services, with some salient age-related differences. For example, young adults require access to adult-level materials as well as to children's collections. They are also less dependent upon parents or other adults to act as intermediaries or to assist with the use of materials. Two major components of reference work with young adults, readers' advisory and school-related information needs, are discussed in this section. Young adults are served by public libraries, school libraries, and, in many cases, college and university libraries. They constitute a prominent service group in these libraries; during 1986-87, one out of every four public library patrons was between the ages of twelve and eighteen.[13] However, only 11 percent of public libraries have an in-house young adult librarian;[14] 51 percent of all public libraries can call upon the assistance of a local or regional young adult coordinator or consultant, who provides services to a number of libraries in a defined system or network.[15]

Adolescence is a time of transition. Public libraries typically purchase duplicate copies of selected titles, making them available in both the adult and juvenile departments. Eighty-four percent of public libraries also offer a section or special collection of materials specifically designated for young adults.[16] The concept of giving young adults a separate library space of their own came into favor during the 1940s and 1950s,[17] but has proven to be very expensive in terms of staffing, and has not decreased the need for duplication of materials among departments. Current thinking judges the separation of services to be developmentally counterproductive; rather than segregating young adults, libraries should assist them in learning adult behavior in an integrated environment conducive to promoting this apprenticeship.

Information Services. School-related queries account for the majority of the informational activities of young adult reference work. Students progressing to junior and then senior high school are faced with assignments of increasing number and complexity. In the school library, the librarian's best ally in providing assignment-related assistance is a good program of bibliographic instruction which is integrated into the school curriculum. In this way, the intent of such assignments—to teach students how to locate and utilize information independently—is directly reinforced by the person most qualified to see that this actually happens. In the public library, librarians have much less control over library-related assignments, though these generate a great deal of their reference activity. For frequently requested topics, many libraries prepare *reference pathfinders*; that is, suggested search strategies which include standard reference tools and their appropriate subject headings. For recurring and popular topics, pathfinders provide a kind of one-on-one instruction in high-use environments where a librarian is not always readily available, and are especially effective for young adults who are too shy to ask for help or who appreciate the opportunity to work independently.

Some public libraries take a more assertive stance by establishing homework hotlines or study services such as peer tutoring programs. Because grades typically become more of an issue at the junior and senior high school levels, and students are increasingly responsible for individual productivity, it is important to establish a library policy for young adult reference services that delineates what the library can and cannot do in terms of homework assistance. Telephone reference, for example, is an amorphous issue; it is difficult to define limits among professionals, let alone explain them to an adolescent. The purpose of a written policy is to serve as a regulating device, designed to keep this burden from being placed upon the shoulders of individual staff members.

Interlibrary loan service also presents special challenges in youth services. In practical terms, tight deadlines and the human tendency to procrastinate, coupled with increased mobility on the part of teenagers, usually suggest that direct reciprocal borrowing from nearby libraries is a more viable option than interlibrary loan for young adults. The reference librarian can assist by providing location information to the patron.

■ ══ ■

10.3
A Delicate Situation

Bill Smith, the librarian at George Washington High School, finds the following note in his mailbox:

> Dear Bill,
>
> Here is a copy of the assignment I have given to my sophomore classes. Each student has a different geographical location to research. I have instructed the students *not* to bother you with questions or requests for help. In fact, I have informed them that they are to finish the work completely *on their own* and that any help they receive from anyone will be considered cheating. I thought I ought to warn you of this in advance before any of them catches you unawares. As always, thanks for your help.
>
> Sylvia Jones
> Social Studies Department

Bill looks over the assignment and observes that the students already possess the general library skills involved, but he is also acutely aware that some small idiosyncrasy in a reference tool could seriously impede the progress of an otherwise conscientious student. For some students, the assignment will become a lesson in frustration rather than in geography. He also knows that some students will feel forced to "cheat" by going to the public library where they can ask for help less conspicuously. How can he convince Sylvia Jones that his reference assistance, and even a dose of bibliographic instruction, will not compromise the integrity of the assignment and that it might even enhance the way students think about and approach their topics?

Ethics and Confidentiality. As a part of growing up, young adults are naturally interested in information that is of a personal or sensitive nature. In the library, they face the prospect of going through an intermediary to find information on topics like sexuality or troubled family relationships. The librarian must be seen as a neutral resource, while appearing sympathetic and understanding. A school librarian may be in the privileged position of knowing the individuals better, of being the trusted counselor. On the other hand, a student in search of sensitive information may prefer to ask for it where anonymity is more likely.

The ability to maintain confidentiality in the patron-librarian relationship, however, is inextricably tied to legal issues, as outlined in the previous section regarding confidentiality and children. In a public library, a written reference policy can provide the opportunity to make an explicit statement regarding open access and the library's commitment to confidentiality. By doing so, the library is released from the *in loco parentis* role and can grant young adults independent and adult status in their pursuit of information. In any case, it is incumbent upon the librarian to find out what local laws or policies govern this issue before stumbling into a compromising situation.

Readers' Advisory. Young adult reference service began largely as an out-of-school, extracurricular effort to emphasize reading guidance in an era when school courses were taught solely from textbooks.[18] This orientation continued even after teachers began expecting students to use outside sources. In libraries without a young adult specialist, the readers' advisory role is often subsumed by the school-related informational role, one with which reference generalists may be more comfortable, and where the techniques and tools more readily translate across age levels.

Readers' advisory service is an aspect of reference work that is of critical importance in the YA arena. Books present young adults with options, allowing them to inspect models of conflict resolution and decision making and, in the process, to develop their own critical thinking skills. Librarians who serve young adults need to know the literature, to be able to suggest titles that are similar to other titles a young patron has enjoyed, and to discuss the issues raised therein. Dorothy M. Broderick admonishes today's librarians with the example of Margaret Edward of the Enoch Pratt Free Library, who required a librarian to read and *orally report* on 300 titles from the New York Public Library's *Books for the Teen Age* before being granted the title of Young Adult Librarian.[19]

The Reference Interview. As young adults begin to move away from the children's department and to ask questions at the adult reference desk, they encounter many librarians who are helpful and friendly, take their needs at face value, and treat them as individuals. They also encounter librarians who are uncomfortable with them, see them as potential problems, and judge their needs to be less serious than those of adults and therefore less important.

Complicating the situation, developmental differences often make it extremely difficult to determine a young person's age. Some young adults still look juvenile, yet consider themselves beyond that stage. Because publishers package most curricular material for the juvenile market, a lot of information very appropriate for adolescents is housed in the children's department. Clearly, navigating between the adult and juvenile departments during the reference process calls for tact and discretion.

During any reference interview, the librarian must determine a patron's actual need, as opposed to the need as it is initially expressed. In the case of young adults, vocabulary and self-concept are still developing.[20] Young adults may not yet possess the analytical skills to identify the components of their information need, or to approach a problem systematically and sequentially. Nevertheless, they have to articulate their needs to a figure of authority in a strange environment.

The librarian must, therefore, take special pains to be approachable, friendly, nonjudgmental, and, above all, not condescending. A patron's reluctance to come forward must also be respected. However, when a question is obviously school-related, it is often possible to ask more pointed, direct questions than one normally would: "Can I ask you what your assignment is? Do you have a copy of it with you?" It is always helpful to rephrase a patron's question to make sure both parties are working under the same assumptions.

Specialized Sources. The young adult librarian has available a number of excellent sources which provide information on a wide variety of reference issues. The Young Adult Services Division of the American Library Association is, in itself, a useful source of information. Several committee-produced lists of recommended book titles are the most well-known of its publications; chief among these is the annual list of *Best Books for Young Adults*. Other lists include titles for special populations (e.g., *Recommended Books for the Reluctant Young Adult Reader*) or on specific topics (e.g., *Outstanding Biographies for the College Bound*). Book-length sources of recommended titles for young adults, such as the time-honored *Books for the Teen Age*, published annually, are also available. Marianne Pilla has compiled *The Best: High/Low Books for Reluctant Readers*, with indexes by reading level and by subject.

Several professional periodicals provide current awareness for YA librarians. The *Voice of Youth Advocates*, edited by Dorothy Broderick, is the only one of these journals with a specific focus on young adult services.

Older Adults

While the other special age groups (children and young adults) have both a body of professional literature and an established separate place in libraries, the elderly often lack recognition as a group with special needs. As the elderly are a fast-growing part of the population, it is likely that their special needs and services will come to the forefront in the next twenty-five years. In the 1980 census, about 11.3 percent of the American population was over 65 years of age. By 2030, it is estimated that the population over 65 will increase by 100 percent and that the population over 85 will increase by 300 percent.[21] It is also anticipated that, because of improved health care, older adults will be more active.

Good reference service for the elderly includes all of the basic components of good reference service for the general adult population, with particular attention to the individual needs of elderly patrons. Reference services for older adults require special planning in several areas. Library agencies serving older populations will need to adapt collection development, delivery of reference services, and interpersonal and communications skills to provide excellent service to older adults. In a report prepared for the U.S. Department of Health, Education and Welfare in the mid-1970s, information specialists identified the following as the most common problems of the elderly: (1) income, money, and Social Security; (2) transportation; (3) housing; and (4) health and nutrition needs.[22] Collections should be developed that deal with these issues both from the point of view of the older adult and from the point of view of their children or other caregivers. It is important to have current directories (local, state, and federal) of services for the elderly, as well as materials that discuss the aging process and how to obtain adequate medical, legal, and psychological help. Libraries can use directories to provide information and referral to appropriate government and private agencies serving the elderly. Sources such as Donald Gelfand's *The Aging Network: Programs and Services* and the *Directory of Resources for Aging, Gerontology and Retirement* are examples of titles that give both a good, current overview of issues associated with the elderly and national sources of services for the older adult. A community resource file should include information about rights organizations; local transportation, housing, and educational and recreational opportunities; tax changes; Social Security; and Medicare. A centralized source of this type of information in a community will prove invaluable to both the older patron and the service providers.

To provide reference services to older adults, it may be necessary to offer remote delivery of materials and services. Certainly the most common form of remote delivery of reference service is by telephone. In libraries where in-person reference service is busy and takes precedence over answering telephoned questions, special provisions must be made to serve the homebound and institutionalized elderly. The general rule of serving walk-in patrons before answering the phone is logical, but may make it difficult for the older adult to use the library. It may be necessary to set up a special phone service for elderly (or disabled) patrons who cannot easily get to the library. Also, it may be helpful to take the reference service to the elderly by including a reference librarian among bookmobile staff for stops at retirement homes, nursing facilities, or senior citizen centers. In this way, questions can be asked and answered in a timely and predictable fashion.

In its guidelines for service to older adults, the Reference and Adult Services Division states that librarians should have a "positive attitude toward the aging process and older adults."[23] Reference librarians need to avoid stereotyping of or condescension to older patrons, and should develop effective communication skills so as to encourage older patrons to ask questions and to ensure that answers are fully understood by the patrons. Special instructional sessions for older patrons may help them to better comprehend and utilize the sources and services of the library. For example, offering instruction about the library's online catalog that is especially tailored for older patrons will create a comfortable atmo-sphere in which patrons can ask questions, and should allow for self-paced practice and reinforcement. It is important to communicate to older adults the reference services that are available to them and to make them feel welcome to use these services. The library can effectively market services of particular interest or consequence to older patrons through library brochures, through specific informational programs held in the library, and through outside agencies. Reference librarians should cultivate communications with other service agencies in the community; often specialists in services to the elderly can provide training for library staff in working with the elderly, and will make appropriate referrals to the library if interagency cooperation is practiced.

Careful assessment of what use older citizens make of a library may reveal a need to publicize existing reference services, or a way to adapt services to meet the needs and capacities of older adults.

Reference Services
to Disabled Individuals

Among the special populations for whom librarians need to develop a full range of reference services are individuals with disabilities. Both legally and ethically, librarians in any setting should evaluate the reference services offered from the perspective of the patron with a disability. This is a challenging task, as there are a myriad of disabling conditions, and in any community served the incidence of any one disabling condition may be relatively low. The general groups considered are individuals with physical disabilities and those with mental disabilities.

Persons with Physical Disabilities

The physically disabled population includes people who are blind, visually impaired, deaf, hearing impaired, or orthopedically impaired. Each of these groups requires some-what different adaptations of reference service. The uniting theme, however, is realistic access to resources and services, so that they are usable to the individual with a physical disability.

Visually Impaired Patrons. Blind and visually handicapped individuals have had the longest tradition of special services from libraries. The Library of Congress developed a special reading room for blind persons in 1897.[24] In the 1930s, the Library of Congress developed a national network of libraries to serve blind persons, and in the mid-1960s other disabled individuals became eligible for this service. Currently, the Library of Congress's service to the blind and physically handicapped is available through public libraries. For eligible individuals, the service includes the loan of talking books, a large-print reference collection of books, magazines, and vertical-file materials, and a system of interlibrary loan and technical assistance available through regional libraries for the blind and physically handicapped. Reference librarians, particularly those in public libraries, should be aware of how to use this network, how to register users for the Library of Congress program, and how to make these services known to persons in the community who would benefit from their use.

In addition to the Library of Congress programs, there are many other programs and agencies whose products and services would be useful in helping the patron with visual impairment to gain access to information. Many vendors distribute large-print books and magazines, and the quality and quantity of recorded materials are increasing. Many larger communities have radio stations for blind people and other disabled individuals, as well as organizations that arrange for recording text and other materials for blind persons. There are several innovative adaptations of microcomputers that may eventually eliminate the need for readers for the blind, except for handwritten materials. The Kurzweil Discover series has an optical scanner that will read aloud a variety of typefaces; as synthetic voice devices improve in tone, computers will allow blind persons to read books on their own. As the cost of these devices is currently high ($10,000 in 1989),[25] prohibiting many individuals from purchasing one, libraries may consider providing access to a computerized reading room. Another Kurzweil product of interest is the Kurzweil Voiceterminal, which translates the spoken word to print. While this product is being developed for office use to replace dictation, it certainly may improve communications for both visually impaired and hearing-impaired individuals.

Hearing-Impaired Patrons. Hearing-impaired individuals have traditionally been less well served by libraries. The language impairment of deaf persons requires both sensitivity and skill on the part of reference staff to provide effective service. Several steps can be taken to provide access for patrons with hearing impairments. First, in the area of collection development, information about hearing impairment, consumer information on products for hearing-impaired individuals, community information, and captioned films and videos, as well as clear signage and appropriate brochures for the hearing impaired about library services, are important.[26] A second step is to provide ways by which the hearing-impaired person can communicate with the reference staff. This could include employing librarians who know American Sign Language (or having an interpreter available by appointment), providing TDD (Telecommunication Devices for the Deaf) machines, which can be attached to a regular telephone, and setting up electronic mail systems and bulletin boards that are accessible to hearing-impaired individuals with personal computers. The third issue in providing reference to the hearing impaired is the publicizing of reference services specifically to the hearing-impaired community, as well as to families and service providers. This is essential so that hearing-impaired persons may understand how they can communicate with librarians and what services and collections the library provides.

Orthopedically Disabled Patrons. Orthopedically disabled persons need materials that aid in locating services, information about their disabling conditions, and current legal and medical information. Such guides as the *Directory of National Information Sources on Handicapping Conditions and Related Services*, or more specialized titles such as *Directory of College Facilities and Services for the Disabled*, will direct patrons to sources of information, advocacy, and services. The focus for the reference librarian should also be on the assessment of the reference department, to see that it is barrier-free. Often, specific information on adaptations to the environment is part of municipal or state building codes or accessibility standards. Librarians need to start by looking at local and state codes and deciding what needs to be done to come into compliance. If building codes do not adequately address issues of physical access for disabled people, advocacy groups may be able to supply information on adapting environments or, if local, be able to help in assessing the library's space.[27] Telephone reference services and communication by computer may help home-bound individuals have access to reference service. It is also important to publicize that the library is accessible to the physically disabled community.

Persons with Mental Disabilities

Generally, there are two groups of individuals who have intellectual impairment. They are the developmentally disabled and the learning disabled. *Developmental disability* refers to significant subaverage intellectual functioning, and is usually measured by IQ. Developmentally disabled individuals have, by definition, an IQ of sixty-nine or less[28] (normal IQ is eighty to one hundred). Persons with *learning disabilities* have a discrepancy between expected and actual performance in spoken, read, or written language and/or mathematics.[29] This means that the individual has a normal or higher IQ and no other impairments, but still cannot perform basic academic tasks. The primary characteristics of both of these conditions are diminished memory, attention span, and capacity to spell and use words and numbers.

Despite a limited ability to manipulate information, individuals with mental disabilities have a right to information, and reference librarians can adapt services to meet their needs. Reference interview sessions will need to be short and focused. The most successful materials should have large print, brief texts, and uncluttered pictures. While children's materials often prove to be good reference tools, mentally disabled adults have the full range of adult concerns, such as vocation, social relationships, sexuality, money management, and parenting; thus, they may need to go beyond the resources of a children's reference collection. With the increase in publishing for adult new readers, the adult reference collection can also include these materials. Because the mentally disabled patron may be slow in processing information, it is important to have useful reference materials that circulate, or space so that the materials may be used for long periods of time in the library.

It is important to provide information about developmental and learning disabilities, including the identification of local and national organizations and agencies that serve the mentally disabled population, so that family and caregivers can understand the conditions themselves as well as make appropriate decisions about care. Reference librarians may offer to create bibliographies and special informational brochures about library services to be used by care providers, special schools, and organizations for mentally disabled individuals.

Reference Services to
Non-English-Speaking Populations

For this discussion, non-English-speaking persons are defined as those whose primary language is not English. *Non-English-speaking* is a term of convenience; in actuality, speaking abilities range from no English-speaking experience at all to high degrees of fluency. Demographically, such individuals fall into three general categories: (1) long-term residents or citizens; (2) immigrants or newly arrived persons, both permanent and transient; and (3) international students attending institutions of higher education. At issue is not only mastery of the English language, but also individual background and experience with the American system of libraries.

Non-English speakers represent every age group and every level of the socioeconomic spectrum, and make use of all types of libraries. In 1980, over fourteen million persons living in the United States (6.2 percent of the American population) were foreign-born;[30] between 1981 and 1987, approximately four million more immigrants arrived in the United States.[31] In 1987, there were 18.7 million Hispanics in this country[32] and 350,000 international students enrolled in institutions of higher education.[33] Clearly, ethnic diversity continues to be a major factor in the composition of the American population.

While types of libraries vary in the exact nature of reference services provided, all libraries should adapt their standard reference services to their non-English-speaking clientele. In providing reference services to non-English-speaking individuals, particular attention should be paid to collection of and access to materials in the language of and/or materials descriptive of major cultures represented in the library's clientele. All types of libraries share the responsibility of provision of reference services to non-English speakers. School library media centers may serve bilingual children, and will need to develop communication skills based on cultural awareness and provide materials in all of the native languages of their students. Academic libraries need to include in their reference programs bibliographic instruction accessible and geared to students for whom English is a second language.

Where the population warrants it, public libraries should also provide access to materials for teaching and learning English and to continuing education opportunities, such as literacy programs, study programs for citizenship, or high school equivalency courses.[34] For example, the Queens Borough Public Library offers a foreign-language books-by-mail service, English as a Second Language (ESL) and literacy courses, and an information and referral service utilizing an automated ethnic information database.[35] In libraries where this kind of comprehensive programming is not feasible, access to such services should be provided by means of referral or liaison work. When possible, both academic and public libraries should also provide bilingual or bicultural reference staff or solicit the aid of volunteer groups for translation purposes or peer support. For instance, international students have been recruited to conduct orientation tours in target languages and to act as peer tutors.[36] At the Denver Public Library, Library Services and Construction Act (LSCA) funds have supported the development of a collection of Vietnamese materials, and a full-time Vietnamese-speaking staff member is on hand to provide assistance.[37]

From this description of reference services, it is obvious that reference services to non-English-speaking groups are more expensive book-for-book and question-for-question than are services to the general American public. However, such services facilitate retention of native languages and traditions while easing integration into the new culture. Such citizens are more quickly in a position to contribute to the economy and the culture of their surroundings and to "pay back" the society which supported their transition.[38]

Specialized Sources

Specialized sources are available to assist in the reference mission, such as the regularly published bibliographies of foreign-language materials in *Booklist*, and Isabel Schon's *Basic Collection of Children's Books in Spanish*. Adela Artola Allen's *Library Services for Hispanic Children*, in addition to providing helpful essays and bibliographic information, contains terminology for librarians with limited Spanish fluency and a table of English/Spanish library-related vocabulary.

Cultural Differences and Reference Services

Libraries, as Americans know them, are unique institutions. In many countries, academic libraries are nothing but vast study halls, or their limited collections are locked away in closed stacks. Access to these warehouses is obtained through the beneficence of retrieval clerks who are not trained librarians. Collections are often noncirculating, and patrons may have to pay fees to check books out. A comparable public library system for the general population may not exist. Reference service is neither provided nor understood in the way that it is practiced in the United States. In support of this type of library service are educational traditions which are often based upon rote learning, where the teacher is regarded as the repository of all knowledge; no independent investigation is required, and may in fact be strongly discouraged.[39]

The characteristics of the American library system are simultaneously wonderful and daunting to many non-English speakers. In these libraries one is permitted direct access to a seemingly unlimited supply of materials and, most exciting of all, is allowed to take books home. On the other hand, open access implies independent negotiation of a confusing and unfamiliar environment. Asking for help does not always seem to be a viable option. From some cultural perspectives, library staff members may be suspect as representatives of the institution and as figures of authority. Librarians may exhibit what appears to be confusing body language, or by their gender or perceived social status be deemed unapproachable. From this vantage point, the patrons must ask questions, not about something they know, but about something they do *not* know, a task which is difficult enough to accomplish when English is one's first language.[40]

■ ══ ■

10.4
In the Words of a Foreigner

In some foreign countries the librarian at the reference desk still possesses the image of the person with the power to claim monopoly of all knowledge, and thus is not to be disturbed. Further, societal demands in some countries require that people of a certain social status, or age, or gender ask nothing but intelligent questions. Thus, with this same perception of the librarian, and the concomitant potential for ridicule, some foreign students will not approach the librarian. And if they have a first [bachelor's] degree, and are large males, they will certainly shy away from the reference desk, abiding by the norm that intelligent people (as shown by possession of a first degree), and mature beings (as shown by size and/ or age), do not ask silly questions, even if this is the only way to get much-needed answers. Sometimes it is not easy for foreign students to realize that certain types of ignorance are acceptable, and that librarians are there to help.

— Kwasi Sarkodie-Mensah
"In the Words of a Foreigner"[41]

The Reference Interview

Fundamentally, the librarian's conduct during the reference interview is no different with non-English speakers than it is with other patrons. The librarian should treat all persons and queries with respect and seriousness. However, with non-English speakers, it is especially important to "understand their timidity; their ignorance of [the] system; their reticence toward public institutions; and their awe."[42] It is crucial to be aware of and to understand both cultural and individual differences. For example, forty-five different political units make up the Latin American population, making the term *Hispanic* hardly descriptive of the very different cultural traditions represented.[43] Furthermore, every cultural group is composed of individuals who have their own unique needs and questions.

It is important to make no assumptions regarding what non-English-speaking patrons know about libraries. Depending upon circumstances, they may not understand the concept of call numbers, be able to decipher commonly used library terms, or know how to distinguish between printed American first names and surnames.[44] In answering reference questions, slang should be avoided and use of the materials explained and demonstrated, giving patrons the opportunity to observe and then to imitate. Whenever possible, the librarian should escort a new patron through to the end of a process, such as locating a book or a magazine on the shelf. It is easy to mistake nods and smiles as signifying comprehension. This pitfall can be avoided by asking questions which allow patrons to communicate more precisely what they do or do not understand. It is also possible to misunderstand body language or perceived gruffness; the librarian must instead concentrate on the intent of the patron's question. After a question is answered, follow-up is especially important and vital to proper closure of the interview.

Reference Services to
Illiterate/Low-Literate Adults

According to the U.S. Department of Education, only about 56 percent of persons aged twenty-one to twenty-five in this country can read and understand newspaper articles and other text materials.[45] Jonathan Kozol estimates that as much as one-third of the adult population in the United States is illiterate or low-literate[46] (see box 10.5). These statistics suggest that delivery of reference service may need to be adapted for significant numbers of adults, in any community, who do not read well. Many community colleges and public and school libraries develop special instructional programs, including GED (high school equivalency), formal Adult Basic Education programs, and special tutoring services for nonreading adults. Reference librarians may be asked to give special tours or conduct bibliographic instruction sessions on how to use basic reference tools such as dictionaries and encyclopedias. Academic libraries often offer remedial help to low-achieving students.

■ ══ ■

10.5

A Third of the Nation Cannot Read These Words

Twenty-five million American adults cannot read the poison warnings on a can of pesticide, a letter from their child's teacher, or the front page of a daily paper. An additional 35 million read only at a level which is less than equal to the full survival needs of our society.

Together, these 60 million people represent more than one third of the entire adult population.

—Jonathan Kozol
Illiterate America[47]

Often libraries choose to offer special services to nonreading adults. One such service is appropriate referral to community agencies or literacy councils which provide testing and tutoring. Some libraries house such services in the library or provide space for tutoring. It is important to collect material explaining tutoring and other services that is written at about the fourth-grade reading level. Libraries also may choose to do special collection development for the new adult reader. This should include coping or basic life skills information (health, consumer, and job information, money management), basic reading skills (materials on a beginning to fourth- or fifth-grade reading level), GED materials (reading level of grades five to seven), and leisure reading.[48] It is important to be aware that adults with reading problems may be hesitant to explain their problems or ask questions effectively, so reference librarians may need to offer materials on several reading levels without being asked by the patron. There are a growing number of vendors of materials for the new adult reader, including the Laubach Foundation and the Literacy Volunteers of America. Educators who specialize in adult basic education can advise librarians of sources of information as well as provide training for reference librarians in interviewing and assessing the needs of the nonreading adult.

Reference Services to
Institutionalized Populations

Individuals are institutionalized for a variety of reasons: punishment, protection, medical purposes, therapy, or rehabilitation. The common element shared by these otherwise disparate individuals is that they are deprived of liberty for some designated period of time. By definition, their lifestyles are restricted due to diminished capacities or to an imposed loss of freedom. Reference service to institutionalized populations has its foundations in the underlying philosophy of public library service itself, which is to provide *all* individuals with opportunities for recreation, self-improvement, and economic betterment.[49] Indeed, the circumstances of institutionalization often necessitate that a major portion of educational activities be self-directed. The classic Carnegie vision of the library as a setting for self-improvement and educational awakening is well suited to such an environment.

In this section, reference services in two predominant types of institutionalized settings are discussed specifically: prison libraries and hospital libraries. The major issues center on management of the services rather than on specialized collection development.

Prisoners

Before discussing reference services in prison libraries, it is important to be aware of the variety of ways in which prison libraries are administered. In some cases, librarians report to prison officials and are part of the prison staff. In other cases, librarians report to outside library agencies which contract with the prison systems for library services. Many libraries are staffed by clerks or inmates. In 1987, only eleven state agencies of correction had library coordinators.[50] State libraries now administer federal Library Services and Construction Act funds earmarked for institutional populations. However, the state library consultants who oversee these funds often have other responsibilities as well, such as supervising library service to blind and physically handicapped populations. Because of these disparities in funding, governance, and staffing, service varies greatly from institution to institution,[51] and librarians work in isolated circumstances.[52]

The role of the prison library has evolved from one of establishing book collections that impart moral values, to one of supporting the prison's educational mission, to one of emulating the public library role by providing a broad range of services based on inmate interests. The latter philosophy, which currently predominates in prison librarianship, supports reference services that include all of the generic public library goals of reference services. In addition, prison library reference services support the underlying goals of the prison mission. Rehabilitative efforts are supplemented by reentry materials, programs of bibliotherapy, reading and discussion groups, and even storytelling. Educational and vocational training programs are supported by access to curriculum-related materials. The library may also be involved in literacy programs and adult basic education programs, which are typically administered by the education department of the institution.

The Change-Based Model of Prison Library Service. Within the field of prison librarianship, there is debate regarding the public library model or, most specifically, whether library service should be based upon inmate *interests* or upon inmate *needs*. At the heart of this argument is disagreement over whether inmates have the same rights to library services, or stand to benefit from them in the same way, as society at large. One approach, coined the "change-based" model by William J. Coyle,[53] defines the prison library mission as restricted to supporting constructive change in the inmate, and delegates the recreational function to prison management. As such, reference services entail only those activities which are broadly educational and which directly promote correctional goals.

Access to Legal Information. A distinguishing characteristic of reference services in prison libraries is an emphasis on access to legal information, which is itself supported by legal mandate. In order to guarantee inmates meaningful access to the courts, states are required to provide free legal counsel, adequate law libraries, or some combination of the two.[54] In most cases, it has been cheaper for states to supply law libraries and designate the most qualified inmates to act as clerks. In Illinois, paralegal personnel teach a course to inmate law library clerks in the use of legal reference materials.[55] Prison law libraries are either integrated with central prison library services, or are established as physically and administratively distinct services. In some correctional institutions, the law library is the only library service available.

Access and Security. Equal access to library service in the prison setting cannot be conceived of in the same way as equal access for the population at large. The concept of access is intricately tied to issues of security. Even in a minimum-security institution, inmates cannot come and go at will. Higher risk populations cannot be allowed to mix with the rest of the population. In a maximum-security prison, where an inmate must always be accompanied by a guard, equal access to library service is an expensive proposition. Prison library staff must be concerned with monitoring behavior as well as with dispensing information, so that problems such as the use of books to pass messages or to hide contraband can be avoided.

Ethics and Confidentiality. Ethical issues also pose challenges to traditional notions of confidentiality in librarian-patron relationships. While librarians may feel little conflict in monitoring library activity for situations that compromise prison security, they may find it more problematic to deal with requests for information that promote the potential for criminal activity once the inmate leaves prison (see box 10.6).

■ ═══ ■

10.6
Aiding and Abetting?

Coyle describes the dilemma of a prison librarian faced with a request for information to which he objected on ethical grounds:

> The inmate in question had used the library quite often and knew his way around. The list of books he submitted included a how-to book on hypnosis, and four titles on alternative methods of adoption — single-parent and overseas adoption, refugee children, black market adoption, and so forth. They were all serious works that might be found in any good public library, but I did a double-take on the list because I knew in connection with a previous incident here, that the inmate has a long record involving procurement and sex offenses against children. The implied purpose of the material was blatant and I couldn't ignore it.
>
> The problem was made worse by the fact that it was an entirely reasonable request as far as meeting our own criteria for inter-library loan; that is, the inmate was specific about what he wanted, the material was informational, and it wasn't locally available. I really didn't know what to do. My dilemma was that I thought it unethical to deny the request, or intimidate the inmate into withdrawing it, simply because of what I knew about him. On the other hand, how could I accommodate a request for material that I knew very well would be used to advance a serious criminal activity?

What would you do?

— William J. Coyle
Libraries in Prisons[56]

Librarians who report to prison authorities may be required to pass judgment about suitable reading material. Those who report to outside library agencies are more likely to adhere to traditional professional standards delineating noninterference.

Hospitalized Persons

This discussion of reference services in hospitals is limited to services to patients, and does not include services to the professional medical community, about which there is much published information. *Hospital* is broadly defined to include general hospitals, long-term care facilities, rehabilitation centers, and mental health institutions.

The descriptions here of patient library services are couched in general terms for the sake of coherence; reference services vary widely from setting to setting. In some hospitals, the "library" is nothing more than a collection of paperbacks located in a central lounge area. In other hospitals, especially those which provide long-term care, library service rivals that of the community public library. The average length of stay in a hospital also has a great impact upon the types of library service that are provided by an institution. A patient who is in a general hospital for two-day minor surgery has very different library needs than the patient who faces an indeterminate stay, for example, in a mental health facility or in a Veterans Administration hospital.

Depending upon the setting, library service to patients may be administered as a free-standing unit or as a service of the same medical library which provides service to medical personnel. Because of staffing limitations, medical libraries housed in hospitals are not always open to patients on a walk-in basis, although patients may be able to obtain a doctor's permission to use the library. Service may also be provided by the outreach programs of local public libraries or in cooperation with library agencies or school districts. For example, Joan Fierberg and others describe the Consumer Health Information Project and Services, a project directed by the Los Angeles County Harbor-UCLA Medical Center in cooperation with the Los Angeles County Carson Regional Public Library.[57] School districts may also be obligated to provide library service to children who are hospitalized for long periods of time.

Reference services for hospitalized persons should include, in addition to the standard informational and readers' advisory services: (1) access to medical information and assistance in the use of medical reference sources; (2) access to materials which support emotional and therapeutic needs (bibliotherapy); and (3) access to materials which support recreational needs. Timely delivery of information and materials is a key element in service to patients. Reference services should be developed with the support and consultation of institution personnel and directed not only to the patients themselves, but also to family members or to others who are part of the patient recovery process.

Access to Medical Information. During discussions with their doctors, most patients and their families are capable of absorbing only the information they are emotionally prepared to accept at that time; access to related medical information allows them to review what their physician has told them when they are better able to deal with it.[58] Patient education is also supported by the current recognition that informed patients who share the responsibility for their care are lower medical risks than are patients who are not exposed to the same kind of educational intervention.[59]

In most hospitals, baseline medical information is dispensed by patient education departments and/or by health care professionals during the process of diagnosis and treatment. Reference services supplement patient education efforts, enabling patients to pursue further information about specific illnesses and conditions, about drugs and various medications, and about forms of treatment. However, unlike the public library environment, in the hospital setting there is an implicit expectation that the information found there is medically sanctioned. Therefore, patients are often allowed only closely prescribed use of medical information; in some hospitals, library materials may be packaged with disclaimer messages.

For example, at the Englewood Hospital Medical Library in New Jersey, whenever possible, books are purchased on approval and are examined by health professionals before payment is allowed. The staff labels all materials with commercially printed stickers which read: "The presence in the patients' library of this volume does not imply an endorsement of its entire contents. Many questions may be stimulated by a reading of this book and should be addressed to your physician."[60]

■ ══ ■

10.7
Patient Rights

Although it is generally recognized that patients should be informed of their condition and prognosis, the exact nature and extent of patient education is a topic which lends itself to debate. What sort of reading material is appropriate for patient consumption? Should physicians screen what their patients are allowed to read? Do librarians have the responsibility or the right to shelter patients from materials—even fiction—which might upset them? What do you think?

Readers' Advisory and Bibliotherapy. Readers' advisory work and bibliotherapy are critically important components of hospital library reference services and, in this setting, often serve the same purpose. Hospitalization is a stressful experience. Reading fiction while hospitalized can provide temporary escape from a traumatic condition,[61] or inspiration, as in the case of the cystic fibrosis patient described by Thelma Kaluzsa who "liked and read books in which the protagonist overcame great obstacles to win."[62] Bibliotherapy also allows patients to confront their conditions through the use of fiction, and it is an especially useful tool in mental health institutions. In a long-term care institution, the library facility itself supports the therapeutic function by being one place where patients can experience unprogrammed activity and the feeling of being persons rather than patients.[63]

Children in Hospitals. When children are hospitalized, they are removed from their familiar home environment, and lack the benefit of an adult intellectual capacity to fully comprehend their circumstances. Appropriate age-level information about their condition, about hospitalization, and about separation can quell many fears.[64] Reference services directed to parents and siblings strengthen familial coping abilities, which in turn aid the young patients.

Ethics and Confidentiality. Confidentiality in the patron-librarian relationship is extremely important, because inquiries and quests for information are likely to be of a highly personal nature. However, in certain institutions, such as some mental health care facilities, patients are confined as a result of legal mandate or are under circumstances in which they are deprived of specific rights in the interests of successful treatment. In such cases, it is incumbent upon library staff to be aware of the restrictions and requirements of their role, which may be governed by legal or institutional regulation. For example, a librarian may be required to inform hospital personnel of a patient's confidences regarding suicide and be obligated to restrict access to material which would enable the patient to take such an action.

Specialized Sources and Organizations. Many specialized sources, such as the bibliography provided by Thelma Kaluzsa in her article on library services to children in hospitals,[65] are available in the literature. More specifically, growing interest in the provision of health information to consumers is evidenced by developments in the organizations and literature which support it. The Consumer and Patient Health Information Section of the Medical Library Association and the American Hospital Association are both committed to exploring the development of these types of services. Two recent books by Alan M. Rees, *The*

Consumer Health Information Source Book and *Developing Consumer Health Information Services*, together describe both how to establish such services and what sources are necessary for their support.

Conclusion

There are several issues to be addressed by librarians who are responsible for ensuring that special groups have equal access to reference services. First, librarians need to acknowledge that reference services do need to be adapted, or at least assessed, in the light of the special patrons' needs and abilities. Librarians need to identify groups within the community to be served that might have obstacles to free access to information. It should be stressed that this assessment needs to go beyond polling or observing users of library reference materials or services. If impediments exist, members of a particular special group often are nonusers of the library. They would be invisible to the librarian who looks only at user groups.

Once groups are identified, librarians need to create a plan of service for meeting the special needs of individuals in each. This plan would include profiling the adaptations needed by each group, assessing the library's ability to meet identified needs, and establishing priorities for actions to be taken by the library. Librarians should plan regular evaluation of special services to keep up-to-date with changes in the special population as well as changes in library technology.

To serve special groups effectively, it is necessary to work with other agencies, either within the community or regional or national organizations, both to identify needs of special users and to design collections and services that meet the groups' information needs. Often library staff will need training to understand how to work with special groups and to become familiar with special reference sources in the collection. The library should have appropriate policies and procedures that enhance access to the library itself, to the library's collection, and to full reference services. Explicit statements against discrimination should be created at the local level. Special adaptations to library procedures should be incorporated in library handbooks or manuals. With children and young adults especially, this should include clear guidelines about access to a full range of library materials and services as well as appropriate discussion of confidentiality.

Librarians should also evaluate the collection to ensure that materials are usable (e.g., talking books for the blind) and useful (i.e., on topics of interest) for the special groups to be served. Collections need to be kept up-to-date, particularly those sources used for information and referral. Accessibility to the physical facility as well as to specific services within the building is another issue to be included when planning to serve special groups.

Good reference service is multidimensional. It is designed to meet the needs of individuals. Librarians plan reference services, develop reference collections, and develop reference skills by anticipating what their community of users might need. To achieve excellence in reference service, this planning process must include appropriate attention to the special needs of groups within the community served.

Notes

1. American Library Association, *Intellectual Freedom Manual* (Chicago: American Library Association, 1989), 14.

2. Ibid., 22-23.

3.   Based in part on a list from Shirley Fitzgibbons, "Reference and Information Services for Children and Young Adults: Definition, Services, and Issues," *Reference Librarian* 7/8 (Spring/Summer 1983): 5-6.

4.   Kieth C. Wright and Judith F. Davie, *Library and Information Services for Handicapped Individuals*, 2d ed. (Littleton, Colo.: Libraries Unlimited, 1983), 129.

5.   Watty Piper, *The Little Engine That Could* (New York: Putnam, 1930), 25p.

6.   Gertrude B. Herman, "What Time Is It in Antarctica?: Meeting the Information Needs of Children," *Reference Librarian* 7/8 (Spring/Summer 1983): 77.

7.   "Children in Crisis: A Cooperative Library and Community Agency Support for Abused and Neglected Youth" (Champaign, Ill.: Lincoln Trail Libraries System, 1990).

8.   "Abused and Neglected Child Reporting Act," Illinois Revised Statutes, 1987, 23: 2054.

9.   Patricia Payne, "Narrowing the Gap Between Library Instruction and Functional Library Literacy," *Reference Librarian* 7/8 (Spring/Summer 1983): 115.

10.   Leslie Edmonds, Paula Moore, and Kathleen Mehaffey Balcom, *An Investigation of the Effectiveness of an Online Catalog in Providing Bibliographic Access to Children in a Public Library Setting*. Unpublished report, 1989.

11.   Linda Ward Callaghan, "Children's Questions: Reference Interviews with the Young," *Reference Librarian* 7/8 (Spring/Summer 1983): 55.

12.   American Association of School Librarians and the Association for Educational Communications and Technology, *Information Power: Guidelines for School Library Media Programs* (Chicago: American Library Association, 1988), 38.

13.   National Center for Education Statistics, *Services and Resources for Young Adults in Public Libraries* (Washington, D.C.: National Center for Education Statistics, U.S. Department of Education, Office of Educational Research and Improvement. CS 88-418k. Data Series: FRSS-28. Survey Report, July 1988), 1.

14.   Ibid., 3.

15.   Ibid., 4.

16.   Ibid., 3.

17.   Mary K. Chelton, "Young Adult Reference Services in the Public Library," *Reference Librarian* 7/8 (Spring/Summer 1983): 35.

18.   Ibid., 32.

19.   Dorothy M. Broderick, "On My Mind," *Voice of Youth Advocates* 11 (August 1988): 116.

20.   David P. Snider, "Eggs to Omelets Without Eggshells," *Reference Librarian* 7/8 (Spring/Summer 1983): 99.

21.   Genevieve M. Casey, *Library Service for the Aging* (Hamden, Conn.: Shoe String Press, 1984), 1.

22.   *Evaluation of Information and Referral Services for the Elderly, Final Report, 1977* (Washington, D.C.: Administration on Aging, Office of Human Development, Department of Health, Education and Welfare, 1977), 79.

23.   Library Services to an Aging Population Committee, Reference and Adult Services Division, American Library Association, "Guidelines for Library Service to Older Adults," *RQ* 26 (Summer 1987): 444.

24.   Steven J. Herman, "Information Center Profile: Library of Congress Division for the Blind and Physically Handicapped," in *Library Services to the Blind and Physically Handicapped*, ed. Maryalls G. Strom (Metuchen, N.J.: Scarecrow Press, 1977), 5.

25.   Edmund L. Andrews, "Computer Recognizes 5,000 Spoken Words," *New York Times*, 28 January 1989, sec. A, p. 36, col. 2.

26.   Wright and Davie, *Library and Information Services for Handicapped Individuals*, 66.

27.   Ibid., 123-24.

28.   Ibid., 93.

29.   Ibid., 100.

30.   *Statistical Abstract of the United States 1989* (Washington, D.C.: U.S. Bureau of the Census, 1989), Table 46.

31.   Ibid., Table 6.

32.   Ibid., Table 20.

33.   Ibid., Table 255.

34.   Robert P. Haro, *Developing Library and Information Services for Americans of Hispanic Origin* (Metuchen, N.J.: Scarecrow Press, 1981), 286.

35.   Renee Tjoumas, "Giving New Americans a Green Light in Life: A Paradigm for Serving Immigrant Communities," *Public Libraries* 26 (Fall 1987): 103-8.

36.   Manuel D. Lopez, "Chinese Spoken Here: Foreign Language Library Orientation Tours," *College & Research Libraries News* 44 (September 1983): 265-69.

37.   "Denver Public Library Reaches Out to Vietnamese Community," *Library Journal* 113 (December 1988): 29.

38.   Leonard Wertheimer, "Library Services to Ethnocultural Minorities: Philosophical and Social Bases and Professional Implication," *Public Libraries* 26 (Fall 1987): 98-102.

39.   Sally G. Wayman, "The International Student in the Academic Library," *Journal of Academic Librarianship* 9 (January 1984): 336-41; Louise Greenfield, Susan Johnston, and Karen Williams, "Educating the World: Training Library Staff to Communicate Effectively with International Students," *Journal of Academic Librarianship* 12 (September 1986): 227-31.

40.   Karen M. Moss, "The Reference Communication Process," *Law Library Journal* 72 (Winter 1979): 48-52.

41.   Kwasi Sarkodie-Mensah, "In the Words of a Foreigner," *Research Strategies* 4 (Winter 1986): 30-31.

42.   Tamiye Fujibayashi Trejo and Mary Kaye, "The Library as a Port of Entry," *American Libraries* 19 (November 1988): 890-92.

43.   Ibid., 890.

44.   Greenfield, Johnston, and Williams, "Educating the World," 230.

45.   *Youth Indicators 1988: Trends in Well-Being of American Youth* (Washington, D.C.: U.S. Department of Education, 1988), 66.

46.   Jonathan Kozol, *Illiterate America* (New York: New American Library, 1985), 4.

47.   Ibid., 4.

48.   Debra Wilcox Johnson with Jennifer Soule, *Libraries and Literacy: A Planning Manual* (Chicago: American Library Association, 1987), 31.

49.   George B. Davis, "The Raison D'Etre for Library Service to Institutional Populations," *Bookmark* 44 (Winter 1986): 94-95.

50.   Rhea Joyce Rubin and Sandra J. Souza, "The Challenge Continues: Prison Librarianship in the 1980s," *Library Journal* 114 (March 1, 1989): 47-51.

51.   *Library Standards for Adult Correctional Institutions*, written by the American Correctional Association/American Library Association (ASCLA) Joint Committee on Institution Libraries (Chicago: Association of Specialized and Cooperative Library Agencies, 1981), 18p., is the most recent set of standards written for prison libraries. Revised standards are currently under development.

52.   Regarding the difficulties of recruiting prison librarians, see Rhea Joyce Rubin, "Keeping Professional Librarians in Prison; or The Problems of Professionalism in Prison Libraries," *RQ* 23 (Fall 1983): 40-46. Regarding preparation for a career as a prison librarian, see Brenda Vogel, "In Preparation for a Visit to a Smaller Planet," *Wilson Library Bulletin* 64 (October 1989): 34-36.

53.   William J. Coyle, *Libraries in Prisons: A Blending of Institutions* (New York: Greenwood Press, 1987), 141p.; William J. Coyle, "Reforming Prison Libraries," *Library Journal* 114 (November 1, 1989): 66-67. A critique of the change-based model can be found in Daniel Suvak, "'Throw the Book at 'em': The Change-Based Model for Prison Libraries," *Wilson Library Bulletin* 64 (October 1989): 31-33.

54.   *Bounds v. Smith*, 430 U.S. 817 (1977).

55.   Thea Chesley, "Library Instruction in Illinois Correctional Institutions," *Illinois Libraries* 70 (December 1988): 659-63.

56.   Coyle, *Libraries in Prisons*, 83.

57.   Joan Fierberg et al., "The Hospital Library as a Focus of Patient Education Activities and Resources," *Bulletin of the Medical Library Association* 71 (April 1983): 224-26.

58.   D. Elizabeth Christie, "A Role for the Medical Library in Consumer Health Information," *Canadian Library Journal* 43 (April 1986): 105-9.

59.   Luke A. Iroka, "Hospital Libraries in Patient's Education," *International Library Review* 20 (1988): 111-14.

60.   Katherine Lindner, "The Evolution of a Hospital Library Patient Education Literature Program," *Patient Education and Counseling* 8 (March 1986): 73-80.

61.   H. A. F. Dudley, "The Place of Literature in Healing," in *Hospital Libraries and Work with the Disabled in the Community*, 3d ed., eds. Mona E. Going and Jean M. Clarke (London: Library Association, 1981), 221-23.

62.   Thelma Kaluzsa, "Library Services to Children in Hospitals," *Top of the News* 42 (Spring 1986): 273-77.

63.   Pam Daniel, "Developing a Plan for Statewide Coordination of Libraries in Mental Health Institutions," *Bookmark* 44 (Winter 1986): 89-93.

64.   See Kaluzsa, "Library Services to Children in Hospitals," for a helpful annotated bibliography of books for children about hospitals and surgery.

65.   Kaluzsa, "Library Services to Children in Hospitals," 275-77.

List of Sources

Allen, Adela Artola. *Library Services for Hispanic Children: A Guide for Public and School Librarians*. Phoenix, Ariz.: Oryx Press, 1987. 216p.

Baskin, Barbara, and Karen Harris. *Books for the Gifted Child*. Vol. 1. New York: R. R. Bowker, 1980. 263p.

Best Books for Young Adults. Chicago: American Library Association, Young Adult Services Division. [Brochure, issued periodically.]

Booklist. Chicago: American Library Association, 1905- . 22 issues/year.

Books for the Teen Age. New York: New York Public Library, 1929- . Annual.

Brooks, Tim, and Earle Marsh. *The Complete Directory to Prime Time Network TV Shows, 1946-Present*. 4th ed. New York: Ballentine Books, 1988. 1,063p.

Carlin, Margaret F., Jeannine L. Laughlin, and Richard D. Saniga. *Understanding Abilities, Disabilities, and Capabilities: A Guide to Children's Literature*. Englewood, Colo.: Libraries Unlimited, 1991. 114p.

Children's Catalog. 15th ed. New York: H. W. Wilson, 1986. 1,298p.

Directory of College Facilities and Services for the Disabled. 2d ed. Edited by Carol H. Thomas. Phoenix, Ariz.: Oryx Press, 1986. 410p.

Directory of National Information Sources on Handicapping Conditions and Related Services. New York: Revisionist Press, 1984. 366p.

Directory of Resources for Aging, Gerontology and Retirement. 2d ed. Edited by Michael E. Gabriel. DeKalb, Ill.: Media Marketing Group, 1986. 400p.

Dreyer, Sharon S. *The Bookfinder: A Guide to Children's Literature About the Needs and Problems of Youth Aged 2 to 15*. 4 vols. Circle Pines, Minn.: American Guidance Service, Inc., 1981-1989.

Fassler, Joan. *Helping Children Cope*. New York: Free Press, 1978. 162p.

Gelfand, Donald E. *The Aging Network: Programs and Services*. 3d ed. New York: Springer Publishing Co., 1988. 341p.

Hauser, Paula, and Gail A. Nelson. *Books for the Gifted Child*. Vol. 2. New York: R. R. Bowker, 1988. 244p.

Index to Poetry for Children and Young People, 1964-1969: A Title, Subject, Author, and First Line Index to Poetry in Collections for Children and Young People. Compiled by John E. Brewton, Sara W. Brewton, and G. Meredith Blackburn III. New York: H. W. Wilson, 1972. 575p. [Supplements cover 1970-75, 1976-81, and 1982-87.]

Kister, Kenneth. *Best Encyclopedias: A Guide to General and Specialized Encyclopedias*. Phoenix, Ariz.: Oryx Press, 1986. 356p.

Lima, Carolyn W., and John A. Lima. *A to Zoo: Subject Access to Children's Picture Books*. 3d ed. New York: R. R. Bowker, 1989. 706p.

Outstanding Biographies for the College Bound. Edited by Mary Ann Paulin and Susan Berlin. Chicago: American Library Association, Young Adult Services Division, 1984. 92p.

Peterson, Carolyn S., and Ann D. Fenton. *Index to Children's Songs: A Title, First Line and Subject Index*. New York: H. W. Wilson, 1979. 318p.

_____. *Reference Books for Children*. Orlando, Fla.: Moonlight Press, 1981. 265p.

Pilla, Marianne Laino. *The Best: High/Low Books for Reluctant Readers*. Englewood, Colo.: Libraries Unlimited, 1990. 100p.

Recommended Books for the Reluctant Young Adult Reader. Chicago: American Library Association, Young Adult Services Division. [Brochure, issued periodically.]

Rees, Alan M., ed. *Developing Consumer Health Information Services*. New York: R. R. Bowker, 1982. 296p.

Rees, Alan M., and Catherine Hoffman. *The Consumer Health Information Source Book*. 3d ed. Phoenix, Ariz.: Oryx Press, 1990. 210p.

Schon, Isabel. *Basic Collection of Children's Books in Spanish*. Metuchen, N.J.: Scarecrow Press, 1986. 240p.

Science Fair Project Index, 1973-1980. Edited by Science and Technology Division, Akron-Summit County Public Library. Metuchen, N.J.: Scarecrow Press, 1983. 723p. [Sequel, covering 1981-1984, published in 1986.]

Strickland, Charlene. *Dogs, Cats, and Horses: A Resource Guide to the Literature for Young People*. Englewood, Colo.: Libraries Unlimited, 1990. 225p.

Voice of Youth Advocates. Metuchen, N.J.: Scarecrow Press, 1978- . Bimonthly.

Winkel, Lois. *The Elementary School Library Collection: A Guide to Books and Other Media*. 16th ed. Williamsport, Pa.: Brodart Co., 1988. 788p.

Additional Readings

Broderick, Dorothy M., ed. *The VOYA Reader*. Metuchen, N.J.: Scarecrow, 1990. 308p.
This reader is a collection of articles from the journal *Voice of Youth Advocates*, which cover major themes in the provision of library service to young adults. It includes discussions of topics such as young adult literature, programming, and censorship and provides insight into the young adult user's perspective on library services.

Casey, Genevieve M. *Library Services for the Aging*. Hamden, Conn.: Shoe String Press, 1984. 168p.
Casey discusses the special needs of the aging population and suggests appropriate library services.

Haro, Robert P. *Developing Library and Information Services for Americans of Hispanic Origin*. Metuchen, N.J.: Scarecrow Press, 1981. 286p.
Much of Robert Haro's advice regarding library services for an individual ethnic group is also pertinent in planning reference service for other minority ethnic groups.

Johnson, Debra Wilcox. *Libraries and Literacy: A Planning Manual*. Chicago: American Library Association, 1987. 38p.

Although it does not address the reference needs of adult new readers directly, this manual will help librarians understand the needs of this population and give guidance for collection development.

Katz, Bill, and Ruth A. Fraley, eds. *Reference Services for Children and Young Adults*. New York: Haworth Press, 1983. 215p. (Also published as *Reference Librarian* 7/8 [Spring/Summer 1983].)

This is a collection of articles specifically addressing issues in reference service for young people. It includes issues for public librarians as well as school library media specialists.

Rees, Alan M., ed. *Developing Consumer Health Information Services*. New York: R. R. Bowker, 1982. 296p.

In addition to covering the development and management of consumer health information programs, this work describes a number of successful programs which are administered by medical and/or public libraries.

Sorenson, Liene S. *Accessible Library Services: Taking Action to Enhance Public Library Services to Persons with Disabilities*. Skokie, Ill.: Skokie Public Library, 1988. 52p.

This book contains chapters dealing with specific components of a program for the provision of library services to the disabled, followed by lists of sources of information, materials, or equipment. It includes directory information for agencies serving the disabled. Although some of the information provided in this source is specific to Illinois, most is applicable to all states.

Vogel, Brenda, ed. "Prison Libraries: Escaping the Stereotype." *Wilson Library Bulletin* 64 (October 1989): 25-38.

Several articles describing the major issues and concerns of the profession are included in this special section on prison libraries, including a statement from William Coyle, proponent of the change-based model of library service.

INFORMATION SOURCES
AND THEIR USE

SELECTION AND EVALUATION OF REFERENCE SOURCES

Reference Sources

Part 1 of this text introduces the variety of services provided by reference departments in all types of libraries. Essential to the provision of services is a carefully selected collection of sources. This chapter introduces the types of sources used most frequently in reference work and discusses reference collection development and maintenance. This includes consideration of the criteria used to evaluate sources as well as the reviewing media and guides to reference books useful in collection development. The remaining chapters in part 2 discuss the characteristics and uses of particular types of reference sources.

What Is a Reference Book?

In considering selection and evaluation of materials for the reference collection, it is helpful first to attempt to characterize the types of materials most commonly included in reference collections, often termed *reference books*. *The ALA Glossary of Library and Information Science* offers the following definitions of *reference book*: "1. A book designed by the arrangement and treatment of its subject matter to be consulted for definite items of information rather than to be read consecutively. 2. A book whose use is restricted to the library building."[1] Marcia Bates terms these definitions "functional" and "administrative."[2] She further clarifies the concept of a reference book by describing in greater detail the arrangement and indexing which typically characterize the presentation of information in reference books. Increasingly, the concept of a reference collection made up of reference *books* is an inadequate characterization of the resources most frequently used by reference librarians. Although printed materials continue to be important, they are supplemented by materials in microform, CD-ROM, and other machine-readable media. All of these are owned by the library, and hence are clearly part of the reference collection, but (as described in chapter 5) it is also appropriate to regard remote online databases as another part of the collection, because they can be accessed from terminals located in the library. In fact, for some sources the librarian may choose to buy only access to online databases, rather than housing the printed or CD-ROM counterpart in the library.

Types of Sources

As noted, one way to categorize reference sources relates to their format: traditional printed format, in microform, in a distributed electronic format such as CD-ROM, or delivered electronically online. Alternatively, it is possible to divide reference sources into two main classes: compilations of one kind or another which furnish information directly; and compilations that refer to other sources containing information, which merely indicate places in which information may be found. In practice, this distinction becomes blurred because sources of the first type often refer to others for fuller information, and those of the second type are adequate for answering some questions. Sources of the first type include encyclopedias, dictionaries, almanacs, handbooks, yearbooks, biographical sources, directories, atlases, and gazetteers; sources of the second type include catalogs, bibliographies, and indexes. Each of these is the subject of one of the remaining chapters in this book. In addition, government publications, which frequently provide unique sources of information, are treated in a separate chapter.

Reference Collection Development and Maintenance

The work of the reference department includes selection of an adequate and suitable collection of reference sources, and arrangement and maintenance of the collection so that it can be used easily and conveniently. Unplanned collection development and neglect of weeding can impair the efficiency of reference services. Records of unanswered questions are one means of identifying deficiencies in the existing collection.

Components of the Collection

Because reference collections now include materials in a variety of formats, the reference librarian must decide whether to acquire particular titles in more than one format. At present, many titles exist in only one format, be it print, microform, or electronic. Others are available in several different formats. For example, to aid in locating residential phone numbers, one can purchase printed phone directories, *Phonefiche* in microform, or a product such as PhoneDisc USA Residential on CD-ROM. Although the different formats may be identical or at least overlapping in content, they may differ in access capabilities.

The greater flexibility of ondisc and online searching has led some to project that there will be increasing migration from print to electronic sources, with libraries cancelling subscriptions to printed indexes, for example, in favor of online or ondisc access. Librarians must weigh such factors as relative costs, amount of use, and likely users and uses in deciding which format(s) to acquire. These decisions must be continuously reviewed as new titles become available in electronic formats.

Reference Collection Development

Increased costs of reference sources and proliferation of formats and titles have focused attention on the importance of a systematic approach to reference collection development. Librarians have more options than ever before in creating a reference collection that is responsive to the needs of the community served. Many of the sources described in this text commonly form the core of a library's reference collection, but other titles in a specific collection will vary depending on local needs.

Decisions in collection development include whether to buy newly published titles, whether to buy new editions of titles already in the collection, whether to continue serials such as indexes, whether to contract with vendors for database access or to acquire CD-ROMs, and whether to coordinate collection development with other libraries to ensure the availability of at least one copy of an expensive set in a particular geographic region. A written collection development policy can provide guidance in making these decisions, and will help in establishing and maintaining an effective reference collection. Sydney Pierce suggests that developing a reference collection development policy requires the reference staff to identify the objectives to be met by the collection and to define the content of the collection: the nature and organization of its different parts, criteria for placing materials in each part, and formats and degree of duplication desired for reference materials.[3] Surveys indicate that many libraries do not have written reference collection development policies.[4] Nevertheless, examples are available in the literature to provide some guidance. Kathleen Coleman and Pauline Dickinson provide a sample policy with the following components: objectives, subject scope of the collection, size of the collection, types of materials included in the collection, responsibility for selection and selection procedures, weeding, and inventory of the reference collection.[5] Additional statements have been collected by Bill Katz.[6]

Maintaining the collection is an ongoing process. To provide accurate information in response to questions regarding current addresses, telephone numbers, and statistical data, for example, it is important to have the latest available edition of a tool in the collection. Publishers' announcements and reviews can alert the librarian to the availability of new titles and new editions. Regular inventory of the reference collection is needed to identify areas that need to be updated or strengthened. Chapter 8 provides more discussion of the evaluation of reference collections.

Arrangement of the Collection

Just as different libraries have somewhat different sets of titles making up their reference collections, there are different possible arrangements of titles. One possibility is to maintain a classified arrangement regardless of type. An alternative is to group types of sources together, creating sections for encyclopedias, biographical sources, directories, indexes, and so forth. Most collections designate a portion of the titles as ready reference, related to the frequency with which they are consulted and the need for rapid access to their contents.

It is difficult to integrate sources requiring special equipment, such as microform readers or computer workstations and CD-ROM readers, with other titles of the same type or in the same subject area. Whatever arrangement is chosen, consideration must be given to ease of use by the library user as well as the reference librarian. Special signage or handouts may be required to orient the library user to the location of particular sections of the collection.

Weeding the Collection

There must be a systematic basis for weeding (i.e., deselection, pruning, deacquisition) as well as for adding new titles to the collection. A reference librarian should discard materials in the same way that they are chosen, by taking into account what is already in the collection and what is actually needed for reference work. Weeding keeps the collection from becoming a depository of out-of-date materials and reduces the danger of giving incorrect information from noncurrent sources. Factors affecting weeding include frequency of use, age of material, physical condition, arrival of a new edition that supersedes a volume already on the shelf, and the need for space. Weeded materials may be placed in the circulating collection or discarded, depending on their possible continuing value to users. For example, old directories might be used for historical research. Different types of materials will require different guidelines for retention. Lynn Westbrook provides guidelines for weeding reference serials,[8] and Bill Katz lists general guidelines for various types of reference sources.[9] For example, Katz notes that almanacs, yearbooks, and manuals are usually superseded by the next edition. However, because the information in each is rarely duplicated exactly, he suggests keeping old editions for at least five years and preferably ten.

Evaluation of Sources

In building the reference collection, the librarian must evaluate the quality of particular sources and their suitability for inclusion in the library's reference collection. While evaluation criteria were originally developed for printed sources, they are also applicable to nonprint sources, such as microforms and databases. It may be more difficult to apply some of the criteria to nonprint sources, however, because nonprint media cannot be examined directly in the same way that one handles printed sources. The criteria covered in this chapter apply to all types of reference sources; chapters 12 through 20 include sections on evaluation of particular types of sources and highlight the criteria of special importance for those types. By considering these evaluation criteria, the librarian will be better able to judge whether a particular source meets the needs of the library and its users and is worthy of purchase using the limited funds available for reference collection development. The focus in this chapter is on evaluation of individual titles. Factors to consider in evaluation of online database vendors are summarized by Carol Tenopir.[10] As Danuta Nitecki explains, the tradition of reviewing databases is not yet well established.[11] Nevertheless, a number of authors have proposed criteria for evaluating CD-ROM and online databases, and these are incorporated in the following discussion.[12]

■ ═══ ■

11.1
Evaluation Criteria

Format
   print/microform/electronic, physical makeup, illustrations

Scope
   purpose, coverage, currency

Relation to similar works
   uniqueness, spinoffs, new editions

Authority
   authorship, publisher/sponsor, sources of information

Treatment
   accuracy, objectivity, style/audience

Arrangement
   sequence, indexing

Special features

Cost

Format

When reviewing printed books, one is concerned with the physical makeup and features of the book, such as binding, paper, typeface, and layout. If a printed source includes illustrations, one must judge their quality and relationship to the text. Printed sources have the advantages of being straightforward to use, predictable in cost, and usable by more than one user if a multivolume set. Disadvantages include the space required to house printed sources, the problem in maintaining currency, and the limitations on search strategies.

Microform formats may prove satisfactory for sources with short entries and alphabetical arrangement, such as bibliographies and directories. Microforms can save space and may be more frequently updated than printed sources. Disadvantages include equipment costs and maintenance, the need for patron orientation, the limit to one user at a time per viewer, and the limitations on search strategies.

CD-ROMs allow complex searching and store large amounts of information. On the other hand, they are generally expensive, somewhat slow to search, and variable in ease of use because interfaces are not standard. They may lack currency, and they require work space for equipment. As with CD-ROMs, online databases support flexibility and complexity in searching and may contain large amounts of information. In addition, they can be updated more frequently than CD-ROMs. Limitations of online access include the unpredictable costs, the need for equipment, and the frequent need for special training to use available search systems effectively. These advantages and disadvantages must be weighed when evaluating a reference source in one or more formats.

Scope

One indication of scope is the statement of purpose, generally found in the preface of printed reference sources. In evaluating a source, it is necessary to judge to what extent the statement of purpose is fulfilled in the text. Has the author or editor accomplished what was intended? Aspects of scope include subject coverage or geographical coverage. Time period coverage is also important for many reference works. How current are the contents? For a serial publication, how frequently is it updated? What is the language of publication? Printed sources can be examined to assess the various parameters that define the work's scope, but evaluations of nonprint sources may have to rely more on documentation, that is, written descriptions that attempt to characterize the coverage of the source. Sample searches can be done to probe various aspects of the scope, but it may be difficult to develop as thorough an understanding of the source's scope as is possible with a printed tool. When the same source exists in different formats, currency may vary. Online sources are often more current than printed sources, which in turn may be more current than CD-ROMs. There are many exceptions, however, so the librarian should investigate relative currency for each source being evaluated.

Relation to Similar Works

A newly published title may have different types of relationships to sources already in the collection. These need to be taken into account in assessing the potential value of the new title to the collection. One obvious category is a new edition of a title already held. In this case, it is necessary to assess the extent of revision in the new edition. Is it sufficient to warrant purchase? Another category is works of similar scope. To what extent is there overlap, and to what extent is there unique information? If there is overlap in content, is information more easily found in the new source? Is it written for a different audience?

Reference book publishers may issue spinoffs from large sets, such as a one-volume physics encyclopedia with articles selected from a multivolume encyclopedia of science and technology. While the one-volume encyclopedia might be useful in a branch library that does not own the parent set, it would duplicate information already found in a collection that contains the original set.

With the availability of machine-readable counterparts, whether online or on CD-ROM, for many printed tools, it is important to assess the extent to which the content in fact corresponds. Often there are differences in time period covered, for example. At times, there is more information in electronic format, because it is easy to store additional information. In some cases, the same database is available from different publishers of CD-ROMs; thus, it is necessary to consider differences in search capabilities and coverage.

Authority

Indicators of authority include the education and experience of the editor(s) and contributors. The reputation of the publisher or sponsoring agency is also an indicator. Certain publishers are well established as sources of quality reference books. Many reference sources include lists of material used in compiling the source. These lists can be used as an indicator of the authority of the work, as well as being leads to additional sources of information. It may be easier to evaluate the authority of printed reference sources, because statements of authorship and lists of references can be easily identified. If a CD-ROM or online database has a printed counterpart, authority can likewise be judged. When there is no printed counterpart, it may be necessary to judge authority from statements presented in the documentation describing the electronic source.

Treatment

Accuracy is important in reference works. How reliable are the facts presented? Objectivity can be assessed by examining the coverage of controversial issues and the balance in coverage given to various subjects. Because reference works can be addressed to particular audiences, it is important to determine who can best use the work—layperson or scholar, adult or child. Reviewing topics on which one has personal knowledge allows one to assess the accuracy and quality of writing. Again, this type of review may be easier to accomplish with printed sources than with those ondisc or online.

Arrangement

Printed and microform sources arrange entries in a particular sequence, such as alphabetical, chronological, or classified. If the sequence is a familiar one, such as alphabetical, the user of the source may be able to find the information sought directly rather than first looking up the location in an index. The flexibility of a reference source is typically enhanced by the availability of one or more indexes offering different types of access to the information. In addition, the text itself may offer leads to additional information, in the form of cross-references to related entries. In general, electronic sources offer many different indexes to the contents of a database. These may allow the reference librarian to answer questions that cannot be answered in a printed source because neither the primary arrangement of entries nor the available indexes offer the needed point of access. For example, while a printed bibliography may allow one to search by author, title, and subject, a publisher index is not likely to be provided. In an online version of the bibliography, however, publisher could be a searchable index, allowing one to locate easily the list of items in the bibliography issued by a particular publisher.

Special Features

One will always be interested in identifying any special features that distinguish a given reference source from others. CD-ROM sources in particular have many possible variations in design, because the databases are sold together with software for searching the contents and displaying the information. A further complicating factor is that many publishers attempt to improve their existing products incrementally by identifying factors that might enhance their usability.[13] Any new developments that make database searching easier and more accessible to users will affect the choice among products. In addition, in the case of electronic sources, one must consider the quality of available documentation, training, and customer support.

Cost

The cost of printed sources and sources in distributed electronic formats (e.g., CD-ROM) are similar in that a copy is acquired for in-house use in the library and the purchase or subscription price buys unlimited access to the contents of the source. In contrast, most pricing of online databases is on a per-use basis. A further complication is that there may be differential pricing of the electronic source, depending on whether the library holds the printed counterpart. In assessing cost, the reference librarian must try to determine if the price is appropriate in relation to the need and the anticipated frequency and length of use. In the case of nonprint sources, costs include purchase and maintenance of the necessary equipment to make the contents accessible. One may also want to consider the costs in terms of the staff support needed to allow users to make use of a nonprint source such as CD-ROM.

Selection Aids

A number of tools are available to assist the reference librarian in the task of evaluating sources for possible inclusion in the library's reference collection. Reviewing sources, varying in frequency from semi-monthly to annual, offer critical reviews of newly published titles. Although most titles reviewed in these sources are in printed format, some include nonprint titles as well. To identify gaps in existing collections, guides to reference sources can be used. These guides are also valuable as aids in identifying likely sources for answering particular reference questions. Both current reviewing media and guides to reference sources are helpful to librarians in developing collections on which effective service is based, but they are no substitute for informed judgment in selection of titles best suited to the library's users. This requires a thorough knowledge of the library's existing reference collection and user needs.

Reviewing Sources

Since it is impossible to examine all books before purchase, several reviewing sources are useful to the librarian in identifying and evaluating new titles. Analyses of these sources demonstrate that they differ in number of titles covered and that each covers some unique titles.[14] Thus, it is worthwhile monitoring several of these sources for reviews of reference sources. One difficulty with reviews is the time lag in appearance of reviews following publication of the book. Generally, the more thorough the review, the longer the time lag. The frequency of publication of the reviewing sources also influences time lag.

Reference Books Bulletin appears in the semi-monthly issues of *Booklist*. It provides long, comprehensive, and evaluative reviews prepared by the American Library Association's Reference Books Bulletin Editorial Review Board or by guest reviewers and revised by the board as a whole.[15] Major new reference sources in English are analyzed at length, and many additional titles, as well as selected revisions of standard works, are also evaluated. Periodic bibliographical essays critically survey specific types of reference sources, such as quotation books. In recent years, an annual review of general encyclopedias has been included. Reprints of *Reference Books Bulletin* are issued annually. Database reviews are included occasionally.

In contrast to the lengthy reviews found in *Reference Books Bulletin*, *Library Journal* includes a section of brief signed reference book reviews in each issue. Books reviewed are generally suitable for public and college libraries. *Choice*, focusing on books suitable for undergraduate collections and published eleven times per year, often reviews more specialized titles than does *Library Journal*. Each *Choice* issue has a section of signed reviews of reference books, and now includes a few reviews of databases. Reviewers are encouraged to compare the title being reviewed with related titles. Since 1938, *Wilson Library Bulletin* has included a regular column on "Current Reference Books," which is currently written by James Rettig of the College of William and Mary. It contains twenty to thirty reviews each month, aimed at the small or medium-sized general library. *RQ* includes critical reviews of reference books and databases in each quarterly issue. There is also a list of books received but not reviewed.

For librarians who do not have ready access to the various current reviewing sources, *Preview*, which began publication in 1988, offers an alternative. Its section on "Reference Resources" is subdivided by subject. Entries come from three different sources: (1) summaries of reviews published in other journals, including the reviewer's name and a citation to the original review; (2) full-length, signed reviews prepared specifically for inclusion in *Preview*; and (3) entries prepared by the editors. There is a section on children's reference materials. Indexes list titles, authors, and nonprint materials. Phyllis Van Orden identifies other sources for reviews of children's reference books.[16]

The most comprehensive source of reviews is *American Reference Books Annual* (*ARBA*). The annual volumes aim to review all reference books published and distributed in the United States and Canada in a given year. Reference sources which are revised on a regular or continuing basis are periodically reassessed. Following most of the reviews are references to additional reviews in selected journals. Arrangement is classified in thirty-seven chapters in four broad categories: general reference works; social sciences; humanities; and science and technology. General reference works are further subdivided by form, such as dictionaries and encyclopedias. Subject areas are subdivided by topic, such as history and law within social sciences. The reviews, which are written by a pool of more than three hundred subject specialists, critically evaluate each work. Each entry includes a full bibliographic citation with price, a description of the reference work, and an evaluation of content. Each volume is indexed by author/title, and by subject. A contributors index with names of reviewers is now also included. Indexes cumulate every five years; to date, cumulations for the periods 1970-74, 1975-79, 1980-84, and 1985-89 are available. The 1990 volume included 1,822 reviews, bringing the total number of reviews since 1970 to 34,942. Since

1981, a selection of reviews from *ARBA* has been published as *Recommended Reference Books for Small and Medium-sized Libraries and Media Centers*, which reprints about one-third of the year's *ARBA* reviews and tags them for type of library (C, P, S to offer guidance to college, public, and school libraries). These sources allow librarians to locate new works in a given field through the subject arrangement, to consult other published reviews from citations provided, and to compare the price and coverage of reference books in a particular subject area.

More selective lists of recommended reference books appear annually in *American Libraries* and *Library Journal*. The list in *American Libraries* is selected by the Reference Sources Committee of the Reference and Adult Services Division of the American Library Association, and appears in the May issue. The list in *Library Journal* is selected by experienced reference librarians, and appears in the April 15 issue. These lists are helpful in identifying outstanding reference books of potential value in many libraries.

Ideally, reviews describe, evaluate, and compare new reference works so that librarians can make informed decisions about whether to purchase the titles for their reference collections. Some researchers who have completed systematic evaluations of the various reviewing tools have expressed dissatisfaction with the content of many reviews. James Sweetland found a general lack of comparison within reviews.[17] Most reviews were generally favorable, with few mixed reviews and even fewer wholly negative ones. Some reviews were descriptive rather than evaluative, and others made recommendations that did not follow from the text of the evaluation. Overall consensus among the reviewing sources covering the same title was low. Nevertheless, while reviews could be improved, they still offer the librarian some basis for assessing new reference works, supplementing the information that can be gleaned from fliers and catalogs distributed by the publishers of reference sources. At present, coverage of printed reference books is more comprehensive than coverage of newer media such as CD-ROM, but the reviewing sources described in this section are trying to be more responsive to the need for reviews of reference sources in all formats.

Guides to Reference Sources

The best-known guide to reference books in the United States is that published by the American Library Association. The *Guide to Reference Books* has served librarians since 1902, with the tenth edition published in 1986. This compilation is frequently referred to by the name of its editor; Alice Kroeger, Isadore Mudge, Constance Winchell, and most recently Eugene P. Sheehy have served in that capacity.[18] The *Guide* provides bibliographic information and descriptions for approximately fourteen thousand English and foreign-language reference works in all fields. Arrangement is in five major parts: Part A—General Reference Works; Part B—Humanities; Part C—Social and Behavioral Sciences; Part D—History and Area Studies; Part E—Science, Technology, and Medicine. Within each part, entries are classified first by subject and then by form. The table of contents displays the subjects in a classified arrangement, and there is an alphabetically arranged author, title, and subject index. A bullet next to a title entry indicates that at least a portion of the source is available online. Entries include complete bibliographic information, publication history where appropriate, notes or annotations, and often a Library of Congress call number.

Two types of publication attempt to make up for the long time lag between editions of the *Guide*. Periodic articles describing new reference sources appear in *College & Research Libraries*.[19] One or more supplements to the *Guide* are published between editions; the supplement for the tenth edition is planned for publication in April 1992.[20] It will include about 4,000 titles published since 1986, and is being compiled by 44 reference librarians from 11 academic institutions, under the editorship of Robert Balay.

The British counterpart to the *Guide to Reference Books* has been edited for a number of years by A. J. Walford. Unlike Sheehy's one-volume format, *Walford's Guide to*

Reference Material appears in three volumes. Volumes in the fourth edition were published in 1980, 1982, and 1987; volume 1 of the fifth edition appeared in 1989. Thus, the three parts differ in their currency. Volume 1 covers science and technology; volume 2 covers social and historical sciences, philosophy, and religion; and volume 3 covers generalia, language and literature, and the arts. Each volume has its own index(es); volume 3 includes a cumulative subject index for the set. Beginning with the fifth edition, volumes have separate author/title and subject indexes. Walford bases the subject arrangement of volumes on the Universal Decimal Classification, with broad subject groupings comparable to those found in the Dewey Decimal Classification. Like the ALA *Guide, Walford's* is international in scope, but it has better coverage of British and European titles.

Although both the ALA *Guide* and *Walford's* seek to encompass works from all subject areas, they cannot cover in depth the works in any particular subject area. For this purpose, the librarian must consult guides to the literature of particular subjects, many of which are identified in a survey by Donald Dickinson.[21] Such works generally serve both as introductions to the subject area and to specialized reference works within each area.

Sample pages from the ALA *Guide* and *Walford's* are reproduced in figures 11.1 and 11.2.

Idioms and usage

Britannica book of English usage. Ed. by Christine Timmons and Frank Gibney. Garden City, N.Y., Doubleday/Britannica Books, 1980. 655p.   **AD53**

Made up in part by excerpts from articles in the *Encyclopaedia Britannica* and partly by new contributions. In three main sections: (1) English today and how it evolved; (2) The basic tools [with subsections on grammar, spelling, pronunciation, words and dictionaries, the library, and abbreviations]; (3) Writing and speaking effectively. Bibliography; index.   PE25.B7

Bryant, Margaret M., ed. Current American usage. N.Y., Funk & Wagnalls, [1962]. 290p.   **AD54**

A handbook which "attempts to bring together the most recent information about frequently debated points of usage in English speech and writing."—*Introd.* Debated points in current usage are discussed with citations to dictionaries, linguistic treatments, and articles in current periodicals, as well as to special investigations made especially for use in this book.   PE2835.B67

Copperud, Roy H. American usage and style: the consensus. N.Y., Van Nostrand Reinhold, [1980]. 433p.   **AD55**

"This book revises, brings up to date, and consolidates two earlier ones: *A Dictionary of Usage and Style* and *American Usage: the Consensus* [1970]."—*Pref.* Compares the judgments of various current dictionaries on disputed points and offers the compiler's own views on those points.   PE1460.C648

Fig. 11.1. Entries from *Guide to Reference Books*, 10th edition, p. 153. Reprinted with permission of the American Library Association.

English Usage

420-3.18
FOWLER, H.W. A dictionary of modern English usage. 2nd ed., revised by Sir E. Gowers. Oxford, Clarendon Press, 1965. xx, (ii), 725p. £5.95; £3.95.

First published 1926.
Some 3,000 entries. A-Z, including *c.* 400 extremely readable articles that embody Fowler's personal recommendations on usage in general and the use of common words. Many brief and more particularized entries on spelling, pronunciation, meaning or phraseology are interspersed. Adopts the Socratic method of teaching by wrong examples. Entry words are sometimes arbitrarily chosen, although a classified guide, under four broad heads (*eg*, 'Out of the frying-pan', on corrections that only make matters worse) precedes in the 2nd ed. In 1926 Fowler had the *O.E.D.*, with its innumerable examples of usage down to his own day, to draw upon, but the new *O.E.D.* supplement will not be completed for some years. Nevertheless the 2nd ed. well preserves the spirit of the original, adding, for example, more portmanteau and modish words (*eg*, 'anti-novel'), and giving more detailed and sympathetic treatment to differences between American and British English.

J.A. Greenwood's *Find it in Fowler; an alphabetical index to the Second Edition* (1965) of H.W. Fowler's 'Modern English usage'... (Princeton, N.J., Wolfhart Book Co., 1969. 113p.) is a detailed key to significant words in Modern English usage. 'Makes the contents of 'Fowler' vastly more accessible' (*Choice*, v.7, no.1, March 1970, p.50).

420-3.18
FOWLER, H.W., and FOWLER, F.G. The King's English. 3rd ed. Oxford, Clarendon Press, 1931 (and reprints). 383p. £2. 95.

Intended as an aid to literary composition. Pt. 1 has chapters entitled Vocabulary, Syntax, Airs and Graces (inversion, metaphor, etc.), and Punctuation. Pt. 2 has sections on euphony, the use of quotation, grammar, meaning, ambiguity and style. Many examples of bad phraseology from newspapers and standard authors are cited throughout.

420-3.18
GOWERS, Sir E. The complete plain words. 2nd ed., revised by Sir Bruce Fraser. London, H.M.S.O. Harmondsworth, Middlesex, Penguin Books, 1973. 332p. £1.

A reconstruction of *Plain words* (1948) and *The ABC of plain words* (1951), first published together as *The complete plain words*. 1954. 'The work is recommended reading in most parts of the (Civil) service'. Mainly concerned with choice and lucidity of expression. 13 chapters and an epilogue (4. Corrections — 5/8. The choice of words: introductory; avoiding the superfluous word; choosing the familiar word; choosing the precise word — 9. The handling of words — 10. Punctuation. Numerous examples of good and bad writing. Bibliography, p.318-20. Index, p.321-32 (subjects in italic; words discussed, in roman). A classic of its kind.

Fig. 11.2. Entries from *Walford's Guide to Reference Material*, Vol. 3, 4th edition, 1987, Generalia, Language & Literature, The Arts, with the permission of Library Association Publishing, London.

For the reference librarian seeking listings of guides to English usage in *Walford's*, there are two entries in the index:

Usage: American English dictionaries, 3/248-9

English dictionaries, 3/243-4

The librarian is directed to volume 3, with pages 248-49 containing entries for American English usage sources and pages 243-44 containing entries for (British) English usage sources.

They appear in separate places because the UDC classification numbers differ somewhat: 420-3.18 for English usage and 420(73)-3.18 for American usage. In this example, the index for the ALA *Guide* is not as helpful, as there is no entry under "Usage." Consulting the table of contents, one finds that "AD Language Dictionaries" is a subsection under "A General Reference Works." Browsing this section, one finds the subheading "Idioms and Usage" where the usage dictionaries are listed. In this case, sources for American and (British) English are intermixed.

The ALA *Guide* and *Walford's* identify many sources likely to be found only in large academic libraries. There are more selective guides to reference books for smaller libraries. One example is *Reference Sources for Small and Medium-Sized Libraries* published by the American Library Association. This compilation, last updated in 1984, has twenty-two sections representing the major subdivisions of the Dewey Decimal Classification and arranged in the order of that classification scheme. It lists about seventeen hundred sources. The first three sections cover general categories of tools (selection aids for reference materials, bibliographies and general sources and encyclopedias), and the remaining sections cover sources for specific subject areas. There is an author/title index at the end. The book includes some titles in microform and online formats, and identifies some titles suitable for children and young adults by a J or Y designation at the end of the annotation. Entries include complete bibliographic information. Christine Gehrt Wynar's *Guide to Reference Books for School Media Centers* includes 2,011 entries in 54 subject categories. These entries cover recommended reference sources in all curriculum areas, providing for a wide range of age and reading levels. Entries include full bibliographic data, descriptions of sources, citations to reviews, and a code for grade level. There is an index of authors, titles, and subjects. In addition to offering broad coverage of general and subject reference works for elementary and secondary school students, Wynar's *Guide to Reference Books for School Media Centers* includes extensive sections on selection aids, study of children's literature, and professional resources for school library media specialists.

Because the widely used guides to reference sources provide only limited coverage of databases, whether online or CD-ROM, there is a need for database directories. Two titles provide very extensive coverage of online databases. The *Directory of Online Databases* lists and briefly describes databases of all types in a wide range of subject areas, covering over four thousand databases available from more than six hundred vendors. There are two complete semiannual issues and two supplements that provide updates in between. Entries are arranged alphabetically, with information on such things as type of database, subjects covered, description of content, producer, vendor, language, geographic coverage, time span, and update frequency. Sample entries appear in figure 11.3. If the database has a related printed publication, this is noted in the content note, as in the entry for *Book Review Digest* shown in figure 11.3. CD-ROM availability is noted at the end of the entry. Indexes cover subjects, database producers, vendors, and telecommunications networks. Using the producer and vendor indexes, one can identify what databases are issued by a particular producer or what databases can be accessed through a particular vendor. A master index covers the names of all organizations, products, and services. The directory can also be searched online through the vendor ORBIT.

Computer-readable Databases: A Directory and Data Sourcebook covers more than six thousand databases of all types, including databases in CD-ROM as well as online. Entries include database name, type of database, language, time span covered, number of records, update frequency, subject coverage, data elements, user aids, database availability, print/microform products, and contact information. Indexes include database producers, database vendors, CD-ROM product, subject, and a master index of names. The directory can also be searched online through DIALOG.

Both directories are useful in identifying available databases covering a particular subject area or containing a particular type of information. The information on producers and vendors indicates how a library can acquire and/or gain access to these databases.

BOOK REVIEW DIGEST℠

Type: Reference (Bibliographic)

Subject: General Interest

Producer: The H.W. Wilson Company

Online Service: WILSONLINE

Content: Contains about 29,000 citations, each with excerpts of reviews, to current reviews of English-language books. Each citation also contains references to the reviews. Covers popular and scholarly works of fiction and non-fiction works, as well as juvenile literature. Sources include over 80 periodicals published in Canada, the U.K., and the U.S. in the humanities, social sciences, and general science. Corresponds to *Book Review Digest*.

Language: English

Coverage: Canada, U.K., and U.S.

Time Span: April 1983 to date

Updating: Twice a week; about 1500 books a month.

This database is also available on CD-ROM.

BOOK REVIEW INDEX

Type: Reference (Bibliographic)

Subject: Social Sciences & Humanities

Producer: Gale Research Inc.

Online Service: DIALOG Information Services, Inc. (File 137)

Content: Contains citations to reviews of books and periodicals carried in approximately 465 journals. Coverage is oriented toward the humanities and social sciences, including literature, fine arts, history, education, and library science. Contains about 1.9 million citations to reviews of approximately 999,000 different publications. Corresponds to *Book Review Index*.

Language: English

Coverage: U.S.

Time Span: 1969 to date

Updating: 3 times a year, about 125,000 records a year

BOOKBASE

Type: Reference (Bibliographic)

Subject: Publishers & Distributors-Catalogs

Producer: IDD Verlag fuer Internationale Dokumentation

Online Service: FIZ Technik (BOOK)

Content: Contains about 33,000 citations to newly announced English- and German-language scientific and technical books, including textbooks, reference books, handbooks, monographs, reports, and conference proceedings. Covers agriculture, biology, business management, chemistry, economics, engineering, ethnology, general science, geosciences, linguistics, mathematics, medicine, physics, political science, and social science.

Language: English and German

Coverage: International

Time Span: 1985 to date

Updating: About 800 records a month

Fig. 11.3. Entries from *Directory of Online Databases*, Vol. 11, No. 3, p. 65. Reprinted by permission of the publisher. Copyright 1990 by Elsevier Science Publishing Co., Inc.

Just as more selective guides to reference books have emerged to serve the needs of the smaller library, there are now more selective database directories. One example is the *Directory of Online Databases and CD-ROM Resources for High Schools*, compiled by Lynn Parisi and Virginia Jones. The compilers tried to include databases with relevance to one or more of the three high school disciplines (social studies, science, English) most likely to prompt research or develop skills compatible with online searching. Entries include a description, scope of the materials covered, intended user, time span covered, and update frequency. There are database name and subject indexes.

While some directories provide descriptions of both online databases and CD-ROMs, other directories concentrate on what might be thought of as "portable" databases. Paul Nicholls identifies several sources of descriptions and evaluations of CD-ROMs.[22] Two of the major directories are the *Directory of Portable Databases* and *CD-ROMs in Print*. The *Directory of Portable Databases* covers databases distributed on CD-ROM, diskettes, or magnetic tape. Types of databases include bibliographic, referral, numeric, full-text, software, graphics, clip-art, photographs, maps, audio/speech, and hypertext. Descriptions indicate the name of the database, producer and vendor names, geographic coverage, time span covered, price, hardware required, subjects covered, type and amount of information, language of data, frequency and format of updating, and software required. Indexes provide various access points to the entries: name, subject, information provider, vendor/distributor, software, corresponding online database, and corresponding printed source.

CD-ROMs in Print covers about fourteen hundred CD-ROMs. Arranged alphabetically by title, each main entry includes hardware requirements, search software, application type, update frequency, price, and CD-ROM player requirements. The directory is updated between editions by listings appearing in *CD-ROM Librarian*. Entries are indexed by distributor, data provider, software provider, publisher, subject, and compatibility with Macintosh computers.

These guides to reference sources and directories of databases serve dual purposes: as collection evaluation checklists and selection tools for reference and collection development librarians, and as aids in reference work to identify appropriate reference sources to use in answering reference questions. In reference work, if the question is unlike one that a reference librarian has answered before, the librarian may not be able easily to identify a likely source without referring to a guide to reference books. These lead-in tools can direct the librarian to one or more sources likely to provide an answer, as previously illustrated by the example on usage dictionaries. The remaining chapters in part 2 consider each type of source in turn, describing their characteristics and appropriate search strategies.

Notes

1.   Heartsill Young, ed., *The ALA Glossary of Library and Information Science* (Chicago: American Library Association, 1983), 188.

2.   Marcia J. Bates, "What Is a Reference Book? A Theoretical and Empirical Analysis," *RQ* 26 (Fall 1986): 37-57.

3.   Sydney J. Pierce, "Introduction," *Reference Librarian* 29 (1990): 1-8.

4.   Mary Biggs and Victor Biggs, "Reference Collection Development in Academic Libraries: Report of a Survey," *RQ* 27 (Fall 1987): 67-79.

5.   Kathleen Coleman and Pauline Dickinson, "Drafting a Reference Collection Policy," *College & Research Libraries* 38 (May 1977): 227-33.

6.   See the sections reprinting reference collection development policies in: Bill Katz, ed., *Reference and Online Services Handbook: Guidelines, Policies, and Procedures for Libraries*, vol. 2 (New York: Neal Schuman, 1986), 67-335.

7.   Eleanor Mathews and David A. Tyckoson, "A Program for the Systematic Weeding of the Reference Collection," *Reference Librarian* 29 (1990): 129-43.

8. Lynn Westbrook, "Weeding Reference Serials," *Serials Librarian* 10 (Summer 1986): 81-100.

9. William A. Katz, *Introduction to Reference Work*, 5th ed., vol. 1 (New York: McGraw-Hill, 1987), 73-76.

10. Carol Tenopir, "Evaluating Online Systems," *Library Journal* 113 (June 1, 1988): 86-87.

11. Danuta A. Nitecki, "The Nontraditions of Database Reviewing," *Library Science Annual* 1 (1985): 42-45.

12. For criteria for evaluating online databases and CD-ROMs, see the following articles: David H. Brunell, "Comparing CD-ROM Products," *CD-ROM Librarian* 3 (March 1988): 14-18; J. A. Large, "Evaluating Online and CD-ROM Reference Sources," *Journal of Librarianship* 21 (April 1989): 87-108; David C. Miller, "Evaluating CDROMs: To Buy or What to Buy?," *Database* 10 (June 1987): 36-42; Paul Travis Nicholls, "Laser/optical Database Products: Evaluation and Selection," *Canadian Library Journal* 45 (October 1988): 296-300; Anne B. Piternick, "Decision Factors Favoring the Use of Online Sources for Providing Information," *RQ* 29 (Summer 1990): 534-44.

13. Steven D. Zink, "Toward More Critical Reviewing and Analysis of CD-ROM User Software Interfaces," *CD-ROM Professional* 4 (January 1991): 16-22.

14. James Rettig, "Reference Book Reviewing Media: A Critical Analysis," *Library Science Annual* 2 (1986): 13-29.

15. Helen K. Wright, "Reference Books Bulletin Editorial Review Board—ALA," in *Encyclopedia of Library and Information Science*, vol. 37, ed. Allen Kent (New York: Marcel Dekker, 1984), 346-52.

16. Phyllis J. Van Orden, "Reviews of Children's Reference Books: Where Are They?," *Reference Librarian* 7/8 (Spring/Summer 1983): 185-89.

17. James H. Sweetland, "Reference Book Reviewing Tools: How Well Do They Do the Job?," *Reference Librarian* 15 (Fall 1986): 65-74.

18. Donald C. Dickinson, "The Way It Was, the Way It Is: 85 Years of the *Guide to Reference Books*," *RQ* 27 (Winter 1987): 220-25.

19. For example, Eileen McIlvaine, "Selected Reference Books of 1989-90," *College & Research Libraries* 51 (September 1990): 431-45.

20. Robert Balay, "Guide to Reference Books," *Choice* 27 (November 1989): 433.

21. Donald C. Dickinson, "A Guide to the Guides: Literary Maps of the Humanities, Social Sciences, and Sciences," *Choice* 21 (November 1983): 383-93.

22. Paul Travis Nicholls, "A Buyer's Guide to CD-ROM Selection: CD-ROM Product Directories and Review Tools," *CD-ROM Professional* 3 (May 1990): 13-21.

List of Sources

American Libraries. Chicago: American Library Association, 1970- . 11 issues per year.

American Reference Books Annual. Edited by Bohdan S. Wynar. Englewood, Colo.: Libraries Unlimited, 1970- . Annual.

Booklist: Including Reference Books Bulletin. Chicago: American Library Association, 1905- . Twice monthly September-June; monthly July-August.

CD-ROM Librarian. Westport, Conn.: Meckler, 1987- . 10 issues per year.

CD-ROMs in Print. Compiled by Norman Desmarais. Westport, Conn.: Meckler, 1991. 450p.

Choice. Middletown, Conn.: Association of College and Research Libraries, 1964- . 11 issues per year.

Computer-readable Databases: A Directory and Data Sourcebook. 7th ed. Edited by Kathleen Young Marcaccio. Detroit, Mich.: Gale Research, 1991. 1,646p. (DIALOG File 230.)

Directory of Online Databases. New York: Cuadra/Elsevier, 1979- . Quarterly. (ORBIT File CUAD.)

Directory of Online Databases and CD-ROM Resources for High Schools. Compiled by Lynn S. Parisi and Virginia L. Jones. Santa Barbara, Calif.: ABC-Clio, 1988. 136p.

Directory of Portable Databases. New York: Cuadra/Elsevier, 1990- . Semiannual.

Guide to Reference Books. 10th ed. Edited by Eugene P. Sheehy. Chicago: American Library Association, 1986. 1,560p.

Guide to Reference Books for School Media Centers. 3d ed. Edited by Christine Gehrt Wynar. Littleton, Colo.: Libraries Unlimited, 1986. 407p.

Library Journal. New York: R. R. Bowker, 1876- . Semi-monthly September-June; monthly July-August.

Preview: Professional and Reference Literature Review. Ann Arbor, Mich.: Mountainside Publishing, 1988- . Monthly.

Recommended Reference Books for Small and Medium-sized Libraries and Media Centers. Edited by Bohdan S. Wynar. Englewood, Colo.: Libraries Unlimited, 1981- . Annual.

Reference Sources for Small and Medium-Sized Libraries. 4th ed. Chicago: American Library Association, 1984. 252p.

RQ. Chicago: American Library Association, 1960- . Quarterly.

Walford's Guide to Reference Material. Edited by A. J. Walford. 3 vols. London: Library Association, 1982-1989. [4th ed. Volume 2 Social & Historical Sciences, Philosophy & Religion, 1982; 4th ed. Volume 3 Generalia, Language & Literature, The Arts, 1987; 5th ed. Volume 1 Science and Technology, 1989]

Wilson Library Bulletin. New York: H. W. Wilson, 1914- . Monthly except July and August.

Additional Readings

Bates, Marcia J. "What Is a Reference Book? A Theoretical and Empirical Analysis." *RQ* 26 (Fall 1986): 37-57.
    Bates notes that reference books have traditionally been defined administratively (e.g., as books that are noncirculating) or functionally (e.g., as books used for reference) rather than descriptively (i.e., in terms of the essential characteristics that distinguish reference books from other books). This article develops and tests a descriptive definition.

Coleman, Kathleen, and Pauline Dickinson. "Drafting a Reference Collection Policy." *College & Research Libraries* 38 (May 1977): 227-33.
    The authors describe the process of developing a reference collection policy, and present a complete sample policy for an academic library reference collection.

Katz, Bill, and Robin Kinder, eds. "The Publishing and Review of Reference Sources." *Reference Librarian* 15 (Fall 1986): 1-336.

This collection of papers examines many facets of reference publishing and reviewing. Of particular interest are the papers in the section on "Reviews and Evaluation of Reference Works," including "Evaluating Reference Books in Theory and Practice" by Norman Stevens; "Reference Book Reviewing Tools: How Well Do They Do the Job?" by James H. Sweetland; and "The Reference Reviewer's Responsibilities" by James Rettig.

Large, J. A. "Evaluating Online and CD-ROM Reference Sources." *Journal of Librarianship* 21 (April 1989): 87-108.

Large provides a clear discussion of the criteria that can be used in evaluating machine-readable sources. In addition to criteria commonly used in evaluation of printed reference works, he identifies criteria associated with databases, online vendors, and telecommunication networks.

Nolan, Christopher W. "The Lean Reference Collection: Improving Functionality through Selection and Weeding." *College & Research Libraries* 52 (January 1991): 80-91.

Nolan develops a series of guidelines for placing sources in reference, focusing especially on the suitability of the items for true reference functions and the expected frequency of use.

Pierce, Sydney J., ed. "Weeding and Maintenance of Reference Collections." *Reference Librarian* 29 (1990): 1-173.

This issue attempts to remedy the limited treatment to date of the topics of weeding and maintenance of reference collections in the library literature. Articles are grouped in three sections. The first considers the impact of differing clientele and objectives on the reference collection, the second deals with policies for reference collection development, and the third covers evaluation and weeding of collections.

Piternick, Anne B. "Decision Factors Favoring the Use of Online Sources for Providing Information." *RQ* 29 (Summer 1990): 534-44.

In developing reference collections, it is helpful to understand the characteristics and capabilities of online sources that make them different from printed sources. This article groups these factors in seven categories: availability, cost, convenience, bibliographic, subject specification, factors relating to information not indexed in printed sources, and special qualifying factors.

Rettig, James. "Every Reference Librarian a Reviewer." *RQ* 26 (Spring 1987): 467-76.

Rettig argues that all reference librarians bear the obligation to get to know the works in their collections as thoroughly as a reviewer must. This article describes this process with respect to reference tools in all formats, relating strengths and weaknesses to the situations that arise in dealing with the information needs posed by the library's users.

DIRECTORIES

Uses and Characteristics

The need for information sources listing people or organizations in a systematic way may first have been met by the production of the *Domesday Book* in 1086 by order of William the Conqueror.[1] Used for tax purposes, this compilation of the wealth and people of England was arranged geographically by county and then by feud within the county.[2] Perhaps this listing was the first directory compiled, providing access to information regarding who held what property, and where that person lived. Now directories cover all topics and geographic areas, ranging from commonly used titles such as *The World of Learning* and the *Encyclopedia of Associations* to unique titles such as *Allergy Products Directory* and the *Whole Horse Catalog*.

Defined by the *ALA Glossary of Library and Information Science* as "a list of persons or organizations, systematically arranged, usually in alphabetic or classed order, giving addresses, affiliations, etc., for individuals, and address, officers, functions and similar data for organizations,"[3] directories are a very important type of reference source. Directories are used to locate organizations, institutions, and people. They are used to verify the name of an organization or the spelling of a person's name, as well as to match individuals with the organizations that can answer their information needs when they have to go beyond the resources of the library. Because directories encompass so many types of organizations, associations, institutions, and individuals, in many libraries they are the most frequently consulted type of reference source.

Evaluation

When evaluating a directory, there are several criteria to consider. First is the *scope* of the directory: what organizations, geographic areas, or types of individuals are included in the directory. The title often gives some insight into the scope of the source; however, more detailed information will be found in the preface, which should be closely examined. It is also important to determine how comprehensive the directory is, within its stated scope. For example, a business directory may include all businesses in the geographic area covered, or only those businesses with an income over a specified dollar amount, or those meeting some other criteria.

The *currency* of the information provided in the directory should also be examined. What is the frequency of publication? How often is the material actually updated? This is an important feature of directories, since they are often used specifically to find the most up-to-date information on an organization, institution, or individual. How the information in the source is updated is also important in determining the *accuracy* of the directory. Many methods are used in updating records: verifying information by telephone, through a form sent in the mail, by public record, or by research staff culling newspapers and journals. Often information on the currency and accuracy of the source is also included in its preface.

The directory's *format* is critical to its effective use by librarians or patrons. One point to consider is the arrangement of the tool. Are the entries clearly arranged and consistent throughout the source? Does the source provide headers at the tops of pages for ease of use? The directory's indexes are a significant factor in providing access to the information it includes. Types of indexes can include, among others, a personal name index, a geographic index, a title or organization name index, and a subject index. Title or organization name indexes may be by actual title or organization name, or by keywords in the title or organization name (see figure 12.1).

```
Pacific Coast Studio Directory  6888
Pacific Design Center—Directory
  [California]  C&SDIP
Pacific Egg and Poultry Association—
  Membership List  3944
Pacific Fishing—Yearbook Issue  2166
Pacific International Trapshooting
  Association—Yearbook  9627
Pacific Island and Australian Aboriginal
  Artifacts in Public Collections in the
  United States of America and
  Canada  IDIP
```

```
Poughkeepsie-Hyde Park-Pleasant
  Valley, New York Cross Reference
  Directory  C&SDIP
[Poultry]; American Silkie Bantam
  Club—Membership List  8742
Poultry Antiquities—Breeders Directory;
  Society for the Preservation
  of  9251
Poultry Association—Membership List;
  Pacific Egg and  3944
Poultry; Computer Software Directory
  for  3650
```

```
Egg Marketing—Directory of
  Processors and Further Processors
  Issue; Poultry &  3979
Egg Marketing—Egg Marketing
  Directory Issue; Poultry &  3980
Egg Marketing—Poultry Distributor
  Directory Issue; Poultry &  3981
Egg and Poultry Association—
  Membership List; Pacific  3944
Egg & Poultry Industries Issue; Poultry
  International—Who's Who
  International in the  3982
```

Fig. 12.1. Example of keyword indexing in *Directories in Print*. Selections from *Directories in Print*, Seventh Edition, 1990, edited by Julie E. Tavell and Charles B. Montney. Copyright © 1990 by Gale Research Inc. Reprinted by permission of the publisher.

Another consideration is the availability of the directory in nonprint format, either as an online database or as a CD-ROM database. There are instances in which an online search is a better choice than trying to locate the information in a paper source. Online databases and CD-ROM products may contain more current information than their printed counterparts. If a source is published annually, but the database has quarterly reloads, the online version may be a more accurate source of information. The online database and CD-ROM can often be searched more efficiently, because some elements or fields of the record are indexed electronically but are not indexed in the print version. One example of this is the *American Library Directory*, which has no personal name index in the printed version, but allows for searching the personal name field in the electronic versions. Searching electronically often allows for keyword searching that the print version cannot provide unless the print version includes a keyword title or name index. The advantage of this technique is that exact names or titles need not be known, but can be found with keyword searching.

Another benefit of online and CD-ROM searching is the ability to combine fields or terms using Boolean logic, a concept discussed further in chapter 5. Boolean logic allows terms to be combined to form a set specific to the library user's needs. For example, when searching for a company name in D&B - Dun's Electronic Business Directory, a large number of matches may occur when keywords are used. Using the Boolean operator "AND," this set can be combined with a geographic location, narrowing the number of hits so the appropriate business can be identified.

An obvious drawback to using electronic sources is the cost involved for online connect time, hardware, and software. This issue of cost must be weighed against the advantages of speed and the currency of information accessed. Each reference department should formulate policies regarding when and how often it is appropriate to use electronic searching.

Selection

The process of selecting directory sources for a reference collection varies greatly from library to library, and depends on many factors. Which directories are included in a collection is based on the community served, on the types of questions asked, and on the number of questions in a particular subject area. For example, research libraries and special libraries may select more international sources than a public library would purchase. Public libraries may be more interested in business sources and telephone directories than a school library. Another factor in selection is the location of the library; this may dictate a concentration of sources dealing with a specific geographic area. Other considerations, related to the library's location, involve what other collections are found nearby, and whether the library has a formal network for the cooperative collection of sources. The budget available to the librarian and the cost of the various directories considered for purchase must also be taken into account. Perhaps the librarian in a smaller library or in a library with funding problems will choose to purchase an annual directory only every other year. Further discussion of the selection process is found in chapter 11.

Important General Sources

Directories of Directories

Directories of directories provide listings and descriptions of various directories. They are a good starting point when the library patron needs a certain directory but does not know the exact title, or when the user wants to know if a specific type of directory exists, such as a directory of a particular occupational group.

Directories in Print gathers information on all types of directories of the United States and Canada that are national or regional in scope. It lists a wide range of directory-type sources, including commercial directories, lists of cultural institutions, directories of trades and professions, rosters of professional and scientific societies, biographical directories, and many other lists and guides on various topics. The common element of these various sources is that they include addresses. Nonprint formats of directories, such as microform collections and databases, are also included. Types of directories not listed in *Directories in Print* include information sources on local clubs and directories of interest only to those in a limited geographic area.

Directories in Print consists of two volumes; a supplement is published between editions of the main set. The supplement gives descriptions of newly published directories and serves as an update to the main edition. Two indexes are provided: a subject index, and a title and keyword index. The main entry portion is arranged by general subject areas; in each of these sections, the entries are listed alphabetically by title of the directory. Each entry describes what the directory covers, language(s) of the text, frequency of publication, and what information the entries in the directory include. Other information given includes how to order the directory, and whether the publication is available online or in any computer-readable format.

Directories in Print is a good starting point when a library patron needs address information on a specialized group of people, such as architects or candy brokers, or on a type of industry, such as the tool or real estate industry. The subject index supports searching under various subject headings to see what directories exist in these areas. The title and keyword index enables the user to browse actual titles of directories arranged by important words in their titles. This index is useful when patrons are searching for a known directory but do not know the complete title, or if they want to browse titles under a keyword to determine what directories are available in that subject area.

Two other sources, similar to *Directories in Print* but different in scope, are *City and State Directories in Print* and *International Directories in Print*. *City and State Directories in Print* has very little overlap with *Directories in Print*, as it lists nearly five thousand state and local directories, rosters, lists, and guides. Subjects covered include restaurant and travel guides, local social service directories, city cross-reference directories, and local association rosters.

International Directories in Print lists over five thousand directories that are either published outside the United States or are international in scope. Subjects covered include business, industrial, scientific, and professional directories. *International Directories in Print* is organized by broad subject areas with geographic, subject, and title and keyword indexes.

Another useful directory of directories is *Organizations Master Index*. This tool lists approximately fifty directories, handbooks, guides, yearbooks, and encyclopedias from various publishers by the names of the organizations found in each of these sources. The sources span broad subject areas, including research centers, foundations, museums, government agencies, national and international associations, religious groups, and political organizations. The scope of geographic coverage is mainly the United States and Canada, although some of the directories indexed provide international coverage.

Organizations Master Index is arranged alphabetically by organization name as the name would appear in its directory listing. Entries are straightforward, providing the organization name, sponsoring or parent organization (when this information is useful), geographic location of city, state or province, and country, and the abbreviated title of one or more sources in which this organization is described. An annotated bibliography at the beginning of *Organizations Master Index* matches this abbreviation with the full bibliographic citation of the source to be consulted.

A useful feature of *Organizations Master Index* is that it identifies the exact source to use for information about an organization, and also, by omission, which sources not to consult. This feature can be a helpful timesaver. *Organizations Master Index* is a good title to check when the library user or librarian needs information on an organization but does not know enough about the organization to decide which directory would contain the needed information. It is also an excellent source to consult when the user's familiarity with various directories is minimal.

Either *Directories in Print* or *Organizations Master Index* would be an excellent first step to consult for finding the appropriate directory needed by a patron. *Directories in Print* allows searching by keyword when the library user is uncertain about whether a directory exists for a particular topic. With *Organizations Master Index*, the user must know the exact name of the organization in order to find information concerning it; there is no keyword access. The two sources vary slightly in approach, in that *Organizations Master Index* is an index to information about organizations and *Directories in Print* is an index to directories of organizations. Directories of organizations often provide the needed information on an organization, so the two sources can be used as different means to the same end.

Library Directories

Directories of libraries and subject collections are valuable sources for identifying the locations, professional staff, and special collections of libraries all over the world. They also provide the added benefit of potentially connecting the library user to information experts in all subject areas and geographic locations.

The main source to consult for basic factual information on libraries in the United States, Canada, and regions administered by the United States is the *American Library Directory*. This two-volume set is a standard tool used by all sizes and types of libraries. Coverage of the directory includes public libraries; college, university, and community college libraries; armed forces and government libraries; law, medical, and religious libraries; and special libraries, which span industry, company, foundation, and association libraries. The directory has been revised annually since 1978; from 1908 to 1978 it was published biennially.

Arrangement of the *American Library Directory* is geographical; entries are arranged by state or province, by city within the state, and then alphabetically within the city. An index by library name is provided. Entries contain a great deal of information: the name and address of the library, the number of staff, income and expenditure figures, library holdings, special collections, automation networks in which the library participates, and branches of the library. This information is obtained either from the library itself or from public sources. The *American Library Directory* also contains a general information section providing, for example, listings of library schools and training courses, libraries for the blind and physically handicapped, libraries which serve the deaf and hearing impaired, and addresses of United States armed forces libraries overseas.

The *American Library Directory* is also available electronically on DIALOG. The online records are identical to those found in the printed format, and all fields are searchable. The entire database is updated annually. A good reason to use the online rather than the printed version of *American Library Directory* is for searching personal names to determine where a particular librarian is located. The printed version has no personal name index, but the online database allows for searching that field electronically. Other indexed fields found in the online format and not in the printed format include publications of the library and subject interest areas of the library.

A directory of library collections that are limited by subject matter or form is the *Directory of Special Libraries and Information Centers*. Collections found in business firms, nonprofit organizations, educational institutions, government agencies, foundations, and holdings of private individuals are within the scope of this directory. This is a good source to consult when trying to find information on a special type of collection rather than on a particular library. The descriptions of the collections, arranged in alphabetical order by name of the library, give name and address of the library or information center, the name of the parent organization, principal subject keyword for the main subject of the collection, the name of the head of the library, the founding date, number of staff, size of the collection, whether the library is automated, and the names of the principal members of the professional staff. Indexes to the directory include a geographic index, a personnel index, and a subject index. These indexes allow the user to locate specific libraries when only a general geographic location is known, to determine where a librarian is located when only the librarian's name is known, or to determine which libraries collect extensively in a specific subject area. This directory is updated annually, with a supplemental volume published between the annual editions.

The format and arrangement of the *Directory of Special Libraries and Information Centers* and the *American Library Directory* differ. Because the *American Library Directory* is geographically arranged with no subject index, it is not possible to search by subject. *Directory of Special Libraries and Information Centers* is arranged alphabetically and includes subject, geographic, and personnel indexes, allowing more access points to the entries.

Another guide to libraries by special book collection is *Subject Collections*, compiled by Lee Ash. Limited in scope to the United States and Canada, this source serves as a directory to special book collections of university, college, and public libraries, special libraries, and museums. It is a useful source when the patron wants to find the names and locations of libraries which have important collections in a specific subject area.

Publishing and Book Trade Directories

Questions concerning addresses and telephone numbers of publishers and various aspects of the publishing business are commonly asked at the reference desk. Publishers directories provide this information and other types of information on the publishing industry on both a national and an international level.

Literary Market Place is the business directory of the American book publishing industry. Published annually, it contains entries related to all aspects of publishing in the United States. Information is found under fifteen main subject groupings, with related sections listed in the table of contents under these groupings. Subjects covered include book publishers, both United States and Canadian, and also those foreign publishers with U.S. offices; book clubs; book distributors and literary agents; book trade organizations and events; and literary awards. Services and suppliers are listed, as well as book manufacturers and paper merchants. Generally, entries include name, address, telephone number, key personnel, and some descriptive information. Indexes to the directory include an alphabetical listing of all companies and personnel in the volume, directing the user to the section number where the full entry is located, and also an index to the various sections of information in the directory, such as jacket design or literary awards. Using the alphabetical index, the patron can find where in the directory a specific company is listed. Using the section index, the user can locate information on companies or services of a specific type.

International Literary Market Place covers information about the publishing world for over 160 countries. This annual source is arranged by country, with information as available from these countries under the various categories of book trade organizations, book trade reference books and journals, publishers, remainder dealers, literary agents, book clubs, major booksellers and major libraries of the country, library and literary associations and prizes, and translation associations and agencies. Because this source is geographically arranged, it is a good source to consult to find the major libraries of a given country, or to see the main publishers of that country listed. One comprehensive index of all entries, by organization name, is provided.

Another source which can be consulted for information on American publishing companies is the publishers volume of the *Books in Print* set. Publishers included are those whose books are listed in the author, title, and subject volumes of *Books in Print*. The first section lists publishers' and distributors' name abbreviations in alphabetical order as they are listed in *Books in Print*. The abbreviated name is followed by the full form of the company's name, International Standard Book Number (ISBN) prefixes, business affiliation, editorial address, telephone number, and ordering/distribution address and telephone number. The next main section of the volume lists publishing companies alphabetically by their full company name, and provides the same information as the entries previously mentioned. The subsequent section is a handy one; it lists publishers and distributors with their toll-free telephone numbers. Following this is a listing of wholesalers and distributors with their ordering information. A geographic index to wholesalers and distributors is provided, allowing the user to see these companies arranged by state. A section of new publishers since the last published edition of *Books in Print* is also provided. The last section is a listing of inactive or defunct publishers. For a complete discussion of all volumes of the *Books in Print* set, see chapter 18.

While *Literary Market Place* deals mainly with the book publishing industry, *American Book Trade Directory* places its emphasis on retailers and wholesalers of books in the United States and Canada. This annual directory of booksellers is arranged geographically by state or province, then by city within the state or province. It lists all types of bookstores, including antiquarian, college, educational, general, mail order, paperback, religious, used, and special subject bookstores. The directory is divided into three main sections: retailers and antiquarians, wholesalers of books and magazines, and book trade information. The section on wholesalers gives information on wholesalers, jobbers, and distributors of trade books and magazines. Also included in this section is a list of national distributors of paperbacks and wholesale remainder dealers. The section on book trade information provides access to information about foreign book dealers and book exporters and importers. Auctioneers and appraisers of library collections are also listed. Entries in *American Book Trade Directory* may be found by consulting either the complete alphabetical index of all entries or the index by type of store, which lists bookstores by the specialty topic comprising at least 50 percent of that store's stock.

Publishers, Distributors and Wholesalers is an online database containing contact information for the entire U.S. book publishing industry. Comprised of eight subfiles, this DIALOG database includes *Books in Print* publishers, association publishers, audiocassette publishers, software producers, microcomputer hardware manufacturers, and book and microcomputer distributors and wholesalers. It was designed to serve as an ordering reference, telephone book, and acquisition guide. Each record provides company name and address, and gives both editorial and ordering information.

The printed counterpart of this database, *Publishers, Distributors and Wholesalers of the United States*, lists approximately fifty-three thousand active publishers, distributors, wholesalers, and software producers and manufacturers in the United States. The main section of the volume is the company name section; arranged alphabetically, it provides company name, the name abbreviation used in many Bowker bibliographies, the ISBN prefix, business affiliation, editorial address and telephone number, ordering/distribution address and telephone number, and imprints with their name abbreviations. Cross-references are provided from imprints and variant names to the main company name. The next section, the key to abbreviations, is useful when a library patron has an abbreviated publisher's name and needs the full name of the company. The ISBN prefix index is arranged numerically by the publishers' and distributors' International Standard Book Number prefix. The corresponding company's full name is then given. The library user can then look in the name index for the full entry. Other sections include a list of publishers' and distributors' toll-free numbers, an index of wholesalers and distributors, a geographic index, and an index of publishers by fields of activity.

Education/Research Directories

Directories of educational institutions, secondary schools, community colleges, universities, and research centers are frequently consulted reference sources, particularly in academic libraries. They are used primarily for addresses of institutions and individuals. More detailed descriptions of programs are found in a source such as the *College Blue*

Book,[4] which is beyond the scope of this chapter. Education and research center directories provide addresses, telephone numbers, and often brief background information on the institution.

Directories of Educational Institutions. The World of Learning is an annually published source of international scope which provides information on learned societies, research institutions, libraries, museums, and universities. Arranged alphabetically by country, it is a good source of information on institutions of higher education in most countries. The general format within each country section uses subject divisions such as academies, learned societies, libraries and archives, museums and art galleries, schools of art and music, and colleges of technology. Under these broad categories, the names of the institutions are listed.

The amount of information provided on a specific institution varies greatly. The minimum amount of information in an entry consists of the address and telephone number of the institution, museum, library, or learned society. The entries can be as detailed as to include the number of teaching staff, number of students, the title(s) of the institution's publication(s), affiliated institutions, and names of faculty members teaching at the institution. The entries for libraries and archives may also include details on the collections. Museum and art gallery entries often include information about the displays or areas of collection. A comprehensive alphabetical index of institutions is provided at the end of the volume.

The universities and institutions of higher education of more than 115 countries and territories, excluding Commonwealth countries, are represented in the *International Handbook of Universities*. Information on more than seven thousand educational institutions is presented by country. General background information on each institution is given in an introductory paragraph. Like *The World of Learning*, entries in the *International Handbook of Universities* vary greatly in the amount of information given. The briefest entry includes address and telephone number, and lists departments of the institution. More complete descriptions include deans' names, number of staff, dates of the academic calendar, admission requirements, fees, the language used for instruction, and the types of degrees and diplomas offered. An index to institutional names lists each institution by its official title, and also lists the institution under the English translation of that title.

Although many similarities exist between *The World of Learning* and *International Handbook of Universities*, there are several reasons why the former is often preferred over the latter. One valuable feature of *The World of Learning* is that it lists the faculty of many educational institutions. Also, *The World of Learning* includes libraries and museums as well as universities. The geographic scope of *The World of Learning* is larger than that of the *International Handbook of Universities*, since it encompasses Commonwealth countries and the latter does not. Also, the information may be more current in *The World of Learning*, since it is published annually and the *International Handbook of Universities* is irregularly published.

While *The World of Learning* is truly international in scope, *Commonwealth Universities Yearbook* serves as the companion to *International Handbook of Universities* to provide full international coverage of institutions of higher education. Giving detailed information about the institutions excluded by *International Handbook of Universities*, namely, members of the Commonwealth of Nations (formerly British colonies), *Commonwealth Universities Yearbook* is an annually published set with information arranged in alphabetical order by country. Within each country section is a narrative about each of the country's universities. Following this general section, the university information is outlined. In addition to standard directory data such as address and telephone number, the teaching staff of the school is listed by department. General information on the institution is then provided, including admission information, first degrees offered, higher degrees offered, fees, dates of the academic year, and publications of the institution. Indexes to the set are found in volume 4. The first index is a general index to organizations and institutions named in this source, as well as to topics discussed (e.g., admissions, degrees) in the essay on each country. The second index is an index to all of the personal names appearing in the entries.

Commonwealth Universities Yearbook is the only one of the international education directories discussed that provides access to entries by personal names.

The *HEP Higher Education Directory* is a listing of accredited institutions of postsecondary education for the United States and its territories. This annual directory has four main parts: a directory portion and three indexes. The directory is arranged alphabetically by state, then alphabetically by institution name. Data provided for each entry includes address, telephone number, size of enrollment, amount of annual fees for undergraduate students, general programs offered, and a list of administrative and academic officers. The first index is of administrators, with their most direct telephone number listed, and a cross-reference to their institution. The second is an index of regional, national, professional, and specialized accreditation status arranged alphabetically by state; a page number is also provided for the institution's main entry. The third index is an alphabetic index of institutions to be used when a patron does not know in which state a college or university is located. Other information provided in this directory includes lists of U.S. Department of Education offices, statewide agencies of higher education, and higher education associations.

For information on primary, secondary, and postsecondary education in the United States, a standard source is *Patterson's American Education*. Included in this directory are entries for thirty-four thousand public, private, and church-affiliated secondary schools; twelve thousand school districts; and seventy-three hundred accredited colleges, universities, and community colleges; and vocational, technical, and trade schools. The main section of *Patterson's American Education* is organized alphabetically by state, then by community. Information found in the listings includes the county name, community population, school district name, total district student enrollment, and a listing of the community schools with their addresses. The second section of *Patterson's American Education* arranges postsecondary schools by discipline and then alphabetically by state. Addresses of the institutions are listed here, although no telephone numbers are provided. This directory is indexed by postsecondary school names only; access to primary and secondary schools depends on the user knowing the town in which the school is located.

Directories of Research Centers. The *Research Centers Directory*, an annual two-volume set, serves as a guide to more than twelve thousand nonprofit research organizations in the United States and Canada. Many types of research facilities fall under the scope of this directory: research institutes and centers, laboratories, experimental stations, and facilities affiliated with universities, hospitals, foundations, and other nonprofit entities. All areas of research are covered here, including agriculture, business, education, the humanities, religion, labor and industrial relations, medicine and life sciences, physical sciences, engineering, and technology. For the purposes of this directory, the term *research* includes fundamental and applied studies, as well as data-gathering and synthesis activities.

Research centers in the fields of life sciences, physical sciences, and engineering are listed in volume 1, while those dealing with private, public, and cultural affairs can be found in volume 2. Entries are arranged alphabetically by research center name within each general subject area. Two indexes are located in volume 2. The first is a subject index which lists general subjects in alphabetical order, followed by corresponding numbers of the entries arranged by the state in which they are located. This is helpful if the library user does not know the name of the research center, but does know the subject area of research conducted by the center. The second index is a keyword index by institution name, which is useful if one or more keywords from the center's name are known, since each center is listed several times, once under each appropriate keyword.

Entries are clearly arranged and provide many details about each research center. After institution name, research center name, address, and telephone and fax number, the director of the center is listed. A second section provides organizational notes, such as when the center was founded, former names of the center, sources of support, number of staff, affiliated centers, and memberships of the center. Next is a section describing research activities and fields within the scope of the institution. Other information provided includes a list of publications of the institution, dates of meetings of the research center, and whether the center has a library collection.

A supplement to this publication appears between the annual editions of the main work. The purpose of the supplement is to list research centers that are either newly formed or that have been recently identified. The arrangement of the supplement is identical to that of the main volumes. It also includes both an institution name keyword index and a subject index.

Broader in scope both geographically and by type of research institution than the *Research Centers Directory*, *International Research Centers Directory* covers all countries (except the United States) and all categories of research, including government, university, independent nonprofit, commercial, and laboratory, as well as organizations which support research. Arranged alphabetically by country, this biennial publication is then organized by the name of the research center. The entries follow the same format as the *Research Centers Directory*, giving general directory information, organizational notes, research activities and field, and publications and services. Three indexes are provided: a name and keyword index, based on research center names; a country index, grouping centers by country; and a subject index, providing access to centers by field of study. The *International Research Centers Directory* provides the same scope of coverage for other countries as the combination of *Research Centers Directory*, *Government Research Directory*, *State Government Research Directory*, and *Research Services Directory* provides for the United States.

As *Research Centers Directory* provides information on university and nonprofit-oriented research institutions in the United States, *Government Research Directory* provides the same type of information for nearly thirty-seven hundred research centers of the United States government. Included in this biennial publication are government research and development centers, test facilities, experiment stations, and laboratories in the areas of agriculture, business, education, energy, engineering, the environment, medicine, the humanities, and basic and applied sciences.

The *State Government Research Directory* is the counterpart to the *Government Research Directory* for approximately 850 state-level research agencies. Geographic scope includes the fifty states, the District of Columbia, and the U.S. territories. Areas of research include agriculture, business and industry, conservation and wildlife, education, environment, health and social services, housing, parks and recreation, transportation, women's rights, and many other areas.

A source outlining information on over four thousand laboratories, individuals, and research firms in the private sector which provide contract or fee-based research services in the United States is the *Research Services Directory*. Services provided include analysis, design, development, experimentation, forecasting, surveys, statistical studies, technical advising, and testing. Fields such as agriculture, biology, business, environmental science, energy, government, humanities, and space sciences are represented. Both the *Research Services Directory* and the *State Government Research Directory* have an irregular publication cycle, and neither is updated annually.

Four of these directories (*Research Centers Directory*, *International Research Centers Directory*, *Government Research Directory*, and *Research Services Directory*) have been combined into a single database, Research Centers and Services Directory, available through DIALOG. This provides the capability of searching on many parts of each directory entry, including names of personnel, publications and services, and research activities. All four directories can be searched simultaneously or the search can be limited to a particular directory.

Foundations and Grants Directories

Foundations and grants directories outline the interests of various foundations and grant-making institutions and the kinds of activities they support. Directories of this type also show which foundations give money to a particular nonprofit entity and how much they give. These are valuable tools in an academic library or in a special library, such as a business or foundation library.

A major source of information on nongovernmental grant-making foundations in the United States is *The Foundation Directory*. It contains entries on over seven thousand of the country's largest foundations. Included in *The Foundation Directory* are those foundations with assets of $1 million or more, or which have annual giving of at least $100,000. Foundation types fall into one of four categories: independent foundations, company-sponsored foundations, operating foundations, or community foundations. The foundations listed in this directory represent over 25 percent of all grant-making foundations.

The Foundation Directory is now published annually, with updated information originating from written reports sent by the foundations, or from the most current public records available. There is, therefore, no longer a need for the supplement that was formerly published between the biennial editions of the directory. The 13th edition includes about 1,200 foundations listed for the first time. To identify new foundations for inclusion, Foundation Center staff monitor journal and newspaper articles and press releases. The new entries are then sent to each foundation for verification.

The Foundation Directory is arranged alphabetically by state, and then alphabetically by foundation name within the state. Entries include the foundation's name and address, funding interests, officers and trustees, and financial data for the last year available. Other information, such as restrictions on giving programs, publications offered by the foundation, and application procedures, is included when applicable.

The Foundation Directory is a good source for a wide range of inquiries regarding foundations. The entries themselves can be used to answer questions regarding what type of support a foundation will give, or for what purposes or activities money will be given. Entries also show the number of grants given by a particular foundation, and specify the grants with the highest and lowest dollar amounts. The introductory pages of *The Foundation Directory* not only describe how to use the directory, but also define types of foundations, discuss overall foundation giving in the United States historically and currently, and analyze trends in foundation giving. Arrangement of the indexes in the directory allows foundations to be studied geographically and also by types of support given. The index to donors, officers, and trustees enables the user to find the foundation connected with a particular individual. The foundation name index cross-references foundations with their state locations. Through the subject index, a patron will find foundations grouped by the purpose and activities for which those foundations give grant money.

The online counterpart to *The Foundation Directory* is much broader in scope than the printed source. This database on DIALOG now includes a formerly separate file, National Foundations, making this a comprehensive directory of more than twenty-five thousand funding sources. Because of the merging of these two files, there are two subfiles: the FULL subfile, which includes the foundations found in *The Foundation Directory* and shows subject descriptors, and the BRIEF subfile, which tends to include smaller foundations giving locally and does not show subject descriptors. This database is updated annually and reflects data available for the current fiscal year.

Taft Foundation Reporter is another useful source of information on grant-making foundations. This source profiles the 500 foundations responsible for 50 percent of all grants awarded by private foundations. Like *The Foundation Directory*, *Taft Foundation Reporter* provides basic information about the foundation, including address, type of foundation, number of grants given (including high and low grants), and areas of funding interest. In addition, it lists sample grants which illustrate the foundation's charitable priorities. A unique feature of *Taft Foundation Reporter* is the inclusion of biographical material on the officers and directors of the foundations, showing place and year of birth, educational background, current employment, corporate affiliations, nonprofit affiliations, and other philanthropic affiliations.

Taft Foundation Reporter is arranged alphabetically by foundation name. Because of the many indexes, foundations can be accessed several ways: by state, by type of grants awarded, and by fields of interest for giving. There are also three types of indexes to individuals affiliated with the foundations: an index to individuals by name, by place of birth, and by college attended.

The Foundation Grants Index is a list of the actual grants awarded by over 470 foundations. This annual publication includes grants of $5,000 or more, most of which are awarded by the 100 largest U.S. foundations. The arrangement is alphabetical by state, with foundations listed alphabetically within each state. The grants are listed in alphabetical order by the name of the recipient organization. These entries include the amount awarded, the name and location of the recipient, for what the grant was used, and the date it was awarded. *The Foundation Grants Index* is a useful tool to determine specific projects for which a foundation has given, to ascertain the current giving trends of a specific foundation, and to assist fund seekers in determining what foundation would be likely to support their projects. Indexes to the main section on grants awarded provide access in a number of ways, including by grant recipient, subject, and recipient categories.

The online version of *The Foundation Grants Index* is available on DIALOG. It includes all information printed in the paper source and more, since it does not represent just one year of awards, but lists grants given by American philanthropic foundations since 1973. As in the printed source, the database includes only grants of $5,000 or more and does not include grants to individuals. Bimonthly updates keep the online source very up-to-date; typically two thousand grants are added or altered per update.

An additional source for matching grant-giving organizations with grant-seeking institutions is the *Annual Register of Grant Support*. Covering a broad scope of grant support programs, this tool outlines programs of governmental agencies, public and private foundations, community trusts, unions, and educational and professional associations. The *Annual Register of Grant Support* is divided into major areas of giving interest: humanities, international affairs and area studies, special populations, urban and regional affairs, education, multiple-discipline sciences, social science, physical science, life science, and technology and industry. These areas are further subdivided into more specific giving areas. Entries for the grant-awarding sources give the name and address of the source, when it was founded, name(s) of program(s), purpose of the program, eligibility, financial data, and number of awards in the past year. Indexes allow the user to find grant-awarding sources by subject, by organization and program, by geographic area (state), or by personnel of the grant-making body. An added feature of this source is an introductory article which describes program planning and proposal writing.

An annual source which matches grant programs with those individuals seeking funding for research projects is the *Directory of Research Grants*. Sponsoring organizations include business and professional organizations, foundations, and governmental agencies. Grant programs are listed alphabetically by the sponsoring organization. These entries provide information on the grant-awarding organization's interests, eligibility requirements, restrictions, application and review procedures, deadlines, and funding history. A subject index allows grant seekers to see a list of funding sources in their areas of interest. An advantage of the corresponding online database on DIALOG is the currency of material. This file is updated monthly; programs are added, deleted, and revised with each update.

The foundation directories discussed here have different approaches. *The Foundation Directory*, *Annual Register of Grant Support*, and *Directory of Research Grants* give mostly information on the foundations themselves, while *Taft Foundation Reporter* and *The Foundation Grants Index* provide examples of actual grants awarded by the foundations. The *Directory of Research Grants* lists institutions giving specifically for research, while the other four directories discussed here have broader giving interests. Sources outlining current funding interests include *The Foundation Grants Index* and the *Annual Register of Grant Support*; these are good sources for determining the most up-to-date giving patterns of major foundations.

Business Directories

Directories of businesses are used to find where a company is located, who is the appropriate contact person at a particular business, general background on a corporation, the correct name of the company, or product information for the company. They also answer questions regarding which companies provide a particular service for consumers and business persons in the community.

The *Standard & Poor's Register of Corporations, Directors and Executives* is an annual directory of over fifty thousand leading public and private U.S. corporations with sales of over $1 million. It is arranged in three volumes, with volume 3 providing indexes to volumes 1 and 2. Volume 1 contains an entry for each corporation in alphabetical order. Entries include addresses and telephone numbers; names, titles, and functions of the company's officers, directors, and other principals; the name of the company's accounting firm, law firm, and primary bank; the stock exchange on which the company's stock is traded; and a description of the company's products and services. Also included in each entry is the company's Standard Industrial Classification (SIC) codes, division names, and subsidiary listings. Volume 2 is an alphabetical listing of directors and executives, naming their affiliations with various companies and giving their business and home addresses. When available, year and place of birth, college attended, and fraternal memberships are also listed. Volume 3 contains indexes by SIC code number, geographic location, and subsidiaries and divisions linked to the parent company. This volume also provides a listing and explanation of the Standard Industrial Classification system, which numbers industries and groups them by type of industry.

Standard & Poor's Register - Corporate is available both online (on DIALOG) and in CD-ROM format. This database corresponds with volume 1 of the paper version of *Standard & Poor's Register of Corporations, Directors and Executives*. Biographical information on key executives is found separately in the online version of volume 2, also available both on DIALOG and on CD-ROM.

Dun & Bradstreet's *Million Dollar Directory* is a five-volume set containing information regarding more than 160,000 U.S. public and privately held businesses. To be included, a business must have a net worth of more than $500,000 and must be a headquarters or a single-location business. Types of businesses include agriculture, mining, construction, manufacturing, transportation, wholesale and retail trade, finance, insurance, real estate, and business services. Hospitals, engineering firms, foreign-owned corporations, and consulting agencies are generally not included. Within the five-volume set, the first three volumes list businesses alphabetically. Volumes 4 and 5 provide indexes by industry SIC code and by geographic location.

Many types of data are provided in each business entry. The entries include headquarters address and telephone number, stock exchange(s) used, company officers and directors, members of the board of directors, and up to six industrial classification (SIC) codes. Information included when available is telex number, whether or not the company is publicly owned, and the company's banking, accounting, and legal firm relationships. Some entries also show the company logo. The *Million Dollar Directory* is searchable online through DIALOG. The database is given annual reloads and contains the same entry information (excluding company logos) as the annually published paper version of this directory. The *Million Dollar Directory* is also available on CD-ROM as Million Dollar Disc.

The *Million Dollar Directory* has a broader scope than *Standard and Poor's Register of Corporations, Directors and Executives*, as it includes businesses with a net worth of over $500,000 rather than the $1 million net worth criterion used by *Standard and Poor's Register*. The *Million Dollar Directory* has more access by indexes, including groupings of businesses geographically and by SIC code. An advantage of *Standard and Poor's Register* is the biographical information for directors and executives, not found in the *Million Dollar Directory*.

Broader in scope than the *Million Dollar Directory*, D&B - Dun's Market Identifiers is a database which includes information on over 2.5 million U.S. companies that have 5 or more employees or $1 million or more in sales. Address, product, financial, and marketing information is provided for public and private companies of a commercial or industrial nature. This DIALOG database is updated quarterly, and it is also available on CD-ROM.

An online database with no printed equivalent is D&B - Dun's Electronic Business Directory (available on DIALOG). This directory of nearly 8.5 million U.S. businesses and professionals is reloaded quarterly, and it covers both private and public businesses of all sizes and types, making it the most comprehensive business directory available. The major industry groups included are agriculture, business services, communication, construction, finance, insurance, manufacturing, mining, professional services, real estate, retail, transportation, and utilities. Information provided for each company includes address, telephone number, SIC codes, and employee size ranges. Dun's Electronic Business Directory is a good source to search when an address is needed for a company but the general geographic location is not known, making it impossible to search in a telephone directory.

A directory providing telephone numbers and addresses only for over 350,000 establishments is the *National Business Telephone Directory*. To be included, a company must have twenty or more employees. Manufacturing and service industries make up most of the entries, with some government and nonprofit organizations, such as universities, museums, hospitals, and public libraries, also included. Entries are arranged in a single alphabetical listing. An added feature is a separate section listing 35,000 of America's most important corporations, the Fortune 500. These companies are arranged alphabetically by parent company, with address and telephone number provided.

Thomas Register of American Manufacturers is an annually published set providing information on products and services of over 145,000 U.S. companies. The set is divided into three main sections: Products and Services (volumes 1 to 14); Company Profiles (volumes 15 to 16); and the Catalog Files (volumes 17 to 23).

The two volumes of Company Profiles list the companies alphabetically, and give brief directory information such as address, telephone number, fax number, and type of product or service offered. More extensive information is listed for some of the companies, giving the chairman or president's name, the subsidiaries and divisions of the company, and a complete product line. When pertinent, cross-references are given to the Catalog Files volumes, which reproduce the actual up-to-date product catalog data for more than fourteen thousand of the companies. These catalogs are arranged alphabetically by company name. The Products and Services volumes provide a subject approach to the *Thomas Register*. Arranged alphabetically by product and service type, manufacturers or sources are then listed alphabetically by state and then by city. Indexes for the entire set include a product index (in volume 14) and a brand name index (in volume 16).

Thomas Register Online, available on DIALOG, is the equivalent of the printed version of *Thomas Register of American Manufacturers*. This database allows the searcher to identify manufacturers of particular products, find trade names of products, develop targeted prospect lists, and find ownership of more than 110,000 active trade names. The database is reloaded annually and is also available on CD-ROM.

The Directory of Corporate Affiliations is an annually published source which matches U.S. companies with their parent corporation or with their divisions, affiliates, or subsidiaries. In a world of mergers and takeovers, this annual publication gives information on who owns whom. Corporations included are those listed on the New York and American stock exchanges, as well as those the stock of which is traded over-the-counter. The first section is an alphabetic index cross-referencing approximately forty thousand affiliates and subsidiaries with their parent companies. The second section lists the parent companies in alphabetical order. Parent company entries include address, telephone number, ticker symbol, stock exchange(s), top corporate officers, and board of directors, followed by divisions, subsidiaries, and affiliates of the parent company. Geographic indexes to all companies and SIC indexes to parent companies are provided.

The online equivalent to this directory is Corporate Affiliations, on DIALOG. Each parent company record contains the complete company hierarchy. Each affiliate record contains that portion of the company's hierarchy in which the affiliate is located. The Corporate Affiliations database is reloaded quarterly, and thus may contain more current information than the printed version.

A source which helps put an individual in touch with the business community of a specific geographic area is the *World Chamber of Commerce Directory*. Published annually, it is arranged alphabetically by state, then by city. Contact person, address, and telephone number of that city's chamber of commerce are given. Other sections include state boards of tourism, convention and visitors bureaus, Canadian chambers of commerce, and United States chambers of commerce abroad. This directory is also a good source of foreign chambers of commerce located in the United States, as well as foreign embassies in this country and United States embassies abroad.

Association Directories

Association directories are an indispensable means of connecting individuals with the appropriate organization for answering their information needs, either on the local, national, or international level. Questions about addresses, telephone numbers, or names of executive officers are frequently asked. Other frequent inquiries include information on publications of the organization, and when or where the organization's annual conference is held. Some association-oriented questions are often best answered by a telephone call to the association. This is also an efficient means (and sometimes the only means) of finding a local chapter of a national association.

The main source to consult for information about United States nonprofit membership organizations of national scope is the *Encyclopedia of Associations: National Organizations of the U.S.* Published annually, this four-volume set contains entries for more than thirty thousand trade, business, and agricultural organizations; educational and cultural organizations; social, health, and public affairs organizations; labor unions; athletic and avocational organizations; Greek societies; fan clubs; and other groups consisting of voluntary members. The first two parts (volume 1, parts 1 and 2) contain details on the organizations themselves, arranged by subject. Volume 1, part 3 is the organization name and keyword index, listing all groups found in this volume or in the *International Organizations* volume of the *Encyclopedia of Associations*. Volume 2 is in two parts: first, the geographic index, which is arranged alphabetically by state and then by city, with association names and addresses listed; and second, the executive index, which lists associations by surname of the chief executive. Also part of this annual publication is volume 3, which is the supplement to volume 1. This supplement gives information on newly found or newly formed associations since publication of the main volume.

The information provided for the various organizations is extensive. Besides the address, telephone number, and acronym of the organization, entries include the founding date of the organization, the name and title of the chief official, number of staff, annual budget of the organization, and the number of members. The main body of the entry, the description of the association, outlines its purpose and activities and states the general type of membership. The frequency and dates of conventions and meetings are included, as well as titles of publications of the organization. Another useful feature is the outlining of the organization's computerized services, including online database searching provided and automated mailing list capabilities.

A companion set to the *Encyclopedia of Associations: National Organizations of the U.S.* is *Encyclopedia of Associations: International Organizations*. Arranged in the same format as the former source, this biennial volume is a guide to international nonprofit membership organizations, national organizations of other countries headquartered in the United States, and international organizations based in the United States. The two-volume set is comprised of one volume of entries and a second volume of indexes. The indexes include a geographic index, an index of names of executive officers, and a keyword index to organization names. The entries are arranged in basically the same format as the entries in the *Encyclopedia of Associations: National Organizations of the U.S.*, but also provide the foreign-language name of the organization, working languages of the organization, and the geographic scope of the organization.

Another set of volumes in the *Encyclopedia of Associations* series is the five-volume set of *Regional, State, and Local Organizations*. These volumes cover all fifty states, divided into five broad geographic areas: Northeastern, Southern and Middle Atlantic, South Central and Great Plains, Great Lakes, and Western. The scope of this set, which is published biennially, encompasses nonprofit membership organizations with interstate, intrastate, state, or local interest. Each volume is arranged alphabetically by state and city, and includes an organization name and keyword-in-name index. Again, entries follow the same format as the other sets in the *Encyclopedia of Associations* series, and include basically the same fields of data.

The *Encyclopedia of Associations* is available electronically on DIALOG. Corresponding to the printed publications of *National Organizations of the U.S.*, *International Organizations*, and *Regional, State, and Local Organizations*, the database is a comprehensive file of about eighty thousand entries. The database is reloaded semiannually. The entire file is also available on CD-ROM as Gale GlobalAccess: Associations. The CD-ROM version offers the *Encyclopedia of Associations* series in its entirety. The CD-ROM format is also updated every six months.

An advantage of searching the *Encyclopedia of Associations* online and on CD-ROM is the access to more current information; the electronic versions are updated twice per year, and the printed version is updated only once per year. Also, personal names can be searched in the electronic versions, but not in the printed editions. Another advantage over the print edition is the ability to search all of the *Encyclopedia of Associations* directories at once, rather than one directory at a time until the appropriate organization is found.

Government Directories

Government directories fall mainly into two categories: those published privately, and those published by governments. This discussion covers only privately published sources; for directories published by government agencies, see chapter 20.

A source which leads one through the labyrinth of governmental structure is the *Worldwide Government Directory*. In this source, every independent country in the world is listed, with information on the top-level officials of its government, as well as the middle-level personnel. Over 50,000 officials are listed for 173 countries. The governmental organization section lists the head of state and cabinet ministers of the executive branch, then lists the legislative bodies, the judiciary, state agencies and corporations, the central bank, and also various branches of each country's armed forces. A section of general data follows; this includes the name of the capital city, official language(s) used, religious affiliations of the population, and the type of local currency. International and regional memberships of the country are provided. There is also a section on the correct form of address for the officials of each country. Following this main entry section is a directory of international organizations, providing address and personnel information on such entities as the World Bank and the United Children's Fund.

For finding information on the executive branch of the U.S. government, Congress, or the related private, nonprofit organizations in the Washington, D.C. area, a useful source is the *Washington Information Directory*. This annual directory is organized by subject, with information grouped into seventeen main topics. Under these main topics, applicable agencies of the federal government, Congress, and private, nonprofit organizations are outlined. Several strategies can be used to find information in the *Washington Information Directory*. To locate an individual, a name index is provided. To locate a particular agency or organization, a keyword index is provided. The table of contents lists the general headings, allowing the user to search also by subject. Subject searching in this directory can help users find agencies with an interest in a given topic, allowing them to browse through the possible options of information sources. Factual information is found in the form of organizational charts and information boxes scattered throughout the text. These boxes outline structures of various departments (e.g., the Navy, the Environmental Protection Agency), and also give access to toll-free numbers and telephone numbers for departmental agencies.

Information on personnel at the federal, state, municipal, and county levels is provided in four directories published by Carroll Publishing Company. The *Federal Executive Directory* includes over eighty-seven thousand entries on both the executive branch of government and Congress. Included are the Executive Office of the President, Cabinet departments, major federal administrative agencies, and congressional offices. The *State Executive Directory* lists executive and legislative officials for the fifty states and the District of Columbia. The *Municipal Executive Directory* provides names, titles, addresses, and telephone numbers of officials in approximately 7,200 cities, towns, townships, and villages. The *County Executive Directory* includes names, addresses, and telephone numbers of primary managers for all U.S. counties. Each one of these directories is updated at least twice per year. All four directories include a personal name index. The *Federal Executive Directory* also includes a department and agency keyword index.

Telephone and Telefacsimile Directories

Telephone directories are an excellent primary source for local information. Typically, a telephone directory is used to find names, addresses, and telephone numbers for individuals and businesses in a specific geographic area. Telephone directories may also provide additional information about a community, such as street maps, local history, calendars of cultural and sporting events, zip codes, shopping guides, and seating charts of auditoriums and stadiums.

The breakup of the monopoly of AT&T in December 1983 led to the emergence of seven main regional telephone companies, each of which produces its own telephone directories: Ameritech, Bell South, Bell Atlantic, NYNEX, Pacific Bell, Southwestern Bell, and U.S. West. One impact of this breakup on libraries is that the telephone books are no longer provided free of charge. Also, there are now seven companies to deal with when ordering telephone books, instead of just AT&T.

An alternative to the purchase of telephone books from these seven regional companies is to purchase *Phonefiche*, telephone directories on microfiche from University Microfilms. With *Phonefiche*, the entire directory is reproduced on microfiche. The microfiche is produced and distributed immediately after the paper version is available, so the information is current. Many different subscription packages are available: categories of cities by various population sizes, packages of all directories for a given state, or for all state capitals, packages for up to fourteen major metropolitan areas, and also for various regions. Individual directories may also be purchased. Some foreign countries (Australia, Canada, China,

Great Britain, and Switzerland) are available; larger academic and public libraries may find these useful.

One advantage of the microfiche versions of telephone directories over the paper copies is the amount of space saved. Nearly 2,600 directories covering 50,000 communities fit into 8 16-inch microfiche trays. This also allows for back issues of directories to be kept, and there is no binding expense. Another advantage of microfiche is that the directories can all be ordered from one source with one subscription payment.

A disadvantage of the microfiche is the resistance many library patrons have to using this format. The microfiche can be difficult to read, and cannot be reproduced without a microfiche printer. Also, there is the consideration of the cost of a microfiche reader and/or printer. For these reasons, many libraries purchase a combination of microfiche for lesser used locations and paper telephone directories for more frequently used cities.

Telephone directories are also becoming available in CD-ROM format. Although this format is currently expensive and requires special equipment, it is faster to consult and can eliminate the need to handle many separate microfiche or printed directories.

The *Toll-Free Digest* is a directory of more than forty-three thousand toll-free telephone numbers from AT&T and other sources. The scope of the *Toll-Free Digest* includes resorts, airlines, auto rentals, railroads, accounting firms, insurance companies, banks, moving and trucking companies, office equipment stores, newspapers, schools, libraries, florists, and department stores. A separate hotel/motel section lists major chains, then specific hotels and motels by state. The main section of the directory lists companies with their toll-free numbers under general subject categories.

The *AT&T Toll-Free 800 Directory* is separated into two directories, the Business edition and the Consumer edition. The directories can be used to purchase equipment or gifts or to make travel arrangements. The directories are both arranged like telephone books, with an alphabetical listing in the white pages section, followed by a subject approach in the yellow pages section, and are updated each year. The *Toll-Free Digest* and the *AT&T Toll-Free 800 Directory* appear to be similar in coverage, although the AT&T directories list more entries. Also, the arrangement of the AT&T directories — with alphabetical as well as subject sections — allows for easier access to the toll-free numbers on those frequent occasions when the user is looking for the number of a specific company.

Facsimile transmission devices (fax machines) give the user the ability to transmit written or printed communication quickly, and are rapidly becoming popular in today's business world. The *National Fax Directory* gives access to over eighty thousand fax numbers for major U.S. companies, law firms, government agencies, media and publishing agencies, financial institutions, leading manufacturers and corporations, and libraries. The directory is arranged in three sections: a subject section, an alphabetical section, and a geographical section, arranged by city within state. Entries include complete address, fax numbers, and voice phone numbers.

Search Strategies

Strategies reference librarians use for finding directory information for patrons are varied, as there is often more than one source which will answer a given information need. An essential component of the librarian's search strategy is a thorough knowledge of available directories, both printed and electronic. The librarian must also be aware of the limitations of the collection and know when it is appropriate to refer the library user to a source outside the collection. The availability of online database searching at the reference desk adds another element affecting search strategy, as an online directory often provides the quickest route to the information needed by the patron.

The first step in establishing a strategy is to determine the patron's actual need. Does this patron really want just the telephone number for a company, or the name of a company officer as well? Will the address of an association suffice, or would the patron also like to know background information on the association? Ascertaining the exact information need of the patron will assist the librarian in choosing the appropriate reference source.

Once the librarian has chosen a directory to consult, there are various ways of using the source. The librarian should already be aware of the directory's basic organization. Many directories are composed of a straightforward alphabetical arrangement of entries. If indexes are provided, they often provide the quickest route to the needed information. Keyword indexes are especially helpful, allowing one to look under a topical term rather than under an exact title or name. A personal name index, if provided, frequently offers the way to find both an individual and the entry for the organization which employs that person. Here again, personal names are more likely to be access points in an electronic database than in a printed source.

When using electronic databases, the key to an efficient and effective search is the librarian's knowledge of the content and structure of the database. This is attained through practice and through a review of database documentation. The librarian should know which fields are searchable and how to combine terms from different fields using Boolean logic to reduce the retrieved entries to the smallest possible number. Otherwise, both time and money will be lost looking at irrelevant records.

The preface of a printed source provides insight into the content, scope, and use of the source. Scanning the preface can help determine whether one is using the proper source for the information needed. The preface often includes a sample entry, with all of the parts of the entry labelled. An example of such a sample entry is shown in figure 12.2, page 273.

In addition to knowing the structure of printed and online directories and understanding the scope of the patron's request, creativity on the part of the librarian is also required. The use of nondirectory sources, tapping the expertise of a colleague, or a telephone call to an association or institution can be important elements of an effective search strategy for locating directory information.

■ ══ ■

12.1

A Sample Directory Search

A library patron had just checked out the book *Summerhill* by A. S. Neill. She had not yet read the book, but thought it had something to do with self-regulated schools in England, and she wanted to know if a center for that type of education existed in the United States. Since the librarian had no knowledge of the information discussed in *Summerhill*, he first located the title in the library's catalog in order to establish subject tracings. The subjects "Education — Experimental methods" and "Free schools" were both used for the title *Summerhill*.

The librarian took these subject headings to check in the name and keyword index of the *Encyclopedia of Associations: National Organizations of the U.S.* Under "Education Experimental Programs," the user was directed to look in *Research Centers Directory*. In the subject index under "Education, Experimental," five centers were listed. After looking at all five entries, the librarian and patron agreed that these were not the type of centers that would be appropriate.

Checking *Encyclopedia of Associations* again, this time under "Free schools," the librarian found that nothing was listed. At this point, he decided to try other terminology to express the same topic. A search under the topic "Alternative Education" in the name and keyword index showed fifteen names of associations. The librarian chose the one most likely to match the patron's needs, and looked up the entry information. Because *Encyclopedia of Associations* groups entries by subject area, the library user was able to choose one or two appropriate associations from the several listed.

Sample Entry

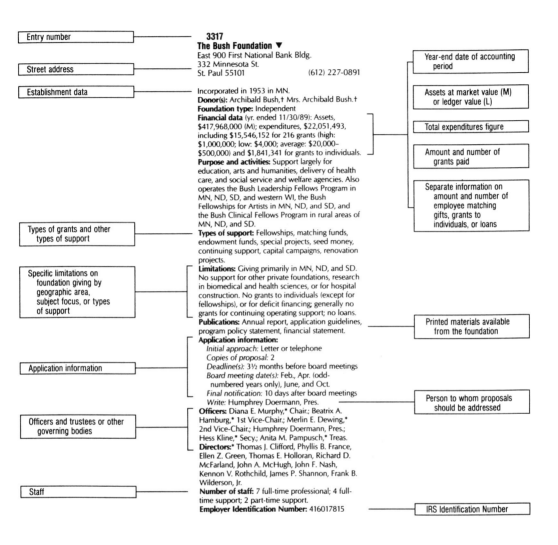

Entry number

3317
The Bush Foundation ▼
East 900 First National Bank Bldg.

Street address
332 Minnesota St.
St. Paul 55101   (612) 227-0891

Year-end date of accounting period

Establishment data

Incorporated in 1953 in MN.
Donor(s): Archibald Bush,† Mrs. Archibald Bush.†
Foundation type: Independent
Financial data (yr. ended 11/30/89): Assets,
$417,968,000 (M); expenditures, $22,051,493,
including $15,546,152 for 216 grants (high:
$1,000,000; low: $4,000; average: $20,000–
$500,000) and $1,841,341 for grants to individuals.
Purpose and activities: Support largely for
education, arts and humanities, delivery of health
care, and social service and welfare agencies. Also
operates the Bush Leadership Fellows Program in
MN, ND, SD, and western WI, the Bush
Fellowships for Artists in MN, ND, and SD, and
the Bush Clinical Fellows Program in rural areas of
MN, ND, and SD.

Assets at market value (M) or ledger value (L)

Total expenditures figure

Amount and number of grants paid

Separate information on amount and number of employee matching gifts, grants to individuals, or loans

Types of grants and other types of support

Types of support: Fellowships, matching funds,
endowment funds, special projects, seed money,
continuing support, capital campaigns, renovation
projects.

Specific limitations on foundation giving by geographic area, subject focus, or types of support

Limitations: Giving primarily in MN, ND, and SD.
No support for other private foundations, research
in biomedical and health sciences, or for hospital
construction. No grants to individuals (except for
fellowships), or for deficit financing; generally no
grants for continuing operating support; no loans.
Publications: Annual report, application guidelines,
program policy statement, financial statement.

Printed materials available from the foundation

Application information

Application information:
Initial approach: Letter or telephone
Copies of proposal: 2
Deadline(s): 3½ months before board meetings
Board meeting date(s): Feb., Apr. (odd-
numbered years only), June, and Oct.
Final notification: 10 days after board meetings
Write: Humphrey Doermann, Pres.

Person to whom proposals should be addressed

Officers and trustees or other governing bodies

Officers: Diana E. Murphy,* Chair.; Beatrix A.
Hamburg,* 1st Vice-Chair.; Merlin E. Dewing,*
2nd Vice-Chair.; Humphrey Doermann, Pres.;
Hess Kline,* Secy.; Anita M. Pampusch,* Treas.
Directors:* Thomas J. Clifford, Phyllis B. France,
Ellen Z. Green, Thomas E. Holloran, Richard D.
McFarland, John A. McHugh, John F. Nash,
Kennon V. Rothchild, James P. Shannon, Frank B.
Wilderson, Jr.

Staff

Number of staff: 7 full-time professional; 4 full-
time support; 2 part-time support.
Employer Identification Number: 416017815

IRS Identification Number

Symbols

▼   Identifies foundations for which in-depth descriptions
     have been prepared for inclusion in the Foundation
     Center's *Source Book Profiles.*
¤   Indicates entries prepared or updated by Center staff
     from public records.

†   Indicates individual is deceased.
(L) Ledger value of assets.
(M) Market value of assets.
*   Officer is also a trustee or director.
☆   Identifies foundations newly listed in this edition.

Fig. 12.2. "Sample Entry" page from *The Foundation Directory*. Reprinted with permission from *The Foundation Directory, 13th Edition*, The Foundation Center, 1990.

Notes

1. Joseph R. Strayer, ed., *Dictionary of the Middle Ages* (New York: Charles Scribner's Sons, 1982), 24: 237-39.

2. Adrian Room, ed., *Dictionary of Britain* (London: Oxford University Press, 1986), 81.

3. Heartsill Young, ed., *The ALA Glossary of Library and Information Science* (Chicago: American Library Association, 1983), 75.

4. *College Blue Book*, 22nd ed. 5 vols. (New York: Macmillan Publishing Co., 1989).

List of Sources

Allergy Products Directory. 2d ed. Menlo Park, Calif.: Allergy Publications, 1987. 130p.

American Book Trade Directory. 36th ed., 1990-91. New York: R. R. Bowker, 1990. 1,880p.

American Library Directory. 43d ed., 1990-91. 2 vols. New York: R. R. Bowker, 1990. (DIALOG File 460.)

Annual Register of Grant Support. 23d ed., 1990. Wilmette, Ill.: National Register Publishing Co., 1990. 1,139p.

AT&T Toll-Free 800 Directory: Business Edition, 1991. Bridgewater, N.J.: AT&T, 1990. 928p.

AT&T Toll-Free 800 Directory: Consumer Edition, 1991. Bridgewater, N.J.: AT&T, 1990. 372p.

Books in Print: Publishers. 43d ed., 1990-91. New York: R. R. Bowker, 1990. 1,007p.

City and State Directories in Print, 1990-91. Detroit, Mich.: Gale Research, 1990. 966p.

Commonwealth Universities Yearbook. 4 vols. London: Association of Commonwealth Universities, 1990.

Corporate Affiliations. Wilmette, Ill.: National Register Publishing Co. (DIALOG File 513.)

County Executive Directory. Washington, D.C.: Carroll Publishing, 1984- .

D&B - Dun's Electronic Business Directory. Parsippany, N.J.: Dun's Marketing Services. (DIALOG File 515.)

D&B - Dun's Market Identifiers. Parsippany, N.J.: Dun's Marketing Services. (DIALOG File 516.)

D&B - Million Dollar Directory. Parsippany, N.J.: Dun's Marketing Services. (DIALOG File 517.)

Directories in Print. 7th ed. 2 vols. Detroit, Mich.: Gale Research, 1990. 1,887p.

Directory of Corporate Affiliations. Wilmette, Ill.: National Register Publishing Co., 1990. 8,999p.

Directory of Research Grants, 1990. Phoenix, Ariz.: Oryx Press, 1990. 1,099p.

Directory of Special Libraries and Information Centers. 14th ed. 3 vols. Detroit, Mich.: Gale Research, 1991.

Encyclopedia of Associations. Detroit, Mich.: Gale Research. (DIALOG File 114.)

Encyclopedia of Associations: International Organizations. 25th ed. 2 vols. Detroit, Mich.: Gale Research, 1990.

Encyclopedia of Associations: National Organizations of the U.S. 25th ed. 3 vols. Detroit, Mich.: Gale Research, 1990.

Encyclopedia of Associations: Regional, State, and Local Organizations, 1990-91. 2d ed. 5 vols. Detroit, Mich.: Gale Research, 1990.

Federal Executive Directory. Washington, D.C.: Carroll Publishing, 1980- .

The Foundation Directory. 13th ed. New York: Foundation Center, 1990. 1,444p. (DIALOG File 26.)

The Foundation Grants Index. 18th ed. New York: Foundation Center, 1990. 1,144p. (DIALOG File 27.)

Gale GlobalAccess: Associations 1991. [CD-ROM]. Detroit, Mich.: Gale Research.

Government Research Directory. 5th ed. Detroit, Mich.: Gale Research, 1989. 1,117p.

The HEP 1990 Higher Education Directory. 8th ed. Falls Church, Va.: Higher Education Publishers, 1990. 583p.

International Directories in Print, 1989-90. Detroit, Mich.: Gale Research, 1989. 1,125p.

International Handbook of Universities. 11th ed. New York: Stockton Press, 1989. 1,302p.

International Literary Market Place, 1991. 25th ed. New York: R. R. Bowker, 1991. 784p.

International Research Centers Directory. 5th ed., 1990-91. Detroit, Mich.: Gale Research, 1990. 1,327p.

Literary Market Place, 1991. New York: R. R. Bowker, 1991. 1,657p.

Million Dollar Directory. 5 vols. Parsippany, N.J.: Dun's Marketing Services, 1990.

Million Dollar Disc. [CD-ROM]. Parsippany, N.J.: Dun's Marketing Services.

Municipal Executive Directory. Washington, D.C.: Carroll Publishing, 1984- .

National Business Telephone Directory. 2d ed. Parsippany, N.J.: Trinet, Inc., 1989. 1,800p.

National Fax Directory 1991. Detroit, Mich.: Gale Research, 1990. 1,741p.

Organizations Master Index. Detroit, Mich.: Gale Research, 1987. 1,120p.

Patterson's American Education. 87th ed. Mount Prospect, Ill.: Education Directories, 1991. 755p.

Phonefiche. [microfiche]. Ann Arbor, Mich.: University Microfilms International.

Publishers, Distributors, and Wholesalers of the United States, 1990-91. New York: R. R. Bowker, 1990. 2,108p. (DIALOG File 450.)

Research Centers and Services Directory. Detroit, Mich.: Gale Research. (DIALOG File 115.)

Research Centers Directory. 15th ed. 2 vols. Detroit, Mich.: Gale Research, 1991.

Research Services Directory. 4th ed. Detroit, Mich.: Gale Research, 1989. 841p.

Standard & Poor's Register of Corporations, Directors and Executives. 3 vols. New York: McGraw-Hill, 1991.

Standard & Poor's Register - Corporate. New York: Standard & Poor's Corporation. (DIALOG File 527.)

Standard & Poor's Register. [CD-ROM]. New York: Standard & Poor's Corporation.

State Executive Directory. Washington, D.C.: Carroll Publishing, 1980- .

State Government Research Directory. Detroit, Mich.: Gale Research, 1987. 349p.

Subject Collections. Compiled by Lee Ash. 6th ed. 2 vols. New York: R. R. Bowker, 1985.

Taft Foundation Reporter. 21st ed. Washington, D.C.: Taft Group, 1990. 847p.

Thomas Register of American Manufacturers. 79th ed. 23 vols. New York: Thomas Publishing Co., 1989. (DIALOG File 535; also available on CD-ROM.)

Toll-Free Digest, 1986-87. Claverack, N.Y.: Toll-Free Digest Co., 1986. 671p.

Washington Information Directory, 1990-91. Washington, D.C.: Congressional Quarterly, 1990. 1,086p.

Whole Horse Catalog. New York: Simon and Schuster, 1985. 250p.

World Chamber of Commerce Directory. Loveland, Colo.: World Chamber of Commerce Directory, 1989. 362p.

The World of Learning. 40th ed. London: Europa Publications, 1990. 1,964p.

Worldwide Government Directory. Bethesda, Md.: Cambridge Information Group, 1990. 912p.

Additional Readings

Grogan, Denis. *Encyclopedias, Yearbooks, Directories and Statistical Sources*. Grogan's Case Studies in Reference Work, vol. 2. London: Clive Bingley, 1987. 170p.
   Although this text is primarily a discussion of British sources, the search strategies and discussions of directories are useful and instructive. Pages 111 to 134 deal with directories.

Grosch, Mary Frances. "Business Reference Sources for the Public Library." *Illinois Libraries* 70, no. 9 (November 1988): 607-13.
   Grosch provides a good bibliography and overview of the major business reference sources, including many business directories.

O'Leary, Mike. "Encyclopedia of Associations Expands Online Reach." *Database* 12 (October 1989): 59-61.
   O'Leary discusses both the print and online versions of this important source, and points out when it is more suitable to use the online database.

Tafel, Linda L. "Dun's Electronic Yellow Pages." *Database* 12 (June 1989): 63-66.
   Tafel provides practical tips on searching this database and useful guidelines for when this is the best source to consult.

Tyckoson, David A. "Telephone Books as Reference Sources." *Booklist* 85 (November 1, 1988): 454-56.
   This article traces how the breakup of AT&T has affected libraries with regard to the collection of telephone directories, and also includes a thorough discussion of the format of telephone directories for each of the regional telephone companies.

ALMANACS, YEARBOOKS, AND HANDBOOKS

Uses and Characteristics

Almanacs, yearbooks, and handbooks are reference works that provide concise factual information about many things: current and historical events; organizations, people, and things; countries and governments; and statistical trends. The information available in these tools is almost always available in other sources. Newspapers and magazines record current events; encyclopedias and history books record historical events; many sources, including directories and encyclopedias, give information about organizations, people, and things; atlases and gazetteers, as well as other sources, give information about countries and governments; and government publications are an invaluable source of statistics and statistical trends.

Almanacs, yearbooks, and handbooks, however, have in common a convenience of use which other tools do not have. They are most often single volumes which summarize and synthesize large amounts of data. For this reason, they can be shelved close to the reference desk and used in the ready reference process. Of course, it does not follow that because these reference works are accessible and easy to use they are the best sources to answer all questions. Reference librarians must evaluate the information needs of patrons and use their knowledge of reference works to determine which type of reference work will supply the most satisfactory answer.

Almanacs first appeared at least seven centuries ago as calendars, containing days, weeks, and months, and astronomical data such as the phases of the sun and moon. In the fifteenth, sixteenth, and seventeenth centuries, almanacs that included astrological predictions became quite popular. Although the first American almanac was published in 1639, the most famous early almanac is Benjamin Franklin's *Poor Richard's Almanack*, which was published from 1733 to 1748. The eighteenth-century American almanac was an annual volume that included a calendar, advice on planting crops, astrological predictions, home remedies, and folk wisdom. The *Old Farmer's Almanac* continues to be published as a surviving example of this type of almanac.

In the nineteenth century, American newspapers began to publish a different kind of almanac. This new type of almanac was oriented to political, historical, and current events,[1] and was more like the contemporary almanacs discussed in this chapter. The newer style of almanac does include some astronomical and calendar data, but it is also, more importantly, a compendium, usually annual, of current and retrospective statistics and facts. Although almanacs can be broad in geographical and subject coverage, many of the best-known general almanacs are biased toward a particular country or state. While the contemporary almanac consists of fact rather than folklore, the most famous general almanacs are still rooted in popular culture, which explains many aspects of their content. Sports, entertainment, practical information such as zip codes and first aid treatment, and business addresses are all included in the contents. An almanac is the place to find answers to questions such as the following:

What is a hurricane?

How many calories are in a tablespoon of butter?

Where was George Washington born?

What is the address of the Special Libraries Association?

Who invented the stethoscope?

What is the population of Houston, Texas?

How many home runs did Willie Mays hit?

Most almanacs are issued annually, and in this respect they are like a yearbook. *Yearbooks*, however, present facts and statistics for a single year, usually the year preceding the publication date, while almanacs also have retrospective facts and statistics. Nomenclature for reference books is not necessarily consistent, of course, and almanacs may be called yearbooks and vice versa. Encyclopedias often issue yearbooks which supplement the main set, but are chiefly the review of a specific year. These yearbooks include a chronology of the year, biographies of newsmakers, obituaries, sports news, current statistical data, and articles about events of the year. A general yearbook such as an encyclopedia yearbook is the place to find information such as these examples:

An obituary for a person who died during the year.

A description of a disaster that occurred during the year.

The winner of an athletic event that happened during the year.

Discussion of a current controversial social problem.

Chronology of a political happening.

A general almanac also provides some of the same information, just as a yearbook supplies answers to some of the same questions as an almanac. The presentation of the information, however, will be different. Obituaries in the encyclopedia yearbook are longer and may include a photograph. Indexes in these yearbooks include personal names, while almanacs index personal names very sparingly. Almanacs do sometimes include signed articles on current social problems, but the yearbook would most certainly have such an article. Print in the yearbooks is usually larger and more readable. This is not to say that encyclopedia yearbooks are preferable to almanacs; they are different and fill different information needs. Almanacs are full of bits of data. A library user who simply wants to know if someone has died in the previous year will be satisfied with the information in the almanac, and the reference librarian aware that almanacs index under "obituaries" instead of personal names can locate the information quickly. The sports fan trying to remember the name of the winning pitcher of the final game of the 1988 World Series will be happy with almanac information. On the other hand, the school child writing a paper about Orel Hershiser (who was that winning pitcher) will be happier with a biography in a yearbook.

Yearbooks that focus on a single topic or theme are also published. They provide information about people, events, and trends in a single area. These yearbooks are similar to another category of reference work, the handbook. The *handbook*, or *manual* as it is sometimes called, is a reference work that serves as a guide to a particular subject. A large amount of information about the subject is often compressed into a single volume. Some of the best-known handbooks are produced for use by practitioners, but are also of value at the reference desk. Later in this chapter, a selection of handbooks, common to many general reference departments, is listed, but this list only gives the reader a small sample of the range of subjects of handbooks. In terms of format, there is really no way to generalize about the content and organization of the handbook, although handbooks often include examples and/or illustrations. For this reason, patrons may wish to look at handbooks themselves. A handbook is specialized, reviewing a particular topic in a factual and comprehensive way. Handbooks provide answers to questions such as these:

Are there any adverse side effects to this drug?

What happened in history on November 23, my birthday?

Is the Sears Tower the world's tallest building?

How do I format a bibliography?

What do I wear to a formal evening wedding?

Evaluation

Evaluation of an almanac, yearbook, or handbook includes consideration of many factors. Accuracy, comprehensiveness and currency of the information, and ease of use are all important to both patron and librarian.

Accuracy

It is surely self-evident that accuracy is the single most important characteristic of works that present factual information. There are several techniques reference librarians can use to test the accuracy and reliability of almanacs, yearbooks, and handbooks. They can read reviews written by knowledgeable reviewers, compare data in different sources, and rely on personal expertise. The long-time reputation of a work is also a guide, but all works should be continually reevaluated. Errors occur in even the most prestigious works. These errors should be corrected in subsequent editions or by addenda.

Indexing

The index in a fact book should be helpful, accurate, and internally consistent in style and terminology, and should complement the overall arrangement of the work. Some year-books include a cumulative index which covers more than the current volume. This is an extremely useful feature, if for instance, the exact date of an event is unknown.

Documentation

Many almanacs, yearbooks, and handbooks are composed, at least in part, of second-hand information. The statistics should be recent and from official sources. Those official sources should be identified, and the identification should be complete enough to lead to the original source where additional information might be located. Reference works without documentation are of questionable reliability.

Comprehensiveness

The importance of almanacs, yearbooks, and handbooks is that they contain a great deal of information about a single subject or many subjects. They should be comprehensive within their stated scope. If they are not, they have little value.

Uniqueness

There is always a certain amount of overlap in reference collections. Since patrons' needs vary in terms of the amount and presentation of information, this overlap can be desirable. Nonetheless, the reference work should provide either unique information or a unique approach to information which is also available elsewhere.

Format

Almanacs, yearbooks, and handbooks should be organized in a logical manner that the user can understand. Because many of these publications are inexpensive, they are sometimes less physically attractive than other types of reference books, but readability is still an important consideration. Currently, some familiar reference works of this type are being marketed as online and/or CD-ROM databases which permit greater flexibility and ease of use. There are several advantages to the electronic formats. They greatly enhance traditional indexing through the use of keyword searching, not just of an index, but of the full (complete) text, which can be searched directly or through Boolean logic. Another advantage is that they can cumulate a number of years, thus eliminating the need to consult more than one source.

Currency

The moment a fact book containing current data is published, it is out of date. For example, the population of the United States increases as this chapter is being written. Within the limitations of their publishing schedules, fact books should be continually updated. This means that annually published editions should reflect change, and that works of this type which do not undergo frequent revision are suspect.

Selection

Reference librarians should select reference works that answer the information demands of library users. Almost every type of library—academic, public, special, and school—can benefit from having one general almanac. A paperbound edition of one of the best known American almanacs costs about ten dollars, and even specialized libraries will have an occasional demand for information in the almanac. It is difficult to imagine a general reference collection in an academic or public library without at least one almanac. Research has also shown that if one almanac is good, several may be better, because various almanacs have unique data and features.[2]

Since almanacs and encyclopedia yearbooks have dissimilar presentations and serve diverse patron requirements, an encyclopedia yearbook is a useful addition to general reference collections. These yearbooks, however, are published to meet the needs of users who will rarely buy a new set of encyclopedias. Therefore, reference librarians, in libraries that routinely acquire the latest revision of major encyclopedias every few years, may decide not to buy yearbooks for every set of encyclopedias. Almanacs and encyclopedia yearbooks consist of information which is more extensively treated in other sources. The decision of whether to rely on the almanac and yearbook to supply information or to purchase these other sources depends on the frequency of demand for more facts in greater depth than the almanac and yearbook supply. To use an example, *The World Almanac* has directories of associations, businesses, and so forth. These directories typically supply the address and number of members of organizations, while the *Encyclopedia of Associations* (discussed in chapter 12) provides more information about more organizations. General reference collections will probably own the *Encyclopedia of Associations*, but small and/or specialized libraries may find that *The World Almanac* meets most of their needs. Librarians in these collections can also use the *Encyclopedia of Associations* online, since this classic reference work is one of an increasing number of reference tools available electronically. Online searching is more economical if occasional use is all that is required. Referral is another way of responding to a request that cannot be answered using the library's collection. The availability of other reference collections and services in a community is a factor in determining which reference books to buy.

Decisions about which of the specialized almanacs, handbooks, and yearbooks to buy is not as easily made as a decision to buy a general almanac. Almanacs, yearbooks, and handbooks tend to offer very good value at a low cost. However, even the least expensive, most useful tool is a poor investment if no one wants the information it contains. Cost, nonetheless, may be a determinant. Some general reference departments in public and academic libraries, as well as many school libraries, can afford to purchase a moderately priced yearbook like the *Statesman's Year-Book*, but not the more expensive *Europa World Year Book*. Currently, the cost of online and CD-ROM databases and the equipment needed to access these databases deters many libraries from acquiring almanacs, yearbooks, and handbooks in these formats. However, changing technology and increased use will probably reduce the cost of reference works in electronic formats. Because they often enable the librarian to provide better service, they may well become commonplace.

Characteristics of the users, such as age, education, and occupation, influence decisions about which works to purchase. Public, academic, and school libraries have some of the same almanacs, yearbooks, and handbooks, but they will be used for different purposes and at different depths.

Important General Sources

The reference collections in most libraries will contain almanacs, handbooks, and yearbooks. In this section, some commonplace examples of these genres are discussed. The examples were chosen because they are likely to be found in general reference collections, rather than collections that are subject-specific, but one should remember that there are, of course, many outstanding subject-specific almanacs, handbooks, and yearbooks.

Almanacs

The World Almanac and Book of Facts began in 1868 as a publication of the *New York World* newspaper, and throughout its history it has been associated with newspaper publishing. The almanac, written in journalistic style, is issued in newsprint and features "The Top 10 News Stories" of the year. Although it prominently bears the date of the following year, the almanac is published annually at the end of November of the preceding year. In major and other election years, i.e., every two years, the cutoff date for news is the November election, and in off years baseball's World Series is the last event covered.[3] For example, the *World Almanac* in an election year includes events through the election which takes place in early November, while in nonelection years the volume will include events only through mid- to late October, when the World Series takes place. A series of colored plates are included in the center of the volume. The plates are of countries' flags, a map of world time zones, and maps of various parts of the world. Millions of copies of *The World Almanac* are sold each year, and it annually appears on the *New York Times'* "Paperback Best Sellers" list in the "Advice, How-to and Miscellaneous" category for a number of weeks. The popularity of the work is probably due as much to the general population's fascination with trivia as it is to this book's value to them as a reference work.

The book has three different indexes: a General Index in the front, a Quick Reference Index on the last page, and a Quick Thumb Index on the back cover of both the paperback and hardcover editions. The General Index consists of topical subject headings, and includes only a few personal names. Earlier in this chapter a series of questions were posed that an almanac could answer. *The World Almanac*'s General Index will easily lead its user to answers to some of these questions. The definition of a hurricane and the calories in a tablespoon of butter can quickly be ascertained through the use of the index, because "hurricane" and "butter," appropriately subdivided by "definition" and "nutritive value" respectively, appear as entries in the General Index. A little more strategy is required to find the answers to the other questions.

■ ══ ■

13.1

Almanac Search Strategy

A library patron wants to know whether George Washington was born at Mount Vernon. The reference librarian can answer this question from *The World Almanac* in a section entitled "Biographies of U.S. Presidents." It can be located most easily by searching the index under a topical subject heading "Presidents of the U.S.," subdivided by "Biography." The user who looks under "Washington, George" finds a series of page references which do not specify the location of biographical information. (George Washington was born at Wakefield on Pope's Creek, Westmoreland County, Virginia, not at Mount Vernon.)

To find the address of the Special Libraries Association, it is necessary to look under "Associations and Societies" or "Addresses, to Find" in the index and then to look at the pages listing associations and societies. The list is arranged by keyword, and the Special Libraries Association is alphabetized under "Libraries, Assn., Special." The inventor of the stethoscope is found by looking at the list of inventions which is indexed under "Inventions." There are three page references to "Houston," subheading "Population" in the index. Each reference refers the user to different statistics about the population of the city, and the user should look at each set of statistics to determine which is the best answer to the particular question. Finally, the number of home runs Willie Mays hit can be found in a chart in the baseball pages of the Sports section. The chart which is titled "All-Time Home Run Leaders" is indexed under "baseball" and the subdivision "home runs." The absence of names in the index can make the almanac more difficult to use. For example, the reference librarian has to know that Willie Mays is a well-known baseball player in order to find information about him. The phrase "noted personalities" is used to index biographical information in the almanac, and brief biographical data is included about categories of people. "Widely Known Americans of the Present," "Noted Black Americans," "Poet Laureates of England," and "Noted Writers of the Past" are but a few of the categories represented. A reference librarian should spend time gaining familiarity with the "Noted Personalities" section in the almanac.

The Quick Reference Index is composed of keywords for some of the most sought-after information in the almanac. Those who understand the organization of the almanac will find this index easier to use than the General Index. The print is larger and the terms more to the point in the Quick Reference Index. The Quick Thumb Index utilizes black marks on the fore-edge of the volume to indicate the location of some sections of the almanac. In the 1991 almanac these sections were the year in review; 1990 elections; science, technology, health; noted personalities; area codes and zip codes; nations; language; vital statistics; and sports. Indexing in *The World Almanac* is similar to the indexing in other fact books, and the librarian who spends time studying this indexing will be rewarded by more efficient use of this type of tool. It seems likely that full-text online searching will soon be available for *The World Almanac*, and this will greatly expand its usefulness. As noted in chapter 15, *The World Almanac* is one of the reference sources in the Microsoft Bookshelf CD-ROM Reference Library.

The World Almanac is a respected reference source that sits next to the telephone at the reference desk in many libraries. Sometimes the almanac is a better-than-average source of information. For instance, the table listing calories is very good (see figure 13.1).

176   Health — Food Values

Nutritive Value of Food (Calories, Proteins, etc.)

Source: Home and Garden Bulletin No. 72; available from Supt. of Documents, U. S. Government Printing Office, Washington, DC 20402

Food	Measure	Grams	Food Energy (calories)	Protein (grams)	Fat (grams)	Saturated fats (grams)	Carbohydrate (grams)	Calcium (milligrams)	Iron (milligrams)	Vitamin A (I.U.)	Thiamin (milligrams)	Riboflavin (milligrams)
Dairy products												
Cheese, cheddar	1 oz.	28	115	7	9	6.1	T	204	.2	300	.01	.11
Cheese, cottage, small curd	1 cup	210	220	26	9	6.0	6	126	.3	340	.04	.34
Cheese, cream	1 oz.	28	100	2	10	6.2	1	23	.3	400	T	.06
Cheese, Swiss	1 oz.	28	105	8	8	5.0	1	272	T	240	.01	.10
Cheese, pasteurized process spread, American	1 oz.	28	82	5	6	3.8	2	159	.1	220	.01	.12
Half-and-Half	1 tbsp.	15	20	T	2	1.1	1	16	T	20	.01	.02
Cream, sour	1 tbsp.	15	25	T	3	1.6	1	14	T	90	T	.02
Milk, whole	1 cup	244	150	8	8	5.1	11	291	.1	310	.09	.40
Milk, nonfat (skim)	1 cup	244	85	8	T	.3	12	302	.1	500	.09	.37
Buttermilk	1 cup	245	100	8	2	1.3	12	285	.1	80	.08	.38
Milkshake, chocolate	10.6 oz.	300	355	9	8	5.0	63	396	.9	260	.14	.67
Ice Cream, hardened	1 cup	133	270	5	14	8.9	32	176	.1	540	.05	.33
Sherbet	1 cup	193	270	2	4	2.4	59	103	.3	190	.03	.09
Yogurt, fruit-flavored	8 oz.	227	230	10	3	1.8	42	343	.2	120	.08	.40

Fig. 13.1. Calorie chart from *The World Almanac*. Reprinted by permission from *The World Almanac & Book of Facts*, 1991 edition, copyright © Pharos Books, 1990, New York, NY 10166.

Derived from a U.S. Department of Agriculture publication, the table includes both a household measure, the tablespoon, and a scientific measure, the gram. Sometimes the information in the almanac is incorrect. As an example, when the Special Libraries Association moved from New York to Washington in late 1985, a change in address did not appear in the almanac until the 1988 (i.e., 1987) edition. Of course, the almanac was not the only reference work which did not have the correct address. Good reference librarians guard against this type of error by updating heavily used reference works. Most of the time the question of whether to use the almanac depends not on accuracy but on the amount of information the patron needs. A general or special encyclopedia or encyclopedia yearbook has more information and a helpful bibliography. In addition, patrons doing research generally prefer to use primary sources or a secondary source which is more detailed than an almanac.

"Information Please" was the name of a famous radio program. The program's listeners attempted to stump a regular panel by submitting questions on a variety of topics. The *Information Please Almanac; Atlas and Yearbook* has been published annually since 1947 by a series of publishers, currently Houghton Mifflin. As is true with *The World Almanac*, the *Information Please Almanac* includes information for the year preceding the year that appears on the title page. In other words, the 1991 almanac provides data up to the end of 1990. A single-page statistical profile of the United States appears before the title page; a table of contents and a comprehensive index follow the title page. The table of contents is reminiscent of the Quick Reference Index in *The World Almanac*, but it is more detailed and begins with a list of special feature articles. The comprehensive index is very similar to *The World Almanac*'s General Index both in style and terminology. The *Information Please Almanac* does appear to include more personal and place names, however. The print in the *Information Please Almanac* is more readable than that in *The World Almanac*. Several colored maps, including a two-page map of the United States, are found in the center of the volume.

Each *Information Please Almanac* has a series of short articles on topics such as health and weather. Some of the topics remain the same and others change from year to year. These short articles, often written by recognized experts, are found throughout the almanac along with pertinent statistical data. The *Information Please Almanac* appears to be more focused toward topics of current popular interest than does *The World Almanac*. It does not, as an example, have a list of calories, but it does give fat and cholesterol counts. The "People" section in the *Information Please Almanac* is comparable to *The World Almanac*'s "Noted Personalities." *Information Please Almanac* also has some material that *The World Almanac* does not have, including a crossword puzzle guide, a section summarizing ideas and beliefs that people have held throughout the ages, and a writer's guide. However, the two almanacs have much in common, and each supplements data found in the other.

An Almanack (commonly called *Whitaker's Almanack*) is the British equivalent of *The World Almanac*. It was founded in London in 1868 by the publisher Joseph Whitaker. The almanac for 1991 has a calendar and astronomical data for 1991, but records events occurring from September of 1989 to August 31 of 1990. A single page toward the front of the almanac called "Occurrences During Printing" gives a brief update for September and October. There is a table of contents in the front of *Whitaker's* and an index at the end. *Whitaker's* has a very extensive index, although personal names are not generally included. The almanac has economic and political information about the whole world, but it emphasizes the United Kingdom in the way that *The World Almanac* and *Information Please Almanac* emphasize the United States. For this reason, it is a useful source for current information about the United Kingdom. As an example, it lists historic landmarks, museums, and monuments, giving when appropriate a brief history, hours open, and admission charge. Other features include sections on British taxation, laws, and passport regulations. The almanac has rather extensive coverage of the British nobility, including a list of the English kings and queens, a list of peers and their heirs, orders of chivalry, and lists of baronetage and knighthoods. American libraries will find *Whitaker's* a valuable guide to the United Kingdom, as well as another source for the wide variety of miscellaneous information common to fact books.

Canadian Almanac and Directory is a highly respected, detailed compilation of facts concerning Canadian education, economy, diplomatic services, government, judicial system, religious organizations, and cultural institutions. A keyword index appears at the end of the volume, which is sent to press in November of the year prior to the date of publication. Unlike the three general almanacs previously discussed, more of the content of the *Canadian Almanac* can be categorized as directory, and it is not as international in scope as *The World Almanac*, *Information Please Almanac*, or *Whitaker's*.

The end of 1989 saw the introduction of a new general almanac, *The Universal Almanac*. This two-color publication is an attractive and easy-to-read work, although the content and indexing are similar to that of *The World Almanac* and *Information Please Almanac*. For that reason, it remains to be seen whether it can find a niche in the publishing market.

There are many almanacs which focus on a particular topic. Some of these could easily be called either handbooks or yearbooks. A few examples of this type of almanac give an indication of the wide variety published. The *International Motion Picture Almanac* is a compilation of biographical, organizational, and statistical information concerning the motion picture industry, primarily in the United States. British, Irish, and Canadian film industries are reviewed, and basic information on the world market is provided. A table of contents and subject index are included. The same publisher also issues another almanac entitled the *International Television and Video Almanac*. This almanac has the type of information about the television and video industries that the previously mentioned almanac has about the motion picture industry. The *Computer Industry Almanac* contains statistical, financial, and general information about computer companies, associations, and people. *The Weather Almanac* is a guide to weather, climate, and air quality in the United States and its major cities. It has statistics, principles, and terminology relating to climate, climate and health, climatic change, and similar topics. Another popular almanac is the *Places Rated Almanac: Your Guide to Finding the Best Place to Live in America*. This almanac rates a group of American cities on climate, housing, health care, crime, transportation, education, the arts, recreation, and economics. It provides considerable data about cities, although the ratings are controversial.

There have been several editions of *The People's Almanac*, which has facts on a surprising variety of topics. The almanacs were written in response to the national interest in trivia and are helpful in answering questions about famous people and their habits. *Library and Book Trade Almanac*, formerly titled *The Bowker Annual of Library and Book Trade Information*, consists of reports written by library and information industry professionals about events of the previous year, topics of current importance, and activities of national associations and government agencies. In addition, it includes statistics, directories, awards, and other information of interest to librarians.

Yearbooks

Britannica Book of the Year updates the *New Encyclopaedia Britannica* (discussed in chapter 16) and is a chronicle of the events of a given year. The updating aspect occupies a relatively small part of the total text, and the majority of each yearbook is, in fact, a review of happenings in the previous year. Additionally, about a third of each volume provides a largely statistical description of the nations of the world, called "Britannica World Data." Besides "Britannica World Data," the *Book of the Year* has one or more feature articles, some special reports, and a lengthy section entitled "The Year in Review." The special reports, which appear in the midst of "The Year in Review," are several-page discussions of topics of current interest, such as reports on "Latin America and the Drug Trade" or "Homelessness."

The "Year in Review" section begins with a number of short biographies and obituaries called "People of [the Year]." These biographies, which often include photographs, are of statesmen, business leaders, poets, artists, athletes, and other people who have been in the news. Another section which also has biographical information is "Britannica Awards."

Biographies are given for the recipients of the awards—people who have demonstrated "excellence in the dissemination of learning for the benefit of mankind."[4] Although biographies in this yearbook are shorter than those in *Current Biography* (discussed in chapter 14), they are often about people who are not in *Current Biography*. The biographies in the *Britannica Book of the Year* will be especially valuable in school libraries and smaller academic and public libraries, because these libraries do not have the large periodical and newspaper collections which are good sources of current biographical information.

After the people section, "Events of [the Year]" is a generally alphabetical set of short articles describing developments in a particular field during the year. Some of the same kind of information that is in the general almanacs is covered in these short articles, but the almanacs include more data and less narrative than does the yearbook. Both almanacs and this yearbook list such things as winners of sporting events, disasters (see figure 13.2), election results, and awards. Articles in the *Book of the Year* are signed, and the contributors are identified.

Natural

January 2–8, U.S. A bone-chilling storm system gripped the Midwest and the East and delivered snow and strong winds that paralyzed much of the South; at least 33 deaths were attributed to the cold weather, 13 of them from exposure.

February 3, Huanuco Province, Peru. Torrential rains unleashed an avalanche of mud and rocks that buried a dozen vehicles and killed at least 30 persons.

Fig. 13.2. "Chronology of Disasters, 1988" from *Britannica Book of the Year, 1989*. Reprinted with permission from the 1989 *Britannica Book of the Year*. Copyright © 1989 by Encyclopaedia Britannica, Inc.

The cumulative decennial index is an important feature of the *Britannica Book of the Year*, because it allows the user to locate information when the exact year is not known. Unlike many almanacs, the index also contains personal names. In the decennial index the date of the yearbook is indicated by boldface followed by a page number. For example, "**89**:14" refers to page 14 of the 1989 yearbook.

The part of the yearbook called "Britannica World Data" provides statistical data on population, employment, education, and geography, as well as brief information about such things as language and government for the nations of the world. It is comparable to *The Statesman's Year-Book*, although it usually is more condensed.

The *Britannica Book of the Year* is a useful reference tool. It is physically attractive and easy to read, and the decennial index, as previously stated, is an excellent feature. The yearbook, however, does have some limitations. Unlike the almanacs, it covers a complete calendar year and is slower to be published than the almanacs. It does not include directories, and, although it does have some retrospective data, the amount of such data is very limited. Because libraries often shelve the *Book of the Year* with the *New Encyclopaedia Britannica*, it is not as accessible as some of the other fact books which are usually shelved at the reference desk. Nonetheless, this as well as other encyclopedia yearbooks help stretch the reference collection, and are valuable in helping students, especially those in junior and senior high school.

Facts on File; World News Digest with Index is a yearbook in the making. It is, as its subtitle implies, a weekly digest of all of the types of information published in newspapers.

Information about political, social, cultural, and athletic events is summarized in the weekly classified digest. Classifications such as "World Affairs," "Finance," "Science," "Arts," and "Sports" are used as headings. Lists of best-selling records, movies, and books are included, as are obituaries of notable people. The digests have references to related stories. Each weekly issue of *Facts on File* is placed in a yearly looseleaf volume which includes a Quick Reference World Atlas. The comprehensive and cumulative index is an important feature of this work. The color-coded index is issued twice a month, with each index superseding the previous one; this index is replaced by a quarterly cumulative index which is in turn replaced by an annual index. The text of *Facts on File* is divided into three columns and further subdivided by letters which appear on the margins. The index (figure 13.3) refers first to the date of the event (not the publication date of *Facts on File*) and then to one of the pages numbered continuously throughout the year, the margin letter, and column number. A citation in the index "3-30, 224C3" refers to page 224, margin letter C, column 3. The date (3-30) in the citation is helpful in identifying the time of an event, but is not necessary to locate a specific item.

President Bush March 30 named prominent black Boston lawyer **Wayne A. Budd** to serve as U.S. attorney for Massachusetts. Budd, a moderate Republican, would replace **Frank L. McNamara Jr.**, who had been forced to resign after he became embroiled in a political controversy involving marijuana-smoking charges against his predecessor. [See p. 69A1] □

BUDAPEST—See *HUNGARY*
BUDD, Wayne A.
  Named US atty for Mass 3-30, 224C3
BUDDHISM
  Tibet unrest 3-5—3-7, martial law
    imposed 3-7, 189E3, G3
  Dalai Lama wins Nobel 10-5, 794A3
  Thai bans Asian WSJ 11-17—11-23,
    965D1

Fig. 13.3. Classified weekly digest with related index entry from *Facts on File 1989*, pp. 224, 1,037. From *Facts on File News Digest*. Copyright © 1989 by Facts on File. Reprinted with permission of Facts On File, Inc., New York.

The importance of the index in *Facts on File* cannot be overstated. Items are indexed under personal names, place names, subject or subjects, and, where appropriate, under title. The same news item is usually indexed in several ways. For instance, an obituary of a business person is indexed under personal name, under the heading "Death" which is subdivided by an alphabetical list of personal names, and under "Business and Industry" subdivided by obituaries. Five-year cumulative indexes are issued for *Facts on File*, which has been published since 1940. An annual bound volume called *Facts on File Yearbook* is also published.

Many of the facts that appear in encyclopedia yearbooks and almanacs also appear in *Facts on File*. A major advantage of *Facts on File* is currency. Because it is issued throughout the year, it is much more up-to-date than other almanacs and yearbooks. Another advantage to the digest is that it can serve as an index to other newspapers and news magazines. Traditionally, newspaper indexes (discussed in chapter 19), if they exist, are slow to be published, and finding a specific bit of news can be time-consuming. Because *Facts on File* gives specific dates for events, it aids a user or reference librarian in locating information in the newspaper. Although news magazines are indexed in periodical indexes, these indexes are not as detailed as the *Facts on File* index. Of course, *Facts on File* does not have the information organized in the concise way that almanacs do. In order to find some information, it may be necessary to consult several years, and this is not as convenient as information in one volume. However, this and other limitations of *Facts on File* are addressed by both online and CD-ROM versions of the news digest.

The CD-ROM *Facts on File* cumulates the full text of the "News Digest" from 1980 to the present, and the database is recumulated annually. The menu for this database offers the following options: Functions, Word, Index, Maps, Date, and Place. The Word option permits keyword searching, including Boolean operators and truncation, of the full-text database, and the Maps option provides access to maps of the United States and the world. Other options allow the user to browse the index, follow cross-references from article to article, and limit the search by date. The online version offers searching capabilities of the full text of *Facts on File* cumulated from 1982. It is updated weekly, and because of publishing and distributing delays, will usually be more current than the paper digest.

At first glance, the *Europa World Year Book* (formerly the *Europa Year Book: A World Survey*) and *The Statesman's Year-Book* seem very similar. They both consist of an initial part on international organizations, followed by an alphabetically arranged part on the countries of the world. They both aim to give a concise but complete description of the organizations and countries. They also both emphasize the political and economic aspects of the world. Each of these yearbooks, however, has unique characteristics.

Europa, published annually since 1960, consists of two thick volumes. Volume 1, usually published in May, contains international organizations and the first part of the alphabetically arranged survey; Volume 2, published in August, contains the second part of the alphabet. International organizations are described in terms of structure, function, and activities. Names of important officials, budget information, and addresses are given. Information about individual countries is divided into three parts: "Introductory Survey," "Statistical Survey," and "Directories." The Introductory Survey includes location, climate, recent history, government, defense, economic affairs, welfare, and education. The brief statistical survey provides summary data about the country.

There are separate directories for government, the press, religion, finance, and other areas (see figure 13.4).

BANKING
(cap. = capital; p.u. = paid up; dep. = deposits; m. = million; res = reserves; brs = branches; amounts in markkaa)

Central Bank
Suomen Pankki/Finlands Bank (The Bank of Finland): Snellman-inaukio, POB 160, 00171 Helsinki; tel. (90) 1831; telex 121224; f. 1811; Bank of Issue under the guarantee and supervision of Parliament; cap. and res 6,335m. (Aug. 1987); Gov. ROLF KULLBERG; 12 brs.

Commercial and Mortgage Banks
Kansallisluottopankki Oy (Kansallis Mortgage Bank Ltd): Erotta-jankatu 19B, 00130 Helsinki; tel. (90) 1631; f. 1985; cap. and res 110m. (1987); Chair. JAAKKO LASSILA; Man. Dir EERO HERTTOLA.
Kansallis-Osake-Pankki: Aleksanterinkatu 42, POB 10, 00101 Helsinki; tel. (90) 1631; telex 124412; f. 1889; cap. and res 6,639m., dep. 53,077m. (Aug. 1988); Chair. AATOS ERKKO; Chief Gen. Man. JAAKKO LASSILA; 468 brs.

Fig. 13.4. Entries from the "Directory of Nations" in *Europa World Year Book*. Reprinted with permission from *Europa World Year Book*.

Entries for some of the industrialized countries include extensive directories of such things as periodicals, banks, and trade unions. The directory also has either a summary of or the complete constitution for each country. The inclusion of this varied information makes the *Europa World Year Book* a one-stop reference work. The yearbook has a short index to territories of the world. There are also tables which make international comparisons of life expectancy, population, gross national product, and other topics. *Europa World Year Book* also includes a page or so of updated information received after the publication was sent to press. Information in the *Europa World Year Book* is obtained from the institutions listed, as well as from many other sources, such as national statistics offices, government departments, and diplomatic missions. Statistical information is also taken from United Nations publications and from *The Military Balance*, which is published by the International Institute for Strategic Studies.

The *Statesman's Year-Book* has been published annually since 1864. As previously stated, it is organized in a manner similar to the *Europa World Year Book*, but in a compact 1,600- to 1,700-page book. It includes information on the general history of the country, its area and population, climate, constitution and government, defense, international relations, economy, energy and natural resources, industry and trade, communications, justice, religion, education, and welfare. It does not have, as *Europa World Year Book* does, a description of the recent history of the country, or the directory information, although it does list the ambassadors from Great Britain and the United States, as well as the country's United Nations ambassador. The *Statesman's Year-Book* does have other special features. There are lists of books about each country. The three indexes — place, product, and name — are helpful in finding specific information or data, and *The Statesman's Year-Book* describes each state in the United States separately, something that the *Europa World Year Book* does not do.

■ ══ ■

13.2
Yearbook Search Strategy

An undergraduate student who was writing a paper on the political history of Grenada since the U.S. invasion in 1983 asked for help at the reference desk of her college library. The reference librarian referred her to the article on Grenada in the *Europa World Year Book*, because this article provides an overview of recent history. He also recommended that the student read the reports on Grenada that have appeared in *Facts on File* since 1983. The library had the CD-ROM edition of *Facts on File*, and the student was able to retrieve all but the most recent news from the disc before looking at the recent paper version. Finally, the librarian also showed the student the bibliography in *The Statesman's Year-Book* of books about Grenada.

As is true for almanacs, there are many yearbooks on special topics. The examples listed under almanacs could as easily be listed under yearbooks. Sometimes special yearbooks update either a special or general encyclopedia. The *McGraw-Hill Yearbook of Science and Technology*, for instance, is an annual review and supplement to the *McGraw-Hill Encyclopedia of Science and Technology* (discussed in chapter 16). The yearbook updates the most recent edition of the encyclopedia and is arranged alphabetically by topic. Entries are written by practitioners and researchers. Bibliographies, cross-references, and an index are also included. Another example, *The World Book Health and Medical Annual*, one of the special yearbooks issued by *World Book Encyclopedia* (discussed in chapter 16), is similar to a general encyclopedia yearbook, but focuses on health and medicine.

Other yearbooks act as reviews of the organization and/or activities of groups. The *Yearbook of American and Canadian Churches* and the *Municipal Yearbook* are examples. These annuals furnish information, such as statistics, directories, facts, and trends, about a specific group, and they are often published as a handbook for the group's members. For instance, the *Yearbook of American and Canadian Churches*, prepared and edited at the National Council of Churches of Christ in the United States, has directories and statistics of religious denominations and affiliated organizations in North America. The *Municipal Yearbook*, which is issued by the International City Management Association to provide factual data as well as a discussion of current trends for city and county officials, has statistical and directory information about local governments in the United States and Canada. The *Municipal Yearbook* also has a section, "References," which is a basic bibliography of books, periodicals, and online data services relevant to local government.

Handbooks

The *Guinness Book of Records*, formerly the *Guinness Book of World Records*, is a famous book of trivia and a useful reference work as well. The first American edition of *Guinness* was published in 1956, and it has appeared annually since that time. This heavily illustrated work is organized into chapters on specific subjects, such as the human being, the living world, and the natural world, and is further subdivided into categories within each chapter. This arrangement facilitates browsing but is less helpful in reference work. The reference librarian will find the subject index essential when using *Guinness*. The subject index, which does not include personal names, lists many specific terms in bold print, in some cases also subdividing the term using normal typeface. The subdivisions are particularly important for terms such as depth, prolific, span, and weight, which are cues to records. A hurdle to using the *Guinness Book of Records* as a reference tool is in understanding what is meant by a *record*. The records in the *Guinness Book of Records* are for every type of extreme: largest-smallest, worst-best, widest-narrowest, oldest-newest, and the like. Reference librarians should thoroughly browse the book to gain a better understanding of what it includes.

While the newspapers regularly report a new record set specifically to be entered in the *Guinness Book of Records*, many of the records are the result of natural phenomena and/or are otherwise independent of record seeking. The book also includes a great deal of miscellaneous information such as definitions, statistics, and history. *Guinness* is normally consulted in order to find records. However, it can be useful occasionally in finding other information, though mostly by accident. The *Guinness Book of Records* is now available in CD-ROM format as the Guinness Disc of Records. This new format, which can be searched by word or phrase, makes the miscellaneous information more accessible. The Guinness Disc of Records includes not only the full text but pictures, sound, and animation, and may be searched using Boolean logic.

Joseph Nathan Kane's *Famous First Facts* is also a book of records. It records "First happenings, discoveries, and inventions in American history."[5] The fourth edition, published in 1981, includes more than nine thousand firsts that pertain to Americans or have occurred in the United States. This venerable reference work is arranged alphabetically by subject. There are cross-references from alternative headings to the heading which is used. Firsts included are quite diverse, from the invention of the tape measure to the first appearance of billiards in America. There are four indexes: by years, days of the month, personal names, and geographical areas. The geographical index is arranged alphabetically by state and, within each state, alphabetically by city. The presence of the indexes means that *Famous First Facts* can be used in several different ways. It can be used to establish historic fact, to identify anniversaries, and to gather information about a specific place or time. The index to days of the month serves as a "book of days" for the United States.

There are several other more general books of days. *Holidays and Anniversaries of the World* is an example of this type of handbook. For each day of the year, it lists birthdates and historical events. The birthdates are arranged chronologically from earliest to most recent, and notable persons born on that date are identified. There is also a religious calendar and an enumeration of international holidays. Names, terms, and events are indexed in a single alphabet. The introductory material in *Holidays and Anniversaries of the World* includes a history of the modern calendar, a glossary and list of time abbreviations, and other uses of time. Some features (a perpetual calendar and a list of wedding anniversary gifts, for example) also appear in almanacs, but the information may vary. A comparison of the information in an almanac with that in *Holidays and Anniversaries of the World* validates this.

The *New York Public Library Desk Reference* is a compilation of information frequently requested at the New York Public Library. "Religion," "Etiquette," "Personal Finance," and "Libraries and Museums" are a few of the chapter headings in this single-volume work. An important feature of *The New York Public Library Desk Reference* is its listing of additional sources of information at the end of each chapter. The source list consists of a directory of related organizations and a bibliography of reference works.

■ ══ ■

13.3
Handbook Search Strategy

A librarian receives a telephone call from a patron who is planning an extended visit to England and wants to know, "How long my dog will be quarantined if I take him with me?" Because the librarian knows that *The New York Public Library Desk Reference* has practical information about travel, she is able to answer the question while the patron is still on the line. The answer (180 days) can be located through the index of *The New York Public Library Desk Reference* by looking under either "Pets" subdivided by "Travel with" or "Travel" subdivided by "With pets."

Another kind of handbook standard in almost all reference departments is the *style manual*. *The Chicago Manual of Style*, one of the most common, is consulted by writers or by librarians helping writers to determine the format of bibliographies and footnotes. Although this is the main reason for its use, the work also includes a considerable amount of other helpful information. It is divided into three parts: "Bookmaking," "Style," and "Production and Printing." The bookmaking section defines and also prescribes the parts of a book and its preparation, including the editorial process. Copyright rules and regulations in the United States and publishing agreements, with examples, are also discussed. The style section is a guide to punctuation, spelling, capitalization, and similar matters, as well as to correct bibliographic forms. The production and printing section is an illustrated description of the physical aspects of bookmaking. *The Chicago Manual of Style* has a glossary of technical terms, a bibliography, and an index. The manual is subdivided into numbered paragraphs. The paragraph numbers appear on the left-hand margin of a page. References in the index, except for tables and figures, are to paragraph numbers rather than page numbers. As noted in chapter 15, *The Chicago Manual of Style* is one of the reference sources in the Microsoft Bookshelf CD-ROM Reference Library.

The Chicago Manual of Style is of use to authors and editors and to librarians who are assisting patrons in the preparation of manuscripts. Patrons often need to use a specific bibliographic style, so additional style manuals may also be needed. The *MLA Handbook for Writers of Research Papers, Themes and Dissertations* and the American Psychological Association's *Publication Manual* are examples of other style manuals that prescribe different bibliographic formats. *A Manual for Writers of Term Papers, Theses and Dissertations*, by Kate L. Turabian, is adapted from *The Chicago Manual of Style*. Other guides for writing are also published. For instance, *The Secretary's Handbook: A Manual for Office Personnel*, by Doris H. Whalen, is a compilation of information useful to the office worker, writer, and student. Punctuation, composition, word usage, and proofreaders' marks are presented in a crisp, concise manner. Examples and exercises complement the text, and there are a glossary and list of reference sources.

There are many handbooks on specialized topics that are of importance in a general reference department. Etiquette books and health and medical manuals are examples of handbooks commonly referred to in general reference departments in both academic and public libraries. In the case of etiquette books, *Emily Post's Etiquette* and one or more of the "Miss Manners" books written by Judith Martin are popular favorites. *Emily Post's Etiquette* has a subject arrangement, divided into categories such as "Forms and Formality" and "Entertaining." It has an excellent index. The "Miss Manners" books are also organized by subject, and are well indexed, but differ from *Emily Post's Etiquette* in that the books consist of letters written to "Miss Manners" and her responses to the letters. Some librarians prefer the formal style of the Post book, but the "Miss Manners" books are in touch with current social issues, and general reference departments can benefit from having both *Emily Post's Etiquette* and one or more of the "Miss Manners" books.

The American Medical Association Family Medical Guide is an example of a medical handbook usually found in a general reference department. This guide, intended for the layperson, has descriptions of many diseases and disorders, as well as aids to self-diagnosis. There are indexes to subjects and drugs. Although the reference librarian should not attempt to diagnose or help a patron diagnose an illness, this type of handbook provides general information about the functioning of the body and helps its user understand a previously diagnosed illness.

The *Physician's Desk Reference* (*PDR*), a handbook intended for physicians, is also at home in a general reference department. It is a compilation of product information on package inserts found in all available prescription drugs. Data complies with Federal Drug Administration (FDA) regulations and is fairly uniform and concise. The *PDR* is alphabetically arranged by trade name of drugs, and access is provided by several indexes at the beginning of the book. There is an index to manufacturers, product names, product categories, and generic and chemical names. The "Product Identification" section of the work shows pictures of the different drugs and aids in verifying the name of a particular drug. The *Physician's Desk Reference* is also available on CD-ROM. The CD-ROM version searches the complete text of the *PDR* under topics such as symptoms, drug brand names, and complications.

These examples are but a few of the many handbooks important in reference work. Many of the best handbooks are subject-specific. The *Standard Handbook for Electrical Engineers* and *CRC Handbook of Chemistry and Physics* are examples of well-known scientific and technical handbooks. *A Handbook to Literature* by C. Hugh Holman and William Harmon, the *Architect's Handbook of Professional Practice*, and the *Handbook of Aging and the Social Sciences* are examples of handbooks from other fields.

Search Strategies

The first step in developing a search strategy is to determine the nature of the question. The books described in this chapter provide simple factual answers. They can also lead the user to other factual sources or in-depth works. Once it has been determined that an almanac, handbook, or yearbook will answer a patron's question, the librarian can draw on a thorough knowledge of the collection to choose the best source. The knowledge comes from previous use of these reference works, and from a continual reexamination, especially when new editions appear. It is important to know not only the strengths and weaknesses, but also publishing schedules, special features, and indexing practices, of every commonly used ready reference source.

Other factors will also influence the choice of source. When current information is needed, frequently updated databases are preferable. If the question involves a nation or region, reference works with a national or regional slant may provide the best answer. It is important, however, to remember that more than one reference work can answer the same question. Sometimes comparing answers in two or more sources may be the best way to serve the patron.

The effective use of almanacs, yearbooks, and handbooks requires both patience and imagination. Successful search strategies can be written down and/or shared with colleagues. "The Exchange," a column in *RQ* which contains "tricky questions, notes on unusual information sources, and general comments concerning reference problems and their solutions,"[6] offers insight into search strategies and identifies novel information contained in familiar sources. Reviews such as those in the "Reference Books Bulletin" section of *Booklist* also aid in the successful use of these sources. New technology can enhance the use of older sources, and an effort should be made to keep abreast of developments. There is no single magic formula to apply to the use of these reference works. This makes using them a challenge, but a rewarding one.

■ ═══ ■

13.4

Locating the Title of a Best Seller

A patron is trying to remember the name of a book he believes was a best seller at some point in the last several years. He knows that it is about physics and thinks that the title includes the phrase "big bang."

This question can be answered in several ways, depending on the sources available to the librarian. *The World Almanac* and *Library and Book Trade Almanac* list best sellers from the previous year, and the librarian may need to consult annual volumes for several years before locating the correct answer. *The World Almanac* indexes best sellers under the heading "Books," while the *Library and Book Trade Almanac* indexes under "Best Sellers." *Facts on File* also lists best sellers on an ongoing basis. Best sellers are listed in the index of the printed version of *Facts on File* under "Literature." The online and CD-ROM versions of Facts on File also can be searched for this information, using the words *big* and *bang* to do a full-text search.

The answer to the question is *A Brief History of Time: From the Big Bang to Black Holes* by Stephen W. Hawking. The answer can be found in the 1990 *World Almanac*, in the 1989-90 *Library and Book Trade Almanac*, and in the 1988 and 1989 *Facts on File*, as well as its CD-ROM and online versions.

Notes

1. "Almanac," in *Encyclopedia Americana* (Danbury, Conn.: Grolier, 1988) 1: 612-13.

2. Julie E. Miller and Jane G. Bryan, "Wealth of Information: A Review of Four 1979 Almanacs," *Reference Services Review* 7 (July/September 1979): 77-78.

3. "Answers to a Manufacturing Task That Aren't in *The World Almanac*," *Publishers Weekly* 227 (March 1, 1985): 66.

4. *Britannica Book of the Year 1986* (Chicago: Encyclopaedia Britannica, 1986), 118.

5. Joseph Nathan Kane, *Famous First Facts*, 4th ed. (New York: H. W. Wilson, 1981), iii.

6. Charles Anderson, "The Exchange," *RQ* 28 (Winter 1988): 146.

List of Sources

An Almanack. Est. by Joseph Whitaker. London: Whitaker, 1868- . Annual.

The American Medical Association Family Medical Guide. Revised and updated. Edited by Jeffrey R. M. Kunz and Asher J. Finkel. New York: Random House, 1987. 832p.

Architect's Handbook of Professional Practice. 11th ed. 4 vols. Washington, D.C.: American Institute of Architects, 1987. (Supplements issued periodically.)

Britannica Book of the Year. Chicago: Encyclopaedia Britannica, 1938- . Annual.

Canadian Almanac and Directory. Toronto, Canada: Copp Clark Pitman, 1848- . Annual.

The Chicago Manual of Style. 13th ed. Chicago: University of Chicago Press, 1982. 738p.

Computer Industry Almanac. New York: Brady, 1987- . Annual.

CRC Handbook of Chemistry and Physics. Boca Raton, Fla.: CRC Press, 1913- . Annual.

Europa World Year Book. 2 vols. London: Europa Publications, 1960- . Annual. (First published in 1926.)

Facts on File; World News Digest with Index. New York: Facts on File, 1940- . Weekly. (DIALOG File 264; also available on CD-ROM.)

Guinness Book of Records. New York: Sterling, 1956-1990. New York: Facts on File, 1991- . Annual. (English edition began publication in 1955.)

Guinness Disc of Records. [CD-ROM]. London: Microsoft Ltd.

Handbook of Aging and the Social Sciences. 3d ed. Edited by Robert H. Binstock and Linda K. George. San Diego, Calif.: Academic Press, 1990. 489p.

Holidays and Anniversaries of the World. 2d ed. Edited by Jennifer Mossman. Detroit, Mich.: Gale Research, 1990. 1,080p.

Holman, C. Hugh, and William Harmon. *A Handbook to Literature*. 5th ed. New York: Macmillan Publishing Co., 1986. 647p.

Information Please Almanac: Atlas and Yearbook. New York: Houghton Mifflin, 1947- . Annual.

International Motion Picture Almanac. New York: Quigley, 1929- . Annual.

International Television and Video Almanac. Edited by Jane Klain. New York: Quigley, 1955- . Annual.

Kane, Joseph Nathan. *Famous First Facts*. 4th ed. New York: H. W. Wilson, 1981. 1,350p.

Library and Book Trade Almanac. New York: R. R. Bowker, 1955- . Annual.

Martin, Judith. *Miss Manners' Guide to Excruciatingly Correct Behavior*. New York: Macmillan Publishing Co., 1982. 768p.

Martin, Judith. *Miss Manners' Guide to Rearing Perfect Children*. New York: Penguin, 1984. 432p.

Martin, Judith. *Miss Manners' Guide to the Turn-of-the-Millennium*. New York: Pharos Books, 1989. 800p.

McGraw-Hill Yearbook of Science and Technology. New York: McGraw-Hill, 1962- . Annual.

The Military Balance. London: International Institute for Strategic Studies, 1959- . Annual.

MLA Handbook for Writers of Research Papers, Themes and Dissertations. 3d ed. Edited by Joseph Gibaldi and Walter S. Achtert. New York: Modern Language Association of America, 1988. 248p.

Municipal Yearbook. Washington, D.C.: International City Management Association, 1934- . Annual.

The New York Public Library Desk Reference. New York: Webster's New World, 1989. 836p.

Old Farmer's Almanac. Dublin, N.H.: Yankee Publishing, 1792- . Annual.

The People's Almanac #3. Edited by David Wallechinsky and Irving Wallace. New York: William Morrow, 1981. 722p. (Earlier editions published in 1975 and 1978.)

Physician's Desk Reference. Oradell, N.J.: Medical Economics Co., 1946- . Annual. (Also available on CD-ROM.)

Places Rated Almanac: Your Guide to Finding the Best Place to Live in America. 3d ed. Edited by Richard Boyer. Englewood Cliffs, N.J.: Prentice-Hall, 1989. 421p.

Post, Elizabeth L. *Emily Post's Etiquette*. 14th ed. New York: Harper & Row, 1984. 1,017p.

Publication Manual of the American Psychological Association. 3d ed. Washington, D.C.: American Psychological Association, 1983. 208p.

Standard Handbook for Electrical Engineers. 12th ed. New York: McGraw-Hill, 1987.

The Statesman's Year-Book. Edited by John Paxton. London: Macmillan, 1864- . Annual.

Turabian, Kate L. *A Manual for Writers of Term Papers, Theses and Dissertations*. 5th ed. Chicago: University of Chicago Press, 1987. 300p.

The Universal Almanac, 1990. Edited by John W. Wright. Kansas City, Kans.: Andrews and McMeel, 1989. 600p.

The Weather Almanac. 5th ed. Edited by James A. Ruffner and Frank E. Bair. Detroit, Mich.: Gale Research, 1987. 811p.

Whalen, Doris H. *The Secretary's Handbook: A Manual for Office Personnel.* 4th ed. New York: Harcourt Brace Jovanovich, 1983. 326p.

The World Almanac and Book of Facts. Edited by Mark S. Hoffman. New York: Pharos Books, 1886- . Annual.

The World Book Health and Medical Annual. Edited by World Book Staff. Chicago: World Book, 1986- . Annual.

Yearbook of American and Canadian Churches. Nashville, Tenn.: Abingdon, 1915- . Annual.

Additional Readings

"Encyclopedia Annuals, Supplements, and Yearbooks: A 1985 Overview." *Booklist* 82 (September 1, 1985): 36-43.
From time to time, "Reference Books Bulletin" in *Booklist* publishes an analysis of encyclopedia yearbooks. Major English-language yearbooks are individually discussed, using the most recent yearbook as an example. The review prior to the review in 1985 was in 1981, and it is possible that another review will appear in the early 1990s.

Grefrath, Richard W. "Eating Clams with Your Fingers: A Survey of Contemporary Etiquette Books." *Collection Building* 6 (Winter 1985): 10-16.
Grefrath has very decided opinions with which the reader may or may not agree. Nonetheless, this article is a useful description and bibliography of contemporary etiquette books.

Grogan, Denis. *Encyclopedias, Yearbooks, Directories and Statistical Sources.* Grogan's Case Studies in Reference Work, vol. 2. London: Clive Bingley, 1987. 170p.
Grogan uses the case study method to illustrate both search strategy and the content of ready reference works. Although the sample questions are oriented to the United Kingdom, the discussion of the search process is informative.

McCulley, Lucretia. "Basic International Reference Sources." *Reference Services Review* 13 (Fall 1985): 31-36.
This is a comparative review of thirteen sources for data about the nations of the world. *Europa World Yearbook* and *Statesman's Year-Book* are included in the survey.

Miller, Julie E., and Jane G. Bryan. "Wealth of Information: A Review of Four 1979 Almanacs." *Reference Services Review* 7 (July/September 1979): 67-78.
Even though the information is very out-of-date, the authors of this article provide an excellent framework for analyzing the organization and content of almanacs.

Rogers, Stephen W. "Did Anything Else Ever Happen on December Seventh? A Review of Books of Days." *Reference Services Review* 14 (Spring 1986): 17-33.
This is a very thorough comparison of the contents of "Books of Days." The author also discusses other reference works, such as encyclopedias and almanacs, which list important happenings on a given date. Examples from different works are given, as well as a summary chart which compares features of the works reviewed.

SOURCES OF BIOGRAPHICAL INFORMATION

Uses and Characteristics

The great nineteenth-century critic, Thomas Carlyle, wrote that "the Life of the lowest mortal, if faithfully recorded, would be interesting to the highest."[1] While it is true that stories in the media about oppressed or underprivileged individuals attract a great deal of interest, it is usually prominent individuals about whom information is requested at the reference desk. Carlyle's larger point, that interest in the lives of others is a universal phenomenon, could be easily verified by reference librarians. In fact, one of the most consistent features of reference work over the years has been the high demand for information about people. Sometimes this information is sought to satisfy curiosity; other times, it is needed for a school assignment or a research project, or to prepare remarks introducing a guest speaker. Among typical questions encountered at a public or academic library reference desk are, "How tall is George Bush?," and "Has George Will won a Pulitzer Prize?" These questions can each be answered with one of the sources to be discussed in this chapter (*Current Biography* and *Contemporary Authors*, respectively), sources which are likely to be found in all college and university library reference collections, and in the reference collections of most large public libraries as well. The second question could also be answered by referring to *Who's Who in America*, which almost all academic and public libraries, as well as some school and special libraries, own.

Questions such as these which require the librarian to find one or two specific facts about an individual are probably the most common type of biographical reference question received in most libraries. Other common requests of this type are for a person's age, place of birth, educational attainments, and career history. Biographical sources which provide this kind of factual information can be called *direct* sources, since they provide the information itself, rather than referring the user, through bibliographic citations, to other sources where the information may be found. Direct sources may offer brief, basic biographical data, as does *Who's Who*, or they may provide lengthy biographical essays about the individuals they include, as do *Current Biography* and the *Dictionary of American Biography*. Although the distinction is not always clear, biographical sources which provide brief data about those individuals they include are generally referred to as *biographical directories*, while those tools offering more detailed information, often in essay form, are usually called *biographical dictionaries*.

There are other questions of a biographical nature, which, unlike the queries mentioned above, may not be answerable by quick consultation of a single source. These questions require the librarian to locate more extensive presentations of a person's life and career, or to find obscure facts about an individual. When the librarian is not sure which source will provide the information requested, or if several direct sources have been tried to no avail, the use of indirect sources is indicated. *Indirect* sources list bibliographic citations leading the user to other works which will contain the information sought. They generally give only enough factual information (such as full name, birth and death dates) to accurately identify each individual listed. Generally, these sources are indexes to other sources, such as *Biography Index*. Some biographical sources are both direct and indirect. *Contemporary Authors*, for instance, gives fairly extensive information about the individuals it includes, and it also often lists other sources where further information can be found.

If biographical reference tools can be divided into two basic types, direct and indirect, it is also possible to divide them into two basic categories: those which supply information about living persons, and those which are about historical figures. The former are called *current*, and the latter are termed *retrospective*. As with direct and indirect sources, some biographical reference tools provide data on both dead and living individuals. However, some major ready reference sources, such as the various "Who's Who" titles, list only persons known to be living at the time of publication, while others include only persons known to have died. It is for this reason that the first question the reference librarian asks a patron usually is, "Do you know if this person is still alive?" Naturally, very recently deceased individuals will still be listed in the latest editions of current sources. It will take some time for those individuals to appear in the newest editions of retrospective sources.

Whether they are retrospective or current, direct or indirect, the scope and coverage of biographical sources vary. The most narrow tools focus on one area of human endeavor, or on one profession or academic field. An example of a source of this type is *Who's Who in Economics*. Other, broader sources cover several related fields. Two well-known sources of this type are the *Directory of American Scholars* and *American Men and Women of Science* (both discussed later in this chapter). A broader class of biographical tool includes prominent persons from all fields who live in a specific country. These titles commonly begin "Who's Who in...." Related retrospective sources of this nature have titles like, "Who Was Who in...." These sources contain brief factual information about prominent persons— living and deceased, respectively—in the given country ("America" or "American" in these titles often means both the United States and Canada, and sometimes Mexico as well). For several Western countries, comprehensive, multivolume retrospective sources which provide fairly lengthy essays on the individuals included have been compiled. Two of these titles, those covering the United States and Great Britain, are discussed in this chapter. Also discussed are obituary sources, which are an important type of retrospective biographical reference tool.

Finally, there are biographical sources which are international in scope. These may be direct sources, such as the *McGraw-Hill Encyclopedia of World Biography*, or they may be indirect tools, such as *Biography and Genealogy Master Index*. Indirect sources, whose purpose is to guide the user to an appropriate source when one is not known, are generally international in their coverage. The relative number of non-American or non-Western persons who are included is a matter which must be examined when evaluating individual tools of this nature.

Evaluation

As with other reference tools containing factual information, biographical sources must be evaluated on their ease of use, the accuracy of the information they provide, and the degree to which they are comprehensive within their stated scope. For current sources, the information provided should be as up-to-date as possible, while retrospective tools, which are often used for research, are more valuable when they give sources for further reading.

Scope

The first question usually asked when evaluating a biographical reference tool is, "Who is included in this work?" This leads immediately to the further question, "What are the criteria for inclusion?" In other words, what is the intended *scope* of the work, and how is it determined whether a specific individual fits within that scope? Generally, biographical sources do not seek to include everyone who meets the most basic criterion indicated by the title (e.g., residents of a certain country, or members of a particular gender, ethnic group, or profession). Rather, they try to include only those individuals in that group who have *reference interest* because of their position, their achievements, or their historical significance.

Comprehensiveness

The scope and the criteria for inclusion are generally spelled out in the book's prefatory material. How the criteria are defined and applied will determine how *comprehensive* the work is within its stated scope. It is important that as many as possible of those individuals who meet the criteria be included, or the reference value of the work will be reduced. Of course, this is not always easy to determine, since criteria often are stated in general terms. *Who's Who Among Black Americans*, for instance, seeks to include blacks who "contribute significantly to American life."[2] *American Men and Women of Science* lists "those who have made significant contributions in their field."[3] "Significant contributions" are difficult to define precisely. However, one can check to see if all individuals who hold comparable positions or with similar accomplishments are included. Also, it can be determined if certain groups or fields of activity are under- or overrepresented. This kind of evaluation is more difficult with retrospective sources, since the importance and even existence of positions and professions change with time, and it requires considerable research to identify individuals who are likely candidates for inclusion.

Whatever criteria are used, it is important that the work's scope and criteria for inclusion be in harmony. If the scope is broad, as in *Who's Who in America*, the criteria must be strictly applied, or not everyone who meets them could possibly be included. On the other hand, if the scope is fairly narrow, then the criteria can be applied more liberally so that the work will be comprehensive within its stated scope. The *Directory of American Scholars*, for instance, summarizes its criteria by stating simply that biographees are "currently active in teaching, research and publishing" in one of the fields covered.[4] This title, therefore, can be expected to list everyone who meets that broad definition, and its success at achieving that goal should not be difficult to evaluate. *Who's Who in America*, likewise, should include everyone who meets its narrower criteria: holder of one of a list of positions stated in its "Standards of Admission" (see figure 14.1, page 300), or one who has demonstrated "significant achievement."[5] How comprehensive it is with regard to the second criterion, however, will depend on how carefully and objectively that criterion is applied. If it is not applied strictly and carefully, uneven rather than comprehensive coverage will be the result. Considering the enormity of this task in a biographical directory which may list anywhere from twenty thousand to eighty thousand individuals, it is strange to see reviewers occasionally criticize a title because one or two individuals deemed important by the reviewer have been missed.

Standards of Admission

The foremost consideration in determining who will be admitted to the pages of *Who's Who in America* is the extent of an individual's reference interest. Reference value is based on either of two factors: 1) the position of responsibility held or 2) the level of significant achievement attained in a career of noteworthy activity. The majority of biographees qualify for admission on the basis of the first factor, a specific position of responsibility. Incumbency in the position makes the person someone of high reference interest. The factor of position includes the following categories:

1. High–ranking members of the legislative, executive, and judicial branches of the United State government. This group includes, for example, members of Congress, cabinet secretaries, chief administrators of selected federal agencies and commissions, and justices of the federal courts.

2. Military officers on active duty with the rank of major general or higher in the army, air force, and marine corps, and of rear admiral or higher in the navy.

3. Specified state government officials. Among them are governors, lieutenant governors, secretaries of state, attorneys general, treasurers, and other selected positions such as president of the state senate, the state university system administrator, and the chief state health officer. This standard includes officials of American territories.

4. Judges of state and territorial courts of the highest appellate jurisdiction.

5. High–level officials of principal cities, based on population. These officials include mayors, police chiefs, school superintendents, and other selected positions.

6. Leading government officials of Canada and Mexico. In Canada, this group includes, as examples, the prime minister, premiers of the provinces, ministers of departments of the federal government, and justices of the highest courts. Examples in the Mexican government are the president and cabinet secretaries of the national government.

7. Principal officers of major national and international businesses as defined by several quantitative criteria.

8. Ranking administrative officials of major universities and colleges. Some of the officers included in this category are president, provost, dean, and selected department heads.

9. Heads of leading philanthropic, cultural, educational, professional, and scientific institutions and associations. These institutions include, for example, selected foundations, museums, symphony orchestras, libraries, and research laboratories.

10. Selected members of honorary organizations such as the National Academy of Sciences, the National Academy of Design, and the Institute of Medicine. This group includes elected fellows of specified organizations, for example, the Royal Society of Canada and the American College of Trial Lawyers.

11. Chief ecclesiastics of the principal religious denominations.

12. Recipients of major national and international awards. A few examples are the Nobel and Pulitzer prizes, the Academy Award, and the American Institute of Architecture Gold Medal for Architecture.

Admission by the second factor—significant achievement—is based on the application of objective criteria established for each field. An artist whose works hang in major museums qualifies for admission for noteworthy accomplishment. The professor who has made important research contributions in his field is of reference interest because of his outstanding achievements. Qualitative standards determine eligibility for every field.

In many instances there is considerable overlap between the two factors used for inclusion in *Who's Who in America*. For example, the head of a major library is in the book because of position, but reaching that responsibility also signifies important achievement. Similarly, a state governor not only holds a position that warrants inclusion; attaining that post also represents significant achievement in the political world. In both cases the reference value of the biographical sketch is significant. Whether the person has been selected because of position or as a mark of achievement, the biographee in *Who's Who in America* has noteworthy accomplishments beyond those of the vast majority of contemporaries.

Fig. 14.1. "Standards of Admission" from *Who's Who in America*. Copyright © 1990-91, Marquis Who's Who, Inc. Reprinted by permission from *Who's Who in America*, 46th Edition, Volume 1, 1990-91.

Accuracy

Of paramount importance in reference work is the *accuracy* of the information presented in the biographical entries or essays. There are basically only two sources of this information, the biographees themselves and writings about those individuals (*secondary sources*). While the biographees are undoubtedly in the best position to provide accurate information, they may rely on memory for some facts (not always reliable), or they may simply omit facts they regard as unfavorable. Most current sources, nevertheless, rely on the biographees for the information they print; some may check secondary sources, when necessary or possible, to verify that information. Retrospective biographical tools must obtain their information either from secondary sources or from the writings and papers of the biographee. The secondary sources used by reputable scholars and publishers are reasonably free of personal bias, but their accuracy is dependent on careful and objective research by their authors. Librarians, when faced with conflicting facts from different biographical sources, can consult other sources to try to determine the truth, or they can choose between the conflicting facts based on the nature and reputation of the titles involved. Either way, it is often difficult to be absolutely sure that one has determined which is the accurate information. In these situations, the librarian must present the conflicting facts to the user and explain why one or the other set of facts is, in the librarian's informed judgment, more likely to be correct.

Currency

A major factor which determines the accuracy of a biographical source is its *currency*. In a highly mobile society, it is difficult to provide biographical information which is absolutely up-to-date. Biographical directories which rely on data provided by the biographees themselves face a dilemma when individuals to be listed do not return their questionnaires. The data from a previous edition might be used, or it may be possible to update that information through research in other sources. Out-of-date information sometimes survives, which could lead to inaccuracies regarding an individual's current position, family status, or address. Comparing entries for the same individual in different biographical tools will occasionally reveal errors of this nature. Publication frequency is another factor in maintaining current information about biographees. Many biographical directories are revised every year or every other year. Their electronic counterparts, when available, are sometimes updated only when a new printed edition is prepared and may, therefore, be no more current than the printed volumes. Biographical dictionaries are revised less frequently, and are more likely to contain out-of-date material. However, dictionaries which are published serially, as are *Contemporary Authors* and *Current Biography*, will often publish entirely new or revised entries on prominent individuals whose earlier entries are dated.

References

Currency plays an important role in evaluating another feature of some biographical sources, the inclusion of *references for further reading*. Generally, sources that provide biographical essays document the information in those essays by listing the sources from which that information was obtained. Some also list sources not used, but which the reader may wish to consult for more extensive information. If these sources are critical in nature, or if they are book-length studies, they can be particularly valuable. However, just as with factual data, one likes these bibliographic citations to be as up-to-date as possible.

Format

Almost as important as the accuracy and currency of the information provided in biographical tools is the *format* in which this information is presented. If a particular title is poorly organized, or if the access points (i.e., indexes, cross-references) to the information are inadequate, the users may never find the information they are seeking, even if it is, in fact, buried somewhere within the book. When one speaks of access points, it is clear that electronic reference tools offer a definite advantage over printed sources. Electronic retrieval, offered in both CD-ROM and dial-up databases, allows one to retrieve biographical entries for persons with common characteristics, such as the same birth date or place, the same educational background or occupation, or even those who have received a particular honor or award. In addition, one can print out full entries or only the parts of entries in which one is interested. A great deal of flexibility is available with this kind of tool, and this flexibility has been used to improve, to some extent, the access points in printed sources. Several printed biographical tools now provide indexes by geographic area and/or occupation. It is doubtful, however, that a printed source could ever offer as many retrieval points as its electronic counterpart.

Electronic searching also permits one to search, simultaneously, entries from many different printed editions or volumes of a specific biographical tool. For instance, in the Biography Master Index database offered on DIALOG, one can search all editions of *Biography and Genealogy Master Index* (1975-present). In similar fashion, on WILSON-LINE's Biography Index (available via dial-up or on a CD-ROM) one can search a database which corresponds to several annual volumes of the printed version. This saves the librarian or user an enormous amount of time, and the references can be printed in one comprehensive list.

Another aspect of a biographical reference tool's format is the ease with which one can interpret the data contained in the individual entries. If a source employs the essay form of entry, ease of interpretation refers primarily to the clarity and grace found in the writing style of the author of a particular entry. As in any written text, the information should be presented in a concise and unambiguous fashion; it should also not be presented in a disorganized or awkward way. In biographical directories, where a great deal of information is packed into brief entries, abbreviations are almost always employed. These, ideally, should be easily interpreted by the user. In any event, a list of abbreviations and their meanings should be included in the work's prefatory material.

Selection

While criteria for evaluating biographical reference sources are fairly objective, selection decisions must be based on the needs of a specific library and its user groups. The amount of money the library can allocate to reference materials, and the uniqueness of the information provided by particular tools, also play a role in the selection process.

Needs of Clientele

Before one selects and purchases a biographical reference tool, several factors must be considered. Perhaps the most important is the *needs of one's clientele*. These needs can be ascertained in several ways (see chapter 11). Generally speaking, users in school and academic libraries need access to as many biographical sources as possible, both dictionaries, for the completion of class assignments, and directories, for finding information about professional colleagues or well-known persons. In special libraries, the latter interest generally predominates; hence, biographical directories will be in the highest demand, particularly directories covering the specific occupation(s) to which the library's users belong. In public libraries, where users of all kinds are served, both types are needed. In smaller public libraries, national sources, like *Who's Who in America* and *Newsmakers*, may suffice, supplemented by the "Who's Who" for that library's region. In academic libraries, large public libraries, and some secondary school libraries, international biographical sources are essential. Current biographical sources will be in demand in all types of libraries; retrospective biographical tools are required in school and academic libraries for research purposes, are used both for general information needs and for research in public libraries, and are less often used in most varieties of special library.

Cost

In any library, the overriding consideration is likely to be cost. Most smaller libraries, of any type, will be unable to afford to purchase *Biography and Genealogy Master Index* ($245 per annual volume and $750-$795 for a five-year cumulation in 1990). Smaller libraries may also elect to purchase the *Concise Dictionary of American Biography* rather than the full twenty-volume set. Even larger libraries, which generally try to be as comprehensive as possible, may be unable to afford to purchase all of the specialized directories available for individual nations, depending instead on the *International Who's Who* and/or *Who's Who in the World* coverage of foreign individuals of note.

Uniqueness

One must also assess the uniqueness of a biographical title before selecting it for one's collection. The two international directories previously mentioned each contain unique entries, but there is also considerable overlap between them with regard to the individuals who are included. Where such overlap exists, many librarians will have to choose to purchase only one of the two or more titles that offer similar coverage. In situations such as this, one must generally rely on reviews in professional journals in reaching a decision.

Important General Sources

Of the many available biographical reference tools, discussion in this chapter focuses on those which, because of their broad coverage, are likely to be heavily used in general reference collections. Information on more specialized sources can be obtained from the guides to biographical reference tools listed in the additional readings for this chapter.

Current Biographical Directories

If there is one biographical source which every library providing reference service is likely to have, it is *Who's Who in America*. Published biennially since 1899, it provides, in the forty-sixth edition, salient biographical facts about approximately 79,400 individuals who, because of their "position and/or noteworthy achievements that have proved to be of significant value to society," have reference value.[6] These general "Standards of Admission" have remained relatively constant during this prestigious work's ninety-year history.[7] Between biennial editions, a *Supplement* providing a number of updated entries and several thousand new entries is published.

As with many reference sources, the "America" in *Who's Who in America* also includes Canada and Mexico. It is important to note that inclusion is based on achievement or position and not simply on wealth or notoriety. Among the twelve types of positions which automatically qualify an individual for inclusion are leading government jobs at the national or state level, high administrative positions in major universities and colleges, and leading positions in large businesses (the full list is printed in the prefatory section of each edition). Persons selected for one edition are generally listed again in succeeding editions (for example, Jimmy Carter and James Watt were still listed in the 1990-91 edition). Possible new listees are identified by careful searching in newspapers and journals. A few individuals, who because of retirement no longer have significant reference value, may be dropped. These individuals are listed in a "Retiree Index," which allows the user to locate an entry for them in an earlier edition. A separate list identifies those who have died since publication of the previous edition.

The information provided for each individual listed is obtained, whenever possible, from the individuals themselves. Each candidate for inclusion is sent a data form and asked to supply the requested biographical facts. If the individual does not respond, the publisher's staff will gather the information as best they can from other sources. The data presented in *Who's Who in America* are arranged in twenty-one data fields (see figure 14.2).

Key to Information

[1] GIBSON, OSCAR JULIUS, [2] physician, medical educator; [3] b. Syracuse, N.Y., Aug. 31, 1937; [4] s. Paul Oliver and Elizabeth H. (Thrun) G.; [5] m. Judith S. Gonzalez, Apr. 28, 1968; [6] children: Richard Gary, Matthew Cary, Samuel Perry. [7] BA, magna cum laude, U. Pa., 1960; MD, Harvard U., 1964. [8] Diplomate Am. Bd. Internal Medicine, Am. Bd. Preventive Medicine. [9] Intern Barnes Hosp., St. Louis, 1964-65, resident, 1965-66; clin. assoc. Nat. Heart Inst., NIH, Bethesda, Md., 1966-68; chief resident medicine U. Okla. Hosps., 1968-69; asst. prof. community health Okla. Med. Ctr., 1969-70, assoc. prof., 1970-74, prof., chmn. dept., 1974-80; dean U. Okla. Coll. Medicine, 1978-82; v.p. med. staff affairs Bapt. Med. Ctr., Oklahoma City, 1982-86, exec. v.p., 1986-88, chmn., 1988—; mem. governing bd. Ambulatory Health Care Consortium, Inc., 1979-80; mem. Okla. Bd. Medicolegal Examiners, 1985—. [10] Contbr. articles to profl. jours. [11] Bd. dirs., v.p. Okla. Arthritis Found., 1982—; trustee North Central Mental Health Ctr., 1985—. [12] Served with U.S. Army, 1955-56. [13] Recipient R.T. Chadwick award NIH, 1968; Am. Heart Assn. grantee, 1985-86, 88. [14] Fellow Assn. Tchrs. Preventive Medicine; mem. Am. Fedn. Clin. Research, Assn. Med. Colls., AAAS, AMA, Sigma Xi. [15] Republican. [16] Roman Catholic. [17] Clubs: Harvard (Oklahoma City); Miami Country. [18] Lodge: KC. [19] Avocations: swimming, weight lifting, numismatics. [20] Home: 6060 N Ridge Ave Oklahoma City OK 73126 [21] Office: Bapt Med Ctr 1986 Cuba Hwy Oklahoma City OK 73120

KEY

[1]	Name
[2]	Occupation
[3]	Vital Statistics
[4]	Parents
[5]	Marriage
[6]	Children
[7]	Education
[8]	Professional certifications
[9]	Career
[10]	Writings and creative works
[11]	Civic and political activities
[12]	Military
[13]	Awards and fellowships
[14]	Professional and association memberships
[15]	Political affiliation
[16]	Religion
[17]	Clubs
[18]	Lodges
[19]	Avocations
[20]	Home address
[21]	Office address

Fig. 14.2. "Key to Information" in *Who's Who in America*. Copyright © 1990-91, Marquis Who's Who, Inc. Reprinted by permission from *Who's Who in America*, 46th Edition, Volume 1, 1990-91.

Abbreviations, which are freely employed, are explained in a "Table of Abbreviations." A few entries conclude with brief, personal thoughts by the biographee, summarizing that individual's goals in life, principles for success, or similar statements. This last feature is a recent addition, apparently designed to add a personal touch to the collection of facts presented in the rest of the entry.

The most frequent use of *Who's Who in America* is to locate information about a specific individual, particularly basic facts such as address, birth date (age), degrees earned, awards received, or positions held. Most of the topics included in the entry will be requested at one time or another. The alphabetical arrangement of listings, with names in bold upper case, makes finding the desired entry fairly simple in most cases. However, one must watch out for names which are very similar, a situation which can lead to confusion or uncertainty as to which is the correct entry. As an example, in the forty-sixth edition, there are *seven* Robert Halls; each, fortunately, has a unique middle name. When middle names are not known, occupation, birth date, or address often helps to distinguish between individuals with the same name. Entries must be read carefully. Often, abbreviations will need to be checked, to be sure that one's hunch regarding them is correct. An asterisk at the end of an entry lets the user know that information in that entry was prepared by the publisher rather than by the biographee. In these cases, frequently changing information, such as address or current position, may not be as up-to-date or accurate as an entry for which the biographee supplied the information.

Who's Who in America is usually the first source to consult when a patron wants basic biographical data on a prominent American. A careful study of the positions that automatically ensure inclusion, along with a good working knowledge of the kind of data that is and is not provided, will give the reference librarian greater confidence that turning to this source will lead to the information requested.

Who's Who in America can be searched quickly and effectively online as well. The three latest editions constitute the DIALOG database Marquis Who's Who. This database is updated quarterly, so the information it contains is more current than the printed source. When searching online, one can combine elements from more than one part of the record, to retrieve, for instance, all members of a particular religious denomination who work in a specific occupation, or all persons who were born in a particular state who have a degree from a specific academic institution (remembering, of course, that these persons must be listed in *Who's Who in America*). Care must be taken, however, when searching geographic, occupational, and other fields in this database: not every individual in a particular occupation or holding a particular position will be indexed under the same term. For instance, one history teacher may enter "educator" on the data form, while another enters "historian." An advantage of searching *Who's Who in America* electronically is that one can choose to display and/or print only certain elements of the record, such as professional data or personal data. This can save much time and expense, if a number of records are printed. Nine formats in all are available as options for printing or displaying individual records in Marquis Who's Who.

Despite its comprehensiveness, *Who's Who in America* cannot list everyone with reference value. Persons of local or regional interest are often omitted. To provide better coverage at this level, Marquis Who's Who publishes four regional biographical directories modeled on *Who's Who in America*, one each for the East, Midwest, West, and South/Southwest. Adjacent areas of Canada (or Mexico) are included in each regional *Who's Who*. Each title lists some twenty to twenty-five thousand persons. Selection criteria are similar and data provided are the same as in the parent title, but overlap with that work is kept to a minimum. For information on business executives, professionals, educators, and government officials at the local and state level, these volumes can be very valuable reference tools. As with *Who's Who in America*, new editions of these regional biographical directories appear roughly every other year. The forty-sixth edition of *Who's Who in America* contains a list of individuals covered in the most recent editions of each of these regional directories.

Marquis Who's Who also publishes *Who's Who of American Women*, a new edition of which has appeared approximately every two years since 1958. The seventeenth edition lists some thirty thousand women (up from twenty-five thousand in the sixteenth edition) who have reference value because of achievement or position held. The entries in *Who's Who of American Women* contain the same personal, educational, and career information found in entries in *Who's Who in America*. Likewise, the criteria for inclusion — achievement and/or position held — are very similar to those of the parent work. Like the regional Marquis titles, *Who's Who of American Women* supplements *Who's Who in America*, although one could look in the former first rather than second when the individual about whom information is requested is an American woman.

Another work which supplements *Who's Who in America* is *Who's Who Among Black Americans*, the sixth edition of which was published in 1990. Since the fifth edition appeared in 1988, this title has been taken over by Gale Research. The sixth edition lists more than seventeen thousand individuals. Both the format and the standards of admission to this work are similar to those used for *Who's Who in America*. Information is generally supplied by the biographee. When compared to other biographical directories, professional athletes seem to have better representation in this work. Entries for blacks in other occupations, and in government, business, and the arts, are more detailed, giving more information, in some cases, than one would find in *Who's Who in America*. The sixth edition has added an obituaries section, which provides complete entries for persons who have died since their names appeared in the previous edition. *Who's Who Among Black Americans* has two very useful indexes, a geographical one and an occupational one. These allow the researcher to determine the numbers of high-achieving blacks in broad career areas or in specific geographical areas.

The British counterpart to *Who's Who in America* antedates its American imitation by some fifty years. First published in 1849, and the first biographical directory of its kind, it bears the simple title, *Who's Who*. As Ann Ricker noted, early editions merely listed nobility and those holding royal court positions; no biographical data were provided.[8] It was in 1897 that *Who's Who* first offered biographical information on those it listed. It also, in that year, broadened its scope to include those who by their abilities (not just by birth or position) had achieved national prominence. It was this expanded scope which provided the model for *Who's Who in America*.[9]

Today's criteria for inclusion in *Who's Who* are simply as stated in the 1990 edition: "the book aims to list people who, through their careers, affect the political, economic, scientific, and artistic life of the country."[10] This scope allows for the listing of a relatively large number of prominent foreigners, both from Commonwealth and from non-Commonwealth countries. The information provided about these individuals is very similar to that provided in *Who's Who in America* (however, the biographee's children's names are not generally given, and sometimes a spouse's name is omitted). The emphasis is on educational background and career history; current addresses are given. Like its American counterpart, avocational interests are also listed. Whenever possible, all data are provided by the biographee.

The arrangement of *Who's Who* is alphabetical by surname. There are no special indexes. Special sections include a list of abbreviations, a list of individuals who have died since the publication of the previous edition, and a section on the royal family, in which very brief biographical data are provided. Unlike *Who's Who in America*, *Who's Who* is published annually. It is indexed both in *Biography and Genealogy Master Index* and in *The Almanac of Famous People*.

Large libraries will purchase current biographical sources covering numerous other countries, in addition to those for North America and for the British Isles. Similar biographical directories in English exist for a number of Western European nations, along with titles covering multination areas such as Scandinavia. Directories in native languages for these countries are also available. There are also current biographical directories for some countries in Asia and Africa, although these tend to be updated less frequently than those for European countries.

Smaller libraries which lack funds for biographical directories for individual countries can rely on an international directory to provide information on a more select group of prominent persons from other parts of the world. The two major current sources are the *International Who's Who*, published annually by Europa, and *Who's Who in the World*, published approximately every other year by Marquis Who's Who. Both titles offer basic biographical data about business, government, religious, educational, scientific, and cultural leaders from many countries.

Who's Who in the World lists, in its tenth edition, about twenty-nine thousand individuals from around the globe, whose position or "notable achievements in their fields" gives them reference value.[11] The format is almost identical to that of *Who's Who in America*, and virtually the same types of data appear in the entries. There is a list of abbreviations employed and a list of rules used to alphabetize complex and compound names. There is, however, no list of those who have died since publication of the previous edition. This is an unfortunate omission, since the question of whether an individual is still alive or recently deceased occurs rather frequently in reference work.

The *International Who's Who* lists fewer persons (about twenty thousand in its fifty-fourth edition) but, because it is published annually, the information in the latest edition will often be more current than that in the latest edition of *Who's Who in the World*. The only clue to selection criteria given in the fifty-fourth edition is that this title provides biographical information about "our most famous and influential contemporaries."[12] Its usefulness in reference work, however, is enhanced by biographical entries for royal families throughout the world and by a list of those who have died (with date of death) since publication of the previous edition. The information provided for individuals listed is often more detailed than that in *Who's Who in the World*, and, frequently, a telephone number as well as a current address is given.

Two more specialized directories are very useful for finding biographical information on contemporary scholars. These are *American Men and Women of Science* and the *Directory of American Scholars*. The seventeenth edition of *American Men and Women of Science*, published in 1989, lists more than 100,000 of "today's leaders in physical, biological and related sciences" (such as mathematics, computer science, and the health sciences). Since its first publication in 1906, it has provided biographical data on more than 290,000 prominent North American scientists and engineers. The purpose of this standard biographical directory is clearly stated in its preface: it is to help scientists learn more about their colleagues and their colleagues' professional and research activities.

Only scientists who "have made significant contributions in their field" are included.[13] These individuals must be actively engaged in scientific work, must have conducted research (which is usually published, but may not be if it is classified), or must have attained a "position of substantial responsibility requiring scientific training or experience."[14] The data given for each scientist is provided by the biographee whenever possible. Personal data given includes birth date and place, marital status, and number of children. Professional data includes education, positions held, professional memberships, and research activities. A current mailing address is also given.

The biographical entries are listed alphabetically in seven volumes. The eighth volume is an index which lists biographees under more than 150 specific disciplines. *American Men and Women of Science* can be searched electronically on DIALOG. Online, each element in the entry is searchable by keyword, so that one can study, in various ways, the geographic, educational, and professional backgrounds, and the research activities and interests of all who are included. The database contains entries only from the most recent edition of its printed counterpart. SciTech Reference Plus, a CD-ROM product from Bowker Electronic Publishing, includes complete data from *American Men and Women of Science*, along with four other scientific databases.

A similar source for the humanities is the *Directory of American Scholars*. This work lists, in its eighth edition (1982), some 37,500 scholars who are "currently active in teaching, research and publishing."[15] While three specific criteria for admission are given, essentially one must have published scholarly works to be listed. The fields covered in the four-volume set include history, English, drama, languages, philosophy, religion, and law, as well as a number of other fields related to these. Each volume covers several fields, but entries in each volume are in one alphabetical list. Each of the four volumes has a geographic index, which gives the name and subject area of biographees who live in the various cities and towns of the United States and Canada. Volume 4 contains an alphabetical index to the entire set, which can be consulted if one does not know the field of activity of a particular individual about whom information is requested.

Each entry provides birth date and place, marital status, number of children, educational background, positions held, honors and awards received, areas of research, titles of important publications, and mailing address. The fact that new editions of this title appear so infrequently makes the current position and address data suspect.

Current Biographical Dictionaries

Since 1940, *Current Biography* has offered librarians and users readable, objective, and carefully researched biographical essays about persons in a broad range of fields "who are prominent in the news."[16] While some of the information presented is obtained from the individuals themselves, the essays are based primarily on articles which have appeared in newspapers and magazines. The style of the essays is analytical within a narrative context. Generally, a chronological overview of the individual's life is given, with the major focus on the contributions, achievements, or events which have brought that person to prominence. Details of the individual's private life (family, appearance, interests) are well integrated with a complete history of his or her public career. Each essay includes a photograph of the biographee, as well as a list of the articles and, occasionally, books upon which the essay is based. For library patrons wanting part or all of a life history without reading a full biography, *Current Biography* is an excellent choice. It is also an excellent choice when a patron is looking for specific biographical data not found in most biographical directories, such as a person's height, dress, or general lifestyle. Although some prominent individuals from other nations are included, most entries are for Americans.

Current Biography is published monthly, from January through November. Each issue contains fifteen to twenty biographical essays, arranged alphabetically, a slightly smaller number of short obituary notices, and a cumulative index for the year's issues to that point. At the end of each year, the essays from the eleven monthly issues are cumulated in one alphabet in the *Current Biography Yearbook*. Each yearbook thus provides essays on approximately 175 to 200 individuals and obituary notices on 125 to 150 prominent persons who died during the year. Generally, obituary notices are restricted to those persons whose biographies appeared in earlier issues of *Current Biography*. Each obituary provides references both to a full-length article in an earlier issue of *Current Biography* and to a *New York Times* obituary. For example, "See *Current Biography* [May] 1963 Obituary *NY Times* p1 + S 23 '89." The yearbook also provides an index by profession for the current year, as well as a cumulative index to yearbooks from the current decade (e.g., 1981-89 in the 1989 yearbook). Indexes covering longer periods are published periodically; the latest covers the period from 1940 to 1985.

Since 1940, a number of individuals whose prominence led to inclusion in *Current Biography* have continued to flourish, leading to new achievements and renewed reference interest in their lives. In these cases, new biographical essays have appeared in *Current Biography* with a note that the earlier essay has now been superseded. While this policy of printing new, updated essays is laudable, it also reveals a weakness of "current" sources such as this, namely that the essays they provide can become outdated within a few years. Until a new essay appears, reference librarians must check other sources for the most recent information about an individual's life and career.

Originally titled "Contemporary Newsmakers," *Newsmakers* was introduced in 1985 by Gale Research, publishers of the excellent and highly successful biographical dictionary, *Contemporary Authors* (discussed later). Following the same general format as its predecessor, *Newsmakers* is designed to complement and supplement *Contemporary Authors* by providing biographical information about prominent individuals who are not writers. Like *Current Biography*, *Newsmakers* covers all fields, from government and business to entertainment and sports. It provides slightly better coverage than does *Current Biography* in certain fields, particularly sports, popular music, and entertainment; business leaders are also well represented. For this reason, it is an important reference source for public libraries, although students at all levels will look in their school and college libraries, also, for information on prominent individuals in the area of popular culture.

Newsmakers is published in three quarterly paperback issues, each containing about fifty entries. At the end of each year, a hardcover cumulated volume is published, which adds about 50 entries to the 150 which appeared in the quarterly issues. The cumulated volume also includes about fifty obituary notices which are longer and more detailed than those provided in *Current Biography*. Two cumulative indexes (1985-) help users to find articles about persons of a particular nationality or occupation anywhere in the set. There is also a cumulative alphabetical index, as well as a cumulative subject index listing entries under subject terms and proper names.

Each entry begins with a listing of personal and career data similar to what one would find in a biographical directory. The main part of the entry, "Sidelights," consists of a narrative and analytical essay on the individual's life and career. The style and content of these essays is similar to what one would find in *Current Biography*. The information is gathered primarily from newspaper and magazine articles, which are cited in the final section of each entry, "Sources." The author's name is provided for each "Sidelights" essay.

As mentioned above, *Newsmakers* excels in its coverage of newsworthy individuals in fields such as sports, theater and television, and popular music, while also covering more traditional fields such as business and government. Although there is overlap between *Newsmakers* and *Current Biography*, having access to both sets increases the reference librarian's chances of finding a well-written, objective account of the life and career of any of the hundreds of individuals whose prominence in a given field makes them likely subjects of reference questions.

Although probably not a favorite reference tool among beginners, due to the fact that it is made up of several separate series, *Contemporary Authors* has proven its worth to reference librarians. One of its strongest assets is that the term *authors* is very liberally interpreted to include not only writers of books, but media writers (i.e., scriptwriters), journalists, critics, musicians, and many individuals whose prominence is primarily in other fields, such as Martin Luther King, Jr. and Paul "Bear" Bryant, but who have also written something of significance. Its coverage is thus much broader than the title suggests. The entire set now includes entries on more than ninety-two thousand individuals. In addition, entries requiring revision are rewritten in a timely fashion. These features make *Contemporary Authors* an obvious first choice for many reference librarians faced with a question about the life or works of a twentieth-century writer.

Contemporary Authors contains three types of entries. "Brief Entries" provide basic personal and career information similar to what might be found in a biographical directory. "Sketches" provide the same data and also include a biographical essay which may extend over several double-columned pages. "Obituaries" are composed of a brief notice of an individual's life and important writings. All three types contain references for further reading or research; generally, these are to full-length biographies, magazine articles, or entries in other reference works. All three types of entries are arranged in one alphabetical sequence for ease of use.

The organization and publication of *Contemporary Authors* are complex. Volumes in the primary ongoing series, or "Original Volumes," appear about twice each year. The second of these semiannual volumes contains a cumulative index to the entire set of *Contemporary Authors* (all series). It is this index which must be checked first in any reference query search, in order to find which, if any, volume in one of the series contains an entry for a given person. The other major ongoing series is the "New Revision" series; volumes in this series are also published at the approximate rate of two per year. In these volumes, all entries are revisions of entries which appeared in the Original Volumes (vols. 45-) or in the "First Revisions" series (vols. 1-44), which is now closed. Two other series are the "Autobiographical" series, wherein writers provide their own analyses of their lives and works, and the "Bibliographical" series, which lists works by and about contemporary writers. Since the two main ongoing series generally list references for further reading and often contain information gathered by personal interview, these last two series merely provide more comprehensive autobiographical and bibliographical information than is usually available in the Original Volumes or the New Revisions series. They would be more useful for the patron pursuing serious research than for the patron merely seeking information about an author's life or writings.

Once one learns the abbreviations used in the cumulative index for the various series, finding the most recent entry on an individual is not difficult. Adding somewhat to the confusion, however, is the fact that references to entries in other Gale Research publications, such as the *Dictionary of Literary Biography*, are also included in the *Contemporary Authors* index. With experience, one learns to regard this practice as an aid to finding additional information rather than as a complicating factor in an already rather complex reference tool.

A Gale Research publication which is comparable to *Contemporary Authors* but which is aimed primarily at children's and young adult librarians and school students is *Something About the Author*. This set offers information very similar to that found in *Contemporary Authors*, such as lists of personal and career facts, and a complete list of writings or other creative products such as filmscripts or recordings. Some entries include lengthy "Sidelights" essays which provide an overview of the person's life and importance in his or her field. The scope of *Something About the Author* includes authors and illustrators of works "created intentionally for children and young adults as well as those written for a general audience and known to interest younger readers."[17] It is heavily illustrated. Several volumes are published each year, and alternate volumes contain a cumulative index to the entire set. Beginning with volume 50, an index of fictional characters, leading the user to entries about their creators, is provided every four volumes.

Retrospective Biographical Dictionaries: Universal

The *McGraw-Hill Encyclopedia of World Biography*, one of the largest modern biographical reference tools, was compiled specifically for students in secondary schools and colleges. The selection of names was made with curriculum needs in mind. Historical outlines of various areas and topics were compiled and reviewed by specialists in each area, and the names of persons associated with those topics and areas were inserted into the outline. It is significant that biographees for this work were chosen "by the standard of representativeness"—whether their lives accurately and meaningfully illuminate particular historical developments in specific parts of the world—rather than "by conventional standards of importance or familiarity."[18] An effort was made to ensure that Asian and African historical figures were well represented among the five thousand names selected for inclusion. It is also a significant and unusual feature of this set that living persons may be included.

This encyclopedia is composed of eleven volumes of text and a twelfth volume containing an index and study guides. Each entry is written by an authority in the field with which the biographee is associated (there are, in all, 884 authors listed in volume 12). Entry length varies from several paragraphs to several pages. Portraits are included whenever possible, and there are numerous other illustrations. Each essay concludes with a "Further Reading" section composed of cross-references to other entries in this set and a short bibliographical essay to lead the student to other published sources (in English).

The *McGraw-Hill Encyclopedia of World Biography* can be used either as an aid to research on a given topic or person or to locate specific facts about an individual. Its topical basis enhances its value for research purposes. The study guides in volume 12, though not very detailed, do allow one to develop a list of persons who were associated with significant events, eras, or historical trends. These trends or events can then be studied by means of the individuals who were involved with them. The bibliographical essays, though now somewhat dated, help the student to locate further sources of background information or to find more detailed scholarly studies about a person or topic. For ready reference purposes, one can be fairly confident that the dates and facts given are accurate, since the authors of each essay have been chosen for their expertise in that area. The index is quite detailed. It lists subjects and corporate names, as well as personal names, and can be used to locate all entries in which a specific individual or topic (e.g., Huguenots) is discussed. Like the study guides, it leads the reader to other entries relevant to the topic.

A more specialized multivolume biographical dictionary aimed at an educated audience is the *Dictionary of Scientific Biography*. Like the *McGraw-Hill Encyclopedia of World Biography*, one of the purposes of this dictionary is to help the user study a topic — in this case, the history of science — through essays on the lives and contributions of eminent persons in that field. The subject areas covered in the *Dictionary of Scientific Biography* are those of the physical and biological sciences and mathematics. Individuals whose primary contributions were in the fields of medicine, technology, or the social sciences are not generally included. The *Dictionary of Scientific Biography* is international in scope, although the history of science in the western world predominates. This imbalance is partially corrected by essays on the history of science in non-Western cultures which were added in the first supplement (volume 15). The second supplement (volumes 17-18) adds essays on twentieth-century scientists who were not included in the original set.

The *Dictionary of Scientific Biography* provides scholarly and very readable essays on several thousand prominent scientists from the past, written by contemporary scientists or historians of science from around the world. Each entry begins with the date and place of the person's birth and death. The essay which follows ranges from one column for more obscure figures to many pages on the most important scientific figures. The essays are all based on extensive study of the relevant primary and secondary literature and constitute, in some cases, a significant contribution to existing knowledge about the individual's accomplishments and importance. The focus is on the career and scientific contributions of each biographee, rather than on details of personal or family life. Each essay is followed by an extensive bibliography, listing published works, locations of papers, secondary literature, and any available bibliographies devoted to that individual.

The index (volume 16) is very detailed. Many subject terms are employed, allowing the user to locate and trace developments in specific scientific areas, such as "fluids" or "retina," in various biographical entries. In addition to subjects and personal names, the index also lists corporate names, such as "Johns Hopkins University," and the names of scientific journals and societies. The index volume also contains "Lists of Scientists by Field." Here entries are listed alphabetically under eight broad headings such as "Astronomy" and "Earth Sciences." Unfortunately, this list is not very useful, because, unlike the main index, the terms chosen are not specific enough to produce a manageable number of entries under each heading.

For libraries where research questions in historical or scientific fields are infrequent, the *Concise Dictionary of Scientific Biography*, published in 1981, can be used instead of the longer set. It contains an entry for each individual included in the *Dictionary of Scientific Biography* and its first supplement. The essay format is preserved for significant figures. In other entries, basic facts of the person's life and career are listed in one paragraph.

For ready reference purposes, two standard sources offering briefer information but more comprehensive coverage are *Webster's New Biographical Dictionary* and the *New Century Cyclopedia of Names*. *Webster's Biographical Dictionary* was originally published in 1943, went through more than twenty updated printings, and was finally thoroughly revised and published in 1983 as *Webster's New Biographical Dictionary*, which is quite different from its predecessor. Of particular importance is the heightened emphasis placed on historical figures from Third World countries. However, the inclusion of more Third World names, along with the reduction in total number of entries from forty thousand to thirty thousand, means that many names that had been in the original edition were dropped from *Webster's New*. Also dropped were useful lists of world leaders and important U.S. government officials, such as Cabinet officers. Consequently, many reference collections will retain both titles on their shelves.

Webster's New offers short, one-paragraph descriptions of the important contributions of approximately thirty thousand persons from the past. Like its predecessor, it provides a syllabic division of each surname, along with a guide to the pronunciation of the name. This pronunciation guide is usually limited to the surname; pronunciations for a long list of given names and titles is provided at the end of the volume. Under each name, in addition to birth and death dates, significant events in the individual's career are described, and the dates of these are given. If appropriate, nicknames and pseudonyms are provided, which is very useful since both are often requested by patrons. *Composite entries* are used occasionally. In these entries, two or more members of a family are treated in one entry. In composite entries, the heading is either the name of the most famous member of the family or the surname by itself. In the case of popes, kings, and other rulers, the composite entry will be headed simply by the common personal name. There are numerous cross-references from variant names, pseudonyms, and titled names to the form of the name under which the entry appears (e.g., "Eliot, George. See Mary Ann Evans"). Lists of abbreviations and pronunciation symbols used in *Webster's New* are provided at the front of the volume.

The *New Century Cyclopedia of Names* is broader in coverage, including entries for places, events, literary works, and fictitious and mythological characters, as well as for important people from the past. As the preface states, it provides "the essential facts about more than 100,000 proper names of every description" of interest to persons "in the English-speaking world."[19] Thus, while many non-Western names are included, they are likely to be those traditionally of interest to British and American citizens. Although now more than thirty-five years old, it is, because of its broad scope, a valuable biographical reference tool. There are times when patrons will be uncertain as to whether the names about which they seek information represent persons who actually lived or mythological or fictitious characters.

Like *Webster's New*, the *New Century Cyclopedia of Names* provides guidance on the pronunciation of surnames, and gives the place and date of the person's birth and death. Some entries are significantly longer than those found in *Webster's*, giving a detailed outline of the person's life and career, including the dates of important events or achievements and a list of significant writings. Shorter entries offer only a summary of the person's importance. Appendixes in volume 3 include a detailed chronological outline of world history, lists of the rulers of many nations, a list of popes, and lists of British prime ministers and U.S. presidents. These lists are very valuable, but those that continue past the mid-twentieth century are out-of-date and must be supplemented by more recent sources.

Retrospective Biographical
Dictionaries: National

United States. The most authoritative source for extensive biographical information about important deceased Americans is the *Dictionary of American Biography*, often referred to simply as the *DAB*. Like *Who's Who in America*, the *DAB* was inspired by a famous British work of the same kind, in this case the *Dictionary of National Biography* (discussed later). The original twenty volumes of the *DAB* were published between 1928 and 1936, and the index was published in 1937. Since that time, eight supplements have appeared; the latest, published in 1988, covers the lives of significant Americans who died during the years 1966 to 1970. The total number of biographical essays in the entire set of 29 volumes now totals 18,110. While in some cases it no longer represents the latest scholarship, the *DAB* is often the best place to begin one's search for information on these historically significant individuals.

Entries are arranged alphabetically by surname in one alphabet throughout the original twenty-volume set; the supplements each contain their own alphabetic arrangement as well. Entirely in essay format, entries all begin with a sentence which gives the birth and death dates, the occupation, and the parents and place of birth of the biographee. Thereafter, they proceed in generally chronological order, with the length and amount of detail provided about the individuals' lives and careers depending both on the importance of the individuals and on the plenitude or scarcity of available information about their lives. The essays are quite readable and vary in length from a couple of paragraphs to several pages; a very few cover more than ten pages. While the focus is on the individual's public life, private and family life are not slighted. All entries have been written by scholars, whose names appear in each volume containing one of their contributions and in the complete list in the index volume. Each entry concludes with a list of sources on which the essay is based; longer entries end with a short bibliographical essay noting important primary and secondary sources. These, of course, are now quite dated and must be updated by reference to more recent bibliographical sources.

The criterion for inclusion in the *Dictionary of American Biography* is that one must have made "some significant contribution to American life in its manifold aspects."[20] In addition, if not born in the original colonies or in the United States, one must have "identified [oneself] with the country and contributed notably to its history."[21] By the 1960s, it was thought by many that the original twenty volumes in particular included too high a percentage of white males, while not sufficiently recognizing the contributions of many women and members of minority groups. This led to the independent creation of retrospective biographical dictionaries devoted solely to one of these groups, some of which are discussed in this chapter.

The entries in the *DAB* may be located through the index to the original twenty-volume set and through the cumulative indexes to the supplements which appear at the end of each supplement. While the indexes to supplements offer only access by name, the index to the original set provides several different types of access to *DAB* entries. In addition to an alphabetical list of all the 13,633 entries in the original twenty volumes, this index contains lists of names by occupation, by state of birth, and by college or university attended. There is also a detailed topical index, allowing the user to investigate numerous events and developments in American history through the biographical essays in the *DAB*. The topical index includes many proper nouns, such as the names of institutions, periodicals and newspapers, and religious and political bodies.

In 1964, a *Concise Dictionary of American Biography* appeared. The third edition, published in 1980, provides, in one volume, brief entries for each individual included in the *DAB* up to 1960. Some entries here offer only basic vital and career facts and a one-sentence summary of achievements. For more important figures, a short essay sums up each life and its significance. This volume will answer many ready reference questions, but those library users interested in full biographical information for research purposes will need to consult the main *DAB* set.

The *National Cyclopedia of American Biography* offers, in its seventy-six volumes, biographical essays on nearly seventy thousand Americans, almost four times the number included in the *DAB*. This work, while lacking the critical approach and scholarly tone of the *DAB*, has many unique and important features. Begun in 1891, it sought from the beginning to include business persons, engineers, inventors, and others who had been neglected in favor of clerics, statesmen, and literary figures in traditional biographical sources. It also sought to include living persons and individuals with regional as well as national eminence. Portraits, some of them full-page, or line drawings (or photographs in recent volumes) accompany each biographical entry whenever possible. Finally, arrangement in each volume is not alphabetical. Rather, biographees are grouped by occupation or area of work; thus, for instance, the sketches of Supreme Court justices of a given period appear together.

Volumes of the *National Cyclopedia of American Biography* appeared in one numbered series until 1926. From that year on, the "Permanent Series," containing essays on deceased persons continued the numbered series, while a new "Current Series," containing essays on living individuals, was published simultaneously, using letters rather than numbers. The last volume in the set, published in 1984, was numbered N-63, indicating that the two series had again merged (and were now closed). Most essays on individuals appearing in the Current Series were revised and transferred to the Permanent Series upon the death of the biographees.

The essays in both series are based on information supplied by the biographees and their families, supplemented by research by the anonymous writer of the essay. The entries vary in length from a one-paragraph sketch to an essay of several pages. There are no bibliographies or suggestions for further reading.

Because of the two series and the lack of an alphabetical arrangement in individual volumes, the index must be used to find specific entries in the *National Cyclopedia of American Biography*. This index, published separately in 1984, covers all seventy-six volumes in the set. There are subject terms and place and corporate names, as well as personal names, in the index, so that information about these can be located in the biographical essays. Thus, the *National Cyclopedia of American Biography* can be used for ready reference questions, such as "Who developed the first liquid India ink?," and also for research into the history of institutions and organizations.

To meet the demand for a more comprehensive, scholarly assessment of American women and blacks, two titles modeled on the *DAB* have been published. The *DAB* provided entries for only eighty-one blacks; the *Dictionary of American Negro Biography* (*DANB*) offers scholarly accounts of the lives of several hundred historically significant blacks.[22] Many of these individuals made important contributions to the (segregated) Negro community, rather than to the white society at large. Some had local rather than national eminence. Together, these entries provide "illustrations of the broad participation of Negroes in the development of the United States."[23]

The signed entries in the *DANB* are the work of more than two hundred contributors. The essays vary in length from one-half page to several pages. Both public and private lives of the biographees are chronicled; for writers, significant works are discussed. Vital facts and family information are generally provided. The essays are very well written, and each concludes with a list of sources upon which the account is based. Arrangement of the volume is alphabetical; no indexes are included.

A larger work, providing scholarly essays on approximately eighteen hundred historically significant American women, is *Notable American Women*. This set was published in two installments: the first three volumes, published in 1971, bear the subtitle "1607-1950"; volume 4, "the Modern Period," focuses on women who died between 1951 and 1975. This last volume was published in 1980. The compilation of this reference work was underwritten by Radcliffe College, and was inspired by that college's important collection of women's studies materials, now called the Arthur and Elizabeth Schlesinger Library. Both the three-volume original set and the supplementary volume were put together under the guidance of impressive scholarly advisory boards. The result is a set with value for ready reference purposes, as well as for research guidance to students of women's history.

Modeled on the *DAB*, each entry in *Notable American Women* contains a fairly lengthy life history (generally a page or two of small print in double columns). Significant personal and career events and achievements are presented in a smooth, easy-to-read narrative. Biographees included must have had American citizenship or have lived here and contributed to American society in a way that transcends purely local significance. Each entry concludes with a list of primary and secondary sources for further research. Numerous vocations are represented among the women whose lives are presented, and, at the ends of both volume 3 and volume 4, indexes by occupation are provided. Both volume 1 and volume 4 contain introductory chapters which offer an overview of women's history during the periods covered (pre- and post-1950, respectively), based largely on the biographical essays themselves.

This title, like the *DAB*, the *DANB*, and the *National Cyclopedia of American Biography*, was published as a reference work and aid to research. However, these works are so well written and engaging that, unlike most reference books, they can also be read simply for pleasure.

An important retrospective source which many will consult, but few will read for pleasure, is *Who Was Who in America*. In 1990 this set numbered nine volumes, each of which reproduces entries from *Who's Who in America* or one of its regional counterparts for individuals who are recently deceased. In addition, an "Historical Volume, 1607-1896," provides entries for important Americans who died before the existence of *Who's Who in America*. This set now lists some seventeen thousand individuals. A new volume is added to *Who Was Who in America* every four or five years. On each of these occasions, a new cumulative index is also published, so that with a single search one can locate an individual entry anywhere in the set. *Who Was Who in America* is often the logical first choice for basic factual data about deceased prominent Americans.

Great Britain. Covering prominent deceased persons from England, Wales, Scotland, and Ireland as well as those from British colonies and non-British citizens who lived in England and contributed to its history, the *Dictionary of National Biography* (*DNB*) was originally published during the period from 1885 to 1901. A year later, a supplement appeared, describing the lives of one thousand individuals who were omitted from the original set or who died in the years during which the *DNB* was published. Since that date, eight other supplements have been published, each of which treats individuals who died during one decade of the twentieth century, up to 1980. Each supplement contains a cumulative index covering the years 1901-date. In an unusual but efficient formula, volume 1 of the *Concise Dictionary of National Biography* serves as an index to the original set and its first supplement, while also giving a brief overview of the life of each individual treated in that set. The second volume of the concise version offers, as of 1990, a brief history for each biographee who died during the period 1901-1970 (this volume is periodically revised); no reference is made to the longer entries in the supplements, but one can generally tell, by the date of death, where the full entry will be. There are no subject or corporate name indexes to the *DNB*. Thus, unlike some other biographical dictionaries, it cannot be effectively used for questions dealing with subjects rather than persons.

As of 1990, the *DNB* offered biographical essays about 36,450 individuals. These essays average about a page in length, although many are shorter and some are much longer (that on Queen Victoria covers over one hundred pages). Each essay describes the life and significance of its subject, including pertinent facts and dates from the subject's personal and public lives. The essays are in general quite readable, although those in the original set are written in a style rather different from today's. All are written by scholars and end with a list of sources upon which the essay is based. These bibliographies are sometimes quite extensive, but, in those cases where personal knowledge played an important role, are quite brief.

Bibliographical references are also sometimes given in the text of the article and not repeated at the end.

For ready reference purposes, *Who Was Who* performs the same service for Great Britain that *Who Was Who in America* provides for the United States. Entries which appeared in *Who's Who* during an individual's life are transferred to *Who Was Who* after that person dies. The date of death is added, and any necessary corrections are made. The first volume of *Who Was Who* covered the period 1897-1916. Since then, the publication schedule has settled into a pattern of one volume every ten years; the latest volume covers the decade 1971-1980. A cumulated index, which includes names from all *Who Was Who* volumes (1897-1980) was published separately in 1981.

Reference librarians in large academic and public libraries will also need to consult retrospective biographical sources for other nations. Descriptions of these can be found in Sheehy's *Guide to Reference Books*.[24]

Indirect Sources

Indirect biographical sources, which tell the user where information about individuals may be found rather than providing that information directly, are helpful in several ways. If librarians are not sure which title is a likely source for the answer to a biographical question, or if they have tried one or several titles without success, they can consult an indirect source to identify relevant and appropriate titles. Or, if the direct sources already checked provide only a partial answer to the question, an indirect source can lead to other titles where more detailed information may be found. Finally, an indirect source is the best place to start a search for information about an individual if a number of different articles or books are requested by a patron who is seeking extensive information or a variety of perspectives. In all these situations, indirect sources serve essentially as indexes to biographical reference tools and to a broader range of biographical literature.

Among indirect biographical sources, *Biography and Genealogy Master Index* (*BGMI*) offers the most comprehensive coverage of current and retrospective biographical sources. In its printed form, it has appeared (as of 1990) in eight base volumes (1981) and annual updates; the annual updates, can, at considerable cost, be replaced by two cumulated indexes covering the years 1981-85 and 1986-90. Online on DIALOG, all are searchable in one database called Biography Master Index. Each annual volume indexes titles published since the compilation of the previous volume. Together, these volumes provide citations to more than six million entries in several hundred biographical sources. These sources are of all kinds: retrospective and current, directories and dictionaries, annual publications and nonserial titles. American biographical tools are the most common, but sources covering other countries are indexed as well. *BGMI* even indexes another indirect source, *Biography Index*.

Of course, many of the six million citations to be found in *BGMI* are duplications, in that they refer the user to a number of similar entries in different works or in different editions of the same work. For instance, an online search for biographical entries about Bob Dylan would produce more than sixty citations, including several for *Who's Who in America* (different editions) and several more for *International Who's Who*, which would give the reader about the same information as the entries in *Who's Who in America*. However, one can find information about Bob Dylan fairly easily; the greatest value of *BGMI* is for locating information about less famous individuals, when the librarian is not sure where to begin the search for information.

In both its print and online versions, *BGMI* lists names exactly as they appear in the indexed sources. Consequently, the same individual may be represented under more than one form of his or her name, such as with and without middle name or initial, or under both given name and nickname. For example, former President Carter is listed under "James Earl" and "James Earl, Jr." in one column, and under "Jimmy," "Jimmy, Jr.," and "Jimmy

Earl, Jr." in another column (see figure 14.3). These variations can be identified in the printed volumes with *careful study*; when searching online, one would need to use the "expand" command to identify them.

Carter, J H *DcVicP 2*
Carter, Mrs. J H *DcWomA*
Carter, J Harmon 1910- *St&PR 87*
Carter, J Howard, Jr. 1930- *St&PR 87*
Carter, J M *DcVicP 2*
Carter, J O *Dun&B 86*
Carter, J Wesley 1940- *St&PR 87*
Carter, Jack *InB&W 85*
Carter, Jack 1922- *HalFC 84*
Carter, Jack 1923- *EncAFC, IntMPA 86, –88*
Carter, Jack 1947- *BioIn 14*
Carter, Jack Franklin 1919- *AmMWSc 86P, –89P, WhoMW 86*
Carter, Jack Lee 1929- *AmMWSc 86P, –89P*
Carter, Jaine Marie 1936- *WhoWor 87*
Carter, Jaine Marie 1946- *WhoAm 86, –88, WhoSSW 84, WhoWor 89*
Carter, James *BioIn 15*
Carter, James 1935- *WhoWor 87*
Carter, James Byars 1934- *WhoSSW 84, –86, –88*
Carter, James C 1931- *WhoAm 86*
Carter, James Cedric 1905-1981 *BioIn 13, –14*
Carter, James Clarence 1927- *AmMWSc 86P, –89P, WhoAm 86, –88, WhoRel 85, WhoSSW 84, –86, –88*
Carter, James Dudley 1938- *WhoFl 85, –87, WhoSSW 84*
Carter, James E 1931- *Dun&B 86, –88*
Carter, James E 1935- *ConAu 22NR*
Carter, James E 1944- *WhoTech 84, –89*
Carter, James Earl 1924- *AmOrTwC, BioIn 14, –15, EncWB*
Carter, James Earl, Jr. *BioIn 13*
Carter, James Earl, Jr. 1924- *Who 85, –88, WhoSSW 84, –86, WhoWor 89*
Carter, James Earl, Jr. 1943- *WhoBlA 85, –88*
Carter, James Edward 1929- *AmMWSc 86P, –89P*

Carter, *WhoAmA 86, –89, WhoE 86, WhoEmL 87*
Carter, Jesse Benedict 1872-1917 *WhAmArt 85*
Carter, Jesse Lee, Sr. 1926- *WhoBlA 85*
Carter, Jessie Anita 1948- *WhoAmW 89*
Carter, Jimmy *PeoHis, WrDr 88*
Carter, Jimmy 1924- *Benet 87, BioIn 13, –14, –15, DcAmC, PresAR, WhoAm 86, WhoAmP 87, WhoEng 88, WhoSSW 88, WhoWor 84, –87*
Carter, Jimmy, Jr. 1924- *WhoAm 88*
Carter, Jimmy Derrel 1951- *WhoSSW 88*
Carter, Jimmy Earl, Jr. 1924- *WhoAmP 85*
Carter, Joan Elizabeth 1937- *WhoBlA 85, –88*
Carter, Joan Lenea 1936- *WhoRel 85*
Carter, Joan P 1943- *St&PR 87*
Carter, Joe *BioIn 15*
Carter, Joe 1951- *WhoAm 88*
Carter, Joe M 1948- *Dun&B 88*
Carter, Joel Steven *Law&B 84*
Carter, Joel William 1932- *WhoWest 87*
Carter, John 1737-1781 *BioIn 14*
Carter, John 1910- *ClaDrA*
Carter, John 1929- *BioIn 13*
Carter, John 1937- *BioIn 13, –14, InB&W 85*
Carter, Sir John *InB&W 85*
Carter, Sir John 1919- *Who 85, –88*
Carter, John A *Dun&B 88*
Carter, John A 1924- *WhoTech 89*
Carter, John A, Jr. 1934- *Dun&B 86*
Carter, John Allen, Jr. 1934- *St&PR 87, WhoAm 88, WhoFl 85*
Carter, John Avery 1924- *WhoAm 86, –88, WhoE 86, –89*
Carter, John B 1934- *Dun&B 86, –88*
Carter, John B, Jr. 1924- *Dun&B 86, St&PR 87*
Carter, John Bernard 1934- *St&PR 87, WhoAm 86, –88, WhoE 85, –86, –89,*

Fig. 14.3. Multiple entries in *Biography and Genealogy Master Index*. Selections from *Biography and Genealogy Master Index* 1986-90 Cumulation, 1990, Volume 1, edited by Barbara McNeil. Copyright © 1990 by Gale Research Inc. Reprinted by permission of the publisher.

Entries in each volume of the printed series are listed alphabetically by surname. Each entry consists of the person's name, birth date (and death date if the citation is to a retrospective source) and an abbreviation for the title where the entry will be found. The user must search the "Bibliographic Key to Source Codes" at the beginning of the volume to find the full title for the work containing the biographical entry represented in the index. The difficulty in using *BGMI* in its printed version is in knowing which volume to search first. If the individual about whom information is requested is deceased, the base set may be the best place to start. However, for someone currently in the news, the latest annual update would be the preferred starting point. In either situation, one may be forced to look through several volumes before locating a citation to an entry for a specific individual.

When access to DIALOG databases is available, an online search is the most effective and efficient way to use *BGMI*. DIALOG's Biography Master Index, File 287, contains the entire *BGMI* set, allowing one to search the base set and all of the annual updates simultaneously. A search of this database will quickly determine if any of the sources indexed contains entries for the individual about whom information is sought. Using the "expand" command, entries for all versions of the individual's name can be located; if a printer is attached to the computer terminal, all citations can be printed out for the convenience of the librarian and the user. In cases in which multiple citations are retrieved (as in the Bob Dylan search), the librarian can advise the patron as to which source appears most relevant to the patron's specific need. Another advantage of searching online is that full titles of publications are displayed, saving the librarian or patron the step of searching through a list of source codes to find this information.

Another Gale Research publication, the *Almanac of Famous People* (formerly titled *Biography Almanac*), offers an alternative to *BGMI* which is less comprehensive but also cheaper and easier to use. The *Almanac of Famous People* is both a direct and an indirect source of information about prominent persons. Based on many of the same sources as *BGMI*, it indexes each source selectively rather than comprehensively, including only those individuals who have achieved fame in some area. While it lists famous persons from all historical eras and places, there is a heavy emphasis upon twentieth-century figures. For each individual listed, brief factual information is provided: birth and death dates, occupation, and a descriptive phrase indicating the person's chief accomplishment. Then, citations to entries in other biographical reference sources are given, in codes similar to those used in *BGMI*. Thus, the briefest of information about an individual may be obtained directly, and, unlike the printed version of *BGMI*, all citations to other biographical sources can be found in one place.

Revised every few years, the fourth edition (1989) lists some twenty-five thousand names and provides references to more than three hundred biographical works. The first two volumes contain the biographical entries. Volume 3 provides three indexes to the names in volumes 1 and 2: a chronological index, listing all entries who were born or who died on each day of the year; a geographic index, listing all names by place of birth or death; and an occupational index, listing individuals by general career titles, such as "actor," "broadcast journalist," and "poet." A quick perusal of the latter two indexes reveals that media personalities, sports figures, and political leaders are heavily represented, and that non-Americans are well represented in *Almanac of Famous People*. For reference purposes, the chronological index may be the most useful; one can use it to find out which famous persons were born on a specific day, such as the patron's birthday.

Both *BGMI* and *Almanac of Famous People* index primarily other reference works, such as biographical directories and biographical dictionaries. For access to biographical information in the general scholarly and popular literature, the best source is *Biography Index*. Produced by the H. W. Wilson Co., publishers of a number of standard indexes in various fields, *Biography Index* appears quarterly with annual and biennial cumulations. It provides references to biographical articles in more than two thousand periodicals, to book-length individual and collective biographies, to entries in reference works, and to other formats such as interviews, obituaries, and book reviews. Biographical articles cited are from periodicals indexed in one of the other Wilson topical indexes. Many of these are of a popular nature, but many citations from scholarly journals are also included. The articles and books indexed in *Biography Index* discuss persons from all historical periods as well as those from the present day.

Arrangement of each issue and cumulation is alphabetical by surname of the individual who is the subject of the article or book cited. Each entry gives the name and occupation of the individual, and many give birth date and, if applicable, death date; this information helps to distinguish the individual from others with the same or a similar name. Citations provide standard bibliographical information, such as author, title, and publication data, as well as year of publication and (for periodical articles) volume and page numbers. There is also an occupational index which lists under each occupation the names of those individuals in that occupation for whom citations to biographical articles or books may be found in that issue or cumulated volume. *Biography Index* is available both in CD-ROM format and for online dial-up searching. The CD-ROM database allows patrons to conduct searches using a menu-driven approach, although the command language normally used by librarians in online searching is also available for the experienced searcher. The major difference between the online and CD-ROM versions of *Biography Index* is currency. The online database is updated twice per week, while new CD-ROM discs are sent to subscribers quarterly. However, if the CD-ROM workstation contains a modem and is hooked up to WILSONLINE, where the online version of *Biography Index* can be accessed, the search on the CD-ROM can be updated immediately online. Both databases begin with July 1984 data, so that the printed volumes must be searched for articles and books indexed before that date.

Obituaries

Obituary articles from national or regional newspapers can be a valuable source of information about prominent, and sometimes not-so-prominent, individuals. To clarify, *obituary articles* are news stories written by newspaper staff, not notices placed in the newspaper by family members. Obituary articles often provide biographical data about persons of regional interest who would not be found in standard biographical reference tools. In fact, obituary articles may, in some cases, be the only readily available published source of information on the lives of such individuals. Most public and academic libraries will have indexes to local and regional newspapers, if these indexes are available in published or printed form.

For prominent Americans and a few individuals from other countries, access to obituary articles is provided by *The New York Times Obituaries Index*. Two volumes of this index have been published to date; the first covers the period from 1858 to 1968, while the second covers 1969 to 1978. These volumes index articles in *The New York Times* which report the death of individuals, provide pertinent facts about their lives, and list important contributions they made during their careers. Specifically, *The New York Times Obituaries Index* lists all names which appeared under the heading "Deaths" in the main index to the newspaper. The total number of names listed in both volumes exceeds 380,000. The second volume also includes reprints of obituary stories for fifty of the most prominent persons who died during the decade 1969 to 1978.

Entries in each volume are alphabetically arranged. Each consists of the name of the deceased and a reference to the year, date, section, page, and column of *The New York Times* where the story is to be found. Some names are listed twice or more; in these cases, there was more than one story (e.g., one on the death and one on the funeral) and all have been indexed.

For obituaries from *The New York Times* since 1978, one can consult *The New York Times Biographical Service*. Many libraries use this monthly service as a biographical reference tool. It reprints biographical articles which appeared in the newspaper during the month covered by each issue. However, since a large proportion of the articles reprinted are obituaries, it can profitably be used to supplement the *New York Times Obituaries Index*. An advantage is that it is a direct source; the articles are right there, saving the user the trouble of going back through past years of the newspaper to find an article. The *Biographical Service* articles are arranged chronologically in each issue. Each monthly issue contains its own alphabetical index; the June issue includes a semiannual index, and an annual index appears in the December issue.

Two other sources of obituaries, one covering the period 1980 to the present and the other first issued for the year 1988, deserve mention. *The Annual Obituary*, the most recently published volume of which covers 1989, provides comprehensive, evaluative essays for some three hundred prominent individuals who died during that year. Coverage is international. Essays are arranged chronologically, by the individual's date of death, but each volume includes an alphabetical index. Following each essay, the pertinent facts of the person's life are given in a paragraph arranged like a "who's who" entry but often considerably longer and more detailed. The *Obituary Index* provides citations to obituary articles in seven prominent American newspapers and in *The Times* of London. Because regional newspapers, such as the *Atlanta Constitution* and the *Boston Globe*, are covered, *Obituary Index* offers unique access to biographical information about deceased individuals who did not attain national prominence.

Search Strategies

The strategy a librarian employs in dealing with a biographical reference question will vary depending on the nature of the reference collection to which the librarian has access. For instance, in a library where online searching in pursuit of an answer to a reference question is not an option, print tools alone must suffice. Similarly, where, for budgetary reasons, sets such as *BGMI* or *Contemporary Authors* are not options, other titles must be used in their place.

Even given identical collections, however, librarians will differ in how they approach the same question. Some will go immediately to a direct source for the answer, while others will search *BGMI* or *Almanac of Famous People* to see where entries about an individual are located. Each reference librarian develops personal strategies for different kinds of questions. Consequently, the strategies outlined here generally suggest more than one possible path to the answer.

Ready Reference Questions

Biographical questions of this kind usually involve straightforward factual questions about an individual's life or career. For instance, the patron may need a date (birth, death, year of graduation, years a certain position was held); a list of degrees, honors, children, or publications; or descriptive information about the individual, such as height, marital status, or current address.

As with any reference question, the first step in dealing with a question of this nature is to get as much information as possible from the patron. Is the person still alive? What nationality is he? Is she an author, politician, scholar, etc.? This information tells the librarian whether to look in a current or retrospective source, and further, what kind of source to use. For instance, in dealing with a request for information about a physicist, two obvious possibilities would be *American Men and Women of Science* and the *Dictionary of Scientific Biography*; which one is used would depend on the answers to the librarian's queries as to the nationality of the physicist and whether the physicist is still alive. For an American physicist of some renown, *Who's Who in America* may also provide the required information.

Of course, a search of *BGMI*, online or in printed form, would be likely to lead to one or more sources where information about the individual can be found. An advantage of this approach is that *BGMI* lists all editions of a title containing entries for that person. In the case mentioned above, if the physicist died quite recently, neither the *Dictionary of Scientific Biography* nor the latest edition of *American Men and Women of Science* would have an entry. *BGMI*, however, would indicate to the librarian which earlier editions of *American Men and Women of Science* contain an entry for the physicist. It may also give the librarian an immediate second source to check should the first not contain the answer.

General Background Questions

General background questions usually arise out of curiosity and a desire for more information about an individual's life and career. The librarian must generally supply a fair amount of descriptive and evaluative discussion, rather than merely a fact or two. The search can often be confined to one or two sources which produce good overviews of the person's life, although sometimes a patron will want references for further reading.

For contemporary figures, two frequent subjects of questions like this are authors and political leaders. For authors, *Contemporary Authors* is the obvious choice; for a writer of books for children or young adults, *Something About the Author* would also be a logical choice. If the author is very well known, an essay about that person's life might be found in *Current Biography*. This source is also good for political figures. The latest yearbook, containing a cumulative index for recent volumes, or the index covering the period from 1940 to 1985, would be the best place to look in this case. As political leaders are often the subjects of magazine articles, the librarian could also consult *Biography Index* to locate articles in periodicals which the library owns.

In cases where neither the patron nor the librarian knows very much about the subject, a search of *Almanac of Famous People* or *BGMI* is the safest place to begin. Here again, the advantages of online searching are apparent. If the name is a common one, or if the patron is unsure of the spelling, as may be the case with a non-English name, the "expand" command on Biography Master Index on DIALOG will display an alphabetically arranged list of names from which the correct one can usually be identified. However, when searching this file, one must always remember that the same person's name may appear in more than one form.

When background information is sought for an historical figure, the first job of the librarian is to try to determine the nationality of the individual. This may lead directly to the *DAB* or the *National Cyclopedia of American Biography*, or to a similar source for another country. If the nationality is not known, it can be found if the person is listed in *Almanac of Famous People*, *Webster's New Biographical Dictionary*, or the *New Century Cyclopedia of Names*; the first-named title will also lead to further relevant sources, while the last-named often provides fairly extensive information. Another good possibility in this situation is the *McGraw-Hill Encyclopedia of World Biography*, since it is international in scope, both current and retrospective in approach, and also often contains rather lengthy discussions of the individuals it includes. General or topical encyclopedias should also be tried for background information on historical figures, if strictly biographical sources fail to produce the needed information. The index should always be used in this situation, in case the individual does not have a biographical entry but is discussed in a topical entry.

Research Questions

When patrons—particularly students at any level—conduct research about a particular individual, they generally need to consult more than one kind of source, such as a reference source for basic information about the person's life and secondary sources, such as books and journal articles, for more detail and an interpretive approach. College students will also be expected to find primary sources, such as correspondence, speeches, or other writings. In this situation, indirect sources such as *Biography Index* are particularly valuable. Also important to consult are those direct sources, such as the *McGraw-Hill Encyclopedia of World Biography*, the *Dictionary of Scientific Biography*, and the *DAB*, which provide extensive evaluative essays and also list sources for further research. For research on a living individual, the patron will find good essays and lists of magazine articles about the individual in *Current Biography* and *Newsmakers*. *BGMI* and *Almanac of Famous People* are less useful, since they index reference works rather than periodical literature, but if the librarian does not find the person sought in any of the sources just mentioned, a search in one of these tools may at least lead to some information.

Research questions are the type of biographical reference queries which most often require the librarian to go beyond the sources discussed in this chapter. Frequently, encyclopedias or specialized biographical dictionaries can be used to get patrons started in their research. In addition, the librarian may suggest that patrons consult the card or online catalog, a topical index, or a specialized bibliography. If the subject's career is or was in a certain field—music, for example—appropriate bibliographies, indexes, and subject headings can be identified which will lead patrons beyond biographical reference materials to the sources they need for their research.

■ ══ ■

14.1

Information about a Rock Group

The reference librarian in the urban public library was initially stumped when two young girls came to the reference desk looking for information about the rock group "U2." Neither girl could think of the names of any of the members of the group, and the librarian in the department most familiar with the musical scene was in a meeting. However, the librarian on duty then remembered that *Biography Almanac* (now *Almanac of Famous People*) sometimes lists individuals by their stage names or the name of their group affiliation. Sure enough, a check of the third edition (the fourth had not yet arrived) listed the names of the group: Adam Clayton; "The Edge" (David Howell Evans); Larry Mullen, Jr.; and "Bono Vox" (Paul Hewson). However, no source for further information was provided.

Now that he had names of individuals, the librarian dialed up Biography Master Index on DIALOG and searched under "U2" and under both the real and stage names of group members. He found several citations. Of the sources indexed, two were in the library's reference room, *Contemporary Newsmakers* (now titled *Newsmakers*) and *Biography Index*. The librarian explained to the girls that *Biography Index* would provide them with citations to articles in other sources, such as magazines, while the *Contemporary Newsmakers* volume would give them information directly. When he checked the 1988 annual cumulation of the latter, he found a five-page article on U2's lead singer, "Bono." The article provided a biographical sketch of Bono and a history of U2, including a discography through 1987. There were also several references to articles in *Rolling Stone*, *Time*, and other sources. The librarian told the girls where these magazines were located, and the girls, after photocopying the article in *Contemporary Newsmakers*, went to find the other sources.

Notes

1. *The Works of Thomas Carlyle* (New York: Charles Scribner's Sons, 1898-1901), 28:86.

2. *Who's Who Among Black Americans*, 6th ed. (Detroit, Mich.: Gale Research, 1990), xi.

3. *American Men and Women of Science*, 17th ed. (New York: R. R. Bowker, 1989), 1:vii.

4. *Directory of American Scholars*, 8th ed. (New York: R. R. Bowker, 1982), 1:vii.

5. *Who's Who in America*, 45th ed. (Wilmette, Ill.: Marquis Who's Who, 1988), 1:viii.

6. Ibid., vi.

7. Ann Ricker, "Who's Who in America," *Reference Services Review* 8 (October/December 1980): 11.

8. Ibid., 8.

9. Ibid., 9.

10. *Who's Who 1990* (London: Adam and Charles Black, 1990), 7.

11. *Who's Who in the World*, 10th ed. (Wilmette, Ill.: Marquis Who's Who, 1990), vi.

12. *The International Who's Who*, 54th ed., 1990-1991 (London: Europa Publications, 1990), v.

13. *American Men and Women of Science*, 17th ed., 1:7.

14. Ibid.

15. *Directory of American Scholars*, 8th ed., 1:7.

16. *Current Biography* 50 (September 1989): 2.

17. *Something About the Author* (Detroit, Mich.: Gale Research, 1989), 57:ix.

18. *McGraw-Hill Encyclopedia of World Biography* (New York: McGraw-Hill, 1973), 1:vii.

19. *New Century Cyclopedia of Names* (Englewood Cliffs, N.J.: Prentice-Hall, 1954), 1:vii.

20. *Dictionary of American Biography* (New York: Charles Scribner's Sons, 1928), 1:vii.

21. Ibid.

22. *Dictionary of American Negro Biography*, eds. Rayford W. Logan and Michael R. Winston (New York: W. W. Norton, 1982), vii.

23. Ibid., viii.

24. Eugene P. Sheehy, ed., *Guide to Reference Books*, 10th ed. (Chicago: American Library Association, 1986), 289-312.

List of Sources

Almanac of Famous People. 4th ed. Edited by Susan L. Stetler. 3 vols. Detroit, Mich.: Gale Research, 1989. (First three editions titled *Biography Almanac*.)

American Men and Women of Science. 17th ed. 8 vols. New York: R. R. Bowker, 1989. (DIALOG File 236.)

The Annual Obituary, 1980- . New York: St. Martin's, 1981-1983; Chicago: St. James Press, 1984- . Annual.

Biography and Genealogy Master Index. 2d ed. Detroit, Mich.: Gale Research, 1980- . Annual. (First edition titled *Biographical Dictionaries Master Index.*)

Biography Index. New York: H. W. Wilson, 1946- . Quarterly, with annual cumulations. (Online on WILSONLINE; also available on CD-ROM.)

Biography Master Index. Detroit, Mich.: Gale Research. (DIALOG File 287.)

Concise Dictionary of American Biography. 3d ed. New York: Charles Scribner's Sons, 1980. 1,333p.

Concise Dictionary of National Biography. 2 vols. London: Smith, Elder & Co., 1903; London: Oxford University Press, 1982.

Concise Dictionary of Scientific Biography. New York: Charles Scribner's Sons, 1981. 773p.

Contemporary Authors. Detroit, Mich.: Gale Research, 1962- . Irregular, generally four volumes per year.

Current Biography. New York: H. W. Wilson, 1940- . Monthly, with an annual cumulative yearbook.

Dictionary of American Biography. 20 vols. and index. New York: Charles Scribner's Sons, 1928-1937. Supplements, 1944- .

Dictionary of American Negro Biography. New York: W. W. Norton, 1982. 680p.

Dictionary of Literary Biography. Detroit, Mich.: Gale Research, 1978- . Irregular.

Dictionary of National Biography. Edited by Sir Leslie Stephen and Sir Sidney Lee. 22 vols. London: Smith, Elder & Co., 1908-1909 (reprint).

Dictionary of Scientific Biography. 18 vols. New York: Scribner, 1970-1980, 1990.

Directory of American Scholars: A Biographical Dictionary. 8th ed. 4 vols. New York: R. R. Bowker, 1982.

International Who's Who. 54th ed., 1990-1991. London: Europa Publications, 1990. 1,772p.

Marquis Who's Who. Wilmette, Ill.: National Register Publishing Co. (DIALOG File 234.)

McGraw-Hill Encyclopedia of World Biography. 12 vols. New York: McGraw-Hill, 1973.

National Cyclopedia of American Biography. 76 vols. and index. New York: J. T. White, 1891-1984.

New Century Cyclopedia of Names. 3 vols. Englewood Cliffs, N.J.: Prentice-Hall, 1954.

New York Times Biographical Service. New York: Arno Press, 1970- . Monthly.

New York Times Obituaries Index, 1858-1968. New York: New York Times, 1970. 1,136p.

New York Times Obituaries Index, 1969-1978. New York: New York Times, 1980. 131p.

Newsmakers. Detroit, Mich.: Gale Research, 1988- . Three issues yearly, with an annual cumulation. (Titled *Contemporary Newsmakers*, 1985-1987.)

Notable American Women: 1607-1950. 3 vols. Cambridge, Mass.: Belknap Press of Harvard University Press, 1971.

Notable American Women: The Modern Period. Cambridge, Mass.: Belknap Press of Harvard University Press, 1980. 773p.

Obituary Index. Westport, Conn.: Meckler, 1989- . Annual.

SciTech Reference Plus. [CD-ROM]. New York: Bowker Electronic Publishing.

Something About the Author. Edited by Anne Commire. Detroit, Mich.: Gale Research, 1971- . Irregular.

Webster's Biographical Dictionary. Springfield, Mass.: G. & C. Merriam, 1980. 1,697p.

Webster's New Biographical Dictionary. Springfield, Mass.: Merriam-Webster, 1988. 1,130p.

Who Was Who, 1897-1980. 7 vols. (in progress). London: Adam and Charles Black, 1929-1985. Irregular.

Who Was Who in America: Historical Volume, 1607-1896. Chicago: Marquis Who's Who, 1963. 670p.

Who Was Who in America, 1897-1989. 9 vols. (in progress). Chicago: Marquis Who's Who, 1942-1989. Irregular.

Who's Who. London: Adam and Charles Black, 1849- . Annual.

Who's Who Among Black Americans. 6th ed., 1990-1991. Detroit, Mich.: Gale Research, 1990. 1,593p.

Who's Who in America. 46th ed., 1990-1991. 2 vols. Wilmette, Ill.: Marquis Who's Who, 1990.

Who's Who in Economics: A Biographical Dictionary of Major Economists, 1700-1986. 2d ed. Edited by Mark Blaug. Cambridge, Mass.: MIT Press, 1986. 935p.

Who's Who in the East. 23rd ed., 1991-1992. Wilmette, Ill.: Marquis Who's Who, 1990. 974p.

Who's Who in the Midwest. 22d ed., 1990-1991. Wilmette, Ill.: Marquis Who's Who, 1989. 730p.

Who's Who in the South and Southwest. 22nd ed., 1990-1991. Wilmette, Ill.: Marquis Who's Who, 1990. 831p.

Who's Who in the West. 22nd ed., 1989-1990. Wilmette, Ill.: Marquis Who's Who, 1989. 784p.

Who's Who in the World. 10th ed., 1991-1992. Wilmette, Ill.: Marquis Who's Who, 1990. 1,218p.

Who's Who of American Women. 17th ed., 1991-1992. Wilmette, Ill.: Marquis Who's Who, 1991. 1,120p.

Additional Readings

"Biographical References Sources: A Selective Checklist." *Booklist* 80 (May 15, 1984): 1,314-27; 80 (June 15, 1984): 1,447-61; 81 (May 15, 1985): 1,309-11.
    The first part of this article provides, in tabular format, basic factual information (format, frequency, etc.) about biographical sources published by Gale Research, H. W. Wilson, St. Martin's, Marquis Who's Who, and R. R. Bowker. Part 2 contains eight subject tables and an annotated list giving similar information for additional biographical tools. Part 3 is an addendum, listing and annotating a smaller number of titles mistakenly omitted from the first two parts.

Cimbala, Diane J., Jennifer Cargill, and Brian Alley. *Biographical Sources: A Guide to Dictionaries and Reference Works.* Phoenix, Ariz.: Oryx Press, 1986. 146p.
    This work is an annotated bibliography of 689 biographical reference works arranged under some 30 subject headings. Annotations range in length from two lines to three paragraphs.

Clarke, Jack. "Biographical Directories, the Fine Line Between Vanity and Pride." *RQ* 22 (Fall 1983): 76-78.
   This brief article provides useful information on "nearly five hundred biographical directories of a questionable reference value that are published irregularly in the United States alone." The goal is to prepare reference librarians to deal with questions about these publications from persons who have been invited to be included in one.

Grogan, Denis. *Biographical Sources*. Grogan's Case Studies in Reference Work, vol. 6. London: Clive Bingley, 1987. 154p.
   Grogan discusses numerous biographical reference sources through 107 cases—scenarios which demonstrate strategies for dealing with a variety of biographical reference questions.

Slocum, Robert B. *Biographical Dictionaries and Related Works*. 2d ed. 2 vols. Detroit, Mich.: Gale Research, 1986.
   This work lists, with brief annotations, some sixteen thousand biographical reference works under three broad headings: "Universal Biography"; "National or Area Biography"; and "Biography by Vocation." Both the table of contents and the subject index are very detailed, allowing one to locate, for example, biographical sources on French musicians. However, many of the specialized sources included in this bibliography will be found only in large research libraries.

Wynar, Bohdan S., ed. *ARBA Guide to Biographical Dictionaries*. Littleton, Colo.: Libraries Unlimited, 1986. 444p.
   This guide reproduces, with necessary updating and some revisions, evaluations which originally appeared in *American Reference Books Annual* (*ARBA*) for 718 biographical dictionaries. Indexes and other indirect sources are excluded. Evaluations include, in many cases, references to reviews in library science periodicals such as *Booklist*, *Library Journal*, and others.

DICTIONARIES

Uses and Characteristics

Dictionaries are used to define words, to verify spelling, syllabication, or pronunciation, to check on usage, or to determine the etymological history of a word. To some degree, they also standardize the language based on current usage.

Dictionaries are consulted chiefly by persons who are writing or editing manuscripts, although they may also be used for puzzle solving, for clarifying the meaning of words in texts, or purely for satisfying intellectual curiosity. Persons outside the library frequently call upon librarians to look in the unabridged dictionaries (which tend to be found mainly in libraries), because these dictionaries are considered to be the ultimate authority for spelling and usage in manuscripts. They also have definitions for words not found in the desk dictionaries used in home and office.

Dictionaries may be either *descriptive*, recording how the language is actually used, or *prescriptive*, advocating how it ought to be used. An example of the prescriptive approach can be found in the entry in Fowler's *Dictionary of Modern English Usage* (second edition), for *inquire*, which says, "There is a tendency, which deserves encouragement, to differentiate *enquir(e)(y)* and *inquir(e)(y)* by using *en-* as a FORMAL WORD for *ask* and *in-* for an investigation, e.g., *They enquired when the Court of Inquiry was to sit*."[1] The *Random House Dictionary of the English Language* (second edition), on the other hand, uses the descriptive approach, giving as its first definition for *inquire*, "to seek information by questioning; ask" and the second definition, "to make investigation." The statement, "Also, *enquire*" is given at the end to indicate that *enquire* can be used as an alternative spelling, but no preference or difference in usage is indicated.[2]

There are proponents of each approach, with those in favor of the descriptive philosophy claiming that language is always changing, and that dictionaries should therefore reflect these changes. This is the philosophy governing the compilation of all major dictionaries today. Those who follow the prescriptive approach say that it is the major role of dictionaries to set standards, support traditional usage, and prevent contamination of the language by slang and jargon. This philosophy was followed by early dictionary compilers, but has now been largely abandoned by the compilers of unabridged dictionaries. Some desk dictionaries and specialized usage dictionaries still maintain the more conservative prescriptive approach.

Kinds of Information Found
in Dictionaries

A basic dictionary contains an alphabetical list of words with their definitions. Usually the linguistic derivation of the word, the part of speech, syllabication and hyphenation, variant spellings, and pronunciation are also indicated. General dictionaries, that is, those covering all subjects, may also have special features, such as gazetteers, lists of proper names, maps, and glossaries of foreign words. These are not central to the purpose of the dictionary, and may be added by the publisher to inflate the size and make the dictionary more attractive to buyers.

Types of Dictionaries

An *unabridged* dictionary attempts to include all the words in the language that are in use at the time the dictionary is compiled. This, of course, is an impossible goal, as no single compilation can ever include every word that is in use at any one time. These dictionaries are large single-volume or multivolume works that sacrifice convenience for comprehensiveness. The necessity for overcoming inconvenience has given rise to the *abridged*, or desk-size, dictionary, a selective compilation often based on a larger dictionary. Desk dictionaries are compiled for a certain level of student use, with the college level being the one in general use by adults. Etymological dictionaries, slang dictionaries, thesauri, dual-language, dialect, and usage dictionaries are specialized types that serve different purposes. Individual titles of these specialized types are discussed later in this chapter.

■ ══ ■

15.1
Specialized Dictionaries

Etymological dictionary. An etymological dictionary gives the history of individual words with linguistic derivation and examples from writings of the past.

Slang dictionary. A slang dictionary defines terms used in ordinary, informal speech. These terms may include jargon, obscenities, or ephemeral words that go in and out of use quickly.

Thesaurus. A thesaurus contains synonyms and antonyms, usually without definitions. Its purpose is to provide writers with alternate or more specific words.

Dual-language dictionary. A dual-language dictionary has two sections, one with English words and their equivalents in a foreign language, and the other with the foreign words and their equivalents in English.

Dialect dictionary. A dialect dictionary gives regional variants and usage for words within a language. It may include some slang.

Usage dictionary. A usage dictionary prescribes how a word should be used, based on the way it has been used in the past.

Evaluation

When evaluating dictionaries, an assessment of their authority and accuracy is essential. More so than most types of reference tool, however, dictionaries tend to be prepared for a specific audience (such as high school students) or to fulfill a specific purpose (such as identifying and defining slang expressions). Therefore, it is also critical to judge the degree to which dictionaries have succeeded in fulfilling their purpose or in effectively meeting the needs of the group to which they are addressed. Here, comparing their scope, format, and ease of use with similar works is often helpful in the evaluation process.

Format

Large unabridged dictionaries are only infrequently published. They do not present many problems in evaluation, because there are so few, and those few are extensively reviewed in the library media. The unabridged dictionary should be a reasonably comprehensive compilation of the words in use in the language at the time of compilation. Current unabridged dictionaries contain between 300,000 and 500,000 entries. They include frequently encountered abbreviations and acronyms, idiomatic expressions, technical terminology, new coinages, nonstandard speech, foreign phrases and loanwords (foreign words that have been incorporated into the English language), and obsolete terms. There may also be lists of synonyms and antonyms, quotations, pictures, and etymologies.

There has been a change in the philosophy of unabridged dictionaries since the eighteenth century, when the first comprehensive dictionaries of English appeared. Early compilers hoped to establish standards of correctness in spelling and usage and to omit anything that was "low" or vulgar.[3] This attitude persisted to the mid-twentieth century, when the realities of language evolution and change convinced dictionary compilers that usage was a more important consideration governing inclusion than an academic standard of correctness. Slang terms and technical jargon now have their place in the unabridged dictionary, and can be used as an indication of the currency of the compilation.

Comprehensiveness, of course, means an almost unmanageable size, so practicality has brought about the abridged, or desk, dictionary. Desk dictionaries must be judged on effectiveness of purpose as stated in the title or introduction. A high-school-level dictionary should include words likely to be used in writing by a high-school student. A college desk dictionary is the level of dictionary used by college students and other adults. A reputable desk dictionary with 50,000 to 150,000 entries is sufficient for most people.

Recent technology has brought into being the CD-ROM reference tool. The chief advantages of the CD-ROM format are the multiple access points and the time saved in computer searching and printing. In dictionaries, the techniques of keyword and Boolean searching (see chapter 5) make it possible to find and search on words in definitions as well as words being defined. Authors whose cited quotations are used as examples can be found, and the citations listed. In works having dated quotations, it is possible to find all the words used within a certain time span. As more CD-ROMs become available, the approaches to dictionary compilation and searching are likely to change to fit the CD-ROM format, and new works that exist only on CD-ROM may be created.

Scope

The scope of a dictionary is stated in its preface or introduction. Dictionaries intended for college-level use should include linguistic derivation and a brief historical definition as well as current usage. Pronunciation guides are a basic necessity in all general-language dictionaries, although it must be borne in mind that standard pronunciation as used by radio and television announcers may not reflect regional variations. Additional lists, such as geographical and proper names, are helpful to the home user who may not have an extensive reference collection, but they are of less use in a library. Illustrations also add interest and information to the dictionary, especially small line drawings accompanying individual definitions. Large color plates are attractive, but not as necessary as the small illustrations.

Comparison with Others of Similar Coverage

To compare two or more dictionaries of the same type, one should pick a group of common words and compare the treatment given to each one in each dictionary. Look for clarity in definitions, accuracy, and comprehensibility in the pronunciation system. There should be verbal examples that explain how the words are actually used. It is a good idea then to pick some uncommon words to test the breadth of inclusion in each dictionary. See if the abbreviations used in the entries are well defined and if the abbreviations list is in an obvious place, such as the bottom of the page. Size of print may also be a consideration for young children and older users.

Authority

It is difficult to judge the qualifications of individual compilers, because general-language dictionaries tend to be compiled by the editorial staffs of publishers. The authority and reputation of the publisher are consequently the most important factors in judging the quality of a dictionary. Publishers' reputations are built on earlier editions or on similar types of publications, and this should be taken into consideration. However, a good first edition does not always mean that the second has been satisfactorily edited and updated. An unknown publisher may put out a very good dictionary, or a well-known publisher can produce a mediocre one. To aid in making a judgment, reference librarians should learn the names of the most authoritative North American dictionary publishers, which are (in alphabetical order): Doubleday (publisher of the "Thorndike-Barnhart" family of school dictionaries), Houghton Mifflin (publisher of the "American Heritage" family of dictionaries), Macmillan, Merriam-Webster (publisher of the "Webster's" family of dictionaries), Oxford University Press, Prentice-Hall (publisher of the "Webster's New World" family of dictionaries), Random House, and Scott-Foresman.[4]

Accuracy

There are two types of accuracy to consider, that of spelling and that of definition. Accuracy in spelling has become a matter of usage rather than academic rule. In evaluating the currency of spelling in a recent dictionary, one should check words that have been modernized, e.g., "airplane" rather than "aeroplane." Dictionaries are frequently used as authorities for such things as hyphenation, although this changes through evolution as well, with formerly hyphenated words becoming one, e.g., "on-line" to "online."

Definitions should reflect the meaning or meanings of words in clear, unambiguous terms. A definition should not use the word being defined or any word based on the same root to explain the meaning. This does not give users any more information than they already have.[5]

Currency

Usage is continually changing. Slang terms can become standard usage, and standard words can take on new connotations that the user did not intend. This is particularly true in areas of popular culture, such as pop music, and in sexual terminology. Explicit definitions of sex words are a problem area in general dictionaries, because publishers are sometimes reluctant to include words that are considered vulgar or obscene. These words are often well defined in slang dictionaries. Writers, in particular, must be careful about current usage in this regard, and they are not well served by an out-of-date dictionary.

Indexing

General dictionaries, because of their alphabetical arrangement, do not require indexes. Indexes are most important in quotation books, because of the variety of approaches that can be used. A good quotation book should have an author index, if the arrangement is not alphabetical by author, and a keyword phrase index. The phrase index is very important, since keywords by themselves cause time-consuming effort when one is following up multiple references only to find out in the end that the desired phrase is not in the book.

Selection

Selection of a new dictionary for an existing collection requires some consideration of the needs of patrons served by the library, the age and condition of the dictionaries already in the collection, and the amount of money that can be put into new acquisitions. There is a natural tendency to replace an outdated edition with a newer one of the same title, but this should not be done automatically, without giving some consideration to new titles in the field that may be just as good or better.

Since desk dictionaries are compiled for certain specific age groups and levels of sophistication, the reference librarian must be aware of this when selecting a specific dictionary. High-school-level dictionaries do not belong in college collections, although students may request them because of familiarity with titles used in high school. College-level dictionaries, however, may be useful in high school libraries, particularly for advanced students. Dictionary buying guides and reviews will indicate the level of specific dictionaries. Scholars and specialists will require specialized subject dictionaries, foreign-language dictionaries, and unabridged compilations such as the *Oxford English Dictionary*.

Unabridged dictionaries may seem expensive initially, but because they are so infrequently issued, experience shows that they will be used until they fall apart. The long useful life of the dictionary will justify the cost. The other types of dictionaries are also heavily used in libraries, justifying the extra cost for a hardbound edition. Paperback dictionaries have limited vocabulary coverage and treatment, in addition to having a shorter shelf life, and are not as satisfactory for library use as the hardbound editions. Smaller dictionaries are vulnerable to theft from reference collections, so it may be necessary to increase security in order to keep them. Also, be wary of dictionaries with the word *illustrated* in the title. These are usually desk dictionaries with attractive pictures added, and a greatly increased price, without any additional text.

Certain standard tools are used over and over again and are considered basic to any reference collection. Library users come to know them by name and expect to find them in any library, whether academic or public. These will be discussed later in this chapter.

There is a confusing proliferation of general English-language dictionaries available from bookstores, supermarkets, and remainder houses. Dictionary publishers themselves frequently publish a number of titles that are similar. One area of confusion is in the designation "Webster" in the title. There is no copyright on the use of "Webster," and anyone can claim to be publishing a dictionary in the direct tradition of Noah Webster himself. Several publishers have a "Webster's Unabridged" that purports to be a great bargain at a greatly reduced price. One should not buy one of these without first examining a copy, as they are, at best, large desk dictionaries. They may also be reissues of older material from other sources.[6]

The best policy when in doubt is to read reviews and stay with the standard titles. Dictionary buying guides that compare several titles, such as *General Reference Books for Adults*, can often clear up the confusion. There are very few bargains in the dictionary world.

Important General Sources

This section focuses on several kinds of dictionaries and related tools which are found in typical school, public, or academic library reference collections. Under each category, a few of the most widely used titles are described. For information on titles not discussed here, the reader can consult one of the guides to dictionaries listed in the additional readings.

Unabridged Dictionaries

There are only three good unabridged, English-language dictionaries: *Webster's Third New International Dictionary of the English Language Unabridged*; *The Random House Dictionary of the English Language*, second edition; and *Funk & Wagnalls New Standard Dictionary of the English Language*.

Webster's Third, originally published in 1961, has been updated periodically by the addition of new words in the form of an addendum, but it is in need of a complete revision. However, it remains the most prestigious dictionary published in North America, and is considered by most users to be the final authority for spelling and definition. In defining usage it has become outdated, and reflects the usage of the 1950s.[7]

When *Webster's Third* first appeared, reviewers complained about permissiveness in the change from a prescriptive to a descriptive philosophy in compiling the third edition. There were scathing reviews in the *New York Times* and in other newspapers and magazines. Some critics also disliked the fact that the biographical section and gazetteer of the previous edition had been omitted. However, these changes just follow in the tradition of change and updating that has gone on since Merriam-Webster bought Noah Webster's copyright in 1843.

■ ═══ ■

15.2

A Prescriptive View

In its review of *Webster's Third New International*, the Washington *Sunday Star* of September 10, 1961, held a staunchly prescriptive view:

It "Ain't" Good

The Merriam-Webster unabridged dictionary, in its first completely new edition since 1934, contains a number of startling revisions. They are revisions likely to shock more than a few of us who happen, for better or worse, to be traditionalists congenitally opposed to change just for change's sake. In that respect, perhaps the most shocking thing in the whole book is that it takes a rather respectful view of "ain't" as a word that is now "used orally in the U.S. by cultivated speakers."

This is certainly a far cry from the dictionary's 1934 edition, which bluntly — and correctly, in our view — brands "ain't" as a "dialectal" and "illiterate" expression employed by people on the fringes of polite society. But now, along with a lot of other vulgarisms that have become respectable, this basically unpleasant, unnecessary and grammatically gauche word has been more or less legitimatized by the Merriam-Webster people.

— James Sledd and Wilma R. Ebbitt
Dictionaries and That Dictionary[8]

■ ═══ ■

15.3

A Descriptive View

A more liberal, descriptive point of view was taken by Norman E. Isaacs, writing in *The Louisville Times* of October 18, 1961:

And Now, the War on Words

As if we do not have enough warring, we have another now on words. It has burst full-blown over the publication of the *Webster's Third New International Dictionary*....

What annoys the traditionalists is Webster's acceptance of words like double-domes, yakking, confabbing, and finalize, to mention only a mere scattering. Presumably, the critics might well sanction such new entries as teaching fellow, carbon 14, traffic island, and even crop duster. Why include such words and set phrases and object to others like litter bug, elbow bending, two-way stretch, or greasy spoon? Are these not also part of the American language?

The *New York Times* shudders over "finalize." I confess to irritation, too. But it must be admitted that it arrives from an established principle that earlier resulted in "colonize" and "clockwise"....

The net is that we have a new dictionary and it will become the accepted authority, despite all the literary hassles that will ensue. It is not a revision of the old unabridged. It has taken 27 years to compile. It includes 50,000 new words and phrases, with another 50,000 new meanings added.

— James Sledd and Wilma R. Ebbitt
Dictionaries and That Dictionary[9]

The first unabridged edition appeared in 1847, with revisions in 1864, 1890, 1909, and *Webster's Second* in 1934. Periodic supplements, the latest called *12,000 Words: A Supplement to Webster's Third New International Dictionary*, are published separately or as an addendum in recent printings. The Merriam-Webster staff is continually collecting citations and examples of language to be added into the addendum with each new printing.

In *Webster's Third*, the first element in an entry is the pronunciation. Etymologies are listed immediately after the pronunciation, followed by the definitions and illustrative quotations. Synonyms are listed at the end of the entry. Three kinds of status labels indicate obsolete, slang, and dialect terms. Pronunciation given is that of educated people, and there is no "preferred" pronunciation listed first.

The Random House Dictionary is the smallest of the three unabridged dictionaries, but it is more current than *Webster's Third*. Its coverage of the language reflects the mid-1980s rather than the 1950s. It is descriptive in its approach, but has numerous usage notes. Valuable features are the inclusion of approximate dates when a word or phrase first entered the language and identification of vocabulary specifically of American origin. The illustrative quotations are made up by the editorial staff and vary in their clarity and usefulness. Because it is so up-to-date, most libraries should have a copy of the *Random House* in addition to *Webster's Third*, and should make it the first choice for recent definitions, spelling, and hyphenations, unless the patron specifically requests *Webster's Third*.

Funk & Wagnalls New Standard Dictionary of the English Language is badly out-of-date, and has not been published since 1965. It was originally published in 1913 as a thorough revision of an earlier work published in 1893. Successive printings had new words inserted in the text and, finally, a supplement of new words. Since 1958, the Funk & Wagnalls name has been used on a desk dictionary published under a succession of titles, the latest being *Funk & Wagnalls New International Dictionary of the English Language*, Comprehensive edition, 1987. It is not comprehensive, however, and has only about half as much text as the *New Standard*.

Etymological Dictionaries

The *Oxford English Dictionary*, second edition, published in the spring of 1989, is a completely updated version of the first edition and its supplements. About five thousand new words and meanings were added, new definitions were added to the old ones, and the old phonetic system devised by Sir James Murray was replaced by the International Phonetic Alphabet. The *OED* is considered the premier source for etymology, and its definitions and quotations take on encyclopedic proportions. It is a massive, scholarly compilation, usually consulted for its extensive etymologies that record the history of words and meanings in use since 1150, and trace their evolution through dated citations, or quotations, from standard literature. It can be used as a quotation dictionary, and often is, particularly by writers and speakers. It has no biographical or geographical material, and no special features outside its main lexicon.

The size of the set (20 volumes) and its approximately $2,000 cost make it a work that is usually only available for consultation in libraries. A two-volume microprint version of the first edition, designed for home use and titled the *Compact Edition of the Oxford English Dictionary*, appeared in 1971. Unfortunately, it requires the use of a magnifying glass, but it is a space saver.

Although the *OED* is compiled in England, American words are well represented. A CD-ROM version is available, and there are plans to convert the total text of the dictionary to a machine-readable database available from a commercial vendor.

The Oxford English Dictionary on Compact Disc, the CD-ROM version, first appeared in 1987, and was an electronic version of the *OED* first edition without the supplements. This meant that the material in the CD-ROM was seriously out-of-date. Presumably future versions of the compact disc will be based on the second edition. As is the case with all CD-ROM products, the advantages of computerized access are keyword and Boolean searching and a variety of customized printouts. Reviewers have complained about the abbreviations system, which has been adapted to accommodate a variety of keyboards that do not support the printed dictionary's diacritical marks.[10] This problem does not occur if a color monitor with graphics capability is used.[11]

Sir William Craigie and James Hulbert's *Dictionary of American English on Historical Principles*, 1938-44, and Mitford Mathews's *Dictionary of Americanisms on Historical Principles*, 1951, cover the historical derivations of words originating in the United States or having a greater currency here than elsewhere. Both are out-of-date (see *Dictionary of American Regional English*).

Desk Dictionaries

Webster's Ninth New Collegiate Dictionary has been highly recommended by reviewers and is considered a classic of its type. The ninth edition represents an extensive revision and updating in both the entries section and the special sections. The publisher, Merriam-Webster, is considered one of the foremost dictionary publishers in the United States, and has an immense citation bank (master collection of words and definitions that is continually enlarged by the addition of new words found by the editorial staff) to draw on for its dictionaries. Their *Collegiate Dictionary* is an adult-level dictionary based on the *Webster's Third New International*, with definitions somewhat simplified and shortened. Many technical, archaic, variant, and esoteric terms found in the parent dictionary are omitted from the collegiate.

The entries include part of speech, pronunciation, inflections, etymology, definitions, and notes on usage and synonymy. The date of the first instance of use of the word is given with a discussion of the current use of the word. Definitions are precise and clear, and there is considerable emphasis on contemporary pronunciation and definitions. Words such as *ain't* are designated "substandard," and four-letter words which are included are labeled "considered obscene" or "considered vulgar." These designations are used sparingly, however. The pronunciation guide is somewhat difficult to use, but there is a short pronunciation key on each right-hand page. There are separate lists of abbreviations and symbols for chemical elements, foreign words and phrases, biographical names, geographical names, colleges and universities, and signs and symbols, and a handbook of style. These are of more use in the home than in the library, where other standard tools provide this information. Illustrations are kept to a minimum.

The Merriam-Webster Ninth New Collegiate Dictionary on CD-ROM, issued in 1989, includes all the text and diagrams from the hard-copy version. In addition, it features a sound recording of the pronunciation of each word that can be activated by the user, and a selection of larger font sizes for visually impaired individuals.

The *American Heritage Dictionary*, second college edition, 1982; *Random House College Dictionary*, revised edition, 1980; and the *Webster's New World Dictionary of American English*, third college edition, 1988, are also popular, authoritative desk dictionaries with many similarities to the *Webster's Ninth* and to each other. It is the opinion of most authorities that 90 percent or so of the lexical content of the leading college dictionaries is roughly the same.[12]

The *American Heritage* is heavily illustrated and is noted for its attractive and easy-to-read page layout. The larger first edition of this dictionary, which appeared in 1969, was noted for its etymologies and for being the first general dictionary to include obscenities. This second edition has briefer definitions and etymologies than that edition or than either the *Webster's Ninth New Collegiate* or the *Webster's New World*. Shortening the definitions and the etymologies was not always an improvement, and many users prefer the original edition. In 1985, Houghton Mifflin published *The American Heritage Dictionary of Indo-European Roots*, a revised version of the appendix in the 1969 edition that lists and defines the ultimate ancestral root and allocates the various words derived from the root to the Indo-European language family, such as Germanic or Latinic, that preceded the English word. It was intended to be a companion volume to the second edition. The *American Heritage*, second edition, emphasizes contemporary usage and is strong in recent scientific and technical terms.

The *Random House College Dictionary* is also based on a well-respected larger dictionary, which first appeared in 1966. Almost all of its material is in a single alphabet, with separate lists only for colleges and universities and for English given names. It follows the descriptive approach of the parent *Random House Dictionary*, and it has excellent usage notes and synonym lists. There are prefix tables for commonly used prefixes, such as *re-* and *pro-*, in their respective alphabetical sections. It has a smaller typeface and is harder to read than the *American Heritage* or *Webster's Ninth New Collegiate*.

Webster's New World Dictionary of American English is highly regarded, and it was completely revised for the third edition. Formerly titled *Webster's New World Dictionary of the American Language*, it is published by Prentice-Hall, a division of Simon & Schuster. It has no relation to the Merriam-Webster line of dictionaries, and has been a separate publication in its own right since 1951. Its major emphasis is on English as it is spoken and written in the United States. The etymologies are particularly good.

High-School-Level Dictionaries

Dictionaries for high school use tend to be abridged, simplified editions of the larger dictionaries intended for adults. High school libraries should also have at least one adult-level dictionary for use by advanced students.

The Concise American Heritage Dictionary is an abridged version of the 1969 *American Heritage Dictionary of the English Language*, and retains many of its features. The definitions have been revised to be simpler and easier to read, and the typeface and the illustrations are larger. Biographical and geographical entries are included in the main alphabet, while etymologies are in a separate appendix. The etymologies are based on those in the parent work. A panel of writers, editors, and speakers determines the usage notes that appear in the text.

This dictionary does not try to be comprehensive, but it is very complete for a concise edition. Many advanced scientific and technical terms which are found in the parent work are excluded, and the meanings for those that remain are considerably rewritten and condensed. The language of the concise edition is simpler and more direct than in the other American Heritage dictionaries. This is a dictionary that can be understood by readers with unsophisticated or limited vocabularies. Pronunciation follows the standard American Heritage system. Usage notes are much more condensed than in the parent dictionary and are less prescriptive. The illustrations are large, excellent, and add considerably to the reader's understanding of words. There are also maps and portraits. This dictionary has been favorably reviewed and is a good buy for the high school library.

Another highly respected dictionary that is suitable for high schools is *The World Book Dictionary* edited by Clarence Barnhart. It is published by World Book, Inc., publishers of the *World Book Encyclopedia*, and is designed to complement the encyclopedia. This title is part of the Thorndike-Barnhart dictionary series, and is a large, annually updated work in two volumes that approaches the size of the unabridged dictionaries. The Thorndike-Barnhart lexicographical file is large and extensive, and the breadth of the dictionary reflects this. It has a large assortment of foreign words and phrases and a selection of British terms. Entries are in simplified language, and obscenities are omitted. The dictionary also has a number of special features, including a lengthy introduction that summarizes the history of the English language, how to write effectively, how to use alternate language systems such as Braille and Morse Code, and how to use the dictionary. This dictionary is well designed and easy to read; its only real drawbacks are the two-volume format and relatively high cost.

In 1990, World Book issued its Information Finder, the complete text and tables from the *World Book Encyclopedia* and *The World Book Dictionary* on CD-ROM. Graphics are not included. The CD-ROM can be searched by subject or keyword, and dictionary definitions can be retrieved for words typed in or highlighted in the text by the user. It will be updated annually.

Foreign-Language/English-Language Dictionaries

The foreign-language/English-language (dual) dictionary is a popular type of reference book that is particularly important in academic reference collections. These dictionaries are generally issued in series by major publishers, and the formats are the same throughout the series. The major publishers are all British, perhaps reflecting a greater concern and expertise with multilingualism in that country.

The Cassell's series, published in England and issued in the United States by Macmillan, are the best known of the dual-language dictionaries for European languages. These handy, one-volume works are large enough to include most of the foreign words and idiomatic phrases that the user is likely to want. The dictionary is divided in half, the first half consisting of the foreign words with English equivalents, and the second half consisting of English words with their foreign equivalents. Slang words, colloquialisms, and pronunciation guides are included. The individual entries give pronunciation, part of speech, definition, inflection, compounds, and idioms. Geographic names are incorporated into the alphabetical listing.

Collins, Oxford University Press, and Cambridge University Press are other highly respected publishers of dual-language dictionaries. Oxford in particular specializes in non-European languages, and has a whole range of dictionaries in African and Asian tongues, as well as in ancient Greek and Latin. Cambridge has a number of multivolume dictionaries that provide a more extensive vocabulary than Cassell's or Collins.

Dictionaries of Slang and Dialect

Slang and dialect dictionaries are compiled because standard dictionaries frequently omit colloquial and vulgar terms or do not define them with enough depth. Dialect dictionaries particularly explore regional differences in spelling, pronunciation, and usage. These types of dictionaries are almost entirely descriptive, with every nuance of meaning considered valid as long as it is used by someone.

The Dictionary of American Regional English is an ambitious scholarly project sponsored by the American Dialect Society and published by the Harvard University Press. The dictionary is scheduled to be completed in five volumes, although as of 1990 only volume 1 had been published. Its purpose is to obtain and document, as comprehensively as possible, a record of regional American English in one thousand selected communities. The dictionary records folk language that is learned at home or in the community rather than from schooling, books, or other sources of formal communication. Vocabularies of in-groups, such as criminals, along with other types of jargon, particularly those of highly specialized or esoteric occupations, are omitted. Included are vocabularies of widespread occupations which involve entire communities or regions, such as farming, lumbering, mining, and homemaking. The language of children's games is included, since it is usually of folk origin, has been preserved orally, and shows great regional differences.

Some of the entries contain deliberately distorted explanatory maps (see figure 15.1) that indicate the frequency and density of the population using the word or phrase by enlarging or compressing the size of the states. In this example, the term *banana pepper* is used by more people in the states of the Mississippi River Valley and farther east, so these states appear larger on the map. Dots indicate the location of individual informants who reported use of the term. A separate map section will be included in the final volume.

banana pepper n **widely scattered exc NEast, West** See Map
A banana-shaped pepper, usu yellow.
1965–70 *DARE* (Qu. I22a, . . *Different kinds of peppers — small hot*) 14 Infs, **esp Sth, S Midl,** Banana pepper; **AL6,** Banana pepper — shaped like a banana and red; (Qu. I22b, . . *Large hot*) 37 Infs, **widely scattered exc NEast, West,** Banana peppers; **CT2,** Banana peppers — built like a banana; hot, long ones; **GA85,** Banana peppers — thicker than a finger; **IL41,** Banana peppers — long, yellow, not too hot; **IL117,** Hot banana peppers; **KY28,** Banana — hots; **OK43,** Banana peppers are sometimes sweet; long but pretty thin, fairly small; (Qu. I22c, . . *Small sweet*) 15 Infs, **esp Sth,** Banana peppers; **AL11,** Banana peppers — green and yellow; **MS59,** White banana pepper; (Qu. I22d, . . *Large sweet*) 19 Infs, **chiefly Missip Valley,** Banana peppers; **LA2,** Called banana pepper in the store — same as wax pepper; **NC81,** Banana peppers — yellow and long, a little hot; **TN26,** Banana peppers — tolerable long yellow pepper.

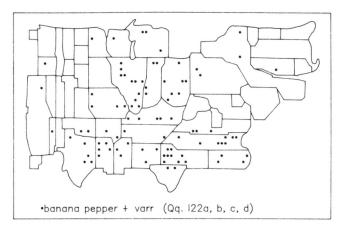

•banana pepper + varr (Qq. I22a, b, c, d)

Fig. 15.1. Entries and map from *Dictionary of American Regional English*. Reprinted by permission of the publishers from *Dictionary of American Regional English*, Volume I, Frederic G. Cassidy, Editor, Cambridge, Mass.: The Belknap Press of Harvard University Press, Copyright © 1985 by the President and Fellows of Harvard College.

Entries are in strict alphabetical sequence, letter by letter. Spelling is based on *Webster's Third New International*. Phrases and compounds are included as well as single words. Parts of speech, pronunciation, etymology, geographic and usage labels, cross-references, dated quotations, and research notes obtained by the dictionary's field workers are included. The field workers were graduate students in English language and linguistics who interviewed 2,777 people in 1,000 communities and phonetically transcribed their speech. The pronunciation key fills thirteen pages, reflecting the importance of exact comprehension of the nuances of regional speech.

The *Dictionary of American Regional English* does not have any current competitors. Two out-of-print dictionaries, Sir William Craigie and James Hulbert's *A Dictionary of American English on Historical Principles*, 1938-44, and Harold Wentworth's *American Dialect Dictionary*, 1944, will be surpassed by the sheer scope and diversity of the newer work when it is completed. The Craigie and Hulbert work is still useful for historical research, however, since it includes some standard words, such as *aborigine*, that do not appear in the *Dictionary of American Regional English*. The Wentworth compilation has been used as a source by the compilers of the *Dictionary of American Regional English*, and will be obsolete when the new compilation is finished.

Slang dictionaries are made up entirely of words used in colloquial speech, and include many terms considered derogatory or vulgar. These words are increasingly found in general dictionaries as well, but the good slang dictionaries are still the handiest source and frequently give better, more complete definitions. The standard in this field is Eric Partridge's *Dictionary of Slang and Unconventional English*, originally published in 1937 and now in its eighth edition. Partridge was Australian, and his compilation emphasizes British slang, but he ranged far over the English-speaking world for his sources. Although many of the words in his dictionary are now found in the *Oxford English Dictionary* with better etymologies, Partridge's dictionary is still considered the most scholarly of the slang dictionaries because of its historical approach and its many quotations with citations to sources. The frequently updated editions keep the dictionary current with recent slang.

American slang has been covered since 1960 by Harold Wentworth and Stuart Berg Flexner's dictionary, now completely revised and titled *New Dictionary of American Slang*, edited by Robert Chapman. It covers all periods of American history, but emphasizes modern slang. Quotations and citations to sources are also an important part of the definitions in this dictionary.

Thesauri and Usage Guides

A *thesaurus* is a very specialized dictionary that deals only with word synonyms (same meaning) and antonyms (opposite meaning). This type of reference book was first developed by Peter Mark Roget, an English doctor, who began the work at age 71 and saw it through 20 editions by the time he was 90. Today the name Roget, like the name Webster, is not copyrighted and can be used by anyone.

The standard thesaurus in the Roget tradition now in use is *Roget's International Thesaurus: Fourth Edition*, published in 1984 by Harper & Row. The distinctive feature of this thesaurus is its arrangement. Words are arranged according to eight primary classes of categories: abstract relations, space, physics, matter, sensation, intellect, volition, and affections. Within these categories, words are grouped by the ideas they convey, with synonyms and antonyms appearing in close proximity. There are many cross-references and no definitions in the usual sense, although the many synonyms serve to make the meaning clear. There is a comprehensive alphabetical index. This thesaurus is used mainly by writers and crossword-puzzle enthusiasts. A writer must already have a good vocabulary and a sense of subtle variations in connotation in order to use it effectively, because connotative meanings are not provided. For example, in figure 15.2, page 340, under *.47 compose*, the user must know that in music *harmonize* and *adapt* do not mean the same thing as *compose*, even though all are listed as synonyms in the same entry, and must understand all three activities in order to convey the correct meaning. It is a good idea to use *Roget's* in conjunction with a standard dictionary that gives definitions, in order to make sure that the synonym selected actually conveys the intended meaning.

.47 compose, write, arrange, score, set, set to
music, put to music; musicalize, melo-
dize, harmonize; orchestrate; instrument,
instrumentate; adapt, make an adaptation; transcribe, transpose.

Fig. 15.2. Definition from *Roget's International
Thesaurus* by Peter Mark Roget. Copyright © 1977
by Harper & Row, Publishers, Inc. Reprinted by
permission of HarperCollins Publishers.

Roget's II: The New Thesaurus, expanded edition, published by Houghton Mifflin in 1988, attempts to overcome this definition problem by providing definitions and illustrative examples and then offering the synonyms side by side in two columns. It does away with the need to use another dictionary for definitions, but does not have the comprehensiveness of *Roget's International* and does not give antonyms. This format has not been as popular with users, who seem to prefer the masses of undefined synonyms provided by the *Roget's International*.

Webster's New Dictionary of Synonyms is entirely in conventional dictionary format. Each entry gives a definition followed by a list of analogous terms (synonyms) and lists of antonyms and contrasted words. Published by Merriam-Webster in 1984, it is both current and comprehensive, although it does not have the sheer quantity of words found in *Roget's International*.

Automated thesauri that are a part of word processing programs are becoming quite popular with both children and adults. Users can point to or click on words to make a window pop up listing synonyms for the highlighted word. They are fast becoming a common writing tool of students and adults alike.

Related somewhat to the thesauri in intent are the usage dictionaries, of which the best known is H. W. Fowler's *Dictionary of Modern English Usage*, which first appeared in 1926. The second edition, published by Oxford University Press, appeared first in 1965. Fowler is entirely prescriptive in his approach, as one would expect, and deals extensively with grammar and syntax. Definitions are supplemented with discussion that analyzes how words should be used and distinguishes clichés and common errors. The intent of this dictionary is to make writers and others aware of the principles of good usage and good writing.

Abbreviations and Acronyms Dictionaries

Abbreviations dictionaries are very important tools in the reference collection, because writers at every level, from journalists to academicians, persist in using abbreviations and acronyms without definitions. Abbreviations are used as a form of literary or bibliographic shorthand, to the confusion of many readers who often cannot remember, or never knew, what they stand for. Some, such as *SPEBSQSA* (Society for the Preservation and Encouragement of Barbershop Quartet Singing in America), have become famous as mind-teasers in their own right.

As is the case with quotation books, it is difficult to have too many abbreviations dictionaries. However, there is one title that is the first choice for abbreviations questions: the *Acronyms, Initialisms, and Abbreviations Dictionary* and its companion, *Reverse Acronyms, Initialisms, and Abbreviations Dictionary*, published annually by Gale Research. This is a multivolume set, and includes abbreviations of periodical titles, acronyms for societies and institutions, and commonly used abbreviations in every subject area. The major disadvantage of such a large compilation is the large number of entries under some abbreviations (see figure 15.3 under *TU*). It is necessary to know the context of the abbreviation in order to select the correct entry.

TU...............	Ivory Coast [*Aircraft nationality and registration mark*] (FAAC)
TU...............	Societe Tunisienne de l'Air [*Tunisia*] [*ICAO designator*]
TU...............	Tanking Unit (AAG)
TU...............	Tape Unit
TU...............	Task Unit
TU...............	Taxicrinic Unit [*Data processing*]
TU...............	Technical Service Unit [*Military*]
TU...............	Technische Ueberwachung [*Technological Supervising*] [*A publication*]
TU...............	Technische Universitat [*Technical University*] [*German*]
TU...............	Technology Utilization
TU...............	Tenebrio Unit [*Endocrinology*]
TU...............	Terminal Unit
TU...............	Texte und Untersuchungen zur Geschichte der Altchristlichen Literatur [*Berlin*] [*A publication*]
TU...............	Thank You [*Communications operator's procedural remark*]
TU...............	Thermal Unit
TU...............	Thulium [*Chemical element*] [*Symbol is Tm*] (ROG)
TU...............	Timing Unit
TU...............	Torah Umesorah - National Society for Hebrew Day Schools (EA)
TU...............	Toxic Unit [*Medicine*]
TU...............	Trade Union
TU...............	Traffic Unit
TU...............	Training Unit [*Army*]
TU...............	Transfer Unconditionally
TU...............	Transfer Unit (AAG)
TU...............	Transmission Unit [*Telecommunications*]
TU...............	Transport Unit (MCD)
TU...............	Transuranium [*Chemistry*]
TU...............	Tritium Unit [*Nuclear energy*]

Fig. 15.3. Entries in *Acronyms, Initialisms and Abbreviations Dictionary*. Selections from *Acronyms, Initialisms and Abbreviations Dictionary*, 1991, Volume 1, edited by Jennifer Mossman. Copyright © 1990 by Gale Research Inc. Reprinted by permission of the publisher.

The *Reverse Acronyms* set reverses the procedure by listing the name of the organization or term and giving the accepted abbreviation. Coverage of these two titles focuses on North America and Western Europe. Gale Research also publishes a separate work, *Periodical Title Abbreviations*, which consists of periodical abbreviations only, but the abbreviations in this work are included in the larger *Acronyms, Initialisms, and Abbreviations Dictionary*. Purchasing the former is an expensive duplication if one already owns the latter, more comprehensive work.

There are many abbreviations dictionaries for specialized subject areas, and abbreviations are also found in general dictionaries and periodical indexes. Large computer databases, such as BIOSIS, have printed lists of the journal abbreviations used in their databases.

Machine-Readable Dictionaries

Several software vendors have produced electronic reference and writing aids. These may be more useful for the home user than for the library, but it is a good idea to be aware of them. One popular system is the Microsoft Bookshelf CD-ROM Reference Library. This is a collection of ten reference books on a single CD-ROM disc, including *The American Heritage Dictionary*, *Roget's II: Electronic Thesaurus*, *Bartlett's Familiar Quotations*, *The World Almanac and Book of Facts*, *The Chicago Manual of Style*, thirteenth edition, *Houghton Mifflin Spelling Verifier and Corrector*, *U.S. ZIP Code Directory*, *Houghton Mifflin Usage Alert*, *Business Information Sources*, a collection of *Forms and Letters*, and a User's Guide and Quick Reference Guide. It is marketed as a tool for writers and is mainly designed to be a memory-resident program used with a word processor. It is for IBM-compatible systems and can be used as a stand-alone application or as a memory-resident program while working in another program. This program has a "quick lookup" feature that operates from keywords and has limited Boolean search capability. Items found can be automatically inserted into the text in the word processor.

The computerized texts do not exactly duplicate the printed sources; some have more information and some less. *The American Heritage Dictionary* does not provide pronunciations, a list of abbreviations, or illustrations. The *Roget's II* gives more possible synonyms than the printed version and changes them to match the grammatical case of the term entered by the user. There are plans for annual updates.

Quotation Books

Quotation questions tend to come from persons writing speeches or essays, or from persons wanting the author, source, or correct wording of a quotation for their own information. Quotations as received by reference librarians are frequently garbled or inaccurate, but a well-indexed quotation book can often solve the problem.

The standard in the vast field of quotation books is *Bartlett's Familiar Quotations*, originally compiled by John Bartlett in Cambridge, Massachusetts in 1855. It is now in its fifteenth edition. Quotations are included on the basis of familiarity and worth, as determined by the editors, and each new edition has quotations added and removed. Bartlett's has a chronological arrangement with authors arranged by birth date and their quotations by date of publication. (See figure 15.4; note that the three authors listed have birth dates within a two-year span, but the dates of their quotations range from 1888 for Thayer to 1936 for Stanislavski. Note also the footnotes for translator and source.) The earliest quotation in Bartlett's is from the ancient Egyptian "Song of the Harper" and the last author quoted is Stevie Wonder (1950-). There is an alphabetical index of authors and an extensive keyword phrase index.

Another good quotation book recently published is *Respectfully Quoted: A Dictionary of Quotations Requested from the Congressional Research Service*. This was compiled by reference librarians in the Library of Congress from the requests that they have received over the years from members of Congress and others in the government. It gathers up a good selection of quotations from government officials as well as from perennially elusive texts. Because it was compiled from a list of actual reference questions, it is likely to include more quotations that have relevance to politics and current affairs than do other quotation books.

There are a number of other highly respected quotation books, some with general coverage and many with coverage of specialized groups such as women or the military. Many of these have insufficient indexes, which makes them less desirable than *Bartlett's* in spite of the fact that they have a good range of quotations. A popular title using a subject arrangement is Stevenson's *The Home Book of Quotations*. This has quotations classified under broad subject terms such as "game" or "garden." Although it has a good phrase index, the author

Santayana — Casement

Konstantin Sergeevich Alekseev
Stanislavski
1863–1938

13   Our type of creativeness is the conception
and birth of a new being—the person in the
part. It is a natural act similar to the birth of
a human being.
      An Actor Prepares [1936],[1] *ch. 16*

14   In the creative process there is the father,
the author of the play; the mother, the actor
pregnant with the part; and the child, the
role to be born.   *Ib.*

Ernest Lawrence Thayer
1863–1940

15 There was ease in Casey's manner as he
        stepped into his place,
There was pride in Casey's bearing, and a
        smile on Casey's face,
And when, responding to the cheers, he
        lightly doffed his hat,
No stranger in the crowd could doubt 'twas
        Casey at the bat.
        Casey at the Bat [1888],[2] *st. 6*

16 Oh! somewhere in this favored land the sun
        is shining bright;
The band is playing somewhere, and some-
        where hearts are light;
And somewhere men are laughing and some-
        where children shout,
But there is no joy in Mudville—mighty
        Casey has struck out.   *Ib. st. 13*

Sir Roger Casement
1864–1916

17   Where all your rights become only an accumulated wrong; where men must beg with
bated breath for leave to subsist in their own
land, to think their own thoughts, to sing
their own songs, to garner the fruits of their
own labors . . . then surely it is braver, a
saner and truer thing, to be a rebel in act and
deed against such circumstances as these
than tamely to accept it as the natural lot of
men.   *Statement from prison [June 29,*
                                          1916]

[1] Translated by ELIZABETH REYNOLDS HAPGOOD.
[2] First printed in the *San Francisco Examiner* [June 3,
1888].
  Yet I'd take my chance with fame, / Calmly let it go at
that, / With the right to sign my name / Under "Casey at
the Bat."—GRANTLAND RICE [1880–1954], *The Master-
piece*

Fig. 15.4. Entries from *Bartlett's Familiar Quotations*, 15th and 125th anniversary edition, copyright © 1980 by Little, Brown and Company.

index can be frustrating because heavily quoted authors are cited by page numbers only, with no further indication of the contents of the quotation. Stevenson is strong on quotations from literature, particularly poetry, and the phrase index makes tracking down this type of question relatively easy. The subject arrangement has little use when a specific quotation is sought. It is difficult to browse through quotes from a single author, as is possible with an author arrangement such as that found in *Bartlett's*.

Some other quotation books cite sources poorly or not at all, giving the user only part of the information sought. The user must also bear in mind that all quotations in English from non-English sources are translations, so there may be variations in wording from one book to another.

Quotation books are beginning to be available in electronic form. *Bartlett's Familiar Quotations* is included in the Microsoft Bookshelf CD-ROM Reference Library. The Quotations Database, with material from *The Oxford Dictionary of Quotations*, is available online through DIALOG. The database includes quotations accompanied by the author's name, birth and death dates, and the source of the quotation. All words from the quotations are searchable, allowing more complete identification of quotations containing particular words or phrases than is possible in a printed quotation book.

Search Strategies

As with all areas of reference work, the strategy of answering dictionary-related questions is often dictated by the nature of the question itself. The questioner may specify the source to be used, for instance, "Please tell me how *Webster's Third* spells this word" or even "Is this word in *Webster's Third*?" Students may come looking specifically for an etymological (or more commonly, an "entomological") dictionary. Librarians soon learn to repress any comments about insects and steer them directly to the *Oxford English Dictionary*.

An interesting problem arises sometimes with regard to the date of the dictionary being used in relation to the information being sought. Editors of manuscript diaries, letters, and personal narratives frequently have to define words found in these manuscripts in the context of the period in which they were written. In this case, a dictionary written during the period in question or a dictionary such as the *OED*, with extensive quotations from the period, may serve better than a modern one.

■ ══ ■

15.4

A Question of Wills

Jane, a graduate assistant working for Professor White in the History Department, came to the reference desk with a problem that had arisen in connection with the manuscript of an eighteenth-century will that the professor was editing for a book. In the will, the deceased had left "a pair of stillyards" to his oldest son, and nothing in the context of the will gave a clue as to what these were. A quick check of the *Webster's Third* and the *Random House Dictionary* proved fruitless, so the reference librarian suggested the *OED*. The *OED* gave two possibilities, both with examples from the eighteenth century (definitions given here are paraphrased from the *OED*):[13]

still-yard, or *stillion*. A stand for a cask used in distilling.

stillyard, or *steelyard*. A balance consisting of a lever with unequal arms, used for weighing. Also ... *a pair of steelyards*.

Although the cask stands could be used in pairs, the more likely answer was the weighing instrument, since it probably was a valuable item and was likely to be mentioned in a will. In this case, it was necessary for Jane to consider the quotations from the eighteenth century, and to make a decision based on the context in which the term in question had originally been found.

Librarians, of course, must work within the limitations of their collections. A representative selection of the sources discussed in the previous section should answer most of the general lexicographical questions that come up. Specialized vocabulary questions may require the use of specialized dictionaries or subject encyclopedias. When more information than a simple dictionary definition is required, or information of a very technical nature is needed, a subject dictionary should be consulted. Scientific and medical terms sometimes require a subject specialist to interpret the dictionary. Telephoned questions, in particular, can be very tricky in this regard, because it is difficult for the nonspecialist to read chemical formulas and unfamiliar terminology to a phone caller. If feasible, it is sometimes better to suggest that the caller consult the books in person or discuss the question directly with a subject specialist.

Librarians soon adopt a strategy such as: first stop, *Webster's Third* or *Random House*; second stop, *OED*; etc., for definition questions. Questions involving quotations can be much more difficult, with a typical strategy involving *Bartlett's* first, followed by a sweep of the quotation books on the shelf one after another until the quotation is located or the available sources exhausted.

Desk dictionaries and thesauri are generally used by library patrons as writing aids while they are in the library, although a desk dictionary by the telephone on the reference desk is handy for librarians answering telephone questions. The use of foreign-language, slang, usage, and abbreviations dictionaries is directly dictated by the question, which may be, "How do you say 'third' in German?" or "What does PMLA stand for?"

There is no substitute for actual use of reference books in enabling a librarian to become familiar with their contents. Browsing through dictionaries or following a subject of interest through several often reveals features that are not indicated by the title. For example, the *Dictionary of American Regional English* is an excellent source for folklore concerning individual wild plants. Unfamiliar terms used in popular song titles and lyrics can be found in Partridge's *Dictionary of Slang and Unconventional English*. Most dictionaries are not used to their fullest capacity. The wise reference librarian knows and uses these valuable tools daily.

Notes

1.   Henry Watson Fowler, *A Dictionary of Modern English Usage*, 2d ed. (Oxford: Oxford University Press, 1983), 287.

2.   *The Random House Dictionary of the English Language*, 2d ed., unabridged (New York: Random House, 1987), 985.

3.   James Root Hulbert, *Dictionaries British and American*, rev. ed. (London: Andre Deutsch Limited, 1968), 99. "The purpose of the dictionary maker then was to present what was correct in the spelling, meaning, and use of words, actually to omit anything that was 'low', and, from the time the dictionaries of Sheridan and Walker appeared, to set a standard of elegance and excellence in pronunciation."

4.   Ken Kister, "The Big Dictionaries: Hoards and Hordes of Words," *Wilson Library Bulletin* 62 (February 1988): 41.

5.   Hulbert, *Dictionaries*, 68: "If I had written: a good definition is one that defines the meaning of a word, I should have dodged the issue or begged the question. The reader would have got no real information, nothing that he did not know before he read my discussion. Yet such slipshod definitions find place in dictionaries."

6.   Kister, "The Big Dictionaries," 41, 43: "Some of our best and worst dictionaries bear the name Webster. The same is true of Roget when it comes to thesauri and synonym dictionaries." The worst of the dictionaries is the heavily promoted *Webster's New Universal Unabridged Dictionary*. This was originally published in 1941 and has been little changed since then.

7.   Kister, "The Big Dictionaries," 40. The supplements are no substitute for a new edition, which will not be forthcoming for at least eight to ten years, if at all.

8.   James Sledd and Wilma R. Ebbitt, *Dictionaries and That Dictionary, A Casebook on the Aims of Lexicographers and the Targets of Reviewers* (Chicago: Scott, Foresman, 1962), 55-56.

9.   Ibid., 79-80.

10. Eric Korn, "Miracles of Miniaturization," *TLS; Times Literary Supplement* (January 13-19, 1989): 34: "The transcription system is an irritant: OEP [Oxford Electronic Press] have decided in the interests of making the system compatible with as many printers as possible, to avoid the use of diacriticals and foreign alphabets (even, shockingly, Greek): consequently the etymological section is full of unrecognizable abbreviations — doubtless there are some printers which are happy to read u《mac》as an instruction to print a long *u* (i.e., U macron) but the human reader has problems. Likewise, a《dotab》is just *a* with a dot above, a《frown》is a picturesque way of saying *â*."

11. Richard A. Bowers, "The Oxford English Dictionary on Compact Disc," *Electronic Library* 7 April 1989): 102.

12. Kenneth F. Kister, *Dictionary Buying Guide, A Consumer Guide to General English-Language Wordbooks in Print* (New York: R. R. Bowker, 1977), 98.

13. *Oxford English Dictionary*, 2d ed. (Oxford: Clarendon Press, 1989) 16: 611, 698, 699, 700.

List of Sources

Acronyms, Initialisms, and Abbreviations Dictionary. Detroit, Mich.: Gale Research, 1960- . Annual.

American Heritage Dictionary. 2d college ed. Boston: Houghton Mifflin, 1982. 1,568p.

American Heritage Dictionary of Indo-European Roots. Boston: Houghton Mifflin, 1985. 113p.

Bartlett, John. *Bartlett's Familiar Quotations*. 15th ed. Boston: Little, Brown, 1980. 1,540p.

Compact Edition of the Oxford English Dictionary. 2 vols. New York: Oxford University Press, 1971.

Concise American Heritage Dictionary. Rev. ed. Boston: Houghton Mifflin, 1987. 818p.

Craigie, Sir William A., and James R. Hulbert, eds. *A Dictionary of American English on Historical Principles*. 4 vols. Chicago: University of Chicago Press, 1938-1944.

Dictionary of American Regional English. Cambridge, Mass.: Harvard University Press, vol. 1- , 1985- .

Fowler, Henry Watson. *A Dictionary of Modern English Usage*. 2d ed. Oxford: Oxford University Press, 1983. 725p.

Funk & Wagnalls New International Dictionary of the English Language. Comprehensive ed. 2 vols. New York: Library Guild, World Publishers Guild, 1987.

Funk & Wagnalls New Standard Dictionary of the English Language. New York: Funk & Wagnalls, 1965. 2,816p.

General Reference Books for Adults: Authoritative Evaluations of Encyclopedias, Atlases, and Dictionaries. Edited by Marion Sader. New York: R. R. Bowker, 1988. 614p.

Information Finder. [CD-ROM]. Chicago: World Book.

Mathews, Mitford M., ed. *A Dictionary of Americanisms on Historical Principles*. 2 vols. Chicago: University of Chicago Press, 1951.

Merriam-Webster Ninth New Collegiate Dictionary. [CD-ROM]. Washington, D.C.: Highlighted Data, 1989.

Microsoft Bookshelf CD-ROM Reference Library. [CD-ROM]. Redmond, Wash.: Microsoft Corp.

New Dictionary of American Slang. Rev. ed. Edited by Robert L. Chapman. New York: Harper & Row, 1986. 485p.

The Oxford Dictionary of Quotations. 3d ed. New York: Oxford University Press, 1979. 907p.

Oxford English Dictionary. 2d ed. 20 vols. Oxford: Clarendon Press, 1989.

Oxford English Dictionary on Compact Disc. [CD-ROM]. New York: Oxford University Press; TriStar Publishing, 1987.

Partridge, Eric. *Dictionary of Slang and Unconventional English*. 8th ed. New York: Macmillan, 1984. 1,400p.

Periodical Title Abbreviations. 7th ed. 2 vols. Detroit, Mich.: Gale Research, 1989.

Quotations Database. New York: Oxford University Press. (DIALOG File 175.)

Random House College Dictionary. Rev. ed. New York: Random House, 1980. 1,568p.

The Random House Dictionary of the English Language. 2d ed., unabridged. New York: Random House, 1987. 2,478p.

Respectfully Quoted: A Dictionary of Quotations Requested from the Congressional Research Service. Washington, D.C.: Library of Congress, 1987. 520p.

Reverse Acronyms, Initialisms, and Abbreviations Dictionary. Detroit, Mich.: Gale Research, 1972- . Annual.

Roget, Peter Mark. *Roget's International Thesaurus: Fourth Edition*. New York: Harper & Row, 1984. 1,316p.

Roget's II: The New Thesaurus. Expanded ed. Boston: Houghton Mifflin, 1988. 1,135p.

Stevenson, Burton Egbert. *The Home Book of Quotations*. 10th ed. New York: Dodd, Mead, 1967. 2,816p.

12,000 Words: A Supplement to Webster's Third New International Dictionary. Springfield, Mass.: Merriam-Webster, 1986. 212p.

Webster's New Dictionary of Synonyms. Springfield, Mass.: Merriam-Webster, 1984. 909p.

Webster's New World Dictionary of American English. 3d college ed. New York: Prentice-Hall Press, 1988. 1,574p.

Webster's Ninth New Collegiate Dictionary. Springfield, Mass.: Merriam-Webster, 1988. 1,563p.

Webster's Third New International Dictionary of the English Language, Unabridged. Springfield, Mass.: Merriam, 1961, 1986. 2,662p.

Wentworth, Harold. *American Dialect Dictionary*. New York: Thomas Y. Crowell, 1944. 747p.

World Book Dictionary. 2 vols. Edited by Clarence Barnhart. Chicago: World Book, 1990.

Additional Readings

Amato, Kimberly, and Karen Moranski. "Oxford English Dictionary: CD-ROM and Second Edition." *Reference Services Review* 18 (Spring 1990): 79-82, 86.
    Amato and Moranski examine the advantages and problems of electronic access to the dictionary through the medium of CD-ROM, and describe the merits of the second edition of the *OED*.

General Reference Books for Adults: Authoritative Evaluations of Encyclopedias, Atlases, and Dictionaries. Edited by Marion Sader. New York: R. R. Bowker, 1988. 614p.
    This is a guide for purchasing reference books for home or library use. "Dictionaries and Word Books," chapter 9, tells what to look for in dictionaries and reviews individual titles.

Hulbert, James Root. *Dictionaries British and American*. Rev. ed. London: Andre Deutsch Limited, 1968. 109p.
    Hulbert gives a short history of English-language dictionaries with a discussion of the features of good dictionaries and how they are used. It is a good background source in spite of its age.

Kister, Ken. "The Big Dictionaries: Hoards and Hordes of Words." *Wilson Library Bulletin* 62 (February 1988): 38-43.

Tips for selecting an unabridged dictionary and an extended review of *The Random House Dictionary*, *Webster's Third New International Dictionary*, and *The Oxford English Dictionary*, first edition, are found in this article.

Kister, Kenneth F. *Dictionary Buying Guide, A Consumer Guide to General English-Language Wordbooks in Print*. New York: R. R. Bowker, 1977. 358p.

Although it is now out-of-date, this is still the most comprehensive guide to English-language dictionaries. It has good critical evaluations.

Pierson, Robert M. *Desk Dictionaries, A Consumer's Guide*. Chicago: American Library Association, 1986. 32p.

This is an updated version of an article that appeared in *Reference Books Bulletin* (December 1, 1983). It contains comparative reviews of desk dictionaries in print.

The Reader's Adviser, A Layman's Guide to Literature. 13th ed. 6 vols. New York: R. R. Bowker, 1986.

Volume 3, chapter 2, "Dictionaries," by Sally M. Roberts, has an annotated list of currently available English- and foreign-language dictionaries.

Sledd, James, and Wilma R. Ebbitt. *Dictionaries and That Dictionary, A Casebook on the Aims of Lexicographers and the Targets of Reviewers*. Chicago: Scott, Foresman, 1962. 273p.

This is a textbook consisting of essays and reviews designed to stimulate discussion and critical thinking about dictionaries. More than half the book is a selection of reviews that appeared after the first publication of *Webster's Third New International*.

16 □

ENCYCLOPEDIAS

Uses and Characteristics

Where can I find information about Napoleon? What does the state flag of Virginia look like? I'm writing a term paper on the arms race; how can I narrow down my topic? What is meant by "free verse"? How is laser technology used for medical purposes? I have to do a report on gerbils; where do I start?

These questions are typical of those posed at many reference desks. It is hard to believe that a single source could possibly satisfy such a broad spectrum of needs, yet encyclopedias are designed to serve just such a herculean function. The *encyclopedia* is an interdisciplinary repository of information, a systematic overview and summary of human knowledge. This knowledge is then organized and packaged in such a way as to be accessible to and retrievable by its users, and to illuminate the relationships and intersections among these innumerable areas of understanding.

The purpose of the encyclopedia form has historically been twofold: (1) to educate; and (2) to inform, although some degree of tension has always existed between these two ideals.[1] Charles Van Doren describes the goals of the editors of *L'Encyclopédie Française*, who proposed that the encyclopedia should primarily serve to teach and only secondarily to inform, as being that the encyclopedia should act primarily as a work of art and only secondarily as a work of reference, and that the ideal reader of an encyclopedia should be the curious average man and only secondarily be the specialist or the student.[2] In contrast to this viewpoint, Jacques Barzun defined the encyclopedia as first and foremost a work of reference, its chief purpose being to supply answers to questions of fact and meaning, and that a didactic intention renders the work "at once tedious and suspect."[3] Current publishing practice reflects a variety of approaches, although *use* of encyclopedias most typically mirrors Barzun's perspective.

Because there are limitations upon the breadth and depth of the information contained in encyclopedias, it is helpful to examine the kinds of questions for which they are most useful. These questions may be categorized by three basic types: fact finding, general background information, and pre-research information.

1. *Fact Finding* (Ready Reference)

When did World War I start? What is the capital of Iowa? The encyclopedia is an ideal hunting ground for answers to ready reference questions. After all, this type of reference source is, by definition, a collection of information about people, places, and things, including numerous facts and figures.

2. *General Background Information*

How is lava formed? How does an electromagnet work? Just as an encyclo-pedia is mined for answers to ready reference questions, it is used to locate explana-tory material or definitions. In providing background information, an encyclopedia also serves as a guide to related topics within its pages or to outside sources of information. For example, information about electromagnets is cross-referenced to information on magnetism and electricity; bibliographies direct the reader to primary sources and to book-length treatments.

3. *Pre-Research Information*

At the novice level, encyclopedias teach research skills — systematic approaches to gathering information. Beyond this level, encyclopedias cannot be considered sole sources of information for research purposes. However, encyclopedias set subjects within a context or a framework, allowing the reader to view the big picture. By becoming aware of the larger issues and the related concepts, users find what they need at this stage of their investigations; they are then in a much better position to develop informed research strategies.

Students often come to the library under admonitions from their teachers not to use encyclopedias. Librarians are therefore burdened with the task of convincing students that using an encyclopedia may be a necessary and very helpful first step, even though it is not appropriate as the only reference for a paper. Similarly, teachers would do well to encourage this kind of pre-research investigation, with the understanding that it will help to direct and strengthen students' subsequent work.

Kinds of Information Contained in Encyclopedias

Encyclopedias provide a systematic overview of *selected* topics of major importance. They deliver a survey presentation, a "snapshot" of how things are and were. As such, encyclopedias are written in an objective rather than an analytical style, imitating the text-book writer rather than the philosopher. In addition to the traditional adult-level, multi-volume general encyclopedia, there are a number of other important types.

Single-Volume Encyclopedias. Single-volume encyclopedias are efficient sources of straightforward, succinct information. They also provide an alternative to multivolume sets for the home user and an inexpensive way for libraries to expand encyclopedia collections. They are usually arranged dictionary-style, without an index. One much-cited standard, the *New Columbia Encyclopedia*, is no longer in print, but is being revised for publication in 1992. The 1990 *Random House Encyclopedia* contains both thematically and alphabetically arranged sections, and includes a 132-page full-color world atlas from Rand McNally. The smaller 1988 *Hutchinson Encyclopedia*, published in Great Britain, contains twenty-five thousand entries and has a distinctly British flavor. A new British title, the 1990 *Cambridge Encyclopedia*, is similar in size and shows conscious attention to international coverage.

Single-volume "desk-top" encyclopedias are extremely inexpensive options which may be especially attractive to the home user. The *Concise Columbia Encyclopedia*, its second edition published in 1989, contains 15,000 entries and sells for $39.95. The *New American Desk Encyclopedia* could also be included in this category, though it is so condensed that it is really suitable primarily as a home reference source rather than as a library research tool.

Encyclopedias for Children and Young Adults. It is typically during childhood that people are introduced to encyclopedias. During these first research experiences, students discover the convenience and accessibility of the encyclopedia format, one which they may later be reluctant to leave. Children's encyclopedia sets are generally based on the same organizational and theoretical principles as their adult-level counterparts; the differences are manifested in such areas as reading level, the percentage and type of illustrative material, and the presence of learning aids and devices.

Within the youth market, encyclopedias are further distinguished from one another by the audience they are intended to serve. Some titles, such as the *New Grolier Student Encyclopedia*, are written for a rather specifically defined age span. Other titles, such as *World Book*, encompass late childhood through the young adult, or even adult, levels. Accommodating such a broad audience is usually accomplished by means of graduated reading levels and user aids, and by targeting topics of interest by age level and writing those articles for that age group. The wide choice of titles and levels allows librarians to cater to the abilities of varied populations and to individual differences.

Subject Encyclopedias. The primary mission of the general encyclopedia is to provide broad scope, a task which can be accomplished only with some limitations on depth. Subject encyclopedias have the luxury of providing in-depth, scholarly coverage of a single subject area or discipline. The multiplicity of available titles allows librarians to customize their reference shelves according to local need. Reference tools such as the *ARBA Guide to Subject Encyclopedias and Dictionaries* and *First Stop: The Master Index to Subject Encyclopedias* are helpful in this kind of collection development as well as in assisting librarians in the identification of appropriate sources when answering questions.

Relatively inexpensive one-volume titles such as the *Cambridge Encyclopedia of the Middle East and North Africa* and *The Encyclopedia of Suicide* facilitate ready reference access to subjects that may not be well represented in the circulating collection. A larger investment allows a library to choose from a growing array of multivolume subject encyclopedias. Mid-sized, two-to-five-volume sets, such as the *Encyclopedia of Psychology* and the *Encyclopedia of Crime and Justice*, provide more thorough coverage than do single-volume titles. Expensive multivolume sets, such as the *McGraw-Hill Encyclopedia of Science and Technology* and the *Encyclopedia of Religion*, add great depth and scholarship to a reference collection.

Encyclopedia Yearbooks and Supplements. Encyclopedia yearbooks function more as a document of the year's major events than as a meaningful method of keeping an encyclopedia up-to-date. For example, the 1990 *Britannica Book of the Year* devotes approximately four hundred pages to describing the major events of 1989, and contains feature stories and articles which update specific portions of the parent set. Departing from typical yearbook format, the last half of this annual publication is comprised of an extremely detailed "World Data" section, which rivals statistical sources of information such as the *Statesman's Year-Book* and other sources discussed in chapter 13. A substantive feature like this section can make a yearbook a unique enough reference tool to consider its purchase for purposes other than as an update of the year's events. Yearbooks can often be purchased singly or on a standing order basis, whether or not a library owns the parent set.

Encyclopedia supplements, as distinguished from yearbooks, are often topically oriented, and may even be unrelated to the parent encyclopedia. For example, World Book's *Science Year* focuses on developments in a single field of endeavor. In order to relate it to the parent set, the volume comes supplied with stick-on cross-references for insertion into the body of the main encyclopedia.

Foreign-Language Encyclopedias. In addition to the obvious—an encyclopedia which is published in another country and in another language—foreign-language encyclopedias are invaluable for obtaining more thorough coverage of other countries and in capturing viewpoints not readily found in English-language publications. Individual sets possess unique traits, as do English-language sets, and they often contain information common to other cultures which is not typically found in American publications. Some sets, such as the *Kodansha Encyclopedia of Japan*, are published in English and can therefore be regarded as subject encyclopedias on other countries. The *Great Soviet Encyclopedia* serves this purpose as well as providing the Soviet perspective on a nearly universal variety of issues.

Evaluation

Like dictionaries, encyclopedias are often published to meet the general information needs of a particular group, such as school children or scholars. Unlike dictionaries, encyclopedias generally contain lengthy essays as well as compact factual discussions. Consequently, the writing style and syndetic structure of encyclopedias assume great importance when one attempts to assess their usefulness. Format, accuracy and objectivity, currency, and ease of use are other issues to keep in mind when evaluating specific titles.

Using Reviewing Tools

In evaluating encyclopedias, librarians justifiably rely upon a core of reputable reviewing sources. Experienced reviewers conduct systematic examinations of new encyclopedias by using standard criteria. Patrons seeking advice about purchasing an encyclopedia can be referred to reviews, particularly to a title such as *Kister's Concise Guide to Best Encyclopedias*, which is addressed to the lay reader. (Commonly consulted encyclopedia reviewing sources are listed at the end of this chapter as additional readings.) A favorite of many librarians, the *Reference Books Bulletin*, appears in each issue of *Booklist* and provides detailed and timely reviews of individual encyclopedia titles on a periodic basis. Once a year, this section features an annual encyclopedia update highlighting the year's changes for each title, and contains a table of valuable comparative statistics (see figure 16.1).

Encyclopedia Summary Chart, 1989						
Encyclopedia	Approx. No of Entries: Excl. Cross-References	No. of Pages	Approx. No. of Illus.	Consumer Price; Excl. Shipping & Handling	School and Library Price 1989; Excl. Shipping & Handling	School and Library Price 1990; Excl. Shipping and Handling
Academic American Encyclopedia 21v.	28,780	9,792	16,800	$800	$660	Same as 1989
Children's Britannica 20v.	4,190 main entries 5,700 capsule articles	6,775	6,200	$303.05	$299	$329
Collier's Encyclopedia 24v.	25,000	19,750	17,600	$1,499.50; $1,799.50 with Collier's Home Educational Program	$899	Not available at this date
Compton's Encyclopedia and Fact-Index 26v.	5,200 + 26,023 Fact-Index entries	11,222	22,513	$699	$539	$499
The Encyclopedia Americana 30v.	52,000	26,965	22,815	$1,200	$995	Same as 1989
Funk & Wagnalls New Encyclopedia 29v.	25,000	13,024	9,153	$135.81	$140	Same as 1989
Merit Students Encyclopedia 20v.	21,000	12,300	20,000	Not availabe to consumers	$579	Not available at this date
The New Book of Knowledge 21v.	4,350+ 4,650 Dictionary Index entries	10,572	23,000	$750	$625	Same as 1989
The New Encyclopaedia Britannica 32v.	64,952 in *Micropaedia,* 680 in *Macropaedia*	32,201	23,082	$1,499	$1,069	$1,089
New Standard Encyclopedia 20v.	17,369	10,680	12,000	$849.50	$499.50	Not available at this date
The World Book Encyclopedia 22v.	25,600	14,052	29,000	$579–$799 (depending on choice of binding)	$549	Same as 1989

Fig. 16.1. "Encyclopedia Summary Chart" from annual encyclopedia update in *Booklist*. Reprinted with permission of the American Library Association, *Booklist*, Oct. 15, 1989, p. 481.

Book-length sources, such as the *American Reference Books Annual* and the Kister guides, profile the salient characteristics and emphases of individual encyclopedias in a single convenient package.

Scope

Focus or Purpose. The purpose of an encyclopedia is defined in terms of audience, content, and the way in which content is presented. For example, *Childcraft* is a topically arranged title for young readers, as opposed to the *Encyclopedia Americana*, which is a full-length, alphabetically arranged title for older students and adults. The focus or purpose of each title is described in its prefatory matter. Good reviewing sources will reveal the less immediately obvious or overtly defined kinds of editorial agendas. For example, some sets emphasize the practical rather than the academic, visual material rather than textual material, or the instructional rather than the simply informational.

Subject Coverage. Ideally, subject coverage should be uniform from discipline to discipline. Some topics are naturally given greater emphasis, based upon factors such as intended audience and scope. Any general encyclopedia published in the United States will devote more space to American history and geography than to the history and geography of another country. However, a general check of proportional length and depth across a representative sampling of subjects can reveal discrepancies and anomalies that are more difficult to justify. The inclusion of contemporary issues is another indicator of both timeliness and uniformity.

Audience. The audience of a general encyclopedia is generally defined in terms of age level. Is a title truly appropriate for the age group it claims to serve? *World Book* gears articles toward the age level most likely to read them. For example, the "Mouse" article is written for younger children, whereas the "Cell" article is written for the more advanced reader.[4] Some publishers use marketing tactics which present their products as being appropriate for all age groups. However, it is very difficult to produce text that can be understood by a nine-year-old and yet not seem diluted or disappointingly brief to an adult.

Arrangement and Style. General encyclopedias are most commonly arranged alphabetically, with additional access provided by cross-references and indexes. Some sets are topically arranged, although that pattern is more typical of single-volume or specialized works. The alphabetical arrangement itself varies between the word-by-word method, where *San Salvador* comes before *sandman*, and the letter-by-letter method, where *sandman* comes before *San Salvador*. In most sets, bibliographies directly follow articles or sections within long articles. In a few titles, such as *Collier's*, the bibliographies are compiled in a separate volume. The length and depth of the bibliographies themselves vary enormously from set to set.

Style of presentation creates further differences among encyclopedias. Titles such as *Collier's* or the *Encyclopaedia Britannica Macropaedia* are characterized by long articles on broad topics. The *Academic American* presents a large number of shorter articles on specific topics. *World Book* features a "study guide" style emphasizing the learning process. The writing style itself deserves close examination. Is the text coherent, readable, and comprehensible? Is it lively and interesting, or is it pedantic?

The organization and presentation of the material in an encyclopedia should enhance rather than interfere with its usefulness and accessibility. Evaluation of these characteristics is ultimately most meaningful within the context of the needs of the local patron population. Most libraries find strength in diversity. By offering a variety of encyclopedia titles, most user needs can be met.

Format

The physical format of an encyclopedia has great impact upon its usefulness. Patrons *do* judge a book by its cover and appearance; they unconsciously select titles based upon such factors as the use of color or the amount of white space on each page. It is revealing to examine the proportion of illustrations in terms of the length of the articles, especially in children's sets. Are the pictures up-to-date? Do the illustrations enhance the text, or do they obviously serve as filler? Is the layout attractive and appealing? Are the user guides clear and easy to follow?

In electronic form, the "cover" of an encyclopedia becomes the hardware itself, the feel of the keyboard, and the appearance of the content on a screen. Initially, electronic encyclopedias contained only the textual portions of their print counterparts, but with rapid developments in optical storage technologies, some publishers are adding pictures and sound, creating an exciting multimedia environment, such as that found in Compton's MultiMedia Encyclopedia.

The user interface, or *user friendliness*, of an electronic encyclopedia has great impact upon its usefulness and accessibility. Just as page headings and other user guides aid the reader in navigating among the volumes of a print set, the means of locating information in an electronic product also must be very obvious in order to work. Format must not interfere with purpose. Given this admonition, it is interesting to observe that online versions of encyclopedias are usually only available through vendors who provide access to a great many online products. A single front-end or software interface is the only pathway to all of the products, whether they are scientific bibliographic databases, corporate annual reports, or general-interest encyclopedias. Without a source-specific friendly interface, the novice user can neither efficiently nor effectively exploit the retrievable nature of electronically stored information, and might be better off using a print product.

In electronic form, every word of an encyclopedia can potentially be accessed, allowing for great flexibility and retrievability. By using Boolean operators to combine concepts, information can be ferreted out in a way that is not possible when using a print set. However, this unlimited accessibility has the potential of being too much of a good thing. Current methods of keyword retrieval make it difficult to discriminate between the more important and the less important occurrences of a term. A subject may appear many times and the information involve an unreasonable number of screens to read. A CD-ROM product, with localized front-end software, can mitigate some of the difficulties of online retrieval by building in controlled vocabulary indexing and allowing the user to leap instantly to cross-references from any article. As a means of determining relevance, Grolier's New Electronic Encyclopedia sorts the retrieved hits in descending order based on the number of times the term appears within an article.

In a high-use environment, many patrons can use a multivolume print encyclopedia at one time. Few libraries can afford to offer multiple online or CD-ROM workstations, enabling the same number of patrons to simultaneously access an electronic version of an encyclopedia. The ability to network CD-ROM workstations cheaply and effectively is only now developing. Evaluating this issue entails examining use patterns in an individual library environment. In an ideal world, funding and space would be available to provide both formats, and selection would be a choice between duplicating titles across formats or offering unique titles in each. One forward-looking solution has been taken by a number of libraries, such as the member libraries of CARL (the Colorado Alliance of Research Libraries): a license for the New Electronic Encyclopedia was purchased so that this source could be made available as an option on the public access catalog. Every online catalog terminal doubles as an encyclopedia![5]

Evaluation of an electronic encyclopedia for an individual library is largely dependent upon understanding the product in terms of its appropriateness for the needs and characteristics of the patron population which will be using it. Without the context of setting, the true value of a title cannot be meaningfully gauged.

Uniqueness

Uniqueness can be measured by two standards. First, an encyclopedia may possess unique features or attributes that distinguish it from other general encyclopedias. For example, the *Britannica Propaedia*, a single-volume hierarchical outline of knowledge, is not matched by anything similar in the field of encyclopedia publishing. Uniqueness can also be measured in terms of an individual library's local encyclopedia collection. The format of an encyclopedia, an emphasis or perspective that is not already represented in a collection, adds dimension and flexibility to that collection.

Authority

An encyclopedia is collectively authored by an editorial staff and by contributors who are considered to be experts in their fields. In an adult-level encyclopedia, the role of the editorial staff is most often one of refining the written work of the expert contributors so that it conforms to editorial goals and standards. Therefore, even the most distinguished of experts is limited by editorial parameters and considerations. Individual credit is generally denoted by the author's name or initials at the end of an article. A separate list of contributors includes each author's full name and current professional position. In some cases, "signed" articles may indicate nothing more than that the text was written by editorial staff and merely reviewed by the subject expert. Careful examination of prefatory material should shed light on the true definition of authorship in an individual encyclopedia.

Accuracy

Accuracy and Reliability of Information. American society is highly susceptible to the notion that the printed word represents gospel truth. Encyclopedias, perhaps more so than other reference sources, are burdened with this expectation. Nevertheless, encyclopedias are written by human beings, not gods; therefore, they inevitably contain errors. Harvey Einbinder made this point most thoroughly in his 1964 exposé entitled *The Myth of the Britannica*,[6] a nearly four-hundred-page long critique of an encyclopedia which had theretofore been held in reverence. Perhaps it is more reasonable to assume that all encyclopedias contain mistakes and that, for evaluation purposes, one looks for titles in which this difficulty is minimized. In any case, accuracy and reliability cannot be assumed.

■ == ■

16.1

The Truth and Nothing But the Truth

Peter was assigned to write a report on George Washington Carver. Now a seventh grader, Peter and his family had just immigrated to the United States the previous summer. Although his command of English was increasing rapidly, this assignment was Peter's first real experience in using library resources. The school librarian showed him how to look up Carver in the 1990 *World Book* and then turned to help another student. Peter copied down Carver's birth and death dates, which were indicated as 1864-1943, and took other notes that he thought were appropriate for his needs.

Peter then noticed other encyclopedia sets next to the *World Book* and decided to give those a try. But when he looked up Carver in the 1990 *Academic American Encyclopedia*, he read that Carver was born a slave in July 1861! Peter was still pondering this discrepancy when the librarian came back to see how he was doing. Together they looked in the 1990 *Britannica Micropaedia*, which indicated a birth date of "c. 1860," and in the 1990 *Encyclopedia Americana*, which reported that the exact date of Carver's birth was not known but was "on or about" July 12, 1861. The librarian explained to Peter that careful records of the birth and death dates of slaves were not always kept. She also expressed disappointment in the treatment of the data in the encyclopedias, yet tried to use it as an opportunity to show Peter that, although they were wonderful sources of information, encyclopedias were not always perfect. She then took him through the steps of locating a book on Carver, which Peter used to supplement the information he had found in the encyclopedias.

Objectivity. Objectivity is a characteristic that is assumed of encyclopedias, yet there are ways to determine if an individual title can truly make this claim. Are both sides of controversial issues represented? Racial and sexual biases are especially evident in language usage and in pictures. These days, however, publishers are more likely to avoid offending anyone, resulting in a noncommittal kind of blandness. Phenomena are described without reporting the different sides of an issue and sometimes without even an indication of the controversial nature of a topic.

Passive bias, an unfortunately common contemporary problem, is evident when, for instance, pictures and examples commonly display men and women involved in stereotypically sex-defined activities.[7] Other clues can be identified by the simple absence of certain kinds of information or in otherwise disproportionate coverage.[8] Biases within a subject area may be more difficult to spot, especially for the lay reader.

Currency

Like cars, encyclopedias begin to lose value, or currency, the moment they are purchased. The economics of publishing a multivolume work make it impossible to achieve comprehensive currency with each annual update. Instead, a percentage of material is revised, but a new annual set does not constitute a totally new edition. The percentage of material revised during each year of this continuous revision process varies from title to title. Kenneth Kister suggests that 10 percent is the minimum percentage to warrant purchase of a new set.[9] Often, text will be revised while bibliographies remain dated. Print sets are also limited by typesetting requirements that allow for minimal changes in pagination.

Without the restrictive burdens of the typesetting process, can one assume that an online or CD-ROM version of an encyclopedia will be updated more frequently? The electronic form certainly liberates editors from tight constraints on length and layout, which affect the ability to maintain currency. For example, the CD-ROM 1988 New Electronic Encyclopedia had ten million words compared to the nine million words in its contemporary print counterpart, the *Academic American Encyclopedia*. Some information that had been dropped from the print version was retained in the electronic version. For example, only in electronic form do the fact boxes in the articles on individual countries include currency exchange rates and the names of heads of state. For reference purposes, then, a librarian might look to an electronic version of an encyclopedia when seeking more complete or more current information. Updating is still limited by economics and editorial priorities, however, and a more frequent schedule of updating for electronic sources cannot be automatically assumed.

Indexing (Access)

Access to the information contained in an encyclopedia is accomplished by means of indexing. In its broadest sense, indexing includes any means by which the reader can be directed to the fullest range of pertinent information. As such, an evaluator should consider such elements as tables of contents, internal cross-referencing, and boxed summaries or study guides.

Most encyclopedias now have a separate analytical index, although these differ in terms of thoroughness and the manner in which subjects are subdivided. In the top half of figure 16.2, the volume and page number for the major reference to "Land reform" are indicated immediately following the main heading; references to land reform in specific locations follow underneath. "Land use" is followed by *see* references to the terms which are used in the index. Children's sets frequently enhance accessibility with the inclusion of an index at the end of each volume. These indexes refer to pages within the volume as well as to related information in other volumes.

Internal cross-references also appear with varying levels of uniformity. In the example at the bottom of figure 16.2, "equestrian arts" and "equilibrium" are followed by clearly indicated *see* references. Within the text of the "equinox" article, the user is expected to understand that the capitalization of "CELESTIAL SPHERE" is to indicate that another article appears under this heading. Some encyclopedias segregate cross-references into a "see also" list at the ends of articles. Other titles provide both internal cross-referencing and separate lists of related articles. Encyclopedias are never guilty of providing too much indexing. Lack of sufficient access is a much more likely possibility, coupled with inaccuracy in indexing.

Land reform 11–26
  Central America **6**–182d
  China **6**–514, 544a
  Cuba **8**–298
  East Germany **12**–641
  Egypt **10**–4, 18
  India **14**–876
  Iran **15**–375, 384
  Italy **15**–570; **27**–288
  Kenya **16**–399
  Korea, South **16**–557
  Latifundia **16**–786
  Latin America **17**–15
  Mexico **18**–821, 823, 825,
    844, 853, 868; **15**–18
  Peru **21**–777, 784
  Philippines **21**–909, 919
  Poland **22**–304
  Puerto Rico **22**–788
  Romania **23**–672
  Russia **24**–17, 18, 21 fol., 36,
    40
  Taiwan **26**–235
  USSR **27**–428o
  Vietnam **28**–110p
  Yugoslavia **29**–722
Land shell (zool.) **24**–693
  Mollusk **19**–332
Land snail 25–82 fol.
  Mollusk **19**–334
Land tax 24–843
Land tenure: *see* Tenure
Land tortoise (zool.): *see* Tortoise
Land use: *see* Land; Urban Planning; Zoning

---

equestrian arts: see RIDING.

equilibrium: see BIOLOGICAL EQUILIBRIUM; CHEMICAL KINETICS AND EQUILIBRIUM; STATICS; STATISTICAL THERMODYNAMICS.

equinox [ee′-kwin-ahks]

The equinoxes are the two points of intersection between the ecliptic (the Sun's apparent annual path) and the celestial equator (the equator of the CELESTIAL SPHERE). The two moments in the year when the Sun is exactly over the equator, and day and night are hence of equal length, are the times of these equinoxes. In the Northern Hemisphere the vernal, or

Fig. 16.2. Example of encyclopedia indexing and cross-referencing. Top half from the *Encyclopedia Americana*, 1989 Edition. Copyright © 1989 by Grolier Incorporated. Bottom half from the *Academic American Encyclopedia*, 1988 Edition. Copyright © 1988 by Grolier Incorporated. Both reprinted by permission.

Selection

The purchase of an encyclopedia is a major investment for most libraries. No matter how good the encyclopedia is, if it is not used, a considerable amount of money has been ill-spent. Therefore, when selecting an encyclopedia, librarians must balance its value to the library's users with the cost of the set. The selection process also must include an analysis of the potential usefulness of an electronic encyclopedia as an alternative to the traditional printed set.

Determining Need in Different Library Settings

The selection of an encyclopedia title depends entirely on local need: who will be using the encyclopedia, and for what purpose will they be using it? A ten-year-old looking for information on earthworms obviously needs a different encyclopedia than a lawyer who is gathering background information on a religious cult and its leader. An elementary school librarian, who encounters many such hunts by ten-year-olds, will have selected from a range of appropriate youth-level encyclopedia titles. On the other hand, a law firm librarian serves many lawyers, but, unless the firm specializes in suits involving religious cults, is not likely to select an expensive title like the *Encyclopedia of Religion* for an in-house collection. The librarians at the city's public library, who serve a diverse range of users and interests, will have selected encyclopedias that should satisfy the initial needs of both these individuals.

This information-seeking audience can be grouped into three general categories: learners, users with general needs, and users with scholarly or specialized needs. In many instances these categories overlap, depending on the individual and the nature of that individual's changing information needs. The lawyer looking for specialized legal information may return to the library on the weekend looking for information to help understand a child's asthma.

Learners. Encyclopedias are most typically marketed to users who can be categorized as *learners*. Everyone is familiar with the television commercials and the glossy brochures warning that children will be educationally deprived if they do not have access to Brand X encyclopedia in their own homes. The ten-year-olds who want to look up earthworms can be regarded as learners. They will want information that is relatively general; they should not be burdened with too much detail regarding the distribution of the chaetae or the shape of the prostomium! These users require text that is clearly written and free from jargon and technical terminology. A graduated vocabulary will enable them to use a wider variety of sources. Learners are not necessarily young children. A college student starting to work on a term paper or a retired person investigating a field of interest are both defined as learners in this context. Finally, learners are excellent candidates for encyclopedias which provide research guides and instructional aids, especially when such users are searching for topic ideas or ways in which to focus an idea.

Users with General Needs. Users with what might be termed *general* needs are interested in finding quick factual information or brief introductory material. Many ready reference queries fit into this framework. Such patrons may not wish to bother with learning aids or other devices; they are primarily interested in ease of use. For this type of need, encyclopedias should be selected which are known for clear layout and simple access to answers, with less emphasis upon lengthy or analytical treatment.

Users with Scholarly or Specialized Needs. For the user with scholarly or specialized needs, an appropriate subject encyclopedia is crucial. A graduate student in education, for example, certainly benefits by becoming familiar with the *Encyclopedia of Educational Research*. The education specialist in that graduate student's university library, understanding the audience served, would have selected such a title for the collection. In a similar fashion, librarians who serve a large Jewish clientele would be likely to select a title like the *Encyclopedia of the Holocaust*.

Clearly, no single encyclopedia title is sufficient to satisfy the differing needs of a library's patron population, unless the library is in a very specialized setting. Because use and audience vary so much, all but the tiniest of libraries should offer more than one title and type of encyclopedia in order to provide adequate service.

Cost

Most general encyclopedia sales are divided between the education market and the retail market. Pricing strategy reflects this two-tiered situation; libraries and schools pay a lower price, but are potential frequent and steady customers. To some degree, the home market is stimulated by titles that commonly appear in libraries. Additional reference books and decorative bindings are often part of the home user package, but add significantly to the base price of a title. Yearbooks and supplements, not necessarily part of the price of the parent set, may have to be purchased separately. The old saying "Let the buyer beware" is certainly pertinent in this complex market.

In a library setting, once an encyclopedia is more than five years old, it may be more misleading than helpful, given patron expectations regarding encyclopedias as sources of new information. Therefore, once an encyclopedia title is purchased, the library is implicitly committed to buying it again within a relatively short period of time. William Katz discusses replacing a set every two to five years, depending upon how much the set is used and upon its own revision cycle.[10] If a library elects not to replace a title after it becomes unacceptably dated, the set should be removed from the reference shelves to prevent misconceptions about its usefulness.

Impact of Format on Costs. When buying a printed encyclopedia, a buyer pays a one-time, often sizable, flat fee which grants undisputed ownership for an infinite number of uses. However, in order to remain current, the library pays this fee all over again within two to five years. Purchasing an encyclopedia in CD-ROM format is similar to purchasing in print format, in that one buys ownership and unlimited use and must consider purchasing anew on a cyclical basis. Some publishers sell CD-ROM product updates at a reduced rate, using a pricing structure which parallels that of the computer software industry rather than that of the book publishing industry. With CD-ROM, however, the purchase of specialized, expensive equipment is also required.

When accessing information from an online encyclopedia, only the bit of information that is retrieved is paid for, an interesting thought when one considers all the pages of a printed encyclopedia that may never be consulted. In addition, online encyclopedias have the potential of being updated much more frequently, without additional cost to the consumer. However, if an encyclopedia is heavily used, the cost of using it online will ultimately be much higher, perhaps prohibitively so. Finally, the price of an encyclopedia in electronic format may not include illustrations which, for reference purposes, really means that the library is paying for a different product.

A comparison of costs for different versions of the Grolier title is illuminating. The print-form 1990 *Academic American Encyclopedia* sold for $660 to schools and libraries. Its CD-ROM counterpart, the 1990 New Electronic Encyclopedia, sold for $395; current subscribers could purchase the update for $125. The networked version cost $1,795 for up to 9 workstations and $3,000 for 10 to 100 workstations. Searching this same text online through DIALOG cost $45 per connect hour plus $.25 per offline print; end users could search it on Dialog's Knowledge Index for a flat $24-per-hour fee. Finally, school rates on Dialog's Classmate Instruction Program allowed students to search the New Electronic for $15 per hour. These great differences in pricing only have meaning in the context of individual reference settings, which is how they must ultimately be judged.

Important General Sources

The discussion in this section focuses on general encyclopedias typically purchased by school, public, or academic libraries. Of the many subject encyclopedias, two major titles which have broad coverage are described. For information on encyclopedias not discussed here, the reader is referred to the titles listed in the additional readings.

Encyclopedias for Children and Young Adults

The *World Book Encyclopedia* is perhaps the most widely used encyclopedia in the United States. Although it is discussed here as a set for young people, it is used by readers from ages nine to ninety because of its readability and its logical organization. This ease of use and general reliability also make it a time-honored favorite of librarians, who trust its usefulness in a myriad of reference situations.

All encyclopedias undergo periodic major revisions; *World Book* did so in 1988, updating 71 percent of its text as well as the typeset and graphic work of the entire set. The 1990 revision contains about 25,600 signed articles in 21 volumes, contributed by over 3,000 individuals who are listed separately in the first volume. *World Book* is also known for its illustrations, which comprise one-third of its space and now number about 29,000, 24,000 of them in color. The use of illustrations is appropriate and imaginative. For example, period art is frequently used to enhance historical articles. The 2,300 maps are also all printed in color.

World Book uses an approach which invites readers. In all but two cases, every article that begins with a given letter of the alphabet is in a single volume. The articles themselves vary in length and complexity, depending upon the audience most likely to read them. Longer articles are written with graduated reading levels, beginning with simpler concepts and moving on to the more sophisticated. Technical terms are used when needed, but are defined within the context of a sentence or within parentheses. Bibliographies follow 1,600 of the longer articles; in many cases the citations have been grouped into two levels based on their ease of use. In addition to textual cross-references, lists of related topics often appear at the ends of articles, and volume 22 contains a detailed 150,000-entry index. *World Book* can cover a lot of territory in reference work; it is commonly purchased for both adult and juvenile departments in public libraries.

Like other titles written for a student audience, *World Book* delivers much of its information in the form of charts and tables and other modules which are visually distinct from the main body of text on a page. This technique serves to summarize or encapsulate complex information, to break up the monotony of the narrative, and to allow for alternative and interesting modes of presentation. For example, in the "Airline" article, logos of the major airlines of the world are colorfully reproduced, a chart contains a chronology of the important dates in airline development, and another table displays the growth of American airlines in terms of numbers of airlines, employees, aircraft, passengers, and cargo-miles. Librarians can use such devices to find quick factual information or to help patrons discover different dimensions of a topic.

Another *World Book* hallmark lies in its role as a teaching and learning tool, making it ideally suited for reference work with students. Each major article concludes with a study aid which contains: (1) an outline of the article (although this particular feature would be more useful if it appeared at the beginning of the article); (2) a list of related entries; and (3) a list of study questions. If appropriate, a reference is made to a corresponding "Reading and Study Guide" in volume 22. Over 200 of these Reading and Study Guides are embedded alphabetically in the index volume. As in the sample shown in figure 16.3, each guide contains suggested topics for study, provides further lists of related books, and indicates other sources of information. Volume 22 also contains a separate student guide to writing, speaking, and research skills.

Reading and Study Guide on Space travel

Topics for study

Compare the advantages and disadvantages of manned and un-manned spacecraft in planetary exploration. Do you think manned expeditions to other planets are feasible? See especially books A, F, G, H, and J below.

How do astronauts and cosmonauts eat, sleep, and exercise on extended space missions? What problems have been posed by weightlessness? What other health problems do human beings face in space travel? See especially books B, C, I, and K below.

What are the advantages of the space shuttle over earlier launch and spacecraft systems? What new capabilities has the shuttle added to space exploration programs? How did the tragic loss of the shuttle *Challenger* and its crew in January 1986 affect the progress of the U.S. space program? See especially books A, C, and K below.

Using a knowledge of current space technology, develop a plan for the construction of an orbiting space station. How would materials be transported from earth? What construction methods would be used? What kind of living and working environment would be provided? What purposes would the space station serve? See especially books E, G, H, I, and J below.

Books to read

Level I

(A) Branley, Franklyn M. *From Sputnik to Space Shuttle*. Crowell Jr., 1986. A history of the development of satellites for communications and exploration. For younger readers.

(B) Cooper, Henry S. *Before Lift-Off: The Making of a Space-Shuttle Crew*. Johns Hopkins, 1987. Follows the selection, training, simulations, and actual flight of the crew of a 1984 space-shuttle launch.

(C) Dwiggins, Don. *Flying the Space Shuttles*. Dodd, 1985. Gives details of a typical flight.

(D) Maurer, Richard. *The NOVA Space Explorer's Guide*. Clarkson N. Potter, 1985. Describes a space shuttle mission, with emphasis on astronomy of the solar system.

(E) Trefil, James S. *Living in Space*. MacMillan, 1981. Considers the difficulties and rewards of future life in a space colony.

Level II

(F) Nicks, Oran W. *Far Travelers: the Exploring Machines*. NASA, 1985. Distributed by the Government Printing Office. Tells the story of the space probes that traveled to Mars, Jupiter, and other parts of the solar system.

(G) Oberg, James E. and Alcestis. *Pioneering Space*. McGraw, 1986. Uses Soviet space logs and diaries to examine the stresses of long-term living in space.

(H) *Pioneering the Space Frontier: The Report of the National Commission on Space*. Bantam, 1986. Projected plans for the United States space program in the next 50 years, including exploration, colonization, and the commercial use of space.

(I) Smolders, Peter. *Living in Space: A Handbook for Space Travellers*. TAB/Aero, 1986. Paperback. Describes life on a space station of the future.

(J) Taylor, L. B. *Commercialization of Space*. Watts, 1987. Discusses the increasing amount of private enterprise in space programs and future uses of space for communications, mining, and energy production.

(K) Torres, George. *Space Shuttle: The Quest Continues*. Rev. ed. Presidio, 1989. Covers U.S. manned space flights, space stations, military use of space, and the Hubble Space Telescope.

Other sources of information

Applied Science and Technology Index under Space flight.

Readers' Guide to Periodical Literature under the heading Space; United States—National Aeronautics and Space Administration.

See also index information under the heading *Space travel*.

Fig. 16.3. Example of a reading and study guide in *World Book*. Excerpted from *The World Book Encyclopedia*. © 1990 World Book, Inc. By permission of the publisher.

Like many encyclopedia publishers, World Book, Inc. now maintains all information in an electronic database, a practice which has revolutionized the updating process. For example, when all references to "Russia" were changed to "U.S.S.R.," 2,284 relevant mentions of the term outside of the main article had to be identified and changed.[11] Using the new technology, World Book developed a CD-ROM product called the Information Finder. Users can search by topic mode, which utilizes terms from the index, or by keyword, using the full power of sophisticated Boolean logic. The latter is most suited for use by librarians or by dedicated users, due to the lack of a software interface which overtly leads an untrained user (or one who does not consult the user manual) through the process. In either search mode, users can instantly access cross-references and view related concepts. Although it does not contain the graphic images of the parent set, Information Finder does include 139,000 dictionary entries which can be accessed at any point during a search.

Compton's Encyclopedia, published by Encyclopaedia Britannica, serves a market very similar to *World Book*'s, encompassing the upper elementary years to the young adult or adult level. *Compton's*, calling itself the "student's encyclopedia," is differentiated by a more specific focus on curricular matters. An attractive layout enhances its accessibility; longer articles contain feature boxes which include definitions of terms, people profiles, and tables of contents. "Fact Finders" direct readers to related articles, bringing together most cross-references rather than embedding them in the text. Only the longer articles are signed; editorial consultants and contributors, with their credentials, are identified at the beginning of the first volume.

In a fashion similar to some of the other youth sets, a "Fact-Index" appears at the end of each volume, which provides additional information as well as indexing the volume's contents and related articles in other volumes. The Fact-Indexes in the 1990 *Compton's* contain about 26,000 capsule articles not found in the body of the encyclopedia, which has about 5,200 articles. Volume 26, the Master Fact-Index, serves as an index to the entire set. By referring to such fact-indexes first, librarians can answer many ready reference questions without having to refer to the main body of the text. On the other hand, an unwitting user (or librarian!) who does not use the indexes first is likely to miss pertinent information.

Each volume of *Compton's* is prefaced by a study aid which groups most of the volume's articles by general subject area, poses topical questions, and refers to the page numbers which have the answers. As such, *Compton's* is more self-contained than *World Book*, providing an in-hand curriculum guide for students, with less emphasis upon external sources of information through the use of bibliographies and search suggestions. Librarians can use the study aids to assist students in selecting topics for projects and reports, especially when more guided or directive assistance is needed.

Compton's is the first encyclopedia to be released in a multimedia version, complete with 15,000 graphic images and CD-quality sound capability. Compton's MultiMedia Encyclopedia is available as a single-user CD-ROM workstation or in a networked arrangement, marketed by Jostens Learning Corporation. The flexible searching capabilities of the electronic format allow the user to zoom in on an area of the atlas, select a highlighted word to get its definition from the integrated Merriam-Webster dictionary, read about Martin Luther King and then hear him speak an excerpt of "I Have a Dream," view full-color illustrations with related text and additional audio and visual information, retrieve articles containing any common phrase entered by the user, or move instantly from the "Topic Tree" to a selected article. Obviously, this kind of capability requires more hardware power than a text-only electronic product, and many libraries may balk at making the commitment.

Merit Students Encyclopedia is another reputable entry in the market which targets students from upper elementary school years to the young adult or adult years. With less emphasis on learning aids, the 1990 *Merit* offers a more traditional encyclopedia layout, containing 19 volumes of text and a final, extremely thorough 140,000-entry index volume. This design supports standard reference use: the index facilitates ready reference activity and the broad coverage allows for more in-depth work. With a much higher proportion of black-and-white illustrations than *World Book* or *Compton's*, *Merit* has a slightly more old-fashioned appearance. Articles are generally signed or otherwise identified when they have been reviewed by a subject specialist. Bibliographies accompany approximately 5 percent of the articles; as in *World Book*, the bibliographies are sometimes divided by level of difficulty. Longer articles are enhanced with a pronunciation guide, definitions of terms, a "fact index," and a brief summary.

The three titles mentioned so far reach an audience which spans a wide range of ages and abilities. None of them, however, is really intended for independent use by the younger student, especially when that student is just starting to learn research skills. Grolier's *New Book of Knowledge* is one of the best known of those that can be used independently by the younger student, and is useful throughout the elementary school years and in some junior high settings. The *New Book of Knowledge* is distinguished by its pleasing appearance, created by a heavy emphasis upon illustrative material, color, design, and layout.

In the 1990 *New Book of Knowledge*, prefatory instructions are written as questions that might be posed by the user, e.g., "How do I look up a poem?" Like *World Book*, the reading level is geared to the grade level at which a subject is usually introduced. Similar to

Compton's, the "Dictionary-Index" located in each volume contains real information in the form of capsule articles which are not duplicated in the main body of the text. Volume 21 contains a comprehensive index to the whole set. Bibliographies appear in a volume entitled *Home and School Reading and Study Guides*, which is written for teachers and parents. Like *World Book* and *Compton's*, the emphasis is on education, and many articles contain study outlines, ideas for projects and experiments, "wonder" questions, and fact boxes. School librarians and teachers can easily take advantage of the *New Book of Knowledge* environment for teaching research skills.

Children's Britannica is the fourth edition of a set first published in Great Britain but now sold in the United States. Written for the middle grades, defined roughly as grades three through eight, the reading level is more suited to the upper end of that range. The set does an admirable job of covering the American scene, yet, unlike other titles, it also offers a unique international perspective not often presented to American students. This trait makes it useful in answering questions about other countries or when trying to find just such a global perspective.

A smaller set than *New Book of Knowledge*, the 1990 *Children's Britannica* contains 19 volumes mostly identical in length (320 pages) and a 631-page "Reference Index." Volume 19 contains a 159-page atlas which is indexed separately; thus, if one looks first at the article on Texas, there is no reference to the map of Texas in volume 19. Maps do not appear in the body of the text except as simple line drawings in some of the articles. Users may not find the atlas; reference librarians must remember to check the separate index. The main index also has brief entries on topics not found in the body of the encyclopedia. *Children's Britannica* has no bibliographies and the articles are unsigned, although a list of writers and authorities is included in the final volume. Compared to the graphic attractiveness of the *New Book of Knowledge*, *Children's Britannica* has a rather unexciting, text-filled appearance. Nevertheless, it remains a reasonably priced, trustworthy source of information.

Encyclopedias are also available for younger children or for a more narrowly defined range of elementary school-age children. For example, the *New Grolier Student Encyclopedia* (which is actually the *Young Students Learning Library* published in a library binding) is similar in appearance to the Grolier's *New Book of Knowledge* with its appealing layout and graphic design, but is less hefty in content and intellectual rigor. The 1990 *New Grolier* contains 3,000 articles and 20,000 index entries as opposed to the 9,000 articles and 85,000 index entries of the 1990 *New Book of Knowledge*.

Like *World Book*, articles in the *New Grolier* begin with simpler material and move on to more complex information. A good choice for the reluctant reader, pages contain no more than two columns of text, though many pages are highlighted by "Information Nuggets" in the sidebar. Natural language phrases, such as "Also Read" instead of "See Also," enhance readability. "Learning by Doing" sections are integrated into the text. For example, when young patrons are looking for science experiment ideas, librarians can consult this set to find the experiments which appear at the ends of science articles.

Alternatives to standard, annually updated comprehensive encyclopedias are also available for children. *Compton's Precyclopedia* and World Book's *Childcraft* are examples of this type. Depending upon the library and the need, these titles may be valuable when serving younger children, when very brief information is required, or for their own unique characteristics and strengths. For example, some libraries select *Childcraft* because each volume covers a single subject area and can be cataloged separately for disperal throughout the reference collection. Thus, the volume on how things work can be shelved in the science and technology section while the volume on holidays and celebrations is shelved with other books on the same topic.

Encyclopedias for Adults

The characteristics that distinguish adult encyclopedias from one another generally center on size and on style of presentation. In terms of length, the *New Encyclopaedia Britannica*, the *Encyclopedia Americana*, and *Collier's* compete as the major full-length titles. The *Academic American Encyclopedia*, *Funk & Wagnalls New Encyclopedia*, and, to some degree, the *New Standard Encyclopedia*, compete as mid-length titles. In terms of style, some titles emphasize long survey articles which put together subordinate related concepts, providing access to these through the index. Other titles are known for short, highly specific articles, which are tied to related concepts through the use of cross-references.

The *New Encyclopaedia Britannica* is regarded by many as the premier English-language general encyclopedia, and certainly the most scholarly. First published in 1768, the *Britannica* is now in its fifteenth edition and is revised annually. Appearing in 1974, this edition ushered in a controversial three-part self-indexing format. A single volume, the *Propaedia*, was designed to serve as an "outline of knowledge" and a topical index to the other two parts. The *Micropaedia* was designated the ready reference portion of the set, and was initially intended to serve as the more detailed index to the *Macropaedia*, which contained the lengthy, more analytical articles. Users' need for a traditional, comprehensive index resulted in the publication of a separate two-volume index with the 1985 revision, along with other significant changes to the organization of the set.

In the 1990 revision, the *Micropaedia* continues to serve as the ready reference part of the set, although 1,300 of the articles are now signed and 1,500 contain bibliographies. The *Macropaedia* articles are followed by lengthy bibliographies; in some cases they can better be described as bibliographic essays. Every article that is in the *Macropaedia* has a corresponding, shorter article in the *Micropaedia*, and in the latter is prefaced with instructions referring the reader to the *Macropaedia* for a fuller treatment of the subject. The 12-volume *Micropaedia* contains about 65,000 articles which average just under 300 words each, in contrast to the 17-volume *Macropaedia* which contains approximately 675 articles, of which about 100 are biographical, averaging 34,000 words each.

The *Propaedia* contains the famous "outline of knowledge," showing relationships within disciplines and corresponding access to the articles in the *Micropaedia* and the *Macropaedia*. This classification scheme is the framework around which the *Britannica* is structured, and can also serve as a study guide for students and other independent learners. The *Propaedia* also includes the list of the 4,262 contributing scholars of signed articles and the 2,603 *Micropaedia* authorities who did not also contribute signed articles. The approximately 202,000-entry index, with over 500,000 references and cross-references, supports detailed access to the *Britannica*.

The small print and illustrations (16,000 in the *Micropaedia* and 7,200 generally larger illustrations in the *Macropaedia*) give a full appearance to the pages and may intimidate the less capable reader. This difficulty is mitigated by helpful guide words in the side margins of the *Macropaedia*. Though in no way comparable to the lavish use of illustrative material in *World Book*, *Britannica* has increased its proportion of illustrations over the years. Approximately half of them are now in color, and the *Macropaedia* includes about 165 color-insert plates. The *Propaedia* contains an insert of acetate overlays displaying the human body.

Because *Britannica* is essentially two encyclopedias, the reader may need to look in several places to find major references to a single topic. However, the *Britannica* focus places information in a larger context and, in the longer survey articles, unifies information rather than subdividing it. As Harvey Einbinder suggests, "major articles possess an intellectual coherence and narrative unity."[12] Thus, information on a country or a state will be located *within* a discussion of the larger region or area. Individual planets are entered alphabetically and treated in several paragraphs in the *Micropaedia*; cross-references direct the reader to the *Macropaedia* article on the solar system (without referring to specific page numbers), where several pages are devoted to coverage of each planet. Practically speaking, college students, who may not typically consult the index first, might miss pertinent information that is buried in the *Macropaedia*. However, this unifying approach is very helpful when the user is grappling with conceptually difficult or amorphous topics.

Textual cross-references in the *Britannica* are indicated by the Latin *q.v.* (*quod vide*, meaning "which see"), a practice which may elude the less frequent user of the set. Periodically, a boxed statement appears mid-text, reminding the user to consult the index first, a good piece of advice given how relatively sparse the internal cross-references are and how comprehensive the index is. Reference librarians must be alert to unwitting patrons who have attempted to look up a term such as "Neptune" alphabetically in the *Macropaedia* and, finding no cross-reference, simply assume that it is not covered at all in the *Britannica*. References are also made from the text and the index to the *Britannica Book of the Year*, which contains the valuable "World Data" section. This section presents current data related to geographic, demographic, and economic issues for 220 countries and regions of the world, as well as tables of comparative statistics on topics ranging from education to health care. However, statistical information is limited in the parent set, so libraries must be sure to maintain a separate subscription to the *Book of the Year*.

Grolier's *Academic American Encyclopedia* is a study in contrast to the *Britannica*. Using a clear, concise writing style, the *Academic American* presents a broad spectrum of information by delivering it in the form of brief articles on specific topics. A typical page in the 1990 revision contains three articles. Cross-references and a good index refer the reader to related topics, but the focus is on information delivery rather than on contextual relationships between fields of knowledge. "Neptune" is entered alphabetically, where the user expects to find it; the article on the solar system is correspondingly brief. Therefore, this set is very efficient when one is looking for factual information; it is less useful when more lengthy background information is needed.

Illustrations are a great strength of the *Academic American*, consuming over one-third of total page space and making this set an excellent starting point when simple diagrams or pictures are called for in reference work. Because it was first published in 1980, it is not saddled with a backlog of outdated illustrations and written material, as are some titles with a long publishing history.

The *Academic American* was one of the first and only titles to be widely available in multiple electronic formats. As the New Electronic Encyclopedia, it is available from commercial online vendors such as BRS, and in CD-ROM format, which includes pictures, for both IBM-compatible and Apple Macintosh computers. In electronic form, the full text can be accessed using Boolean search techniques; in CD-ROM format, the software interface allows for instant access to cross-references and the use of features such as notetaking and windowing. A "bookmark" feature enables the user to designate links between places in the text other than the editorially designated cross-references. A school version of the CD-ROM Encyclopedia includes an online tutorial, practice exercises, and subject-specific teacher's guides.

The *Encyclopedia Americana*, one of the "big three" along with *Britannica* and *Collier's*, is well known for its emphasis on American history, geography, and biography, and a strong coverage of science and technology. The attention to North America does not detract from an impressive coverage of other parts of the world. In fact, the 1990 *Americana* is second in comprehensiveness only to *Britannica* and emulates it in other ways. The format is a mix of lengthy survey articles and the shorter, specific articles so useful in answering ready reference questions. As such, it is like a smaller version of the *Britannica* arranged in a single continuous alphabet. In the reference setting, it might be selected for use with patrons who have difficulty with the *Britannica* format, but who need fuller treatment than that given in a title like the *Academic American*.

The longer articles in the *Encyclopedia Americana* are signed, and many include bibliographies. The extremely detailed index subdivides broad topics, compensating for a rather restrained use of internal cross-references. Although the *Americana* has a well-deserved reputation for accuracy and thoroughness, it lacks the visual sparkle of other sets. The bland layout and more scholarly tone unfortunately limit its appeal with younger users.

The 1990 *Collier's Encyclopedia*, smallest of the three large sets, is written in an engaging, accessible style, yet delivers scholarly depth and coverage. Most articles are signed by acknowledged authorities; over five thousand contributors and advisers are listed at the front of the first volume. Longer overview articles predominate, although there are short ones where appropriate. Both the size and tone of *Collier's* make it highly suitable for student use in school and public library reference settings.

Distinguishing *Collier's* from most other adult-level encyclopedias is the unusual placement of the bibliographies. Rather than appearing at the ends of articles, they are compiled separately in a classified arrangement in the index volume. References to the bibliographies are made from the text and from index entries. Although the purpose of this arrangement is to promote related reading and study, many users never find the bibliographies. The index itself, at 400,000 entries, is extremely comprehensive. Knowing this, the reference librarian may choose to try *Collier's* first when looking for detailed information, such as geographic details on a map. The accessibility provided by this index, the readable text, and the visual appeal of the illustrations and layout have made *Collier's* a popular title.

Unlike the other encyclopedias discussed in this chapter, *Funk & Wagnalls New Encyclopedia* is sold in supermarkets, although libraries can order it directly from the publisher. The supermarket image, however, has no bearing upon the quality of this set, which delivers a high return for its purchase price in terms of authority and currency. Most of the articles are written by editorial staff with the assistance of expert consultants; however, nine hundred scholars contributed signed articles to the 1989 revision. The 1989 *Funk & Wagnalls* is also noted for a strong global and unbiased presentation.

Because *Funk & Wagnalls* is neither as detailed nor as scholarly in tone as other adult titles, and because article content progresses from general information to the more specific, it is suitable for those as young as junior high age. The reference librarian would also select it to assist someone who has no background in a subject or who wants basic introductory information. As in *Collier's*, bibliographies are collected at the end of the set and are referred to within the text. Perhaps economy is achieved in part by saving on illustrative material; most pictures are in black and white, and the set has fewer illustrations than do other general encyclopedias.

The *New Standard Encyclopedia*, like *Funk & Wagnalls*, is sold primarily to the home consumer market, although not through the supermarket route. Written for an audience spanning age ten through the adult years, the 1990 *New Standard* favors short article treatment, using long articles for broad subject areas. Articles are written by the editorial staff, and then reviewed by subject specialists for accuracy. The careful editing and an emphasis on practical information make it useful in answering reference questions from students and from the less capable adult reader. Unlike any set mentioned in this chapter, this one did not traditionally have a separate index volume, instead using a system of intensive cross-referencing within the text. The 1989 update, however, was extended from seventeen to twenty volumes and, for the first time, included a separate analytical index.

Subject Encyclopedias

Although a thorough treatment of subject encyclopedias is beyond the scope of this chapter, two multidisciplinary titles, the *McGraw-Hill Encyclopedia of Science and Technology* and the *International Encyclopedia of the Social Sciences*, are discussed because of their importance in general reference work and as illustrations of more specialized encyclopedias.

Unparalleled in its coverage, the scope of the twenty-volume *McGraw-Hill Encyclopedia of Science and Technology*, last revised in 1987, encompasses seventy-seven major subject areas in the fields of science and technology. Designed to guide the reader from general overview information to the more specific, broad survey articles cover the whole of a discipline (e.g., "chemistry") or a major subject area (e.g., "airplane"). There are no separate biographical and historical articles, however. Cross-references from the longer articles lead the reader to those that are more restricted in scope. Most articles, both short and long, have bibliographies. A separate two-part index is made up of a traditional analytical index of 150,000 entries, preceded by a topical index which displays article titles grouped according to the 77 major subject areas.

Although an impressive group of experts contributes to this monumental work, the signed articles are intended for the nonspecialist. This avoidance of technical terminology is more evident in the longer survey articles. The smaller, more specific articles often presume background knowledge; a user may need to be guided back through the introductory material. Still, the thrust of this set is definition and description; it is thus highly suitable at the high school and undergraduate levels.

What the *McGraw-Hill* does for subject coverage in the fields of science and technology, the *International Encyclopedia of the Social Sciences* does for the fields of the social sciences. However, the *International* is written for a higher level, more scholarly audience. In its original version, as the *Encyclopaedia of the Social Sciences* (published between 1930 and 1935), it was the first comprehensive encyclopedia covering the entire domain of the social sciences. The *International* was published in 1968 to complement rather than to revise the earlier set. The newer seventeen volumes cover the disciplines of anthropology, economics, geography, history, law, political science, psychiatry, psychology, sociology, and statistics. Six hundred biographical entries list works written both by and about individuals; in 1979, a biographical supplement was added. Arranged in conventional alphabetical order, additional access is provided by cross-references and the index.

The articles in the *International* were contributed by distinguished scholars, and are enhanced by extensive bibliographies. Many articles were written by more than one contributor. For example, the twenty-page article on urban revolution is comprised of three parts, each written by a different scholar. The *International* favors the survey approach, grouping subordinate concepts in a single overview article. Topical articles emphasize analytical and comparative issues. This perspective is especially evident when a single concept is common to different disciplines and therefore has varied meanings, depending on the context. In these cases, two or three specialists were assigned to write a part of the article, each discussing the concept as it applies to a single discipline. This practice accurately reflects the nature of the social sciences, where ideas and meanings are not as easily defined and differentiated as they are in the physical and life sciences. The tone and style of these two subject encyclopedias also mirror the differences between the disciplines. The *International* articles are more essay-like; the *McGraw-Hill* articles are more definitional. Although more than twenty years old now, the *International Encyclopedia of the Social Sciences* remains a standard of scholarship and authority.

Search Strategies

Finding answers in encyclopedias involves first understanding the various access points, something which becomes automatic with practice and experience. The modes of access generally remain constant. However, as has been demonstrated, individual titles structure those modes in different ways. Understanding the structural arrangement of a particular title is an implicit first step. Is it alphabetically or topically sequenced? Do tables of contents appear at the beginning of the longer, more general articles? Is the index in a separate volume? Are the cross-references flagged within the text in some way, or are they listed at the ends of articles? What does the prefatory matter at the beginning of the encyclopedia have to say regarding search strategy for that particular title?

In the *World Book* preface, it is suggested that most information can be found by using the alphabetical arrangement of articles and cross-references. If this strategy is not successful, the reader is advised to refer to the index.[13] Other sets advise the reader to start immediately with the index volume. For comprehensive coverage, the reader must consult both text and index. Cross-references, no matter how good, will never be as thorough as a true index.

A crucial aspect of developing search strategies for encyclopedias lies in understanding their place within a larger framework. Encyclopedias are very often used as intermediate tools; a search strategy may start with an encyclopedia and then move on to other tools and sources, including those suggested by the encyclopedia's bibliographies. Good follow-up in the reference interview ensures that a search does not end prematurely in an encyclopedia when further information may be needed.

Perhaps the best way to demonstrate search strategy is by using a few cases, or examples, involving the kinds of key information needs — fact finding, general background information, and pre-research — described at the beginning of this chapter. Some of the case descriptions overlap, both in terms of the type of need and the methodology used to solve the problem. This ambiguity mimics real life; genuine questions and their answers are not easily compartmentalized. As one need is satisfied, it may evolve into another type of need, and the reference query is then renegotiated and fine-tuned.

As a caveat, it is important to stress that these cases serve to illustrate plausible search patterns and strategies and, as such, demonstrate only one path out of many which might be selected. In the same vein, sample encyclopedia titles are named to add verisimilitude. Each case is expressed as a reference question after it has been negotiated in the reference interview. When relevant, the age and specific need of the patron are also indicated. The first cases are simple and straightforward; subsequent cases are more complex.

Fact Finding

- When did Desmond Tutu win the Nobel Peace Prize?

    In a title like *Compton's*, this information is simply and readily supplied directly in the Fact-Index, in a subheading under Tutu's name. The main article on Tutu in any encyclopedia would also certainly supply this information.

- Is there a system of youth hostels in the United States similar to the system of youth hostels in Europe? (undergraduate student)

    When looking under "Youth Hostels" in a title such as *Merit Students Encyclopedia*, both within the text and the index there is a reference from "Youth Hostels, American" to an article entitled "American Youth Hostels." The article indicates the name of an organization from which the student can get further information. The librarian assists the student in looking in a directory for the current address of the organization.

- Who starred in the television show *Gunsmoke*? (teenage trivia buff)

    This student has already looked in an encyclopedia under "Gunsmoke" without success. The librarian demonstrates how checking the index reveals references to articles on television programming and Westerns. The article on Westerns not only has the names of the stars, but a picture of them as well. If the patron is interested in further information, a biographical source may be the next step, or a book-length history of the genre.

- Do you have a map of Copenhagen? (adult patron in a small public library)

    Small libraries are unlikely to have street maps of foreign cities or to have atlases at this level of detail. Investigating encyclopedias is a bit frustrating because the indexes generally refer to Copenhagen within the article on Denmark; on the map of Denmark, Copenhagen is nothing more than a big black dot. Knowing this, the librarian still thinks that it might be worth looking in a title like the *Academic American*, known for concise entries on specific subjects and for an emphasis upon illustrative material. Sure enough, "Copenhagen" is an entry in its own right, accompanied by a small city map. Follow-up with the patron is essential to ensure that this map is sufficient; the geographical sources of a larger library may be necessary.

- Who was the first woman senator who did not "inherit" the job but was elected in her own right?

    After spending some time looking through encyclopedia indexes under headings like "Senate" and "Women" and finding no entry matching this query, the librarian realizes that the answer can only be found by reading through a lot of text, if it indeed can be found without already knowing the woman's name. Instead, the librarian dials into an online encyclopedia and searches the text by using the Boolean operator "AND" to tie together the terms *first, elected, woman,* and *senator.* Within moments the answer emerges, showing Nancy Landon Kassebaum as the first elected woman senator, although Hattie Wyatt Caraway was elected to a second term after having first been appointed to complete her late husband's term.

General Background Information

- I need to find out how a camel's hump works and what it is for (fifth-grade student working on a school assignment).

    Looking up "camel" alphabetically in a title like *Children's Britannica*, the student finds an article on camels which gives a good description of the camel's system of food and water storage. When the librarian directs the student to the index entry, they discover further references to such relevant items as adaptation, the desert, and transportation. By pulling in these additional pieces of information, the student creates a more interesting report, going beyond how it works and really explaining what it is for.

- I'd like some information about the Indianapolis 500—the names of past winners, the kinds of cars they drove, how the race got started, things like that (adult armchair racing enthusiast).

    Almost any adult-level general encyclopedia will provide this information, if not in an article solely on the Indy 500, then referenced by the index to a survey article with a title like "Automobile Racing." The name of the most recent winner may not appear in even the newest encyclopedia, however, so the librarian will need to refer the patron to that information in a current almanac or in a periodical or newspaper index.

- Can you help me find out how divorce is regarded and treated by the major western religious traditions? (undergraduate student)

    To find information which most closely represents the point of view of each religious perspective, the student agrees with the librarian's suggestion that individual religion-based encyclopedias might prove more fruitful than general encyclopedias. They look under "divorce" in *First Stop: The Master Index to Subject Encyclopedias* and find references to the page numbers of specific entries in several pertinent titles such as the *Encyclopedia Judaica* and the *New Catholic Encyclopedia.*

- I need some information about decibel levels. In terms of human hearing, what is a "high" level? A "low" level? (parent who is tired of a teenaged child's loud music)

  The article on decibels in a specialized encyclopedia like the *McGraw-Hill Encyclopedia of Science and Technology* turns out to be too technical for the patron to really understand, and lacks an explanation of relative decibel levels. However, the entry in the index volume refers to an overview article entitled "Loudness." The information there is easier to understand because it is more general, and it also describes decibel ranges. Best of all, a chart displays decibel levels of some common sounds such as whispering, street noises, and jet planes. The article concludes with cross-references to information on hearing and acoustic noise and with a bibliography of further sources which the patron makes note of. The librarian next leads the patron to a medical encyclopedia to look for information on hearing damage and loss.

Pre-Research Needs

- I have to pick an extinct animal and write a report on it. Can you help me find an animal and some information about it? (fourth-grade student)

  In a set like the *New Grolier Student Encyclopedia*, there is no article entered alphabetically under "extinct." Looking in the index, the student's eye is caught by the entry "Extinct Birds," which refers to an article entitled "Birds of the Past." After skimming this survey article, the student selects the dodo bird, which is described as having been killed off by settlers in the 1600s. Back in the index volume under "dodo," the student finds references to other articles within the set. Knowing the student to be a competent reader, the librarian also checks the *Children's Britannica*, which has a separate article on dodo birds and other material within articles referred to by the index. If the student needs still more information, the catalog can be checked for books in the library's collection.

- I'd like to write my term paper on astrology, but I'm not supposed to write it just on how to tell someone's horoscope. Also, my teacher isn't convinced that there are enough reputable sources of information on this topic. (high school student)

  Checking in an encyclopedia with study aids, like *World Book*, the librarian finds a study guide on astrology in the index volume. The guide suggests several specific topics which are suitable as subjects for term papers, from historical surveys of astrology to possibilities for empirical experimentation. The accompanying bibliography lists a variety of recommended sources which should satisfy the student's teacher.

- I'd like to spend some time learning about the various schools of philosophy and about a few of the important philosophers. I don't know where to start — can you help me? (retired adult)

  The *Britannica Propaedia* contains a section called "The Branches of Knowledge," which includes an outline covering the history of philosophy, its nature and divisions, and the major philosophical schools and doctrines. Integrated within the outline are references to specific articles in the *Macropaedia*. From these references, the patron can read overview material, select which schools of philosophy and philosophers to learn about, read those articles, and then cull the bibliographies to pursue the subject further.

■ ━━ ■

16.2
The Future

- I've just purchased a compact digital disc of *The Last Emperor*,[14] a 1987 movie release about the last Chinese dynastic emperor, who reigned at the beginning of the twentieth century during the establishment of the Republic. I'd like to find out more about him and his English tutor, Sir Reginald Johnston, in the context of the time period. (undergraduate student working on a research project)

> This question has come into the library's viewphone reference ser-
> vice. The patron is sitting at a home computer workstation and is logged
> into the library's information network. The librarian, using the patron's
> password, boots up an electronic hypermedia encyclopedia so that it
> appears on the home screen as well as the reference desk screen. The
> patron does not know the emperor's full name, so the librarian begins the
> search with a few keywords like *China*, *emperor*, and *last*. In this way, they
> locate the emperor's Chinese and anglicized names and the name of the
> dynasty. By selecting these individual terms, the patron brings up audio
> pronunciation of the Chinese names and a picture of the emperor. The
> librarian gives further suggestions regarding the use of the encyclopedia
> before hanging up to answer another call.
>
> After reading brief biographical information, the patron selects a map
> of the Forbidden City and looks at a few pictures, then resizes the map to
> see where the Forbidden City lies in relationship to the rest of Beijing.
> Back in the text, the patron selects the name of the emperor's English
> tutor, Sir Reginald Johnston, and brings up a window with his photograph
> and biographical information. Using a notetaking feature, the patron
> copies bibliographies into a personal file and makes other notes and
> observations. These notes can later be linked to the digitized video file of
> the movie, so that this supplementary information will be directly accessi-
> ble from selected images.
>
> Some of the items from the bibliography are also available in elec-
> tronic form, and the patron selects these citations to continue the search
> in a subject encyclopedia on China and in a biographical dictionary. How-
> ever, Johnston's autobiography,[15] written in 1934, is not yet available in
> electronic form, so the user exits from the reference tools and checks the
> online catalog. The library does have a copy in its print collection, which
> can be held at the circulation desk or sent in the mail. Tired of sitting in
> front of a computer screen, the patron welcomes the chance for a leisurely
> walk to the library.

Notes

1.   Bohdan S. Wynar, "Encyclopedias and Yearbooks," in *Introduction to Bibliography and Reference Work: A Guide to Materials and Sources*, 4th rev. ed. (Littleton, Colo.: Libraries Unlimited,
1967), 159-72.

2.   Charles Van Doren, "The Idea of an Encyclopedia," *American Behavioral Scientist* 6 (September
1962): 23-26.

3. Jacques Barzun, "Notes on the Making of a World Encyclopedia," *American Behavioral Scientist* 6 (September 1962): 7-14.

4. *World Book Encyclopedia* (Chicago: World Book, 1989), I:v.

5. Patricia B. Culkin, "Rethinking OPACS: The Design of Assertive Information Systems," *Information Technology and Libraries* 8 (June 1989): 175.

6. Harvey Einbinder, *The Myth of the Britannica* (New York: Grove Press, 1964), 390p.

7. June Engel and Elizabeth Futas, "Sexism in Adult Encyclopedias," *RQ* 23 (Fall 1983): 29-39.

8. Henrietta W. Smith, "Missing and Wanted: Black Women in Encyclopedias," *School Library Journal* 34 (February 1988): 25-29.

9. Kenneth F. Kister, "Questions and Answers About Encyclopedias," in *Best Encyclopedias: A Guide to General and Specialized Encyclopedias* (Phoenix, Ariz.: Oryx Press, 1986), 1-17.

10. William A. Katz, "Encyclopedias: General and Subject," in *Introduction to Reference Work*, 5th ed., vol. 1 (New York: McGraw-Hill, 1987), 191-92.

11. Peter Mollman, Senior Vice President, World Book Publishing, in a talk given on Tuesday, June 27th, 1989, at the program "Encyclopedia Publishing in the 1990's and Beyond," sponsored by the Editorial Board of the *Reference Books Bulletin*, American Library Association Annual Conference, Dallas, Texas.

12. Harvey Einbinder, "The New Britannica: Pro and Con," *Library Journal* 112 (April 15, 1987): 50. Less strident here than in *The Myth of the Britannica*, both Einbinder and the *Britannica* have modified their perspectives over the years.

13. *World Book Encyclopedia* (Chicago: World Book, 1989), I:ix.

14. *The Last Emperor*, Bernardo Bertolucci, director; Jeremy Thomas, producer; Mark Peploe with Bernardo Bertolucci, screenplay (Columbia Pictures, 1987).

15. Reginald F. Johnston, *Twilight in the Forbidden City* (London: Victor Gollancz Ltd., 1934), 486p.

List of Sources

Academic American Encyclopedia. 21 vols. Danbury, Conn.: Grolier, 1988. (BRS File AAED.)

ARBA Guide to Subject Encyclopedias and Dictionaries. Edited by Bohdan S. Wynar. Littleton, Colo.: Libraries Unlimited, 1986. 570p.

Britannica Book of the Year. Chicago: Encyclopaedia Britannica, 1938- . Annual.

Britannica Macropaedia, *Britannica Micropaedia*, and *Britannica Propaedia*. *See New Encyclopaedia Britannica*.

Cambridge Encyclopedia. New York: Cambridge University Press, 1990. 1,488p.

Cambridge Encyclopedia of the Middle East and North Africa. New York: Cambridge University Press, 1988. 504p.

Childcraft: The How and Why Library. 15 vols. Chicago: World Book, 1989.

Children's Britannica. 4th ed. 20 vols. Chicago: Encyclopaedia Britannica, 1990.

Collier's Encyclopedia. 24 vols. New York: Macmillan Educational Co., 1990.

Compton's Encyclopedia and Fact-Index. 26 vols. Chicago: Encyclopaedia Britannica, 1990.

Compton's MultiMedia Encyclopedia. [CD-ROM]. San Francisco: Britannica Software.

Compton's Precyclopedia. 16 vols. Chicago: Encyclopaedia Britannica, 1988.

Concise Columbia Encyclopedia. 2d ed. Irvington, N.Y.: Columbia University Press, 1989. 920p.

Encyclopaedia Britannica Macropaedia, *Encyclopaedia Britannica Micropaedia*, and *Encyclopaedia Britannica Propaedia. See New Encyclopaedia Britannica.*

Encyclopedia Americana. International ed. 30 vols. Danbury, Conn.: Grolier, 1989.

Encyclopedia Judaica. 16 vols. New York: Macmillan, 1971.

Encyclopedia of Crime and Justice. 4 vols. New York: Free Press, 1983.

Encyclopedia of Educational Research. 5th ed. 4 vols. New York: Free Press, 1982.

Encyclopedia of Psychology. 4 vols. New York: Wiley, 1984.

Encyclopedia of Religion. 16 vols. New York: Macmillan, 1987.

Encyclopedia of Suicide. New York: Facts on File, 1988. 434p.

Encyclopedia of the Holocaust. 4 vols. New York: Macmillan, 1989.

Encyclopédie Française. 21 vols. Paris: Comité de l'Encyclopédie Française, 1935-1966.

First Stop: The Master Index to Subject Encyclopedias. Edited by Joe Ryan. Phoenix, Ariz.: Oryx Press, 1989. 1,582p.

Funk & Wagnalls New Encyclopedia. 29 vols. New York: Funk & Wagnalls, 1989.

Great Soviet Encyclopedia. 31 vols. New York: Macmillan, 1971-1983.

Hutchinson Encyclopedia. 8th ed. London: Hutchinson, 1988. 1,273p.

Information Finder. [CD-ROM]. Chicago: World Book.

International Encyclopedia of the Social Sciences. 18 vols. New York: Macmillan; New York: Free Press, 1968-1979.

Kodansha Encyclopedia of Japan. 9 vols. New York: Kodansha, 1983.

McGraw-Hill Encyclopedia of Science and Technology. 6th ed. 20 vols. New York: McGraw-Hill, 1987.

Merit Students Encyclopedia. 20 vols. New York: Macmillan Educational Co., 1990.

New American Desk Encyclopedia. New York: New American Library, 1989. 1,374p.

New Book of Knowledge. 21 vols. Danbury, Conn.: Grolier. Annual.

New Catholic Encyclopedia. 17 vols. New York: McGraw-Hill, 1967-1979.

New Columbia Encyclopedia. 4th ed. New York: Columbia University Press, 1975. 3,052p.

New Electronic Encyclopedia. [CD-ROM]. Danbury, Conn.: Grolier.

New Encyclopaedia Britannica. 15th ed. 32 vols. Chicago: Encyclopaedia Britannica, 1990.

New Grolier Student Encyclopedia. 22 vols. Danbury, Conn.: Grolier, 1989.

New Standard Encyclopedia. 20 vols. Chicago: Standard Educational Corp., 1990.

Random House Encyclopedia. Rev. ed. New York: Random House, 1990. 2,912p.

Science Year: The World Book Annual Science Supplement. Chicago: World Book, 1965- . Annual.

Statesman's Year-Book. London: Macmillan, 1864- . Annual.

World Book Encyclopedia. 22 vols. Chicago: World Book, 1990.

Young Students Learning Library. 22 vols. Middletown, Conn.: Weekly Reader Books, 1988.

Additional Readings

American Reference Books Annual. Edited by Bohdan S. Wynar. Englewood, Colo.: Libraries Unlimited, 1970- . Annual.
General encyclopedias that are updated annually are reviewed by *ARBA* in three-, four-, and five-year cycles. The initial review includes historical information; subsequent reviews point out significant changes in scope and format.

ARBA Guide to Subject Encyclopedias and Dictionaries. Edited by Bohdan S. Wynar. Littleton, Colo.: Libraries Unlimited, 1986. 570p.
This specialized *ARBA* guide contains signed reviews of selected subject dictionaries and encyclopedias that would be useful in all types of libraries. Coverage includes titles which were published within eighteen years prior to the compilation of this source.

First Stop: The Master Index to Subject Encyclopedias. Edited by Joe Ryan. Phoenix, Ariz.: Oryx Press, 1989. 1,582p.
This handy tool is a keyword and broad subject index to nearly 40,000 topics contained in 430 subject encyclopedias, dictionaries, handbooks, comprehensive textbooks, and other reference sources.

General Reference Books for Adults: Authoritative Evaluations of Encyclopedias, Atlases, and Dictionaries. Edited by Marion Sader. New York: R. R. Bowker, 1988. 614p.
Within a large section devoted to encyclopedias, multipage reviews cover a broad range of criteria. Each review also contains a facsimile reproduction of a page from the title under consideration. The coverage includes encyclopedias appropriate for both young adult and adult audiences.

Kister, Kenneth F. *Best Encyclopedias: A Guide to General and Specialized Encyclopedias.* Phoenix, Ariz.: Oryx Press, 1986. 317p.
The first chapter of this book — "Questions and Answers About Encyclopedias" — stands alone as a superb introduction to the encyclopedia form itself and to the process of choosing an encyclopedia. This chapter is followed by lengthy reviews of general encyclopedias and brief descriptions of a host of specialized encyclopedias.

Kister, Kenneth F. *Kister's Concise Guide to Best Encyclopedias*. Phoenix, Ariz.: Oryx Press, 1988. 108p.

This compact guide, with its down-to-earth advice, is primarily directed to the lay reader. Each review contains a "Facts" section and an "Evaluation" section; detailed information is provided concerning how each title may be purchased.

Reference Books Bulletin Editorial Board of the American Library Association. *Purchasing an Encyclopedia: 12 Points to Consider*. 3d ed. Chicago: American Library Association, 1990. 48p.

Reference Books Bulletin editor Sandy Whiteley delineates twelve sensible criteria to use in evaluating encyclopedias. Reviews of ten general encyclopedias follow this introductory essay.

Reference Books Bulletin Editorial Board of the American Library Association. *Reference Books Bulletin*. Chicago: American Library Association, 1983- . 22 issues/year.

RBB is a separate publication that appears in each issue of *Booklist*, which is published twenty-two times a year. In addition to an "Annual Encyclopedia Update," *RBB* occasionally features longer reviews of individual encyclopedias, evaluating the substantive changes and developments which have occurred over an extended period of time.

Reference Books for Young Readers: Authoritative Evaluations of Encyclopedias, Atlases, and Dictionaries. Edited by Marion Sader. New York: R. R. Bowker, 1988. 615p.

Identical in format and style to Sader's *General Reference Books for Adults*, this work's coverage reflects age-appropriate titles. If titles are suitable for both adult and youth audiences, reviews appear in both volumes, but are written with the different audiences in mind. Both volumes contain a lengthy discussion entitled "What to Look for in Encyclopedias."

GEOGRAPHICAL SOURCES

Uses and Characteristics

Geographical sources are most often used to answer locational questions: "Where is Palatka in Florida where my aunt lives?" or "Where is the location of yesterday's plane crash?" While these are the types of questions asked most often, readers should not have the false impression that location is "geography." Geographers study spatial problems involving environmental issues, regional planning, medical geography, political geography, mapping, and the general relationship between humans and their physical world. While it is beyond the scope of this chapter to discuss specialized works in geography, readers are encouraged to pursue further studies if they should find themselves in charge of administering even a small geography collection or acquiring materials in geography.

The publications discussed in this chapter represent the basic sources used in an average academic library or large public library. Additional sources are referred to for larger academic libraries that have more resources.

Because most librarians will not be able to answer all geographical questions using the sources in their own collections, they should identify the closest large collection of geographical and cartographic materials in the state or region. David Cobb's *Guide to U.S. Map Resources* is the most comprehensive listing of such collections in the United States, providing information on nearly one thousand individual map collections. The geographic and cartographic collections in this guide are the locations to which one can direct questions requiring more detail or expertise than one's own library can provide.

Librarians must always justify the cost of their materials, and geographical sources have suffered in the library environment because of their cost, size, and storage requirements. Quality atlases, which may cost well over $100, create an added burden on budgets that are usually already overstretched. The recent increase in the number of quality atlases makes it even more difficult for the reference librarian to make choices among geographic materials. While it may be impossible to purchase all of the different atlases, an alternative solution might be to purchase one or two titles annually, which would build a well-rounded collection in several years.

Any oversized books, and particularly geographic sources and maps, present obvious storage problems for the average reference department. The increasing availability of maps and atlases through the U.S. Government Printing Office's depository library program (see chapter 20) has exacerbated this problem. All too often, oversized atlases are filed on bottom shelves only to be forgotten. The acquisition of oversized atlases is more cost effective if they are stored (preferably horizontally) on middle shelves where they can be seen and used more frequently. Almost all maps, especially oversized maps, present a unique problem for the library, as they require specialized storage equipment. Ideally, large atlases should be stored on oversized atlas shelves, and maps should be placed in either vertical or horizontal cases designed specifically for map storage. Unfortunately, these may be luxury items for some libraries. Maps can always be placed in large flat boxes and stored on top of filing cabinets to provide protection from light and dust. If a library's collection of maps grows to several hundred, metal map cases are the alternative of choice.

The primary purpose for the majority of geographical sources is to help one locate places. All of the sources described in this chapter locate something, tell something about a location, or show how to get there. Another general characteristic of geographical sources is that they usually deal with a time period, either current or historical. While currency is very often important, historical and out-of-date information is often critical to a reference question as well. In addition, some geographical sources deal with thematic or subject information. Examples of thematic information are a population atlas, a geologic map, or a map of deforestation.

General locational questions can be grouped into three categories: current events, recreation, and business. Current events are one of the strongest reasons for maintaining current geographical sources. Just as last night's talk-show novel will be requested in the library the next day, so too will information on yesterday's volcanic eruption, earthquake, revolution, or similar human or physical disaster. The world has become more global than ever, and the media have brought the world's crises and disasters into the living room. It is the library's role to provide additional information on this global society. Current detailed geographical sources are one important means by which to do so.

Recreation has become an important part of many lives, and travel is now more common than it was in the past. The result is that a larger segment of the population is interested in information, not only on the local state or national park, but also on cities and regions all over the world. The amount of travel literature available today is more than any library can possibly accumulate, but an attempt should be made to provide a collection of travel literature for patron demands.

Finally, business travel has also become more common, and the information required to answer these questions is related to travel literature. This particular type of travel requires more information on cities and detailed information regarding things like hotels and restaurants.

Another category of questions concerns historical geography. This can be divided into genealogy, military history, and place name changes. All three of these areas are covered in many specialized sources that cannot be described in this chapter. Many of the genealogy questions are specific. For example, the user may want a map of the town where an ancestor lived in southern Germany in 1864. Few libraries can provide this information, so this question requires referral to a more specialized map collection. However, many times a quality atlas or an older atlas in the collection may indeed show the location of the town. The most valuable asset in answering any of these questions may be a late nineteenth- or early twentieth-century atlas. Age should not be a primary criterion when weeding geographical sources, as historical sources are especially valuable for some questions. Most historical atlases provide some treatment of military history, and there are also large atlases that restrict themselves to a particular war or country (the American Civil War, for example), if more specialized information is needed. Similarly, place name changes can present a special problem for the general reference librarian; Eastern Europe presents particularly difficult challenges no matter how many sources the library has. Again, older atlases are very good sources for changing place names. Gazetteers, which list place name locations, are also discussed later in this chapter.

The types of geographical sources to be considered in this chapter include maps, atlases, gazetteers, travel literature, and a few general sources. Maps are purposely listed first, because too many libraries tend to forget them, for reasons already mentioned. Nevertheless, maps generally provide more detailed information on a specific area, and provide more comprehensive thematic coverage, than do atlases. The advantage of atlases, however, is that they can provide the whole world in one volume at a nominal cost. Individual atlases may cover many types of subjects and offer basic reference information on geology, the oceans, space, or the historical geography of a particular country. Gazetteers are also important reference tools, for they provide information on geographical place names. Some gazetteers simply provide precise locational information, such as latitude and longitude; others describe the locations and give information on population, climate, economy, and notable tourist attractions. The titles comprising travel literature have grown considerably in the last few years because of the travel patterns of society. Fortunately, there are many good options available from which libraries and individuals can choose. The section covering other geographical sources briefly describes the genre of titles that relate to geography. Examples include data related to climatic information, political/geographical information on individual countries, mileage guides, and geographical dictionaries.

Evaluation

Although atlases may be evaluated using criteria applicable to other reference books, there are specific criteria unique to atlases that should be reviewed. Maps too must be evaluated differently than other reference sources. The criteria to be considered when evaluating atlases and maps include: scale and projection, color and symbols, publisher/authority, indexing, and currency.

Scale and Projection

Scale and projection are the two most common characteristics that make cartographic materials different from all other library materials. These two concepts are very difficult for many persons to understand, and are oftentimes difficult to explain. Essentially, *scale* is the ratio of the distance on the map to the actual distance in the real world on the face of the earth. Maps must be drawn to scale so that accurate comparisons may be made between the map and the corresponding distance on the earth. This scale may be given as a verbal scale (1 inch equals 4 miles); a representative fraction (1:253,440); or a graphic scale or bar scale normally found below the map. The verbal and representative fraction examples here are the same, since there are 253,440 inches in 4 miles. Scale is the most important element of a map, as it defines the amount of information that can be shown as well as the size of the geographical area (see figure 17.1). Maps are generally classed by scale: large-scale maps are normally 1:100,000 or larger; medium-scale maps are between 1:100,000 and 1:1,000,000; and smaller-scale maps are 1:1,000,000 or smaller. Note the cartographic aberration that, as the number increases, the scale is considered smaller rather than larger, and vice versa.

A good map or atlas will always identify the scale, and the librarian must decide the appropriate scale for the user or library. Topographic maps, with large scales of 1:50,000, are excellent sources for geographical place names, but would be the wrong choice for someone looking for a country's administrative boundaries. Very little geographical area would be shown on a 1:50,000-scale map; such a tool is very detailed in the amount of data it shows. A more appropriate scale for administrative divisions would be 1:250,000 or even 1:500,000. It is important that maps in an atlas not vary their scales greatly. Quality atlases make an attempt to map nations and states at similar scales. An inferior atlas may show each U.S. state on its own page, which leads the user to believe that all states are "page-size." Similar examples should be carefully reviewed when looking at world atlases.

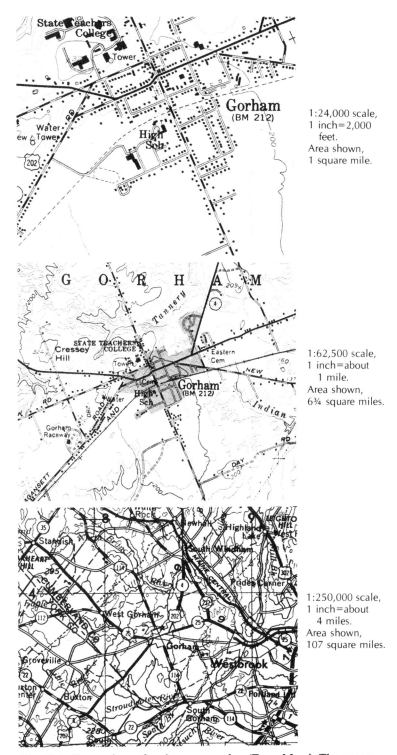

1:24,000 scale,
1 inch=2,000
  feet.
Area shown,
1 square mile.

1:62,500 scale,
1 inch=about
  1 mile.
Area shown,
6¾ square miles.

1:250,000 scale,
1 inch=about
  4 miles.
Area shown,
107 square miles.

Fig. 17.1. Comparison of various map scales. (From Morris Thompson, *Maps for America*, U.S. Department of the Interior, 1987.)

Map projection is one of the most complicated fields of cartography, and scholars continue to argue the value of one projection over another. Suffice to say that when a circular globe is drawn onto a flat piece of paper (*projected*), there will be some distortion and unavoidable error. Certain projections are better suited to large-scale maps and others to small-scale maps. Furthermore, some projections are preferred for their mapping characteristics (e.g., equal area, navigation, and least distortion). The map user should be aware of these distortions. Having a current globe for reference obviates the degree of distortion on many maps and in many atlases. One of the well-known examples of distortion is the "large" Greenland on the Mercator projection world map. Find such a map and compare it to a globe to see how projections can slant one's understanding of the earth. It is difficult for the average user, or librarian, to be aware of the many characteristics of the various projections used. A recent title by Mark Monmonier and George Schnell, *Map Appreciation*, provides an expert and clear explanation of this mapping concept.[1]

Color and Symbols

Color is used on maps in many different ways and for different purposes. The simplest of maps uses color to show political boundaries: for example, France, green; Germany, yellow; and Italy, blue. Color is also used on many government maps to show standard types of information. The U.S. Geological Survey, for example, uses five basic colors on its topographic maps. Brown is used to show contours, or altitude lines, their elevations, and certain unverified altitude bench marks. Blue is used to show lakes, rivers, canals, and other waterways. Black is used to show roads, buildings, railroads, and other human impact upon the land. Green is used to display vegetation, such as woodland, vineyards, and orchards. Red is another "culture color," showing road classifications for major highways, some administrative boundaries, and built-up areas in the center of many cities.

Color may also be used to show land heights, ocean depths, or gradients on a thematic map. An example of the latter might be the use of color shading to show population distribution from an inner city to its suburbs. Many atlas maps use color to show the varying land heights in a country or across Europe, for example. Usually, deeper colors are used to show the highest land, with pastel shades used to show lowlands and coastal plains. Another subtle use of color is the use of shading that creates shadows along the eastern side of mountains, assuming a light source from the northwest. The results create an easy-to-read relief map. Figure 17.2 shows the relationship between shaded relief and contour elevations. Excellent examples of this map type are the many country maps produced by the Central Intelligence Agency and distributed by the U.S. Government Printing Office.

Symbols on a map allow the map to communicate its information to the reader. It is also important that users not expect too much from a map. The map can only communicate effectively when it is not cluttered. The amount and type of symbology are controlled by the scale of the map. To state the obvious, a map of Chicago will show far more detail and symbols for that city than will a map of Illinois. A successful map differentiates between geographic features. For example, there should be a clear indication of the difference between such things as roads and railroads, external and internal boundaries, rivers and canals. Each map or atlas should provide a key or index to its symbols. The first question that should be asked of a map may be: "Is it too cluttered?" A map that attempts to provide too much information can be as misleading as a map that shows very little.

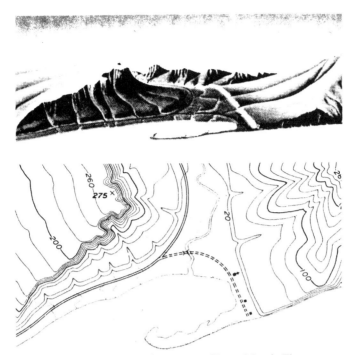

Fig. 17.2. Shaded relief and contours. (From Morris Thompson, *Maps for America*, U.S. Department of the Interior, 1987.)

Publisher/Authority

As with any area of publishing, there are reputable map and atlas publishers and those that are less so. On the whole, there are very few publishers who do not produce quality products, because they face a marketplace that has become far more qualified to evaluate their products. Nevertheless, it continues to be important for librarians to be familiar with the literature and to study reviews of maps and atlases, as they would for other reference materials.

With very few exceptions, national mapping agencies (see *Worldwide Directory of National Earth-Science Agencies*[2]) produce high-quality, current, authoritative maps for their countries. These national mapping agencies, such as the Geological Survey in the United States, the Ordnance Survey in Great Britain, and the Institut Géographique National in France, are a source of quality mapping products at reasonable costs for their countries—but are often overlooked.

Commercial map products are more difficult to evaluate if the librarian is not familiar with the firm or its products. The major U.S. firms that produce both maps and atlases are Rand McNally, C. S. Hammond, and the National Geographic Society. The number of smaller firms producing high-quality products is growing rapidly, and includes such companies as DeLorme, Raven, Northern Cartographic, ADC, and many others. The international market is equally prolific, although several large firms again stand out. There is John Bartholomew in Scotland, Kummerly & Frey of Switzerland, and Michelin of France. Numerous smaller firms also produce maps, especially city maps of individual foreign countries. While quality maps are available from many sources, it is prudent to purchase materials from established, reputable dealers.

Indexing/Place Names

The heart of an atlas or a map is the map itself. By analogy, then, the brain is the index or guide to that atlas or map. An atlas without an index to the maps, their locations, and the place names is of questionable value as a reference tool. Similarly, a map of a city without an index to its streets or geographical features is equally suspect. How is the index to be used? Does the index locate the feature on the map with grid references or exact coordinates, as well as references to page number? Does the index include all of the place names on the map? Does the index include not only cities and towns, but also national parks, administrative divisions, and mountains? It is important to find an atlas/map that does index as many of these features as possible. One must realize that a publisher's higher priced atlas or map is usually the best buy, because it offers more information.

Currency

After scale, currency is probably the most important criterion for any geographical source material. Because the world is changing so rapidly, it is imperative that libraries be able to provide current information. A world atlas that is five years old portrays enough obsolete information that it should be used only for historical purposes. So many changes occur annually: place name changes, new roads, railroad abandonment, boundary changes, new dams, and power lines. There are also many subtle changes that occur within cities that can be shown only on the most detailed of maps. Examples of these changes are the growth of the city's boundaries, its suburbs, and redevelopment projects, including the replacement of old buildings with new.

Selection

Geographical sources vary extensively. Each library must determine the needs of its users and the community that it is trying to serve. A large academic library will require a greater complexity of geographical sources for its users than will a smaller, rural public library. The academic library may require several world atlases as well as selected national atlases to supplement its map collection, while a small public library may be satisfied with a new world atlas every three years. No library can satisfy all its users all the time, and it is imperative that librarians communicate among themselves to become aware of expertise that is available to them. This may be especially important with geographical sources, as very few libraries have large, comprehensive collections in this area.

The library must also decide, within its collection development guidelines, whether it will collect for ready reference materials or develop a more comprehensive collection for in-depth research purposes. A ready reference collection may consist of only 100 titles,[3] while research collections may include tens of thousands of maps and hundreds of atlases. The basic collection is the focus in this chapter; there are many sources one can refer to for the development of larger collections.

Finding appropriate selection tools for geographical sources is perhaps the most difficult task in this area of collection development. While *Publishers Weekly*, *Choice*, and others include atlas reviews, it is not possible to use only the standard sources for current awareness of geographical sources. As in other fields, there is a specialized literature of unique publications. The most current and comprehensive listing of new publications appears in *base line*, the newsletter of the American Library Association's Map and Geography Round Table.[4] Published six times annually, this small newsletter contains information in each issue on new publications. Other publications useful for selection purposes are included in the List of Sources for this chapter.

Two useful guides provide additional sources of information. David Cobb's *Guide to U.S. Map Resources* (with over 950 entries) is the most comprehensive, up-to-date source describing U.S. map collections. It provides information on special collections and area and subject strengths, as well as addresses, telephone numbers, and so forth. Libraries are encouraged to review this volume to locate the nearest research library map collection and to develop contacts for interlibrary loan and assistance on research questions. A *Geographical Bibliography for American Libraries* is another superb collection of sources in the many fields of geography. Its many contributors have provided a significant bibliography to aid libraries in identifying, selecting, and securing publications of value in geography for their respective collections. A valuable section, "For School Libraries," recommends titles for elementary and secondary schools. Each entry is annotated, and a useful index provides access to authors, short titles, and subjects.

The choice of format is quickly becoming a dilemma for those using geographical sources. Maps and atlases are now being offered as print publications, on diskette, and as CD-ROM. With these formats come the demands for additional library equipment, such as personal computers with hard disk drives, CD-ROM drives, and color printers. Two specific computer disk programs that are highly recommended for reference purposes are PC-Globe and PC-USA. These systems are produced by PC-Globe, Inc. of Phoenix, and are specifically geared to the educational market. These automated mapping tools, and others that are being planned, provide the library with enhanced graphics capabilities. These systems bring together a variety of federal information (such as population census data, economic statistics, and agricultural commodities data) and can produce those items in country or state formats. The PC-USA disk allows further subdivision of this information by various regions in the United States. The major limitation of most of these systems at present is their inability to interact with other data that a library might have and wish to map. It is, however, only a matter of time before many of these systems become interactive and allow data to be imported and exported to fit the particular specifications for any library query. They are reasonably priced (about $75) and provide high-resolution color graphic maps that can be reproduced for applications such as term papers. Essentially, they provide a variety of international and domestic document information in map form, and are early examples of what may be expected throughout the decade of the 1990s. Additional software options are too specialized and highly priced at this time for general reference use.

Important General Sources

As mentioned earlier in this chapter, categories of geographical sources that librarians find useful in reference work include atlases, travel guides, gazetteers, and maps. In this section, major publishers of maps and travel guides and their products are discussed, along with a selection of the most useful gazetteers and geographical dictionaries. Three distinct types of atlases are identified, and a few of the best available titles of each type are described. Finally, mention is made of some important geographical sources that do not fit into any of these categories.

Maps

Even though individual maps may present storage problems, libraries should not forego them entirely in favor of atlases. The major disadvantage of the atlas map is its small scale and inability to depict many geographical regions with sufficient detail. Local detail is usually provided only through individual maps, unless one is fortunate enough to live in a large metropolitan area that has its own street atlas. Some of the sources for maps that should be collected and included in all library collections are described here.

The U.S. Geological Survey (USGS) is the national agency officially responsible for domestic mapping. It produces maps at many scales, prints maps for other agencies of the federal government, and produces maps on printed paper as well as in digital formats. Libraries should focus on providing coverage of the local area at various scales to show varying amounts of detail. Libraries may request the free state indexes and other information for their states by calling 1-800-USA-MAPS. This number may also be used to ask any questions regarding maps or map products. All libraries should purchase maps covering their cities or towns at the following scales: 1:250,000 (one sheet); 1:100,000 (one to two sheets); 1:24,000 (one to six sheets). These maps provide valuable information on topography, drainage systems, transportation, woodland coverage, and other physical and cultural features. Libraries located in coastal cities or near the Great Lakes are encouraged to contact the National Ocean Survey in Rockville, Maryland for information on nautical charts of their local areas. These charts are valuable for boaters, fishermen, and others interested in the coastline environment.

A variety of commercial sources also produce local maps which are useful when answering reference questions on local streets, public buildings, schools, and so forth. Companies such as Rand McNally, American Map Co., and Champion Maps produce numerous local maps for local government agencies and chambers of commerce. Libraries should always maintain contacts with local tourism offices for new publications, including maps, and regular visits to local bookstores also can provide information on new maps.

Some of the most important, and often overlooked, sources for local information are local governments and regional agencies. Most municipal governments and regional agencies produce maps for planning and engineering studies. Sadly, many of these items are simply discarded once they are out-of-date. It is important to maintain contacts with these agencies, as their discards can be a valuable source of information for libraries. While maps and aerial photographs are not always free, these items are usually available for reasonable reproduction costs. Besides the usual chamber of commerce maps, libraries are encouraged to seek out aerial photographs and maps showing neighborhoods, school districts, and parks, as well as examples of out-of-date maps to show the growth or decline of certain sections of their cities.

Atlases

Atlases, like maps, can be divided into three groups: current, historical, and thematic. Current atlases are needed for up-to-date information on geographical and political changes in the world. Historical atlases are necessary for the study of boundary changes, military campaigns, and early exploration. Thematic, or subject, atlases, emphasize a specific subject or region. Examples include national atlases, population atlases, and geological atlases.

General World Atlases. The two finest general world atlases available today are the *Times Atlas of the World* and *The New International Atlas*. The *Times* is regarded as the finest English-language world atlas, providing balanced geographic coverage. Its 123 map pages, produced by the highly respected firm of John Bartholomew, provide excellent regional maps to answer all but the most specialized reference questions. This atlas is divided into three general sections: an introductory section including general physical information and thematic world maps; a series of regional maps showing political and physical features; and a final section which is a large index-gazetteer with over 200,000 names. Locations are indexed by map page, a map-page referencing system, and by latitude and longitude.

The New International Atlas is the result of an international collaborative effort by scholars around the world. One of its advantages is the use of shaded relief, which makes it easier for readers to interpret mountains and highland regions. It also includes a section on the population of cities and towns with more than 50,000 inhabitants, and an introductory section of excellent oceanographic maps. Its gazetteer of over 160,000 names provides geographical coordinates and map locations.

Historical Atlases. The *Times Atlas of World History* broke a long tradition of Euro-centricity, or emphasis on the history of Europe, by presenting a more balanced view of history which is worldwide in conception. The maps begin with one showing human origins, move through the early civilizations, and conclude with a group entitled "The age of global civilization," which takes users into the 1980s. It is the first historical atlas to incorporate new mapping techniques and to include information on social history and cultural achievements of different civilizations. It also provides an index to historical place names and a glossary giving supplementary information about some individuals, peoples, and events.

The *New Cambridge Modern History Atlas* is volume 14 of the *New Cambridge Modern History*. Its approach is more traditional, but its value is in its regional approach to history. It contains geographical maps showing political, ecclesiastical, and military developments over time. It also includes a useful subject index.

The *Historical Atlas of the United States* provides a unique and current perspective on America's history. In addition to hundreds of maps, this atlas incorporates more than 450 photographs, 80 graphs, and 140,000 words of text. It is an interesting volume that interweaves the historical timeline of U.S. history throughout the chapters: Land; People; Boundaries; Economy; Networks; and Communities. The atlas also includes a useful bibliography and index. This atlas will soon become one of the major sources for the study of American history.

Kenneth Martis's *Historical Atlas of Political Parties* offers a wealth of information in a political atlas. Its multicolored maps, combined with judicious text and tables, provide an authoritative record and geographical understanding of American political history.

Many other historical atlases concentrate on either particular periods in history or particular regions. Examples of the former are Martin Gilbert's *Atlas of the Holocaust* and the *Times Atlas of the Second World War*. Regional atlases are appearing with greater frequency today. Gerald Hanson's *Historical Atlas of Arkansas*, Iwo Pogonowski's *Poland, A Historical Atlas*, and Michael Crowder's *Historical Atlas of Africa* are examples of the proliferation of this atlas type that librarians should be aware of.

Thematic Atlases. The *National Atlas of the United States of America* is included in this category because it focuses on a specific nation. Even though this atlas has long been out-of-print (and federal government shortsightedness has prevented a new edition), it provides a cornucopia of knowledge about the United States through its many statistical and graphic maps. While much of the economic and social information is now out-of-date, many of the sections (for instance, general reference maps, landforms, climate, and history) are still valuable for reference purposes.

We the People: An Atlas of America's Ethnic Diversity is an excellent graphic and textual explanation of the social context of America's population. Using 1980 census data, this atlas successfully reveals the distribution patterns of the ethnic populations that are so important to the evolution of America. The atlas examines these populations primarily in terms of counties and larger cities and towns. The atlas also includes an appendix showing the estimated size and percentage of groups in each state's ancestries and another showing ethnic population data for states and counties.

The *Atlas of North America* is included here, not for its regional perspective, but rather for its unique blend of traditional maps and satellite imagery. Library users often ask for examples of satellite imagery and how it may be used. This atlas, with its numerous examples of remote sensing, is an excellent source for answering such questions. It includes examples of black-and-white, natural-color, and infrared images. The atlas also includes geographical information on North America, making it a valuable regional reference source as well.

There are numerous titles available in thematic atlas publishing, and a library's budget and collection development goals will define the depth of coverage in this area. Examples of additional titles are Michael Kidron and Dan Smith's *The War Atlas*, John Keegan and

Andrew Wheatcroft's *Zones of Conflict: An Atlas of Future Wars*, and Patrick Moore's *The New Atlas of the Universe*.

A new genre of thematic atlases has recently appeared, and represents a new trend in atlas publishing. These atlases usually focus on a theme or historical time period. They are further characterized by their textual commentary, illustrations, photographs, and a relative paucity of maps. These books are more aptly described as popular histories illustrated with maps rather than atlases. Nevertheless, for the less specialized library they can offer an economical option, by combining a historical volume and maps. Examples of these titles include Nicholas de Lange's *Atlas of the Jewish World*, *Atlas of the Christian Church*, Frances Robinson's *Atlas of the Islamic World since 1500*, and Donald Matthew's *Atlas of Medieval Europe*.

Gazetteers

Gazetteers may be the most often used geographical reference source. A *gazetteer* is usually a list of geographical names and/or physical features, either appended to an atlas or published as a separate volume. There are two types of gazetteers: locational and descriptive. *Locational* gazetteers usually provide information precisely locating the feature either by atlas page and grid index, or by even more precise latitude and longitude on the earth's surface. *Descriptive* gazetteers may provide some or all of the above information, but then also describe the place. Such a description may include such features as a brief history, commodity production, population, and altitude.

Almost every atlas includes a gazetteer as an appendix used to locate the place names in that volume. Therein lies its limitations. Atlas gazetteers are useful for locating major towns, cities, administrative divisions, and physical features. Questions requiring information on those cities beyond the scope of the normal world atlas will require a more detailed volume, such as a gazetteer.

The standard library gazetteer in the past has been the *Columbia-Lippincott*. While its 130,000 entries make it one of the most comprehensive descriptive gazetteers, it has really become too outdated (1961) to be used for current reference. Nevertheless, its value for historical information (including its historical editions) will continue to be significant for many reference questions.

Similar in format, as it provides descriptive information for locations, is *Webster's New Geographical Dictionary*. This has become the best choice for American libraries, although it is restricted by having less than fifty thousand entries. Its inclusion of maps and lists of administrative divisions for major countries and U.S. states makes it the most useful world gazetteer available today.

A re-entrant (last edition was 1965) into the gazetteer market is *Chambers World Gazetteer*. This English publication has fewer entries than *Webster's* (733 pages versus 1,376), yet it often offers more information in its descriptions for geographical locations. The maps in *Chambers* are decidedly inferior to those in *Webster's*, showing only administrative divisions and no major cities.

The newest, and potentially most valuable, gazetteer is the U.S. Geological Survey's *National Gazetteer of the United States of America*. When completed, this series of gazetteers will have a single volume for each state and presumably another one or two for territories and possessions. It is being published as a part of the Survey's Professional Paper Series, and each volume will have the number designation "1200" followed by the two-letter code for the subject state. The series is available to depository libraries as a separate item, and is for sale from the USGS to all other libraries. These gazetteers are derived from the National Geographic Names Data Base. This database includes names found on various maps and public documents, but excludes railroads, streets, and roads. These gazetteers will become the most comprehensive listing of geographical information for each state as soon as they are published. Their detail can be illustrated by comparing the Indiana volume, with 23,000 entries, to *Webster's*, which has approximately 47,000 entries to cover the whole world.

Another important series of gazetteers for foreign names is the series of foreign-country volumes produced by the U.S. Board on Geographic Names and published by the Defense Mapping Agency. Similar to the USGS gazetteers, these are locational gazetteers providing a latitude/longitude location for geographic places. These are the best volumes for locating any place-name information for foreign countries. Most of these titles have been distributed to libraries through the Government Printing Office depository library program.

Two additional titles that will be found in many libraries are worth noting. The Reader's Digest *Guide to Places of the World* is a general descriptive gazetteer with excellent illustrations and maps. The *Rand McNally Commercial Atlas and Marketing Guide* contains a wealth of economic information in addition to large maps for each state. It is noted in this context, for it has long been considered an unofficial gazetteer for the United States. The 1990 edition includes over 128,000 principal cities, towns, and inhabited places. Furthermore, each entry includes information on population, elevation, zip code, airlines, railroads, and so forth.

Travel Guides

Travel literature is proliferating at an unprecedented rate today, as publishers attempt to provide sources for a large number of travelers, both domestic and international. It is becoming difficult for libraries to decide among a multiplicity of choices for travel guides to various regions of the United States or to individual foreign countries. There is also considerable duplication, as publishers try to take advantage of a growing market. The traditional areas of Europe, the Caribbean, and the United States are the mainstays of the travel industry, but many firms are now trying to produce new guides for Eastern Europe and the Soviet Union as expectations for expanded travel in these areas increase.

Two recent articles in *Publishers Weekly*, entitled "The World in the '90s" and "A Round-up of 1990 Travel Books,"[5] are the best summaries to date on the travel literature available from numerous publishers. Although these articles concentrate on foreign travel, there are numerous references to U.S. travel sources. An article by Jean Crichton on U.S. travel sources provides a comprehensive listing for this literature.[6]

Carolyn Anthony's article provides an interesting division of travel literature into four general categories.[7] First are the popular annuals—Fodor, Frommer, Birnbaum, Mobil—that cover all topics, including passports, restaurants and hotels, and car rentals. Most of these guides are revised annually by local authorities and provide reliable, up-to-date information on restaurants, accommodations, and sightseeing. They usually provide current pricing for a variety of budgets. A second group—"Let's Go" from the Harvard Student Agencies, "Shoestring Guides" from Lonely Planet, and business traveler guides—is aimed at a particular group or type of traveler. These guides may be for the more adventurous traveler looking for out-of-the-way locations. Alternatively, they may be written for special groups such as students and budget travelers, business travelers who intend to extend their stays for short vacations, or upscale travelers looking for premier accommodations and sightseeing. Third, there is a growing literature for the specialized traveler—guides to museums, cathedrals, pubs, and similar tourist attractions. Guides in this category include "maverick" guides, trail guides, diving and snorkeling guides, and so forth. One of the notable examples in this category is the *Smithsonian Guide to Historic America*. Finally, there is a resurgence in the literary travel book, for the armchair tourist who enjoys taking an imaginary trip, or to satisfy curiosity.

Other Geographical Sources

Geography has supplementary reference sources, which contain information not found in the atlases, gazetteers, and maps discussed previously. The *Standard Highway Mileage Guide* is essential for answering such questions as "How far is it from Boston to Syracuse?" The *Mileage Guide* should really be supplemented by a current road atlas such as the annual *Rand McNally Road Atlas*. The *Standard Highway Mileage Guide* contains over 800,000 index mileages between 1,300 major U.S. and Canadian cities.

Background Notes is compiled by the U.S. Department of State. It is a series of brief, authoritative pamphlets on selected countries and geographical entities, and includes information on history, geography, culture, government, politics, and economics. These pamphlets also include base maps (easily photocopied) for each country, which show major cities, rivers, railroads, roads, and airports. The series now totals approximately 170 titles, which are updated about every two years.

A geographic encyclopedia is useful for any reference collection. Many specialized terms developed as the lexicon of this field are not included in standard dictionaries. Audrey Clark's *Longman Dictionary of Geography* is a compact volume incorporating terms from both physical and human geography, including definitions for terms such as *bathymetric*, *gobolala*, *portulano*, and *zymogenous*. Similarly, *The Weather Almanac* provides information on U.S. weather and weather fundamentals (see chapter 13).

Search Strategies

Geographical sources should be used when the question asked involves location. Such questions could be as simple as, "I need to know where Beethoven was born" and/or "Could I have a map showing Beethoven's birthplace?" They may also be more complicated, such as a request for information on the distribution of radioactive waste from a specific nuclear arsenal or power plant. Both cases require maps and other reference sources as well, which may be more easily accessible in a smaller library where all of these sources are grouped together. Reference librarians must become thoroughly familiar with basic mapping concepts, such as scale and projection, and must understand how these concepts are represented in general and historical maps. This knowledge will allow the librarian to focus on finding the needed information, without having to struggle to interpret mapping symbols.

Map reference also requires a reference interview process. Most users are unfamiliar with the resources of the map collection and, therefore, generally ask for maps of a much larger area rather than for a map of a specific area that they would really prefer. For example, a map librarian may encounter a genealogist requesting a map of Germany, when the patron really needs a detailed map of the outskirts of Hanover, Germany. Too often, users ask for general maps because they do not know the resources of the library, and are not sufficiently questioned by the librarian so that they can be helped to use those resources correctly. It is frequently important to converse with the patron to better define the query so that the appropriate map can be retrieved. Similarly, patrons will often use an atlas to attempt to locate a particular place name; if they fail to find it, they may leave, believing that the library does not have the answer. Again, a little discussion with the patron would probably lead the librarian to choose a gazetteer, with considerably more place names of an area, to provide the answer to such a question.

One of the more difficult concepts for many map users to accept is that it may be possible to use a map of a larger area to answer a question for a smaller one. This is especially important for those libraries that do have large, detailed collections of maps for foreign countries. An example would be a question on the location of Angel Falls, Venezuela. While the collection may not contain maps of Venezuela, a map of northern

South America or of the whole of South America may provide the correct location. Similarly, patrons may ask for a small map of a particular country, but be shown only a wall-size map which is too large. Again, using the above example, a map of South America may be able to provide a Venezuelan map for the patron at a smaller size for their use.

A "sliding-scale" concept should be used when answering geographic reference questions. The reference interview allows the librarian to ask specific questions to define the appropriate type of map to be used to answer the question. For example, suppose a patron asks for a railroad map of Europe. While the library has such a map, further questioning reveals that the patron is really looking for railroads in Germany, and additional questions reveal that he really wants to know if there is a subway system in Berlin. That question is probably going to require a different map than a railroad map of Europe. It is useful if librarians can let their minds "slide" through the various kinds of maps in the collection as the discussion with the patron progresses. Patrons often have not defined their questions before they approach the library; thus, it is important for the librarian to assist in the clarification of questions so that appropriate and correct reference sources can be used to answer them.

■ ══ ■

17.1
A Map of Oberweis

A patron entered the map library one afternoon to inquire if the library had any maps of Germany, as she was tracing her family history. A brief reference interview revealed that she was really looking for a detailed map that would show the town of Oberweis. The librarian first checked the gazetteer in the *Times Atlas of the World*, only to discover that this town was not listed. Two additional world gazetteers were also consulted, the *Columbia-Lippincott* and *Webster's New Geographical Dictionary*, with no success. It became apparent that this was a small village which would require a specialized place name gazetteer usually available only in research collections. Fortunately, the librarian had access to such tools in the collection, and the town was located in *Müllers Grosses Deutsches Ortsbuch*, which included a brief description of the village. An additional source, *Gazetteer to AMS 1:25,000 Maps of West Germany*, volume 2, also listed Oberweis and provided locational information: latitude/longitude and an individual map number for libraries having this map series. The patron not only found the location of the small village, but was able to view a detailed map (1:25,000) revealing the plan of the town. This map provided the patron with the necessary information to locate her family's birthplace.

Notes

1. Mark Monmonier and George A. Schnell, *Map Appreciation* (Englewood Cliffs, N.J.: Prentice-Hall, 1987), 15-25.

2. U.S. Geological Survey, *Worldwide Directory of National Earth-Science Agencies and Related International Organizations* (Washington, D.C.: Superintendent of Documents, 1981) (Geological Survey Circular 834), 87p.

3. David A. Cobb, "Developing a Small Geographical Library with Special Emphasis on Indiana," *Focus on Indiana Libraries* 26 (Fall 1972): 114-20.

4. American Library Association, Map and Geography Round Table, *base line*, 1980- . Six times per year.

5. Carolyn Anthony, "The World in the '90s," *Publishers Weekly* 237 (January 19, 1990): 20-30; Karole Riipa, "A Round-up of 1990 Travel Books," *Publishers Weekly* 237 (January 19, 1990): 38-56.

6. Jean Crichton, "Travel USA," *Publishers Weekly* 237 (May 4, 1990): 17-28.

7. Anthony, "The World in the '90s," 20-30.

List of Sources

Atlas of North America: Space-Age Portrait of a Continent. Washington, D.C.: National Geographic Society, 1985. 264p.

Atlas of the Christian Church. Edited by Henry Chadwick and G. R. Evans. New York: Facts on File, 1987. 240p.

Background Notes. Washington, D.C.: U.S. Government Printing Office, 1954- . Irregular.

Chambers World Gazetteer. 5th ed. Edited by David Munro. Cambridge: Chambers, 1988. 733p.

Clark, Audrey N. *Longman Dictionary of Geography: Human and Physical*. Essex, England: Longman, 1985. 724p.

Columbia-Lippincott Gazetteer of the World. New York: Columbia University Press, 1952, with supplement 1961. 2,148p.

Crowder, Michael. *Historical Atlas of Africa*. Essex, England: Longman, 1985. 156p.

Gazetteer to AMS 1:25,000 Maps of West Germany. 3 vols. Washington, D.C.: U.S. Army Map Service, 1954.

A Geographical Bibliography for American Libraries. Edited by Chauncy D. Harris. Washington, D.C.: Association of American Geographers, 1985. 437p.

Gilbert, Martin. *Atlas of the Holocaust*. New York: Pergamon, 1988. 256p.

Guide to Places of the World. 1st ed., reprinted with amendments. London: Reader's Digest Association, 1988. 735p.

Guide to U.S. Map Resources. 2d ed. Compiled by David A. Cobb. Chicago: American Library Association, 1990. 495p.

Hanson, Gerald T. *Historical Atlas of Arkansas*. Norman, Okla.: University of Oklahoma Press, 1989. 142p.

Historical Atlas of the United States. Washington, D.C.: National Geographic Society, 1988. 289p.

Keegan, John, and Andrew Wheatcroft. *Zones of Conflict: An Atlas of Future Wars*. New York: Simon and Schuster, 1986. 158p.

Kidron, Michael, and Dan Smith. *The War Atlas: Armed Conflict—Armed Peace*. New York: Simon and Schuster, 1983. 124p.

Lange, Nicholas de. *Atlas of the Jewish World*. Oxford: Phaidon, 1984. 240p.

Martis, Kenneth C. *The Historical Atlas of Political Parties in the United States Congress, 1789-1989*. New York: Macmillan, 1989. 518p.

Matthew, Donald. *Atlas of Medieval Europe*. New York: Facts on File, 1983. 240p.

Moore, Patrick. *The New Atlas of the Universe*. London: Mitchell Beazley, 1984. 271p.

Müller, Friedrich. *Müllers Grosses Deutsches Ortsbuch....* Wuppertal, Germany: Post- und Ortsbuchverlag, 1982-1983. 1,194p.

The National Atlas of the United States of America. Washington, D.C.: U.S. Geological Survey, 1970. 417p.

The National Gazetteer of the United States of America. Washington, D.C.: U.S. Geological Survey, 1982- . (Professional Paper 1200).

The New Cambridge Modern History Atlas. Cambridge: Cambridge University Press, 1970. Reprinted with corrections, 1978. 319p.

The New International Atlas. Chicago: Rand McNally, 1990. 520p.

PC-Globe. [computer disks]. Phoenix, Ariz.: PC-Globe, Inc., 1989.

PC-USA. [computer disks]. Phoenix, Ariz.: PC-Globe, Inc., 1989.

Pogonowski, Iwo. *Poland, A Historical Atlas*. New York: Hippocrene Books, 1987. 321p.

Rand McNally Commercial Atlas and Marketing Guide. Chicago: Rand McNally, 1876- . Annual.

Rand McNally Road Atlas. Chicago: Rand McNally, 1926- . Annual.

Robinson, Frances. *Atlas of the Islamic World since 1500*. New York: Facts on File, 1982. 238p.

Smithsonian Guide to Historic America. 12 vols. Washington, D.C.: Stewart, Tabori & Chang, 1989- .

Standard Highway Mileage Guide. Chicago: Rand McNally, 1987. 638p.

The Times Atlas of the Second World War. Edited by John Keegan. New York: Harper & Row, 1989. 254p.

The Times Atlas of the World. 7th ed. London: Times Books, 1989. 227p.

The Times Atlas of World History. 3d ed. Edited by Geoffrey Barraclough. London: Times Books, 1989. 358p.

We the People: An Atlas of America's Ethnic Diversity. New York: Macmillan, 1988. 315p.

The Weather Almanac. 5th ed. Edited by James A. Ruffner and Frank E. Bair. Detroit, Mich.: Gale Research, 1987. 811p.

Webster's New Geographical Dictionary. Springfield, Mass.: Merriam-Webster, 1988. 1,376p.

Worldwide Directory of National Earth-Science Agencies and Related International Organizations. Washington, D.C.: U.S. Geological Survey, Superintendent of Documents, 1981. (Geological Survey Circular 834). 87p.

Additional Readings

American Library Association, Map & Geography Round Table. *base line*, 1980- . Six times per year.
    This newsletter provides current information on cartographic materials, other publications of interest to map and geography librarians, meetings, related governmental activities, and map librarianship.

American Library Association, Map & Geography Round Table. *Meridian*, 1988- . Semiannual.
    Meridian provides reviewed articles, book reviews, mileposts, and forthcoming events for those interested in maps and map librarianship.

Cobb, David A. "Reference Service and Map Librarianship." *RQ* 24 (1984): 204-9.
    This article defines both the uniqueness of map reference service as well as the many similarities it shares with general reference service.

Larsgaard, Mary Lynette. *Map Librarianship: An Introduction*. 2d ed. Littleton, Colo.: Libraries Unlimited, 1987. 382p.
    This text constitutes the most comprehensive description of map librarianship, including information on collection development, cataloging, reference, and care of maps. The appendixes provide useful information for those just beginning to work with maps.

Maizlish, Aaron, and William S. Hunt. *The World Map Directory, 1990-91: A Practical Guide to U.S. and International Maps Available Today*. Santa Barbara, Calif.: MapLink, 1990.
    MapLink is a retailer and wholesaler of maps. This catalog, updated approximately every two or three years, was developed out of their database of map titles. It is arranged by the Library of Congress four-digit LC code, making it easy to locate maps for geographical regions.

Monmonier, Mark, and George A. Schnell. *Map Appreciation*. Englewood Cliffs, N.J.: Prentice-Hall, 1988. 431p.
    Written by two geographers, this book provides an excellent explanation of the different types of maps (such as photomaps, population maps, political maps, and computer maps).

Parry, R. B., and C. R. Perkins. *World Mapping Today*. London: Butterworths, 1987. 583p.
    This book offers a unique combination of text, graphic indexes, cartobibliography, and source of information on mapping.

Seavey, Charles A. "Map Collection Development Planning: Mapkeeper and Library Administrator Working Together Can Tailor a Rational Acquisition Policy." *Information Bulletin* (Western Association of Map Libraries) 15 (1984): 268-79.
    This is an excellent article for the librarian wishing to develop a collection development policy for the map collection.

Special Libraries Association, Geography and Map Division. *Bulletin*, 1947- . Quarterly.
    This journal presents original articles on research problems, technical services, and other aspects of cartographic and geographic literature.

Western Association of Map Libraries. *Information Bulletin*, 1969- . Three times per year.
    This lively journal includes articles, many announcements, and news regarding new maps, atlases, and other related publications.

BIBLIOGRAPHIES AND
LIBRARY CATALOGS

Uses and Characteristics

A knowledge and an understanding of bibliographic sources are essential skills for librarians in all types of libraries. From the rare book librarian who seeks to discover the author of a fragment of an early printed book to the children's librarian who wants to know if there are any good children's books on woolly mammoths, all types of librarians use bibliographies to answer many of the questions they encounter during any given work day.

Indeed, many of the most challenging questions, both reference and professional, that a librarian faces deal with bibliographic puzzles. A patron cannot find a particular book on the shelf. The librarian must then determine the following:

1. Do the library's records show that the library owns that book?

2. If not, is the patron looking for a book that really exists, that is, has actually been published?

3. Is the patron's information correct, or only partially correct? For example, could the author's name be a pseudonym or perhaps misspelled, thus rendering the search of the catalog fruitless?

4. If the information is not completely correct, did the patron get the information about the book from a printed source, or orally, from someone who might have garbled the information?

In other words, what path can or should the librarian take in order to recreate the information in correct form or to verify that the information is correct? A seemingly simple question—Does this library own this book?—may turn into a puzzle requiring the skills of a legendary detective.

This example illustrates the use of bibliographies to verify or identify a title. Other uses of bibliographies concern the selection of materials for the use of patrons in a particular library. Librarians combine their knowledge of the needs of library patrons with a continual evaluation of the effectiveness of the library collection in order to create a well-rounded collection which is actively used. This requires thorough perusal of sources listing books which cover particular subjects and which are currently available for purchase.

Types of Bibliographies and Catalogs

The term *bibliography* refers to a list of works, whether complete or selective, compiled upon some common principle, such as authorship, subject, place of publication, or printer.[1] The bibliographic sources covered in this chapter are arranged by one or more of these organizing principles, depending on the intended scope of the publication.

Another definition of *bibliography* concerns the systematic description and history of books, their authorship, printing, publication, editions, and so on.[2] Material falling under this definition is often termed *historical bibliography*, and lies outside the scope of this chapter.

National bibliographies exist to list comprehensively the materials published in a particular country. The scope of the work may be enlarged to include works about the particular country or works in the language of that country, regardless of the place of publication. National bibliographies are often, but not always, published under the auspices of a national library or other agency which is charged by law with the receipt by legal deposit of copyrighted materials. Current national bibliographies often appear weekly, or monthly, with annual and/or multiyear cumulations. In many cases, retrospective national bibliographies, which give a record of a country's publishing history over a long period of time, have also been compiled.

Trade bibliographies, on the other hand, are commercial publications which exist to provide to the book trade the information required for the selection and acquisition of published materials. Usually the materials included in trade bibliographies are *trade books*: those intended for sale to the general public and which would generally be available for purchase in bookstores. Other nontrade publications, such as textbooks, government documents, encyclopedias, or dissertations, are not listed in trade bibliographies, but may appear in the national bibliography of the country in which they are produced. The predominant form of trade bibliography is the in-print listing, such as *Books in Print*. The purpose of this type of publication is to show which titles are currently available from the publisher. In another form, trade bibliographies such as *Weekly Record* provide up-to-date lists of books as they are published.

Library catalogs list the material held in the collection of one library. Previously, this type of bibliography was most often a photoreproduction of the cards in that library's card catalog. Now, with the advent of machine-readable catalog copy, catalogs are accessible online, and are also available on microform, CD-ROM, or other nonpaper format.

Union catalogs reflect the holdings of more than one library. Such shared cataloging networks as OCLC and RLIN may be considered union catalogs for their member libraries. The geographic area covered by union lists may vary from a local area to the entire nation. In the case of union lists of serials, it is quite common to find not only the lists of libraries holding a particular title, but also a record of which volumes each library holds.

Bibliographies of bibliographies are general in scope and are used to identify bibliographies on a specific subject. These sources are a good starting place when trying to locate a list of works on a specific subject.

Kinds of Information Contained in Bibliographies

The data elements in a bibliography entry depend largely on the intent of the publication. Current national bibliographies exist in part to facilitate the international exchange of cataloging data in standardized format. Therefore, one would expect to find subject headings, contents notes (when appropriate), and suggested classification numbers in these listings, in addition to author, title, and publication data. Also, name entries would be in standardized form, with appropriate *see* references from alternate forms of the name.

Because trade bibliographies are produced for the use of book dealers, they contain information which is essential to the business person, but is not always found in other types of bibliographies. Examples include price, availability information, publishers' addresses, and International Standard Book Number (ISBN). The ISBN is a code number assigned by the publisher to each volume. It is used by acquisitions departments and booksellers to provide unique identification of a particular work. There will be, for example, different ISBNs for the hardbound and paperback versions of the same title. The ISBN consists of country code, a publisher code, and a title code.

In general, the newer, computer-produced lists tend to give the most complete information. This can be seen in the records in OCLC, RLIN, and the *National Union Catalog Register*, which give not only cataloging data but also ordering information such as price and ISBN.

Use of bibliographies will depend on the type of information needed. If one needs simply to verify the existence of an item, a source giving short entries may be sufficient. If one needs both to identify and to locate copies, a union list is necessary. If the intent is to purchase materials, information such as price and ISBN are required.

Evaluation

Evaluation of general bibliographies and library catalogs is primarily concerned with the following criteria: scope of the bibliography; arrangement of the contents; frequency of publication; and currency of the included material. These criteria are used to evaluate the bibliography itself. Additional criteria are to be considered when choosing a bibliography for inclusion in a collection, and these are discussed in the section on selection.

Scope

The scope of any reference tool is of primary importance when evaluating its usefulness. The scope of the bibliography should be stated by the compilers in the preface or introduction to the reference source. Furthermore, any exclusion of materials, by such factors as place of publication, language, time, type of material, format, or subject, should also be noted. The librarian will need to make frequent use of the introductory material, because this type of information is not always immediately apparent simply from the entries themselves. For example, the *Union List of Serials* does not contain entries for newspapers, a fact not readily discernible simply by scanning the listings.

Reading the introductory material is essential, but it may not be completely effective. Commercial publishers may not be too eager to point out the limitations of their publications, and the introductions to national bibliographies are often in a language unfamiliar to the librarian. Therefore, it is essential to consult guides to the tools of reference work which give clear and concise descriptions of the coverage, accuracy, intent, and scope of the bibliographic sources. Sheehy's *Guide to Reference Books* and *Walford's Guide to Reference Material*, its British counterpart, serve this purpose. (These sources are discussed more fully in chapter 11.) Other, more specialized tools exist for specific types of bibliographies, and a selection of these tools is listed in the "Additional Readings" section at the end of this chapter.

When a bibliography or catalog includes coverage dates in its title, the librarian must learn what those dates mean. In some cases, the dates may indicate the years in which the items were published. In the case of the *National Union Catalog*, the dates mean the years in which cataloging copy was reported to the Library of Congress. The title of the printed catalog of the New York Public Library includes the dates 1911-1971. Here 1911 refers to the date of the founding of the library, and has no relation to the dates of the publications listed in the catalog.

Similarly, the word *international* may be included in a title merely as a selling point. The true geographical coverage of an international or regional work must be determined by reading introductory material and examining the contents for depth of inclusion from the countries covered. The coverage may be uneven, or spotty entries from a few countries may be added to justify the use of the word *international*.

Arrangement

The titles discussed in this chapter vary widely in the primary form of arrangement. Some catalogs have author, title, and subject entries in separate alphabetical sequences. *Dictionary catalogs* interfile all three types of entries in a single alphabetical listing. A *classified subject* approach arranges the contents by subject according to a classification scheme. Practically any combination of arrangement and subarrangement is possible, but in any case, indexes, which complement the primary arrangement, are essential to enhance the effectiveness of access. Any of these arrangements may be helpful at a given time, depending on the user's need. In reference work, the librarian needs to be aware of the possible arrangements and to make the appropriate choice of tools depending on the information at hand and the information to be located.

Frequency

Frequency of publication is especially important when dealing with publications used for selection or acquisition of current material. Sometimes the same title has different frequencies in different formats. *Books in Print*, for example, is published annually with one midyear supplement. More frequent updating is available in the quarterly cumulations of *Books in Print on Microfiche*, the bimonthly cumulations of the Books in Print Plus on CD-ROM, or the monthly updates of the online version available through access to DIALOG and BRS. For retrospective bibliography, frequent publication is not necessary, although a cumulated index covering a number of years is extremely valuable.

Currency

Currency refers to the delay—or lack thereof—between the date of publication of the material and the time at which it is entered in the bibliography. Obviously, book trade publications offer the most current information. National or regional bibliographies produced in countries where there is no formal system of deposit of published materials, and bibliographies produced in developing countries, where the production of a national bibliography is a major undertaking considering the resources of the country, have perhaps the greatest problem with currency. In regions such as Eastern Europe and Africa, where prompt book orders are necessary in order to obtain one of the few copies produced before the title goes out of print, national bibliography entries are rarely produced fast enough to be of help in acquisitions. Librarians must rely on the services of book jobbers in the region and other means to supplement information obtained in national and trade bibliographies.

Selection

The selection of a particular title depends on the mission of the library and the collection development policies of the library units using the bibliographic tools. These library units may well stretch across administrative/budgetary divisions in the library. Thus, the reference department may be called upon to purchase a title which is more frequently used by catalogers or subject bibliographers than by reference librarians; yet all concerned feel the title should be in the reference department because of the use of the material by so many different departments in the library: acquisitions, cataloging, interlibrary loan, reference, and subject bibliographers. Reference librarians can be encouraged by the knowledge that all sources are eventually used for reference purposes. Often reference library budgets are increased in anticipation of this demand on their monetary resources.

Many of the sources discussed in this chapter would be found in most libraries. Such current American sources as *Books in Print* and *Cumulative Book Index* (*CBI*) are essential tools for selection and acquisition purposes in both public and academic libraries of all sizes. National and trade bibliographies of foreign countries, however, are most often found in large research libraries. Nevertheless, large public libraries maintaining foreign-language collections for ethnic minority users would frequently need at least some of these foreign sources, particularly in-print lists.

Most often, the choice is fairly clear-cut; only one source will fill a particular need. Therefore, the most frequent decisions to be made involve choice of format — paper versus microform or online access — number of copies, and the retention of those copies.

The selection of format involves weighing several factors concerned with use of the item. Paper and microform versions have identical contents, but the microform version saves space and may last longer in an historical collection. Often a microform version is updated more frequently than its paper counterpart. The paper copy is easier to use and can be used by more people at one time. Unless networked, the CD-ROM and online versions limit the number of simultaneous users, but allow sophisticated searching by keyword or other points of access as well as Boolean searching techniques.

Cost must be considered when selecting which form of a bibliography or catalog to purchase. So many factors come into the equation that it is hard to generalize; each library's situation is unique. The use of online access and CD-ROM format involves the purchase of supporting equipment in addition to the cost of the bibliography itself. The exact cost of online access, with its connect charges and per-citation pricing, is difficult to anticipate and thus budget for. Moreover, the paper versions of such H. W. Wilson products as *Bibliographic Index* and *CBI* are sold on a service basis, under which the price depends on the size of a library's book budget. In some cases, the cost of a CD-ROM or online product is discounted if the library also subscribes to the paper version. Relative costs are discussed further in chapters 5 and 11.

Retention of copies to provide for an historical perspective on publishing is common in a large academic library. In other cases, when libraries require payment of lost book fees to reflect the actual price of the book at the time of its publication, historical information is needed for accounting purposes. However, the choice of format may confuse the issue. Suppliers of CD-ROM versions tend to require return of the previous disc when a new one is issued. If a subscription is cancelled, contracts often require return of the last disc. The provision of online access does not provide for archival coverage, although Books in Print Online (in 1991) covers 1.5 million titles that are in print, forthcoming, or declared out-of-print since 1979. To assure a retrospective collection, a library should acquire either a microform or a paper copy of the same title acquired on disc or used online.

Important General Sources

This section includes discussion of those bibliographic compilations that provide the most comprehensive coverage of published books and/or serials. For the United States, both current and retrospective sources are described, while for the United Kingdom and France, only current bibliographies are included. Works providing information about materials currently available from commercial publishers (in-print lists) are discussed, as are a few of those that offer lists of recommended works in a particular area or for a specific group of users. The printed catalogs of a few of the world's largest libraries, as well as a selection of bibliographies of bibliographic materials, are also discussed.

United States Bibliography

There is no official list of books published in the United States. The retrospective coverage of publishing in the United States must be pieced together by using several sources, some produced by commercial publishers and some by individuals. In addition, the products and services of the Library of Congress and shared cataloging networks such as RLIN and OCLC are becoming the dominant elements in the provision of bibliographic control in the United States.

A reference librarian needs a thorough knowledge of these bibliographic sources in order to choose which tool to use to answer a bibliographic question (see figure 18.1). In answering the question, the librarian may need to look at several tools, and may well find pieces of the bibliographic puzzle in each of several sources. Therefore, a knowledge of these sources will assist the librarian in deciding which tools to examine first, and, in some cases, may narrow the search to only one tool which will give a particular type of information. For example, a bibliographic description of a book published in 1857 might be found in the *National Union Catalog*, but the price is likely to be found only in Roorbach's *Bibliotheca Americana*.

```
              CHRONOLOGY OF AMERICAN RETROSPECTIVE BIBLIOGRAPHY

                           1492    1639    1800    1820    1830    1839   1861    1871

Sabin, J.  Biblotheca Americana ......(1492)———————————————————————————(1868)

Evans, C. American Bibliography .................(1639)—(1800)

Shaw, R.  American Bibliography ........................(1800)—(1819)

Shoemaker, R. Checklist of American ..........................(1820)–(1829)
              Imprints...

Checklist of American Imprints ........................................(1830)—(1839)

Roorbach, O.  Bibliotheca Americana ..........................(1820)——————————(1861)

Kelly, J.  American Catalogue of Books ......................................(1861)—(1871)


                           1876    1899    1910    1928    1977    Present

American Catalogue ..................(1876)——————————(1910)

United States Catalog ........................(1899)——————————(1928)

Cumulative Book Index ...............................................(1928)————————

American Book Publishing Record ......(1876)—————————————————————————(1977)
       Cumulative
```

Fig. 18.1. Timeline of major sources for American bibliography.

United States Retrospective Bibliography (to 1876)

Charles Evans's *American Bibliography*, which lists books, pamphlets, and periodicals published in the United States from 1639 through 1800, is the most important of the bibliographies covering this period. The titles included are arranged in chronological order by date of publication. Every effort was made to include all publications and to give a complete bibliographic description of each item. Each volume includes an index of authors and anonymous titles and a list of printers and publishers. The fourteenth volume, published in 1959, provides a cumulative author-title index to the whole set. The references in the index are to the item numbers assigned to each entry. Library locations are given for each item listed.

A microform set of the full texts of the nonserial titles listed in this work is available from Readex Microprint Corp. The microforms are filed in order by the item numbers in the Evans bibliography. Records for these microform copies have now been entered in the OCLC database, so the possibility of an increase in requests for materials, both locally and through interlibrary loan, exists. Figure 18.2 shows a typical entry from the *American Bibliography*. Note the Evans number to the left of the entry.

37339   DWIGHT, TIMOTHY   1752–1817
        A DISCOURSE, DELIVERED AT NEW-HAVEN, FEB. 22, 1800; ON THE CHARACTER OF GEORGE
        WASHINGTON. . . .
            Printed by Thomas Green and Son, New-Haven: 1800.   pp. 55.   8vo.
        Cover title: "Dr. Dwight's discourse, Feb. 22, 1800. Also, Gen. Washington's Farewell
        address."   AAS, BA, BPL, CHS, CSL, GˡL, HEH, JCB, LCP, LOC, MFM, MHS, NL, NYPL, NYSL, PL,
                                                                 PˡU, RU, WC, WL, YC.

Fig. 18.2. Entry from *American Bibliography*, showing "Evans number." Reprinted by permission of publisher from Evans, *American Bibliography*, Peter Smith Publisher, Inc.: 1941, Gloucester, Mass.

Ralph R. Shaw and Richard H. Shoemaker continued the Evans bibliography with *American Bibliography: A Preliminary Checklist for 1801-1819*. This twenty-three volume set includes nineteen annual volumes and four additional volumes containing addenda, as well as author, title, publisher, and geographic indexes. Library locations for copies are given whenever possible. A microform reprint set of the contents is also available, with the titles arranged by the Shaw-Shoemaker numbers. The series continues with Shoemaker's *Checklist of American Imprints for 1820-1829* and *A Checklist of American Imprints for 1830-* .

Orville Roorbach's *Bibliotheca Americana ... 1820-61* and James Kelly's *American Catalogue of Books ... Jan. 1861 to Jan. 1871* are trade bibliographies listing books published during the periods covered. They are alphabetical lists by author and title and give publisher and price information. Neither title is as complete or as accurate as one would like, but they are the only general bibliographies which cover the period.

Joseph Sabin's *Bibliotheca Americana* is an extremely valuable bibliography of books relating to America from its discovery to 1868. It lists books, pamphlets, and periodicals published in the Western hemisphere as well as elsewhere. Sabin differs from the titles discussed previously in that the emphasis is on complete bibliographic description. Therefore, contents notes and varying editions are frequently included. The entries also often give locations of copies and references to reviews.

United States Retrospective Bibliography (since 1876)

The *American Book Publishing Record Cumulative, 1876-1949* and *American Book Publishing Record Cumulative, 1950-1977* are relatively recent publications that have the same type of arrangement and scope. The main arrangement is by Dewey Decimal Classification with separate volumes for fiction and juvenile fiction. These volumes are followed by author and title indexes. They do not include periodicals, government publications, theses, or some other types of publications. The information in these bibliographies is taken from many sources and the great value of the cumulation is the unique subject access combined with multiyear coverage.

The *American Catalogue* covers the period 1876 to 1910 in volumes spanning varying numbers of years. Each volume is a record of books in print at the time of publication, and each provides author, title, and subject access. *United States Catalog* was an in-print list published in four editions from 1899 to 1928.

Current United States Bibliography

Current bibliographical sources are heavily used in any library. They serve as selection and collection development aids for acquisitions and reference staff. In addition, reference librarians use them for reference questions, including verification and identification of bibliographic citations.

Cumulative Book Index (*CBI*) is sold by H. W. Wilson on a service basis under which the index is priced according to the library's expenditures for books. To obtain a price quote, the librarian fills out an order form providing the library's annual expenditures for books during the last three fiscal years. *CBI* has been published continuously since 1933, with coverage from 1928. Each volume is a listing of works in the English language that are published anywhere in the world, although it is most complete for the United States. A subscription includes eleven monthly paperbound issues (no issue is published in August). The eleven monthly issues include quarterly cumulations in March, June, September, and December. Additionally, there is a permanent annual clothbound cumulation. *CBI* is arranged by author, title, and subject in one alphabet.

Information provided for each publication includes full bibliographic description, price, ISBN or ISSN, and Library of Congress card number. Each volume also contains a list of publishers and their addresses. *CBI* is the most inclusive bibliography currently published of works in English, and its dictionary arrangement makes it the easiest to use for verification of titles, authors' names, and other publication information.

Until 1957, multiyear cumulations of *CBI* were published; from 1957 through 1968, cumulations were biennial. Since 1969, only annual cumulations have been published. Access to *Cumulative Book Index* online through WILSONLINE, on CD-ROM, or by magnetic tape allows one to search the equivalent of all volumes from 1982 to the present simultaneously. In addition, the online and CD-ROM versions of *CBI* provide out-of-print status for both clothbound and paperback editions, whenever the publisher has made this information available.

The *Weekly Record* is a record of approximately eight hundred titles published or distributed in the United States during the week covered. It is arranged by main entry and has no subject access. Each entry contains full cataloging information, including both Dewey and LC classifications. From 1872 until 1974, the *Weekly Record* was published as part of *Publishers Weekly*, the standard book trade journal. *Weekly Record* contains the most recent information for American books, but its lack of a subject approach limits its usefulness as a selection tool.

The monthly *American Book Publishing Record* cumulates the cataloging records originally published in *Weekly Record*, but it is arranged in a classified order by the Dewey Decimal Classification number. Other sections list fiction, juvenile fiction, and mass-market paperbacks. Author and title indexes complement the classified arrangement. A subject guide is also included.

Current Bibliographies from Great Britain and France

The *British National Bibliography (BNB)* is an example of a true national bibliography. Its content is based on the books deposited with the copyright office and, as such, is a record of the books published in the country. It is published weekly, with cumulations covering varying periods of time. There is an annual cumulation. The arrangement is by Dewey Decimal Classification with author, title, and subject indexes. The author/title indexes have been cumulated in a microfiche edition which provides access to publications from 1950 through 1984 in one alphabet. A CD-ROM version is also available.

The *BNB* provides full bibliographic description, provided by the British Library, and such essential ordering information as ISBN and price. It also includes CIP records, which makes it a source of information for forthcoming publications. *CIP* stands for *Cataloging in Publication*, "a publication cataloging program through which participating publishers provide galley proofs or front matter of their books to the national library or other central- ized cataloging agency, where a bibliographic record is prepared and returned to the publisher.... Originating in the Library of Congress in 1971, the program is now internation- ally operational."[3]

The current national bibliography of France is the *Bibliographie Nationale Française* (until 1990, *Bibliographie de la France*). This title has been continuously published since 1811, although the frequency, arrangement, and supplements have varied through the years. It is now published bi-weekly. A CD-ROM version covers the period since 1975. The primary arrangement is by Universal Decimal Classification, and there are author and title indexes in each issue. A cumulated author and title index is provided annually. The Universal Decimal Classification (UDC) began as a French translation of the Dewey Decimal Classification. It retains the same basic arrangement, but is much more detailed than Dewey.

In-Print Lists

In-print lists include titles that are currently available from publishers. Because books may remain in print for a number of years, the current list can also be useful for identifying material published much earlier. In reference work, in-print lists are often used to determine if an announced book has been published, if a later edition of a work has been published, or what volumes of a series are still in print.

Books in Print (BIP) is an annual listing of books available from American publishers. It is a multivolume set with separate author and title sections. Each entry includes price, ISBN, publisher, and other ordering information. A separate volume lists publishers and their addresses. The 1990-91 edition includes a volume listing out-of-print and out-of-stock titles. The lists are compiled from information provided by the publisher. Thus, *BIP* is a list of what publishers report is in print at a given moment. Since data is collected from thousands of sources, errors of omission and commission are not uncommon. No attempt is made to standardize the form of an author's name. It is, therefore, possible to have a single author listed in more than one form, so one must be careful when searching the author volume.

Subject Guide to Books in Print arranges the contents of *Books in Print* according to the Library of Congress subject headings assigned to the book. Although *BIP* and the *Subject Guide* are separate publications, most libraries subscribe to both titles, for each is necessary for acquisitions and reference work.

There are three companion titles to *BIP*, each of which adds unique features to the main set. The annual volumes of *BIP* are supplemented by *Books in Print Supplement* which appears approximately six months after the main volumes. The supplement also includes separate author, title, and subject listings. *Paperbound Books in Print*, the second title, provides order information for American paperbacks. Most of these are not listed in *Books in Print*, so it is frequently necessary to search both titles to determine the availability of an item. *Forthcoming Books* is a bimonthly supplement which lists new books in print as well as books projected to be published within the next several months. This title is not only useful for selection and ordering, but is also frequently used to confirm that a requested title has *not* yet appeared.

Books in Print on Microfiche has been available since 1972, and is most frequently seen in bookstores. The microfiche is fully updated four times a year and includes forthcoming titles for the next six months. The information is also available online, updated monthly, or on CD-ROM, updated bimonthly, both of which allow searching by keyword (not just the *first* word in the title) or ISBN. The entire contents of *Books in Print, Books in Print Supplement, Subject Guide to Books in Print, Paperbound Books in Print, Forthcoming Books*, and other Bowker titles are now available in a single CD-ROM product called Books in Print Plus. Cumulative quarterly updates make this the largest, most current, in-print list available.

Publishers' Trade List Annual (*PTLA*) is a collection of publishers' catalogs bound together in alphabetical order. Because each publisher must pay a fee for having its catalog included, there are major publishers whose catalogs do not appear in *PTLA* but whose publications do appear in *BIP* (where there is no fee for listing). In reference work, publishers' catalogs are frequently used to verify authors and titles of books appearing in series. This is necessary, for example, when a reader has used one book in a series and wants to know what other titles have been published in the same series. *PTLA* now includes an index to publishers' series which leads from the series title to the publisher's name. The appropriate catalog can then be consulted to locate a list of titles in that series.

Publishers' Catalogs Annual is a microfiche collection of United States and Canadian publishers' catalogs. It is now larger than *PTLA*. Each collection contains catalogs not in the other, and there are still catalogs which appear in neither collection. In 1989, *Publishers' Catalogs Annual* included over 1,300 publishers, while *PTLA* included approximately 850 publishers. However, *PTLA* provided the series index and an index to publishers by field of activity.

Whitaker's Books in Print (until 1989, *British Books in Print*) is published annually, and lists titles available in the United Kingdom. It is arranged by author, title, and subject in one alphabet and includes a list of publishers and their addresses. Unlike its American equivalent, it does list some government publications. *Whitaker's Books in Print* is available on microfiche with complete quarterly updates, on CD-ROM, and online on DIALOG with monthly updates.

Foreign in-print lists are invaluable for verifying titles for selection or interlibrary loan purposes, as well as for locating publishers' addresses. The French books-in-print list is *Les Livres Disponibles*, an annual publication with books listed in separate author, title, and subject volumes. Another useful reference tool, *International Books in Print* is now published annually. This title lists books published in English in non-English-speaking countries. It can be used, for example, to verify an English-language work published in Denmark. Its list of publishers and their addresses contains some which are difficult to locate elsewhere.

Library Catalogs

Hundreds of published library catalogs have appeared over the years, but only a few of the largest can be discussed here. In reference work, library catalogs are used most often for verification purposes, but those which include a subject approach can also be used as subject bibliographies. The catalogs of some special libraries also include article-level indexing for periodicals in the fields covered.

Few new printed library catalogs are appearing. Because publishing costs have made printed library catalogs prohibitively expensive, these catalogs are now more likely to appear in a nonprint format such as microfiche. Several large national library catalogs are available in microfiche, allowing a much wider distribution than would be possible in book form.

United States. Whether one is the sole librarian in a small public library or one of many reference librarians in a large academic library, one needs to be familiar with the *National Union Catalog* and its publishing history.

National Union Catalog began as the actual card catalog of the Library of Congress. Later, when increased access to the card catalog was deemed desirable, depository (duplicate) sets of cards were distributed to and maintained by large libraries throughout the United States. The first printed book catalog version of the card set, *The Library of Congress Catalog: A Cumulative Catalog of Books Represented by Library of Congress Printed Cards*, was published in 1942 under the sponsorship of the Association of Research Libraries. This set represented cataloging done at the Library of Congress, at some libraries of government departments, and at libraries which were participating in the cooperative cataloging program. The catalog reproduced cards printed from 1898 to July 31, 1942. Its supplement included cards produced from August 1, 1942, to December 31, 1947; the next cumulation was the *Library of Congress Author Catalog ... 1948-1952*. In 1953, the scope was enlarged to include cataloging entries and holdings information of additional contributing North American libraries, and the title of the catalog was changed to *National Union Catalog* (*NUC*).

The publication of the Library of Congress catalogs has continued to the present with additional title changes reflecting variations in scope, frequency, and format. Figure 18.3, page 406, demonstrates the patterns of publication and the scope of the sections. For a more extended description of the publishing history of the *NUC*, see the entry for it in Sheehy's *Guide to Reference Books*.[4]

The large, retrospective set of *NUC* now in use is the *National Union Catalog Pre-1956 Imprints*. For this set, the entries are photocopies of catalog cards. Location symbols for research libraries in the United States and Canada are added to the bottom of the card.

NUC Pre-56 Imprints is an author, or main entry, catalog. Cross-references are included, but subject headings are not. Furthermore, only selective added entries are included. Thus, a knowledge of the cataloging code which governs the choice and form of the main entry is necessary in order to use *NUC* effectively. For almost all entries in *NUC Pre-56*, this means using the American Library Association's *Cataloging Rules for Author and Title Entries*, 1949 edition. For example, general rule 92 stated, "Enter an institution (using the latest name) under the place in which it is located."[5] Similarly, many subdivisions of government were entered first under the largest unit of government, with subdivisions for the successive layers of government structure. Subsequent cataloging codes have allowed for entry under the smallest subdivision of a government agency that can logically stand alone, and for entry directly under the name of the institution.

Because the set was published over a period of twelve years, supplementary volumes were necessary almost immediately. The supplementary volumes (volumes 686 to 754) add titles identified after publication began and add locations to those titles published earlier. *NUC-Pre 56* was continued as the *National Union Catalog* through 1982. Five-year cumulations, except for the years 1978 to 1982, have been published. Beginning in 1983, *NUC Books* has been published in microfiche only. This set replaces the following Library of

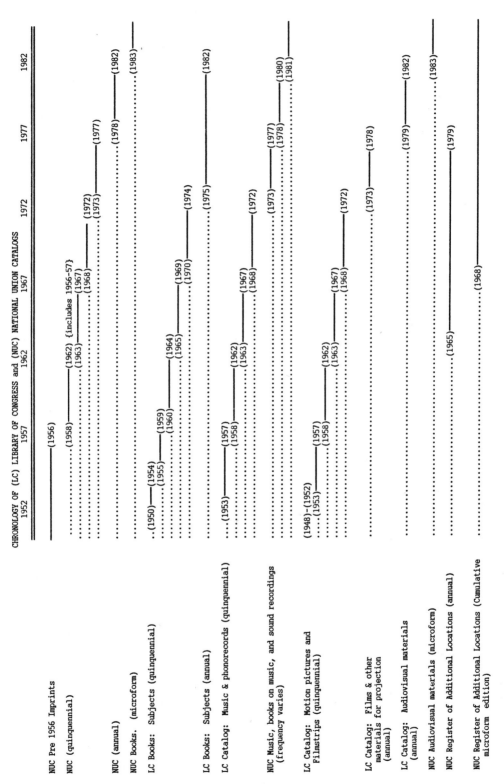

Fig. 18.3. Timeline for components of National Union Catalog.

Congress book-form publications: *National Union Catalog, Monographic Series, Subject Catalog*, and the *Chinese Cooperative Catalog*. In the microfiche edition, full bibliographic records appear only once, in the register, and they are numbered sequentially. Separate indexes for names, titles, subjects, and series provide the access points to the register. The indexes provide a brief catalog record and the item number under which the full record can be found in the register. "Index entries, arranged in alphabetical order, are briefer than the register records, but will frequently provide sufficient bibliographic information to complete a search."[6] The full record in the register provides full cataloging information as well as information such as ISBN, price, and suggested Dewey Decimal Class number. With this arrangement, the indexes can be cumulated without having to reprint the full record. As of 1990, there is a 1983-1987 and a 1988-1989 cumulation for each index.

For interlibrary loan purposes, the *NUC Register of Additional Locations* (*RAL*) contains additional location symbols of libraries contributing bibliographic records to the *NUC* since 1968. "Updated quarterly, *RAL* now includes more than forty million locations with about three million new location symbols added each year."[7] The entries are arranged by the LC card number which is part of the *NUC* entry.

The *National Union Catalog: Books* provides bibliographic records for books, pamphlets, manuscripts, map atlases, monographic microform publications, and monographic government publications. Its scope is not limited by date, language, or place of publication.[8] Records for all non-roman-language materials are in romanized form only. The Library of Congress announced in 1990 that with the publication of the 1990 edition, the *National Union Catalog: Books* will no longer include records for books from the following bibliographic utilities: OCLC, Inc., the Research Libraries Information Network (RLIN), and Western Library Network.

The National Union Catalogs of the Library of Congress also include the following titles in microfiche: *National Union Catalog: Audiovisual Materials* and *National Union Catalog: Cartographic Materials. Music, Books on Music, and Sound Recordings* became a microfiche publication in 1990. *The Music Catalog: 1981-1990*, "a ten-year cumulation, will include MARC records from both the Library of Congress and the National Union Catalog: Books database, and it will include new data for 1990 never published" in the predecessor publication.[9] The *National Union Catalog of Manuscript Collections*, a printed publication, "includes entries for personal papers, records of public and private organizations, and other materials of historical importance or research potential."[10]

The *Dictionary Catalog of the Research Libraries* of the New York Public Library is the largest of the many American library printed catalogs. One of its greatest values is that it includes added entries (e.g., title and coauthor) and subject cards as well as main entries. This kind of catalog can be used to verify an incomplete reference by title, for instance, and then the *National Union Catalog* can be used to locate copies. It should be noted that this catalog does not use Library of Congress subject headings. New York Public Library headings are published in *Subject Headings Authorized for General Use in the Dictionary Catalogs*.

Great Britain and France. The British Library's *General Catalogue of Printed Books to 1975* (*BLC*) is the title of the latest edition of this catalog. Editions published before the establishment of the British Library in 1972 were known as the *British Museum Catalogue*. As of 1991, supplements have been published, bringing the coverage through 1987. This catalog is an invaluable source of bibliographic data because it lists the holdings of one of the world's largest libraries. Because the British Library is a depository for all material copyrighted in the United Kingdom, its catalog is the most complete record of such publications.

The catalog is arranged by main entry in one alphabetical sequence. Most entries are personal authors, but corporate author and title entries are included where necessary. It should be noted that serials are included, but they are listed under "periodical publications." Newspapers are not included, but the British Library has published a catalog of its newspaper library.[11]

The completeness of the bibliographic description provided varies a good deal, depending on when the book was cataloged. In the supplements, complete MARC (machine-readable cataloging) records are the rule. Figure 18.4 shows entries from the *BLC to 1975* and its 1986-87 supplement illustrating the differences in format and amount of information given. Note that the newer entries give complete catalog information.

LEMON (Abraham) Report of the proceedings upon a criminal information against A. Lemon, T. Turner, B. Wilson, J. Webster, J. R. Mulleneux, and C. Rowlinson, for a conspiracy and riot at the Theatre Royal, Liverpool ... at the Summer Assizes for ... Lancaster ... 14th September 1810 ; taken in short hand by Mr. Farquharson. *Liverpool*, 1810. 8°.   1131. d. 18.

LEMON (Alfred D.) *See* Cumming (j. g.) The great Stanley ... A narrative ... illustrated from Manx scenery and antiquities, by A. D. L., *etc.*
1867. 8°.   10816. bb.27.

LEMON (Anthony)

—— Postwar industrial growth in East Anglian small towns: a study of migrant firms, 1945–1970. *Oxford*, [1975].
ISBN 0 901691 12 7   P. 805/202. (12.)

   pp. 40; maps. 30 cm. (University of Oxford. School of Geography. Research papers. no. 12 ISSN 0305 8190.)

□

LEMON, Anthony
   Apartheid in transition / Anthony Lemon. – Aldershot : Gower, 1987.
   [410]p : ill ; 22cm. – Includes bibliography and index.
       0–566–00635–9   YC.1987.a.8439
   White voters and political change in South Africa, 1981–1983 / A. Lemon. – Oxford : School of Geography, University of Oxford, 1984.
   40p : ill,maps ; 22cm. – (Research paper ; 32). – Bibliography: p39–40.
       B86–26660   P.805/202

LEMON, Charles
   A leaf from an unopened volume, or, The manuscript of an unfortunate author : an Angrian story / by Charlotte Brontë ; newly transcribed and edited by Charles Lemon. – Haworth : Brontë Society, 1986.
   xvi,66p : ill,facsims,1geneal.table ; 21cm.
       0–9505829–2–1   YC.1986.a.4005

LEMON, Daphne Violet
   The stars in Orion : Tuapeka then and now / Daphne Lemon. – Dunedin : J. McIndoe, 1979.
   64 p. : maps.
       0–908565–89–5   X.800/43123

Fig. 18.4. Entries from British Library *General Catalogue of Printed Books to 1975* and from 1986-87 supplement. Reprinted by permission of Bowker-Saur Ltd. (London, England).

A subject approach to the catalog has been provided under the title *Subject Index of the Modern Works Added to the Library*, which has appeared in multivolume sets published from 1906 to 1985. These indexes exclude "pure" literature and personal names, which are included in the *General Catalogue*. The early catalogs are rather difficult to use because the material is arranged in very broad subjects which are then subdivided. The subjects are in alphabetical rather than classified order.

Beginning in 1989, the British Library's *General Catalogue of Printed Books to 1975* is being converted to CD-ROM. The project is expected to take two years and will be the first such retrospective conversion. It is important to remember that such conversion does not merely change the form of the catalog, but also enhances use of the catalog by making almost all elements of the entries searchable.

The *Catalogue Général des Livres Imprimés* from the Bibliothèque Nationale in Paris is the most important source for French publications. It is an alphabetical list of books by personal author only. It does not include entries for anonymous works, serials, or works of corporate authorship. The catalog was published from 1897 to 1981, so there is a great difference in the dates of coverage in different parts of the alphabet. Even in the volumes published after 1960, nothing is included which was published after 1959. A supplement covering 1960 to 1969 has been published which includes entries for corporate authors and anonymous works as well as for personal authors. Because of the unevenness in coverage over time, the Bibliothèque Nationale has recently published a microfiche supplement which brings the original publication up to 1959.

Serial and Newspaper Sources

Nothing is more confusing to the neophyte than the term *serial*. It simply means a publication that is issued in successive parts and is intended to be published indefinitely. Types of serial publications include annuals, magazines, journals, yearbooks, and newspapers. Irregular serials are issued irregularly at unspecified intervals. The term *periodical* refers to a serial with a distinctive title.

Two types of sources are discussed in this section. Some are lists of titles that are currently being published. Others are union lists which include the location and holdings of each title listed. In these examples, *location* means a library in the United States or Canada; *holdings* means a record of which volumes or years each library owns.

Retrospective and Union Lists. The *Union List of Serials in Libraries of the United States and Canada* (*ULS*) lists alphabetically by main entry serials published before 1950. While the holdings information is limited to libraries located in the United States and Canada, the serials may be published in any country, making this work international in its coverage. Each entry includes a detailed publication history of the title and notes any variation which has occurred in the title. *ULS* contains no newspapers and very few government publications. Figure 18.5 illustrates a typical entry from *ULS*. Note the library locations and the holdings shown. The symbols used are the same as those used in the *NUC*.

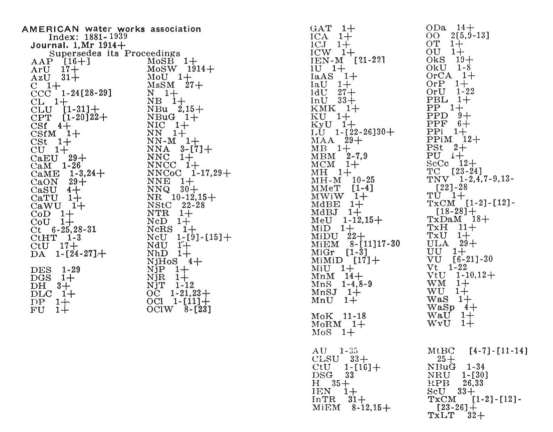

Fig. 18.5. Entry from *Union List of Serials*. Reprinted with permission of The H. W. Wilson Co., 1965.

New Serial Titles (*NST*), continues the *Union List of Serials*. Its first cumulation covers serials which began publication from 1950 to 1970. Since that time there have been several multiyear cumulations and the title continues to appear on a regular basis. In 1981, *NST* expanded its entries to include complete cataloging information; the entries are produced from OCLC tapes and are the reproduction of the OCLC record (see figure 18.6).

Journal (American Water Works Association)
Journal / American Water Works Association. —
Vol. 40, no. 1 (Jan. 1948)-   — [New York,
N.Y.] : The Association, [c1948-
 v. : ill. ; 23-28 cm.
Monthly.
Title from cover.
Imprint varies: Denver, CO,
Supplements accompany some numbers.
Indexes:
Vols. 32 (1940)-47 (1955) (includes index to former title). 1 v.;
v. 48 (1956)-57 (1965). 1 v.
 Annual special no. published separately with title: AWWA
 ... buyers' guide and publications catalog.
 Running title: Journal AWWA
 Continues: Journal of the American Water Works As-
sociation.
 ISSN 0003-150X = Journal - American Water Works As-
sociation.
 1. Water-supply engineering—Periodicals.   I. American
Water Works Association.   II. AWWA ... buyers' guide and
publications catalog.   III. Title: Journal AWWA.
TD201.A512   86-641260
               628.1'05—dc19
                                                           AACR 2
CSt DLC ICRL InU KMK MChB MoSU PU
RPB-S

Fig. 18.6. Entry from *New Serial Titles*, published by the Library of Congress, Washington, D.C.

American Newspapers, 1821-1936 is similar in format to the *ULS*, in that it lists locations in the United States and Canada and gives a complete bibliographic description of each title. Entries are arranged by place of publication. Detailed holdings for each location are included. Because there has been no supplement, other titles must be used to identify more current holdings and to locate descriptions of titles which began publication after 1936.

Newspapers in Microform: United States and *Newspapers in Microform: Foreign Countries* are union lists for Canadian and United States libraries. In addition to listing libraries where the newspapers can be consulted or borrowed, the source for purchasing microform copies is indicated. Both of these titles, as well as *American Newspapers*, are arranged by the place of publication of the newspaper. A title index is provided.

The *United States Newspaper Program National Union List* is a microfiche product listing American newspapers held by libraries in the United States. The list is created from the information included in the OCLC Online Union Catalog, and it first became available in 1985. The arrangement of the list is alphabetical by title; indexes by date, intended audience, language, and place of publication are included. The most current information is available online through OCLC.

Current Lists. *Ulrich's International Periodicals Directory* is a guide to currently available periodicals. The arrangement is by broad subject area with a title index. Entries include the information needed to order the title: publisher, address, price, and International Standard Serial Number (ISSN). In addition, frequency, beginning date, circulation, and telephone number are usually included. *Ulrich's* has several other features which increase its usefulness in the reference collection. Each entry lists the indexes and online databases that index the contents of the periodical. This feature allows the librarian or user to locate the complete citation for an article in a periodical by identifying the index or database where that citation can be found. Another valuable feature is the list of cessations, which lists periodicals which have ceased publication since the previous edition. Since 1988, *Ulrich's* has incorporated *Irregular Serials and Annuals* in its coverage and title, thus providing publication and ordering information for most directories, almanacs, and yearbooks. *Ulrich's Update* is a quarterly update provided free with the purchase of *Ulrich's*.

Ulrich's is available electronically through DIALOG and BRS as well as on Ulrich's Plus CD-ROM. Ulrich's on Microfiche is also available. The online version is updated monthly, and the CD-ROM and the microfiche versions have quarterly cumulated updates. Ulrich's Plus CD-ROM includes the same information as the directory, but the CD-ROM search software allows for searching on many parts of the entry. It is possible, for instance, to compile lists of periodicals by zip code or by price.

Newspapers currently published in the United States and Canada are listed in the *Gale Directory of Publications and Broadcast Media*. This directory had been published annually since 1880, until 1982, as *Ayer Directory of Publications*. Because it has been published for such a long time, back volumes are an excellent source for historical information on American newspapers. In addition to newspapers, the *Gale Directory* includes information about magazines, journals, college publications, radio and television stations, and cable. *Ulrich's*, since it is international in scope, lists more periodicals than the *Gale Directory*, but it does not include newspapers or broadcast media.

The *Gale Directory* is published in three volumes. The first two volumes are arranged geographically, with the titles listed alphabetically under the place of publication. In addition to information which can be used for ordering, such as address and price, the entries include information specific to newspapers, such as circulation figures, number of columns, size, and advertising rates. The third volume includes statistical tables, indexes, and maps. In addition to the title and keyword index, there are seventeen different subject or type listings, such as Jewish publications, free newspapers, and radio format. Tables are provided showing statistics by type of publication and geographical region. The maps section includes maps for individual states and provinces, and shows the cities and towns in which the titles listed in the directory are published.

Bibliographies of Bibliographies

Bibliographies of bibliographies are usually general in scope and are used to identify bibliographies on a specific subject. The major titles of the genre are Theodore Besterman's *World Bibliography of Bibliographies* (often referred to as Besterman) and *Bibliographic Index*. Besterman includes more substantial bibliographies, but it is not current. *Bibliographic Index* is current and provides information appropriate to any level of inquiry.

Besterman lists separately published bibliographies only. It is international in scope and is arranged by subject. The last volume of this five-volume work is an index including authors, titles, and subjects. The last edition covers material through 1963. It has been supplemented by Alice F. Toomey's *World Bibliography of Bibliographies, 1964-1974*. The supplement is compiled from Library of Congress printed cards, and is arranged by subject, based on the Library of Congress subject headings.

Bibliographic Index is a subject index to bibliographies which have been published in books, pamphlets, and over 2,600 periodicals. The H. W. Wilson Company began publishing the index in 1937. It currently appears with two paperbound issues and a permanent annual clothbound cumulation, which includes four additional months of coverage. This is an excellent source for beginning a search for scholarly and/or popular works in many subjects. *Bibliographic Index* includes material published in English and other Western European languages. Each entry gives complete information on the bibliography and tells if it is annotated. The arrangement is by Library of Congress subject headings. Coverage online through WILSONLINE begins with 1984.

Recommended Lists

Recommended lists complement other types of bibliographies by providing a qualitative evaluation of the contents listed or by offering indexing by criteria not used in other types of bibliographies. The primary examples are lists of fiction and nonfiction by age level or difficulty and lists of fiction by topic. Neither of these functions is accomplished by the card catalog or traditional bibliographies. For example, finding books on astronomy written for the layperson in a collection which contains both technical and nontechnical works can be extremely time-consuming. Often annotated, the lists are used by both library patrons and librarians for the selection of books for purchase or in the selection of books for recreational reading or research.

Designed for the "non-specialist,"[12] *The Reader's Adviser* includes annotated bibliographies in broad subject areas. Most books listed are in print; only major works in a subject are listed if they are out-of-print. The current edition, published from 1986 to 1988, has five volumes covering British and American literature, world literature in English translation, philosophy, religion, Bible, science, technology, medicine, arts, history, and social sciences. Volume 6 provides name, title, and general subject indexes to the entire set.

The H. W. Wilson Company publishes several catalogs often referred to as the "Standard Catalogs." These are lists of books aimed at particular audiences, such as schools or children. Two of the most useful are the *Public Library Catalog* and the *Fiction Catalog*. The first lists adult, nonfiction, in-print titles arranged by Dewey Decimal Classification, and includes annotations. The *Fiction Catalog* is an annotated bibliography arranged by author with title and subject indexes. With this catalog it is possible to identify novels about specific places or historical periods, for example. Another popular use is to locate novels set in a particular location or to locate genre fiction, such as spy novels or murder mysteries.

Search Strategies

Verification is necessary when trying to identify, and eventually to locate, a given item. Often the bibliographic information presented by a library user to the reference librarian is so incomplete that a good deal of ingenuity must be used to locate a copy. The sources of incomplete citations can vary from partial information gathered from a chance reference on a talk show to a poorly constructed bibliography in a scholarly book. Practice and experience make the process easier, but there are a number of factors to keep in mind when deciding where to start.

If the incomplete citation lacks a date, it is best to start looking in a cumulated list that will allow searching a number of years simultaneously. Electronic databases such as OCLC and RLIN are often useful in cases like this. Unfortunately, a citation lacking a date frequently also lacks some other important element.

As an example of a question when neither date of publication nor author is known, suppose a patron is looking for a book he read in the "late '30s" called *Heroes of the Air*. If the title cannot be found in the local catalog, a bibliography must be used. The *NUC* would seem a logical place to look to both identify and locate a copy. However, because the *NUC* is a main entry catalog only, books there are listed only under author—a piece of information that is lacking. In this case, a search in *CBI* or *American Book Publishing Record* will provide the author's name: Chelsea Curtis Fraser. After identifying the author, one can go to the *NUC* to locate a copy.

Another example of an incomplete citation is a request for Louise Holborn's *The Legal Status of Political Refugees, 1920-1938*, 1938. In this case, a search of bibliographic utilities, *CBI*, and *American Book Publishing Record* is unproductive. Figure 18.7 shows the result of a search of *NUC*.

Holborn, Louise Wilhelmine, 1898–
    The legal status of political refugees, 1920–1938, by Louise W. Holborn ...

    (*In* American journal of international law. Concord, N. H., 1938. v. 32, p. 680–703)

    1. Refugees, Political. 2. Asylum, Right of.

                                           A 39–258

Carnegie endow. int. peace.   Library
  for Library of Congress   [JX1.A6 vol. 32]

                           (2)   (341.05)

NH 0453042   NNCE DLC

Fig. 18.7. Entry from *National Union Catalog, Pre-1956 Imprints*. Reprinted with permission.

This cataloging record shows that the requested item is actually an article published in the *American Journal of International Law*. While this is an unusual case, it points out the importance of verification. In most libraries, it is the journal title which should be searched, because most libraries will not catalog articles as separate works.

In selecting the bibliography or catalog to use for verification, the librarian needs to keep in mind the purpose of the tools. National bibliographies usually list material *published* during the time period covered. Most library catalogs list material *cataloged* during the stated time. Thus, a title published in 1850, but not cataloged and reported to the *National Union Catalog* until 1965, will not appear in *NUC* until the 1963-67 cumulation.

Using *New Serial Titles* presents some of the same concerns. That is, a serial which began publication in 1975 may very well not appear until the 1981-85 cumulation. In addition, the librarian needs to keep in mind the changes in rules of entry which have occurred over time. The examples given in figures 18.5 and 18.6 show the same serial title cataloged at different times.

■ ═══ ■

18.1
Art and Error

A reference librarian is asked to locate a book of essays called *Modern Textual Editing*, published in 1970. Since the librarian must both complete the citation and find a library location, a title search of the OCLC database is the most logical place to start. In this case, the title search produces no hits. A search in *NUC* 1968-72 is also unproductive. At this point, the librarian should begin to consider the possibility that the information at hand is either wrong, or incomplete, or both. If the title is correct and is the main entry, one would expect to find it in one of the two sources already checked. If the book has a main entry other than the title (personal or corporate author, for example), it cannot be found by title in the *NUC*.

The librarian now needs to consider a subject search, and must find a source which will have both title and subject listings for books published in 1970. There are several possibilities, including *Books in Print* and *American Book Publishing Record* for the appropriate year, but the only one which has all approaches in one alphabet is *CBI*.

As might be expected, the title is not found in *CBI*; so the subject approach is used. The librarian follows the *see* reference, "Textual criticism see Criticism, textual," to the appropriate heading. Under "Criticism, textual — addresses, essays and lectures," there is only one item:

> Gottesman, R. and Bennett, S.B., eds. *Art and Error: Modern Textual Editing*. Bloomington, Indiana University Press, 1970.

With the title corrected and the editors' names added, a search of OCLC easily locates copies of the book.

Notes

1. *Random House Dictionary of the English Language*, 2d ed. unabridged (New York: Random House, 1987), 203.

2. *Oxford English Dictionary*, 2d ed. (Oxford: Clarendon Press, 1989), 2:169.

3. Heartsill Young, ed., *ALA Glossary of Library and Information Science* (Chicago: American Library Association, 1983), 37.

4. Eugene P. Sheehy, ed., *Guide to Reference Books*, 10th ed. (Chicago: American Library Association, 1986), AA123-31.

5. *A.L.A. Cataloging Rules for Author and Title Entries*, 2d ed. (Chicago: American Library Association, 1949), 151.

6. *Access CDS 1990* (Washington, D.C.: Library of Congress Cataloging Distribution Service, 1990), 22.

7. Ibid., 24.

8. Ibid., 23.

9. Ibid., 24.

10. Ibid., 25.

11. British Library, Newspaper Library, Colindale, *Catalogue of the Newspaper Library*, Colindale. 8 vols. (London: British Museum Publications, Ltd., 1975).

12. *The Reader's Adviser*, 13th ed. (New York: R. R. Bowker, 1986), 1:xiv.

List of Sources

American Book Publishing Record. New York: R. R. Bowker, 1960- . Monthly.

American Book Publishing Record Cumulative, 1876-1949. 15 vols. New York: R. R. Bowker, 1980.

American Book Publishing Record Cumulative, 1950-1977. 15 vols. New York: R. R. Bowker, 1979.

American Catalogue ... 1876-1910. 8 vols. in 13. New York: Publishers' Weekly, 1880-1911.

American Newspapers, 1821-1936. New York: H. W. Wilson, 1937. 791p.

Ayer Directory of Publications. Philadelphia: Ayer, 1880-1982. Annual.

Besterman, Theodore, comp. *A World Bibliography of Bibliographies and of Bibliographical Catalogues, Calendars, Abstracts, Digests, Indexes, and the Like*. 4th ed. 5 vols. Lausanne, Switzerland: Societas Bibliographica, 1965-1966.

Bibliographic Index: A Cumulative Bibliography of Bibliographies. New York: H. W. Wilson, 1937- . Eleven issues per year, with quarterly and annual cumulations. (Online on WILSONLINE.)

Bibliographie Nationale Française. Paris: Bibliothèque Nationale, 1990- . Biweekly, with annual indexes. [Title varies: 1811-1989, *Bibliographie de la France*]. (Available on CD-ROM.)

Books in Print. New York: R. R. Bowker, 1948- . Annual, with semiannual supplements.

Books in Print on Microfiche. New York: R. R. Bowker. Annual, with quarterly cumulated updates.

Books in Print Online. New York: R. R. Bowker. (DIALOG File 470, BRS File BBIP.)

Books in Print Plus. [CD-ROM]. New York: R. R. Bowker.

British Library. *General Catalogue of Printed Books to 1975*. 360 vols. London: K. G. Saur, 1979-1987. (Available on CD-ROM.)

British Library. *General Catalogue of Printed Books 1976-1982*. 50 vols. London: K. G. Saur, 1983.

British Library. *General Catalogue of Printed Books 1982-1985*. 26 vols. London: K. G. Saur, 1986.

British National Bibliography. London: British Library, 1950- . Weekly, with annual cumulative volumes. (Available on CD-ROM.)

Cumulative Book Index, A World List of Books in the English Language. New York: H. W. Wilson, 1933- . Eleven issues per year, with quarterly and annual cumulations. (Online on WILSONLINE; also available on CD-ROM.)

Evans, Charles, comp. *American Bibliography; A Chronological Dictionary of All Books, Pamphlets, and Periodical Publications Printed in the United States of America from the Genesis of Printing in 1639 Down to and Including the Year 1800.* 14 vols. Chicago: printed for the author, 1903-1959.

Fiction Catalog. 11th ed. New York: H. W. Wilson, 1986. 951p.

Forthcoming Books. New York: R. R. Bowker, 1966- . Bimonthly. (Online as part of Books in Print Online; also available on CD-ROM as part of Books in Print Plus.)

France. Bibliothèque Nationale. *Catalogue Général des Livres Imprimés: Auteurs.* 231 vols. Paris: Impr. Nationale, 1897-1981.

France. Bibliothèque Nationale. *Catalogue Général des Livres Imprimés: Auteurs-Collectivités-auteurs-Anonymes, 1960-1969.* 27 vols. Paris: Impr. Nationale, 1972-1978.

France. Bibliothèque Nationale. *Catalogue Général des Livres Imprimés, 1897-1959, supplement sur fiches.* Paris: Chadwyck-Healey France, 1986. 2,890 microfiche.

Gale Directory of Publications and Broadcast Media. Detroit, Mich.: Gale Research, 1989- . Annual.

Guide to Reference Books. 10th ed. Edited by Eugene P. Sheehy. Chicago: American Library Association, 1986. 1,560p.

International Books in Print, English-language Titles Published Outside the U.S.A. and the United Kingdom. Munich, Germany: K. G. Saur, 1979- . Annual.

Irregular Serials and Annuals: An International Directory. New York: R. R. Bowker, 1967-1987. Irregular.

Kelly, James, comp. *The American Catalogue of Books (Original and Reprints), Published in the United States from Jan. 1861 to Jan. 1871.* 2 vols. New York: Wiley, 1866-1871.

Les Livres Disponibles. Paris: Cercle de la Librairie, 1971- . Annual.

National Union Catalog, Pre-1956 Imprints. A Cumulative Author List Representing Library of Congress Printed Cards and Titles Reported by Other American Libraries. 754 vols. London: Mansell, 1968-1981.

National Union Catalog of Manuscript Collections. 1959/61- . Washington, D.C.: Library of Congress, 1962- . Annual.

National Union Catalogs in Microfiche. Washington, D.C.: Library of Congress, 1983- . Frequency varies. Includes: *National Union Catalog: Audiovisual Materials, National Union Catalog: Books, National Union Catalog: Cartographic Materials, National Union Catalog: Music, Books on Music, and Sound Recordings,* and *National Union Catalog Register of Additional Locations.*

New Serial Titles: A Union List of Serials Commencing Publication after Dec. 31, 1949. Washington, D.C.: Library of Congress, 1953- . Monthly, with cumulations.

New York. Public Library. Reference Department. *Subject Headings Authorized for General Use in the Dictionary Catalogs.* 5 vols. Boston: G. K. Hall, 1960.

New York. Public Library. Research Libraries. *Dictionary Catalog of the Research Libraries ... , 1911-1971.* 800 vols. New York: The Library, [1979-1983].

Newspapers in Microform: Foreign Countries, 1948-1983. Washington, D.C.: Library of Congress, 1984. 504p.

Newspapers in Microform: United States, 1948-1983. 2 vols. Washington, D.C.: Library of Congress, 1984.

Paperbound Books in Print. New York: R. R. Bowker, 1955- . Frequency varies. (Online as part of Books in Print Online; also available on CD-ROM as part of Books in Print Plus.)

Public Library Catalog. 9th ed. New York: H. W. Wilson, 1989. 1,138p.

Publishers' Catalogs Annual. [microfiche]. Alexandria, Va.: Chadwyck-Healey, 1979- .

Publishers' Trade List Annual. New York: R. R. Bowker, 1873- . Annual.

Publishers Weekly, The Book Industry Journal. New York: R. R. Bowker, 1872- . Weekly.

Reader's Adviser: A Layman's Guide to Literature. 13th ed. 6 vols. New York: R. R. Bowker, 1986-1988.

Roorbach, Orville Augustus, comp. *Bibliotheca Americana ... 1820-61*. 4 vols. New York: Roorbach, 1852-1861.

Sabin, Joseph, comp. *Bibliotheca Americana. A Dictionary of Books Relating to America, from Its Discovery to the Present Time*. 29 vols. New York: Sabin, 1868-1892; Bibliographic Society of America, 1928-1936.

Shaw, Ralph R., and Richard H. Shoemaker, comps. *American Bibliography; A Preliminary Checklist for 1801-1819*. 23 vols. New York: Scarecrow, 1958-1983.

Shoemaker, Richard H., comp. *Checklist of American Imprints for 1820-1829*. 10 vols. New York: Scarecrow Press, 1964-1971. Continued by *A Checklist of American Imprints for 1830- *. Metuchen, N.J.: Scarecrow Press, 1972- .

Subject Guide to Books in Print. New York: R. R. Bowker, 1957- . Annual.

Subject Index of the Modern Works Added to the Library. London: British Library, 1906-1985.

Toomey, Alice F., comp. *A World Bibliography of Bibliographies, 1964-1974: A List of Works Represented by Library of Congress Printed Cards. A Decennial Supplement to Theodore Besterman, A World Bibliography of Bibliographies*. 2 vols. Totowa, N.J.: Rowman and Littlefield, 1977.

Ulrich's International Periodicals Directory, Now Including Irregular Serials and Annuals. 29th ed. 3 vols. New York: R. R. Bowker, 1990. Updated quarterly by *Ulrich's Update*. (DIALOG File 480, BRS File ULRI; also available on CD-ROM as Ulrich's Plus.)

Union List of Serials in Libraries of the United States and Canada. 3d ed. 5 vols. New York: H. W. Wilson, 1965.

United States Catalog: Books in Print. 4 vols. New York: H. W. Wilson, 1899-1928.

United States Newspaper Program National Union List. 3d ed. Dublin, Ohio: OCLC, 1989. 55 microfiche.

Walford's Guide to Reference Material. 4th ed. 3 vols. London: Library Association, 1980-1987.

Weekly Record. New York: R. R. Bowker, 1974- . Weekly.

Whitaker's Books in Print. London: Whitaker, 1874- . Title varies: 1962-1988, *British Books in Print*. (Online on DIALOG as File 430; also available on CD-ROM.)

Additional Readings

Beaudiquez, Marcelle, ed. *Inventaire Général des Bibliographies Nationales Rétrospectives = Retrospective National Bibliographies, an International Directory*. Munich, Germany: K. G. Saur,
1986. 189p. (IFLA Publications, no. 35.)

This volume lists retrospective national bibliographies worldwide, with the exception of the Soviet
Union and the countries of Eastern Europe. The introduction includes a valuable discussion of retrospective bibliographic control as well as definitions of different types of bibliographies.

Bell, Barbara L. *An Annotated Guide to Current National Bibliographies*. Alexandria, Va.: Chadwyck-
Healey, 1986. 407p.

This bibliography lists and annotates the current national bibliographies of 108 countries. It
includes substitutes, when possible, where no true national bibliography exists. In addition, it identifies
countries for which no bibliography could be located.

Gorman, G. E., and J. J. Mills. *Guide to Current National Bibliographies of the Third World*. 2d rev.
ed. London: Hans Zell Publishers, 1987. 372p.

Annotations are provided for 12 regional and 98 national bibliographies for 152 developing
countries. Every effort has been made to identify some source of bibliographic information for each
country, even if it is not an official publication. The chapter entitled "Third World National Bibliographies and International Standards" gives an overview of the current status and problems of such
bibliographies.

Kilton, Thomas D. "National Bibliographies — Their Treatment of Periodicals and Monographic
Series." *Serials Librarian* 2 (Summer 1978): 351-70.

This article presents the results of a study of the major national bibliographies of Western Europe,
the United States, Canada, Mexico, Australia, and New Zealand with regard to their inclusion of
periodicals and series. The author provides a chart for each bibliography showing whether the
bibliography lists this type of material.

Krummel, D. W. "Guides to National Bibliographies: A Review Essay." *Libraries and Culture* 24
(Spring 1989): 217-30.

Krummel discusses the history and current state of universal bibliographic control and provides a
critical review of the latest publications on retrospective bibliography.

Nelson, Bonnie. *A Guide to Published Library Catalogs*. Metuchen, N.J.: Scarecrow Press, 1982.
342p.

Nelson's guide describes hundreds of library catalogs and includes a general subject index to them.
The introduction provides a short history of published catalogs, and is particularly valuable for its
excellent advice on how to use them.

INDEXES AND ABSTRACTS

Uses and Characteristics

Indexes and abstracts are systematic listings of works that tell where information can be located. While the library's catalog is an essential tool for identifying titles in the collection, additional indexes are needed in reference work to reveal more fully the contents of the library's collection. For example, the catalog can confirm that the library holds a particular journal title, but a periodical index is needed to identify the authors and subjects of articles in the journal. Other indexes can locate individual poems, plays, short stories, essays, and news stories.

Abstracts present a summary of content. Most abstracts are descriptive, but a few abstracting services contain evaluative abstracts, including the abstractor's critical comments, in the summary. Many abstracting services at present rely on author abstracts (or translations thereof) rather than having staff abstract the articles. Although indexes and abstracts existed prior to 1900, there has been a dramatic growth in their number in the twentieth century, reflecting the growth in periodicals and other publications that they index and abstract.

Recent volumes and current issues of newspapers and periodicals provide the most up-to-date information on many subjects; older volumes provide a record of past ideas and events. Indexes and abstracts are used to verify references, to develop bibliographies of publications by a particular author or on a particular subject, and to provide current awareness by performing subject searches on an ongoing basis. They can also be used to answer some factual questions, such as locating a person's address by using the author affiliation information often included as part of an index entry.

Evaluation

Reference librarians carry out evaluation of indexes and abstracts as part of the reference collection development process and as they use the tools in reference work. Important characteristics to consider are format (print, CD-ROM, or online), scope, authority, accuracy, arrangement, and any special features that enhance effectiveness or ease of use.

Format

As explained in chapter 5, many indexes and abstracts now exist in machine-readable form. Many of the databases that were accessible in the 1970s and 1980s only by searching remote vendors online are now also available on CD-ROM. A few titles exist only online or on CD-ROM. The printed format may still lend itself best to browsing, especially for abstracts, but the machine-readable forms usually have much more powerful search capabilities, with more access points and the possibility of refining searches through using Boolean logic to combine terms. Because most databases do not cover the literature prior to the mid-1960s, searches of indexes and abstracts for older literature must rely on the printed versions. While most databases contain the same records as their printed counterparts, some databases include more or combine the records from several printed counterparts in a single database. Thus in comparing alternative formats for a particular index or abstract, the librarian should study available documentation to determine the extent of correspondence between the content of each format as well as to understand the search capabilities of each.

The readability of entries is important, whether the index is in printed or in CD-ROM form. Indexes vary in type size, use of boldface, and other aspects of presenting entries. Heavy use of abbreviations may make the entries hard to interpret without frequent reference to lists of abbreviations and symbols elsewhere in the set.

Scope

Several characteristics define the scope of indexes and abstracts. The time period covered does not necessarily coincide with the period of publication because the publisher may go back and index some older material valuable to the users of the index. For example, *Science Citation Index* has now extended its coverage back to 1945, although it originally began publication in the 1960s. Related factors are the frequency of publication and cumulation. Frequency of publication also affects currency; a monthly publication is likely to be more current than a quarterly publication. Frequency of cumulation affects the ease with which retrospective searching can be done. If an index is semimonthly but cumulates only annually, for example, then many individual issues must be searched until the annual cumulation is issued. An advantage of searching indexes and abstracts online or on CD-ROM is that the contents are automatically cumulated.

Frequency of update may vary among the different formats. The librarian should take this into account when deciding which format to consult in verifying references for recently published articles. Another factor affecting currency, common to all formats, is the time lag in indexing (and abstracting, when abstracts are present). Generally indexes relying on keyword indexing can be produced more rapidly than those requiring indexing and abstracting of documents by trained staff. Comparing the date of the index issue with the date of publication of items indexed provides an indication of the time lag.

Types of materials covered are another aspect of scope. Indexes and abstracts differ in the number of publications covered and in the extent to which particular titles are covered. General periodical indexes tend to index all substantive articles from the periodicals selected for indexing, while subject-specific indexes and abstracts are more likely to index selectively from a much larger list of periodicals, with indexers identifying those articles of most relevance to the subject scope of the service. Some indexes and abstracts are more inclusive in the types of articles indexed, indexing such things as letters to the editor and editorials, while other services restrict their coverage to research articles.

Most of the indexes and abstracts discussed in this chapter are devoted to a particular type of publication: periodicals, newspapers, dissertations, or pamphlets. More specialized services devoted to indexing and abstracting the literature of a discipline often try to encompass many different types of publications to provide more comprehensive coverage in one source. Other differences arise if there are restrictions on place and language of publication of the source materials. Some indexes and abstracts cover only English-language material, while others try to identify material relevant to a particular subject area in any language and from any part of the world. There may also be differences in the level of material covered. Some indexes of science materials may focus on the popular science literature while others cover the scholarly research literature. In printed indexes and abstracts, introductory matter may provide a clear statement of materials covered. For machine-readable databases, it is necessary to rely on database descriptions found in directories or in documentation provided by the database producer or vendor.

Authority

Considerations in assessing the authority of indexes and abstracts are the reputation of the publisher or sponsoring organization and the qualifications of the editorial staff. Publishers of indexes include commercial firms, professional associations, and government agencies. The H. W. Wilson Company is probably the best-known commercial firm and has a well-deserved reputation for the quality of its indexes.

Accuracy

While quality of indexing and accuracy of bibliographic citations are important in printed indexes and abstracts, they are even more critical in machine-readable databases where "dirty" data may result in missed references due to inaccurate or incomplete information in the records for items indexed and abstracted. Because an important function of indexes and abstracts is to provide leads to published sources, bibliographic data must be accurate and complete to allow the item sought to be located in the library's catalog or requested through interlibrary loan. The quality of indexing is determined by its depth and accuracy. Depth can apply to both author and subject indexing. Are all authors associated with an indexed item included in the author index? Are all major facets of the content of the article represented by entries in the subject index? Accuracy can also apply to both author and subject indexing. Author names should be spelled correctly. Unfortunately indexing guidelines for some indexes and abstracts dictate that only initials of given names be retained, even when a fuller form of the name appears on the original publication. This can make it difficult when searching authors to distinguish between different authors who share a common surname and initials. Accuracy of subject indexing depends on the indexer's ability to represent the content of a publication using terminology drawn from the controlled vocabulary to be used in indexing. Cross-references should be included where needed to go from a form not used to the proper form or to link related terms. Some indexes include augmented titles, where the indexer supplements the original title with additional terms to characterize the article's content more completely. Abstracts should provide an accurate summary of the original article's content.

Arrangement

Arrangement of entries determines one possible approach to the items indexed. While indexes generally employ an alphabetical arrangement, abstracts often appear in a classified arrangement that makes it easier to browse entries for related material. If additional indexes are present, they offer other access points to the publications indexed. In printed sources access points are generally limited to subject, author, and (occasionally) title, but indexes and abstracts in machine-readable form generally offer many additional options for searching, such as keywords from title and abstract, journal title, and author affiliation.

Special Features

When indexes and abstracts are evaluated, any special features that enhance their usefulness should be noted. Examples include a list of periodicals or other sources indexed and a published list of subject headings. The list of sources indexed is helpful in providing a clear indication of the materials covered as well as complete bibliographic information for those not available locally. This can be helpful in acquiring documents, whether ordering copies for inclusion in the library's collection or making requests through interlibrary loan. A published list of subject headings can help in formulating more effective search strategies in both the printed and machine-readable indexes and abstracts, because the user can see a comprehensive list of terms available to the indexer and thus have a better chance of locating the appropriate terms under which to search. This is especially the case for those lists of subject headings that include scope notes or instructions for indexers, explaining how particular terms are to be used in indexing (and hence in searching).

Selection

Indexes and abstracts are often expensive reference tools, no matter what format is selected. Selection of titles for a particular collection must take into account the characteristics of that collection as well as the needs of users for access beyond what is already provided by the library's catalog.

Directories of periodicals can be used to identify available indexes and abstracts. *Ulrich's International Periodicals Directory*, described in chapter 18, has a section on abstracting and indexing services, with entries for a few general services and cross-references to many more subject-specific services with entries elsewhere in the directory. In addition, for each periodical listed in the directory, *Ulrich's* provides an indication of the indexes and abstracts that include the periodical in their coverage—meaning inclusion of at least some of the periodical's articles as entries in the index or abstract. EBSCO Publishing has issued *The Index and Abstract Directory: An International Guide to Services and Serials Coverage*. The directory provides information on more than 750 indexes and abstracts. Section 1 provides a complete listing, by subject, of all serial titles in the EBSCO Publishing database that have index and abstract coverage. Section 2 lists bibliographic information for the indexes and abstracts together with an alphabetical list of the serials that a particular service covers. Three indexes provide access by title, subject of indexes and abstracts, and ISSN. *Magazines for Libraries* provides descriptions for many of the more widely held titles in its section on abstracts and indexes. The directories of databases and CD-ROMs described in chapter 11 provide good coverage of indexes and abstracts in machine-readable form.

Needs of Users

Indexes and abstracts selected for a particular library collection should reflect the types of information and publications to which library users wish to gain access. They should allow more complete use of the local collection as well as identification of publications of possible value available elsewhere. General periodical indexes and newspaper indexes could be useful in libraries of all types. Selection of periodical indexes devoted to particular subject areas will reflect the subject interests of the library's users. Citation indexes, with their emphasis on scholarly literature, will be of most use in academic and special libraries. Indexes to special types of materials, with the exception of *Vertical File Index*, are also likely to be found most often in academic and special libraries. Selection of indexes to reviews should reflect user demand for this information. Indexes to literary forms can prove useful wherever collected works and anthologies make up part of the collection. Fortunately the availability of so many indexes and abstracts in machine-readable form has meant that access to at least a portion of most indexes is possible online even if the library does not have a subscription to the printed version. The availability of CD-ROM versions has complicated the selection decision, because now the library can acquire many indexes in printed form, CD-ROM, or both. Where librarians feel that the increased cost of CD-ROM can be justified by the increased power of searching and convenience to the user, then this format is likely to take its place in all types of library collections.

Cost

The discussion of alternative formats in chapter 11 identified a number of factors affecting the cost of using indexes and abstracts in the various formats — in print, on CD-ROM, or online. While the price of a particular format is usually not affected by whether or not the library has access to other formats, some publishers of indexes and abstracts offer discounted pricing on a second format if one format is already part of the library's collection. For example, users of the citation indexes online have lower charges if they are also subscribers to the printed citation indexes. The same differential pricing may also apply to CD-ROM: the index publisher could charge more for the CD-ROM to a library that did not hold the printed version or that decided to cancel the printed version in favor of the CD-ROM. A complete analysis of cost factors for each format has to take into account subscription prices for printed and CD-ROM versions, binding and shelving costs for printed copies, equipment costs for using CD-ROM or online databases, and charges for online searching. The tradeoffs may be different for different indexes as each publisher develops its own pricing policy.

In a discussion of cost of indexes, it is important to describe the service basis of charging for many of the indexes published by the H. W. Wilson Company. To make the indexes available to the widest possible audience, the printed versions of many Wilson indexes are priced so that each subscriber is charged according to the amount of service provided. For periodical indexes such as *Business Periodicals Index*, *General Science Index*, *Humanities Index*, and *Social Sciences Index*, subscribers pay an amount determined by the number of indexed periodicals they hold. A library holding only a small proportion of the indexed periodicals would pay less than a library holding most of the titles. For some book indexes, such as *Book Review Digest*, the price of the index paid by a particular library reflects that library's expenditure for books. The concept underlying this approach is that the users of a library with a large collection derive more benefit from the index than the users of a library with a small collection.

Uniqueness

Uniqueness relates to both the coverage and arrangement of the indexes and abstracts being considered for selection. While overlap in sources indexed is one indicator of the degree of uniqueness of indexes, the access points and search capabilities provided by the indexes must also be considered. Two indexes could cover many of the same periodicals, but the subject indexing provided may give the user different ways of approaching the content in each. Thus examination of overlap in materials covered must be supplemented by an assessment of the approaches provided to those materials by the different indexes.

Important General Sources

This chapter describes some of the most widely held general periodical indexes, newspaper indexes, broad subject periodical indexes, citation indexes, indexes for special types of materials, indexes of reviews, and indexes for different literary forms. Because most abstracting services are devoted to the literature of a specific subject area, they lie outside the scope of this chapter.

General Periodical Indexes

General periodical indexes are held by all types of libraries. They index periodicals covering current events, hobbies, popular culture, and school curriculum related areas. The *Readers' Guide to Periodical Literature* has filled this need since 1900. The main body of the index consists of subject and author entries to articles from about 200 periodicals arranged in one alphabet (see figure 19.1). Since 1976 each issue has included a listing of citations to book reviews, arranged by author of the book reviewed, following the main body of the index. An *Abridged Readers' Guide* covering sixty-five periodicals selected from those in the unabridged edition is available for use in school and small public libraries.

FREEDOM OF INFORMATION ACT *See* Freedom of information
FREEDOM OF RELIGION *See* Religious liberty
FREEDOM OF SCIENCE *See* Science, Freedom of
FREEDOM OF SPEECH
 See also
 Blasphemy
 Freedom of the press
 Libel and slander
The Atwater flag sting. N. Hentoff. il *The Progressive* 53:12-14 N '89
Behind the flag-burning firestorm [Supreme Court decision] M. Barone. il *U.S. News & World Report* 107:28 Jl 3 '89
Burn, baby, burn! [Supreme Court ruling on flag burning] *National Review* 41:13-14 Ag 4 '89
The campus: "an island of repression in a sea of freedom". C. E. Finn. *Commentary* 88:17-23 S '89
The Court and the flag decision. W. F. Buckley. *National Review* 41:54 Ag 4 '89
The 'crime' of flag burning [Supreme Court to review case] M. Garbus. il *The Nation* 248:369-70 Mr 20 '89
Dial-a-porn, find-a-lawyer [Supreme Court rulings] A. L. Sanders. il *Time* 134:56 Jl 3 '89
Don't ban the banners [stadiums] R. Telander. por *Sports Illustrated* 71:100 O 30 '89
The dynamics of flag-burning [Supreme Court decision] J. M. Wall. *The Christian Century* 106:643-4 Jl 5-12 '89
Faith and flag-burning [discussion of July 5-12, 1989 article, The dynamics of flag-burning] J. M. Wall. il *The Christian Century* 106:757-9 Ag 16-23 '89
A fight for Old Glory [Supreme Court rules flag burning is not a crime] T. Jacoby. il *Newsweek* 114:18-20 Jl 3 '89
The flag and freedom of speech [Supreme Court decision] *America* 161:3 Jl 1-8 '89
Flag-burning & other modes of expression. W. Berns. *Commentary* 88:37-41 O '89
Flag desecration legislation. *Congressional Digest* 68:193-224 Ag/S '89
Flag-saving [Supreme Court ruling] *The Nation* 249:229-30 S 4-11 '89
Free speech on the campus. N. Hentoff. il *The Progressive* 53:12-13 My '89

FREELANCE WRITING
The four P's for free lancers. V. Buchan. *The Writer* 102:30 S '89
Freelance writers claim nonpayment by 'Inside books'. C. Reid. *Publishers Weekly* 235:25 Je 30 '89
A specialist in many fields. G. Stern. *The Writer* 102:17-19 My '89
Spring training for writers. J. McCollister. *The Writer* 102:7-8 Ap '89
Three surefire ways to write and sell nonfiction. S. S. Baker. *The Writer* 102:11-13 Mr '89
You may be an expert and not know it. C. A. Smith. *The Writer* 102:26-7 Ja '89
FREEMAN, ARTHUR M.
 "Woulda/coulda/shoulda": how to avoid no-win thinking [excerpt] il *Ladies' Home Journal* 106:124+ O '89
FREEMAN, BRIAN M.
 about
The workingman's man at the takeover table. C. Tucher. il por *Business Week* p62 S 4 '89
FREEMAN, CAROLYN
 about
23 years of outrageous water bills spur two sisters to fight city hall. (P.S.: they won!). S. Percy. il pors *Good Housekeeping* 209:52+ O '89
FREEMAN, CHARLES W.
The Angola/Namibia accords. *Foreign Affairs* 68:126-41 Summ '89
FREEMAN, CLAIRE
 about
Claire Freeman takes oath as asst. secretary of HUD. il por *Jet* 77:8 D 4 '89
FREEMAN, DAVID, 1941-
High on Kauai. il *Vogue* 179:396+ Mr '89
FREEMAN, HAROLD P.
 about
Dr. Harold P. Freeman. D. C. Lyons. il pors *Ebony* 44:60+ Ag '89
FREEMAN, JOHN W.
The good life [cover story] il pors *Opera News* 54:8-12 D 23 '89
Records. See issues of Opera News
The subject is Rose [cover story] il pors *Opera News* 53:8-13 Mr 18 '89

Fig. 19.1. Entries from *Readers' Guide to Periodical Literature*, 1989 cumulation. Reprinted with permission of The H. W. Wilson Company.

Extensive cross-references lead the user from a term not used to the proper term (for example, Freedom of science, *See* Science, Freedom of) and from a term to related terms (for example, Freedom of speech, *See also* Blasphemy, Freedom of the press, Libel and slander). Specific aspects of a subject are indicated by subdivisions under the main heading (such as Freedom of the press — International aspects). Under authors and subjects, titles are arranged in alphabetical order by the first word, disregarding initial articles. Under personal names, titles *by* an author precede those *about* him or her. When titles are not sufficiently descriptive of an article's content, supplementary notes are added in brackets following the original title. Subdivisions of a subject are arranged alphabetically under the subject, with geographical subheads following the other subdivisions in a separate alphabet. The instructions for use explain how to locate reviews of ballet, dance, motion pictures, musicals, opera, phonographs, radio programs, television programs, theater, videodiscs, and videotapes, as well as how to locate the index entries for fiction, poems, and short stories. The subject headings try to make use of common language, so that users can easily find the topics sought.

Readers' Guide is published semimonthly in March, April, September, October, and December and monthly in January, February, May, June, July, August, and November. There are quarterly cumulations and an annual bound cumulation. Since 1952 the Committee on Wilson Indexes of the American Library Association's Reference and Adult Services Division has advised the publisher on indexing and editorial policy for *Readers' Guide* as well as other Wilson indexes.[1] To keep the number of titles covered at a manageable size and reflective of popular interests, coverage changes over time as new periodicals are included and others are dropped.

In the 1970s a few other general periodical indexes were introduced. Examples are *Access: The Supplementary Index to Periodicals*, an author and subject index to more than 150 periodicals not indexed in *Readers' Guide* but commonly held by libraries; and *Magazine Index*, an author and subject index on microfilm covering about twice as many periodicals as *Readers' Guide*.

During the 1980s the H. W. Wilson Company introduced a number of additions to the *Readers' Guide* family, and competitors emerged with new products taking advantage of optical disc technology. Wilson's *Readers' Guide Abstracts* provides summaries of many of the articles indexed in *Readers' Guide* and can be purchased on microfiche, CD-ROM, or print, or accessed online. Selection of articles for abstracting is based on the substantive nature of the article, currency and topicality, reference value, and relevance to school and college curricula. *Readers' Guide Abstracts* is issued ten times per year in print with two semiannual cumulations and eight times per year on microfiche. Coverage on microfiche dates from 1984 and in print from 1988. The abstracts are arranged under the subject headings used in *Readers' Guide*, with the most recent articles listed first. Cross-references to related subjects are provided. The CD-ROM version has quarterly updates, while the online version on WILSONLINE has indexing updated twice weekly and abstracting updated weekly. Search capabilities on the WILSONDISC CD-ROM version range from simple browsing to Boolean searching, using the same commands found on the online system WILSONLINE. In fact a CD-ROM search can be updated online by connecting to WILSONLINE from the CD-ROM workstation. *Readers' Guide to Periodical Literature* is also now available online and on CD-ROM with coverage beginning in 1983.

In 1985, Information Access Company, publishers of *Magazine Index*, introduced InfoTrac, using optical disc and microcomputer technologies to provide access to indexing for periodical articles. They now market a family of databases on CD-ROM, with products ranging from those for school libraries to those intended for large academic and public libraries.[2] They have expanded their offerings online to include Magazine Index with coverage from 1959-1970 and 1973 to the present, Magazine ASAP (full text of over 120 magazines) with coverage beginning in 1983, and Academic Index (indexing of more than 400 scholarly and general interest periodicals) with coverage beginning in 1976. University Microfilms International and EBSCO have introduced general periodical indexes (with abstracts) on CD-ROM. University Microfilms International publishes Periodical Abstracts Ondisc covering 450 periodicals. Virtually all of the indexed publications are available on microform from UMI as subscriptions and backfiles as well as photocopies of individual articles. If a library also subscribes to General Periodicals Ondisc, users can retrieve the full text of articles from 150 of the journals covered by Periodical Abstracts Ondisc. Magazine Article Summaries covers 200 periodicals, somewhat more than the printed publication of the same name. It is also available online through BRS as Popular Magazine Review Online. These competing products continue to change their coverage and search capabilities, so librarians need to follow these developments to determine which approaches to providing access to general periodicals best meet the needs of the library's users and which are affordable.

Although not as widely held and used as indexes covering recently published literature, indexes covering nineteenth century periodicals are helpful supplements to *Readers' Guide*. *Nineteenth Century Readers' Guide to Periodical Literature* indexes — by author, subject, and illustrator — fifty-one periodicals published in the 1890s, mainly general and literary with some from special fields. Supplementary indexing for fourteen of the periodicals makes indexing coverage complete for each title from 1890 to the time when it was added to the list of one of the other Wilson indexes. *Poole's Index to Periodical Literature* covers the period 1802-1881 in the original set, with five supplementary volumes bringing coverage up to 1906. It is a subject index to 470 American and English periodicals. Entries give article title, author, abbreviated title of periodical, volume, and page reference. The date can be determined from the chronological conspectus given in the beginning of each volume. It is valuable for the long period and large number of titles covered.

Newspaper Indexes

General periodical indexes such as *Readers' Guide* include coverage of the major news magazines and thus offer some access to information on current events at the national and international level. Many library users also want access to newspaper coverage of national and international topics as well as regional and local news. The impact of technology on newspaper indexing has been considerable: well-established newspaper indexes are now supplemented with indexes and abstracts available on CD-ROM or online as well as the full text of many newspapers available online. These changes have made it possible to make much fuller use of newspapers in answering reference questions, especially those on current events.

The best-known printed newspaper index is the *New York Times Index*. Because it includes abstracts of articles appearing in the newspaper, it can be used alone for a basic overview of the news, or it can be used to locate full articles in the original newspaper. Abstracts are classified under appropriate subject, geographic, organization, and personal name headings. They are sufficiently detailed that they may answer some questions without reference to the original *Times* articles. Headings are arranged alphabetically and entries under them are arranged chronologically. Each entry is followed by a reference (date, section, page, and column) to the item it summarizes. Entries indicate if the original article includes illustrations or other special material. Cross-references are used to identify related material. In addition to serving as an index to the *New York Times*, the index can also be used to locate discussions of particular events in other newspapers that lack their own indexes. The *New York Times Index* can be used to identify the date of an event, and the corresponding issue of the local newspaper can be consulted for its discussion of that event. Issues appear semimonthly, with quarterly and annual cumulations. Because of the time lag in indexing, the index is not helpful in locating articles on very recent events.

Other newspaper indexes have been issued on microfilm, CD-ROM, and online. The *National Newspaper Index* is available in all three formats and provides indexing coverage of three newspapers beginning with 1979 (*New York Times*, *Wall Street Journal*, *Christian Science Monitor*) and two others beginning with 1982 (*Los Angeles Times*, *Washington Post*). *NewsBank Index*, an index to the microfiche of articles drawn from more than 450 U.S. newspapers, is now available on CD-ROM as the NewsBank Electronic Index. It provides good regional coverage, including such titles as the *Bangor* (Maine) *News*, the *Belleville* (Illinois) *News-Democrat*, and the *Bellevue* (Washington) *Journal-American*. Newspaper Abstracts Ondisc covers major U.S. newspapers including the *New York Times*, *Atlanta Constitution*, *Boston Globe*, *Christian Science Monitor*, *Chicago Tribune*, *Los Angeles Times*, *Wall Street Journal*, and the *Washington Post*. A version is also available online through DIALOG. Alexa Jaffurs compares the coverage and search capabilities of the CD-ROM newspaper indexes as of 1989.[3]

At present many newspapers are available in full-text online. If the newspaper is not covered in a printed or CD-ROM index, then this is the only option for locating articles. Even if other forms of indexing exist, it may be more efficient to do an online search, particularly when the topic is one that may not be easy to find in a controlled vocabulary index or even in a CD-ROM index that searches headlines and brief abstracts. Systems offering full-text searching of newspapers include NEXIS, VU/TEXT, and DataTimes.[4] In searching full-text files, it is important to use the most specific and unique words possible and to narrow the search by other criteria (such as date range) if possible. Full-text files generally do not predate the 1980s. Some full-text newspapers are now also being distributed on CD-ROM.

Broad Subject Periodical Indexes

When the scope of a library's periodical collection exceeds that of the coverage of a general periodical index, the library should acquire one or more additional indexes. Most of the widely held titles are published by the H. W. Wilson Company, but one index commonly found in public and academic libraries is published by Public Affairs Information Service, Inc. Formerly titled *Public Affairs Information Service (PAIS) Bulletin*, *PAIS International in Print* now incorporates both the *Bulletin* and the *PAIS Foreign Language Index*. It appears monthly, with quarterly and annual cumulations. English-language sources are supplemented with material published in French, German, Italian, Portuguese, and Spanish. Entries include English-language abstract-like notes and indications of special features, such as maps, charts, tables, and bibliographies. Its scope includes public policy, business, legal, economic, social science, and related literature. Compilers try to identify the public affairs information likely to be most useful to legislators, administrators, the business and financial community, policy researchers, and students. The listings encompass printed materials in all formats: periodical articles, books, government documents (drawn from national and state governments and intergovernmental organizations), and the reports of public and private organizations. Indexing of periodicals is selective; about 1,400 periodicals are scanned to identify articles within the scope of *PAIS*. In introducing a library user to this index, it can be helpful to point out the types of publications indexed, as different strategies may be needed to locate periodicals, books, and documents in the library's collection.

The emphasis in *PAIS* is on factual and statistical information. An effort is made to represent the full range of positions on controversial subjects. The subject entries are drawn from a controlled vocabulary, *PAIS Subject Headings*, which includes more than eight thousand subject headings and cross-references displaying relationships among terms. Entries can appear under either subject or geographical headings, both of which may be subdivided. An author index is provided in the annual bound volume for entries that have either a personal or a corporate author. The Key to Periodical References gives the abbreviated journal title, the full title, the frequency, price, and ISSN of the journal, as well as the address of the publisher. The Directory of Publishers and Organizations gives the abbreviated name, the full name, and address. PAIS can also be searched on CD-ROM and online through DIALOG and BRS with coverage from 1972. The CD-ROM is updated quarterly, while online updates are made monthly.

The H. W. Wilson Company now publishes many indexes to periodicals in a variety of subject areas, supplementing the coverage of general periodicals provided by *Readers' Guide*. One or more of these indexes are likely to be found in academic, public, and special libraries, with the choice depending on the subject strengths of the collection and interests of the library's users. They are all limited to English-language periodicals, but include some titles published outside the United States. Selection of periodicals for indexing is accomplished by subscriber vote, with an emphasis on the reference value of the periodicals under consideration. There is also an effort to give consideration to subject balance. As explained in the section of this chapter on selection of indexes, several of these indexes are priced on a service basis. The subscriber's periodical holdings determine the annual subscription rate. Each issue has a list of periodicals indexed with order information. A well-developed system of cross-references aids the search for articles on specific subjects in a particular index. Each of these indexes is available on CD-ROM with coverage for the past few years. In addition they can be searched online through WILSONLINE and, as of 1991, through BRS.[5]

Four of the broad subject indexes are described in this section.[6] *Humanities Index* has author and subject entries to articles from 345 periodicals in one alphabet and a separate listing of citations to book reviews. Subject fields indexed include archaeology and classical studies, art and photography, folklore, history, language and literature, performing arts, philosophy, and religion and theology. As found in *Readers' Guide*, coverage includes reviews of plays, operas, ballets, dance, musicals, motion pictures, videotapes, television and radio programs as well as works of fiction, drama, and poetry. The index is published quarterly with a bound annual cumulation. Coverage on CD-ROM and online begins in 1984.

Social Sciences Index has author and subject entries to articles from 350 periodicals in one alphabet and a separate listing of book reviews. Subject fields indexed include anthropology, area studies, community health and medical care, economics, geography, international relations, law and criminology, minority studies, planning and public administration, police science and corrections, policy sciences, political science, psychiatry, psychology, social work and public welfare, sociology, and urban studies. The index is published quarterly with a bound annual cumulation. Coverage on CD-ROM and online begins in 1983.

General Science Index has only subject entries to articles from 109 periodicals, followed by a separate listing of book reviews. Although "general science" suggests a somewhat narrow field of coverage, subject fields indexed include astronomy, atmospheric science, biology, botany, chemistry, computers, earth science, environment and conservation, food and nutrition, genetics, mathematics, medicine and health, microbiology, oceanography, physics, physiology, and zoology. The index is published monthly except June and December, with a bound annual cumulation. Coverage on CD-ROM and online begins in 1984.

Business Periodicals Index also has only subject entries to articles from 345 periodicals, followed by a separate listing of book reviews. Subject fields indexed include accounting, advertising and marketing, banking, economics, finance and investments, industrial relations, insurance, international business, management and personnel administration, occupational health and safety, printing and publishing, public relations, real estate, regulation of industry, transportation, and other specific industries. The index is published monthly except August with a bound annual cumulation. Coverage on CD-ROM and online begins in 1982.

Citation Indexes

The periodical indexes described thus far allow the user to find articles written by the same author or indexed under the same subject heading. Citation indexes allow the user to locate items based on a different type of relationship: the links created when authors cite earlier works by other authors (or even some of their own previously published works). The primary use of a citation index is to find, for a particular publication known to the searcher, later items that have cited it. The Institute for Scientific Information publishes three indexes that allow the user to carry out such searches in broad subject areas: *Science Citation Index*, *Social Sciences Citation Index*, and *Arts & Humanities Citation Index*. Coverage includes journals and chapters in some multiauthored books. They are all structured in the same way, with four indexes: a Source Index, Citation Index, Permuterm Subject Index, and Corporate Index. The Source Index provides complete bibliographic information for each article indexed in a particular issue. It is arranged by author name, with cross-references from coauthors to first authors. Figure 19.2 shows some sample entries from the Source Index. In addition to bibliographic and author address information, the entries in *Social Sciences Citation Index* and *Arts & Humanities Citation Index* contain a complete list of the references included in the source item's bibliography. To find complete journal titles, the periodicals list elsewhere in the volume must be consulted to translate from abbreviated to full journal titles. The Source Index is used to find articles by known authors that have been published during the time period covered by the index.

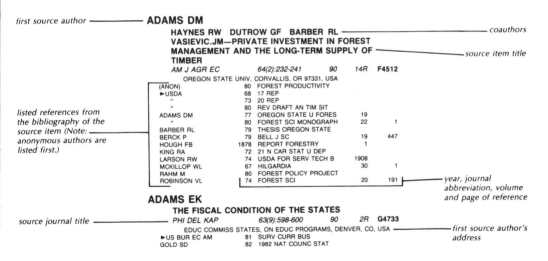

Fig. 19.2. Entries from "Source Index," *Social Sciences Citation Index*. Reprinted by permission of Institute for Scientific Information.

Figure 19.3, page 430, shows sample entries from the Citation Index. Entries are made for any author's work cited during the period covered by the index. In the example, an article by G. Renoux, published in 1973 in the *Bulletin of the World Health Organization*, was subsequently cited by A. Thelin writing in the *Scandinavian Journal of Social Medicine* in 1980. Cited publications can be of all types and from any time period. The Source Index must be consulted to get complete bibliographic information for the citing articles. Codes are used to indicate the type of source item (e.g., E = editorial) where applicable. The Citation Index is used to go from older, known publications to the more recent, related articles that cite them. Using the Citation Index, terminology problems may be avoided because earlier published works can be used to represent concepts or topics of interest. Citing publications are assumed to be related in some way to those earlier cited publications. Only first authors are listed in the Citation Index entries, so the first author of multiauthored papers must be known to use the paper as a starting point in the Citation Index.

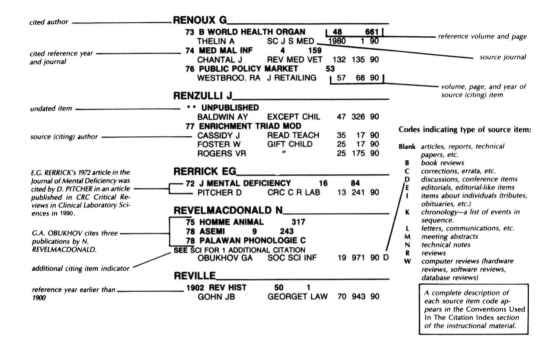

Fig. 19.3. Entries from "Citation Index," *Social Sciences Citation Index*. Reprinted by permission of Institute for Scientific Information.

Figure 19.4 shows sample entries from the Permuterm Subject Index. This is derived from keywords appearing in source article titles. The Source Index must be consulted to get complete bibliographic information for the articles. In the figure, it can be determined that V. H. Freeman wrote an article with a title including the keywords "aide," "case," "course," "training," and "volunteer." This index is especially useful for searching newly coined terms that may appear in article titles but may not yet be used in other indexes as subject headings. When using the Permuterm Subject Index, it is necessary to begin with one term and then to scan the secondary terms found below the entry point to identify articles of interest. Because there is no vocabulary control (although some cross-references are provided), it is necessary to look for synonyms and variant spellings.

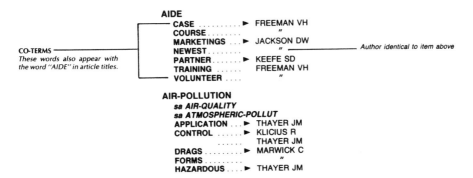

Fig. 19.4. Entries from "Permuterm® Subject Index," *Social Sciences Citation Index*. Reprinted by permission of Institute for Scientific Information.

The fourth index is the Corporate Index. It provides access to authors and their works by corporate or academic affiliation. It is arranged by geographic location and then by organization name. States of the United States appear in one alphabetical listing, followed by a separate list of other countries. There is also a list of organizations with cross-references to the geographic list. The Source Index must be consulted to get complete bibliographic information for the articles located in the Corporate Index. This index can be used to find articles of interest when a corporate or academic institution is known to sponsor work on the topic.

All three citation indexes are international in scope, covering many journals published outside the United States as well as the major U.S. titles in each subject area. Source articles in languages other than English include a language code preceding the English translation of the title. *Science Citation Index* now covers the period back to 1945 with two ten-year cumulations (1945-1954, 1955-1964), five five-year cumulations (1965-1969, 1970-1974, 1975-1979, 1980-1984, 1985-1989), annual cumulations, and bimonthly issues for the current year. *Social Sciences Citation Index* now covers the period back to 1956 with one ten-year cumulation (1956-1965), four five-year cumulations (1966-1970, 1971-1975, 1976-1980, 1981-1985), annual cumulations, and current issues covering four-month intervals. *Arts & Humanities Citation Index* has annual volumes for the period 1976-1988 and semiannual volumes beginning in 1989. All three indexes are available with more restricted time coverage online (SciSearch from 1974, Social SciSearch from 1972, and Arts & Humanities Search from 1980). For the time period covered, however, these sources can be searched much more easily online. Coverage is also more current online since updates are made weekly. CD-ROM editions are now available for *Science Citation Index* and *Social Sciences Citation Index*. In addition to search capabilities found in print, the CD-ROMs have a "related record" feature, enabling the user to find articles related to a known article. Relatedness is determined within the program by the number of references the articles share (a technique known as bibliographic coupling), rather than by having keywords in common.[7] SciSearch has added author abstracts beginning in 1991.

Indexes for Special Types of Materials

The indexes discussed thus far in this chapter provide good coverage of periodicals and newspapers, but are not helpful for gaining access to some other special types of materials that may be important in certain library collections. Academic library users frequently want access to dissertations; public and school library users often want to locate pamphlets on particular topics. Indexes devoted to these and other special types of materials, such as conference proceedings and research reports, can be useful for both collection development and reference work. This section describes the indexes for dissertations and pamphlets. Other indexes to special materials are described in more specialized guides to reference sources, such as the sections on conference literature, patents, and technical reports in *Using Science and Technology Information Sources.*[8]

Students have been earning doctoral degrees in American universities for 130 years. Research for the doctorate is described in a dissertation, many of which are deposited with University Microfilms International (UMI) in Ann Arbor, Michigan, to enable their use outside of the institution in which the research was originally completed. UMI has developed several reference tools to aid librarians in providing more effective access to the dissertation literature. Printed tools include *Comprehensive Dissertation Index* (*CDI*) and *Dissertation Abstracts International* (*DAI*). *CDI* attempts to list every doctoral dissertation accepted in North America since 1861. The original set covers the period 1861-1972. This has been followed by a ten-year cumulation (1973-1982), a five-year cumulation (1983-1987), and annual supplements. The set includes some coverage of dissertations accepted at universities outside North America. Figure 19.5 shows sample entries taken from the 1988 supplement.

PREVAILING
PLANNING AND ADMINISTRATION GUIDELINES: A DELPHI STUDY BASED IN THE **PREVAILING** SITUATION OF LIBRARIES WITH RESEARCH PUERTO RICAN MATERIALS.— MUNOZ-SOLA, HAYDEE (D.L.S. 1985 COLUMBIA UNIVERSITY) 509p. 49/03A, p.369 **DEV88-09396**

PRICES
DEVELOPMENT OF A DECISION-MAKING MODEL FOR SELECTION OF SERIAL TITLES IN LATIN AMERICAN UNIVERSITY LIBRARIES: A SOLUTION TO INCREASING **PRICES** OF PERIODICAL PUBLICATIONS (SOFTWARE).— GONZALEZ-FERNANDEZ, JORGE LUIS (ED.D. 1987 GEORGE PEABODY COLLEGE FOR TEACHERS OF VANDERBILT UNIVERSITY) 220p. 48/08A, p.1919 **DEV87-23887**

PRICING
TOP: TUNING AN OPTION **PRICING** MODEL USING A KNOWLEDGE-BASED APPROACH.— KIM, SUNG KUN (PH.D. 1988 NEW YORK UNIVERSITY, GRADUATE SCHOOL OF BUSINESS ADMINISTRATION) 134p. 49/05A, p.983 **DEV88-14675**

PRIMACY
RESONANCE, INFORMATION, AND THE **PRIMACY** OF PROCESS: ANCIENT LIGHT ON MODERN INFORMATION AND COMMUNICATION THEORY AND TECHNOLOGY.— MILLER, GORDON LYNN (PH.D. 1987 RUTGERS THE STATE UNIVERSITY OF NEW JERSEY - NEW BRUNSWICK) 256p. 48/07A, p.1566 **DEV87-23276**

PRINCIPAL
RELATIONSHIP BETWEEN THE COMMITMENT AND ROLE OF THE ELEMENTARY SCHOOL **PRINCIPAL** IN REGIONS I, III AND V IN THE STATE OF FLORIDA REGARDING MEDIA AND THE QUALITY OF THE SCHOOL MEDIA CENTER.— HYATT, BETTY JO (ED.D. 1987 THE FLORIDA STATE UNIVERSITY) 150p. 48/07A, p.1569 **DEV87-23133**

PRIORITIES
A TEST OF THE INCREMENTAL MODEL OF FEDERAL BUDGETING: LIBRARY OF CONGRESS PROGRAM **PRIORITIES** FY 1961-1981.— HANNA, MARCIA KATHLEEN (PH.D. 1988 THE UNIVERSITY OF WISCONSIN - MADISON) 457p. 49/05A, p.985 **DEV88-05420**

PRIVATE
THE ADMINISTRATION AND ORGANIZATION OF **PRIVATE** AND PUBLIC MULTICAMPUS UNIVERSITY LIBRARIES: A STUDY OF SELECTED CASES.— SCHWARTZ, RUTH (D.L.S. 1987 COLUMBIA UNIVERSITY) 320p. 48/08A, p.1920 **DEV87-24091**

Fig. 19.5. Entries from *Comprehensive Dissertation Index*, 1988 Supplement. The dissertation titles contained here are published with permission of University Microfilms Inc., copyright © 1988, by University Microfilms Inc., and may not be reproduced without their prior permission. (Full text copies are available from UMI.)

Titles are arranged by keyword in broad subject categories in the sciences or the social sciences and humanities (for example, library and information science is one category within the social sciences). Entries give the full dissertation title, author, degree, date, institution, number of pages, a reference to the location in *DAI* where an abstract can be found, and an order number if it is available from UMI. Because dissertations usually have quite specific titles, this form of subject access works reasonably well. However, the lack of vocabulary control means that the user must identify any likely synonyms for the topic of interest to do a complete subject search. If the author is known, the author index can be used to identify the title of the dissertation.

DAI is published monthly in two parts (A — The Humanities and Social Sciences and B — The Sciences and Engineering) and includes abstracts of doctoral dissertations submitted to UMI by participating institutions in North America. A third section (C — Worldwide) is published quarterly and includes abstracts of dissertations in all disciplines from many institutions throughout the world. About 550 institutions cooperate in sending dissertations to UMI. Most dissertations from outside North America are not available from UMI; those available are also listed in section A or B. A list of participating institutions is included in each issue of *DAI*. Copies of dissertations may be purchased from UMI in microform or paper copies. Entries in *DAI* are grouped by author-selected subject, then alphabetically by author within subject. Each issue contains a keyword index and an author index to gain access to the classified abstracts.

While *CDI* cumulations can make the task of searching several years for dissertations somewhat easier than searching year by year, the availability of *CDI* and *DAI* in machine-readable form on CD-ROM and online has considerably enhanced the search capabilities. The online database includes abstracts published since July 1980 as well as citations to dissertations back to 1861 in a single database. Subject access is enhanced for those dissertations with abstracts since every word in the abstract is searchable in addition to the title keywords searchable in the printed indexes. Dissertation Abstracts Ondisc has the same coverage as the online database and also allows keyword searching.

Vertical File Index is a subject index to current pamphlets and other inexpensive paper-bound items published in English in the United States or Canada. Selected nonbook materials such as charts, posters, and maps for classroom use are also listed. Under subject headings, entries are arranged alphabetically by the title of the pamphlet. Entries contain bibliographic and ordering information and many include an annotation. Each issue now includes a supplementary section, titled "References to Current Topics," that contains selected periodical citations to subjects of current interest. Each issue also includes a separate title index. *Vertical File Index* is issued monthly except in August. A subject index published in quarterly and semiannual numbers cumulates the subject headings used in preceding issues of the current volume. The index is useful in acquiring and organizing vertical file material. Coverage beginning with 1985 is available online on WILSONLINE.

Indexes of Reviews

Reference librarians are often asked to assist the user in locating reviews of books or nonprint materials, such as films and software. While periodical indexes such as *Readers' Guide* can sometimes help with such requests, it may be more efficient and effective to use indexes specifically designed for this purpose.

The two tools most often used to locate book reviews are *Book Review Digest* and *Book Review Index*. *Book Review Digest*, with coverage since 1905, provides excerpts of and citations to reviews of current fiction and nonfiction in the English language. Book reviews appearing in 95 selected periodicals in the humanities, social sciences, and general science from the United States, Canada, and Great Britain (e.g., *Canadian Literature*, *Political Science Quarterly*, *New Scientist*) as well as library reviewing media are included. Certain types of books (government publications, textbooks, technical books in the sciences and law) are excluded, but books on science for the general reader are included. Not all books reviewed in the indexed periodicals are included in *Book Review Digest*. To qualify for inclusion a book must have been published or distributed in the United States or Canada. A work of nonfiction must have received at least two reviews, a work of fiction for children or young adults must have received at least three reviews, and a work of fiction for adults must have received at least four reviews. All books reviewed in the *Reference Books Bulletin* section of *Booklist* are included, even if that is the only review received. Reviews must have appeared within eighteen months after a book was published, and at least one review must be from a journal published in the United States or Canada. Excerpts from reviews accompany many of the citations to the original reviews, with more excerpts included for books of unusual importance or of a controversial nature.

The main body of *Book Review Digest* consists of listings in alphabetical order by the last name of the author (or by title when title is the main entry). Citations include bibliographic information, price, classification according to the Dewey Decimal Classification (for nonfiction titles), and subject headings from *Sears List of Subject Headings*. A descriptive note, including age or grade levels for juvenile books, precedes the excerpts and review citations. The excerpts and review citations are arranged by the names of the journals in which the reviews appeared. Both the name of the reviewer and the approximate number of words in the complete review are included as part of the citation to a review. A Subject and Title Index is included in each issue. Fiction for adults is listed under "Fiction themes." Fiction and nonfiction for children and young adults are listed under the headings "Children's literature" and "Young adult literature," respectively. *Book Review Digest* is published monthly except February and July, with a bound annual cumulation. Coverage on CD-ROM and online begins in 1983.

Because of differences in coverage and inclusion policies, *Book Review Index* often can identify one or more reviews of many books that *Book Review Digest* will not include. *Book Review Index* provides access to reviews of books and periodicals appearing in more than 500 publications and indexes reviews as soon as they appear. It covers reviewing journals (such as *Booklist*), national publications of general interest (such as *Newsweek*), scholarly and literary journals (such as *American Anthropologist*), daily and weekly newspapers, British and Canadian publications, and specialized journals from various subject areas. *Book Review Index* includes citations for reviews of any type of book that has been or is about to be published and is at least fifty pages long, though poetry and children's books may be shorter. All reviews in the journals indexed are cited. Citations for reviews of periodicals are included if the reviewer evaluated the publication as a whole. The definition of "review" used in compiling the index is broad; "annotations and brief listings are cited if they provide a critical comment, a detailed description of the contents, or a recommendation regarding the type of library collection a book is suited for."[9] Entries in the main section of *Book Review Index* include the author's or the editor's name, the title being reviewed, an abbreviation identifying the reviewing source, the date and volume number of the source, and the page number on which the review appears. Reviews of reference works, periodicals, and books for children and young adults are coded to allow them to be distinguished easily (using *r*, *p*, *c*, and *y*). The title index, which follows the main body of the book, can be used to identify the main entry where the review citation will be found. A listing of all periodical abbreviations together with the full title appears in the front matter of each issue. In contrast to *Book Review Digest*, *Book Review Index* has neither a subject index nor digests of the book reviews indexed. *Book Review Index* has six bimonthly issues that cumulate every four months and annually. There is a master cumulation for the twenty-year period 1965-1984. The entire run of *Book Review Index* can be searched online through DIALOG.

Entries for reviews of the *Encyclopedia of Southern Culture* listed in *Book Review Digest* and *Book Review Index* are shown in figures 19.6 and 19.7. *Book Review Digest* includes citations to reviews from *Booklist*, *Library Journal*, and *New York Review of Books*. The 1989 cumulation of *Book Review Index* identifies eleven reviews (listed under the first editor's name as the entry point, rather than title), in periodicals ranging from *Esquire* and *Southern Living* to *Wilson Library Bulletin*. As can be seen, the periodical titles are quite abbreviated, so the listing of periodical abbreviations may need to be consulted to decipher such entries as UPBN (*University Press Book News*).

ENCYCLOPEDIA OF SOUTHERN CULTURE; Charles Reagan Wilson & William Ferris, coeditors; Ann J. Abadie & Mary L. Hart, associate editors; sponsored by the Center for the Study of Southern Culture at the University of Mississippi. 1634p il $59.95 1989 University of N.C. Press
    975 1. Southern States—Civilization—Dictionaries
    ISBN 0-8078-1823-2   LC 88-17084

"This volume of 1,300 entries is divided into 24 major sections (e.g., 'Agriculture,' 'Environment,' 'Ethnic Life,' 'Industry,' 'Media,' 'Violence,' 'Women's Life'). These sections vary in length from 36 pages ('Language') to 131 pages ('History and Manners'). Each section begins with an overview essay written by the Encyclopedia's consultant for that section. This essay is followed by alphabetically arranged thematic articles (usually 1-3 pages) and then by brief (often a page or less), alphabetically arranged topical-biographical articles. . . . The topics treated range from the . . . specific (Fried Chicken, Mint Julep, Dukes of Hazzard, Foxfire, the magazine Southern Living, Lost Cause Myth, Kentucky Derby, Snake Handlers, Texas Rangers, and specific cities, sports, universities, and ethnic groups) to the broad (Painting and Painters, Film, Indians, Population, Civil War, Industrialization, Country Music, and Health). All entries are signed and end with a bibliography." (Booklist) Indexes.

———

"The Encyclopedia's definition of the South is a cultural one: wherever southern culture is found. While the focus is on the 11 states of the Confederacy, the work also encompasses midwestern and Middle Atlantic border states, even southern outposts in Chicago, Detroit, and Bakersfield. . . . This compendium has no contemporary rival. The Encyclopedia of Southern History [BRD 1980], an alphabetically arranged volume of usually brief articles, treats a much narrower range of topics. . . . This well-written work is recommended for public and academic libraries where there is interest in American studies through a regional perspective; some high school collections may find it appropriate too. In addition to its usefulness for scholars and students, general readers with an interest in the South will find it an irresistible book in which to browse."
Booklist 86:97 S 1 '89 (850w)

"This monumental reference work analyzes in both broad strokes and minute detail all things southern. . . . While the sections on literature and music are among the longest, there are excellent sections on black life, folk life, social class, violence, etc. Two of the most fascinating, 'history and manners' and the 'mythic south' discuss all things quintessentially southern—barbeque, chitterlings, fried chicken, mint juleps, and moon pies—or viewed as southern—good old boys and girls, moonlight-and-magnolias, and rednecks. . . . A worthy complement to the Encyclopedia of Southern History [BRD 1980], this is a stunning achievement in the field of regional reference works and bargain priced to boot."
Libr J 114:72 Jl '89. Brian E. Coutts (250w)

N Y Rev Books 36:13 O 26 '89. C. Vann Woodward (7200w)

Fig. 19.6. Entry from *Book Review Digest* 1989. Reprinted with permission of The H. W. Wilson Company.

Wilson, Charles R - *Encyclopedia of Southern Culture*
  r AB - v84 - Ag 7 '89 - p428
  r Antiq - v136 - O '89 - p756
  yr BL - v86 - S 1 '89 - p97
  r BW - v19 - Jl 30 '89 - p3
  r Econ - v312 - S 23 '89 - p109
  r Esq - v112 - O '89 - p49
  r LJ - v114 - Jl '89 - p72
  r NYTBR - v94 - S 17 '89 - p3
  r S Liv - v24 - O '89 - p88
  r UPBN - v1 - S '89 - p11
  r WLB - v64 - O '89 - p133

Fig. 19.7. Entry from *Book Review Index* 1989. Cumulation, 1990, edited by Neil E. Walker and Beverly Baer. Copyright © 1990 by Gale Research Inc. Reprinted by permission of the publisher.

Although book reviews are likely to be the types of reviews most often sought, library users may also be interested in locating reviews of other types of materials such as nonprint media (film and video, filmstrips, audio) and computer software. *Media Review Digest* (*MRD*) is an annual index to and digest of reviews, evaluations, and descriptions of all forms of nonprint media appearing in 132 periodicals and reviewing services. The 1988 volume of *MRD* includes about forty thousand citations to reviews and descriptions of films, video-cassettes, videodiscs, filmstrips, records and tapes, slides, transparencies, illustrations, globes, charts, media kits, and games. Primary emphasis is placed on instructional and informational media. Sections cover film and video, filmstrips, audio, and miscellaneous. Materials reviewed are listed alphabetically by title or other main entry. Entries include descriptive and cataloging information, audience level indications, review sources, review ratings (an indication of how positive or negative the original review was), and review digests (brief extracts from the original reviews). Indexes to the review listing include a video index (alphabetical list of titles available in video format), a general subject index for a broad subject approach using about ninety subject headings, an alphabetical subject index using Library of Congress subject headings, a reviewer index to evaluators of feature films, and a geographical index to foreign feature films.

Software Reviews on File is published monthly with excerpts of software reviews appearing in over 300 computer magazines. Indexing includes program names, categories of software, software publishers, and hardware for which the programs are designed. Indexes cumulate each month, with the January-December index covering the entire volume. Software covered ranges from computer games to sophisticated business programs. Entries include publisher, price, system requirements, publisher's description, and review extracts with an indication of review source and date.

Indexes for Different Literary Forms

Library collections in school, public, and academic libraries generally include many collected works: poetry anthologies, collections of plays or short stories, and collections of essays. Unless the contents of these volumes are analyzed during the cataloging process and the analytical entries made searchable directly in the library's catalog, the user of the catalog cannot easily determine whether the library holds an anthology that includes a particular play, short story, poem, or essay. The H. W. Wilson Company publishes three indexes that provide access to the contents of collections by author and subject: *Essay and General Literature Index*, *Play Index*, and *Short Story Index*. *Essay and General Literature Index* is an author and subject index to essays published in collections, with particular emphasis on materials in the humanities and social sciences. It is published semiannually, with an annual cumulation. Five-year cumulations are also published. Each issue includes a list of books indexed and a directory of publishers and distributors. *Essay and General Literature Index* is arranged in one alphabet and includes author entries, subject entries, and occasional title entries under significant phrases. Each entry includes the author and title of the essay together with brief information about the collection and the pages where the essay can be found. Entries under the name of a person follow the sequence: person's own works, works about the person's life (listed under the subdivision "About"), and criticism of an individual work (listed under the subdivision "About individual works"). It is available on CD-ROM and online from 1985.

Play Index is published at several-year intervals. The most recent volume, *Play Index, 1983-1987*, indexes 3,964 plays that were published during the period 1983-1987. The index covers both individual plays and plays in collections, written in or translated into English. Plays are tagged with *c* for children (through grade six) or *y* for young people (grades seven through ten), when those designations apply. The contents are in four parts. Part I is an author, title, and subject index, part II provides a cast analysis, part III has a list of collections indexed, and part IV provides a directory of publishers and distributors. In part I the most complete information is found under the author entries, which include name of the author, title of the play, a brief descriptive note, the number of acts and scenes, the size of the cast, and the number of sets required. For separately published plays, bibliographic information is given; for plays in collections, the name of the collection is identified. Title entries give the name of the author, and subject entries give the name of the author and title of the play. This tool can be used to identify plays meeting certain requirements, such as subject and cast composition, as well as to identify one or more collections containing a play when the title or author are known.

   Short Story Index appears annually, with five-year cumulations (the most recent covering 1984-1988). The 1990 volume indexes 5,035 stories published in 1989. About 80 percent of the stories appeared in 257 collections and the remainder appeared in periodicals indexed in *Humanities Index* and *Readers' Guide*. Part I contains the index to short stories, with author, title, and subject entries. As in *Play Index*, the author entry provides the most complete information on where the story can be found. The stories in periodicals are indexed only by authors and title. Subject entries include access through theme, locale, narrative form, and genre (for example, science fiction). Part II is a list of collections indexed, part III is a directory of publishers and distributors, and part IV is a directory of periodicals.

   All three of these indexes to literary forms may be helpful in collection development as well as in reference, since order information is given for the indexed collections. Reference librarians often annotate the lists of collections in these indexes to indicate holdings and location information. This saves the user a step, because the library's catalog does not have to be consulted to determine this information once the collection containing an essay, play, or short story of interest has been identified.

   Indexes to poetry anthologies are comparable to the indexes to collections in providing author, title, and subject indexing. In addition indexes like *The Columbia Granger's Index to Poetry* also index poems by first line, since that may be the information the patron remembers rather than the poem's title. The most recent edition of *The Columbia Granger's* indexes anthologies published through June 30, 1989. As noted in the introduction, it can answer such questions as: "Where can I find a poem whose title is the only thing about it I remember? What is the title of a poem whose first line I know? Where can I find some good poems on a subject I have to talk or write about next week?"[10] More than one hundred thousand poems, drawn from almost four hundred anthologies, are indexed in this edition. Several of the anthologies are collections of poetry translated from other languages. The list of anthologies has forty titles starred as recommended for first purchase. There are three indexes: title and first line, author, and subject. Titles and first lines are arranged in one alphabetical listing. Titles are distinguished by initial capital letters on the important words and all first line entries are followed by the title of the poem, if there is a title. Entries in the title and first line index include the author of the poem and an abbreviated symbol for each anthology that includes the poem. This must be checked in the List of Anthologies to find the complete bibliographic information. Starting from the author or subject index involves two more steps, since each leads to the titles of poems that in turn must be looked up to find the symbols for the anthologies prior to turning to the list of anthologies. Because the most recent edition does not cover all anthologies indexed in the previous editions, the latter should be retained to allow access to poems found only in older anthologies.

   Just as other types of indexes now have a CD-ROM format, indexes to literary forms are now available on CD-ROM. One example is CD-CoreWorks from Roth Publishing. The CD-ROM provides access to over 1,300 poetry collections, over 1,500 essay collections, over 300 short story collections, and 860 plays. It can be searched by title words, authors, first line words, translators, keywords, and play characters; Boolean logic can be used to combine search criteria. Citations retrieved refer to the source book title and page number. If a library does not have the collected works listed as part of its collection, copies of these works on microfiche can be purchased from the same publisher who produces the CD-ROM.

Search Strategies

The reference interview is an important part of assisting library users in accessing indexes and abstracts. Many users may be familiar with only the *Readers' Guide* and ask for it by name. If the library does have other indexes and abstracts available, it is important to determine the subject of interest and direct the user to the most appropriate indexes for the subject and type of material desired. The same phenomenon may occur in libraries with indexes on CD-ROM: because they are the most visible, they may be used even if other indexes in the collection would provide more appropriate sources for a particular search.

If a library user is in search of an article that is known to have appeared in a certain periodical, but for which no other information is available, the librarian can consult either a cumulative index for the specific periodical (if one is available) or an index or abstract that covers the periodical. The entry for the periodical in *Ulrich's International Periodicals Directory* provides notations to indicate coverage by indexes and abstracts. *The Index and Abstract Directory* provides comparable information. Some periodicals also include information about where they are indexed in the issues themselves. Joseph Marconi's *Indexed Periodicals: A Guide to 170 Years of Coverage in 33 Indexing Services* provides retrospective indexing information.[11] DIALOG Journal Name Finder is a helpful tool for identifying coverage of journal titles in online databases available on DIALOG. Records include a listing of the journal title as it appears in a database (such as a particular indexing or abstracting service), the DIALOG database (file) number in which the title is found, and the number of records in the file for that journal title. Because many indexes and abstracts only cover periodical titles selectively, it may be necessary to look in more than one index to find the particular article sought. Indexes also differ in time lag for indexing the same article where there is an overlap in coverage.

For the first-time user of an index, some instruction may be necessary. Although introductory material in the index should explain the scope and arrangement of entries and provide examples of searches, it may be more efficient for the librarian to tell the user the essential information directly as users may not be willing to take the time to read through the instructions. This is also an opportunity to advise on search strategy, such as beginning with the most specific heading and proceeding to more general headings as needed. The purpose of cross-references should be explained. It may also be necessary to explain how to interpret the various components of a bibliographic citation as well as how to locate materials in the library's collection. If citations contain abbreviations, then the librarian should point out the section of the index where these abbreviations are interpreted.

Chapters 4 and 5 provide additional discussion of search strategies of indexes and abstracts in printed and machine-readable form. Knowing the scope of the various indexes and abstracts is essential in selecting the most appropriate source(s) when verifying a citation or searching for information on a subject. Familiarity with the approaches to subject indexing used in each index or abstract is necessary to select the source(s) most likely to have the terminology required in searching a particular subject. If the librarian is unfamiliar with the topic sought, it may be necessary first to check reference books such as encyclopedias and dictionaries to develop a list of related terms under which to search. As noted in chapter 4, indexing vocabularies are not standardized, so it may be necessary to reformulate a subject search in checking multiple indexes and abstracts. Access to online and CD-ROM sources, as well as printed indexes with keyword indexes, allows the use of terms appearing in titles and/or abstracts in addition to terms selected from controlled vocabularies.

■ ═══ ■

19.1

Not in My Backyard

A college student in an environmental policy class has asked for help in finding information on the "NIMBY syndrome." The professor has listed it as one of several possible topics for a paper that is to compare the attitudes of environmental activists with those held in other sectors such as government and industry. A quick check using a keyword search on NIMBY in the online catalog yielded nothing. The librarian then turned to the latest edition of the *Acronyms, Initialisms and Abbreviations Dictionary*[12] and learned that NIMBY stands for "Not in My Back Yard," with the supplementary note "i.e., garbage incinerators, prisons, roads, etc." Looking for a more detailed definition, he also checked the *Third Barnhart Dictionary of New English*[13] and found a definition for "nimby": "opposition by a community or a group within a community to the establishment in its midst of a public facility which it regards as undesirable, such as a prison, a waste dump, a shelter for the homeless, or a drug rehabilitation center." The definition indicated that the term could be used with regard to both environmental and other issues, but no synonyms or related terms were given.

The librarian decided to begin by looking in *Readers' Guide to Periodical Literature*, where a few articles were found under NIMBY syndrome in periodicals such as *The Mother Earth News, Omni, The Christian Century, Time, National Wildlife*, and *Environment*. While the student felt that these would be a useful starting point for her research, particularly the article in *Environment* by John H. Gervers titled "The NIMBY Syndrome: Is It Inevitable?" (from the October 1987 issue), she hoped to find some more scholarly sources. Checking *Social Sciences Index, General Science Index*, and *PAIS International in Print* with the NIMBY syndrome heading yielded nothing. The librarian explained that the student might have more success checking CD-ROM sources that allowed searching on keywords from article titles since NIMBY syndrome was not yet an established subject heading except in *Readers' Guide*. He noted that the Permuterm Subject Index in the citation indexes also allows keyword searching. In addition the student could use known relevant articles as starting points for searches in the Citation Index. Since the student had never used *Science Citation Index* before, the librarian spent some time showing her how to use the various parts. NIMBY did appear as a keyword in the Permuterm Subject Index. The librarian showed the student how to go from the author names listed under keywords in the Permuterm Subject Index to the Source Index to get full bibliographic information for the articles, such as S. Robinson's "Resource Recovery and the NIMBY Syndrome," in *Water Engineering & Management*. They also looked up "Gervers JH, 87" in the Citation Index and found a citing article that they then checked in the Source Index for full bibliographic information. The article, "Siting America's Geologic Repository for High-Level Nuclear Waste — Implications for Environmental Policy," by J. Lemons and C. Malone in a 1989 issue of *Environmental Management* sounded promising even though it did not have the phrase NIMBY syndrome in the title.

The librarian showed the student the CD-ROM workstations and suggested some databases to check — Newspaper Abstracts Ondisc, PAIS, Applied Science & Technology Index — searching on the word NIMBY. After completing her search on these databases, the student returned to the reference desk with some printouts for help in locating the articles she had found. The librarian reviewed how to

(Box 19.1 continues on page 440.)

Box 19.1 — *Continued*

use the library's database of journal and newspaper holdings. He explained that articles not held locally could be requested through interlibrary loan. The student was especially interested in one of the abstracts located through the search on Newspaper Abstracts Ondisc, briefly summarizing an article from the January 20, 1991, issue of the *Boston Globe* with the headline "Author Charts Rise of NIMBYs." It reported that Kent E. Portney, a Newton, Massachusetts, resident, had written a book about the not-in-my-backyard, or NIMBY, syndrome. The student wondered whether the book had already been published. The librarian found no entry for the book in the most recent edition of *Books in Print*, but did find the needed information in *Forthcoming Books*,[14] which listed the title as *Siting Hazardous Waste Treatment Facilities: The Nimby Syndrome* and gave the publisher, ISBN, and expected publication date (February 1991). The student took down the information, saying she would contact the publisher to determine whether the book was now available. Satisfied that she had a number of good leads to material on her topic, the student headed for the library's periodical section to locate the actual articles.

Notes

1.   Charles R. Andrews, "Cooperation at Its Best: The Committee on Wilson Indexes at Work," *RQ* 24 (Winter 1984): 155-61.

2.   Carol Tenopir and Timothy Ray Smith, "General Periodical Indexes on CD-ROM," *CD-ROM Professional* 3 (July 1990): 70-81.

3.   Alexa Jaffurs, "Newspapers on CD-ROM: Timely Access to Current Events," *Laserdisk Professional* 2 (May 1989): 19-26.

4.   Joseph A. Puccio, *Serials Reference Work* (Englewood, Colo.: Libraries Unlimited, 1989), 164-66.

5.   Carol Tenopir, "Wilson Branches Out," *Library Journal* 116 (March 1, 1991): 73-74.

6.   Other Wilson indexes devoted to broad subject areas but not discussed in this chapter include *Applied Science & Technology Index*, *Art Index*, *Biological & Agricultural Index*, *Education Index*, *Index to Legal Periodicals*, and *Library Literature*. *Biography Index* is described in chapter 14 and *Bibliographic Index* is described in chapter 18.

7.   Frances A. Brahmi, "SCI CD Edition: ISI's New CD-ROM Product," *Medical Reference Services Quarterly* 8 (Summer 1989): 1-13.

8.   Ellis Mount and Beatrice Kovacs, *Using Science and Technology Information Sources* (Phoenix, Ariz.: Oryx Press, 1991), 189p.

9.   "Introduction," *Book Review Index* 26 (September-October 1990): vii.

10.   "A Key to the World of Poetry," *The Columbia Granger's Index to Poetry*, 9th ed., edited by Edith P. Hazen and Deborah J. Fryer (New York: Columbia University Press, 1990), v.

11.   Joseph V. Marconi, *Indexed Periodicals: A Guide to 170 Years of Coverage in 33 Indexing Services* (Ann Arbor, Mich.: Pierian Press, 1976).

12. *Acronyms, Initialisms and Abbreviations Dictionary*, 15th ed. (Detroit, Mich.: Gale Research, 1990), 2,313.

13. *Third Barnhart Dictionary of New English* (New York: H. W. Wilson, 1990), 343.

14. *Forthcoming Books* 26 (February 1991): 618.

List of Sources

Abridged Readers' Guide to Periodical Literature, 1935- . New York: H. W. Wilson, 1936- . Monthly except June-August, with quarterly and annual cumulations.

Academic Index. Foster City, Calif.: Information Access Company. (DIALOG File 88, BRS File ACAD; also available on CD-ROM.)

Access: The Supplementary Index to Periodicals. Evanston, Ill.: John Gordon Burke, 1975- . Three issues per year with annual cumulation.

Arts & Humanities Citation Index, 1976- . Philadelphia: Institute for Scientific Information, 1978- . Semiannual.

Arts & Humanities Search. Philadelphia: Institute for Scientific Information. (DIALOG File 439, BRS File AHCI.)

Book Review Digest. New York: H. W. Wilson, 1905- . Monthly except February and July, with quarterly and annual cumulations. (Online on WILSONLINE; also available on CD-ROM.)

Book Review Index. Detroit, Mich.: Gale Research, 1965- . Bimonthly with annual cumulations. Twenty-year cumulation, 1965-1984. (DIALOG File 137.)

Business Periodicals Index. New York: H. W. Wilson, 1958- . Monthly except August, with quarterly and annual cumulations. (Online on WILSONLINE and BRS; also available on CD-ROM.)

CD-CoreWorks. [CD-ROM]. Great Neck, N.Y.: Roth Publishing.

The Columbia Granger's Index to Poetry. 9th ed. Edited by Edith P. Hazen and Deborah J. Fryer. New York: Columbia University Press, 1990. 2,082p.

Comprehensive Dissertation Index, 1861-1972. 37 vols. Ann Arbor, Mich.: University Microfilms International, 1973. Supplemented by ten-year cumulation 1973-1982, five-year cumulation 1983-1987, and annual supplements. (Online as part of DIALOG File 35, BRS File DISS.)

DIALOG Journal Name Finder. Palo Alto, Calif.: Dialog Information Services, Inc. (DIALOG File 414.)

Dissertation Abstracts International. Ann Arbor, Mich.: University Microfilms International, 1938- . Monthly with annual cumulated author and subject indexes. (Online as part of DIALOG File 35, BRS File DISS.)

Dissertation Abstracts Ondisc. [CD-ROM]. Ann Arbor, Mich.: University Microfilms International.

Essay and General Literature Index, 1900- . New York: H. W. Wilson, 1934- . Semiannual with bound annual and five-year cumulations. (Online on WILSONLINE; also available on CD-ROM.)

General Periodicals Ondisc. [CD-ROM]. Ann Arbor, Mich.: University Microfilms International.

General Science Index. New York: H. W. Wilson, 1978- . Monthly except June and December, with quarterly and annual cumulations. (Online on WILSONLINE and BRS; also available on CD-ROM.)

Humanities Index. New York: H. W. Wilson, 1974- . Quarterly with annual cumulations. (Formerly *International Index*, 1907-1965; *Social Sciences and Humanities Index*, 1965-1974.) (Online on WILSONLINE and BRS; also available on CD-ROM.)

The Index and Abstract Directory: An International Guide to Services and Serials Coverage. Birmingham, Ala.: EBSCO Publishing, 1989- . Biennial.

Magazine Article Summaries. [CD-ROM]. Topsfield, Mass.: EBSCO Subscription Services.

Magazine ASAP. Foster City, Calif.: Information Access Company. (DIALOG File 647, BRS File MSAP.)

Magazine Index. [microfilm]. Foster City, Calif.: Information Access Company, 1976- . Monthly. (DIALOG File 47, BRS File MAGS; also available on CD-ROM.)

Magazines for Libraries. 6th ed. Edited by Bill Katz and Linda Sternberg Katz. New York: R. R. Bowker, 1989. 1,159p.

Marconi, Joseph V. *Indexed Periodicals: A Guide to 170 Years of Coverage in 33 Indexing Services*. Ann Arbor, Mich.: Pierian Press, 1976. 416p.

Media Review Digest, 1970- . Ann Arbor, Mich.: Pierian Press, 1971- . Annual.

National Newspaper Index. [microfilm]. Foster City, Calif.: Information Access Company, 1979- . Monthly. (DIALOG File 111, BRS File NOOZ; also available on CD-ROM.)

New York Times Index. New York: Times, 1913- . Semimonthly with quarterly and annual cumulations.

NewsBank Electronic Index. [CD-ROM]. New Canaan, Conn.: NewsBank.

NewsBank Index. New Canaan, Conn.: NewsBank, 1982- . Monthly with quarterly and annual cumulations.

Newspaper Abstracts Ondisc. [CD-ROM]. Ann Arbor, Mich.: University Microfilms International. (Also online as part of DIALOG File 603.)

Nineteenth Century Readers' Guide to Periodical Literature, 1800-1899 with supplementary indexing, 1900-1922. Edited by Helen Grant Cushing and Ada V. Morris. 2 vols. New York: H. W. Wilson, 1944.

PAIS Foreign Language Index. New York: Public Affairs Information Service, 1972-1990.

PAIS International. New York: Public Affairs Information Service. (DIALOG File 49, BRS File PAIS.)

PAIS International in Print. New York: Public Affairs Information Service, 1991- . Monthly with annual cumulations.

PAIS on CD-ROM. [CD-ROM]. New York: Public Affairs Information Service.

PAIS Subject Headings. 2d ed. Edited by Alice Picon and Gwen Sloan. New York: Public Affairs Information Service, 1990. 536p.

Periodical Abstracts Ondisc. [CD-ROM]. Ann Arbor, Mich.: University Microfilms International.

Play Index. 1949- . New York: H. W. Wilson, 1953- . Irregular with multiyear volumes.

Poole's Index to Periodical Literature, 1802-1881. Rev. ed. 2 vols. Boston: Houghton, 1891. Supplements, January 1882-January 1907. 5 vols. Boston: Houghton, 1887-1908.

Popular Magazine Review Online. Topsfield, Mass.: EBSCO Subscription Services. (BRS File PMRO.)

Public Affairs Information Service Bulletin. New York: Public Affairs Information Service, 1915-1990. Annual cumulations.

Readers' Guide Abstracts, 1984- . New York: H. W. Wilson, 1986- . Ten issues per year with semiannual cumulations. (Online on WILSONLINE and BRS; also available on CD-ROM.)

Readers' Guide to Periodical Literature, 1900- . New York: H. W. Wilson, 1905- . Seventeen issues per year with quarterly and annual cumulations. (Online on WILSONLINE and BRS; also available on CD-ROM.)

Science Citation Index, 1945- . Philadelphia: Institute for Scientific Information, 1961- . Bimonthly with annual and five- or ten-year cumulations. (Available on CD-ROM.)

SciSearch. Philadelphia: Institute for Scientific Information. (DIALOG Files 34, 432, 433, 434; ORBIT File SCIS.)

Short Story Index, 1900- . New York: H. W. Wilson, 1953- . Semiannual with annual and five-year cumulations.

Social Sciences Citation Index, 1956- . Philadelphia: Institute for Scientific Information, 1973- . Three times per year with annual and five-year cumulations. (Available on CD-ROM.)

Social Sciences Index. New York: H. W. Wilson, 1974- . Quarterly with annual cumulations. (Formerly *International Index*, 1907-1965; *Social Sciences and Humanities Index*, 1965-1974.) (Online on WILSONLINE and BRS; also available on CD-ROM.)

Social SciSearch. Philadelphia: Institute for Scientific Information. (DIALOG File 7, BRS File SSCI.)

Software Reviews on File. New York: Facts on File, 1985- . Monthly, with annual cumulation of indexes.

Ulrich's International Periodicals Directory, Now Including Irregular Serials and Annuals. 29th ed. 3 vols. New York: R. R. Bowker, 1990. Updated quarterly by *Ulrich's Update*. (DIALOG File 480, BRS File ULRI; also available on CD-ROM as Ulrich's Plus.)

Vertical File Index, 1932/34- . New York: H. W. Wilson, 1935- . Monthly except August. (Online on WILSONLINE.)

Additional Readings

Bailey, Charles W., Jr., Jeff Fadell, Judy E. Myers, and Thomas C. Wilson. "The Index Expert System: A Knowledge-Based System to Assist Users in Index Selection." *Reference Services Review* 17 (Winter 1989): 19-28.
　The authors describe development of an expert system to assist library users in selecting appropriate indexes and abstracts, in both printed and CD-ROM formats, to meet their information needs. The Index Expert seeks to capture certain aspects of the reference librarian's expertise and make this knowledge available to the user whenever it is needed.

Cleveland, Donald B., and Ana D. Cleveland. *Introduction to Indexing and Abstracting*. 2d ed. Englewood, Colo.: Libraries Unlimited, 1990. 329p.
The authors describe the types of indexes and abstracts, indexing and abstracting methods and procedures, and index evaluation. The book includes a glossary and a bibliography.

Garfield, Eugene. *Citation Indexing: Its Theory and Applications in Science, Technology, and Humanities*. New York: Wiley, 1979. 274p.
Eugene Garfield, who originally developed the *Science Citation Index*, covers many aspects of citation indexing including the design and production of a citation index, the citation index as a search tool, and applications of data from citation indexes in citation analysis.

Grogan, Denis. *Periodicals and Their Guides*. London: Clive Bingley, 1987. 114p. (Vol. 4 in Grogan's Case Studies in Reference Work).
The fifty-eight cases in this volume have been chosen to demonstrate how abstracting and indexing services are used to exploit the information found in periodicals and newspapers. The cases include examples of terminological problems in subject searching, the difficulties of composite topics, the advantages and disadvantages of online and manual searching, author searching, and the use of citation indexes.

Jaffurs, Alexa. "Newspapers on CD-ROM: Timely Access to Current Events." *Laserdisk Professional* 2 (May 1989): 19-26.
This article provides a comparison of three indexes to newspapers on CD-ROM: Newsbank Electronic Index, National Newspaper Index, and Newspaper Abstracts Ondisc. Features of each are described, including coverage and cost, system requirements, and search capabilities.

Neufeld, M. Lynne, and Martha Cornog. *Abstracting and Indexing Career Guide*. 2d ed. Philadelphia: National Federation of Abstracting and Information Services, 1986. 63p.
This guide provides answers to such questions as: What is "abstracting and indexing"? Who uses abstracts and indexes? What do abstractors and indexers do? Who hires abstractors and indexers? What education do abstractors and indexers require? Appendixes include descriptions of the American Society of Indexers, the Indexing and Abstracting Society of Canada, and the National Federation of Abstracting and Information Services.

Noras, Sibylle R. "All the News That's Fit to Screen — The Development of Fulltext Newspaper Databases." *The Australian Library Journal* 38 (February 1989): 17-27.
The author reviews developments in full-text newspaper databases and their implications for researchers, management, and librarians. She describes U.S., Canadian, British, and Australian newspaper databases and online vendors.

Puccio, Joseph A. *Serials Reference Work*. Englewood, Colo.: Libraries Unlimited, 1989. 228p.
This book is intended as a practical guide to the tools and techniques of serials reference work. Of particular interest are chapter 5 on periodical indexes and abstracts and chapter 12 on newspaper indexes and abstracts.

Rowley, Jennifer E. "Printed versus Online Indexes." *The Indexer* 13 (April 1983): 188-89.
Rowley presents a concise summary comparing the major features of indexes in printed versus online format. Many of the features listed for online indexes apply to indexes on CD-ROM as well.

Tenopir, Carol, and Timothy Ray Smith. "General Periodical Indexes on CD-ROM." *CD-ROM Professional* 3 (July 1990): 70-81.
This article examines products available from EBSCO Electronic Information, the H. W. Wilson Company, University Microfilms International, and Information Access Company, explaining the coverage and features of their CD-ROM offerings covering general periodicals.

GOVERNMENT DOCUMENTS AND STATISTICS SOURCES

Uses and Characteristics

Government documents are used in virtually every library, regardless of its type, size, or location. These documents are authoritative, comprehensive, inexpensive, and easy to obtain. They are used by statisticians, social workers, teachers, politicians, parents, gardeners, scientists—in short, by everyone who ever has a need for information.

Government documents are officially defined as: "Informational matter which is published as an individual document at Government expense, or as required by law."[1] In practice, government documents are publications which may be in the form of books, periodicals, microfiche, microfilm, tapes, compact discs, or other formats, and which are published by or for a government agency (municipal, local, state, federal, foreign government, or intergovernmental organization). They may be the official records of the agencies, as in the case of the *Congressional Record*, the *Federal Register*, and *U.S. Reports*,[2] or they may be technical reports which make available the results of government-funded research. Some are administrative publications, such as *Informing the Nation*[3] (General Accounting Office) and the Annual Report of the Department of Energy;[4] others are statistical, such as the *Statistical Abstract of the United States* (Bureau of the Census) and *Business Statistics*[5] (Bureau of Economic Analysis). They can be as esoteric and technical as *Theoretical Atomic Physics for Fusion*[6] (Department of Energy), or they may be of general interest, as in the case of *Health Consequences of Involuntary Smoking*[7] (Surgeon General).

Government publications clearly encompass many different kinds of materials aimed at all types of audiences. The U.S. Government Printing Office (GPO) is the largest printing house in the world. Included among its publications are many reference sources which are essential in all libraries, as well as some with limited application and of interest only to larger academic or special libraries. This chapter focuses on the most important reference sources from the U.S. government, along with several nongovernmental titles which are important reference sources for use with government documents.

As noted, the distinguishing characteristic of a government document is that it is published by or for a government agency. This fact affects the way librarians evaluate, select, and use this material. Strategies for answering questions pertaining to government information and statistics and the most important reference sources for each type of question are discussed later in this chapter.

445

Organization of Documents

Federal government publications are unique in that they generally fit into a classification system which is determined by the federal government. The Superintendent of Documents classification system (hereafter called the SuDoc system) is based on issuing agency rather than subject arrangement. Class numbers are assigned based on agency, subagency, and publication type. For example, the SuDoc number for the *County and City Data Book*, C3.134/3:C83 is constructed as follows:

C	Department of Commerce
3.	Bureau of the Census
134/	*Statistical Abstract of the United States*
3:	Supplement
C83	*County and City Data Book*

The SuDoc number is assigned by a GPO classifier and, once assigned, is used in many standard bibliographies (*Monthly Catalog of United States Government Publications*, *PAIS International in Print*, *CIS/Index*). Use of this system enables the library user to go from the bibliography or index directly to the shelf list or to the shelf to find an item. It permits browsing of an agency's or subagency's publications and allows a user who is familiar with the system to locate easily the same or similar items in another library which uses those class numbers. For the librarian, it can eliminate one step in the cataloging process and get the book to the shelf more quickly. As an alternative, documents can be classified using Dewey Decimal or Library of Congress numbers, and can be integrated into the reference or circulating collections. The classification system chosen will, to some extent, determine how the collection is used and whether reference service is provided mainly by documents specialists or by general reference staff.

Uses of Documents

The way in which reference librarians use documents is no different from the way in which they use other reference tools. It is affected by the classification system chosen, which will segregate documents from other materials if they are in SuDoc or integrate them if they are in Dewey Decimal or Library of Congress classifications. The classification and location of government documents will determine whether they are used mainly by a specialist in a documents department, by a subject specialist, or by a general reference librarian. In many larger libraries, it will be a combination of all three. Because documents are often indexed only by highly specialized indexes (*CIS*, *Monthly Catalog*), there is usually an instructional component to documents reference work. It is important to be able to interpret all of the essential parts of the citations presented in such indexes. The indexes tell the user if a title is a depository item, through use of a special symbol (.) and item number, and whether a title is part of a series or subseries. It is often more desirable to assist and instruct the user in the process of using an index to identify a document than to locate the document and the needed information. By doing so, the user gains skill in that process and will be able independently to find additional information or use those skills on another occasion. This process requires more time on the part of the librarian, but is a worthwhile and rewarding aspect of documents librarianship.

In many cases, patrons use documents to do statistical or legislative reference work. The nature of these inquiries means that a user may need some interpretive help from the librarian. It is necessary to be very familiar with the appropriate reference tools in order to maximize the help given to the patron.

Another major category of reference use of documents is for bibliographic verification, or supplying bibliographic information. The question may take the form of: "What is the *Serial Set* volume number of House Document 91-102?" or "What series includes the title: '*Housebat Management*?'" The sources used to answer such questions are unique to government documents and must be mastered so they can be easily used when the occasion arises.

Evaluation

In most cases, a government document reference source on any subject is the final and sole authority; it cannot be compared with similar sources for currency or accuracy. Because the federal government is the largest collector of statistical data in the world, most trade publishers get their data from government documents, repackage it, perhaps abridge or enhance the data, offer the data in an electronic medium, or add unique features such as expanded indexing, cross-tabulations, and analyses. Nevertheless, the fact remains that the original sources are government documents, so evaluation depends mainly on comparing features, format, and ease of use rather than accuracy or currency of information. There will be instances when, because of space constraints, librarians may choose to store reports in microform rather than on paper. They may also need to offer data in a CD-ROM or diskette version which is more flexible and user-friendly than the paper product, in order to meet user demands. In those cases, a trade edition may be preferred to the original document.

Similarly, government-funded research, as reported in the research and development literature, and records of government operations in administrative reports, present unique and original information. Librarians may again have a choice of paper, microfiche, or electronic formats. They also have an opportunity to choose commercially published sources which analyze factual data or present additional information. Examples of these types of enhancements are: *Politics in America*,[8] which goes beyond basic information from the *Official Congressional Directory* to present facts about congressional districts, as well as voting analyses; and *C Q Weekly Report*, which gives background information about issues rather than just the bare facts as presented by congressional committee reports and hearings.

An example of a basic government document source which is available in multiple formats is the *Monthly Catalog of United States Government Publications*. The paper edition is discussed later in this chapter in the section on catalogs and bibliographies. It is also available on computer tape, for cataloging purposes, as well as in microform, online, and on CD-ROM. While the basic *Catalog* is well indexed by title, title keyword, author, SuDoc number, series, report number, contract number, and subject, the electronic editions have the added flexibility of allowing for the use of Boolean logic and free-text searching of the entire entry.

The ultimate choice of edition and format is individual and depends, to a large extent, on a library's available space, its budget for equipment, facilities already in place, and user needs. For a complete discussion of electronic formats, see chapter 5.

Selection

The enormous variety of government publications requires librarians to employ several different strategies for identifying and selecting documents that will meet the needs of their users. In similar fashion, there is more than one method of acquiring government documents, once they have been selected. This section describes both selection and acquisition processes commonly employed by librarians in obtaining government publications.

Identification

Selection of government documents has a formal and an informal component. In the formal sense, a librarian may make regular use of nongovernmental selection tools, such as *Government Publications Review*[9] or *Library Journal*,[10] which regularly review new documents, and *Government Reference Books*, a biennial publication which is an authoritative, annotated guide to reference publications issued by U.S. government agencies during the two-year period covered by each volume. One can also use bibliographies from the Government Printing Office which list but do not review or annotate titles. These include: *New Books*, *GPO Sales Publications Reference File*, *Subject Bibliographies*, and *U.S. Government Books*, as well as newsletters or new book lists from various agencies (e.g., *Library of Congress Information Bulletin*,[11] *Census and You*[12]). The reference librarian can build a collection based on Gladys Sachse's *U.S. Government Publications for Small and Medium-Sized Public Libraries*[13] or *The Federal Depository Library Manual*.[14] In an informal sense, sometimes the best and only way to select new documents is to be attuned to the needs and tastes of library users and to be aware of current events. Simply by carefully reading a daily paper and listening attentively to the media when they hear the phrase "in a government study released yesterday," librarians can identify the information sources which will be of the most interest to their patrons. Depending on the expectations of users, a librarian may anticipate a request for facts or for the full text of the material cited in such oblique references. In many cases, a letter or telephone call to the appropriate agency will procure the information required and/or a copy of that recently released study. While the basic sources can be easily identified and are, for the most part, discussed later in this chapter, the less common sources that patrons of a particular library want will have to be identified through the librarian's alertness and sensitivity to their needs.

Acquisition

Just as identification of documents is a multifaceted activity, so is acquisition. Again, because documents are published by or for a government agency, their acquisition may, depending on the situation, be either more or less complicated than the process of acquiring trade publications. In the approximately fourteen hundred U.S. Federal Depository Libraries, acquisition is a very straightforward business. Through the depository program, the Government Printing Office makes thousands of federal publications available to libraries at no charge. There are at least two depositories in each congressional district. Included are public, university, college, and special libraries. Most are *selective depositories*, meaning that the documents librarian has the opportunity to select categories or types of items from various agencies. In contrast, a *regional depository* receives all materials available on deposit, and acts as a resource library for selectives in its region, as well as for other nearby libraries which are not federal depositories. Depending on the categories of items which a library has pre-selected, current documents are sent on a regular schedule. In a depository library, alternative methods of acquisition are a consideration only for multiple copies or replacements and for titles which were not pre-selected. In those cases, and for nondepository libraries, the following procedures can be applied.

Titles that are sold by the Government Printing Office can be identified in *GPO Sales Publications Reference File (PRF)*, a quarterly microfiche listing of titles in print and for sale by the GPO. The librarian can easily determine the in-print status and price of a publication. In order to purchase from the GPO, the library must be able to prepay the order, a routine which can be facilitated by establishment of a GPO deposit account on which the GPO draws and to which the library makes deposits to maintain a minimum balance. Libraries may also purchase through vendors, in the same way they would order trade publications. In addition, with little effort and no expense, it is frequently possible to obtain free copies of some publications by sending a request directly to an agency. Most standard government reference sources are available only as sales items from the GPO, but titles which are less in demand, which are printed in smaller quantities, and which may have special use in a particular situation, can sometimes be obtained directly from the issuing agency at no charge.

Important General Sources

Government-produced reference sources fall into many of the categories treated elsewhere in this text, such as directories, fact books, catalogs, and indexes. Other tools are unique to the world of government publications, because they provide comprehensive coverage of the legislative and regulatory activities of the government. Statistical reference tools are also treated in this chapter, since many of the most important general sources of this type are compiled and published by the government.

Guides

Guides to government documents are useful to librarians who need to know when to use a particular type of source and how to use it. For example, when a patron needs to know details about an eighteenth-century report, a legislative document from the 100th Congress, or thirty years of data on the Gross National Product, and the librarians are uncertain about which source to consult for help in answering those questions, they would turn first to a guide to documents. This is analogous to consulting Sheehy's *Guide to Reference Books*,[15] reading the annotations, and then choosing the source most likely to contain the answer to the question. The guides provide information about the government in general, publication practices of various government agencies, and details about coverage of important reference sources.

Joe Morehead's guide, *Introduction to United States Public Documents*, its fourth edition due in 1992, is a basic introductory text. It presents the bibliographic structure of federal government publications and covers both current and historical reference sources. Morehead provides information about the government, the Government Printing Office, the Superintendent of Documents, and the depository library system, all of which is fundamental to understanding why documents sources are indispensable and how documents are acquired and organized. This guide also provides detailed information on how to use the most important reference tools for technical report literature, as well as those for legislative and administrative publications. Coverage includes statistical, geographic, audiovisual, and electronic sources. Appendixes include a list of online databases and a list of abbreviations and acronyms.

United States Government Publications by Anne Boyd and Rae Rips, and *Government Publications and Their Use* by Laurence Schmeckebier and Roy Eastin, while older publications, are still extremely useful guides. Because so much of the reference work done with government publications involves historical research using original documents, there will always be a need for these guides, which provide complete and useful descriptions of basic bibliographic, administrative, and legislative sources from earlier historical periods.

A recently published guide, *Tapping the Government Grapevine*, by Judith Schiek Robinson, is an excellent introduction to documents librarianship and documents usage. It presents, in an extremely clear and readable format, basic information on government agencies, their functions and publications, how to use reference services, and how to administer a documents collection. The graphics, flowcharts, examples, and bibliographies make this book as attractive as it is useful.

Catalogs and Bibliographies

Catalogs and bibliographies are used in reference work for a variety of reasons. First, they can be used as an aid to selection of new books for the library. Librarians can browse the catalog for new titles or new editions and can use the catalog to supply bibliographic or ordering information for new titles. Second, catalogs are used as an index or guide to the collection. That is, when librarians want to know if the library owns a document on a particular topic, or need to know whether the government has published in a subject area, they can consult these sources as a guide to their own collections as well as a guide to all titles cataloged by the Government Printing Office.

The most basic of all catalogs is the *Monthly Catalog of United States Government Publications*. The *Monthly Catalog* (for a sample entry, see figure 20.1) serves as the most complete record of titles cataloged by the Superintendent of Documents. The *Catalog* has been published since 1895 and underwent a significant change in format in July 1976. Since that time, entries have been in a standard cataloging format, and now present complete bibliographic information along with depository item numbers. The *Catalog* is organized by SuDoc number; hence, agency publications are listed together. Indexes by author, title, title keyword, subject, series/report number, and SuDoc number are published in each monthly issue, and are cumulated semiannually and annually. Each index has specific uses. The subject index, which employs Library of Congress subject headings, is used by inquirers who want to know if the government has published anything on a particular subject, such as grizzly bears, forest fires, or trade with Kuwait. Title and author indexes are usually used to verify a bibliographic citation or to identify a title when only part of the relevant information is known. Series/report number indexes help to draw together reports on a similar topic by a single agency.

The *Monthly Catalog* is used for identification of titles, for ordering information, and as a primary access tool to any library's documents collection. In a library in which government documents are not typically cataloged and entered into a card catalog or online catalog, the *Monthly Catalog* provides access to the library's collection. The *Monthly Catalog* is available on deposit in the traditional paper format, and can be purchased on CD-ROM from many publishers. It can be searched online through DIALOG or BRS, and records can also be accessed through OCLC. The CD-ROM format provides flexible searching, and is particularly useful in libraries in which documents are not integrated into an online catalog. The *Monthly Catalog* includes an annual *Serials Supplement* which lists periodicals, annuals, and other regular serials and a *Serial Set Supplement* (listing House and Senate Committee reports and documents).

GPO Sales Publications Reference File (*PRF*) is a microfiche catalog (48x reduction) listing all sales publications from the Superintendent of Documents which are in print, forthcoming, or recently out-of-stock. It is a useful selection too, but is more important as a reference aid for supplying order information for library patrons or librarians who want to purchase documents. It is revised bimonthly with monthly updates. Microfiches are arranged by GPO Stock Number, SuDoc number, and keyword. Each entry includes the entire bibliographic information. It can also be searched online through DIALOG.

Subject Bibliographies, which number over 250, are irregularly revised lists of sales titles which range from anthropology to zoology, and include reference books, pamphlets, audiovisuals, monographs, and periodicals. Entries are alphabetical by title, and include date, pagination, SuDoc number, order information, and (in some cases) an annotation. For reference usage, the *Subject Bibliographies* present a concise list of titles on a topic, including many current and some older sources. Their limitation is that they cover only in-print sales publications, and thus omit many unpriced titles that could be found through the *Monthly Catalog*.

SAMPLE ENTRY

Monthly Catalog descriptive cataloging entries follow the precepts of the *Anglo-American Cataloguing Rules*, 2nd ed., 1988 revision, the Library of Congress Rule Interpretations, the *GPO Cataloging Guidelines*, and the several pertinent OCLC format documents. All name and series authorities are in AACR2 format, and are established through the Library of Congress Name Authorities Cooperative Project (NACO). The subject headings used in the GPO cataloging are derived from the *Library of Congress Subject Headings*, 11th ed.

The following sample entry is an artificial, composite record, designed to illustrate the major features of a *Monthly Catalog* bibliographic citation.

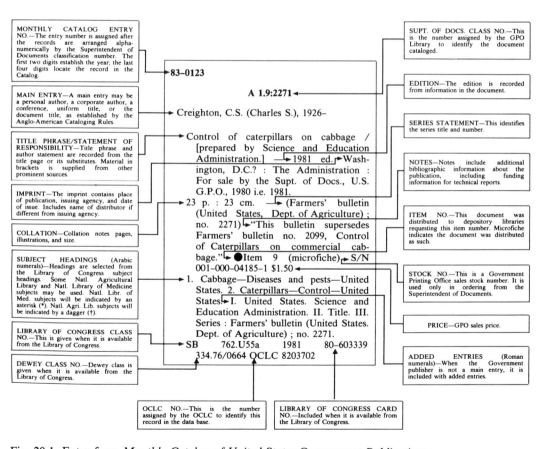

Fig. 20.1. Entry from *Monthly Catalog of United States Government Publications*.

Since 1982, the Superintendent of Documents has also published *U.S. Government Books*, an annotated list of popular monographs and periodicals which are for sale, and *New Books*, a bimonthly, unannotated list of titles placed on sale during the preceding two months. Both include ordering information and order forms and are used primarily for current awareness.

The federal government produces specialized indexes to provide access to reports published as a result of government-funded or contract research. The most general and comprehensive is *Government Reports Announcements and Index* (*GRAI*). A typical question arises when a patron has what appears to be a citation to a research report from a government agency and wants to know how to obtain a copy. If there is no indication that the title is available from the Government Printing Office, or if a search of the *Monthly Catalog* or the *PRF* does not turn up information on availability, it is appropriate to search *GRAI*. Through use of the keyword, personal author, corporate author, or report/accession number indexes, the user is referred to a complete bibliographic citation with all relevant report numbers, a very detailed abstract, subject descriptors, and the price for a microfiche or paper copy. Abstracts are presented in a broad subject arrangement. Reports indexed in *GRAI* are available for purchase from the National Technical Information Service (NTIS). *GRAI* can be searched online (as NTIS) through DIALOG and BRS, and is available on CD-ROM as well. In addition to *GRAI*, there are more focused indexes, such as *Energy Research Abstracts*,[16] *Scientific and Technical Aerospace Reports*,[17] and *Selected Water Resources Abstracts*.[18] Their organization and usage are similar to those of *GRAI*, but their subject coverage is narrower, and periodical citations may be included along with the references to research and development reports. They, too, may be searched online through DIALOG.[19]

Periodical Indexes

Government periodicals are indexed by many indexes which treat these documents in the same way they would cover any other periodical. Examination of the list of periodicals indexed by such sources as *Readers' Guide*,[20] *PAIS International in Print*,[21] *Education Index*,[22] or *Current Index to Journals in Education*[23] will reveal that government documents are well represented. There are, however, many useful but less well-known periodicals that are indexed only by more specialized indexes. Examples of these specialized indexes are the *Index to U.S. Government Periodicals* and the *American Statistics Index*. The *Index to U.S. Government Periodicals*, published by Infordata, is a quarterly index to approximately 175 federal periodicals which offer articles of reference and research value. It covers a small percentage of all periodicals published by the government and does not include abstracts, but the coverage ranges from technical to popular journals for a special audience, and the subject indexing is quite good. This index is used in situations when the user needs current periodical articles on subjects relating to government operations and/or policies, but finds that a general index like *Readers' Guide* does not include enough material that is issued by the government. The *Index to U.S. Government Periodicals* provides author and subject access (see figure 20.2 for examples of citations). The list of periodicals indexed includes SuDoc numbers. *American Statistics Index* is an example of a highly specialized index to the hundreds of daily, weekly, monthly, quarterly, semiannual, and annual statistical reports produced by the government which are not easily accessed. This title is discussed more fully in this chapter's section on statistical sources.

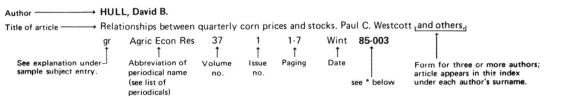

SAMPLE AUTHOR ENTRY

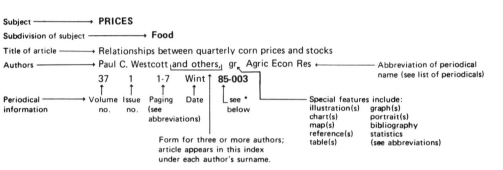

SAMPLE SUBJECT ENTRY

* Microfiche identifying number for ordering this periodical from Index to U.S. Government Periodicals under title CURRENT U.S. GOVERNMENT PERIODICALS ON MICROFICHE, in the 1985 series. Contact Index to U.S. Government Periodicals, c/o Infordata International Inc., 175 E. Delaware Place, Suite 4602, Chicago IL 60611, regarding price and availability of individual articles, issues, titles and subscriptions.

Fig. 20.2. Entry from *Index to U.S. Government Periodicals*.

Factual/Directory Information

The official handbook of the federal government, the *United States Government Manual*, has been published annually since 1935. The *Manual* provides descriptions and, in some cases, organization charts (see figure 20.3, page 454) for legislative, judicial, and executive agencies and offices, as well as for independent boards, commissions, committees, and quasi-official agencies. Entries give information on dates of establishment, key personnel, major subagencies, and programs and services.

Another basic government handbook which covers most government offices is the *Official Congressional Directory*. It can be thought of as a directory published for the *use* of Congress rather than *about* the Congress. A major portion of this handbook provides biographical and directory information about senators and representatives and their offices and committees. In addition, this title presents directory information for all major departments and many smaller agencies in which members of Congress may have some interest. The *Government Manual* presents useful descriptions of agencies and their programs, but the *Congressional Directory* usually provides more detailed directory information, with names, addresses, and telephone numbers. If a patron wants to know the address of the Government Printing Office, for example, one can consult either the *Manual*

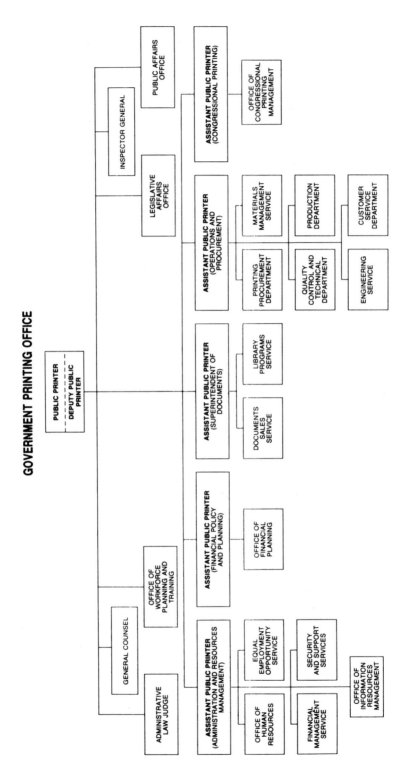

Fig. 20.3. Organization chart from *United States Government Manual*.

or the *Directory*. If a user wants to know when the GPO was established or how the Depository Library Program is administered, one must consult the *Manual*. On the other hand, if a very fine breakdown of the subagencies and names of department and section heads is required, turn to the *Congressional Directory*.

Various other directories are published commercially. Some are descriptive, such as the *Washington Information Directory* and the *Congressional Staff Directory*. Both include brief information about the programs or purpose of an agency, as well as the address, telephone number, and directors' names. The *Washington Information Directory* also covers nongovernmental agencies which have relevance to the government; these might include associations, lobbying groups, and foundations. Other directories provide only names, addresses, and telephone numbers, as does the *Federal Executive Directory*. This is updated bimonthly, is well indexed by keyword and personal name, and is indispensable as a source for the most current names, telephone numbers, and addresses of government agencies and their employees.

In addition to these comprehensive directories, individual agencies publish their own handbooks or manuals which give the user more detailed information about the programs, services, and organization of an agency, or provide factual material for reference purposes. An example of the first type is the *Social Security Handbook*, which tells what the Social Security Administration programs encompass and how to apply for benefits. Examples of the second type are *General Information Concerning Patents* (U.S. Patent and Trademark Office) and *Occupational Outlook Handbook* (Bureau of Labor Statistics). The former describes the process of patenting, in a question-and-answer format. The latter provides detailed descriptions of various occupations and careers. It informs the user about preparation for that career, salary expectations, job descriptions, and where to get additional information. These are only a few examples of an enormous variety of sources for factual, ready reference questions such as: "How can I determine if my invention is already patented?" or "Do I need a master's degree to be a medical technologist?" or "Who is the representative from my congressional district, and how can I contact him or her?"

Legislative Documents

There are many steps in the process by which a bill becomes a public law. At each step along the way, there will be congressional committee documents associated with the legislation. When a bill is introduced, it is printed with a number which designates its congress and a sequential number for the House or Senate Bill or Resolution. If there are hearings on the bill, the transcript of the *Hearings* will be published. There may also be a *Committee Print* with additional relevant background information. If the bill is then reported out of committee, there will be a printed *Report*. In addition, the House and Senate may order publication of special *Documents*, which are sometimes annual titles for special purposes (e.g., *Economic Report of the President*). The House and Senate Reports and Documents are published collectively as the *U.S. Serial Set*.

Guides and Indexes. A major component of reference work dealing with federal documents is legislative reference. A typical question might involve a simple request for a known primary document, such as a Public Law or a House Resolution, or it could be an inquiry as to whether there have been hearings on a particular topic, or whether a bill ever became a law. The process of tracking legislation from the introduction of a bill to the passage of a law has been made very straightforward by several excellent commercial publications. Most notable is the *CIS/Index* (figure 20.4, page 456), published since 1970 by Congressional Information Service, Inc. *CIS/Index* provides access to all of the types of congressional publications mentioned above. A very comprehensive index by subject and name directs the user to a numbered abstract. That citation gives complete bibliographic information, details for purchase, and SuDoc classification number, followed by a detailed abstract with page references. Source documents as cited in the abstracts are also available from the publisher on microfiche. *CIS/Index* is available from the publisher on CD-ROM as the Congressional Masterfile 2 which covers the period from 1970 to date, and it can also be searched online through DIALOG. CIS also produces Congressional Masterfile 1, a CD-ROM which provides access to congressional papers from 1789 to 1969.

SAMPLE ABSTRACT

The following sample entry shows the information contained in a typical abstract.

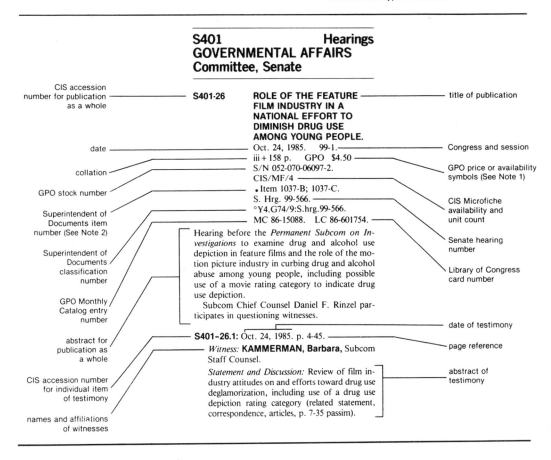

Fig. 20.4. Abstract from *CIS/Index*. Reprinted with permission of Congressional Information Service (Bethesda, MD). All rights reserved.

An equally useful but quite different index is the *Congressional Index* from Commerce Clearing House. This is a looseleaf service, updated weekly. It is particularly valuable as a place to find the current status of legislation. The status tables indicate, by bill number, whether hearings have been held and reports issued, and follow through with information and dates on votes, vetoes, and public law number. The *CIS/Index* provides abstracts of congressional committee publications, but *Congressional Index* is more timely and covers all pending legislation, providing useful information even when no publications are issued after a bill's introduction and referral to committee.

If library users want discussion or background information, but not necessarily primary documents from Congress, then they can consult *C Q Weekly Report* and *C Q Almanac*. These publications from Congressional Quarterly, Inc. cover Congress, the Supreme Court, the presidency, and politics. The *C Q Weekly Report* discusses major legislation, events, and issues, and cites primary documents. It also furnishes roll call votes. At the end of the year, that information from the *Weekly* is reorganized by subject and summarized in chronological order in the *Almanac*. The *C Q Weekly Report* and *C Q Almanac* provide the user with a well-organized, succinct, and readable account of congressional, presidential, and judicial consideration of major issues affecting national politics.

Primary Sources. Once users have read about legislation in the Congressional Quarterly sources, or have identified sources in *CIS/Index* or *Congressional Index*, they can move on to read the actual primary documents. These should be available in a paper or microfiche format in most depository libraries. They will include: *Congressional Record*, the verbatim transcript from the floor of Congress; congressional bills, the form in which legislation is introduced; committee hearings, again verbatim transcripts; committee prints; and reports and documents, which comprise the *U.S. Serial Set*. Bills that pass and become public laws are first printed separately as "Slip Laws," then compiled into the *United States Statutes at Large*, and finally are codified in the *United States Code*. (For a complete discussion of the legislative process and the associated publications, see any of the guides cited earlier in this chapter.)

Regulatory Documents

Executive departments and agencies are empowered by Congress to issue rules and regulations which implement Acts of Congress. These administrative rulings, as well as presidential documents, proposed rules, and notices, are published daily in the *Federal Register*. Proposed rules are published to give interested citizens a chance to comment. For instance, there might be a proposed change for designating nonsmoking areas in public buildings. Notices can be announcements of meetings, opinions, or other miscellaneous information, such as the availability of an environmental impact statement or a research grant (see figure 20.5, page 458). Final rules and regulations, and presidental Executive Orders and proclamations, are then incorporated into the *Code of Federal Regulations* (*CFR*). The *CFR* is divided into 50 titles, such as Transportation, the Environment, Communications, and Occupational Safety and Health. Each title is revised once a year, with one-fourth of the *CFR* being issued each calendar quarter.

When a library user needs up-to-date regulations for an agency and its programs, the research starts in *CFR*. By using the index to *CFR*, the user identifies the relevant title and section and notes the status of regulations as of the latest *CFR* edition for that title. Then the *LSA-List of CFR Sections Affected* is consulted to determine if there are rules and regulations more recent than those in the last edition of *CFR*. If the relevant title and section appear in the *LSA*, the user will be referred to a page number in the *Federal Register* which has updated information for that *CFR* section. In figure 20.5, the entry shows that 47 *CFR* 73 — that is, *CFR* title 47, section 73 — has been affected; in this case, specific information about a rule is explained. In order to locate items in the *Federal Register* which do not update the *CFR*, or if the correct *CFR* section is unknown, consult the monthly index to the *Federal Register*, which is arranged by the name of the agency that issued the rules, proposed rules, or notices. As an alternative, the librarian can search the *Federal Register* on DIALOG, where all regulations issued since the latest *CFR* edition can be identified in one search. The *Federal Register* is now also available on CD-ROM.

47 CFR Part 73

[MM Docket No. 89-381; RM-6739]

Radio Broadcasting Services; Amarillo, TX

AGENCY: Federal Communications Commission.

ACTION: Final rule.

SUMMARY: The Commission, at the request of Amarillo Community Broadcasting Company, allots Channel 265C1 to Amarillo, Texas, as its eighth local FM service. *See* 54 FR 37702, September 12, 1989. Channel 265C1 can be allotted to Amarillo in compliance with the Commission's minimum distance separation requirements without the imposition of a site restriction. The coordinates for Channel 265C1 at Amarillo are North Latitude 35-12-30 and West Longitude 101-50-00. With this action, this proceeding is terminated.

DATES: Effective October 22, 1990; The window period for filing applications will open on October 23, 1990, and close on November 23, 1990.

FOR FURTHER INFORMATION CONTACT: Andrew J. Rhodes, Mass Media Bureau, (202) 634-6530.

SUPPLEMENTARY INFORMATION: This is a synopsis of the claimant's Report and Order, MM Docket No. 89-381, Commission's adopted August 21, 1990, and released September 5, 1990. The full text of this Commission decision is available for inspection and copying during normal business hours in the FCC Dockets Branch (Room 230), 1919 M Street NW., Washington, DC. The complete text of this decision may also be purchased from the Commission's copy contractors, International Transcription Service, (202) 857-3800, 2100 M Street, NW., Suite 140, Washington, DC 20037.

List of Subjects in 47 CFR Part 73

Radio broadcasting.

PART 73—[AMENDED]

1. The authority citation for part 73 continues to read as follows:

Authority: 47 U.S.C. 154, 303.

§ 73.202   [Amended]

2. Section 73.202(b), the Table of FM Allotments is amended under Texas by adding Channel 265C1 at Amarillo.

Federal Communications Commission.

Kathleen B. Levitz,

Deputy Chief, Policy and Rules Division, Mass Media Bureau.

[FR Doc. 90-21173 Filed 9-7-90; 8:45 am]

BILLING CODE 6712-01-M

Fig. 20.5. Notice in *Federal Register*.

Statistical Sources

The federal government is the most important statistics-gathering agency in the world. Data gathered and published covers every topic from production and consumption of agricultural commodities to daily and annual rainfall at weather reporting stations. A librarian can quickly and easily determine how many persons were arrested last year, by race and sex, as well as how many high school graduates went on to college. If an event can be counted, chances are that the government has reported it. This section reviews the most important sources for finding basic facts, as well as the guides that assist individuals in using more specialized sources. It is essential to remember that, to protect confidentiality of information, published data from the government never identifies individuals or individual companies by name. The confidentiality provision sometimes results in suppression or deletion of data if it could possibly be used to identify characteristics of an individual.

Guides. Since 1973, the most comprehensive and easy-to-use guide to federal government statistics has been the *American Statistics Index* (*ASI*). Like other indexes from Congressional Information Service, Inc., *ASI* consists of two complementary parts: Index and Abstracts. A sample abstract is shown in figure 20.6. The user first consults the subject

Sample Abstract—Individual Publication

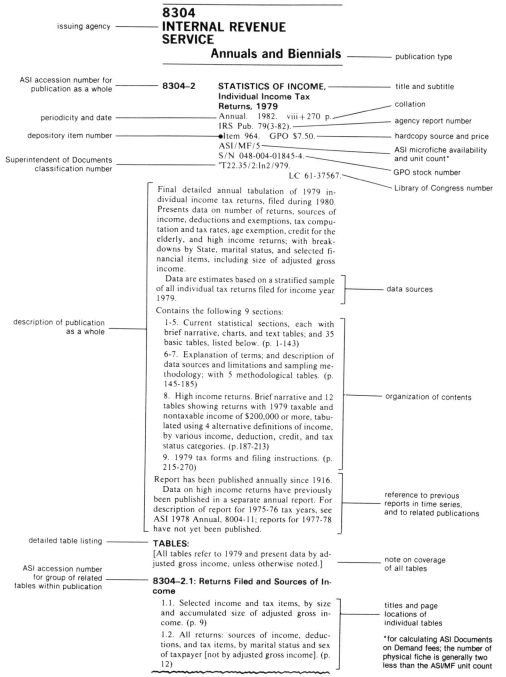

issuing agency ——————— **8304**
INTERNAL REVENUE SERVICE
Annuals and Biennials ——————— publication type

ASI accession number for
publication as a whole ——————— **8304–2**   STATISTICS OF INCOME, ——————— title and subtitle
Individual Income Tax
Returns, 1979 ——————————————— collation
periodicity and date ——————— Annual.   1982.   viii + 270 p.
IRS Pub. 79(3-82). ————————————— agency report number
depository item number ——————— ●Item 964.   GPO $7.50. ——————— hardcopy source and price
ASI/MF/5 ———————————————————— ASI microfiche availability
and unit count*
Superintendent of Documents
classification number ——————— S/N 048-004-01845-4.
ᵀT22.35/2:In2/979. ————————————— GPO stock number
LC 61-37567. ——————————————— Library of Congress number

description of publication
as a whole ——————————— {

Final detailed annual tabulation of 1979 individual income tax returns, filed during 1980. Presents data on number of returns, sources of income, deductions and exemptions, tax computation and tax rates, age exemption, credit for the elderly, and high income returns; with breakdowns by State, marital status, and selected financial items, including size of adjusted gross income.

Data are estimates based on a stratified sample of all individual tax returns filed for income year 1979. ——————— data sources

Contains the following 9 sections:

1-5. Current statistical sections, each with brief narrative, charts, and text tables; and 35 basic tables, listed below. (p. 1-143)

6-7. Explanation of terms; and description of data sources and limitations and sampling methodology; with 5 methodological tables. (p. 145-185)

8. High income returns. Brief narrative and 12 tables showing returns with 1979 taxable and nontaxable income of $200,000 or more, tabulated using 4 alternative definitions of income, by various income, deduction, credit, and tax status categories. (p.187-213) ——————— organization of contents

9. 1979 tax forms and filing instructions. (p. 215-270)

Report has been published annually since 1916.

Data on high income returns have previously been published in a separate annual report. For description of report for 1975-76 tax years, see ASI 1978 Annual, 8004-11; reports for 1977-78 have not yet been published. ——————— reference to previous reports in time series, and to related publications

detailed table listing ——————— **TABLES:**
[All tables refer to 1979 and present data by adjusted gross income, unless otherwise noted.] ——————— note on coverage of all tables

ASI accession number
for group of related ——————— **8304–2.1: Returns Filed and Sources of Income**
tables within publication

1.1. Selected income and tax items, by size and accumulated size of adjusted gross income. (p. 9) ——————— titles and page locations of individual tables

1.2. All returns: sources of income, deductions, and tax items, by marital status and sex of taxpayer [not by adjusted gross income]. (p. 12)

*for calculating ASI Documents on Demand fees; the number of physical fiche is generally two less than the ASI/MF unit count

Fig. 20.6. Abstract from *American Statistics Index*. Reprinted with permission of Congressional Information Service (Bethesda, MD). All rights reserved.

index, or one of several indexes by category (for example, by race, by country, by sex), or, if possible, the title index. The subject indexing is fairly broad, but includes useful cross-references and suggests related headings. In the index, the user identifies a content note that seems to describe the needed data. From the index, the user is referred, by abstract number, to the complete citation in the companion abstract volume. Notice that in addition to a very detailed abstract which describes data in the report, the citation includes complete bibliographic information, with the SuDoc classification number and depository item number. *ASI* is an indispensable reference tool. It is necessary to use this index in order to make full use of all of the annual, monthly, weekly, and daily statistical publications, as well as press releases and newsletters which may contain data. Many publications listed are available on deposit to depository libraries. Complete text of all cited reports can be purchased from the publisher in a microfiche edition, or a library can elect to purchase only nondeposit documents on microfiche. The microfiche editions are arranged by abstract number, making the fiches quite easy to find and use. Because the citations and notes are so comprehensive in *ASI*, this index can also be used effectively as a bibliographic verification source for government publications. *ASI* can be searched online through DIALOG.

A companion guide for statistics published by nonfederal agencies is *Statistical Reference Index (SRI)*. This index began in 1980. It is used in exactly the same way as *ASI*, but its coverage is quite different. If a user needs more data from an individual state, or data from an analytical study or opinion poll, or statistics from an industry organization rather than from the federal government, this is the index of choice. Data found through *SRI* will often supplement that found using *ASI*. It is also possible to purchase source documents on microfiche from the publisher, arranged by abstract or accession number. *Index to International Statistics (IIS)*, another index from the same publisher, provides information about statistical publications from intergovernmental agencies. *IIS*, *SRI*, and *ASI* are available on one CD-ROM as the Statistical Masterfile. This can be purchased in a current edition covering 1989 to date, or a retrospective edition which dates from the beginning of each index through 1988.

An additional guide which is less specific in its indexing and does not include detailed abstracts, but which has much broader coverage, is *Statistics Sources*. It does cover the most useful sources from the U.S. government, and has the advantage of also referring to nongovernment and United Nations titles.

Primary Sources. When librarians can afford only one statistical source, they are likely to choose the *Statistical Abstract of the United States*. *Statistical Abstract*, published annually, summarizes statistical data from most government and some nongovernment sources. To gain access to these tables, start with the subject index in the back. Subjects are arranged by broad headings with more specific subheadings. Since 1987, references are to table numbers rather than to page numbers. In over fifteen hundred tables (for a sample table, see figure 20.7), there are economic, social, agricultural, demographic, and political data on topics such as births, unemployment, voter registration, foreign aid, and welfare. In many cases, the data is sufficient to answer a reference question, but the *Statistical Abstract* can also be used as a guide to more detailed or earlier information. For more detail, use the source notes provided with each table to identify the titles where the data originally appeared. For earlier information, it is sometimes possible to use notes at the beginning of many tables which cite related data tables in *Historical Statistics of the United States, Colonial Times to 1970*. The two-volume set of *Historical Statistics* compiles data from the earliest time it was available, and presents comprehensive source notes, definitions, and a detailed subject index.

No. **19.** Resident Population—Selected Characteristics: 1790 to 1988

[**In thousands, except as indicated.** Excludes Armed Forces abroad. For definition of median, see Guide to Tabular Presentation. See also *Historical Statistics, Colonial Times to 1970*, series A 73–81 and A 143–149]

DATE	SEX		RACE					Hispanic origin [1]	RESIDENCE [2]		Median age (years)
					Other						
	Male	Female	White	Black	Total	American Indians and Alaska Natives	Asian and Pacific Islanders		Urban	Rural	
1790 (Aug. 2) [3]	(NA)	(NA)	3,172	757	(NA)	(NA)	(NA)	(NA)	202	3,728	(NA)
1800 (Aug. 4) [3]	(NA)	(NA)	4,306	1,002	(NA)	(NA)	(NA)	(NA)	322	4,986	(NA)
1850 (June 1) [3]	11,838	11,354	19,553	3,639	(NA)	(NA)	(NA)	(NA)	3,544	19,648	18.9
1860 (June 1) [3]	16,085	15,358	26,923	4,442	79	(NA)	(NA)	(NA)	6,217	25,227	19.4
1870 (June 1) [3]	19,494	19,065	33,589	4,880	89	(NA)	(NA)	(NA)	9,902	28,656	20.2
1880 (June 1) [3]	25,519	24,637	43,403	6,581	172	(NA)	(NA)	(NA)	14,130	36,026	20.9
1890 (June 1) [3]	32,237	30,711	55,101	7,489	358	(NA)	(NA)	(NA)	22,106	40,841	22.0
1900 (June 1) [3]	38,816	37,178	66,809	8,834	351	(NA)	(NA)	(NA)	30,160	45,835	22.9
1910 (Apr. 15) [3]	47,332	44,640	81,732	9,828	413	(NA)	(NA)	(NA)	41,999	49,973	24.1
1920 (Jan. 1) [3]	53,900	51,810	94,821	10,463	427	(NA)	(NA)	(NA)	54,158	51,553	25.3
1930 (Apr. 1) [3]	62,137	60,638	110,287	11,891	597	(NA)	(NA)	(NA)	68,955	53,820	26.4
1940 (Apr. 1) [3]	66,062	65,608	118,215	12,866	589	(NA)	(NA)	(NA)	74,424	57,246	29.0
1950 (Apr. 1) [3]	74,833	75,864	134,942	15,042	713	(NA)	(NA)	(NA)	96,468	54,230	30.2
1950 (Apr. 1)	75,187	76,139	135,150	15,045	1,131	(NA)	(NA)	(NA)	96,847	54,479	30.2
1960 (Apr. 1)	88,331	90,992	158,832	18,872	1,620	(NA)	(NA)	(NA)	125,269	54,054	29.5
1970 (Apr. 1) [4]	98,926	104,309	178,098	22,581	2,557	(NA)	(NA)	(NA)	149,325	53,887	28.0
1980 (Apr. 1) [5]	110,053	116,493	194,713	26,683	5,150	1,420	3,729	14,609	167,051	59,495	30.0
1983 (July 1) [6]	113,919	120,365	199,849	28,056	6,379	1,524	4,855	16,649	(NA)	(NA)	30.8
1984 (July 1) [6]	115,022	121,455	201,290	28,457	6,730	1,559	5,172	17,251	(NA)	(NA)	31.1
1985 (July 1) [6]	116,160	122,576	202,769	28,870	7,097	1,594	5,504	17,865	(NA)	(NA)	31.4
1986 (July 1) [6]	117,370	123,737	204,326	29,303	7,478	1,629	5,849	18,521	(NA)	(NA)	31.7
1987 (July 1) [6]	118,539	124,880	205,827	29,748	7,845	1,664	6,181	19,173	(NA)	(NA)	32.1
1988 (July 1) [6]	119,738	126,069	207,377	30,202	8,228	1,699	6,529	19,831	(NA)	(NA)	32.3

NA Not available. [1] Persons of Hispanic origin may be of any race. [2] Beginning 1950, current definition. For explanation of change, see text, section 1. [3] Excludes Alaska and Hawaii. [4] The revised 1970 resident population count is 203,302,031; which incorporates changes due to errors found after tabulations were completed. The race and sex data shown here reflect the official 1970 census count while the residence data come from the tabulated count; see text, section 1. [5] The race data shown for April 1, 1980 have been modified; see text, section 1 for explanation. [6] Estimated.

Fig. 20.7. Table and notes from *Statistical Abstract of the United States*.

For a broad range of statistical data on states, counties, and cities, consult the *County and City Data Book* and the *State and Metropolitan Area Data Book*, both published approximately every five years by the Census Bureau. In both cases, data items are presented for major topics, such as population, housing, retail trade, crime, agriculture, education, and employment, for similar geographic areas (states, counties, standard metropolitan statistical areas, and cities with population over 25,000). The *Data Books* are published irregularly, and time coverage for the data items is inconsistent, depending on the source of the data. For example, economic data may be from the latest quinquennial Economic Census (1982 or 1987), while population data is from the latest Current Population Survey (annual) or the Decennial Census (1980 or 1990). *County and City Data Book* is also available on CD-ROM, which allows the user to manipulate and format data in ways not possible with the printed version.

The *U.S. Census of Population* has been conducted every ten years since 1790. It is the official count of the population of the United States, conducted for the purpose of congressional apportionment. The census questionnaire has a small number of questions asked of all persons and additional questions asked of a sample of the population. In effect, it provides a representative picture of the United States population, reporting data on age, race, sex, household relationships, income, employment, nativity, and disability. The publications give benchmark data from which estimates and projections can be drawn. Estimates and projections based on that benchmark data, and data drawn from an annual sample of the population, are later reported in *Current Population Reports*. Typically, a large research library will have the complete set of decennial census products in its collection, while a smaller library might choose only those which cover its own and neighboring states. The *1980 Census of Population and Housing* is currently being replaced by the *1990 Census*, which will be available in a variety of formats, including paper, microfiche, computer tape, and CD-ROM. Specific use, space, staff, budget, and equipment, as well as availability from the Government Printing Office, will determine which format works best in a particular library.

In contrast to the Census Bureau, which presents a portrait of the United States in the Decennial Census, other agencies record and publish data on specific events, such as divorces, crimes committed, bushels of corn harvested, motor vehicle deaths, or housing permits issued. Data will be found in such titles as *Digest of Education Statistics*,[24] *Agricultural Statistics*,[25] *Uniform Crime Reports*,[26] and *Vital Statistics of the United States*.[27] It is not necessary at this point to describe each title, except to point out that the data in these and other publications is accessible through the *Statistical Abstract of the United States* and *American Statistics Index*.

Data on foreign countries can sometimes be found in the *Statistical Abstract*. The *Abstract* presents very basic demographic and economic data, sometimes as it relates to the United States (export/import, foreign aid, immigration). More detailed information for a particular country can be found in that country's own version of the *Statistical Abstract*. These are filmed and sold by Congressional Information Service as a set (*Current National Statistical Compendiums*).[28] For comparative data, a title that presents data for many countries in one source is needed. Examples of that type of work are: *United Nations Statistical Yearbook*, *United Nations Demographic Yearbook*, or yearbooks from other intergovernmental organizations, such as the World Health Organization or the Food and Agriculture Organization.

Search Strategies

As a rule, reference librarians should consider using government documents to answer questions that ask for facts about a government agency and its programs or personnel. Numerous directories are available from the government and from commercial publishers (see also chapter 12); beyond those, very detailed information will be found in an agency's own directory or annual report. If a patron asks who is the Surgeon General of the United States, the first choice is the most up-to-date directory in the collection: probably the *Federal Executive Directory*, which is updated bimonthly. This will be the best source, particularly if the person occupying that position changed within the past year. If, however, the patron wants to know who was the Surgeon General during World War II, it is necessary to use an older edition of the *United States Government Manual* or the *Official Congressional Directory*. If the patron wants to know who worked for the Surgeon General in several subagencies, one would use the *Congressional Directory*. If the patron wants to know when the Surgeon General's office was established and if it was ever organized differently, one would consult the *Government Manual*.

For statistical data, there is almost always an appropriate governmental source. The data will be reliable, complete, and usually up-to-date. It is always appropriate to start by trying the *Statistical Abstract of the United States*. Use the *Abstract* for complete data and as an index to other sources. Remember that, as its title implies, it is an abstract; that is, the data tables presented are condensed from other sources, which are always traced through source notes. In addition, notes will frequently guide the user to *Historical Statistics of the United States, Colonial Times to 1970* for earlier data. If statistics are not found through these or other basic sources, such as *County and City Data Book* or *State and Metropolitan Area Data Book*, the librarian in a large library will consult *American Statistics Index*. Keep in mind that a statistic has to be collected in order to be reported. Poorly defined requests such as "the number of alcohol users" will have to be refined to data requests like "the per capita consumption of alcohol" or "the number of alcohol-related motor vehicle accidents."

Legislative reference service must be accomplished by using commercial indexes such as *CIS/Index* and *Congressional Index*. Many users will find that the Congressional Quarterly products give them sufficient details to help them understand and trace a particular piece of legislation, but a large library will also have the primary documents, including bills, reports, documents, hearings, prints, debates, and laws. All the source documents are best accessed through the nongovernmental indexes previously mentioned. Suppose a patron wants to know the current status of legislation to change the minimum wage. *Congressional Index* will identify, by subject, the bill number, provide a brief summary, and tell if hearings were held and if the bill was reported. If the patron needs historical background and wants to know who supported the legislation, use *C Q Weekly Report*. To find an abstract of relevant hearings with page references and names of witnesses, the *CIS/Index* is the best choice.

When looking for documents on a particular subject, start the search in the *Monthly Catalog*. Specialized lists are published as *Subject Bibliographies*, and periodical articles are found through the *Index to U.S. Government Periodicals*. If the subject sounds as though it might involve government-funded research, try to find citations in *Government Reports Announcements and Index*.

If the patron has a report number and wants to identify the document, try to determine the origin of the alphabetic part of the number (e.g., PHS for Public Health Service, EIA for Energy Information Administration, NTSB for National Transportation Safety Board). Knowing the issuing agency will help determine if the report is more likely to be administrative or research. Administrative reports can be identified by using the *Monthly Catalog*, while research and development reports will be identified in *GRAI*. Both of these sources include report number indexes. If the patron has a SuDoc number with no date, try the online version of the *Monthly Catalog* or an OCLC search. If the patron supplies a date, go to that year of the *Monthly Catalog* and consult the SuDoc number index. If the report is too old, and there is no SuDoc number index, use the number to determine the issuing agency and consult the agency index. There may be occasions when a patron knows only a common or unofficial name for a report, such as the "Warren Report" or the "Plum Book." There is a specialized index which gives the correct name of such reports along with the complete bibliographic citation: *Popular Names of U.S. Government Reports*.[29]

Government documents are treated like any other material by most indexes and catalogs. In general, one can expect to find documents along with commercial publications by using general indexes such as *PAIS International in Print* and shared cataloging networks like OCLC. Even though a document originates and is distributed by the government, it should be cataloged and used like any other material in the library collection. It should not be viewed as being particularly difficult or even different simply because of its origin. There was a time when users who wanted government publications had to deal with a card catalog containing dozens of drawers and thousands of cards that all began U.S. −, or had to limit their searches in printed catalogs to the *Monthly Catalog*, which had only limited indexing. Those difficulties are now mitigated by excellent commercially published indexes and by keyword access through online databases, CD-ROM catalogs, and online bibliographic databases. The key point to remember is that if it can be investigated, counted, legislated, or regulated, the government has probably published something about it. With improved indexing and new technology, these government publications are now easily accessible.

■ ═══ ■

20.1

Tracking Current Legislation

A patron wants to know the current status of legislation to improve the ailing savings and loan industry. There has been a great deal of media coverage, so the librarian knows this legislation is currently under consideration. To identify the legislation by bill number, and obtain a brief description, she turns to *Congressional Index*. The subject index in volume 1 covers "Financial Institutions," with the subheading "Federal Deposit Insurance Corporation — improvements." Bill number H-1278 is described in volume 2 under "House Bills" as a bill to reform the federal savings and loan insurance system. The librarian then consults the section called "Status of House Bills," in volume 2. This provides a chronological listing of all action on this bill, including hearing dates, vote tallies, and report numbers. She is also able to determine that this bill passed and is now identified as Public Law 101-73.

After the patron is presented with these facts, he decides he would like to read the reports and transcripts of the hearing. The report numbers provided in *Congressional Index* are sufficient to identify the reports and enable the librarian to find a copy in her library's microfiche version of the *U.S. Serial Set*. She then identifies hearings on this bill using *CIS/Index*. She consults the index under "Savings and Loans" or "Federal Deposit Insurance Corporation" and examines the abstracts to see which cites H.R. 1278. The abstracts identify the hearings, which are titled *Financial Institutions Reform, Recovery and Enforcement Act of 1989*.

If the numerous volumes of hearings and reports had proven to be more than the patron needed to know or had time to read, the librarian could have used the *C Q Weekly Report* to get a summary of the issues involved in this legislation. The correct index heading is "Banks and Banking." Useful subheadings include "Legislative summary," "Highlights," and "Major Issues."

The question in box 20.1 illustrates that there are many approaches to the same question. It is important to understand the patron's specific information needs and tailor the search accordingly. Also, keep in mind that choosing the correct subject heading in various indexes requires some creativity and use of cross-references.

Notes

1. 44 U.S.C. §1901.

2. *United States Reports* (Washington, D.C.: U.S. Supreme Court, 1790-). Annual.

3. U.S. Congress, Office of Technology Assessment, *Informing the Nation* (Washington, D.C.: U.S. Government Printing Office, 1988), 333p.

4. U.S. Department of Energy, *Annual Report* (Washington, D.C.: U.S. Government Printing Office, 1978-). Annual.

5. U.S. Bureau of Economic Analysis, *Business Statistics* (Washington, D.C.: U.S. Government Printing Office, 1986).

6. M. S. Pindzola, *Theoretical Atomic Physics for Fusion* (Washington, D.C.: U.S. Department of Energy, 1989), 7p.

7. U.S. Public Health Service, Office of the Surgeon General, *The Health Consequences of Involuntary Smoking* (Washington, D.C.: Public Health Service, 1986), 359p.

8. *Politics in America* (Washington, D.C.: Congressional Quarterly, 1981-). Biennial.

9. *Government Publications Review* (Elmsford, N.Y.: Pergamon, 1973-). Bimonthly.

10. *Library Journal* (New York: Bowker Magazine Group, 1871-). Monthly.

11. U.S. Library of Congress, *Library of Congress Information Bulletin* (Washington, D.C.: U.S. Government Printing Office, 1943-). Monthly.

12. U.S. Bureau of the Census, *Census and You* (Washington, D.C.: U.S. Government Printing Office, 1988-). Monthly. (Formerly *Data User News*.)

13. Gladys Sachse, *U.S. Government Publications for Small and Medium-Sized Public Libraries* (Chicago: American Library Association, 1981), 195p.

14. U.S. Government Printing Office, *The Federal Depository Library Manual* (Washington, D.C.: U.S. Government Printing Office, 1985, revised 1990).

15. Eugene P. Sheehy, *Guide to Reference Books*, 10th ed. (Chicago: American Library Association, 1986), 1,560p.

16. *Energy Research Abstracts* (*ERA*). Oak Ridge, Tenn.: U.S. Department of Energy, Technical Information Center, 1976- . Semimonthly with annual indexes.

17. *Scientific and Technical Aerospace Reports* (*STAR*). Washington, D.C.: U.S. National Aeronautics and Space Administration, 1963- . Semimonthly with annual indexes.

18. *Selected Water Resources Abstracts* (*SWRA*). Springfield, Va.: National Technical Information Service, 1968- . Monthly with annual index.

19. *Energy Research Abstracts* is part of DOE Energy (DIALOG Files 103, 104); *Scientific and Technical Aerospace Reports* is part of Aerospace Database (DIALOG File 108); *Selected Water Resources Abstracts* is online as Water Resources Abstracts (DIALOG File 117).

20. *Readers' Guide to Periodical Literature* (New York: H. W. Wilson, 1905-). Monthly.

21. *PAIS International in Print* (New York: Public Affairs Information Service, 1991-). Monthly. (Formerly *Public Affairs Information Service Bulletin*, 1915-1990.)

22. *Education Index* (New York: H. W. Wilson, 1932-). Monthly except July and August.

23. *Current Index to Journals in Education* (Phoenix, Ariz.: Oryx Press, 1969-). Monthly.

24. *Digest of Education Statistics* (Washington, D.C.: U.S. National Center for Education Statistics, 1962-). Annual.

25. *Agricultural Statistics* (Washington, D.C.: U.S. Department of Agriculture, 1936-). Annual.

26. *Uniform Crime Reports* (Washington, D.C.: U.S. Federal Bureau of Investigation, 1930-). Annual.

27. *Vital Statistics of the United States* (Washington, D.C.: U.S. Government Printing Office, 1937-). Annual.

28. *Current National Statistical Compendiums* (Washington, D.C.: Congressional Information Service, 1970-). Annual.

29. Bernard A. Bernier, Jr. and Karen A. Wood, comps., *Popular Names of U.S. Government Reports* (Washington, D.C.: Library of Congress, 1984), 272p.

List of Sources

Agricultural Statistics. Washington, D.C.: U.S. Department of Agriculture, 1936- . Annual.

American Statistics Index (ASI). Washington, D.C.: Congressional Information Service, 1973- . Annual, with monthly supplements. (DIALOG File 102.)

Boyd, Anne Morris. *United States Government Publications*. 3d ed. revised by Rae Elizabeth Rips. New York: H. W. Wilson, 1949. 627p.

C Q Almanac. Washington, D.C.: Congressional Quarterly, 1945- . Annual.

C Q Weekly Report. Washington, D.C.: Congressional Quarterly, 1946- . Weekly.

CIS/Index. Washington, D.C.: Congressional Information Service, 1970- . Annual, with monthly supplements. (DIALOG File 101.)

Code of Federal Regulations. Washington, D.C.: National Archives and Records Service, 1949- . Revised annually.

Congressional Index. Chicago: Commerce Clearing House, 1937- . Weekly throughout session.

Congressional Masterfile, 1 and 2. [CD-ROM]. Washington, D.C.: Congressional Information Service.

Congressional Record. Washington, D.C.: U.S. Congress, 1873- . Daily when Congress is in session.

Congressional Staff Directory. Mt. Vernon, Va.: Staff Directories, Ltd., 1959- . Biennial.

County and City Data Book. Washington, D.C.: U.S. Bureau of the Census, 1988. 795p. and appendixes. (Available on CD-ROM.)

Current Population Reports. Washington, D.C.: U.S. Bureau of the Census, 1946- . Irregular.

Digest of Education Statistics. Washington, D.C.: U.S. National Center for Education Statistics, 1962- . Annual.

Federal Executive Directory. Washington, D.C.: Carroll Publishing, 1980- . Bimonthly.

Federal Register. Washington, D.C.: National Archives and Records Administration, 1936- . Daily. (DIALOG File 669; also available on CD-ROM.)

General Information Concerning Patents. Washington, D.C.: Patent and Trademark Office, 1989. 42p.

Government Reference Books. Littleton, Colo.: Libraries Unlimited, 1970 (covers 1968/69)- . Biennial.

Government Reports Announcements and Index (GRAI). Springfield, Va.: National Technical Information Service, 1946- . Bimonthly. (BRS File NTIS; DIALOG File 6.)

GPO Sales Publications Reference File (PRF). Washington, D.C.: U.S. Government Printing Office, 1977- . Bimonthly, with monthly supplement. (DIALOG File 166.)

Historical Statistics of the United States, Colonial Times to 1970. 2 vols. Washington, D.C.: U.S. Bureau of the Census, 1975.

Index to International Statistics (IIS). Washington, D.C.: Congressional Information Service, 1983- . Annual, with monthly supplements.

Index to U.S. Government Periodicals. Chicago: Infordata International, 1971- . Quarterly.

Monthly Catalog of United States Government Publications. Washington, D.C.: U.S. Government Printing Office, 1895- . Monthly. (DIALOG File 66.) Supplemented annually by *Serials Supplement* and *Serials Set Supplement*. (BRS File GPOM, DIALOG File 66; also available on CD-ROM.)

Morehead, Joe. *Introduction to United States Public Documents*. 4th ed. Englewood, Colo.: Libraries Unlimited, 1992. (in press)

New Books. Washington, D.C.: U.S. Government Printing Office, 1982- . Bimonthly.

Occupational Outlook Handbook. Washington, D.C.: U.S. Bureau of Labor Statistics, 1949- . Biennial.

Official Congressional Directory. Washington, D.C.: U.S. Government Printing Office, 1887- . Biennial.

Popular Names of U.S. Government Reports. 4th ed. Compiled by Bernerd A. Bernier, Jr. and Karen A. Wood. Washington, D.C.: Library of Congress, 1984. 272p.

Robinson, Judith Schiek. *Tapping the Government Grapevine: The User Friendly Guide to U.S. Government Information Sources*. Phoenix, Ariz.: Oryx Press, 1988. 193p.

Schmeckebier, Laurence F., and Roy B. Eastin. *Government Publications and Their Use*. 2d rev. ed. Washington, D.C.: The Brookings Institution, 1969. 502p.

Social Security Handbook. Washington, D.C.: Social Security Administration, 1960- . Irregular.

State and Metropolitan Area Data Book. Washington, D.C.: U.S. Bureau of the Census, 1986. 697p.

Statistical Abstract of the United States. Washington, D.C.: U.S. Bureau of the Census, 1878- . Annual.

Statistical Masterfile. [CD-ROM]. Washington, D.C.: Congressional Information Service.

Statistical Reference Index (SRI). Washington, D.C.: Congressional Information Service, 1980- . Annual, with monthly supplements.

Statistics Sources. 14th ed. Edited by Jacqueline Wasserman O'Brien and Steven R. Wasserman. 2 vols. Detroit, Mich.: Gale Research, 1990.

Subject Bibliographies. Washington, D.C.: U.S. Government Printing Office, 1975- . Revised irregularly.

U.S. Census of Population. Washington, D.C.: U.S. Bureau of the Census, 1790- . Decennial.

U.S. Government Books. Washington, D.C.: U.S. Government Printing Office, 1982- . Triennial.

U.S. Serial Set. Washington, D.C.: U.S. Congress, 1817- .

Uniform Crime Reports. Washington, D.C.: Federal Bureau of Investigation, 1930- . Annual.

United Nations Demographic Yearbook. New York: United Nations, 1948- . Annual.

United Nations Statistical Yearbook. New York: United Nations, Statistical Office, 1948- . Annual.

United States Code. 1982 ed. 17 vols. Washington, D.C.: U.S. Government Printing Office, 1983.

United States Government Manual. Washington, D.C.: National Archives and Records Service, 1935- . Annual.

United States Statutes at Large. Washington, D.C.: U.S. Government Printing Office, 1789- . Annual.

Vital Statistics of the United States. Washington, D.C.: U.S. Government Printing Office, 1937- . Annual.

Washington Information Directory. Washington, D.C.: Congressional Quarterly, 1980- . Annual.

Additional Readings

Hernon, Peter, and Charles R. McClure. *Public Access to Government Information*. 2d ed. Norwood, N.J.: Ablex, 1988. 524p.
    Hernon and McClure focus on administration of a documents collection, provision of public access, new technologies, government information policies, and education for documents librarianship, rather than how to use specific sources.

McIlvaine, Betsy. *A Consumers', Researchers', and Students' Guide to Government Publications*. New York: H. W. Wilson, 1983. 115p.
    This guide looks at how documents sources can be used to answer typical reference questions.

Ondrasik, Allison. *Data Map 1989*. Phoenix, Ariz.: Oryx Press, 1989. 787p.
    Data Map 1989 is a detailed subject index and bibliographic guide to the most commonly used federal government, commercial, and international statistical sources. It is a useful one-volume guide for a library that does not use *American Statistics Index*, *Statistical Reference Index*, or *Index to International Statistics*.

Robinson, Judith Schiek. *A Subject Guide to U.S. Government Reference Sources*. Littleton, Colo.: Libraries Unlimited, 1985. 333p.
    The scope and purpose of selected popular titles are presented in a broad subject arrangement. This revision of Sally Wynkoop's *Subject Guide to Government Reference Books* is clearly presented and well-indexed, and includes new printed sources.

Ross, John M. *How to Use the Major Indexes to U.S. Government Publications*. Chicago: American Library Association, 1989. 37p.
    The text clearly shows, in a step-by-step process, how to use six major reference services: *American Statistics Index*, *CIS Annual*, *CIS Legislative Histories of U.S. Public Laws*, *Index to U.S. Government Periodicals*, *Congressional Record*, and *Monthly Catalog*.

Sears, Jean L., and Marilyn K. Moody, eds. *Using Government Publications*. 2 vols. Phoenix, Ariz.: Oryx Press, 1985, 1986.
    This work presents a subject and agency approach to sources and information in the first volume, and information on statistical searches and special techniques (such as patent, treaty, and archival records searches) in the second.

Spencer, Michael D. G. *Free Publications from U.S. Government Agencies: A Guide*. Englewood, Colo.: Libraries Unlimited, 1989. 123p.

Spencer's guide is arranged by broad subject heading, then by agency. Information included describes each agency, and its publications and how to obtain them. The author also includes bibliographic information, when possible, on each agency's own publications list.

AUTHOR/TITLE INDEX

Entries in this index include all titles from the "List of Sources Discussed" in chapters 10 through 20. Entries have been made for authors, editors, compilers, and titles. The page numbers referring to the bibliographic information in the lists of sources discussed are set in italics. This format allows one to distinguish references to bibliographic materials from references to text. Names of databases (CD-ROM and online) are not italicized, while titles of printed and microform works are italicized. Articles at the beginning of titles have been omitted in most cases. Entries are arranged in accordance with the word-by-word principle of filing, with acronyms filed as words.

SUBJECT INDEX

Use this index to locate topical discussions in the text of the terms listed. An attempt has been made to index all substantive discussions, however brief, of these terms. However, for general terms such as "CD-ROM databases" and "DIALOG," the many occurrences in part 2 are not indexed here. For discussion of specific databases, consult the author/title index.

Terms chosen for this index are both those used by the authors and those the reader is most likely to use. In some cases, for the convenience of the reader, terms are listed both as direct entries and as subentries under a broader term.